Why Violence?

Why Violence?

Leading Questions Regarding the Conceptualization and Reality of Violence in Society

William E. Thornton

Lydia Voigt

Dee Wood Harper

CAROLINA ACADEMIC PRESS

Durham, North Carolina

Library of Congress Cataloging-in-Publication Data

Thornton, William E., 1946-
 Why violence? : leading questions regarding the conceptualization and reality of violence in society / William E. Thornton, Lydia Voigt and Dee Wood Harper.
     p. cm.
 Includes bibliographical references and index.
 ISBN 978-1-59460-867-4 (alk. paper)
 1. Violent crimes. 2. Victims of violent crimes. 3. Violence. I. Voigt, Lydia. II. Harper, Dee Wood. III. Title.

 HV6493.T48 2012
 303.6--dc23   2012021818

Carolina Academic Press
700 Kent Street
Durham, North Carolina 27701
Telephone (919) 489-7486
Fax (919) 493-5668
www.cap-press.com

Cover photo credits:
Burning police car © Jen Grantham; battered woman © Don Bayley; riot police © Brandon Laufenberg; World Trade Center ruins © Terraxplorer; crime scene © Denis Tangney Jr.; child in war zone © MShep2; handgun © Guven Demir. All images are from iStockphoto.

Printed in the United States of America

Contents

List of Boxes, Images, Figures and Tables

Preface

Why Violence? Leading Questions Regarding the Conceptualization and Reality of Violence in Society presents a comprehensive discussion of violence that is organized around overarching questions that have perplexed human beings since time immemorial. The book begins with the question of what is the meaning of *violence*. The relative ubiquity and ambiguity of the term has made it difficult to find a definition of violence that captures its complexity and often contradictory forms of expressions. Violence refers to various acts such as homicide, rape, robbery, and assault as well as collective violence, war, and terrorism; it may be found in our homes, workplaces, schools, places of worship, and communities both locally and globally. In everyday life the concept of violence seems to draw its significance more from the ways it is used to label certain types of behavior and certain types of people or countries than from the ways it is applied to describe concrete phenomenon. As a consequence, the concept is typically used as a pejorative or negative "summary symbol" serving mainly as an emotional intensifier, which creates mistrust or fear of others. Through its ubiquitous and ambiguous application, violence has become the quintessential metaphor that we all live by; it is symbolically ingrained in our language, thinking, and behavior. Due to its lack of specificity and function as a symbolic intensifier, it has lent itself to being politically exploited. As a result of the challenges associated with violence, its study calls for a very cautious and critical approach.

Why Violence? explores the many manifest ways in which violence is understood in contemporary society, ranging from popular perceptions to scientific claims. It covers age-long questions such as why some human beings, under certain circumstances, react in violent or aggressive ways and others do not and why some social forces/institutions tend to encourage or exacerbate violence and others do not. The book also treats questions that have not conventionally been associated with violence such as: why are acts of social injustice, environmental degradation, and gross abuse of power not considered acts of violence per se? In this sense, the book serves to fill a gap in the literature by raising not only the enduring questions of violence, but also new questions about the conceptualization and reality of violence. For example, should the recent financial crisis stemming from mass fraudulent acts that have adversely affected the lives of millions of people be considered acts of violence? Should homeless populations be considered victims of violence? Should unchecked and blatant air and water pollution be considered forms of violence? Unlike many books on violence that focus on narrow depictions of certain types of perpetrators, this book widens the list of potential perpetrators and includes consideration of a broad spectrum of victims of violence.

In addressing the leading questions about violence, the book introduces readers not only to the complexities associated with violence and violence studies, but also to state-of-the-art thinking and associated research/knowledge-base on violence. It provides a critical analysis of the interplay between popular questions of why there is a "disconnect" between the public's understanding of violence, including official responses to violence and scientific evidence. The most current theories and research evidence from the biological, psychological, sociological, and criminological viewpoints are presented and critically considered with respect to their relative strengths and weaknesses and potential for finding solutions to the problem of violence. The book begins with the question *Why Violence?* and ends with the question *Why not peace?*

A companion reader to the book, *Violence: Do We Know It When We See It?* (Harper, Voigt, and Thornton, 2012), comprised of original works from leading experts on violence from around the world, addresses a wide spectrum of interpersonal, institutional, and structural forms of violence and serves to illustrate key elements of this book. Together, *Why Violence?* and its companion reader explore multiple socially manifest and latent expressions of violence, including the symbolic ways in which violence is understood in contemporary society. The books cover topics ranging from common parlance, everyday perceptions and myths to governmental proclamations and scientific claims.

Special thanks must be expressed to Leo Barrile and Rae Taylor, who have contributed to the chapters in this book that deal with corporate violence and violent victimization, respectively. We would also like to thank our many colleagues who have written on the topic of violence over the years and have inspired us in ways that would be difficult to enumerate in a few words. Finally, we would like to extend our appreciation to everyone at Carolina Academic Press for their support on this project.

Why Violence?

Chapter 1

What Is the Meaning of Violence?

Violence is a conceptual enigma wrapped in a social paradox. Few concepts are so widely used, representing such a broad range of meanings and interpretations, and referring to such a vast spectrum of phenomena. While much violence is invisible, our society seems to be oversaturated with violence. It has countless forms of expression and appears in all social settings—in our homes, workplaces, schools, places of worship, and in communities as well as in recreational sports, entertainment, and across all levels of public and private institutions. It signifies many different things to people in different historical periods and in different cultural contexts. It conjures up lots of images of reality and is frequently associated with other actions, behaviors, events, or concepts such as crime, terrorism, and war. For example, it has been argued that violence is explicitly or implicitly a form of justice — expressed as punishment, retaliation, resistance, or revenge (Black, 1983).

Violence has been noted not only for its ubiquity (pervasiveness) and ambiguity (lack of clarity and uncertainty), but also its political exploitation (Imbusch, 2003). In fact, particular acts of violence may be considered legitimate and illegitimate at the same time, usually depending on who is applying the label and who is being labeled (Apter, 1997; Barak, 2003; 2007). For instance, during the war with Iraq, people in the U.S. referred to Iraq's military defense arsenal as weapons of "mass destruction" while referring to their own as "peacekeepers." Tony Platt (1992) comments that "the happy combination of relatively vague descriptive content, coupled with a negative moral and emotional connotation, makes the word violence ideal for use in polemic discourse" (pp. 187–188).

While violence is mainly known for its pejorative connotation and association with destructive and lethal consequences, the creation of fear, and as a cause of social disorganization and anomie, it is also used to respond to or rectify a problem (or justify action) and to bring upright consciousnesses together. For instance, politicians are always fighting violence with violence (e.g., "war on crime" or "war on terrorism"). In fact, the distinction between the legitimate and illegitimate use of violence is often blurry. Ray Surette (2007) observes: "In today's media the distinction between the crime fighter and the criminal has all but disappeared in regard to who initiates violence and how much force is used" (p. 113).

Since the concept of violence lacks concrete specificity and often functions to emotionally charge and politically define debates or the legitimacy of actions, it is important to approach any discussion of violence cautiously. This chapter, which serves to introduce this book, considers some of the most enduring questions related to the phenomenon of violence and explores multiple socially manifest and latent expressions of violence, including the symbolic ways in which violence is understood in contemporary society. We review violence topics ranging from common parlance, everyday perceptions and common myths to governmental proclamations and scientific claims.

Common Definitions

Violence is one of those "elephant" concepts that everyone recognizes when he or she sees it, but is hard-pressed to define it. Indeed, no single definition of violence has been proffered that meets with broad agreement. No definition successfully captures the complexities of its many forms and contexts. In everyday speech the term is used very generally and is often interchanged with other terms such as aggression, anger, hate, physical injury, and killing. Most English dictionaries draw the origins of violence from the Latin root words *violentus* or *violentia* (meaning physical force) and *violare* (meaning violation of the law). The definition of violence as physical force is one that is most commonly used.

Violence as Physical Force

The initial entry for violence in the *Oxford Dictionary* is: "The exercise of physical force so as to inflict injury on, or cause damage to, persons or property." At first glance, this definition may appear to be adequate, but on careful scrutiny it turns out to be too narrow. The definition implies the *direct* application of force as well as physical contact between the aggressor and victim or object. As a result, it leaves out many acts of violence. For instance, this definition of violence would exclude robbery. Under this definition the mere pulling of the trigger of a gun in a homicide may not itself suggest "physical force," yet given the consequences of such an act, it would not make sense to exclude the use of a gun (whether in a robbery or homicide) from a definition of violence. It is important to note that it does not take "physical force" per se to initiate a computer command to expel a guided missile (Alvarez and Bachman, 2008), yet this, too, is considered a violent act in terms of its consequences. The typical dictionary definition, as it stands, also omits the act of suicide since the aggressor and the victim are one and the same.

An important question, which is raised in connection with its definition in the context of physical force, is whether definitions of violence should include both physical and nonphysical injury/harm. Some scholars make a strong argument that both physical and nonphysical injury, such as psychological damage, should be included in definitions of violence. General bias against recognizing nonphysical forms of injury (thus denying victimization and ultimately justice) has been associated with cases of abuse such as intimate partner abuse (Bartol and Bartol, 2005). The United States military has only recently recognized brain injuries as "real" injuries in its award of the Purple Heart Medal for valor (Garamone, 2011).

Broader definitions of violence, such as "all types of behavior either threatened or actual that result in or are intended to result in the damage or destruction of property or the injury or death of an individual," are also problematic (Moyer, 1983, p. 1618). They encompass not only the different classes of homicide (premeditated, negligent, accidental, and justifiable), but also psychological or nonphysical harm and aggressive behaviors found in sports such as football or hockey. These broad definitions may actually be too inclusive, subsuming behaviors that may not be considered violent, per se.

Violence as Violation

Defining violence as violation, i.e., "to fail to keep or observe the law or to violate the law," however, is also not without complications. First, most legal violations are not violent; this is also true of violations of the criminal code—most criminal offenses are not violent. Second, there are many forms of violence that remain outside the law and are unsanctioned. Even by invoking legality in the definition of violence as physical force, e.g., by adjusting the version above to read: "all types of [*illegal*] behavior either threatened or actual, that result in the damage or destruction of property or in the injury or death of an individual" (Moyer, 1983, p. 1619), many forms of violence would still escape this legal definition.

Under this type of definition, the Nazi Holocaust, which resulted in the deaths of over six million people, would be considered "nonviolent" on the grounds that the acts constituted legal policies of the time. Currently, there are many forms of violence that are *not* part of any legal or criminal code, for instance, a wide range of regulatory violations committed by corporations, businesses, and public officials resulting in public injury and even deaths (e.g., safety violations, toxic waste dumping, and political corruption and human rights violations) (Geis, 2007; Barrile and Sloan, 2012).

In addition to the issue of legality, debates over what is necessary to include or exclude in various definitions have involved many other considerations including whether such definitions should take into account *intentionality* and considerations of subjective or emotional context, i.e., whether such acts are *instrumental* (means to an end) or *expressive* (emotionally motivated actions). Some definitions, for example, incorporate emotional qualities such as anger, hate, rage, or vehemence, along with physical force. However, this does not solve the problem of eliminating acts that should be considered violent by definition, e.g., the physical injury/killing perpetrated by a gunman or killer-for-hire, whose action may be calculated and instrumental (i.e., for monetary gain), would still be excluded from such definitions, particularly if intentionality is not factored in. According to most codes of law, intentionality plays an important role in determining degree of responsibility or liability. Unintentional violent acts generally carry lesser penalties or may be excused from criminal liability.

Levels of Violence

The complex issues associated with violence have led to a large variety of definitions offered over the decades. For example, a well-known definition of violence is: the "threat, attempt, or use of physical force by one or more persons that results in physical and non-physical harm to one or more persons" (Weiner, Zahn, and Sagi, 1990, p. xiii); this definition focuses attention exclusively on harmful acts committed by and to human beings.[1] Peter Iadicola and Anson Shupe (2003, p. 23) have expanded this definition by going beyond action by individuals and groups to add the institutions and structural foundations of society that results in harm. For them, "violence is any action or structural arrangement that results in physical or nonphysical harm to one or more persons." Under this definition the alleged public negligence leading up to the levee breech and widespread flooding associated with the aftermath of Hurricane Katrina (in New Orleans, in 2005) would be defined as a violent act. Increasing environmental degradation/destruction is being viewed as a form of violence stemming from institutional and structural levels of society (Pinker, 2011, pp. 375–377).

The question of level of violence, i.e., whether it is understood as an interpersonal, institutional, or structural problem, has been raised as an important consideration. Researchers have noted that most definitions tend to focus attention on interpersonal forms of violence and fail to include institutional and structural forms of violence (Barak, 2003; Iadicola and Shupe, 2003; Iadicola, 2012). This results in selectively reserving the label of violence for only certain forms of violence while keeping other forms relatively invisible or hidden from public purview, such as the type of harm and suffering, both physical and nonphysical, that comes from official denial (Cohen, 2001) or discriminatory social policies or institutional practices or through political indifference and inaction that leaves people homeless or without adequate medical care (Barak, 2007).

---

1. Iadicola (2012) also extends his definition to include animal victimization, which seems to be drawing more attention as a form of violence recently. It is interesting to note that we may be seeing a reversal of collective consciousness, e.g., the first Society for the Prevention of Cruelty against Animals established in New York (1866) historically predates the establishment of the Society for the Prevention of Cruelty to Children (1874) (ASPCA, 2011; Peck, 1989).

Interpersonal Violence

Interpersonal violence refers to acts of violence that occur between and among individuals interacting in a wide range of contexts of daily, private living. While some forms of violence in varying degrees may be allowed or tolerated (e.g., sibling violence, parents spanking children, sports violence, or accidental violence), interpersonal violence such as the main forms of criminal violence (e.g., homicide, rape, robbery, and assault) is typically considered illegitimate and illegal. In legal cases involving interpersonal violence the official victim is the state.

Interpersonal violence is the form of violence that the public knows most about. It is this type of violence that receives the most attention by public authorities as well as experts, and it is the most pervasive form portrayed by the mass media. As a result common definitions of violence usually focus on interpersonal expressions of violence and the majority of theories or causal models of violence typically address questions related to interpersonal acts of violence dealing largely with individual motivations of violent perpetrators. By focusing chiefly on micro-level or interpersonal forms of violence, however, public attention is deflected from other macro-level types of violence (e.g., state or political forms of violence). Thus, our typical understanding of violence, including our theories of the causes of violence tends to be personalized, resulting in a general failure to see larger social influences.

Institutional Violence

Institutional violence refers to acts of violence that emanate in the context of definitions and patterns of interactions and relationships within the social milieu of the fundamental institutions in society (such as the family and familial organizations, school and educational organizations, workplace and economic organizations, place of worship and religious organizations, and the state and the political/legal and public agencies or organizations). Institutionalized violence may be an implicitly acceptable way of interacting, which is a part of a long-standing tradition that is not usually treated as illegitimate. Some cases of institutional violence may not even be thought of as violence. For instance, forced intercourse in the context of a marital union may not be regarded as a form of criminal rape (see Easteal, 2012). Gross negligent homicide committed by a corporation's violation of safety rules or a public official's corruption that leads to the violation of human rights may be treated differently than similar acts committed by private individuals. For instance, complaints of personal injury by corporations are generally handled by civil courts and are usually subject to lesser penalties than matters that are brought before criminal courts. In the context of schools, examples may include ignoring abusive treatment of students by school authorities or even medicating students to keep them complicit and still or failing to offer an adequate education through discriminatory educational practices (e.g., tracking some students to succeed and others to fail). In the context of religious institutions, acts may range from violations of trust to abuse in the name of religion and religious-based terrorism (see Vollman, 2012). In the context of the military, acts may range from hazing of recruits to war crimes, such as the torture and killing of civilians or non-civilian enemy populations. Examples may also be found on the broader community level when there is political and public disregard shown for residents' needs in low income areas, which lack an infrastructure that adequately supports a community, i.e., the living spaces of truly disadvantaged populations that lack job opportunities, transportation, adequate housing, adequate schools, adequate child care, adequate health care, and other social services. In the context of State or political institutions, examples may include human rights violations by persons in authority or implementation of policies that work against certain groups by violating their fundamental human rights. These include detainment policies pertaining to "illegal" immigrants or, for instance, President Bush's suspension of the Davis-Bacon Act of 1931, which established minimum pay scales on Federal contracts following Hurricane Katrina that allowed contractors in New Orleans to pay less than the average minimum wage of the region to migrant workers brought in to help in the cleanup efforts.

Structural Violence

Structural violence refers to acts of violence that have been accepted as being necessary for the maintenance of the overall established pattern of organization of society. Iadicola and Shupe (2003) refer to this form as the "violence of the status quo." These acts of violence are authorized and are considered instrumental in protecting the fabric of society; and, therefore, they are officially acknowledged as legitimate. This form of violence is used to defend and reinforce the hierarchical patterns of society, which determine the power relationships across all spectrums of society. The maintenance function of structural violence is so important that it is rationalized and protected both physically (by the military and police forces) and psychologically (by dominating political ideology and philosophy).

Even though structural violence is believed to be an essential part of the established patterns of society and indispensable to people's survival, it often results in disproportionately affecting members of the more disadvantaged populations of society adversely. It is used to reinforce and maintain a hierarchy of inequality, often disregarding the basic needs and rights of people. According to Iadicola and Shupe (2003) structural violence is the most fundamental form of violence, affecting all other expressions of violence because it is rooted in the basic organizational structure of society and power-defining arrangements. Structural violence is accomplished through policies and laws that are enforced informally and formally, affecting both the extension and denial of civil, criminal, and basic human rights of people. Iadicola and Shupe (2003) point out that structural violence may include violence by either commission or omission. Poverty and homelessness in the context of affluent societies such as the U.S. represent archetypical illustrations of structural violence.

Iadicola and Shupe (2003) argue that violence is ultimately a form of power. The defining role of structural violence emerges at the global, systemic echelons of power (i.e., systems of stratification representing the transnational political economy) (Iadicola and Shupe, 2003; Iadicola, 2012). International structural violence serves the primary function of establishing and reinforcing the power relationships or balance of power in the world (see Mosher, 2012). Relative degree of power determines how violence in the international sphere is interpreted and responded to (e.g., whether weapons are considered "peacekeeping" devices or threats of "mass destruction"). The levels of violence are interconnected and re-produced across all spheres of relationships (structural, institutional, and interpersonal). The highest level of international structural violence, which determines the world order and balance of power, is reproduced between nations as well as within societies of the world, across all levels of relationships.

The Social Construction of Violence in Society

Even though violence is ubiquitous and appears on all levels, we still know very little about the nature of our perceptions or mental images of violence or how these images are created, developed, or changed. Questions, such as how do we come to know what is acceptable or unacceptable, what is criminal or noncriminal, what is normal or abnormal, what is moral or immoral, or what is legitimate or illegitimate use of violence, have interested human beings since antiquity. Emile Durkheim, one of the founding fathers of sociology and criminology, observes that it is important to understand that criminal behavior, including violent behavior, is not inherently legitimate or illegitimate, criminal or noncriminal, in and of itself. Rather, certain types of behavior are labeled criminal or violent or unacceptable by collective decision and definition of a group. For example, he states: "We must not say that an action shocks the common conscience because it is criminal, but rather that it is criminal because it shocks the common conscience" (1893/1960, p. 81). Durkheim uses killing to illustrate his point: The act of taking the life of another human being receives many responses depending on the social context. For instance, the three contextual sets below suggest possibilities of various interpretations or justifications for the act of killing, which may lead to different responses to perpetrators or victims or the act in general:

- Social roles (e.g., police officer v. private citizen)
- Social situations (e.g., defending one's life v. being angry v. seeking revenge)
- Social conditions/events (e.g., time of war v. time of peace).

Durkheim further claims that no known society is exempt from crime, including violent crime. Trying to envision a society in which violent and other criminal acts are no longer committed, he speculates: "Assuming that this condition could actually be realized, crime would not thereby disappear; it would only change its form, for the very cause which would thus dry up the sources of criminality would immediately open up new ones" (1895/1938, p. 67). It is important to point out that his reference to a change in form includes a change in social perception or collective consciousness. Once a particular type of behavior is no longer socially defined as criminal or violent another may take its place. Durkheim imagines a "Society of Saints," suggesting that behavior that would be normal under ordinary circumstances in ordinary society would be repugnant and become intolerable in a Society of Saints.

Our seemingly natural categorization of what constitutes violence and our spontaneous reactions to violence and violent offenders as well as our responses to crimes and criminals are actually consistent with the typical range of definitions and response norms that are determined by our social milieu (Quinney, 1970). This leads to the question: What is the process of social definition? Peter Berger and Thomas Luckmann (1967) in their seminal work, *The Social Construction of Reality*, argue that this question stems from a more fundamental sociological problem.

The theory of "the social construction of reality" suggests that there is no single "objective" or universally held definition of reality. Rather, there are many different and often competing realities, each defined by a different group or public. For example, the problem of violence concerns many different groups or publics, and represents a multiplicity of perspectives, values, experiences, and interpretations. The same empirical evidence or objective indicators, whether about society or violence, can be used to support a variety of interpretations of reality. For example, fluctuations in the rate of violent crimes may be variously interpreted as indicative of variations in:

- Laws and public policies (e.g., three-strikes laws)
- Law enforcement patterns (e.g., directed patrols of violence-hotspots)
- Public perceptions of safety and security (e.g., fear of crime and violence victimization)
- Economic conditions (e.g., connecting unemployment patterns and violence trends)
- Illicit drug use (e.g., linking cause of violence with drug use)
- Gun availability (e.g., inadequate background checks prior to sale of weapons)
- Mental health issues (e.g., lack of programs to treat mental illnesses)
- Mass media images of violence (e.g., oversaturation of violence in the media)
- Demographic patterns (e.g., the relative proportion of young men in the population).

Even this small sample of topics suggests a broad spectrum of interpretations that may be linked with understanding a particular change in the rate of violence. Each interpretation may be associated with a certain socially defined design or system of meanings that may be superimposed on "empirical facts" or data that otherwise may have no meaning. Indeed, there are different realities for the different segments of the population who hold particular perspectives or interpretations. For example, a very different set of facts and social reality including common explanations or causes is associated with linking violence with the availability or use of guns than connecting violence with certain economic conditions. Each socially defined interpretation or perspective is based on certain sets of assumptions about human behavior and society and is expressed with select data, reference to particular behaviors/actions/situations, carefully chosen concepts, and language or metaphors that evoke different emotions and reactions (see Whitt, Corzine, and Huff-Corzine, 2012).

Given all the possibilities for divergent interpretations, one may wonder whether consensus is even possible in society. Yet, there is relative social consensus from time to time. For example, while there may be vigorous debate over the validity and reliability of official crime statistics, such as the accounts of crimes known to the police that are compiled and distributed annually by the FBI in *Uniform Crime Reports* (UCR), there is still relatively widespread support for the continued collection and analysis of these data. Even though there are recognized shortcomings of UCR data (e.g., the UCR's relatively limited definition of criminal violence and measurement of violent offenses), most people agree that UCR statistics are indicators of certain realities. Moreover, the statistics may be associated with certain types of behaviors or reactions on all levels (i.e., individual, institutional, and structural levels). For instance, certain rates of violence may inspire the creation of national commissions to study the problem and to recommend solutions that may be followed by sweeping social changes, reconstruction of national policies and procedures, or enactment of new laws (e.g., *U.S. National Commission on the Causes and Prevention of Violence*, 1969) or they may provide justification for state and local intervention policies or official decisions such as hiring more law enforcement personnel or increasing the operating budgets of law enforcement agencies. These statistics may also affect individual prevention tactics such as avoiding walking alone at night or carrying a gun for protection. Accordingly, the violent crime rate may be perceived as real with real consequences. Such generalized agreement may be referred to as *consensual reality*.

It is worth noting that consensual reality is rooted in public opinion and is not dependent on any criterion of truth (Berger and Luckmann, 1967). For instance, social reactions to UCR information depend on the extent to which people or certain groups accept the reality of the statistics and can identify with the perceived consequences. Consensual reality is both socially and psychologically significant. It represents the primary form of operative reality that most people have. Indeed, according to Berger and Luckmann (1967) the social construction of reality is fundamentally based on agreement. They divide consensual reality into two main types: informal and formal.

Informal Consensual Reality v. Formal Consensual Reality

Informal consensual reality refers to "truths" as found in common sense data (including accumulated traditions, anecdotes, folklore, and myths), personal experiences, and certain episodes. Most of us believe and act on whatever we have learned to be true from our family, friends, communities, and society in general. In other words, we do not have to be a victim of a violent crime, or even to have known someone who was, to have attitudes or knowledge about violence or violent crime and criminal justice. We obtain our knowledge and form our perceptions and attitudes in the course of our daily interactions.

Our common sense data sources also include vicarious experiences. Vicarious experiences may be understood as interpersonal communication between individuals and the mass media. The mass media, especially television and the internet, play a significant role in the formation of our images of the nature and extent of violence in society, including our understanding of laws and the criminal justice system, or even our own personal sense of risk of victimization (see Ostertag, 2012). The point has been made that "vicarious knowledge of crime may constitute a form of indirect victimization" (Skogan and Maxfield, 1981, p. 164). Surette (2007) writes: "More than ever before, an individual today can experience crime and criminal justice through the media and come away with the sensation of an actual experience" (pp. 23–24).

For many people, despite the ubiquity of the internet and its ability to mobilize thousands of people, television still serves to authenticate news or events in the larger world. Television allows unprecedented large numbers of people (who may be geographically, ideologically, and epistemologically very distant) to share social events. Thus, television events often constitute the main common experience related to violence that people in general may have. News of a sensational occurrence of violence or violent event portrayed on television (such as the September 11th, 2001 [9-11] terrorist attack on the World Trade Center towers in New York City) may represent one of the most widely shared common referent to violence that different groups around the globe share. The exact nature and extent of media influences on our general consensual reality or common stock knowledge is still poorly understood (see Taylor, 2012).

Formal consensual reality originates from individuals connected with institutions generally regarded as authorities or experts. The formal definitions of reality are distinguished from the informal types primarily by their presumably more systematic or scientific nature. Often, formally constructed reality is believed to be neutral or objective in character. This point, however, has been widely debated (e.g., Chambliss, 1984; Brownstein, 2000). The experts may come from all the major sectors of society (e.g., religious, political/governmental, economic, and scientific or academic institutions). Expert testimony comes in many different forms, including government reports and statistics; published books and articles; internet, television, and newspaper interviews; and documentaries. Experts in one field are usually acknowledged by experts in others. Even though "expert" knowledge has its critics and admitted relative strengths and weakness, most people treat expert knowledge and opinions as being more valid and reliable than lay information. Of course, this does not suggest that there is no competition for dominance among the different experts from different institutions. In fact, rivalry among various experts in promoting their respective perspectives and social definitions of violence is vigorous.

No matter how neutral or unbiased certain groups or experts claim to be, their special interests underlie their perspective and construction of reality. Scientific communities as well as the wide range of scientists who study violence (e.g., criminologists, sociologists, psychologists, and public health researchers) are also subject to the principle of consensual reality. "Scientific reality," regardless of which discipline is represented, constitutes a unique kind of social construction of reality with its own sets of facts, concepts or symbols, theories, and specially constructed knowledge. Indeed, the presence of scientific knowledge in the mix of social definitions and knowledge-base related to violence, itself, represents a cultural contingency. Not all cultures have such a large number of widely diverse scientists (e.g., criminologists) represented in their cultural distribution of knowledge pertaining to violence. It is important to underscore, however, that the same social dynamics characterize scientific knowledge regarding violence. Agreement is fundamental to the construction of reality among the various scientific communities, with each offering rival theories and evidence and making various "scientific claims" about violence based on their respective disciplines and unique theoretical paradigms or perspectives. Thomas Kuhn (1962/1970) in his celebrated book, *The Structure of Scientific Revolutions*, argues that scientific claims of various scientific communities are validated more by *social support* or agreement (i.e., as expressed in specific disciplinary paradigms or perspectives including accepted theories and methodologies or fundamental assumptions that bind members of a particular scientific community) than by empirical evidence (p.124).

Common Stock Knowledge

General consensual reality or common stock knowledge may be diffused across a society by such characteristics as social class, age, sex, occupation, political preference, place of residence, race and ethnicity, and religion. Public interest groups of all sorts produce their own perspectives and interpretations of reality or "socially segregated sub-universes of meaning" (Berger and Luckmann, 1967, p. 45). The number and variety of definitions of reality that emerge, which may be equally embraced by various interest groups or publics, may be described in terms of the "social distribution of knowledge" (p. 46). The different sets of assumptions, concepts, facts, values, and priorities of people and groups comprise their respective definitions of reality, which often compete with other definitions of reality, thus leading to "rival definitions of reality" (p. 120).

Henry Brownstein (2000) in his book, entitled *The Social Reality of Violence and Violent Crime*, writes:

Ultimately, public opinion, public policy, and public practice with regard to violence are the products of claims making. Claims are made through stories that are told by governmental officials, the media, and other social actors with a stake in the meaning given to violence in order to support a representation of violence that is favorable to their own values and interests (p. 10).

How much social support is necessary for a particular definition or interpretation to be accepted by the broader society? What effects does the relative power of rival interest groups with their respective claims have on the diffusion of certain perspectives on problems such as violence? Such questions are crucial to an understanding of the social construction of violence (Best, 2001; Potter and Kappeler, 2006). Similar to Durkheim, Herbert Blumer (1971) argues that social problems such as violence are not inherently problems, but are made into problems by our collective defining processes determined by the social life cycles of particular social problems. Blumer (1971) suggests that our current social problems, including the problem of violence, are defined as such only after passing through a number of stages, for example:

- *Emergence:* Making the public aware of the problem (e.g., through an explosive event [such as the 9-11 attack], which is usually widely covered by the mass media, or brought to the attention of the public by widely-known cultural or political celebrities, such as the President of the United States);

- *Legitimization:* Demonstrating evidence (in the form of cases, statistics, research results) of the gravity and extent of the problem;

- *Mobilization:* Building social support and interest and getting different publics to place a priority on committing attention and resources to addressing the problem;

- *Formation of Official Plans:* Engaging groups (representing experts from both the public and private sectors) in finding/recommending solutions and developing a plan of action (e.g., recommending new legislation or new policies);

- *Implementation of Official Plans:* Enacting new laws, establishing new agencies or restructuring organizations, and instituting new policies and programs; and then

- *Redefinition of the problem:* Beginning the cycle over again.

Over the past century, various types of violence have socially cycled through the stages and have emerged at the top of the national agenda of social problems, e.g., violence as a problem of immigration; or violence in connection with organized crime, juvenile delinquency, collective movements, illicit drugs, guns, hate crimes, school violence, and terrorism; or violence as expressed in child abuse, intimate partner homicides, and serial murders, to name a few. Some violence problems have cycled multiple times, often with a different point of emphasis or thematic connection, e.g., terrorism as a problem of national defense; terrorism as a problem of national intelligence information and predictability; and terrorism as a problem of homeland security.

Cultural Indicators of Violence: Language and Metaphors

Language as a key indicator of culture may also suggest ways particular societies approach violence. Does the way we speak affect our thoughts and behavior? More specifically, does violent rhetoric ultimately lead to violent behavior? This question has been raised in connection with the Tucson, Arizona, January 8, 2011, shooting of Gabrielle Giffords and the vitriolic comments posted on Sarah Palin's (former governor of Alaska and Republican vice-presidential candidate in 2008) Web site and *Facebook* sites, which featured "cross-hairs" over Representative Giffords' district in Arizona in a political advertisement that made reference to "reloading" for the political battle ahead (Berman, 2011). It has been alleged that this type of violent rhetoric may have possibly been a precursor of the subsequent shooting. This question leads to the larger question of the affects of the metaphors of violence in our society and their symbolic use or abuse, particularly in the political arena.

George Lakoff and Mark Johnson (2003) write that "the essence of a metaphor is understanding and experiencing one kind of thing in terms of another" (p. 5). Typically when we think of a metaphor, we think of a literary tool; we also usually consider metaphors to be a part of poetic or literary language rather than ordinary, everyday language. Lakoff and Johnson, however, argue that metaphors are pervasive in our daily lives not just in expressions of language, but also in our thoughts and actions and, thus, they play a very important role in structuring our everyday realities. Violence as a common metaphor is ubiquitous in most cultures and is usually an integral part of the everyday patterns of communication.

Indeed, violence has become the quintessential metaphor that we all live by. It is symbolically ingrained in our language, thinking, and behavior. Violence metaphors are part of our daily interactions. For example, we employ the metaphor of violence, particularly the metaphor of war, to structure many of our daily experiences such as making an argument or participating in a debate, expressing love, developing a plan of action, or describing social policies. For instance, an argument may be described as a *battle of wits*. Arguments are *won* or *lost*. Parties to an argument are typically referred to as *opponents*. They *attack* the weak points of arguments or they *counterattack arguments*. And, if a position does not work, a *new line of attack* is considered. Even love is often described in terms of a battle (e.g., we *fight to win* the love of our beloved). Planning regardless of the institutional context (e.g., a military unit, a government agency, a business enterprise, or a university) is usually framed in military terms. For example, when we speak of "strategic planning," we often refer to the relative *strengths, weaknesses, opportunities* and *threats, mobilizing resources, combating challenges*, and *forming tactics* or *action plans*. Social problems and policies, particularly those that make it to the national level, are also frequently described using the metaphor of war. For instance, over the decades U.S. presidents have declared not only foreign wars, but also domestic wars (e.g., recall President Kennedy's War on Delinquency, Johnson's War on Poverty, Nixon's War on Cancer, Regan's War on Drugs, G.W. Bush's War on Terrorism, and the numerous presidents who have over the decades declared wars on crime). The presidential elections are also frequently portrayed in terms of the metaphor of war. In the 2012 presidential election there have been references to the *battleground states* (with references to candidates "fighting" over various states to "win" a majority of electoral college votes); *ground war* (referring to time candidates put into small political activity, i.e., meeting people and shaking hands); and *air war* (referring to media coverage serving to bombard the public with candidate's position on issues and distortions of opponents messages) (Voigt and Thornton, 2011).

What is important to note here is that many of our daily interactions and activities are characterized by metaphors of violence (e.g., fighting, destroying, and attacking). In this sense the metaphor of violence is a cultural metaphor that we all encounter in our daily lives. It structures our relationships, especially those relationships that have competitive elements. Indeed, it is worth underscoring that while most verbal battles do not result in physical battles; many physical battles are preceded by verbal battles. For example, David Luckenbill (1977) in his well known article, "Criminal Homicide as a Situated Transaction," notes that over 40% of murders include an offensive interchange between an offender and victim. According to the *Uniform Crime Reports* (2010), when the circumstances of murder are known, 42% of victims are killed during arguments (FBI, 2011).

It is also important to emphasize that framing such social activities as arguing, planning, or loving in terms of the metaphor of war or violence may have the effect of focusing our attention to certain aspects while hiding certain other aspects of these activities. For example, when we approach an argument in war terms, we may fail to see other possibilities, such as considering an argument in terms of compromise or taking less extreme positions or an alternative framework, e.g., structuring an argument in terms of a rational activity by stating a premise, citing supporting evidence, drawing a logical conclusion, and serving the purpose of enhancing understanding.

Lakoff and Johnson (2003) maintain that the most critical aspect of metaphors is that they are experienced and they have consequences in reality. On a micro-level, metaphors not only represent an individual's way of looking at reality, but also may give license for individual action. On the macro-level, metaphors not only frame the leading issues, but they also provide support or justification for political action such as legislative enactments or policy changes or social interventions by public agencies. Political use of conventional metaphors of war or violence, both old and new, can define reality in terms of selected issues and ideas, serving to highlight some features of reality and hide others.

The general uncertainty or ambiguity associated with the concept of violence as well as its catchall and ubiquitous nature has contributed to its use (or abuse) as a *pejorative label,* which is typically connected with threatening, destructive, lethal, and often illegitimate connotations, rather than its employment as a referent to concrete phenomenon. Peter Imbusch (2003) persuasively argues that violence employed as a negative label usually plays the role of a "summary symbol" and commonly serves the function of an "intensifier." Anyone or anything that is summarily labeled as "violent" is immediately held in contempt or is feared and assumed to be pathological as well as illegitimate or illegal.

Moreover, pejorative labels usually apply exclusively to "others" and not to ourselves or those who occupy positions of authority. Labels such as criminal, crazy, immoral, and violent are generally reserved for less powerful individuals and groups in society (Reiman, 1990). State agencies such as the criminal justice system or the mental health system or schools typically generate and apply various labels as mechanisms of social control and as justification for intrusive action (e.g., incarceration or commitment to a treatment facility). The public knows much more about those who are labeled than those who do the labeling. Most people accept these labels uncritically. In fact, however, those who are socially or politically powerful are usually in advantaged positions to inflict their metaphors or labels on others who are in less powerful positions (Weber, 1978).

For instance, most political and economic ideologies may be couched in terms of certain metaphors that typically work to justify certain actions and veil certain dehumanizing conditions or coercive aspects. Thus, for example, those who support our nation's military involvement or war in a particular area may be more likely to use metaphors and terms that sanitize war such as "collateral damage" rather than "civilian causalities." Or, on the domestic front, violence may be presented as stemming from impoverished, "disorganized" neighborhoods or "broken" families, giving politicians justification for certain intervention policies, such as relocating families or assigning custody of children to the state. When metaphors such as the one that links disorganized neighborhoods with violence are employed, the public at large may be prevented from considering ways to empower or build neighborhood capacity and social capital.

Power also determines the degree of responsibility as well as the type of response that is given to certain acts of violence. Typically, government officials who commit acts of corruption or who violate human rights are rarely held criminally liable. Corporate CEOs who are responsible for consciously making business decisions that result in harmful consequences or the loss of lives are more likely to be dealt with by the civil courts and fined rather than by criminal courts and imprisoned. The same pattern may be observed among sovereign states — global power determines what is ultimately labeled by the global community as legitimate and illegitimate uses of force and violence. Nation states utilize violence and violence labels for their own political benefit and to amplify certain realities and underplay other realities (e.g., Giddens, 1985).

Similarly, by focusing on violence metaphors and making violence the object of scientific study, including criminological investigation, researchers may wittingly or unwittingly disregard the roots of peace and cooperation. For example, some biological and evolutionary theories of human violent behavior have been criticized for minimizing mitigating factors and for ignoring human nonaggressive, cooperative, and peaceful tendencies. Focusing on violence may have the effect of preventing both researchers and the public, especially those who believe that aggression or violence is natural and, therefore, inevitable, from working toward peace.

Various metaphors underlying the construct of violence are able to influence perceptions as well as actions in ways that many people may not even be aware of. For instance, if violence itself is defined in terms of a *disease*, attention may be drawn to finding a cause of the disease or identifying a *cure* or instituting a *prevention* program. On the other hand, if violence is defined as a crime, the emphasis may be on *control* or *deterrence* and may lead to legislating stiffer penalties or building more prisons. Again, when reviewing various definitions or theories of violence and applications of violence labels, it is important to note that they often expose us to certain aspects of human social relationships, while blinding us to others. It is also worth noting that a particular bias may impede our ability to understand the full nature of human beings, the nature of society, and the role of violence metaphors in structuring how we think about and respond to events and actions or even how we relate to one another.

Moreover, it is not a metaphor's accuracy/validity or falsity that is the critical factor of consideration, but the level of awareness and the conclusions that follow from it and the actions that are ultimately sanctioned by it. The main problem that emerges from this is that the public is a great deal more conscious of the ideological scripts and rhetorical summaries connected with responding to "violence with violence" or "peace through war and conflict" instead of "peace through cooperation or compromise or conflict resolution" or "peace through meeting the needs of people."

Hence, what often appears to be people's spontaneous reaction to violence may actually be reflective of the typical range of metaphors and labels and their associated scripted response norms that are historically and culturally defined and mediated. What people in their social milieu consider unacceptable violence has varied over historical periods and across cultures. For example, infanticide, slavery, burning people at the stake, and cruelty as entertainment are relatively rare today and considered unacceptable in most parts of the world (Pinker, 2011).

Mass Media Images v. the Reality of Violence

The mass media, including print and electronic, is an important agent in the diffusion of all types of information pertaining to violence, especially violence metaphors. For example, reporting of violent crime news (including print, online, and television news), while certainly not just a contemporary concern, has been studied with regard to how it affects people's estimates and interpretations of the prevalence of violence or violent crime in society. It has been found that the frequency and nature of violent crime coverage by the media affect people's own assessment of safety, level of fear, and accommodation or reactive behavior (Surette, 2007). The media also affect people's appraisal of the criminal justice system, and consequently, how they vote (Dowler, 2003).

In addition, the media, including entertainment media, shapes people's understanding of the nature of violence. For instance, the media places primary attention on criminally motivated interpersonal acts of physical force rather than on harmful acts emanating from institutional or structural levels. The public is much more attuned to individual motivating factors associated with violence than any contributing social forces. Evidence gathered over the years indicates that the amount of violent crime depicted in the media grossly over represents rare and extreme violent acts and generally bears little relationship to official counts of violent crime (e.g., as reported in *Uniform Crime Reports* [UCR]) (Rapping, 2003). Over-reporting of violent, sensational crimes may signal to the public that all crime is on the rise, when in fact this may not be the case (Surette, 2007). While violent crime, especially the rate of homicide, has been steadily decreasing in the U.S. since 1993, the typical public perception is that violent crime is rising (Saad, 2007; Sourcebook of Criminal Justice Statistics Online). George Gerbner and his associates note that the more time that individuals spend watching television daily, the more likely they believe that violence is rampant and on the rise and the more fearful they are of being victims of violent crimes (Gerbner, et al., 1994).

The public, however, often fails to realize just how selective the media is in reporting news, especially violent crime news. Historical and contemporary studies have consistently revealed that the print and electronic news services are literally the gatekeepers of the news by selecting and filtering stories (Fishman, 1979; Muraskin and Domash, 2007). The more sensationalistic and violent the criminal event, such as acts of terrorism, school shootings, and gang shootings, or any mass shooting, particularly when body counts are high, the more likely the criminal event will get the greatest journalistic coverage (Duwe, 2000).

Just as the media may affect public perceptions of the amount of criminal violence in society, so, too, it may affect public images of typical violent events, offenders, and victims. Almost without exception, *violent interpersonal crimes*, especially homicides, are disproportionately represented in media depictions of violence in the United States (Muraskin and Domash, 2007). Inconsistencies between the official accounts of violent crime and media reporting have raised questions regarding the causal connection between media images and public beliefs about violence in society (National Institute of Mental Health, 1982; Gerbner, et al., 1986; Gerbner, et al., 1994; Bushman and Anderson, 2001; Reiner, 2002; Peelo, et al., 2004). The argument proffered is that people accept the media's version of violence (especially as reported in the news media) because most people have minimal or no direct experiences with violent offenses, violent offenders, or victims of violence during their lives.

What a lot of people do not realize is that what appear to be crime waves, often involving violence, are a special kind of "social awareness of crime," referring to the "continued and heavy coverage of numerous occurrences, which journalists report as a single topic"

(Fishman, 1979, p. 534). Crime news themes allow reporters or journalists to make a single incident or relatively few incidents part of a larger phenomenon. Themes have longer life spans than individual incidents and as a result can be part of longer range assignments and news planning efforts. Crime themes, especially violent crime themes, facilitate the development of special in-depth coverage of an incident. Crime news is cheap and easy news because it is always available, easy to obtain, and easy to develop and spin. As a result it has become a mainstay in media reporting.

An example of a violent crime wave, which appears from time to time, may be school shootings. Despite a common perception that it is on the rise, the number of school shootings has not significantly increased in the U.S. in the past 10 years, and, in fact, most types of school crimes have decreased since the early 1990s (Lawrence, 2007). Although highly publicized in the media, school shootings amount to a very small number of students being affected by these shootings. Yet, *looping* or repetitive or recycled coverage of school shootings as, for example, demonstrated by the immense coverage of the 1999 Columbine High School shootings in Littleton, Colorado, has provided the media with a "newsworthy" theme that has been covered over and over again and expanded through linkage with other subjects such as youth crime or gun control (Killingbeck, 2001).

Crime news themes can also be further developed around some broader public issues such as enforcement or legislative, political, and community responses to the problem. In the case of school shootings, immense efforts have focused on the suspected causes of school violence at the individual, school, and neighborhood level. The United States Secret Service, for example, developed a profile of school shootings and shooters (Vossekuil, et al., 2000). Most states have passed legislation creating weapons-free or safe-school zone statutes. Schools have cooperated with juvenile court officials such as probation officers to share information regarding students with official (criminal) records and developed zero tolerance policies for possessing weapons and/or drugs and engaging in any violent activities on campus. Schools around the country have also revised their school safety plans and they have target-hardened their facilities with metal detectors and surveillance cameras. Many have also hired school resource officers to coordinate their safety plans.

On December 14, 2012, Adam Lanza, killed 25 people (20 of whom were children aged 6-10) and himself at Sandy Hook Elementary School in Newtown, Connecticut. This incident is considered to be the second deadliest school shooting in U.S. history following the 2007 mass shooting at Virginia Polytechnic Institute. The Sandy Hook shooting has rekindled the national debate on gun control. Even though President Obama has called for a ban on assault weapons and has formed a workgroup to find ways to reduce gun violence, public opinion polls and recent spikes in gun sales suggest that many Americans may still be leery of supporting strict gun control legislation (Time, January 14, 2012, pp. 14-15). The incident along with the resurgence of the debate on gun control that it sparked has been receiving a steady stream of extensive media coverage.

In 2005, during Hurricane Katrina, the mass media played a particularly crucial role in formulating national and international public opinion regarding crime, particularly violent crime, taking place in New Orleans. The media created a social construction of reality regarding perceptions of crime, crime control, and public safety during and immediately after Katrina struck New Orleans. Despite minimal information regarding crime due to a temporary hiatus in the crime reporting functions of the police, particularly during the emergency phase of the storm, the national and international news reporting agencies overwhelmingly painted a picture of a city out of control with stories of murder, rape, armed robbery, pedophilia, looting, and images of marauding criminal gangs. While violent crimes and other crimes did occur during and after this disaster, normative behavior by far characterized the unfolding events. However, violent crimes were made to appear rampant through use of media looping, i.e., repetitive and exaggerated coverage of selected events. The negative portrayals of violence in the aftermath of Katrina, however, left an indelible image of a crime-ridden city, effecting perceptions of dangerousness and stereotypic connections of poverty and crime, and reinforcing an image of a city that hope has forgotten (Thornton and Voigt, 2006).

One of the main consequences of violent crime waves is that this type of reporting dramatically increases the public's level of fear. Heavy reporting of violence by the mass media can generate what has been referred to as a "moral panic," i.e., "a condition, episode, person or group of persons that emerges to become defined as a threat to societal values and interests" (Cohen, 1972, p. 9). Some moral panics may be of short duration, but others may produce wide-spread public opinions as well as be associated with legal and social policy changes that have longer-term effects (Cohen, 1972; Jenkins, 1998; Burns and Crawford, 2006; Weitzer, 2007).

Surette (2007) suggests that the role and relative impact of mass media on public perceptions and understanding of crime, violence, and criminal justice in the twenty-first century must be considered with respect to several important points, including:

- The main goals of the media is to create mediated images, which are indistinguishable from reality
- In the United States the mass media is mainly motivated and determined by the marketplace. The underlying assumption is that the time honored method of getting the attention of large numbers of people quickly is to follow the common adage: "If it bleeds it leads!"
- The public cannot depend on governmental agencies to enforce truth and accuracy in reporting

From the perspective of mass media, violence, especially violent crime, is a highly valuable, profitable commodity.

Competing Perspectives on Violence

Violence information, attitudes, and perceptions are communicated to us daily both formally and informally across our society. However, certain elite groups in our society (i.e., groups that have relatively greater power and legitimacy than other groups), not the majority of citizens, are more likely to determine which social problems/issues overall gain notoriety and official support (Blumer, 1971). This is true of how the problem of violence has been defined and approached by our society historically (Quinney, 1970; Weber, 1978; Brownstein, 2000; Barak, 2003; Alvarez and Bachman, 2008).

The experts on violence (such as crime experts, terrorist experts, and war experts) in our society are numerous and represent a large spectrum of perspectives. The government, mass media, and the various interest/reform groups with sufficient power and means to lobby for their interests select the violence problems that will receive the greatest public attention or traction. Convergence on an issue (either in the form of support or nonsupport) is part of the process of the social construction of violence, especially regarding what aspects of violence reach crisis proportions, such as school violence or drug violence, as well as what issues reach the top of the public or political agenda.

While there may be sharing of information and occasional congruence in general orientation, the various perspectives on violence represent unique sets of goals, motivations, and activities as well as unique types of experts, organizational entities, and hierarchy of leadership. Ultimately, different perspectives may be associated with certain definitions and metaphors of violence along with distinct uses of knowledge and information. Even though the perspectives operate independently, they frequently compete with one another for resources and general public attention and acceptance of their respective construction of the reality of violence in society.

To facilitate our understanding of the nature of competition among violence experts and to enhance our appreciation of the fundamental differences among certain violence/crime experts regarding the significance of various definitions or social constructions of violence, we will review four broad areas of competing conceptualizations of violence: (1) the criminal justice perspective, (2) the public health perspective, (3) the human rights perspective, and (4) the commercial/commodity perspective. It is important to underscore that the perspectives as described here represent only a small sample of some of the broad categories of perspectives on violence that compete for attention on a daily basis.

Criminal Justice Perspective

For nearly half a century the problem of violence (excluding military violence) in the United States has been considered to be primarily a criminal justice issue. The President's Commission on Law Enforcement and Administration of Justice (1968) defined violence in terms of criminal violence (i.e., homicide, rape, robbery, and assault). Since the 1930s, the FBI's *Uniform Crime Reports* (UCR) has provided the official annual measure of these violent crimes in the United States. Brownstein aptly notes: "Violent crime has largely become a proxy for all violence. The public and its social representatives have constructed the social meaning of violence in terms of violent crime" (2000, p. 10).

The criminal justice system (CJS) is comprised of federal, state, and local criminal justice agencies (including law enforcement or police agencies, courts, and correctional institutions including treatment/rehabilitation centers and other specialized programs). While data gathering activities are conducted (e.g., *Uniform Crime Reports*), information is not the main focus of the criminal justice system. The primary goal of the criminal justice system is to maintain laws and social order and to ensure the public's safety and well-being. The governmental divisions and agencies, which deal with crime-related cases and problems, including violent crimes, are usually part of larger social welfare and public service networks at the local, state, and federal levels.

The criminal justice system's primary focus on interpersonal acts of violence (i.e., homicide, rape, robbery, and assault) much to the exclusion of other forms of violence, particularly institutional or structural forms of violence, has been debated for nearly a century. In an effort to address public criticisms regarding its relatively narrow definition of violent crimes, the criminal justice system has expanded its attention to include some special initiatives on the control of intimate partner and domestic violence as well as violence related to offenses such as drug use/distribution, gang activities, and sexual misconduct—especially offenses against young people. For example, at the law enforcement level, the police have tried making mandatory arrests for domestic violence offenders; they have also focused on proactive arrests for high-risk repeat offenders and engaged in directed patrols of drug and gun violence-hotspots. In addition, many states have enacted various laws that harshly penalize sex offenders and/or require them to register and be monitored (Megan's Laws) (Worrall, 2008). At the court level, tough sentences have been handed down for career offenders using mandatory three-strikes laws (for a third felony), selective incapacitation (i.e., more lengthy incarcerations for select violent offenders), and sentencing enhancements (e.g., longer sentences for use of a gun in a crime). Through the use of involuntary civil commitment, dangerous sex offenders, after serving their time in prison, may be involuntarily committed to a mental facility if it is determined that they are not cured and are a danger to the community (Worrall, 2008, p.140).

The criminal justice system employs a myriad of professionals and government personnel. Most of the professionals are law enforcement officers, judges, attorneys, justice administrators, corrections officers, probation and parole officers, social workers, counselors, forensic experts, laboratory technicians, coroners, and a large assortment of bureaucrats and organizational staff. The researchers/academics (e.g., criminologists) who are employed in the criminal justice system are typically referred to as "applied" practitioners; they usually function as researchers, evaluators, and consultants.

Since funding and program support are determined by governmental and legislative bodies, the criminal justice system cannot be discussed apart from the political establishment. Consequently, the criminal justice system comprises a sizeable set of governmental officials who, together, have an important impact on politics and the social definition of crime and especially of violence in the United States. Federal, state and local governments of the United States spend over two and one half billion dollars annually for criminal justice at the local, state, and federal levels (U.S. Department of Justice, 2009).

As noted earlier, the primary definition of violence promoted by the criminal justice system, which is expressed in terms of the four types of interpersonal acts of violence (i.e., homicide, rape, robbery and assault), is in fact the definition/perspective on violence that is most widely distributed in the United States. In summary, the identifying key points of the criminal justice perspective on violence include the following:

- The criminal justice system (CJS) emphasizes interpersonal attacks.
- The CJS mode of intervention is mainly reactive.
- CJS personnel focus on offender's intentions, motivations, and background. Restorative Justice (RJ), which focuses on the injury resulting from violence and gives equal weight to victim, offender, and community needs, is still marginally recognized as an alternative to the CJ perspective (Sullivan and Tifft, 2005).
- Greater weight is given to incidents resulting in serious injury (Moore, 1995).
- Solutions are mainly based on *control,* especially through *incapacitation* and *deterrence.*

Public Health Perspective

Violent acts according to the public health (PH) perspective are considered *health* problems and are typically viewed as intentional injuries as opposed to unintentional injuries. In essence, the PH approach is a research and prevention oriented science concerned with a variety of types of violence (Green, 2002). Evidence of PH responses to violence within the national health agenda began to appear in the 1980s and continue to the present time. The Centers for Disease Control (CDC) created the Violence

Epidemiology Branch in 1983, which later was integrated into the Division of Injury Epidemiology and Control (DIEC). Supporters of the PH model argue that violence should be viewed as a public health issue because of the detrimental effects that it has on individual's health and well-being and on the very social fabric of a society. The PH approach, which focuses mainly on the *prevention* of interpersonal violence, stems from the formal recognition given in 1984 when Surgeon General C. Everett Koop stated: "Violence is every bit as much a public health issue for me and my successors in this century as smallpox, tuberculosis, and syphilis were for my predecessors in the last century" (Green, 2002). Koop's interest stimulated the Surgeon General's Workshop on Violence and Public Health in 1985, which brought violence to the forefront of public attention and encouraged all healthcare professionals to respond. There are several factors that have contributed to the recognition and acceptance of the idea that violence should be treated as a *disease* and addressed from a PH perspective:

- With advances in the prevention and treatment of many infectious diseases, homicide and suicide concomitantly rose in the rankings in the U.S. as the leading causes of death. For example, from 1985 to 1991, homicide rates among 15–19 year-old males increased 154 percent, and were especially acute for young Black males. Given the advances in medicine to "cure" many of the earlier infectious diseases, public health practitioners believed that prevention of violence, like certain other types of diseases that kill large numbers of people (e.g., heart disease, stroke, and cancer), largely depends on *behavioral modifications* in life style (Dahlberg and Mercy, 2009, p. 1).

- Several early landmark studies highlight the impact of the PH influence on violence control in the U. S. The Surgeon General's Report, *Healthy People* (1979), which received wide national attention demonstrated the advances made in the health of Americans over a 100 year period and noted 5 key areas (including control of violence in an effort to improve the health of children, adolescents, and young adults) where further gains could be made using the PH model. *Promoting Health/Preventing Disease: Objectives for the Nation* (U.S. Department of Health & Human Services, 1980) also got a national press by focusing on its objectives to significantly reduce violence by 1990 in: (1) the number of child-abuse injuries and deaths; (2) rate of homicide among black males 15–24 years old; (3) rate of suicide among 15–24 year olds; (4) number of privately owned handguns; and (5) improvements in the reliability of data on child abuse and family violence. In 1985, the *Report of the Secretary's Task Force on Black and Minority Health* brought the national spotlight on the PH perspective on violence when it "identified homicide as a major cause of the disparity in death rate and illness experienced by African Americans and other minorities relative to non-Hispanic whites" (Dahlberg and Mercy, 2009, p. 2). Moreover, the *Report of the Secretary's Task Force on Youth Suicide* (1989), which was also nationally discussed, described the scope of the problem of youth suicide going back three decades. With overwhelming evidence of various patterns of violence, relatively clear objectives and target populations, and a strong call for action on the part of the health professional community on all levels, including the AMA, the PH movement appeared to effect changes heretofore not seen.

Beginning in 1992 the CDC shifted its PH focus from describing the parameters of violence to prevention efforts, particularly in approaching the problem of youth violence and homicide. Through a series of evaluation studies produced over several decades, public health professionals have demonstrated that significant reductions in aggressive and violent behavior could be achieved with "applied, skill-based violence-prevention programs that address social, emotional, and behavioral competencies, as well as family environments" (Dahlberg and Mercy, 2009, p. 5). These achievements, which are published in *Youth Violence: A Report of the Surgeon General* (2001), include the identification of the risk factors that lead young people to gravitate toward violence as well as the factors that protect youth from perpetrating violence within and across various domains (e.g., peer group, family, school, and community) and the corresponding effective research-based preventive strategies (Dahlberg and Mercy, 2009, p. 5).

The relative success of the PH approach in addressing the problem of youth violence stimulated the application of the PH approach to other types of violence, including sexual violence and intimate partner violence. As an example, in 1994 the CDC and National Institute of Justice (NIJ) collaborated on one of the first national surveys to measure the incidence, prevalence and economic costs associated with intimate partner violence, sexual violence, and stalking (Tjaden and Thoennes, 2000). As a result of the research, in the same year, Congress passed the Violence Against Women Act (Title IV of the Violent Crime Control and Law Enforcement Act), which created rape prevention and education programs across the U.S. and Puerto Rico and also stimulated local demonstration projects in the intervention and prevention of domestic violence (Dahlberg and Mercy, 2009).

The Centers for Disease Control and Prevention's (CDC) National Violent Death Reporting System (NVDRS) compiles as well as combines data gathered from medical examiners, coroners, police, crime labs, and death certificate registrars. First initiated as a pilot study by Harvard University School of Public Health, the NVDRS, which is overseen by the CDC, currently operates in seventeen states across the United States. This dataset, with associated analysis and body of studies, provides a significant source of information on violence-precipitated deaths in the country.

The attention generated by the PH approach to violence in the United States has paved the way for international efforts along the same path. In 1996, the World Health Assembly adopted Resolution WHA49.25, "declaring violence a major and growing public health problem across the world" (Krug, et al., 2002, Introduction). The goals of the report were to raise awareness globally and to show that violence is preventable and that public health can play a crucial role in addressing its causes and consequences. Specific objectives were to: (1) describe the magnitude and impact of violence throughout the world; (2) describe key risk factors; (3) review and evaluate types of intervention and policy responses; and (4) make recommendations for action at local, national, and international levels (Krug, et al., 2002, Introduction).

In summary, the key identifying points of the public health (PH) perspective include the following:

- The PH perspective is essentially based on a *disease* model.
- The PH perspective focuses mainly on *prevention* (rather than on control or deterrence), with an emphasis on primary prevention (i.e., preventing the first offense) although secondary (i.e., immediate response to violence), and tertiary preventive measures, which are more policy-oriented (i.e., addressing institutional and structural causes), are also considered important.
- The emphasis is on reducing the risk factors, of which there are three types: (1) institutional/structural and cultural (e.g., familial or neighborhood factors or governmental/policy factors), (2) criminogenic commodities (e.g., guns), and (3) situational (e.g., drug use) (Prothrow-Stith, 1991).

- The PH perspective challenges the moral value about who should be blamed for the problem of violence, resulting in a more favorable disposition regarding the needs of victims of violence and particularly a restorative justice approach.

Human Rights Perspective

Since the Holocaust, the protection of human rights has emerged as an international norm. However, human rights are defined in various ways. A commonly referenced definition of human rights is contained in Articles 1 and 2 of the Universal Declaration of Human Rights (UDHR), as adopted by the General Assembly of the United Nations on December 10, 1948.

- Article 1 states that "All human beings are born free and equal in dignity and rights. They are endowed with reason and conscience and should act towards one another in a spirit of brotherhood."

- Article 2 lays down that "Everyone is entitled to all the rights and freedoms set forth in this Declaration, without distinction of any kind, such as race, colour, sex, language, religion, political or other opinion; national or social origin, property, birth or other status. Further, no distinction shall be made on the basis of the political, jurisdictional or international status of the country or territory to which a person belongs, whether it is independent, trust, non self governing or under any other limitation of sovereignty."

The UDHR supports the concept that there are certain universal human rights that the international community has accepted. Beyond the obvious rights flowing from the UDHR, distinctions are made between positive and negative rights due all individuals. Positive rights are those rights that require the state to be proactive in providing basic rights such as a right to food, healthcare, or safety. Negative rights are those rights that require the government to refrain from some action such as torture, executions, and genocide (Harrelson-Stephens and Callaway, 2007, p. 7). It is in this latter category that various forms of overt and covert (e.g., starvation) violence almost beyond human comprehension has been perpetrated by various governments and/or by their insurgents. Human rights scholars and international organizations such as the United Nations have attempted to measure and document human rights abuses around the world, including violent offenses such as extrajudicial killing, torture, disappearance, and political imprisonment (Cingranelli and Richards, 2005); political terror (Gibney and Dalton, 2007); and all forms of human rights violations including violence in more than 150 countries (Amnesty International, 2011a).

While no category or group of individuals is exempt from human rights violations, particularly violence, the most disadvantaged and marginalized populations (i.e., people affected by the deep-rooted inequalities of race, gender, age, and poverty) are often the most victimized by the physical consequences of events such as natural disasters, civil unrest, revolutions, war, and the like. They are also the most vulnerable to being victims of neglect and corruption of public officials who disregard basic human rights needs (Walsh, Thornton, and Voigt, 2010, p. 127).

Gender based repression is a universal form of humans rights violations in the world (e.g., rape, slavery and sex trade of women and children, and female circumcision/genital mutilation). It was not until 1979 that the international community began to address the specific legal needs of women in the United Nations Convention on the Elimination of All Forms of Discrimination against Women (Callaway and Harrelson-Stephens, 2007,

p. 177). However, many human rights abuses continue to the present time. For example, the conflict in Darfur, Sudan has led to some of the worst human rights abuses imaginable, including systematic and widespread murder, rape, torture, abduction, and displacement of large numbers of people. Mass rapes of Darfur women and girls show that the suffering and abuse endured by these women goes far beyond the actual rape. There is a devastating and ongoing impact on the health of women and girls who face a lifetime of stigma and marginalization from their own families and communities. A residual, and planned, effect of the rapes by the perpetrators, serves not only to inflict fear in and to dehumanize the women themselves, but also to disintegrate the communities to which they belong (Amnesty International, 2011a).

While certainly recognized as an international problem, particularly associated with conditions in developing third-world countries, the human rights perspective on violence is not generally thought of in the context of the modern post-industrial world. Yet, evidence of corruption (including political corruption) and human rights violations may be found everywhere (see Kalb, 2012).

For example, Quigley (2007) writes "that the civil and human rights perspective on Hurricane Katrina indicates that the people left behind when Katrina hit are being left behind now and will likely be left behind again" (p. 955). He addresses a virtual cornucopia of human rights violations, many existing in New Orleans prior to the disaster, that were brought to light, further exacerbated, or otherwise expanded and facilitated by events that took place as a result of Katrina. Many of his examples and case studies underscore the fact that corruption is intimately linked to the struggle for human rights, especially in the post Katrina reconstruction period with the exploitation and abuse of many people in New Orleans (and the region). The most disadvantaged and marginalized populations were the most victimized not only by the physical consequences of the disaster itself, but also by public officials and criminals who preyed upon the most vulnerable (p. 1005). With respect to the billions of dollars appropriated by the United Sates Congress to rebuild the city and region, he notes that "There has been little accounting of where the money has gone, but even the briefest visit to the Gulf Coast reveals that the money has not reached the people in need ..." (p. 1011). Quigley reinforces what others have observed, i.e., that the "International Human Rights laws ... have created a new and important perspective on the ongoing impact of Katrina" (p. 1005).

George Edwards (2006) documents the link between the possible corruption of public officials and international human rights abuses. He concludes that the United States has an obligation not to violate international human rights laws and not to allow others to engage in such breaches. Moreover, he notes that "State and local governments also carry the burden of ensuring human rights protections" (p. 416). He further claims that "multi-national corporations, local companies, and private individuals as non-state actors also share this responsibility" (p. 416). Edwards also observes that corruption, including human rights abuses and violations, in post-Katrina New Orleans has been, at a minimum, facilitated by governmental entities at all levels—local, state, and federal or through the corrupt actions of their representatives—in blatant disregard for the well-being of the people they are charged to protect.

Unfortunately not much attention has been given to egregious cases of corruption and serious human rights violations. For instance, a content analysis conducted by Patrick Walsh, William Thornton, and Lydia Voigt (2010) of five hundred internet articles spanning 2005 to 2007 using the phrase "Hurricane Katrina fraud" or "Hurricane Katrina corruption" disclosed that the number of articles concerning the fraudulent acts of individuals obtaining monies from federal programs and charities far outpaced the number of articles related to the fraudulent activities of individuals in positions of authority, e.g., stealing from within or through a federal program (79% versus 21%, respectively). For example, the search was four times more likely to produce news articles about recipients of Oprah Winfrey's "Angels" houses, who continued to file for Federal Emergency Management Administration (FEMA) housing vouchers, or about persons fraudulently applying for $2000 FEMA debit cards for displaced persons as opposed to producing articles concerning corrupt practices of public officials or improper administration of federal programs or the utilization of bribes to secure contracts or other acts of malfeasance that adversely affected the lives of hundreds of thousands of people and cost the public several billions of dollars.

The connection of corruption at all levels with the violation of human rights is critically important to make. If corruption is treated as a form of violation of human rights subject to official criminal prosecution, this may influence public attitudes and actions. With greater public awareness of the damage that corruption causes, public concern and support of programs and campaigns to prevent it are more likely to manifest themselves. Unfortunately, despite strong rhetoric, the political will to control and enact most anti-corruption programs has been low. Identifying the specific links between corruption and human rights violations may persuade key actors from all sectors (e.g., public officials, parliamentarians, judges, prosecutors, law enforcement officials, lawyers, business people, bankers, accountants, the media, and the public-at-large) to take a stronger stand against corruption. It is important to underscore that a suspension of human rights is never justified at any level.

Commercial/Commodity Perspective

The commercialization and commoditization of violence as a perspective is not typically discussed in the literature on violence, yet it significantly affects our understanding of violence in society as well as our response to violence. Our economic dependence on violence is astounding in terms of the breadth and scope of activities and the sheer amount of money that is implicated. The profit-making commercial entities/activities that are related to violence represent a very broad range. For example, businesses devoted to producing crime-related information and other media products may include publications and mass media presentations that exploit crime, especially violent crime, by sensationalizing criminal and violent behavior (e.g., books and journals; paperback crime novels; television crime programming including crime news, reality programs, and other entertainment shows; video/computer games; and movies as well as many associated thematic products, such as toy action figures). Public opinion polls regarding crime and violence, for example, are not only conducted by non-profit entities, but also by for-profit entities that conduct political polls that are used for political campaigns. Even some services such as corrections/treatment are offered by for-profit companies. In fact this is an area that has experienced a great deal of growth in the private for-profit sector. (Correctional Corporation of American [CCA] manages about 75,000 inmates including adults and juveniles at all security levels in more than 60 facilities, 44 of which are company owned in 19 states and the District of Columbia) (CCA, n.d.). In addition to the privatization of corrections, thousands of private vendors and companies supply all sorts of equipment and services to criminal justice facilities, such as institutional furniture and supplies, institutional clothes and uniforms, and security equipment. Private security companies comprise another rapidly expanding area. Currently in the United States, the funding for private security personnel exceeds the combined total of federal, state, and local law enforcement expenditures. Moreover, the private security workforce is greater than the combined total of sworn law enforcement personnel (Benson, 1997; The Law Enforcement-Private Security Consortium, 2005, p. 37; Florquin, 2011).

The security and crime-related industrial/commercial enterprises include the multi-billion dollar security and surveillance industry (e.g., alarms, detectors, and electronic monitoring services). The private security industry provides equipment and services for public and private agencies, and commercial, corporate, and industrial establishments. Likewise, so-called private military companies (PMC), in the past referred to as mercenaries, carry out many different missions and jobs, contracting out their services to foreign governments and even the U.S. Department of State. The PMC industry is estimated to be worth over $100 billion a year (Singer, 2003; Private Warriors, 2005).

Finally, another source of protection against crime and violence comes in the form of insurance coverage. Insurance companies also profit from fear of crime and especially violence in society. There are different types of "crime" insurance, which provide protection to businesses for the loss of money, securities, property and personal injury of patrons, clients, and employees from crimes. Since the 9/11 terrorist attacks against the United States, many insurance carriers now provide insurance to protect from loss that is caused by terrorists' attacks against businesses. To protect themselves, and to limit the insurance industry's exposure to terrorism related losses, shortly after 9/11 Congress passed the Terrorism Insurance Act of 2002 (P.L. 107-297 formerly H.R. 3210). The law is designed to make sure that insurance carriers can continue to insure businesses for coverage against risks from terrorism. There are, however, several limitations built into the act that protect insurance companies for excessive losses: "the terrorist act must have been committed by an individual(s) acting on behalf of a foreign person or interest, or if the terrorist act was committed as part of a war declared by Congress, or if the terrorist act does not result in property or insurance losses in excess of $5 million dollars" (Pastor, 2007, p. 575).

The gun industry in the United States is huge. The United States is not only the most heavily armed nation in the world, it is also one of the largest weapons producing countries globally. No one knows the exact number of guns in the hands of private citizens in the U.S. Estimates of gun ownership range from 200 to 300 million, depending on the source (e.g., Worrall, 2008; NRA, 2010). Various surveys show that as many as 40 to 50 million households have a gun and at least 40 percent of the adult population owns a gun (Cook and Ludwig, 1997; Carroll, 2005; Agresti and Smith, 2010). We do know, however, the number of guns manufactured and sold by legitimate companies for non-military sales in the U.S. each year. The Bureau of Alcohol, Tobacco and Firearms (ATF) tracks these figures yearly. It is estimated that the number of manufactured guns rise by about 4.5 million each year in the U.S. In 2010, for example, there were 5,403,714 guns (pistols, long guns, and miscellaneous firearms) manufactured by approximately 190 U.S. gun companies; in 1999, there were 4,070,236 guns manufactured; over the 11 year period there was a 33 percent increase in gun manufacture (ATF, 1999–2010). The year 2009 was the first time the gun industry produced more than 5 million firearms since 1994, and it was the largest number manufactured since 1980, when 5,645,131 guns were made (Thurman, n.d.). The legal retail sale of guns is estimated to average about $3.5 billion annually in inflation-adjusted dollars, going back to the mid-1990s. One source indicates that the legal sale of new guns in the U.S. was at a record high number of about 9 million in 2009 (Shapiro, 2011). However, these figures do not take into account millions of used guns sold through gun shows and unlicensed dealers and other private citizens (Shapiro, 2011). Additionally, imported firearms are a big business for the U.S. firearms market, which add to the number of guns produced each year. In 2010, there were 2,508,888 firearms imported, with Brazil being the largest importer (697,350 guns in 2010) (Thurman, n.d.).

Firearm sales tend to rise for a number of reasons, including the public's perception of high crime rates, fears of terrorism, vulnerability during natural disasters, or fear of gun control measures, which might affect the ability of people to purchase guns. Historically, it appears that the American gun industry over the years has reaped the benefits of special protections from both Congress and many state legislatures. For instance, except for the prohibition of the production of machine guns, short-barreled shotguns, other military-style weapons, the civilian market had no real restrictions in terms of gun design and performance in the U.S. until 1994, when legislation was passed to band the manufacture of assault weapons and ammunition magazines that hold more than 10 rounds (Wintemut, 2002). However, many of the restrictions have been lifted since 2004 (NRA-ILA, 2011). As an industry spokesman notes, "Solid business practices, continuous anti-gun vigilance, and consumer-driven new products are the benchmark for continued success" (Thurman, n.d.).

The foregoing discussion only serves to highlight some of the entrepreneurial, commercial, corporate, and industrial areas that depend on violence (especially keeping criminal violence among the leading social problems in the nation) for their own survival. The for-profit industrial/economic implications of war and production of armament is also nothing short of staggering. The qualifications and background of the various types of violence experts in the commercial sector are altogether different from those experts representing the other perspectives. For example, the commercial complex employs some research scientists/criminologists and some criminal justice/military professionals; but, overall, it depends largely on professionals from various product development areas/fields, industrial/business management, marketing and sales, and customer relations. Most activities, even those involving research, security and corrections, are centered on profit motives and incentives. Again, the bottom-line is that violence is a highly valuable, profitable commodity on which significant networks of public and private establishments/institutions depend for their respective survival.

The Scientific/Criminological Construction of Violence

The *scientific construction of violence* entails a very special kind of definition of violence and construction of reality! Scientific definitions of violence necessitate an emphasis on systematic observations and empirically documented phenomena that are subject to measurement and questions of *reliability* (referring to issues of consistency from knower to knower and from time to time) and *validity* (referring to questions of accuracy in measuring what we think we are measuring).

In the United States *scientific* crime-related, especially violence-related, research and the generation of data and information on all facets of crime and violence is part of an enormous research/information infrastructure and institutional network unlike any other in the world. The main focus of these research and information generating entities is to develop, verify, and disseminate authoritative, scientific information and knowledge about violence, including criminal violence, and the social response to such behaviors/actions/events. Collecting information; producing statistical summaries; conducting scientific investigations and verification studies; developing and testing hypotheses, typologies, and theories; and preparing reports and sets of recommendations comprise the main sorts of activities of these various entities. The typical organizations or institutions that devote their efforts to the creation and dissemination of knowledge pertaining to violence include both public and private non-profit information and research generating institutions, such as government agencies (e.g., the FBI's UCR, the National Institute of Justice Statistics, or the Centers for Disease Control and Prevention's National Violent Death Reporting System, NVDRS) and a wide range of research centers (e.g., the Violence Policy Center), private foundations, special topic research centers (e.g., the Center for the Study and Prevention of Violence), as well as universities and colleges across the nation.

Most of the research that is conducted on violence, especially criminal violence, is carried out by criminologists. *Criminology,* which may be defined as an interdisciplinary field that relies on the scientific method to study crime phenomena including violence, is the field of study that produces the largest number and greatest variety of research and theory that pertains to criminal violence and other forms of violence in the U.S. While there are many perspectives even within the field of criminology, the dominate emphasis is on bringing "scientific" understanding to the nature and extent of the problem of crime including the problem of violence and separating myths from facts and perceptions from reality. Criminology includes the study of the patterns of crime and victimization, the causes of crime, social responses to crime, and crime prevention and control. Thus, the sub-areas of criminology include: *law, measurement, victimology, crime typologies,* and *etiology,* as well as the study of the *criminal justice system and the public order* (Voigt, et al., 1994).

Violence and the Law

Criminologists have disagreed over the question of whether to limit the field of criminology to legal violations (e.g., focusing studies of violence exclusively on criminal homicide, rape, robbery, and assault) or to extend the scope of study to include other forms of violence, which may not be illegal at the time of occurrence. There are forms of violence that result in individual injury or destruction of property (e.g., corporate violence such as toxic waste dumping or selling harmful products to third world nations) that are typically not treated as criminal offenses and do not fall under the criminal code, but rather may be treated under the civil code. Today, most criminologists support a broad approach to the study of criminology and topics such as violence that extends well beyond the laws of any one nation or transnational codes to include patterns of behavior/actions/events that may not be obvious to most people or well understood. For example, *cyber violence* (referring to mediated violence in electronic space) for which laws have not yet been fully drafted and for which the severity and deadly consequences are still largely unforeseen, will require greater awareness and understanding on the part of law makers and law enforcement agents in order to adequately prevent its real consequences (e.g., electronically manipulating computerized passageways that causes mass train collisions across state and national boundaries) or to identify and respond to the originators or perpetrators of violence that may be unknown and unlikely to be tracked down (Wall, 2007).

The Measurement of Violence

Among the greatest challenges in the study of violence is determining the actual amount of violence in society. We simply do not know how much violence occurs. Most acts of violence go either undiscovered or unreported. In addition to the fact that many acts of violence are not reported or are selectively reported, statistics are subject to the organizational definitions and politics of the various agencies that collect the data. For instance, the statistics/indicators reported in Uniform Crime Reports (UCR), the National Crime Victimization Survey (NCVS), or the National Center for Health Statistics (NCHS) are all subject to their respective organizational definitions and policies. Each has its own set of strengths and weaknesses. For example, one of the drawbacks to the data provided by the UCR regarding the amount of violence in society is that it mainly focuses on criminal homicide, rape, robbery, and assault; certain types of violence such as political corruption that results in injury and loss of lives are less likely to come to the attention of local law enforcement authorities. When it comes to statistics related to specific subsets of criminal violence, such as serial murder or other forms of violence such as terrorism or war or workplace violence, there are other agencies that collect and disseminate relevant information (e.g., data related to war is reported by the U. S. Department of Defense and data related to workplace violence is reported by the Bureau of Labor Statistics).

One of the great challenges associated with the study of violence is that there is no general repository of information regarding violence in society. As a result, different forms of violence present varying degrees of difficulty in obtaining data. For this reason criminologists often must conduct studies using their own derived datasets.

Since, the criminological or scientific study of violence necessitates conceptual clarity and precise measurement, rarely is the general form of violence the subject of attention in scientific investigations. In fact, the police reports of criminal violence as defined by the UCR index categories of violence are among the most common operationalizations (empirical definitions) of violence in our society. For instance, many criminologists, who study the history of violence or international trends of violence, empirically define or operationalize the concept using homicide as a proxy. However, it is important to note that distinct forms of violence such as rape or robbery suggest very different types of perpetrators, victims, perpetrator/victim relationships, fact patterns, motivations or causes, and solutions or responses.

Violence Victims

Until recently most of the emphasis in the field of criminology has been on the offender. It was not until the 1970s that the field of *victimology* (i.e., the study of victim-offender relationships) became an area of concentration for criminologists. It was during this time that the National Crime Victimization Survey (NCVS) was introduced as an alternative data set to the UCR. However, even with this alternative data set, which employs different strategies of gathering information and includes much more information regarding victims, the emphasis has still remained largely focused on criminal forms of violence as defined by the UCR. The main benefits of the NCVS include additional information on victims and public perceptions of criminal justice as well as studies on various subtopics of violence such as intimate partner violence and sexual assaults.

Violence Typologies

Criminologists have long sought to find a violence typology, i.e., an organizing device for categorizing large amounts of information into mutually exclusive categories (as in the biological system of taxonomy or the chemical periodic table). A number of typologies have been suggested. However, to date, there has not been a universally accepted typology of violent offenses, motivations, and victim or offender profiles offered. Some typologies are based on legal or semi-legal definitions of criminal violence. Additional typologies have been developed based on information related to such factors as the seriousness of the offense, the psychological characteristics of the offender, the motivations of the offender, the victim-offender relationship, and the career patterns of the offender. For example, rapists may be classified as sadistic, power control, or opportunistic (Groth and Birnbaum, 1979); rampage school shooters have been categorized into three types, traumatized, psychotic, and psychopathic (Langman, 2009); and workplace violence has been categorized into intrusive violence, consumer-related violence, relationship violence, and organizational violence (Vaughan, 2002, p. 6).

The Etiology of Violence

Criminologists have been seeking the causes of crime, especially violent crime, for at least 200 years. During that time many competing theories and paradigms have been offered. Theories basically represent speculative guesses about some aspect of the phenomenon under study. More advanced theories are usually stated in some logical framework, about why and how certain behaviors or events occur. Moreover, theories are statements of relationships among facts that have some basis in empirical and experimental testing. Based on their logical framework and supporting empirical base, theories of violence address questions of why and how violent behaviors or events occur.

"What causes violence?" is a very difficult question to answer. It is important to keep in mind that each form of violence refers to actions that differ significantly in a number of ways. As noted earlier, each form of violence (e.g., rape, mass murder, child abuse, or terrorism) suggests unique sets of aggressors and victims with varying motives and emotional states, different social contexts or situations, varying social definitions or response patterns, as well as different strategies of research or sources of data.

The relative strengths and weaknesses of different explanations are mainly determined by scientific merit, with propositions and theories supported or dismissed on the basis of the *reliability* (i.e., referring to the degree of consistency of findings) and *validity* (i.e., the degree of certainty in accuracy of measurements) of evidence. Since no perspective has the market on truth, all the perspectives taken together enhance our understanding of the problem of violence. Theories of violence are extremely important and must not be taken for granted because they underlie the fundamental ways in which violence is defined and how we respond to it and, ultimately, what we think of one another.

Causal models of criminal violence, derived from the field of criminology, are among the most numerous. This may be due to the great cultural popularity of crime topics, the relative ease of obtaining crime data (police reports and statistics), and the specificity of legal definitions (i.e., criminal codes). However, critical attention must be given to the underpinning assumptions of the nature of human beings and society, the operationalization or empirical definition of key variables, the relationship between the theory and supporting research, and the appropriateness of generalizations or ethical application of results. For instance, some researchers vaguely make violence equivalent with all crime (including public order and property offenses). By today's standards, such vague references are considered scientifically useless. Nonetheless, when reviewing criminological theories and research, one must be mindful of the limiting effects of certain definitions of violence upon generalizations and policy applications.

The history of criminology suggests that no one theory has been able to explain violence. As a result, many rival etiological theories of violence, or one of its more specific forms, have been developed from a wide variety of disciplines and perspectives, including biological, psychological, sociological, and humanistic or conflict approaches. Since no one vantage point or theoretical perspective can claim superiority, the development of a more holistic, critical analysis of the complexity of the subject matter of violence is essential in fostering understanding that can lead to effectively addressing human needs and ultimately improving the quality of life on earth.

Criminology, the Criminal Justice System, and the Political Order

Another integral part of criminology is the scientific investigation of the criminal justice system (CJS) including the study of its major components: (1) law enforcement, (2) courts, and (3) corrections. Since it is the criminal justice system (including practitioners such as police, prosecutors, judges, probation officers, and correction personnel) that actually responds to most acts of interpersonal violence and deals with violent offenders, criminologists' vigilance over its functions and operations is vital. Every aspect of the criminal justice system has been widely studied and analyzed by criminologists.

Criminologists working from the humanistic and conflict perspective have been particularly vigilant over criminal justice system practices and the law and order orientation of the field. They have been especially critical of mainstream criminology for its selective attention to interpersonal violence with relatively minor consideration of institutional and structural patterns and causes of violence. Their work has been successful in exposing some of the dangers of this biased treatment of violence, which contributes to public un-awareness of significant acts of violence including the violation of human rights, environmental degradation, and endangerment of all living creatures on earth (Friedrichs and Friedrichs, 2002; Platt and O'Leary, 2003; Agozino, 2004; Wollford, 2006; Roth, 2010).

For example, public opinion is often formulated without full understanding of the many complexities related to empirical evidence and scientific research surrounding various national debates of key issues related to the administration of justice, such as capital punishment. In is interesting to note the historical pattern of fluctuation of public opinion related to capital punishment. The Gallup Poll measurement of public perceptions, i.e., opinions for and against the death penalty go back to 1936 (which registered 59% in favor and 38% against) and extend to the present. Over this particular poll's 75-year history the lowest point of 42 percent in favor and the highest point of 47 percent against were registered in 1966; the highest point of 80 percent in favor was registered in 1994 and the lowest point of 13 percent against was registered in 1995 (Gallup Poll, 2011). According to the most recent Gallup polls,[2] conducted in October 2011, the level of support for capital punishment (61%) represents the lowest point of those in favor and the highest point of those against (35%) in 11 years (2001–2011). With the exception of this most current poll, the trend over this period has been relatively stable trend averaging 65.4 percent in favor and 29.4 percent against. These trends have remained stable despite

---

2. The Gallup Poll measurement of the level of support, i.e., percent for/against the death penalty for 2001–2011 are: 2001 (68/26); 2002 (70/25); 2003 (64/32); 2004 64/31); 2005 (64/30); 2006 (67/28); 2007 (69/27); 2008 (64/30); 2009 65/31); 2010 (64/29) 2011; (61/35) (Gallup Poll, 2011).

vigorous debate and scientific evidence on different aspects of the arguments, such as evidence suggesting that the death penalty is applied unfairly. For example, there is evidence suggesting that arbitrary differences in trial procedures may be related to trial outcomes (Bohm, 2012a; 2012b; Innocence Project, n.d.; Culbert, 2008); there is also evidence of racism and wrongful conviction (Hawkins, 2006; Bedau, 2009).

At the end of 2010, 36 states and the Federal Bureau of Prisons held more than 3,158 people under sentence of death in the U.S. Of those sentenced to death, approximately 55 percent were white, 42 percent were black, and 14 percent were Hispanic. Twelve states executed 46 inmates during 2010; of those executed, 28 were white, 13 were black, and 5 were Hispanic (Snell, 2011). From 1977 to 2010 there have been 1,234 executions in the U.S. (57% white, 35% black, 7% Hispanic, and the remainder representing other races) (Snell, 2011). Illinois abolished the death penalty in January 2011, replacing it with a sentence of life without parole (Death Penalty Information Center, 2011).

Globally, support and use of the death penalty has been declining. According to Amnesty International (2011b), of the total 58 countries that have to date retained the death penalty, the United States is 5th (with 46 executions, which represents a decline from 2009) on the list of reported number of executions in 2010 following China (which executed more than the total for the rest of the world), Iran, North Korea, and Yemen. The U. S. is 8th on the list of reported number of inmates sentenced to the death penalty (with 110 sentenced in 2010) following China, Pakistan, Iraq, Egypt, Nigeria, Algeria, and Malaysia. One hundred and thirty nine (139) countries in the world (two-thirds of the total) have abolished the death penalty in law and practice; 30 of these countries have abolished the death penalty during the past decade.

In many countries of the world (e.g., all of the countries in the European Union), the death penalty is regarded as a human rights violation. The U. S. position on capital punishment stands contrary to the position of other Western industrial nations of the world and most of its allies, which may have significant political and economic consequences (Amnesty International, 2011b; Bohm, 2012a).

Debunking Violence Myths

As we have seen, there are numerous challenges associated with defining violence, such as its ambiguous and ubiquitous nature. Violence means different things to different people. Its meaning varies depending on cultural contexts or historical periods. Violence has many forms of expression and appears in many social situations. In addition, violence not only appears to be an extensive part of our patterns of communication and daily metaphors (e.g., "love as war," "argument as war," "social policy as war"), but it is also perceived as a pervasive part of our social life.

Imbusch (2003) claims that its ambiguity as well as its apparent ubiquity is what allows the concept of violence to be so easily applied to such a wide range of cultural phenomena and used for political purposes. It is significant to point out that certain applications of violence metaphors can simultaneously mean different things and may fulfill contradictory purposes. Ironically, violence has been associated with both disintegrative and integrative functions and consequences (Barak, 2007). For example, high levels of violent crime in a specific community may be correlated with anomie, normlessness, and social disintegration (Shaw and McKay, 1969). Yet these same types of violent acts may also work to mobilize and bring a community together (Durkheim, 1895/1938). Georg Simmel (1908/1983) argues that conflict, even high intensity conflict, does not always result in "breakdown" or "change" as is often claimed; but, rather, it may serve to maintain the social order and existing hierarchy. Violence often plays a role in both creating a new social order and in the destruction of the social order. It is amazing that violence can be viewed both as a problem and a solution. The pervasive use and application of violence in both sanctioned (lawful) and unsanctioned (unlawful) ways and the fact that both the creation and the destruction of the social order can involve violence raises the question of how its legitimacy is determined.

Iadicola and Shupe (2003) maintain that violence is fundamentally an issue of inequality and human freedom. They argue that those individuals who are in positions of power are given legitimate authority to employ violence and those who lack position and power are prohibited from using violence, and, if they do, they are subject to heavy punishments and labels such as "criminal," "insane," or "enemy" and they are considered to be dangerous threats to the social order.

Ironically, globalization, the most recent vestige of postindustrial capitalism, has created the conditions for the development of unprecedented wealth and prosperity. Yet at the same time, it has caused an unparalleled polarization of affluent and disadvantaged populations, the exacerbation of injustices and human rights violations, and the escalation of international structural violence. Iadicola and Shupe (2003) point out that globally, assuming that the population on earth stands at about 5.5 billion, approximately 15 percent of the world's wealth is divided among 5 billion people or 90 percent of the population, while 85 percent of the wealth is apportioned among only 500 million inhabitants or 10 percent of the world's population. It is difficult to reconcile the contradiction that exists from the fact that in the wealthiest of nations (i.e., in the U.S.) millions of people, including one of five children, live in dire poverty with significant numbers who are homeless and hungry (Rank, 2005).

These types of social and economic contradictions and uncertainties of the modern world are reflected in the ambiguity or ambivalence connected with violence. Imbusch (2003) claims that the contemporary world is faced with a great paradox: "The modern age with its democratic-rational institutions has created better chances for the realization of humanity, nonviolence, and peacefulness; but, at the same time, it has vastly increased the potential of violence through new technologies, the greater social distance between members of society, and the development of a science of repression of human nature" (p. 35).

This paradox stems from the ambivalence surrounding violence, making us vulnerable to *metaphorical blindness*[3] that works to distract us from certain realities of violence and prevents us from seeing the problem of violence for what it is, critically understanding its nature, and doing something to address it. Five forms of metaphorical blindness to avoid include the following:

(1) *We must avoid accepting the belief that violence stems primarily from individual pathology rather than institutional and structural causes*: By assuming that violence is caused by individual abnormality, insanity, and defective personality traits or by explaining violence exclusively with respect to inborn qualities, we are blinded from seeing social injustices and other root social structural causes of

---

3. The five forms of metaphorical blindness have been inspired and adapted from Wilhelm Heitmeyer and John Hagan's (2003) discussion of "thematic traps" (p. 8).

violence. Moreover, by focusing our attention on individual causes of violence and blaming certain types of individuals or groups and by ignoring or disregarding institutional/structural forms of violence, we offer people in authority positions a pretext for moral self-exculpation or license to selectively impose repressive policies. For example, as a result of our typical emphasis on interpersonal criminal violence or "street violence"; we know relatively little about institutional or structural forms of violence, such as corporate violence or governmental corruption and human rights violations, for which data are not readily available. Yet, the harm both in terms of lives lost and cost as a result of violent actions or inactions committed by corporations and the government far exceeds any costs associated with street violence.

(2) *We must avoid accepting sensational images of violence as typical representation of reality*: By sensationalizing the most rare and extreme forms of violence (e.g., serial murders) and using pejorative violence labels such as "insane" or "depraved" (serving to intensify emotions), we are drawn to certain narrow realities, which tend to blind us from other aspects of the problem, generating fear and ultimately affecting or disaffecting our personal and collective responses to the problem of violence. The media, which both produces and reinforces sensationalistic images of violence in order to get quick audience attention, plays a significant role in creating collective awareness of the most esoteric elements of violent acts, giving the impression that extreme forms of violence are common. Thus, while murder is relatively infrequent when compared with other acts of violence (e.g., assaults), it is more likely to be reported, especially when there are multiple victims (i.e., the more victims, the more media coverage) (Duwe, 2000). As a result, the fear of homicide, especially stranger-perpetrated homicide, far exceeds the reality. While most of us fear being victimized by strangers, we miss the evidence suggesting that we are at greater risk of being victimized by acquaintances or relatives than by strangers.

(3) *We must avoid accepting over-generalizations of violence in everyday life*: By creating the impression that violence is ubiquitous and that there are hardly any areas of our social existence where violence is not present in some form or fashion and by reinforcing the notion (especially by the media) that violence is lurking all around us all of the time, we are prevented from seeing and appreciating the more peaceful and cooperative side of human nature and social interactions. For example, even though the immediate aftermath of Hurricane Katrina is associated with looting, violence, and the breakdown of law and order, it is worth remembering that most people acted peacefully and orderly throughout these very trying times (Thornton and Voigt, 2006).

(4) *We must avoid accepting social stereotypes of the normalcy of violence*: By stereotyping the expressions of violence in certain social contexts or among particular individuals, neighborhoods, or even nations as part of some natural stage of de-velopment, we blind ourselves to its harmful effects and fail to find solutions. For instance, when we accept violence, such as fighting among siblings, e.g. among brothers, as normal by trivializing it with sayings like "boys will be boys" or when we disregard calls for safety measures or protection from violence in some neighborhoods on the assumption that violence is a "way of life" there, we erroneously communicate and support the idea that in some social contexts or areas of society, violence is normal and that it is insolvable. We often treat violent outbreaks in developing nations in a similarly dismissive manner. These types

of perceptions may lead to selective patterns of responses to crime and violence in our society and globally.

(5) *We must avoid accepting the reification of violence metaphors:* By substituting violence metaphors for reality and using violence metaphors such as "peace through war," we further fall prey to accepting violence as the dominating feature of our natural condition, which we cannot alter. As a result we have little confidence in finding other alternatives and are prevented from considering or searching for more "peaceful" solutions or even seeing or acknowledging the results of scientific evidence to the contrary. Most of us cannot imagine a world in which violence is not the main way of preserving our safety and well-being. Yet, there is overwhelming evidence that peaceful alternatives as illustrated in "conflict resolution" or "political resolution" strategies are successful and more lasting than violent resolutions (Fisher and Ury, 2006). While we may, upon occasion, even quote the eloquent statement by Mohandas Gandhi that: "we must be the change we hope to see in the world," suggesting that we must practice peace in order to achieve peace in the world, we still depend on violence to bring about peace.

All of these forms of metaphorical blindness are associated with perpetuating distorted understanding of real events that eventually become collectively transformed into violence myths (e.g., the myth that violence is necessary for peace). Victor Kappeler and Gary Potter (2005) describe violence myths as "powerful constructions of reality" because they frequently operate on an unconscious level and have persuasive and motivating power, which can undermine scientific evidence and fly in the face of facts (p. 2).

Violence myths gain their power from reflecting our rich cultural heritage, including deeply embedded symbols and metaphors, and amplifying our own personal values and beliefs. Often we are not conscious that violence myths are at work or that violence metaphors organize our views of perpetrators, victims, and the proper operation of public institutions such as the criminal justice system. For example, when we think of violent offenders, we exclude ourselves, our families, our friends, or even public officials from the realm of possible suspects—we usually think of "others" very different from ourselves.

In our review of the social construction of violence, we have found that most of what we all know about violence includes interpersonal forms of criminal violence, particularly as reported by the *Uniform Crime Reports* (UCR). Yet, we know relatively little about any other forms of violence, such as harms resulting from violations of human rights. We have also learned that the media often distorts crime information. For instance, violent crime waves are really not about any surges in the incidence of violent crimes, but more about how they are reported (you may recall that a *crime wave* is defined as heavy and sensational coverage of a crime, which is selected by the editorial board as a "news theme," giving the impression that the occurrence of the particular crime has dramatically risen).

Once select elements of violent events become transformed into violence myths, they are entered into the collective consciousness. Over time and through repeated reinforcement, violence myths become larger than life and function to shape our thoughts and response patterns and, ultimately, the social construction of the reality of violence in society. Kappeler and Potter (2005) claim that what makes violence myths unique is that the society's mythmakers represent a large variety of entities and actors, which may take interchangeable roles, e.g., sometimes the government is the mythmaker and the media or special interest groups respond to the official myth or vice versa. Moreover, violence myths also vary with respect to their general intent and consequences. For instance, some myths may result in the enactment of laws that criminally label certain types of behavior or people or they may lead to repressive policies or they may just fall by the wayside. Some myths may function to serve the vested interests of particular groups in society, while others may have no apparent purpose.

This book, which elaborates on all of the key points of this introductory chapter, is designed to challenge readers to deconstruct the meaning of violence by providing a critical consideration of the topic of violence in society, giving special attention to distinguishing violence facts from myths. The book is organized around some of the most enduring questions related to violence. In addressing these questions, we review the history and patterns of violence in society, we critically evaluate theories and scientific evidence, we question stereotypes and simplistic explanations, and we challenge simple solutions. Remember that things are rarely simple and seldom what they seem.

References

Agozino, B. (2004). Imperialism, Crime and Criminology: Towards the Decolonization of Criminology. *Crime, Law and Social Change*, 41, 343–358.

Agresti, J.D., and Smith, R.K. (2010). *Gun Control Facts*. Retrieved from: http//www.justfacts.com/guncontrol.asp.

Alvarez, A., and R. Bachman. (2008). *Violence: The Enduring Problem*. Thousand Oaks, CA: Sage Publications, Inc.

American Society for the Prevention of Cruelty to Animals. (ASPCA). (2011). History. Retrieved from: www.aspca.org/aboutus/history.aspx.c.

Amnesty International. (2011a). Sudan: *Rape as a Weapon of War*. Retrieved from: http://www.amnestyusa.org.

Amnesty International (2011b). Death Sentences and Executions 2010. Retrieved from: http://www.amnesty.org.

Apter, D. (1997). *The Legitimization of Violence*. New York: NYU Press.

Barak, G. (2007). *Violence, Conflict, and World Order: Critical Conversations on State-Sanctioned Justice*. Lanham, MD: Rowman & Littlefield Publishers, Inc.

Barak, G. (2003). *Violence and Nonviolence: Pathways to Understanding*. Thousand Oaks, CA: Sage Publications.

Barille, L.G., and Sloan, N. (2012). Corporate Violence: The EPA's Criminalization and Control of Environmental Destruction. In Dee Harper, Lydia Voigt and William E. Thornton (Eds.), *Violence: Do We Know It When We See It?* Durham, NC: Carolina Academic Press, 323–340.

Bartol, C. R., and Bartol, A.M. (2005). *Criminal Behavior: A Psychosocial Approach*. Upper Saddle River, NJ: Pearson Prentice Hall.

Bedau, H.A. (2009). Racism, wrongful convictions, and the death penalty. *Tennessee Law Review*, 76, 615–624.

Benson, B. (1997). *Privatization in Criminal Justice*. National Institute of Justice, Office of Justice Programs.

Berger, P., and Luckmann, T. (1967). *The Social Construction of Reality*. New York, NY: Doubleday.

Berman, J. (January 9, 2011). Sarah Palin's 'Crosshairs' Ad Dominates Gabrielle Gifford's Debate. Retrieved from: http://abcnews.go.com/Politics/sarah-palins-crosshairs-ad-focus-gabrielle-giffords-debate/story?id=12576437.

Best, J. (2001). The diffusion of social problems. In J. Best (Ed.) How *Claims Spread: Cross-national Diffusion of Social Problems.* New York, NY: Aldine De Gruyter, 1–18.

Black, D. (1983). Crime as Social Control. *American Sociological Review,* 48, 34–45.

Blumer, H. (1971). Social Problems as Collective Behavior. *Social Problems,* 18, 298–306.

Bohm, R.M. (2012a). *Deathquest.* Boston: Anderson Publishing.

Bohm, R.M. (2012b). Racial Discrimination and the Death Penalty in the United States. In D.W. Harper, L. Voigt, and W.E. Thornton (Eds.). *Violence: Do We Know It When We See It?* Durham, NC: Carolina Academic Press, 305–316.

Brownstein, H. H. (2000). *The Social Reality of Violence and Violent Crime.* Boston, MA: Allyn and Bacon.

Bureau of Alcohol, Tobacco, and Firearms (ATF). (1999–2010). *Annual Firearms Manufacturing and Export Report, 1999–2010.* Retrieved from: http://www.atf.gov. firearms/stats/index.htm.

Bureau of Justice Statistics (Executive Summary). (1993). *Correctional Populations in the United States, 1980–1993.* U.S. Department of Justice, Office of Justice Programs. Retrieved from: http://www.druglibrary.org/schaffer/govpubs/corr93.html.

Burns, R., and Crawford, C. (2006). School Shootings, the Media, and Public Fear: Ingredients for a Moral Panic. *Crime, Law and Social Change.* 32(2) 147–168.

Bushman, B.J., and Anderson, C.A. (2001). Media Violence versus Public Misinformation. American *Psychologist,* 56(6/7) 477–489.

Callaway, R.L., and Harrelson-Stephens, J. (2007). Gender-Based Repression. In R.L. Callaway and Harrelson-Stephens, J. (Eds.) *Exploring International Human Rights.* Boulder: Lynne Rienner Publishers, 177–179.

Carroll, J. (2005). *Gun Ownership and Use in America.* Retrieved from: http://www. gallup.com/poll/20098/gun-ownership-use-america.aspx.

Chambliss, W. (1984). *Criminal Law in Action.* New York, NY: Macmillan.

Cingranelli, D.L., and Richard, D.L. (2005). *The Cingranelli-Richards (CIRI) Human Rights Data Set.* Version 2005.10.12. Retrieved from: www.humanrightsdata.org.

Cohen, S. (1972). *Folk Devils and Moral Panics.* London: MacGibbon and Kee.

Cohen, S. (2001). *States of Denial: Knowing about Atrocities and Suffering.* Cambridge, UK: Polity Press.

Cook P.J., and Ludwig, J. (1997). *Guns in America: Results of a Comprehensive National Survey on Firearms Ownership and Use.* Summary Report. Washington, DC: Police Foundation.

Correctional Corporation of America (CCA). (n.d.). Retrieved from http://ccc.com/facilities/.

Culbert, J.L. (2008). *Death Certainty: The Death Penalty and the Problem of Judgment.* Stanford, CA: Stanford University Press.

Dahlberg, L.L., and J. A. Mercy. (2009). History of violence as a public health issue. *AMA Virtual Mentor,* 11(2), 17–172 (printed pdf page numbers used in text). Retrieved from: http://www.cdc.gov/violenceprevention/pdf/history_violence-a.pdf.

Death Penalty Information Center. (2011). *The Death Penalty in 2011: Year End Report.* Retrieved from: http://www.deathpenaltyinfo.org/documents/2-11_Year_End.pdf

Dowler, K. (2003). Media consumption and public attitudes toward crime and justice: The relationship between fear of crime, punitive attitudes and perceived police effectiveness. *Journal of Criminal Justice and Popular Culture,* 10(2), 109–126.

Durkheim, E. (1893/1960). *The Division of Labor in Society.* Translated by G. Simpson. Glencoe, IL: Free Press.

Durkheim, E. (1885/1938). *The Rules of the Sociological Method.* Translated by S. Solovay and J. Mueller, edited by G. Catlin. New York, NY: Free Press.

Durkheim, E. (1887/1951). *Suicide.* Translated by J. Spaulding G. and Simpson. New York, NY: Free Press.

Duwe, G. (2000). Body-count Journalism: The Presentation of Mass Murder in the News Media. *Homicide Studies,* 4(4), 364–399.

Easteal, P. (2012). Violence against Women: Colliding "Realities." In D.W. Harper, L. Voigt, and W.E. Thornton (Eds.). *Violence: Do We Know It When We See It?* Durham, NC: Carolina Academic Press, 27–40.

Edwards, G. (2006). International Human Rights Law Violations Before, During and After Hurricane Katrina: An International Law Framework for Analysis, *Thurgood Marshall Law Review,* 31(2), 353–424.

Federal Bureau of Investigation (FBI). (2011). Crime in the United States, 2010. Uniform Crime Reports, Washington, DC: Retrieved from: www.fbi.gov.

Fishman, M. (1979). Crime Waves as Ideology. *Social Problems,* 25, June, 531–543.

Fisher, R., and Ury, W. (2006). *Getting to Yes: Negotiating Agreement Without Giving In.* New York, NY: Penguin Press.

Florquin, N. (2011). A Booming Business: Private Security and Small Arms. Retrieved from: http://www.smallarmssurvey.org/publications/by-type/yearbook/small-arms-survey-2011.html.

Friedrichs, D., and Friedrichs, J. (2002). The World Bank and Crimes of Globalization: A Case Study. *Social Justice,* 29, 13–36.

Gallup Poll (2011). Death Penalty. Retrieved from: www.gallup.com/poll/1606/death-penalty.aspx.

Garamone, J. (2011). DOD Issues Purple Heart Standards for Brain Injury. Armed Forces Press Service, April 30.

Geis, G. (2007). *White-Collar and Corporate Crime.* Upper Saddle River, NJ: Prentice Hall.

Gerbner, G. L., Gross, N., Signorielli, and Morgan, M. (1986). *Television's Mean World Violence Profile,* Number 14–15. Philadelphia, PA: Annenberg School of Communications, University of Pennsylvania, September.

Gerbner, G., L. Gross, N., Morgan, M. and Signorielli, N. (1994). Growing up with television: The cultivation perspective. In B. Jennnings and D. Zillman (Eds.). *Media Effects,* Hillsdale, NJ: Erbaum, 17–41.

Giddens, Anthony. (1985). *The Nation State and Violence.* Cambridge, UK: Polity Press.

Gibney, M., and Dalton, M. (2007). The Political Terror Scale. In R.L. Callaway and J. Harrelson-Stephens (Eds.). *Exploring International Human Rights*. Boulder: Lynne Rienner Publishers.

Glaze, L. (2010). United States Bureau of Justice Statistics. *Correctional Populations in the United States*, 2009. Retrieved from: http://bjs.ojp.usdoj.gov/content/pub/pdf/cpus09.pdf.

Glaze, L. (2011). United States Bureau of Justice Statistics. *Correctional Populations in the United States*, 2010. Retrieved from: http://bjs.ojp.usdoj.gov/content/pub/pdf/cpus10.pdf.

Green, M.B. (2002). *Encyclopedia of Public Health*. Retrieved from: www.encyclolpedia.com/topic/violence.aspx.

Groth, N., and Birnbaum, H.J. (1979). *Men Who Rape: The Psychology of the Offender*. New York: Plenum.

Harper, D., Voigt, L., and Thornton, W. E. (2005). *Neighborhoods and Murder: New Orleans 1940–2000*. European Society of Criminology, Krakow, Poland.

Harrelson-Stephens, J., and Callaway, R.L. (2007). What are Human Rights? Definitions and Typologies of Today's Human Rights Discourse. In R.L. Callaway and J. Harrelson-Stephens (Eds.). *Exploring International Human Rights*. Boulder: Lynne Rienner Publishers, 4–10.

Hawkins, B. (2006). Capital punishment and the Administration of Justice: A Trial Prosecutor's Perspective. *Judicature*, 89, 258–261.

Heitmeyer, W., and J. Hagan. (2003). Violence: The difficulties of a systematic international review. In W. Heitmeyer and J. Hagan (Eds.), *International Handbook of Violence Research*. Boston, MA: Kluwer Academic Publishers, 3–12.

Iadicola, P., and A. Shupe. (2003). *Violence, Inequality, and Human Freedom* (2nd Ed). New York, NY: Rowman & Littlefield Publishers, Inc.

Iadicola, P. (2012). Violence: Definition, Spheres, and Principles. In D.W. Harper, L. Voigt, and W.E. Thornton (Eds.). *Violence: Do We Know It When We See It?* Durham, NC: Carolina Academic Press, 7–26.

Imbush, P. (2003). The concept of violence. In W. Heitmeyer and J. Hagan (Eds.), *International Handbook of Violence Research*. Boston, MA: Kluwer Academic Publishers, 13–40.

Innocence Project (n.d.). Retrieved from http://www.innocenceproject.org.

Jenkins, P (1998). *Moral Panic: Changing Concepts of the Child Molester in Modern America*. New Haven, CT: Yale University Press, 207–231.

Kalb, J. (2012). Guantanamo Continued. In Dee Harper, Lydia Voigt and William E. Thornton (Eds.), *Violence: Do We Know It When We See It?* Durham, NC: Carolina Academic Press, 323–340.

Kappeler, V. E., and Potter, G.W. (2005). *The Mythology of Crime and Criminal Justice* (4th Ed.). Long Grove, IL: Waveland Press, Inc.

Killingbeck, D. (2001). The role of television news in the construction of school violence as a 'Moral Panic.' *Journal of Criminal Justice and Popular Culture*, 8(3), 186–202.

Krug, E.G., Dahlberg, L.L., Mercy, J.A., Zwi, A.B., and Lozano, R. (2002). *World Report on Violence and Health*. Geneva, Switzerland: World Health Organization.

Kuhn, T. S. (1962/1970). *The Structure of Scientific Revolutions*. Chicago, IL: University of Chicago Press.

Lakoff, G., and M. Johnson. (1980/2003). M*etaphors We Live By*. Chicago: University Press.

Langan, P.A. (2002). Recidivism of Prisoners Released in 1994. Bureau of Justice Statistics Special Report, U.S. Department of Justice, NCJ 193427.

Langman, P. (2009). Rampage School Shooters: A Typology. *Aggression and Violent Behavior*, 14, 79–86.

Lawrence, R. (2007). *School Crime and Juvenile Justice*. New York: Oxford University Press.

Luckenbill, D. (1970) Criminal Homicide as a Situated Transaction. *Social Problems*, 24, 176–186.

Mills, C. W. (1956). *The Power Elite*. NY: Oxford Press.

Moore, M. (1995). Public Health and Criminal Justice Approaches to Prevention. In M. Tonry and D. F. Farrington (Eds.). *Building a Safer Society: Strategic Approaches to Crime Prevention*. Chicago: University of Chicago Press, 237–262.

Mosher, J. (2012). War, Taxonomy, Mythology, Reality. In D. Harper, L. Voigt and W.E. Thornton (Eds.)., *Violence: Do We Know It When We See It?* Durham, NC: Carolina Academic Press, 289–301.

Moyer, K. (1983). Violence. In S.H. Kadish (Ed.), *Encyclopedia of Crime and Justice*. New York, NY: Macmillan, 1618–1623.

Muraskin, R. and Domash, S.F. (2007). *Crime and the Media: Headlines versus Reality*. Upper Saddle River, NJ: Prentice Hall.

National Center for Injury Prevention and Control. (1993). *The Prevention of Youth Violence: A Framework for Community Action*. Atlanta, GA: Centers for Disease Control and Prevention.

National Institute of Justice, Office of Justice Programs. (2000). United States Department of Justice, Centers for Disease Control and Prevention.

National Institute of Mental Health. (1982). *Television and Behavior: Ten Years of Scientific Progress and Implications for the Eighties,* Volume I, Summary Report. Rockville, MD: U.S. Government Printing Office.

National Rifle Association (NRA). (2010). *Firearms Fact Card, 2010*. National Rifle Association, January 20, 2010. Retrieved from: http://www.nraila.org/Issues/FactSheets?Read.aspx?ID=83.

National Rifle Association Institute for Legislative Action (NRA-ILA) (2011). *Automatic Firearms and the Assault Weapon Issue*. Retrieved from: www.nraila.org/issues/factsheets./read.aspx?ID=238.

Ostertag, S.F. (2012). News Construction of Urban Violence: Fear and the Making of the Prototypical Criminal. In D.W. Harper, L. Voigt, and W.E. Thornton (Eds.). *Violence: Do We Know It When We See It?* Durham, NC: Carolina Academic Press, 165–176.

Pastor, J. F. (2007). *Security Law and Methods*. Boston: Elsevier, Inc.

Peck, E. (1989). Criminal Approaches to Family Violence, 1640–1980. In L. Ohlin and M. Tonry (Eds.). *Family Violence*. University of Chicago Press, 19–58.

Peelo, M., Francis, B., Soothill, K., Pearsen, J. and Ackerley, E. (2004). Newspaper Reporting and the Public Construction of Homicide. *British Journal of Criminology,* 44(2), 256–78.

Pew Center on the States. (2011). *State of Recidivism: The Revolving Door of America's Prisons.* Washington, DC: The Pew Charitable Trusts, April.

Pinker, S. (2011). *The Better Angels of Our Nature: Why Violence Has Declined.* New York, NY: Viking Press.

Platt, T. (1992). The Concept of Violence as Descriptive and Polemic. *International Social Science Journal*, 132, 185–191.

Platt, T., and O'Leary, C. (2003). Patriot Acts. *Social Justice*, 30, 5–21.

Potter, G., and Kappeler, V. (2006). *Constructing Crime: Perspectives on Making News and Social Problems.* Long Grove, IL: Waveland Press.

President's Commission on Law Enforcement and the Administration of Justice. (1967). *The Challenge of Crime in a Free Society.* Washington, DC: U.S. GPO.

Private Warriors (2005). *Interview with Peter Singer. Frontline, PBS.* Retrieved from: http://www.pbs.org/wgbh/pages/frontline/shows/warriors/interviews/singer.html.

Prothrow-Smith, D. (1991). *Deadly Consequences.* New York, NY: Harper Collins.

Quigley, W. (2007). Thirteen Ways of Looking at Katrina: Human and Civil Rights Left Behind Again, *Tulane Law Review*, 81(4), 955–1017.

Quinney, R. (1970). *The Social Reality of Crime.* Boston, MA: Little, Brown.

Rank, M. R. (2005). *One Nation Underprivileged: Why American Poverty Affects Us All.* NY: Oxford Press.

Rapping, E. (2003). *Law and Justice as Seen on TV.* New York, NY: New York University.

Reiman, J. (1990). *The Rich Get Richer and the Poor Get Jail.* NY: Macmillan.

Reiner, R. (2002). "Media made criminality: The representation of crime in the mass media." In M. Maguire, R. Morgan and R. Reiner (Eds.). *The Oxford Handbook of Criminology.* Oxford, UK: Oxford University Press, 376–416.

Roth, D.L. (2010). International Financial Institutions, Corruption and Human Rights. In M. Boersma and H. Nelen (Eds.). *Corruption & Human Rights: Interdisciplinary Perspectives.* Cambridge, Intersentia, 177–196.

Saad, L. (October 22, 2007). *Perceptions of Crime Problem Remain Curiously Negative: More See Crime Worsening Rather Than Improving.* Gallup. Retrieved from: http://www.gallup.com/poll/102262/percerptions-crime-problem-remain-curiously-negative.asp.

Shapiro, L. (2011). One Constant: American Gun Industry Thrives. Retrieved from: http://www.huffingtonpost.com/2011/01/11/gun-industry-thrives_n_807360.

Shaw, C.R., and McKay, H. (1969/1942). *Juvenile Delinquency in Urban Areas.* Chicago: University of Chicago Press.

Simmel, G. (1908/1983). *Conflict and the Web of Group Affiliation.* Translated by Kurt Wolff and Reinhard Bendix. New York, NY: The Free Press.

Singer, P. (2003). *Corporate Warriors: The Rise of the Privatized Military.* Cornel University Press.

Skogan, D., and Maxfield, M. (1981). *Coping with Crime.* Thousand Oaks, CA: Sage.

Snell, T.L. (2011). Capital Punishment, 2010—Statistical Tables. U.S. Department of Justice, Bureau of Justice Statistics, NCJ 236510

Sourcebook of Criminal Justice Statistics Online. (2010). Table 2.33 Attitudes toward levels of crime in the U.S. Retrieved from: http://www. Albany.edu/sourcebook/pdf/12332010.pdf.

Sullivan, D., and Tifft, L. (2005). *Restorative Justice: Healing the Foundation of our Everyday Lives.* Monsey, NY: Willow Tree Press, Inc.

Surette, R. (2007). *Media, Crime, and Criminal Justice: Images, Realities, and Policies* (3rd Ed.). Belmont, CA: Thomson Wadsworth.

Taylor, R. (2012). Victim Blame and the Media: The Portrayal of Femicide in Newspaper Stories. In D.W. Harper, L. Voigt, and W.E. Thornton (Eds.). *Violence: Do We Know It When We See It?* Durham, NC.: Carolina Academic Press, 181–199.

The Law Enforcement-Private Security Partnership. (2005). *Operation Partnership: Trends and Practices in Law Enforcement and Private Security Collaborations.* U.S. Department of Justice, Office of Community Oriented Policing Services.

Thornton, W. E., and Voigt, L. (2006). *Media Construction of crime in New Orleans: Hurricane Katrina and Beyond.* Paper presented at Southern Sociological Society Meetings, March, New Orleans, LA.

Thurman, R. (n.d.). *U.S. Firearms Industry Today.* Retrieved from: http://www.shootingindustry.com/firearmsreport10.pdf.

Time. (January 14, 2013). Arms Race. The U.S. Is a Global Outlier on Gun Laws. Will Newtown Change Anything?, 181(1), 14–15.

Tjaden, P., and Thoennes, N. (2000). *Full Report of the Prevalence, Incidence and Consequences of Violence against Women: Findings from the National Violence against Women Survey.* Washington, D.C.: National Institute of Justice, Office of Justice Programs, United States Department of Justice, Centers for Disease Control and Prevention.

U.S. Department of Justice. (2009). Bureau of Justice Statistics, 2006 *Justice Expenditure and Employment Extracts.* NIC 224394. Retrieved from: http://www.Ojp.usdoj.gov/bjs/pub/sheets/cjee06.

U.S. Department of Health, Education, and Welfare. (1979). *Healthy People. The Surgeon General's Report on Health Promotion and Disease Prevention.* Washington, DC: U.S. Government Printing Office.

U.S. Department of Health and Human Services. (1980). *Promoting Health/Preventing Disease; Objectives for the Nation.* Washington, DC: U.S. Government Printing Office.

U.S. Department Health and Human Services. (1985). *Report of the Secretary's Task Force on Black and Minority Health.* Washington, DC: U.S. Government Printing Office.

U.S. Department of Health and Human Services. (1986). U.S. Department of Justice. *Surgeon General's Workshop on Violence and Public Health Report.* Washington, DC: Health Resources Service Administration.

U.S. Department of Health and Human Services. (1989). *Report of the Secretary's Task Force on Youth Suicide.* Washington, DC: U.S. Government Printing Office.

U.S. Department of Health and Human Services. (2001). *Youth Violence: A Report of the Surgeon General.* Centers for Disease Control and Prevention, Substance Abuse and Mental Health Services Administration. National Institutes of Health for the National Institute of Mental Health. Washington, DC: U.S. Government Printing Office. Retrieved from: http://www.surgeogeneral.gov/library/youthviolence/youvioreport.htm.

U. S. National Commission on the Causes and Prevention of Violence. (1969). Washington, DC: U.S. Government Printing Office.

Vaughan, B. (2002). Defining Violence at Work: A New Typology. In M. Gill, B. Fisher, and V. Bowie, (Eds.). *Violence at Work: Causes, Patterns and Prevention.* Portland, Oregon: Willan Publishing.

Voigt, L., Thornton, W.E., Barrile, L., and Seaman, J.M. (1994). *Criminology and Justice.* New York: McGraw Hill.

Voigt, L., and Thornton, W.E. (2011). *The Rhetoric and Politics of Violence.* Washington, DC: American Society of Criminology.

Vollman, B. (2012). Pedophilia and the U.S. Catholic Church: Victimization and Its Effects. In D. W. Harper, L. Voigt, and W.E. Thornton, (Eds.). *Violence: Do We Know It When We See It?* Durham, NC: Carolina Academic Press, 345–361.

Vossekuil, B., M. Reddu, R Fein, R. Borum, and W. Modzelski. (2000). *Safe School Initiative: An Interim Report on the Prevention of Targeted Violence in Schools.* (Washington, DC: United States Secret Service.

Wall, D.S. (2007). *Cybercrime: The Transformation of Crime in the Information Age.* Cambridge, UK: Polity Press.

Walsh, P.D, Thornton, W.E., and Voigt, L. (2010). Post-Hurricane Katrina and Human Rights Violations in New Orleans, Louisiana. In M. Boersma and H. Nelen (Eds.). *Corruption & Human Rights: Interdisciplinary Perspectives.* Cambridge: Intersentia.

Walmsley, R. (2009) World Prison Population List (8th Edition). London's Kings College. International Center for Prison Studies. Retrieved from: http://www.prisonstudies.org/info/downloads/wppl-8th_41.pdf.

Weber, M. (1978). *Economy and Society.* San Francisco, CA: University of California.

Weiner, N.A., Zahn, M.A. and Sagi, R.J. (1990). *Violence Patterns, Causes, Public Policy.* San Diego, CA: Harcourt Brace Jovanovich.

Weitzer, R. (2007). The social construction of sex trafficking: Ideology and Institutionalization of a Morale Crusade. *Politics and Society,* 35(3), 447–475.

Whitt, H.P., Corzine, J., and Huff-Corzine, L. (2012). The Social Construction of Suicide, Suicide Rates, and the Suicidal Act. In D.W. Harper, L. Voigt, and W.E. Thornton (Eds.). *Violence: Do We Know It When We See It?* Durham, NC: Carolina Academic Press, 205–218.

Wintemute, G.J. (2002). Where Guns Come From: The Gun Industry and Gun Commerce. Retrieved from: http://futureofchildren.org/publicaitons/journals/article/index.xml?journalid+42&articleid=165&sectionid=1058.

Woolford, A. (2006). Making Genocide Unthinkable: Three Guidelines for a Critical Criminology of Genocide. *Critical Criminology,* 14, 87–106.

World Health Organization. (2009). *Violence against Women.* Retrieved from: http://www.who.int/mediacentre/factsheets/fs239/en/.

Worrall, J.L. (2008). *Crime Control in America: What Works.* Boston, MA: Pearson.

Youth Violence is a Public Health Issue (2001. Retrieved from: http://odphp,osophs.dhhs.gov/pubs/prevrpt/01spring/spring2001pr.htm.

Chapter 2

The Measurement of Violence

Violence-related statistics have become part of our daily lives. The measurement of violence and quality of factual information related to violence is of vital importance to all of us. Violence information and statistics not only create interesting news headlines and political platforms, they underlie our social responses and solutions to the problems of violence, in all of its manifestations. Scientific studies of violence ultimately rest on the foundation of two great pillars, facts and theories to explain facts. For example, criminologists need accurate data on the nature, extent, location, and distribution of violence and other criminal behavior in society. Without valid and reliable data of this kind, the various theories developed to explain and understand violence will be seriously flawed. The critical importance of accurate reliable information cannot be overstated. We cannot stress enough that violence-related statistics form the basis of our images and understanding of violence in society. These statistics are used to support or disconfirm causative theories as well as to justify certain policies and social responses including evaluations of their effectiveness. Ultimately, these statistics affect our peace of mind (or level of fear) and how we relate to one another.

Official systematic collection as well as analysis of crime data including violent crimes committed in society, however, is historically a relatively recent advent. Over 180 years ago, the famous Belgian statistician, Adolphe Quetelet, in his noted book, *Research on the Propensities for Crime at Different Ages* (released in 1831, the first publication of its kind and forerunner of our current *Uniform Crime Reports*) not only was the first to summarize crime statistics in France (which was the first country to collect such information) with regard to age, sex, race, social class, literacy, and residence, but also he was the first to make predictions based on area and trait analyses of crime statistics. Quetelet, however, was careful to make his predictions on the basis of crime rates (i.e., the number of crimes in a particular area divided by a standard unit of population) rather than attempting the impossible task of predicting individual crimes. Quetelet concluded that the best general predictor of crime commission in general is age (1831/1984, p. 64) claiming that criminal activity sharply declines after the age of 25.

Amazingly, many of Quetelet's findings continue to be borne out by contemporary analyses of the patterns of crimes across different geographic locations world-wide. He was also the first to observe that the "sum total of crimes committed will probably remain unknown forever," and consequently that all official accounts "will be more or less defective" (p. 17). Therefore, he warned that interpretations must be extremely cautious, since there is an inherent relationship between "offenses known and judged and the unknown sum total of offenses committed." While our modern statistical procedures and techniques, by comparison, may be more refined and our forecasts of crime patterns more precise, our predictions are still limited by the unknown nature of the sum total of offenses committed. Given that most crimes lie hidden, we will never know with certainty whether a particular recorded rise in crime rates represents truly more criminal activity or is just the result of more effective policing or crime reporting and our presumably greater awareness of it. In other words, is a rise in violent crime statistics due to a real increase in violence or is it a function of more efficient record keeping, more intense enforcement strategies, greater deterrence policies, enactment of new laws, or changes in public perceptions? For example, certain forms of violence, which have not been legally recognized in the past, may appear to have increased as a result of a more expansive definition (e.g., since rape by legal definition did not include rape by spouses or among males, its redefinition in many jurisdictions has resulted in increases in incidents). Even a slight change in the way that crimes are legally defined, reported or responded to by police or the public will have an effect on our official crime rates. Part of the reason why so many people believe that crime is rising may be due to the historically unprecedented amount of information about violence and crime across our society. According to recent Gallup polls, over two-thirds of Americans perceive that crime is rising even though, according to the *Uniform Crime Reports*, crime rates in the United States are at a twenty-year low (Jones, 2010).

Over the last several decades the United States and other countries have been undergoing revolutionary transformations in information technology and communications resulting in greater efficiency in data collection and analysis and accessibility of information, which has been associated with an information explosion. This recent transformation of information and its explosive growth has had a significant effect on the quality and quantity of violence-related information and ultimately on the social construction of the reality of violence. Billions of dollars are spent annually on the collection, analysis, and dissemination of crime, particularly violence data across the globe.

There are many sources of data used to measure different types of violence in the United States and in the world. Criminologists and other social scientists have only recently, since World War II, come to recognize that crime and violence are not unique to one country, but exist globally and that solutions to the many types of interpersonal, institutional, and structural forms of violence can mainly be informed by accurate information. A statement made by Nelson Mandela in the Foreword to the World Health Organization's *World Report on Violence and Health* (2002) is especially poignant.

> The twentieth century will be remembered as a century marked by violence. It burdens us with its legacy of mass destruction, of violence inflicted on a scale never seen and never possible before in human history. But this legacy—the result of new technology in the service of ideologies of hate—is not the only one we carry, or that we must face up to. Less visible, but even more widespread, is the legacy of day-to-day individual suffering. It is the pain of children who are abused by people who should protect them, women injured or humiliated by violent partners, elderly persons maltreated by their caregivers, youths who are bullied by other youths, and people of all ages who inflict violence on themselves (Krug, et al., 2002, Foreword).

The World Health Organization (WHO) study of global violence, which examines interpersonal and collective violence, seeks first to measure the magnitude and impact of fatal and non-fatal violence globally, using a variety of innovative measures well beyond just national official crime statistics (e.g., police reports) including sources such as mortality data (e.g., death certificates), morbidity data (e.g., hospital or other medical records), self-reported data (e.g., victimization and perpetration), and economic data (e.g., costs of treating violence related injuries). The study also seeks to accomplish several other objectives including describing key risk indicators for violence, measuring the impact of types of intervention and their effectiveness, and making recommendations for action and policies at local, state, and international levels (Krug, et al., 2002, Introduction).

As the WHO study suggests, there are unique sources of data available to study violence in all cultures, although availability and quality of the data varies from country to country. However, given that professionals now include criminologists and other social and physical scientists, medical practitioners, legal scholars, and criminal justice practitioners, it should come as no surprise that individuals who study violence employ a variety of research methodologies based on their respective disciplinary orientation. The use of one technique over another depends on the goals of the research, e.g., to show violence in the form of human rights violations in a particular country or to show trends in instrumental murder as a crime in a particular country.

The use of existing statistical and archival data, e.g., national official crime statistics collected by different countries and international organizations such as the United Nations, are used to make inferences or generalizations about violent crime trends, particularly interpersonal violence, in a particular country or between countries. Countries such as the United States, Canada, Australia, Great Britain, and Japan collect national crime statistics on a regular basis. However, many countries do not collect consistent (or any) statistical data on crime or violence.

Internationally, the crime of homicide or murder generally serves as the universal proxy for "violence." It is not uncommon to see comparisons made between countries based on homicide volumes and rates, which may not at all be comparable for any number of reasons, such as variations in legal classifications and reporting/data collection methodologies (Pakes, 2004, pp. 19–23). In fact, it is often difficult to compare rates or trends of violence, using indicators such as murder, from city to city and state to state even in our own country. It is important to remember that making comparisons between countries in terms of violence must be done cautiously. As noted by Fairfield and Dammer, "the fact is that a nation's way of administering justice reflects deep-seated cultural, religious, economic, political, and historical realities. Learning about the reasons for these different practices can give us insight into the values, traditions, and cultures of other systems" (2001, p. 9).

We shall begin by reviewing different sources of information and statistics pertaining to violence. Along the way, we will note some of the benefits of various sources of information and also some of the methodological flaws as well as the theoretical and policy implications. As we shall see, the impact of violence statistics on us, and the effect of the information revolution in the past few decades on our estimates of violence in the United States and globally are still, in many ways, unknown and subject to many interpretations.

The Measurement of Violence in the United States

The U.S. Department of Justice administers two statistical programs to measure the magnitude, nature, and impact of crime including violent crime in the nation: The *Uniform Crime Reports* (UCR) and the *National Crime Victimization Survey* (NCVS). Each of these programs produces information about characteristics associated with violent crime and property crime. We will focus our attention on violent crimes. Given that the UCR and NCVS programs are conducted for different purposes, use different methods, and focus on different aspects of crimes, the information they produce together presents a more comprehensive picture of violent crime in our country (FBI, 2011, The Nation's Two Measures).

Uniform Crime Reports

The oldest consistent source of information on violent crime in the United States is the *Uniform Crime Reports* (UCR). When first conceived in 1927 at the annual convention of the International Association of Chiefs of Police (IACP), the goal was to obtain systematic and comparable reports on the volume of different types of crimes from all city, county, and state police agencies in the nation. The first report, entitled, *Uniform Crime Reporting: A Complete Manual for Police*, was released in 1929; it offered standardized definitions of crimes in various categories and provided guidelines where police agencies could prepare monthly and annual reports so that a national crime picture could be produced (Voigt, et al., 1994, p. 68).

In 1930, by act of Congress, the Federal Bureau of Investigation (FBI) took charge of the reporting program, created a national clearing house for the monthly and annual reports and published the first edition of the UCR, with reports from 400 police agencies. The number of police agencies participating in the UCR as of 2010 was over 18,000 (FBI, 2011, Summary of UCR Program). Published annually the UCR, *Crime in the United States*, has been completely online on the FBI's Web site (www.fbi.gov) since 2005. The site contains several major types of information of interest to criminologists and other researchers who study violence as well as to the public. This information usually originates from a "call for service" complaint in which a law enforcement officer responds to an alleged criminal event, and makes a determination as to whether a crime has actually occurred. Through subsequent investigation, the initial determination may change, e.g., decision that a crime did not occur or upgraded to a more serious offense. Discretion in law enforcement as well as political decisions regarding the reporting of crimes may affect estimated volumes (total number of crimes) and rates (crimes per 100,000 population).

The UCR reports crime counts for the nation as a whole, as well as for regions, states, counties, cities, towns, tribal law enforcement, and colleges and universities. The UCR is best known for its computation of annual violent and property crime rates. The *rate* is based on the number of crimes known to the police for a given year, divided by the "estimated" U.S. population for a given year and then multiplied by 100,000. The population figure is based on census data, which is collected every ten years. The estimates vary in quality depending on which part of the decade the computations are made, a criticism often made of the UCR. Another problem stems from the fact that the population estimates are based on the number of "residents." Populations such as tourists and transients are excluded by the UCR. Cities such as Atlanta, Boston, Chicago, Miami, and New Orleans attract millions of tourists each year. Since the rate of crime is affected by population size, such a sizable omission can distort the reality of crime. The city of New Orleans, after Hurricane Katrina, lost about one third of its population driving the murder rate up substantially, well above the national level (VanLandingham, 2007). The New Orleans Police Department spent considerable time trying to make the case to residents and the local newspaper, *The Times-Picayune*, that the murder rate was inflated, because of the population count, which was reputed to be larger than official counts (Ripley, 2006; Konigsmark, 2006).

Several types of crime data are collected by the UCR including:

(1) *Offenses known to law enforcement* in eight offense categories (i.e., criminal homicide [murder and non-negligent manslaughter], forcible rape, robbery, aggravated assault, burglary, larceny-theft, motor vehicle theft, and arson). These offenses are referred to as Part I Offenses. The FBI further classifies these offenses into broad categories: "violent crime" (i.e., homicide, rape, robbery and assault) and "property crime" (i.e., burglary, larceny-theft, motor vehicle theft, and arson). These offenses comprise serious offenses, which occur regularly, concern people the most, and therefore are most likely to be reported. Part II Offenses include 21 other crimes, which are less serious and less likely to be reported (e.g., forgery, fraud, vandalism, drug abuse violations, and sex offenses).

(2) *Arrest statistics* (i.e., the number of persons arrested and rates of arrest per 100,000 population) in the Part I categories, plus arrest estimates for the Part II offenses. The UCR further breaks down arrests by age, sex, race and ethnicity, and by population density of reporting areas (e.g., cities, suburban areas, and rural areas).

(3) *Clearance rates* are indicators of police efficiency in solving crime (see Riedel, 2012). The *clearance rate* is defined as the percent of all index offenses known to the police that are "cleared" by the arrest of the suspected perpetrator who is charged with the commission of an offense and turned over for prosecution or by exceptional means. When it not possible for the police to arrest an offender, the agency can clear the offense *exceptionally* by meeting certain conditions including identifying the offender, having enough evidence for making an arrest, knowing the offender's exact location, and encounters a problem beyond their control for making an immediate arrest. Examples of exceptional clearances include the death of an offender or the victim's refusal to cooperate with the

---

Box 2.1 UCR Definition of Violent Crimes

Criminal Homicide: (a) Murder and non-negligent manslaughter: the willful (nonnegligent) killing of one human being by another. Deaths caused by negligence, attempts to kill, assaults to kill, suicides, and accidental deaths are excluded. The program classifies justifiable homicides separately and limits the definition to: (1) the killing of a felon by a law enforcement officer in the line of duty; or (2) the killing of a felon, during the commission of a felony, by a private citizen. (b) Manslaughter by negligence: the killing of another person through gross negligence. Deaths of persons due to their own negligence, accidental deaths not resulting from gross negligence, and traffic fatalities are not included in the category Manslaughter by Negligence.

Forcible rape:* The carnal knowledge of a female forcibly and against her will. Rapes by force and attempts or assaults to rape, regardless of the age of the victim, are included. Statutory offenses (no force used—victim under age of consent) are excluded.

Robbery: The taking or attempting to take anything of value from the care, custody, or control of a person or persons by force or threat of force and/or by putting the victim in fear.

Aggravated assault: An unlawful attack by one person upon another for the purpose of inflicting severe or aggravated bodily injury. The type of assault is accomplished by the use of a weapon or by means likely to produce death or great bodily harm. Simple assaults are excluded.

Source: FBI, 2011: Offense Definitions.
  * Changed as of January, 2012 (see p. 57).

---

prosecution after identification of the offender. In reporting year 2010, 47.2 percent of violent crimes (overall) were cleared, including murder (64.8%), forcible rape (40.3%), robbery (28.2%), and aggravated assault (56.4%) (FBI, 2011, Offenses Cleared).

(4) *Expanded offense data* consists of collected data on violent and property crime offenses beyond the count of how many crimes are known to the police. Depending on the type of offense, these details may include information such as the type of weapon used and other information about the crime. For the crime of murder, for example, expanded data include *supplemental* information (referred to as *Supplemental Homicide Data*) regarding the age, sex, and race of the murder victim and offender; the type of weapon used in the murder; the relationship of the victim to the offender; and the circumstances surrounding the incident. These data also include information about *justifiable homicide.* Since these killings are determined by the police to be justifiable, they are tabulated separately from murder and non-negligent manslaughter. The *Supplemental Homicide Data* program requests reporting agencies to provide complete supplementary homicide data for each murder they report to the UCR program. Given that murder is often considered to be a universal proxy for violent behavior, it has been studied more than any other violent crime both in the United States and in other countries (e.g., UNODC, 2011a). According to the *Supplemental Homicide Data* results, of the 12,996 incidents of murder in 2010, the majority of victims were male (77%) (Expanded Homicide Data [EHD], Table 1); 50 percent were black, 47 percent were white, 3 percent represented other races, and for 152 victims race was unknown (EHD, Table 2). The overwhelming majority of offenders were male (90%) (EHD, Table 3); 53 percent were black, 45 percent were white, 2 percent other, and for 4,224 offenders race was unknown (EHD, Table 3). Single

victim/single offender accounted for 48 percent of all murders (EHD, Table 4) and most incidents involved a firearm (68%) (EHD, Table 8). Of the murders for which the circumstance surrounding the murder was known, 42 percent of victims were murdered during arguments (including romantic triangles). Felony circumstances (e.g., rape, robbery, burglary, etc.) accounted for 23 percent of murders. Circumstances were unknown for 36 percent of reported homicides (EHD, Table 12). Law enforcement reported 665 justifiable homicides in 2010. Of those, law enforcement officers justifiably killed 387 felons, and private citizens justifiably killed 278 people during the commission of a crime (EHD, Tables 14 and 15). In 2010, in incidents of murder for which the relationships of murder victims and offenders were known, 53 percent were killed by someone they knew (intimate partner, family member, acquaintance, neighbor, or friend) (EHD, Table 10). Of the female murder victims for whom the relationships to their offenders were known, 38 percent were murdered by their intimate partner (EHD, Tables 2 and 10). The relationship of murder victims and offenders was unknown in 44 percent of murders (EHD, Table 10). Figure 2.1 depicts *Murder by Relationship* for 2010 showing that murder victims are more likely to be killed by someone they are acquainted with rather than by strangers, when such data is available.

(5) *Characteristics of sworn officers and civilian law enforcement personnel* is another source of data included in the UCR (FBI, 2011, Police Employees). A total of 14,744 city and county law enforcement agencies provide information on the number of full-time law enforcement employees in 2010. In the nation's cities, the average number of full-time law enforcement officers is 2.3 per 1,000 population. Cities with less than 10,000 population report the largest officer-to-individual rate among city population groups (FBI, 2011, Police Employees). A separate UCR publication, *Law Enforcement Officers Killed and Assaulted*, provides information on line-of-duty deaths and assaults on local, state and federal police (www.fbi.gov/about-us/cjis/ucr/ucr).

NIBRS, Redesign and Changes in the UCR

Although the UCR has remained virtually unchanged over the years, in the 1980s the International Association of Chiefs of Police and the National Sheriff's Association called for a major redesign of the UCR system, outlined in the final report, *Blueprint for the Future of the Uniform Crime Reporting Program*, released in 1985. While the redesign embraced the revolution in computer information systems, the major change in the UCR was the establishment of the National Incident-Based Reporting System (NIBRS) in 1989, which involved a reporting system where each reporting law enforcement agency reports on each individual crime incident and on each individual arrest. Under the traditional system, the UCR only reports summary counts of offenses. NIBRS was originally designed to employ fifty-two data elements organized around six types of data elements: administrative, offense, victim, property, offender, and arrests; however it can capture data up to 57 elements (see Box 2.2). Additional incident-based information has been built into the system over the years including: (1) bias-motivated offenses (1990); (2) presence of gang activity (1997); (3) data on law enforcement officers killed and assaulted (2003); and (4) data on cargo theft (2005) (UCR, 2011, About the UCR Program). While the original UCR focuses on the eight violent and property crimes (formerly known as Index Offenses), NIBRS has forty-six Group A offenses representing twenty-two categories

Figure 2.1

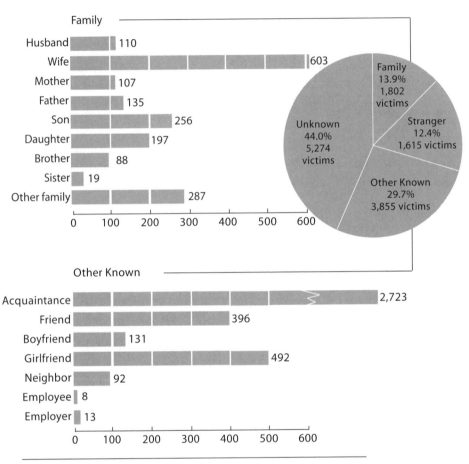

Expanded Homicide Data Figure
Murder by Relationship[1]
Percent Distribution,[2] Volume by Relationship, 2010

1 Relationship is that of victim to offender.
2 Due to rounding, the percentges may not add to 100.0.
NOTE: Figures are based on 12,996 murder victims for whom supplemental homicide data were received, and includes the 5,274 victims for which the relationship was unknown.

of crime (including violent offenses such as homicide, robbery, forcible sex offenses, assault, and kidnapping/abduction). The FBI began accepting NIBRS data from a few law enforcement agencies in 1989, but participation has been limited based on a department's data processing resources. As of 2007, the FBI has certified 31 state UCR programs for NIBRS participation. Ten of those states submit all their data to NIBRS and 9 states are in various stages of testing NIBRS. There are a number of positive changes in the eventual shift of the UCR to NIBRS for the study of violent crime, including: (1) expanded offense definitions for all violent offenses, particularly rape (e.g., forcible rape

Box 2.2 NIBRS Group A Offenses and Data Elements

Group A Offenses

Arson	Gambling offenses	Motor vehicle theft
Assault offense	Betting/wagering	Pornography/obscene
Aggravated assault	Operating/promotion/	material
Simple assault	assisting gambling	Prostitution offenses
Intimidation	Gambling equipment	Prostitution
Bribery	violations	Assisting/promoting
Burglary/breaking &	Sports tempering	prostitution
entering	Homicide offenses	Robbery
Counterfeiting/forgery	Murder/nonnegligent	Sexual offenses, forcible
Destruction/damage/	manslaughter	Forcible rape
vandalism of property	Negligent homicide	Forcible sodomy
Drug/narcotic offenses	Justifiable homicide	Sexual assault with an
Drug/narcotic violations	Kidnapping/abduction	object
Drug equipment violations	Larceny/theft offenses	Forcible fondling
Embezzlement	Pocket picking	Sexual offenses,
Extortion/blackmail	Purse snatching	non-forcible
Fraud offenses	Shoplifting	Stolen property offenses
False pretenses/swindle/	Theft from building	Weapon law offenses
confidence game	Theft from coin-operated machine	
Credit card/ATM fraud	Theft of motor vehicle parts/	
Welfare fraud	accessories	
Wire fraud	All other larceny	

Data Elements

Administrative segment
1. ORI Number
2. Incident number
3. Incident date/hour
4. Exceptional clearance indicator
5. Exceptional clearance date

Offense segment
6. UCR offense code
7. Attempted/completed code
8. Alcohol/drug use by of Victim
9. Type of location
10. Number of premises entered
11. Method of entry
12. Type of criminal activity
13. Type of weapon/force used
14. Bias crime code

Property segment
15. Type of property loss
16. Property description
17. Property value
18. Recovery date
19. Number of stolen motor vehicles

20. Number of recovered motor vehicles
21. Suspected drug type
22. Estimated drug quantity
23. Drug measurement unit

Victim segment
24. Victim number
25. Victim UCR offense code
26. Type of victim
27. Age of Victim
28. Sex of victim
29. Race of victim
30. Ethnicity of victim
31. Resident status of victim
32. Homicide/assault circumstances
33. Justifiable homicide circumstances
34. Type of injury
35. Related offender number
36. Relationship of victim to offender

Offender segment
37. Offender number
38. Age of offender

39. Sex of offender
40. Race of Offender

Arrestee segment
41. Arrestee number
42. Transaction number
43. Arrest date
44. Type of arrest
45. Multiple clearance indicator
46. UCR arrest offense code
47. Arrestee armed indicator
48. Age of arrestee
49. Sex of arrestee
50. Race of arrestee
51. Ethnicity of arrestee
52. Residence status of arrestee
53. Disposition of arrestee under 18

Source: FBI, 2011.

Table 2.1 Violent Crimes in the U. S. by Volume and Rate per 100,000 Inhabitants, 1990–2010

Year	Population	Violent Crimes Volume/Rate	Murder Volume/Rate	Rape Volume/Rate	Robbery Volume/Rate	Assault Volume/Rate
1990	249,464,396	1,820,827/ 729.6	23,438/ 9.4	102,555/ 41.1	639,271/ 256.3	1,054,863/ 422.9
1991	252,153,092	1,911,767/ 758.2	24,703/ 9.8	105,593/ 42.3	687,732/ 272.7	1,092,739/ 433.4
1992	255,029,699	1,932,274/ 757.7	23,760/ 9.3	109,062/ 42.8	672,478/ 263.7	1,126,974/ 441.9
1993	257,782,608	1,926,017/ 747.1	24,526/ 9.5	106,014/ 41.1	659,870/ 256.0	1,135,607/ 440.5
1994	260,327,021	1,857,670/ 713.6	23,326/ 9.0	102,216/ 39.3	618,949/ 237.8	1,113,179/ 427.6
1995	262,803,276	1,798,792/ 664.5	21,606/ 8.2	97,470/ 37.1	580,509/ 220.9	1,099,207/ 416.3
1996	265,228,572	1,688,540/ 636.6	19,645/ 7.4	96,252/ 36.3	535,594/ 201.9	1,037,049 391.0
1997	267,783,607	1,638,096/ 611.0	18,208/ 6.8	96,153/ 35.9	498,534/ 186.2	1,023,201/ 382.1
1998	270,248,003	1,533,887/ 567.6	16,974/ 6.3	93,144/ 34.5	447,186/ 165.5	976,583/ 361.4
1999	272,690,813	1,426,044/ 523.0	15,522/ 5.7	89,411/ 32.8	409,371/ 150.1	911,740/ 334.3
2000	281,421,486	1,425,486/ 506.5	15,586/ 5.5	90,178/ 32.0	408,016/ 145.0	911,706/ 324.0
2001	285,317,480	1,439,480/ 504.5	16,037/ 5.6	90,836/ 31.8	423,557/ 148.5	909,023/ 318.6
2002	287,973,924	1,423,677/ 494.4	16,229/ 5.6	95,235/ 33.1	420,407/ 146.1	891,402/ 309.5
2003	290,788,976	1,383,676/ 475.8	16,528/ 5.7	93,883/ 32.3	414.235/ 142.5	859,030/ 295.4
2004	293,656,842	1,360,088/ 463.2	16,148/ 5.5	95,089/ 32.4	401,470/ 136.7	847,381/ 288.6
2005	296,507,061	1,390,745/ 469.0	16,740/ 5.6	94,347/ 31.8	417,438/ 140.8	862,220/ 290.8
2006	298,754,819	1,435,951/ 480.6	17,318/ 5.8	94,782/ 31.7	449,803/ 150.6	874,048/ 292.6
2007	301,290,332	1,421,990/ 472.0	17,157/ 5.7	91,874/ 30.5	447,155/ 148.4	865,804/ 287.4
2008	304,374,846	1,392,629/ 457.5	16,442/ 5.4	90,479/ 29.7	443,574/ 145.7	842,134/ 276.7
2009	307,006,550	1,325,896/ 429.4	15,399/ 5.0	88,241/ 28.7	408,742/ 133.1	812,514/ 264.7
2010	308,745,538	1,246,248/ 403.6	14,748/ 4.8	84,767/ 27.5	367,832/ 119.1	777,901/ 252.3

Source: FBI 1991; FBI 2011: Violent Crime, Table 1.

including forcible sodomy, sexual assault with an object); (2) greater specificity of data (e.g., breakdowns regarding victims, injuries, involvement of weapons); (3) inclusion of attempted versus completed crimes; (4) the ability to better analyze relationships between variables such as offenses, victims, offenders, and arrestees (FBI, 2011; Hagan, 2010, pp. 105–110; NACJD, about NIBRS; Blueprint, 1985).

Other recent developments in the UCR program include: (1) the collection of crime data on human trafficking as stipulated in the William Wilberforce Trafficking Victims Protection Reauthorization Act of 2008; (2) the collection of data on crimes motivated by "gender and gender identity" bias crimes and "crimes directed against juveniles" under the Matthew Shepard and James Byrd, Jr. Hate Crime Prevention Act of 2009; (3) the eventual expansion of race categories from four (White, Black, American Indian or Alaska Native, and Asian or Other Pacific Islander) to five (adding Native Hawaiian or Other Pacific Islander); and (4) changing the ethnicity categories from "Hispanic" to "Hispanic or Latino Origin" and from "Non-Hispanic" to "Not of Hispanic or Latino Origin"). And, to deal with criticisms regarding the availability of the crime data, the FBI through the UCR Redevelopment Project (UCRRP) plans to decrease the time to analyze and release/publish crime data, and to develop more data query ability on the internet for public usage (FBI, 2011, About the UCR Program).

Trends in Violent Crimes from the UCR

The UCR classifies violent crime as being composed of four offenses (i.e., murder and non-negligent manslaughter, forcible rape, robbery, and aggravated assault). Violent crimes defined by the UCR are "those offenses, which involve force or threat of force" (FBI, 2011). Operating under the Hierarchy Rule, "which requires that only the most serious offense in a multiple-offense criminal incident be counted," the descending order of the four violent crimes is murder and non-negligent manslaughter, forcible rape, robbery, and aggravated assault. Thus, if an incident involves both murder and rape, only the crime of murder is reported to a respective law enforcement agency and would be counted.

Table 2.1 displays the volume (total number) and rate of violent index crimes reported from 1990 through 2010. Comparisons generally show a significant drop in the overall total violence crime rate during the past twenty years. The 2010 estimated violent crime rate, 403.6 per 100,000 inhabitants, represents a 45 percent decrease when compared to the 1990 violent crime rate, 729.6 per 100,000 inhabitants. Particularly interesting as an indicator of violence is the crime of murder. The *volume* of murder decreased from 23,438 in 1990 to 14,748 in 2010, with an accompanying *rate* decrease from 9.4 murders per 100,000 to 4.8 murders per 100,000, a decrease of about 49 percent. Criminologists have been trying to explain the dramatic drop in major crime rates starting in the 1990s, the longest and deepest reduction since World War II. The declines, according to many experts, occurred without any warning and, to the contrary, predictions were that there would be the very opposite, an explosion in crime in the mid-1990s (Levitt, 2004; Zimring, 2007). There have been various theories and explanations for the drop, especially in violent crimes like murder, including: (1) more proactive/aggressive policing; (2) tougher gun control laws; (3) unprecedented economic gains, (4) demographic changes resulting in terms of a drop in high-risk population of teens to 29 year olds, and (5) increases in incarceration (e.g., Zimring, 2007; Gilmore, 2007). Unfortunately, while these, and other factors, may have led in some way to the drop in violent crime in the 1990s and beyond, we cannot point to definitive research supporting these hypotheses. Criminologist, Frank Zimring, in his book, *The Great American Crime Decline* (2007), sums it up this way:

Even with so much good news on law enforcement and the economy, much of the great American crime decline could be a cyclical phenomenon, unrelated to public policy changes or new approaches to police work (Gilmore, 2007). Whatever else is known about crime in America, the most important lesson of the 1990s was that major changes in rates of crime can happen without major changes in the social fabric (p. 206).

National Crime Victimization Survey (NCVS)

The limitations in police-reported crime statistics first received national attention with the creation of the President's Commission on Law Enforcement and the Administration of Justice in 1965. Acknowledging the flaws in police crime reports, the Commission funded three initial surveys of crime victims. The first national victimization survey was carried out for the Commission by the National Opinion Research Center (NORC) of the University of Chicago in 1967, and involved questioning a random cross-section of approximately 33,000 persons in 10,000 households. Survey respondents were asked whether they or any member of their household had been the victim of an "Index" crime (excluding homicide, but including forcible rape, armed robbery, and assault) during the past year, and "whether the crime had been reported" and, if not, the reason for not reporting" (President's Commission, 1967, p. 21). The survey approach to crime measurement was designed to avoid the discretionary, organizational, and political factors that produce selectivity in official police records. The victim surveys also included information regarding unreported crimes. The initial surveys sponsored by the President's Commission confirmed that the rate of victimization as reported by randomly selected persons greatly exceeds the rates reflected in both national and local police reports. According to the NORC national survey, for instance, rates from victim reports exceed UCR rates for violent crimes (e.g., forcible rapes were 3.5 times higher and aggravated assaults 2 times higher). The results from the other victimization surveys conducted in specific cities such as Washington D.C. were even more dramatic, with victim-reported violent crimes seven times higher than recorded by law enforcement agencies (p. 21).

Such discrepancies led to the establishment of the annual national crime victimization surveys, formerly published in National Crime Survey, and now in National Crime Victimization Survey (NCVS). National crime victimization surveys have been published yearly since 1973 by the Bureau of Justice Statistics' (BJS) NCVS, which provides a detailed picture of crime incidents, victims, and trends. The BJS publishes numerous focused reports based on the survey results in the annual report, *Criminal Victimization in the United States*. The National Archive of Criminal Justice Data at the University of Michigan archives the NCVS data files, which allows researchers to conduct their own studies. The BJS completed a major methodological redesign of the survey questions in 1993 to better discover crime and broaden the scope of crimes measured. The new survey collects detailed data on the frequency and nature of the violence crimes of rape, sexual assault, personal robbery, aggravated and simple assault, as well as property crimes of household burglary, theft, and motor vehicle theft. It does not measure homicide. Twice a year, the U.S. Census Bureau interviews household members in a nationally representative sample of approximately 43,000 households (about 76,000 people). Approximately 150,000 interviews of persons age 12 and older are conducted annually. The NCVS collects data on crimes perpetrated against individuals and households and whether or not those crimes were reported to law enforcement. The actual survey includes information about *victims* (age, sex, race, ethnicity, marital status, income, and education level); *offenders* (sex, race, approximate age); *victim-offender relationship* (intimate partners, family members, acquaintances, or strangers); and *crime occurrence* (time and place of event, use of weapons, nature of injury, and economic consequences). There are also questions addressing the experiences of victims with the criminal justice system, self-protective measures used by victims, and possible drug use by offenders (FBI, 2011, The Nation's Two Measures).

Historically, the NCVS was created to complement the UCR crime reporting program, so there are many similarities. As much as the differences in data collection methods allow, both programs provide measures of violent crimes (i.e., rape, robbery, and aggravated assault) and property crimes (i.e., burglary, theft, and motor vehicle theft). There is, however, a major difference between the UCR and the NCVS in the *type* of data collected. The NCVS obtains estimates of *crimes reported to the police as well as crimes not reported to the police*. The UCR collects information on *reported crimes only*. According to victims interviewed in the latest NCVS, about 50 percent of violent crimes were reported to the police in 2010 (Truman, 2011). Another difference between the two crime measures is that the NCVS collects data on nonfatal crimes reported and not reported to the police against persons age 12 and older and produces national rates of personal (and property) victimization. The NCVS excludes, but the UCR includes, homicides, arson (a possible violent crime), commercial crimes (including robberies of commercial establishments such as gas stations, convenience stores, and banks), as well as crimes against children under age 12. The UCR program until recently has recorded rapes in which the victims are females; the NCVS has included both sexes (FBI, 2011, The Nation's Two Measures). And, as has been noted by law enforcement officials and women's advocates, the UCR definition of rape "the carnal knowledge of a female, forcibly and against her will" excludes cases that involve oral or anal penetration or penetration with an object, and also excludes rapes that occur when a victim is drugged or intoxicated. However, as a response to these criticisms of the narrow definition of rape, the FBI expanded the definition of rape as of January, 2012, which now covers several forms of sexual assault and includes male rape. The new definition of rape is: "The sexual penetration, no matter how slight, of the vagina or anus with any body part or object, or oral penetration by a sex organ of another person, without the consent of the victim." It also includes "any gender of the victim or perpetrator, and includes instances in which the victim is incapable of giving consent because of temporary or permanent mental or physical incapacity, either due to the influence of drugs or alcohol or because of age. Physical resistance of the victim is not required to demonstrate lack of consent" (FBI, January, 2012). Most state rape statutes already contain the broader definition of rape. As noted by Susan Carbon, Director of the Justice Department's Office of Violence against Women, "This sends a powerful message that … rape is rape." And it's rape even if you're a man" (Markon, 2012, p. A-2). The change will no doubt have a significant effect on the volume and rate of rapes reported in the FBI's UCR Summary Reporting System. Thousands of sexual assaults that have occurred in the United States each year have not been reflected in the Uniform Crime Reports because of the archaic definition of rape. The former definition has been misleading the public about the prevalence of rape and has resulted in fewer local resources devoted to apprehending rapists and helping rape victims (Goode, 2011, p. A-5).

The NCVS definition of rape is "forced sexual intercourse including both psychological coercion as well as physical force, and includes vaginal, anal or oral penetration as well as incidents where penetration is from a foreign object such as a bottle." Attempted rapes, including verbal threats of rape, are also included in the definition (Criminal Victimization in the U.S., 2008; 2010, Glossary).

If we understand the strengths and limitations of each of the programs, the information provided in the UCR and NCVS can give us a better understanding of violent crime trends and the nature of violent crime in the U.S. In particular, the NCVS and the development of comprehensive data on violent crime victims has led to the rise of a new subfield within contemporary criminology, *victimology*. Victims have for too long been a secondary subject in criminology. We discuss the dynamics of violence on victims in Chapter 7 and see that crime victimization, like many hotly debated social issues, is fertile ground for misconceptions and political manipulation.

Select Findings from NCVS

The NCVS provides current as well as trend data about violent crime victimization in the United States. In 2010, 40,974 households and 73,283 individuals were interviewed by the NCVS. U.S. residents aged 12 and older experienced an estimated 3.8 million violent crimes, of which 1.4 million were serious violent victimizations. The volume of violent victimizations decreased from about 4.3 million in 2009 to about 3.8 million in 2010, a decline of 12 percent. The overall victimization rate for violent crimes (rape/sexual assault, robbery, aggravated and simple assault) decreased from 17.1 in 2009 to 14.9 victimizations per 1,000 persons in 2010, a 13 percent decline. The greatest decrease of all violent victimizations was for the crime of simple assault, which has declined by 15 percent. Somewhat of an aberration is the increase in 2010 in the volume and rate of rape/sexual assault. When 2010 is compared to 2009, the change in volume is 49.6 percent and the change in rate is 48.5 percent; although as noted by the NCVS, "care should be taken in interpreting this increase because the estimates are based on a small number of cases reported in the survey" (Truman, 2011, p. 2). Long term decreases in rape and sexual assault victimizations from 2001 to 2010 show a significant decline in volume of 24.1 percent and decline in rate of 32 percent. Between the years 2001 and 2010 the rates of all major violent victimizations based on NCVS data declined; the rate of overall violent victimizations declined by 40.5 percent and the rate of serious violent crimes decreased by 40.6 percent (pp. 2–3).

Other significant findings from the 2010 NCVS include the following:

- From 2001 to 2010, weapon violence (26% to 22%) and stranger-perpetrated violence (44% to 39%) declined.

- Between 2001 and 2010, about 6 percent to 9 percent of all violent victimization was committed with firearms. This percentage has remained stable since 2004.

- After a slight decline from 2001 to 2008, the percentage of victims of violent crimes who suffered an injury during the victimization increased from 24 percent in 2008 to 29 percent in 2010.

- About half (50%) of all violent crimes were reported to the police in 2010.

- Males (15.7 per 1,000) and females (14.2 per 1,000) had similar rates of victimization during 2010.

- Strangers were offenders in about 39 percent of all violent victimizations in 2010, a percentage that has declined from 44 percent in 2001. Females knew their offenders in 64 percent of violent victimizations against them and males knew their offenders in 40 percent of violent victimizations against them in 2010. (Offenders known to both male and female victims were most often identified as friends or acquaintances).

- The percentage of female victims (22%) of intimate partner violence was about 4 times that of male victims (5%) (Truman, 2011, pp. 1–19).

**Table 2.2 Number of Criminal Victimizations and Percent Changes,
by Type of Crime, 2001, 2009, and 2010**

Type of Crime	Number of Victimizations 2001	Number of Victimizations 2009	Number of Victimizations 2010	% Change 2001–2010	% Change 2009–2010
Violent Crime (Overall Total)	5,743,820 (25.1)*	4,343,450 (17.1)	3,817,380 (14.9)	-33.5% (-40.5)	-12.10% (-12.7)**
Serious Violent Crime (Incl. Rape, Robbery, Aggravated Assault)	2,101,100 (9.2)	1,483,050 (5.8)	1,394,310 (5.4)	-33.6% (-40.6)	-6.0% -6.7
Rape/Sexual Assault	248,250 (1.1)	125,920 (0.5)	188,380 (0.7)	-24.1% (-32.0)	+49.6% (48.5)
Robbery	630,690 (2.8)	533,790 (2.1)	480,750 (1.9)	-23.8 (-31.7)	-9.9% (-10.6)
Assault (Overall Total)	4,864,890 (21.2)	3,683,750 (14.5)	3,148,250 (12.3)	-35.3% (-42.0)	-14.5% (-15.2)
Aggravated Assault	1,222,160 (5.3)	823,340 (3.3)	725,180 (2.8)	-40.7% (-46.9)	11.9% (-12.6)
Simple Assault	3,642,720 (15.9)	2,860,410 (11.3)	2,423,060 (9.5)	-33.5% (-40.4)	-15.3% (-15.9)

Source: National Crime Victimization Survey, 2001, 2009, 2010 adapted from Truman, *Criminal Victimization, 2010*, September 2011, NCJ 235508, p. 2–3.
* Victimization rate (per 1,000 persons age 12 or older for violent crime).
** Percent change in victimization rate.

The NCVS also provides historical trend data on violent crime victimization going as far back as 1973. Adjustments made by NCVS take into account methodological changes and the redesign of the survey in 1993 as well as the inclusion of select UCR data such as homicide, not collected by the NCVS. Figure 2.2 reports violent crime rates for the crimes of rape (excluding sexual assault), robbery, aggravated and simple assault, collected from the NCVS, and homicide (collected by UCR) for the years 1973 to 2009 (BJS, *Violent Crime Rate Trends*).

Figure 2.2 shows that the historical patterns of violence based on adjusted violent victimization rates for overall violent crimes have been decreasing significantly beginning in 1997 (victimization rate of 39 per 1000 persons age 12 and older), which has continued to drop through 2009 (victimization rate of 17 per 1000) and 2010 (victimization rate of 15 per 1000, which is not included on Figure 2.2).

The NCVS and UCR: True Crime Stories?

Two researchers, Michael Rand and Callie Rennison (2002) collaborated on an article entitled, "True crime stories: Accounting for differences in our national crime indicators," in which they discussed the pros and cons of the NCVS and UCR in relation to gauging crime in America. They noted, as we have, that each of these programs are conducted

Figure 2.2 Violent Crime Rates

Adjusted victimization rate
per 1,000 persons age 12 and over

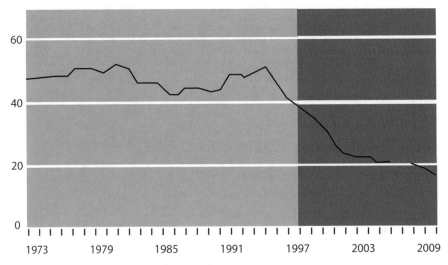

Source: Bureau of Justice Statistics: *Key Facts at a Glance,* http://bjs.ojp.usdoj.gov/content/glance/viort.cfm.

for different reasons, use different methods, and focus on somewhat different aspects of crimes, in our case, violent crimes. What we do know from both indicators is that violent crime certainly occurs in the United States, whether we examine the victim's perspective or that of law enforcement. At the time of their article, in 2002 violent crime while still declining had begun to stabilize after decreasing significantly. Both measures, they note, are efficient and practical, and, in fact, other countries have copied our approach and collect information from both victims and law enforcement agencies. We cannot say that one measure is better than the other. Both measures are the better measure for what they are intended to measure. Indeed, violent crime must be examined from a number of perspectives in order to understand it. For example, Rand and Rennison note:

> The UCR provides information on the amount of crime reaching law enforcement, and can help inform police departments of manpower needs. The NCVS provides a national picture of what people are experiencing, what proportion of crime does not reach the police, the characteristics associated with offenses, and the consequences and costs of crime (2002, p. 51).

The Bureau of Justice Statistics has developed a technique to compare types of violent crime commonly found in both programs. The technique involves removing crimes against children under age 12 and commercial robberies from the UCR, removing simple assault and crimes not reported to law enforcement from the NCVS, and adding homicides to the NCVS (Rand and Rennison, 2002, p. 47). Figure 2.3 is based on a recent chart from the Bureau of Justice Web site that presents four measures of serious violent crime from the NCVS and UCR for the years 1973 through 2009. The top curve shows the overall NCVS estimate of *Total Violent Crime* (rape, robbery, and aggressive assault, with homicide data added from the UCR) whether or not they were reported to the police. The curves labeled "Victimizations Reported to the Police" and "Crimes Recorded by the Police"

Figure 2.3 Four Measures of Serious Violent Crime

Offenses in millions

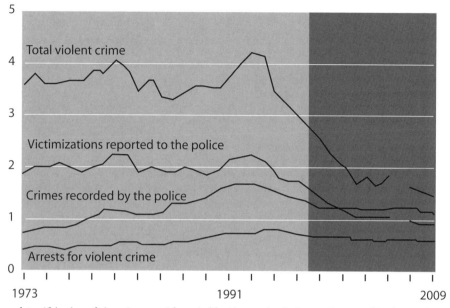

Source: http://bjs.ojp.usdoj.gov/content/glance/tables/4meastab.cfm*Source:* Bureau of Justice Statistics: *Key Facts at a Glance,* http://bjs.ojp.usdoj.gov/content/glance/cv2.cfm.

present data modified to eliminate, as is best possible, incongruous elements. These data show, respectively, NCVS victims of violent crime who indicate that they reported violent crime to the police and the UCR estimate of reported violent crime. Although each measure is different, both the NCVS and UCR generally show that violent crime in the United States has been declining since the mid-1990s, but certainly remains a serious problem (BJS, Four Measures of Serious Violent Crime; Rand and Rennison, 2002, pp. 50–51). As Rand and Rennison note, despite drops in violent crime, these two measures tell us that violent crime in the U.S. remains pervasive and that "this is evident whether we consider the victim's perspective or that of law enforcement." The researchers further note that "independent measures of a social issue are valuable and, since about half of all violent crime is not reported to the police, the NCVS is the only national forum that victims have to inform us about crimes they are reluctant to report to the police" (p. 51). In addition they claim that the UCR is also valuable in that it is the only source that provides national crime and other data by state and city reported to law enforcement agencies throughout the United States. They conclude that: "Together, the measures enhance our understanding of crime" (p. 51).

Self-Report Inventories

Another approach to the measurement of violence involves eliciting "confessions" of violent criminal behavior from surveys or questionnaires and interviews. Respondents are given the assurance that their honest disclosures will be kept in strict confidence. With a few exceptions, self-report studies have been limited to surveys of high school students

**Table 2.3 2009 Self-Report Survey of Violent Activity of
50,000 High School Seniors**

Offense	% Engaging in Offenses	
	Committed once	Committed more than once
Hit Instructor	1.4	2.3
Got in serious fight	6.4	5.4
Used weapon to steal	1.8	1.8
Involved in group fight	8.5	7.5
Hurt someone badly (medical care)	6.3	5.7

Source: Johnson, Bachman, and O'Malley, 2010.

in an attempt to measure the volume of "hidden delinquency," some of which is violent. Since many violent crimes are known only to those persons who commit them, self-report studies (SR) provide another estimate of *hidden violent criminality*. Decades of results from various self-reports reveal that the amount of hidden crime and delinquency is quite large. While most of the research has generally shown that property type crimes are the most prevalent, violent offenses such as fights, weapons use, and other forms of interpersonal violence are consistently reported (e.g., Hindelang, 1971; Gold, and Reimer, 1975; Bachman, O'Malley and Johnson, 1978; Thornton and James, 1979; Thornton and Voigt, 1984; Elliott, Huizinga, and Ageton, 1985; Johnson, Bachman, and O'Malley, 2010). Self-report survey questions relating to violence might ask:

1. How many times in the past year have you hurt someone badly enough to require medical care?

2. How many times in the past year have you engaged in a gang fight?

3. How many times in the past year have you used force to steal something from someone?

4. How many times in the past year have you hit a teacher or supervisor?

5. How many times in the past year have you participated in a serious fight?

Results from the Monitoring the Future (MTF) project, an ongoing study of the drug use, behaviors, attitudes, and values of American secondary school students, college students and young adults conducted by researchers at the University of Michigan's Institute for Social Research, uses a self-report inventory to measure select delinquent/criminal behaviors, some including violence. Each year, since 1975, a total of about 50,000 8th, 10th, and 12th grade students have been surveyed (www.monitoringthefuture.org). Table 2.3 reports the 2009 findings from high school seniors asking their involvement in select offenses involving interpersonal violence during the past 12 months. While relatively small percentages of youth report engaging in violent behavior, results suggest these behaviors do indeed occur (Johnson, Bachman, and O'Malley, 2010).

While most criminologists have supported the use of self-report studies because they provide useful supplementary data on violent crime and the characteristics of persons who report their own criminal involvements, these studies suffer from a number of methodological and conceptual deficiencies including: (1) reliability and validity problems, (2) lack of large national samples, (3) inconsistent questions over different administrations of the surveys, and (4) almost exclusive focus on juveniles with few adult samples (Junger-Tas and Marshall, 1999; Kirk, 2006). Some self-report studies have been conducted by criminologists with adult populations such as drug users (O'Donnell et. al., 1976; Tittle and Villemez, 1977), incarcerated adult offenders to obtain information about their offending patterns over time (e.g., Greenwood and Abrahamse, 1982; Horney and Marshall, 1992), and adult criminal career offense admissions (Petersilia, Greenwood, and Lavin, 1977). These studies generally look at individual offending frequency, offering further insight into the relationship of violence crimes, known to the police and hidden violent criminality.

Other Sources of Data on Violence

In addition to standard types of data on criminal violence, as collected by law enforcement, such as the Uniform Crime Reports, the National Crime Victimization Survey, and self-report studies, other data collected by different government agencies, professional and private organizations, and specialty groups provide useful information about: (1) the magnitude and impact of violence; (2) understanding which factors increase the risk for violent victimization and perpetration; and (3) the effectiveness of possible violence prevention programs (Krug, et al., 2002, p. 7).

It is important to remember, as discussed in Chapter 1, that it is difficult to arrive at any single definition of violence and efforts to develop comprehensive typologies or classification systems of violence fail to include all the nuances of the concept. At best, broad categories based on the characteristics of those committing the violent act, e.g., self-directed violence (suicide), interpersonal violence (e.g., single perpetrator or several perpetrators), and collective violence (e.g., state, organized political groups, terrorist organizations) impact the type of data collected on violence. Here, further categorization focusing on the nature of the violent acts (e.g., physical, psychological, sexual, and deprivation or neglect), similarly dictate what type of data is collected (Krug, et al., 2002, pp. 5–7).

It is beyond the parameters of this chapter to discuss all the possible sources of data on violence; however, in Box 2.3, we include a selection of agencies and organizations that collect data on different aspects of violence of interest to researchers as well as practitioners.

As we have seen with violent crime data, comparing official UCR data with unofficial crime victimization data is challenging, but possible; however, comparing and linking violence data *across* different sources is very difficult. Data about violence is collected from a wide variety of different organizations, both within the United States, and in the world, that operate independently from one another. While efforts have been made in recent years, especially from international organizations such as the United Nations and the World Health Organization to standardize certain measures of violence, there is still a lack of uniformity comparing data across communities and countries (Krug, et al. 2002, p. 9).

National Institute for Occupational Safety and Health (NIOSH)

NIOSH is part of the Centers for Disease Control (CDC) in the Department of Health and Human Services and "is the federal agency responsible for conducting research and making recommendations for the prevention of work-related injury and illness"

Box 2.3 Types of Data and Potential Sources for Collecting Violence Information

Types of Data	Data Sources	Examples of Information Collected
Crime	Police records, judiciary records, crime laboratories	Calls for service, incident reports, types of offenses, characteristics of offenders, relationships between offender and victim, circumstances of violent event
Mortality	Death certificates, vital statics registries, medical examiners' or coroners' reports or mortuary reports	Characteristics of the decedent, cause of death, location, time, manner of death
Morbidity and other health data	Hospitals, clinics or other medical records	Diseases, injuries, information on physical mental reproductive health, presence of alcohol or drugs
Self-reports	Surveys, interviews, special studies, focus groups, media	Victimization reports, delinquency and crime perpetration, exposure to violence in home or community, attitudes, beliefs, behaviors, cultural practices
Community	Population records, local government records, other institutional records, program, institutional or agency records	Population counts and density, levels of income and education, unemployment rates, divorce rates and family structure, institution-related data such as labor statistics on workplace violence, and economic studies on the costs of certain crimes to society
Special research/ Scientific investigation	Research and special studies conducted by public and private research institutes/ centers and universities	Analysis of patterns and trends of various types of violence, correlation studies, studies of causes of violence, development of profiles and classification systems and predictive models, studies of the quality and use of other data sources, and analysis of law enforcement activities, and policy effectiveness
Policy and legislative	Government or legislative records	Laws, institutional policies and practices

Source: Modified/Adapted from Krug, et al., 2002, Table 1.1, p. 8.

(http://www.cdc.gov/niosh/about.html). Part of its broad based initiative is to reduce the incidence of occupational violence in the U.S.; and, to this end, NIOSH conducts, funds, and generates research on risk factors and prevention strategies related to workplace violence in numerous settings such as offices, factories, warehouses, hospitals and other health care settings, convenience stores, law enforcement agencies, prisons, and retail settings including studies of: (1) non-fatal violence such as assaults, (2) fatal violence such as homicide; (3) domestic violence; and (4) reduction of robberies and violence in high-risk businesses. NIOSH coordinates its efforts dealing with workplace violence with

Table 2.4 Homicide Cause of Death — ICD Codes: E960–E969

E-Code	Cause of Death
E960	Fight, brawl, rape
E961	Corrosive, caustic substance
E962	Poisoning
E963	Hanging, strangulation
E964	Submersion (drowning)
E965	Firearms and explosives
E966	Cutting and piercing instruments
E967	Pushing from high places
E968	Other
E969	Late effect of injury

Source: U.S. Department of Health and Human Services. October 2007, ICD DHHS pub. No. PHS01-1260). Washington, D.C.

the Departments of Justice and Labor. Chapter 3 in the book discusses many of these types of violence.

The National Center for Health Statistics (NCHS)

NCHS, which is also part of the CDC in the Department of Health and Human Services, is the federal agency responsible for the use of the International Statistical Classification of Diseases and Related Health Problems (ICD-10-CM) (http://www.cdc.goc/nchs/icd10cm.htm). Homicide is the only violent offense that NCHS reports, making homicide the only violent offense for which there are two local and national reporting systems (i.e., NCHS and UCR). Information is collected through the use of standardized death certificates that are completed by some designated official such as a coroner or medical examiner. NCHS claims complete coverage since 1933, no estimates are used. Mortality data are "a fundamental source of demographic, geographic, and cause of death information" and extremely useful for comparing the crime of homicide for geographical areas in the United States consistently over time and for tracking mortality trends for the crime with other countries (http://www.cid.gov/nchs/deaths.htm). Cause of death is classified according to categories in the International Classification of Diseases (ICD-10), as shown in Table 2.4. The ICD is copyrighted by the World Health Organization (WHO), which owns and publishes the classification system, giving it the ability to be used in international comparisons of homicide deaths.

The CDC and NCHS and respectively the World Health Organization based on requests on how to classify deaths and injuries as a result of September 11, 2001 terrorist attacks on the U.S. formed an ad hoc workgroup on the Classification of Death and Injury Resulting from Terrorism and developed terrorism codes designed to fit the ICD classifications. To classify the death or injury as terrorist-related, the incident must be designated as such by the Federal Government, not by any other person such as a medical examiner or coroner or the nosologist, a person who classifies diseases or who inputs the code on the death certificate (http://www.cdc.gov/nchs/icd/terrorism_code.htm). The newest ICD-10 classification for death and injury resulting from terrorism, U01-02, *Terrorism Assault (Homicide)*, includes: "Assault-related injuries resulting from the unlawful use of force or violence against persons or property to intimidate or coerce a government, the civilian population, or any segment thereof, in furtherance of political or social objectives" (http://www.cdc.gov/nchs/icd/terrorism_code_appendix1.htm).

Bureau of Labor Statistics (BLS)

The Bureau of Labor Statistics produces the *BLS Annual Census of Fatal Occupational Injuries* (CFOI) including workplace violence, such as homicides, suicides and assaults. Workplace violence accounted for 18 percent of all work-related fatal occupational injuries in 2010; homicides are annually among the top four causes of fatal workplace injuries for all workers (http://www.bls.gov/iif/oshfaq1.htm). CFOI reported 506 work-related homicides for employed victims age 16 or older who were killed while at work or on duty (excluding deaths by accident). Contrary to popular opinion, most work-related homicides result from robbers and other assailants in the work place rather than from disgruntled co-workers, spouses or acquaintances. Of the 506 homicides that occurred in 2010, 65 percent were committed by robbers and other assailants, 25 percent were committed by work associates, and 10 percent were committed by relatives and other personal acquaintances. Work-related homicides have decreased more than 50 percent from 1994 to 2010 (http://www.bls.gov/iif/oshwc/cfoi/work_hom.pdf_).

The BLS also tracks nonfatal occupation injuries in the workplace by industry. For example, for the years 2003 through 2007, nearly 60 percent of all non-fatal assaults and violent acts by persons occurred in the health care and social assistance industry (e.g., hospitals, nursing homes, and residential care facilities). However, about three-quarters of these were assaults by health care patients or residents of a health care facility. Of the 16,840 assaults in 2007, the most common victims were nursing aids, orderlies, and attendants (Janocha and Smith, 2010, p. 7). Chapters 3 and 7 discuss work-related violence in more detail.

Cross Cultural Comparisons of Violence

The cross cultural study of violence has evolved both within the field of comparative criminology, defined as the cross-cultural study of all aspects of crime and criminal justice, and as a separate area of study by international organizations such as the United Nations and the World Health Organization, and others focusing on the globalization of human rights and special types of violence including gender-based repression, exploitation of children, torture, and political corruption and violence. The breadth of data available since the advent of the Internet has allowed researchers to tap into data sources on every imaginable type of violence, difficult, if not impossible to obtain in the past. As noted earlier, some of these studies dealing with violence rely not just on official statistics, but also on other sources of data such as victimization studies, public health statistics, and other specialized unofficial data. The amount of international data on crime and violence is, unfortunately, somewhat disorganized, spread around on a number of different national and international Web sites, and requires some research effort depending on the area of interest.

Comparative methodology to study crime globally can be classified into several categories including: (1) comparative analysis of official statistics and archival data, (2) comparative studies employing various standardized techniques (e.g., interviews and self reports); (3) comparative case studies; (4) comparative historical analysis; and (5) comparative content analysis of theoretical and popular literature. The use of one technique over another depends on the goals of the research and the logistical problems associated with different methodologies, including sample selection, validity, reliability testing, financial limitations, and the level of national or international support. As is the case with the use of any methodology employing official data collected by criminal justice agencies to make inferences or generalizations about crime trends in a particular country or between countries, numerous problems exist in this type of data collection. Countries that do collect national crime data are plagued by the same reporting problems that the United States faces when official agents collect and interpret data. Discretion in law enforcement as well as political decisions regarding the reporting of crimes may affect reported volumes and rates. Legal categories or definitions of crimes and the operation of criminal justice systems vary from country to country, making comparisons extremely difficult. In some countries, attempted crimes are counted as crimes, while in other countries they are not.

United Nations Office on Drugs and Crime (UNODC)

UNODC, which was established in 1997 through a merger between the United Nations Drug Control Program and the Centre for International Crime Prevention, operates in all regions of the world through an extensive network of field offices. Headquartered in Vienna, UNODC includes more than 50 field offices covering more than 150 countries. The organization assists member states in their fight against violent activities including illicit drugs, human trafficking, migrant smuggling, organized crime, and terrorism. UNODC also engages in research and analytical work to increase knowledge and understanding of drugs and crime issues with special emphasis on fostering an evidence-based policy and operational decision-making approach in addressing these problems. As one of its mandates, the UNODC collects information on global crime and criminal justice through the United Nations Survey of Crime Trends and Criminal Justice (UN-CTS) as well as from other sources including international crime victimization surveys and other specialized sources. The UNODC promotes and facilitates internationally comparable victim surveys, particularly in developing countries, and recognizes that these surveys are needed to make up for deficiencies in police and criminal justice data in the measurement of violent and nonviolent crime. In 1998, the UNODC was given another mandate to collect data about the world drug problem in order to have accurate information for dealing with international drug control. Beginning in 1999, the publication *Global Illicit Drug Trends* was published providing data and estimates from world governments and other international institutions on global illicit drug markets. This annual study was merged into a more comprehensive work, *World Drug Report* in 2004, and continues to be published annually, with the most recent edition published in 2011. The newest edition, *World Drug Report 2011*, available online, examines statistical trends for transnational drug markets in opium/heroin, coca/cocaine, amphetamine-type stimulants, and marijuana (UNODC, 2011b). This report and another recent publication, *Global Report on Trafficking in Persons* (2009), both confirm that virtually every country in the world is affected by these crimes. Human trafficking is the acquisition of people by improper means such as force, fraud, or deception, with the aim of exploiting them, including the sexual exploitation of women and children. The UNODC Web site provides access to all their data, reports and other publications (http://www.unodc.org).

United Nations Surveys of Crime Trends and Operations of Criminal Justice Systems

Efforts have been made to measure trends in world crime, obviously including violent crimes such as murder, rape, robbery, and assaults. The United Nations Surveys of Crime Trends and Operations of Criminal Justice Systems (UN-CTS) (formally known as the United Nations *World Crime Surveys*), which was begun in 1978, is currently comprised of eleven surveys, 1970–1975, 1975–1980, 1980–1986, 1986–1990, 1990–1994, 1995–1997, 1998–2000, 2001–2002, 2003–2004, 2005–2006, and the latest, the Eleventh CTS, 2007–2008. Results of the Twelfth UN-CTS (2009) will soon be available (http://www.unodc.org). As noted on the United Nations Office on Drugs and Crime (UNODC) Web site, the major goal of the UN surveys "is to collect data on the incidence of reported crime and the operations of the criminal justice systems with a view of improving the analysis and dissemination of that information globally" (UNODC Web site). Various statistics are reported to the United Nations based on surveys on crime levels for police recorded incidents, including violent crimes such as homicides, rapes (sexual violence), robbery, assaults, kidnapping, trafficking in persons, and property crimes (theft, motor vehicle theft, burglary, and illicit trafficking in cultural property). Other information on criminal justice trends reported to authorities, e.g., formal contacts with police, persons prosecuted and persons convicted are included for respective countries. Cross-national UNODC crime statistics are now available for over 120 countries for all the surveys on the UNODC Web site and detailed analyses are available for the more recent data collection period from 2003–2008.

The UNODC/HEUNI publication, *International Statistics on Crime and Justice* (Harrendorf, Heiskanen, and Malby, 2010) provides a comprehensive analysis and discussion of global responses to the UN-CTS surveys analyzing violent crime as well as other crimes for an eleven year period from 1996–2006. The first article by Steven Malby on "Homicide" (specifically intentional homicide—the intentional killing of a person by another) utilizes both UN survey data, i.e., police recorded homicides, as well as public health data, i.e., documented cause of death by assault, to gauge global homicide levels. His results indicate that the highest homicide rates are found in the Americas (particularly South and Central America and the Caribbean) and Africa; and the lowest levels generally being in European countries (Malby, 2010, p. 7). He suggests these differences in rates may be linked not only to the problems of organized crime, drug trafficking and gang activity but also significant data challenges in the accuracy of reporting homicides in some developing countries such as Africa, which no doubt affects cross national comparisons (p. 8). Another article by Markku Heiskanen, "Trends in Recorded Crime" (2010), examines the prevalence rates for the traditional violent crimes of rape, robbery, assault, and kidnapping as well as burglary and motor vehicle theft. He reports that for the 11-year period of the study, rapes and robberies have slightly increased and assaults have increased considerably in the countries as a whole; however, there are significant differences among countries. West, Central, and Southern Africa, for example, show the highest rates of reported major assaults; differences in assaults between North America and West and Central Europe are small. With respect to rapes, Southern Africa, Oceania, and North America have the highest reported rape rates, and Asia the lowest (p. 22).

Table 2.5 World Homicide Rates by Region

Source: UNODC Homicide Statistics (2011a). Bars represent population weighted average homicide rate (per 100,000 population), with high and low estimates.

UNODC Global Study on Homicide

The United Nations Office on Drugs and Crime (2011a) conducted a new study on global homicide based on a variety of sources of data, including official criminal justice data from the UN-CTS and public health data resulting in a dataset, which includes data from 207 countries. The study examined intentional homicide, "unlawful death purposefully inflicted on a person by another person." Deaths due to civil conflict, recklessness or negligence or deaths considered justifiable by penal law were excluded in the study (p. 15). The study estimated that worldwide, 468,000 homicides occurred in 2010, with 36 percent taking place in Africa, 31 percent taking place in the Americas, 27 percent in Asia, 5 percent in Europe, and 1 percent in Oceania (p. 9). The total volume of worldwide homicides results in a global homicide rate of 6.9 per 100,000 population (p. 19) (see Table 2.5). Results indicate that young males, particularly those in Central and South America, the Caribbean and Central and Southern Africa, have the highest risk of becoming victims of intentional homicide. Globally, about 83 percent of both victims and perpetrators of homicide are men (p. 63). Females run the greatest risk of being murdered because of domestic violence, killed by intimate partners or family members. In Europe, for example, over half of the female victims were killed by a family member (p. 58).

The recent increase in homicide rates in Central America and the Caribbean are said to be at a "near crisis point" according to this study and the key reason for rising murder rates are the greater prevalence of firearms (with about 75 percent of the homicides committed with guns, compared to 21 percent in Europe). In fact, based on UNODC figures for 108 countries, accounting for over 50 percent of the world's homicides, approximately 199,000 out of a total of 468,000 homicides, 42 percent were committed using firearms (p. 39). Closely connected to the firearms homicides especially in the Americas is the operation of gangs and organized criminal groups involved in drug trafficking and the perpetration of other forms of violence (pp. 39–42).

UNODC examines the relationship between homicide and levels of development of countries, which includes various "indicators of social and economic progress, the rule of law, economic trends and the impact of the recent economic crisis on crime in different countries" (p. 29). The study finds, for example, a strong relationship between *low* levels of economic development, e.g., the connection of wide income disparity with *higher* homicide rates. Countries that have wide income disparities have homicide rates almost four times higher than more equal [equitable] societies" (p. 30). Likewise, strong economic growth, as measured by Gross Domestic Products (GDP), in countries is conversely linked with decreases in homicide rates as has been the case in the Former Soviet Union after stability gradually emerged in the late 1990s (p. 34). Of particular interest to criminologists is the finding of the *Global Study on Homicide* that sudden changes in the economic conditions of countries (e.g., declining GDP, higher consumer price index, and greater unemployment) can increase homicide rates and other violent and property crimes. Connected to economic stability, covered in the study, is the finding that long-term economic and social development in a country "requires democratic governance rooted in the rule of law."[1] UNODC reports that countries that have increasing homicide rates generally have weak rule of law and conversely, countries with relatively strong rule of law have lower homicide rates (p. 34). The financial crisis of 2008–2009, it was discovered, corresponds to increases in homicides in select countries in the study such as Central and South America, Costa Rica, and Thailand (pp. 35–37). It is cautioned, however, that these economic variables, and others, alone are not the only factors that influence homicide and other violent (and property crimes). UNODC further cautions that "certain measures of development have been analyzed in isolation from these other variables; development factors alone are not sufficient to account for variations in homicide rates between countries" (p. 36).

Global Crime Victimization Surveys

The launch of the National Crime Victimization Survey in the United States in 1972 implemented by the National Opinion Research Center and initiated earlier by President's Commission on Law Enforcement and the Administration of Justice is often thought of as one of the first large scale self-report crime victimization surveys. This and earlier pilot victimization surveys in the 1960s in the U.S. have demonstrated the validity of the self-report methodology as a viable way to complement official statistics and also a way to get some data on crimes not reported to the police. In the same general timeframe, or perhaps earlier, victimization surveys were being conducted in other countries. In 1970, Finland conducted what may be the first national victimization survey partnering with the Gallup Poll. The Netherlands launched a government sponsored crime survey in 1973 and Australia administered its first victimization survey in 1975 followed by other countries such as Sweden in 1978–79, and Israel in 1979. The first British Crime Survey was conducted in England, Wales and Scotland in 1982 and continues to provide information on trends in crime victimization and the nature of those crimes by the self-report method (*UNODC, 2010: Manual on Victimization Surveys*, pp. 1–3). Other countries including Canada, Italy, and Switzerland have initiated their own victimization surveys over the years. A specialized survey, *The International Violence against Women Survey* (IVAWS) project was started in the late 1990s coordinated by HEUNI, Statistics Canada and UNICRI and involved several countries including Australia, Costa Rica, the Czech Republic, Denmark, Greece, Hong Kong, Italy, Mozambique, the Philippines, Poland, and Switzerland

---

1. Rule of law is measured in the study by the World Bank Rule of Law Index (ROLI), which "captures perceptions to the extent to which agents have confidence in and abide by the rules of society, and in particular the quality of contract enforcement, property rights, the police, and the courts as well as the likelihood of violence" (The United Nations, 2011).

(UNODC, 2010: *Manual on Victimization Surveys*, pp. 1–3 and pp. 198–199; Johnson, et al, 2008).

As the body of data from various victimization surveys around the world was developed and as the techniques were refined and somewhat standardized, scholars from around the world began to use this information for cross cultural studies and comparisons. However, as is the case with international comparisons of official crime statistics collected from law enforcement agencies, similar problems of comparability with differences in crimes exists for comparative crime victimization surveys. The UNODC in conjunction with the United Nations Economic Commission for Europe (UNECE) published a *Manual on Victimization Surveys* to help "develop methodological guidelines at the international level for the design of national victimization surveys." The manual provides assistance to countries for the construction and administration of self-reported criminal victimizations and addresses in detail the problems of international comparability of major crimes, including violent contact crimes such as robbery, physical assault, and sexual offenses, as well as other factors such as weapons use, physical injury, and victim-offender relationships, and confidence in law enforcement, feelings of safety and socio-demographic variables (see Table 2.6) (UNODC and UNECE, 2010, p. 12).

Table 2.6 Key Topics for International Comparability

Reports of Crimes and Victimization	Property Crime			Contact Crime/Violent Crime			No Crime Specified
	Household Burglary	Theft of Vehicles	Other Theft	Robbery	Physical Assault	Sexual Offences	
Measure of victimization in the past 12 months	X	X	X	X	X	X	
Measure of repeat victimization in the past 12 months	X	X	X	X	X	X	
Reporting to the police	X	X	X	X	X	X	
Crimes involving weapons				X	X	X	
Victims with physical injury				X	X	X	
Victim-offender relationship				X	X	X	
Public confidence/ Trust in police						X	X
Feelings of safety						X	X
Basic socio-demographic variables						X	X

Source: United Nations Office on Drugs and Crime (UNODC) and United Nations Economic Commission for Europe (UNECE). 2010. *Manual on Victimization Surveys*. Geneva: UN.

International Crime Victimization Survey (ICVS)

The first ICVS was launched in 1989 and surveys have subsequently been administered in 1992, 1996, 2000, 2004/2005, and 2009 (results not yet released). In the beginning, the IVS focused on developed countries; however, with involvement of the UNODC and UNICRI, the surveys expanded to include developing countries and Eastern Europe. European criminologists initiated the ICVS with the main objective being to advance international comparative criminological research beyond the reliance on police recorded official data and to develop estimates of criminal victimizations for international comparisons. As of 2005, 140 surveys have been conducted in over 78 different countries and over 300,000 participants were interviewed about their victimization experiences in the respective countries (van Dijk, Mayhew, and Killias, 1990; Background to ICVS, http://rechten.uvt.nl/icvs; UNODC and UNECE, 2010, p. 3).

The most recent report, *Criminal Victimisation in International Perspective* (van Dijk, van Kesteren, and Smit, 2007; http://rechten.uvt.nl/icvs/pdffiles/ICVS2004_05.pdf) describes the 2004–2005 victimization surveys administered in 30 countries, including the majority of developed nations, and 33 capital or main cities of developed and developing countries; current results are compared to earlier survey findings. Results in this report also include 2005 findings from the *European Survey on Crime and Safety* (EC ICS). The International Crime Victim Survey (ICVS) covers 10 conventional crimes, including the violent crimes of robbery, sexual offenses, and assaults/threats, including use of a weapon. As with the American NCVS, homicide is not a crime covered on the international victim survey. In terms of the violent contact offenses — robbery, assaults, and sexual offenses — populations in main cities experienced higher rates of violent crime than those living in the country. Johannesburg, South Africa, for example, has victimization rates for assault and threats, including those with weapons, of over 10 percent per year (van Dijk, van Kesteren, and Smit, 2007, p. 14). Generally, about 3 percent of respondents at the country level reported that they were victims of assault with force or threat of force; higher than average rates exist in Northern Ireland, Iceland, England and Wales, the Netherlands, New Zealand and the U.S. (4% and above); levels were the lowest in Italy, Portugal, Hungary, and Spain (below 2%). Assault rates in developing countries tended to be higher (mean about 6%) (p. 80). Robbery was comparatively low in almost all countries with differences between developed countries small. Mexico had the highest risk for robberies; Japan, Italy, Finland, Germany, Austria and the Netherlands, the lowest. In main cities, the highest annual victimization rate for robbery was in Buenos Aires, with a victimization rate of 10 percent. Similarly, all rates of participating countries and cities from Latin America are comparatively high (p. 73). About 1.7 percent of women reported sexual victimizations, (grab, touch or assault for sexual reasons) and on average .5 percent of males. The survey reveals that approximately one in a hundred females in the U.S., Iceland, Sweden, North Ireland, Australia, Norway, England and Wales and Switzerland reported such offenses. In instances where the offender was known, 11 percent were ex-intimate partners, 17 percent were colleagues/bosses, 8 percent were current intimate partners, and 16 percent were close friends. In about 80 percent of the reported cases, there was only one perpetrator; in 8 percent of the cases three or more offenders committed the crime. Weapons such as guns or knives were used in 8 percent of reported sexual offenses (pp. 76–79).

World Health Organization (WHO)

The World Health Organization (WHO) was created in 1948 and is the "directing and coordinating agency for heath within the United Nations system" (World Health Organization Web site). In recent years, WHO through its research agenda, publications, and programs has stressed that violence in all its manifestations represents a major health problem throughout the world and "threatens the lives and physical and mental health of millions of people, over-burdens health systems, undermines human capital formation, and slows economic and social development" (Violence Prevention Alliance, 2010, p. 2). WHO has been on the cutting edge of many international studies dealing with a wide range of violence, most recently dealing with areas such as intimate partner violence, child abuse and neglect, youth violence, and sexual violence (e.g., Krug, et al., 2002; Garcia-Moreno, et al., 2005; WHO/London School, 2010).

In 1996, the Forty-Ninth World Health Assembly adopted Resolution WHA49.25, "declaring violence a major and growing public health problem across the world ... The Assembly drew attention to the serious consequences of violence both in the long-term and short-term—for individuals, families, communities, and countries, and stressed the damaging effects of violence on health care services" (Krug, et al., 2002, Introduction). As a result, the World Health Organization launched the first comprehensive review of the problem of violence from a global perspective in the *World Report on Violence and Health* (Krug, et al., 2002). While the study focuses on the role of public health in terms of prevention, causes and consequences of a vast spectrum of violence (e.g., *self-directed violence*—suicide, suicide attempts, and self-abuse, *interpersonal violence*—youth violence, intimate partner violence, sexual violence, child maltreatment and elder abuse, and *collective violence*—war and other forms of armed conflict and state perpetrated genocide, repression and torture), the work provides one of the first truly global efforts to describe the magnitude and impact of major categories of fatal and non-fatal violence.

To accomplish this goal, WHO uses several types of data, including *mortality data* from the World Health Organization's Global Burden of Disease project (Murray and Lopez, 1996; Murray, et al., 2001), comprised of WHO member countries grouped into six regions: African Region, Region of the Americas, South-East Asia Region, European Region, Eastern Mediterranean Region, and Western Pacific Regions. Deaths and non-fatal injuries are categorized to one underlying cause using the guidelines of the International Classification of Diseases (ICD), e.g., homicide, suicide, war related injuries, legal intervention, and all intentional injury (Krug, et al., 2002, pp. 257–258). In addition, the *World Report on Violence and Health* uses hundreds of other surveys and special studies of fatal and non-fatal violence from all over the world focusing on the above noted types of violence. One of the things that WHO attempts to do in this report and other research is to make violence data more comparable for international research. This is particularly important, for example, in intimate partner violence where it is often not possible to distinguish between physical, sexual and psychological violence from culture to culture. Guidelines have been used, for example, for both defining and measuring intimate partner violence and sexual assault to improve comparability among studies. WHO has also developed guidelines addressing the ethical and safety issues involving research on violence against women (e.g., Saltzman, et al., 1999; Basil and Saltzman, 2002).

WHO Multi-Country Study on Women's Health and Domestic Violence against Women

Another international study conducted by the World Health Organization presents the results of a study on domestic violence and women's health, which was conducted in ten countries with 24,000 respondents. The study used trained teams of interviewers and standardized data collection techniques, which allowed the results to be analyzed across different settings and internationally. Findings show that intimate partner violence is the most common form of violence in women's lives, much more so than assault or rape by strangers or acquaintances. The report offers a wide range of interventions to change attitudes and challenge the inequities and norms that perpetuate the violence (Garcia-Moreno, et al., 2005). More recent studies have expanded the number of countries in the survey (Garcia-Moreno and Watts, 2011).

Bureau of Justice Statistics (BJS)

The BJS International Justice Statistics Web site (http://bjs.ojp.usdoj.gov/content/ijs.cfm) is an invaluable resource for obtaining data about global violence including: (1) links to BJS publications; (2) select justice statistics from the United Nations; (3) United Nations participating research institutes; (4) United Nations Data Collections; (5) international data sets from the National Archive of Criminal Justice Data (NACJD) (http://www.icpsr.umich.edu/icpsrweb/NACJD/index.jsp); (6) official country Web sites devoted to that country's statistical agency or department responsible for justice, public safety and/or law; (7) World Justice Information Network (WJIN.net); (8) International Criminal Police Organization (INTERPOL) — source of select published statistics; and (9) National Institute of Justice International Center — gateway to international activities within the Office of Justice Programs and host of NIJ International Library and Global Criminal Justice Links (http://www.nij.gov/international/welcome.htm).

Conclusion

This chapter reviews the different sources of data, information and statistics pertaining to violence. Admittedly, we have only scratched the surface in trying to measure some commonly known types of violence. Most of the information in this chapter is focused on criminal violence, which is globally pervasive, yet still varied based on cultural nuances. Violence, as has been noted, is a conceptual enigma. The concept of violence is literally universally applied, representing a broad range of meanings and interpretations and referring to a vast spectrum of phenomena — everything from interpersonal assaults to international combat.

In this chapter we mainly review the measures of overt violence as documented in official statistics collected by law enforcement agencies (all over the world), which record known and reported types of violent crimes, with homicide perhaps being a proxy for violence in many people's minds representing the ultimate form of violence, the killing of another human being. Ironically, violent crimes including homicide have been declining in the United States, something criminologists and other experts did not predict, and, are unable to definitively explain. Ideally criminologists would like to have an exhaustive enumeration of all violent crimes, but this ideal is unattainable for a variety of reasons, the chief one being that the great majority of crimes, perhaps with the exception of murder, go undetected, unreported, and unrecorded. Thus what we know about the volume of violent crimes and characteristics of perpetrators is only the tip of a huge iceberg, and the tip cannot be assumed to be similar to the portion that lies beneath the surface.

Criminologists, like scientists in other fields, however, are constantly striving to improve and refine their measures and to devise new approaches to investigate the patterns and forms of violence. Creation of unofficial measures of violence such as victim surveys, used in many countries including the U.S., has expanded the parameters of our measurement of some violent crimes. International studies of violence and comparative studies of different legal codes and criminal justice systems have grown as a result of greater access to data/information. Currently several large bodies of data exist, which allow comparisons, albeit cautious ones of violence trends in many developed and developing nations around the world. Such organizations as the United Nations, World Health Organization, and INTERPOL have conducted major surveys on violent crimes and violence in general. Greater sharing and exchange of international information, ideas, and solutions has facilitated our understanding of the violence in society. Whether the problem of violence is addressed on a global level or on a local community level, solutions are unlikely to be found in isolation looking only at isolated situations or using isolated incidents.

References

Bachman, J., O'Malley, P.M. and Johnson, J. (1978). *Youth in Transition*. Ann Arbor, MI: University of Michigan, Institute for Social Research.

Background to the International Crime Victim Victims Survey (ICVS). Retrieved from: http://rechten.uvt.nl/icvs/background_to_the_international.htm.

Basil, K.C., and Saltzman, LE. (2002). *Sexual Violence Surveillance: Uniform Definitions and Recommended Data Elements: Version 1*. Atlanta, GA: Centers for Disease Control and Prevention, National Center for Injury Prevention and Control.

Blueprint for the Future of the Uniform Crime Reporting Program (Blueprint). (1985). Final Report of the UCR Study. U.S. Department of Justice, Bureau of Justice Statistics, Federal Bureau of Investigation.

Bureau of Justice Statistics (BCJ). *Key Facts at a Glance. Violent Crime Rate Trends*. http://bjs.ojp.usdoj.gov/content/glance/viort.cfm.

Bureau of Justice Statistics (BCJ). *Key Facts at a Glance. Four Measures of Serious Violent Crime*. http://bjs.ojp.usdoj.gov/content/glance/cv2.cfm.

Criminal Victimization in the United States, 2008 — Statistical Tables (March 2010). *National Crime Victimization Survey (NCVS)*, U.S. Department of Justice, Bureau of Justice Statistics, NCJ 227669. Retrieved from: www.bjs.gov.

Elliott, D.S., Huizinga, D. and Ageton, S. (1985). *Explaining Delinquency and Drug Use*. Beverly Hills, CA: Sage.

Fairfield, E., and Dammer, R.D. (2001). *Comparative Criminal Justice Systems*. Belmont, CA: Wadsworth.

Federal Bureau of Investigation (FBI). (1991). *Crime in the United States, 1990*. Uniform Crime Reports, Washington, DC: U.S. Government Printing Office.

Federal Bureau of Investigation (FBI). (2010). *Crime in the United States, 2009*. Uniform Crime Reports. Washington, DC: Retrieved from: www.fbi.gov.

Federal Bureau of Investigation (FBI). (2011). *Crime in the United States, 2010*. Uniform Crime Reports. Washington, DC: Retrieved from: www.fbi.gov.

Federal Bureau of Investigation (FBI). (January 6, 2012). Attorney General Eric Holder Announces Revisions to the Uniform Crime Report's Definition of Rape. Retrieved from: www.fbi.gov.

Garcia-Moreno, C., and Watts, C. (2011). Violence against Women: An Urgent Public Health Policy. Bulletin of the World Health Organization. Retrieved from: http://www. Who.int/bulletin/volumes/89/1/10-085217/en/.

Garcia-Moreno, C., Jansen, HAFM, Ellsberg, M., Heise, L, and Watts, C. (2005). *WHO Multi-Country Study on Women's Health and Domestic Violence against Women: Initial Results on Prevalence, Health Outcomes and Women's Responses*. Geneva: World Health Organization.

Gilmore, J. (Feb.16, 2007). *New Research Reveals Historic 1990s U.S. Crime Decline*. Retrieved from: http://www.eurekalert.org/pub_releases/2007/-02/uoc-nrr021207.pdf

Global Report on Trafficking in Persons. 2009. United Nations Office on Drugs and Crime (UNOC). Retrieved from: http://www.unodc.org.

Gold, M., and Reimer, D.J. (1975). Changing Patterns of Delinquent Behavior among Americans 13 through 16 Years old: 1967–1972. *Crime and Delinquency Literature*, 7, 483–517.

Goode, E. (2011). FBI's Definition of Rape too Narrow, Critics Say. New Orleans: *Times-Picayune*, September 29, 2011, A-5.

Greenwood, P.W., and Abrahamse, A. (1982). *Selective Incapacitation*. Santa Monica, CA: Rand Corp.

Hagan, F. (2010). *Research Methods in Criminal Justice and Criminology*. Upper Saddle River, NJ: Prentice Hall.

Harrendorf, S., Heiskanen, M., and Malby, S. (2010). *International Statistics on Crime and Justice*. HEUNI and UNODC. Retrieved from: http://www.unodc.org/documents/data-and-analysis/Crime-statistics/International_Statistics_on_Crime_and_Justice.pdf.

Heiskanen, M. (2010). Trends in Police-Recorded Crime. In S. Harrendorf, M. Heiskanen, and S. Malby (Eds.). *International Statistics on Crime and Justice*, HEUNI and UNODC, 21–35.

Hindelang, M.J. (1971). Age, sex and the versatility of delinquent involvement. *Social Problems*, 18, 527–535.

Horney, J., and Marshall, I. H. (1992). An Experimental Comparison of Two Self Report Methods in Measuring Lambda. *Journal of Research in Crime and Delinquency*, 29 (1), 102–121.

Ismaili, K. (2011). Thinking about Criminal Justice Policy: Process, Players and Politics. In K. Ismaili (Ed.) *U.S. Criminal Justice Policy: A Contemporary Reader*. Ontario: Jones and Bartlett Leaning, 1–16.

Janocha, J.A., and Smith, R.T. (Aug. 30, 2010). *Workplace Safety and Health in the Health Care and Social Assistance Industry, 2003–07*. United States Department of Labor, Bureau of Labor Statistics. Retrieved from: http://www.bls.gov/opub/cwc/sh20100825ar01p1.htm.

Johnson, H., Ollus, N., and Nevala, S. (2008). *Violence against Women: An International Perspective*, HEUNI, Springer.

Johnston, L. D., Bachman, J. G., and O'Malley, P. M. (2010). *Monitoring the Future: Questionnaire responses from the nation's high school seniors, 2009*. Ann Arbor, MI: Institute for Social Research, p.388. Retrieved from: http://www.monitoringthe future.org/datavolumes/2009/2009dv.pdf.

Jones, J. M. 2010. *Americans still perceive crime as on the rise*. Retrieved from: http://www.gallup.com/poll/144827/Americans_Perceive_Crime_Rise.aspx.

Junger-Tas, J., and Marshall, I.H. (1999). *The Self Report Methodology in Crime Research*. Washington, DC: Bureau of Justice Statistics, NCJ 17873.

Kirk, D. (2006). Examining the Divergence across Self-Report and Official Data Sources on Inferences about the Adolescent Life-Course of Crime. *Journal of Quantitative Criminology*, 22, 107–129.

Konigsmark, A.R. (Dec. 8, 2006). Crime Takes Hold of New New Orleans. *USA Today*. Retrieved from: http://www.usatoday.com/news/nation/2006-11-30-orleans-crime-cover_x.htm.

Krug, E.G., Dahlberg, L.L., Mercy, J.A., Zwi, A.B., and Lozano, R. (2002). *World Report on Violence and Health*, Geneva: World Health Organization. Retrieved from: http://www.who.int/violence_injury_prevention/violence/world_report/en/index.html.

Levitt, S.D. (2004). Understanding Why Crime Fell in the 1990's: Four Factors that Explain the Decline and Six that Do Not. *Journal of Economic Perspectives*, 18(1) 163–190.

Liberman, A.M. (2009.) Advocating evidence-generating policies: A Role for the ASC. *The Criminologist*, 34(1), 1–5.

Malby, S. (2010). Homicide. In S. Harrendorf, M. Heiskanen, and S. Malby (Eds.). *International Statistics on Crime and Justice*, HEUNI and UNODC, 7–19.

Markon, J. (2012). FBI Changes Its Definition of Rape. New Orleans, La.: *The Times-Picayune*, January 7, 2012, A-2.

Murray, C.J.L., et al. (2001). *The Global Burden of Disease 2000 Project: Aims, Methods and Data Sources*. Geneva: World Health Organization, (GPE Discussion Paper, 36).

Murray, C.J.L., and Lopez, A.D. 1996. *The Global Burden of Disease: A Comprehensive Assessment of Mortality and Disability from Diseases, Injuries, and Risk Factors in 1990 and projected to 2020*. Cambridge, MA, Harvard School of Public Health, (Global Burden of Disease and Injury Series, Vol. I).

National Archive of Criminal Justice Data (NACJD). Retrieved from: http://icpsr.umich.edu/icpsrweb/NACJD/NIBRS/.

O'Donnell, J.A. (1976). *Young Men and Drugs: A Nationwide Study*. Rockville, MD: National Institute of Drug Abuse.

Pakes, F. (2004). *Comparative Criminal Justice*. Cullompton, Devon: Wilan.

Petersilia, J., Greenwood, P.W., and Lavin, M. (1977). *Criminal Careers of Habitual Felons*. Santa Monica, CA: Rand Corporation.

President's Commission on Law Enforcement and Administration of Justice. (1967). *The Challenge of Crime in a Free Society*. Washington, DC: U.S. Government Printing Office.

Putting women first: Ethical and Safety Recommendations for research on domestic violence against women. Geneva, World Health Organization, 2001 (document WHO/FCH/GWH/01.01).

Quetelet, A. (1831/1984). *Research on the Propensity for Crime at Different Ages*. Trans. By S.F. Sylvester. Cincinnati: Anderson.

Rand, M.R. and Rennison, C.M. (2002). True Crime Stories? Accounting for Differences in Our National Crime Indicators. In D. Cork and M. Cohen (Column editors, Window on Washington). *Chance: A Magazine of the American Statistics Association*, 15(1) 47–51. Retrieved from: http://bjs.ojp.usdoj.gov/content/pub/pdf/tcsadnci.pdf.

Riedel, M. (2012). Getting Away with Murder: A Review of Arrest Clearances. In D.W. Harper, L. Voigt, and W.E. Thornton (Eds.). *Violence: Do We Know It When We See It?* Durham, NC: Carolina Academic Press, 249–271.

Ripley, A. (March 21, 2006). Crime Returns to the Big Easy. *Time U.S.* Retrieved from: http://www.time.com/time/nation/article/0,8599,1175489,000.html.

Saltzman, L.E., Fanslow, J.L., McMahon, P.M., and Shelly, G.A. (1999). *Intimate Partner Surveillance: Uniform Definitions and Recommended Data Elements, Version 1.0*. Atlanta, GA: National Center for Injury Prevention and Control, Centers for Disease Control and Prevention.

Sygnatur, E.F., and G.A. Toscano. (2000). Work-related Homicides: The Facts. *Compensation and Working Conditions*, Spring, 3–8.

Thornton, W., and James, J. (1979). Masculinity and Delinquency Revisited. *British Journal of Criminology*, 19, 223–241.

Thornton, W., and Voigt, L. (1984). Television and Delinquency: A Neglected Dimension of Social Control. *Youth and Society*, 15, 445–463.

Tittle, C.W., and Villemez, W.J. (1977). Social Class and Criminality. *Social Forces*, 56, 474–502.

Toscano, G.A. and Sygnatur, E.F. (2000). Work-Related Homicides: The Facts. Compensation and Working Conditions, Spring, 3–8. Retrieved from: http://www.bls.gov/opub/cwc/archive/spring2000art.pdf.

Truman, J.L., and Rand, M.R. (October, 2010). *Criminal Victimization, 2009. National Crime Victimization Survey*. U.S. Department of Justice, Bureau of Justice Statistics. NCJ 231327. Retrieved from: http://bjs.ojp.usdoj.gov.

Truman, J.L. (September 2011). *Criminal Victimization, 2010*. National Crime Victimization Survey. U.S. Department of Justice, Bureau of Justice Statistics. NCJ 235508. Retrieved from: http://www.bjs.gov.

U.S. Department of Justice. (2000). *The Nation's Two Crime Measures*. Fact Sheet NCJ-122795. Retrieved from: www.fbi.gov.

United Nations. (2011). *The United Nations Rule of Law Indicators, Implementation Guide and Project Tools*. Retrieved from: http://www.un.org/en/events/peacekeeping/2011/pub-licaitons/on_rule_of_law_indicators.pdf.

United Nations Office on Drugs and Crime and United Nations Economic Commission for Europe (UNODC and UNECE). (2010). *Manual on Victimization Surveys*. Geneva:

United Nations. Retrieved from: http://www.unodc.org/unodc/en/data-and-analysis/Manual-on-victim-surveys.html.

United Nations Office on Drugs and Crime (UNODC). (2011a). *2011 Global Study on Homicide.* Retrieved from: http://www.unodc.org/documents/data-and-analysis/statistics/Homicide/Globa_study_on_homicide_2011_web.pdf.

United Nations Office on Drugs and Crime (UNODC). (2009). *Global Report on Trafficking in Persons.*

United Nations Office on Drugs and Crime (UNODC). (2011b). *World Drug Report 2011.* Retrieved from: http://www.unodc.org/unodc/en/data-and-analysis/WDC-2011.html.

United Nations Office on Drugs and Crime (UNODC). *United Nations Surveys on Crime Trends and the Operations of Criminal Justice Systems (CTS).* Retrieved from: http://www.unodc.org/unodc/en/data-and-analysis/United-Nations-Surveys-on-Crime-Trends-and-the-Operations-of-Criminal-Justice-Systems.html.

Van Dijk, J.J.M., Mayhew, P. and Killias, M. (1990). *Experiences of crime across the world: Key findings from the 1989 International Crime Survey.* Deventer: Kluwer Law and Taxation.

Van Dijk, J.J.M., van Kesteren, J.N. and Smit, P. (2007) *Criminal Victimization in International Perspective: Key Findings from the 2004–2005 ICVS and EU ICS.* The Hague: Boom Legal Publishers. Retrieved from: http://rechten.uvt.nl/icvs/pdffiles/ICVS2004_05.pdf.

VanLandingham, Mark. J. (2007). Murder Rates in New Orleans, La, 2004–2006. *American Journal of Public Health*, 97, 1614–1616.

Violence Prevention Alliance. (n.d.). Retrieved from: http://www.who.int/violenceprevention/en/.

Voigt, L., Thornton, W.E., Barrile, L., and Seaman, J.M. (1994). *Criminology and Justice.* New York: McGraw Hill.

World Health Organization (WHO). Retrieved from: http://www.who.int/about/en/.

WHO Multi-Country Study on Women's Health and Domestic Violence against Women. (2005) Summary Report of Initial Results on Prevalence, Health Outcomes, and Women's Responses. Geneva: World Health Organization.

World Health Organization (WHO)/London School of Hygiene and Tropical Medicine. (2010). *Preventing Intimate Partner Violence and Sexual Violence against Women: Taking Acton and Generating Evidence.* Geneva: World Health Organization.

Zimring, F. (2007). *The Great American Crime Decline.* Oxford University Press.

Chapter 3

Interpersonal Violence

As noted in the previous chapters, interpersonal violence refers to acts of violence that occur between and among individuals interacting in a wide range of contexts of daily, private living. Interpersonal violence is the form of violence that is most commonly discussed in the literature on violence; it is the form that we know most about. This chapter reviews various types of interpersonal violence beginning with legally defined forms of criminal violence that are included in the Uniform Crime Reports (UCR) and then the chapter examines expressions of interpersonal violence in institutional settings.

Criminal Violence

When we speak of violence we typically refer to interpersonal acts of violence such as homicide, rape, robbery, and assault, which are known as *criminal violence*. In our society it is criminal violence that is associated with violence in general and that most people are aware of and fear. Acts such as homicide, rape, robbery, and assault bring individuals face-to-face with offenders in interpersonal violent transactions. These types of crimes, while relatively rare in terms of actual incidents occurring in comparison with property crimes (e.g., shoplifting, burglary, auto theft, and white-collar fraud or embezzlement), nevertheless attract considerable attention in our society. In fact, it is the rarest and most heinous forms of violent crimes such as mass murders or serial killings that we are most familiar with and that come to our minds when we think about violence in society. Consider the following three cases:

Case one:

On January 8, 2011 Representative Gabrielle Giffords was shot in Tucson, Arizona by Jared Louhner, who in addition to seriously injuring Giffords also shot to death six other individuals, including a nine year old child and a federal judge; 14 others were wounded. Twenty three year old Jared from all indications seemed like an ordinary young man, somewhat withdrawn, a little nerdy, who liked music and played the saxophone (Cloud, 2011, p. 32).

Case two:

On February 12, 2010 Dr. Amy Bishop, a neuroscientist with a Harvard Ph.D. and professor in the Biology Department at the University of Alabama at Hunstville, was arrested in the shooting of six of her colleagues (three killed and three severely wounded) at a departmental faculty meeting after finding out that she had been denied tenure at the university (Dewan, et al, 2010, p. 2).

Case three:

On April 16, 2007 Seung Hui Cho, a 23 year old student at Virginia Technical University, left his dormitory armed with a 9 mm pistol and a 22 caliber handgun. He entered a coeducational residence hall that housed 895 people and shot to death a 19 year old female freshman and a 22 year old male resident assistant. About two hours later, Cho entered an engineering classroom about a half a mile from the initial shooting site. He chain-locked the front doors from the inside and made his way to the second floor. Cho killed another 30 people in four different classrooms and wounded at least 15 others before turning the gun on himself. Another 60 students were injured as they leapt from the windows of their classrooms (cited in Hickey, 2010, p. 20).

When we hear of someone like Jared Loughner, Amy Bishop, or Seung Hui Cho, we immediately look for an explanation or label to explain such seemingly incomprehensible acts. We wonder whether these offenders represent some recognizable *violent type*. Following each of these cases, there have been speculations of some causative type of mental illness or mental disorder. Over the years, psychiatrists, psychoanalysts, and forensic psychologists have produced a vast array of literature on profiles or predictors of violent criminal behavior. However, none of these profiles or predictors has proven to be definitive. Clinical *predictions of dangerousness* are generally problematic because they are difficult to test or support with evidence. In reality the overwhelming majority of people representing the profile characteristics of dangerousness never commit serious violent acts much less such heinous acts as described above. Often psychiatrists and psychologists are faced with professional ethical dilemmas due to pressure placed on them to "over predict" individual dangerousness from past behaviors. Basing predictions on past patterns of behavior often leads to erroneous conclusions because mitigating circumstances or environmental factors may be ignored (Monahan, 1981).

As we noted in Chapter 1, the *social construction of reality* about violent crime concerns many different groups and publics, and represents a multiplicity of perspectives, values, experiences, and interpretations. The mass media, for example, selectively reports the most sensational of violent crimes; cases with multiple bodies are more likely to be reported (Duwe, 2000). Journalists often provide extensive details of the offenders, their lives, and the events leading up to the crimes and offer endless commentary from a variety of "experts" about the prevalence and causes of these crimes. From media accounts and also our daily interpersonal exchanges of observations and ideas with family, friends and acquaintances, an *informal consensual reality* or understanding often develops about violent crime types, i.e., speculations regarding those types of people most likely to commit such violent, heinous crimes. In addition, a prototype, archetype or stereotype of a "violent type" of individual or offender is often created by the media, which becomes self-perpetuating when similar crimes occur. So called rhetorical constructions of these violent types are often used including terms such as *predator, rampage killer, crazy, pathological, psychopathic*, and *psychotic* (Spitzberg and Cadiz, 2002; Surette, 2007, p. 40). Some of these terms have their roots in various scientific theories of violent crime causation (see Chapters 8–9) while others are part of our cultural lexicon of labels, which are applied to the outrageous acts of violence such as mass murder in which several people are killed at one point in time.

Likewise, *formal consensual reality* about violent crime originates from persons representing the scientific community (e.g., criminologists, psychologists, psychiatrists, and sociologists) as well as other various official spokespersons representing the society at-large (e.g., the criminal justice or public health systems, governmental or public sectors, and a wide spectrum of community and religious establishments) generally regarded as authorities or experts. The *formal* parameters of reality are usually distinguished from the informal types primarily by their presumably more systematic or scientific nature. However, even scientific crime experts from different fields (e.g., biology, psychology, and sociology) compete among themselves for dominance in terms of having their explanations and typologies of violence accepted and cited in both the scientific literature and popular media. This also holds true for all other experts across society.

Currently the dominate view of violence in the United States is the criminal justice perspective. The primary definition of violence promoted by the criminal justice system, which is expressed in terms of the four types of interpersonal acts of violence (i.e., homicide, rape, robbery, and assault), is in fact the definition/perspective on violence that is most widely distributed and recognized in the U. S. Violent crimes are by definition interpersonal in nature involving perpetrators and victims and they have in common the element of the infliction (or attempted infliction) of physical/psychological injury and/or death to the victim.

Homicide

The taking of a human life quite possibly represents one of the most heinous of crimes known to humankind. Yet the circumstances surrounding a killing, including the mental state of the perpetrator and the role of the victim, determine the severity of the penalty that we place on the murder act.

The Law

Any unlawful taking of a life of another is classified under the generic heading homicide. The two principle types of homicide are: *murder* and *manslaughter*. In most states, murder is divided into first-degree and second-degree. *First-degree murder* generally means murder with "premeditation and deliberation" and killings committed during the course of certain felonies, usually "inherently dangerous" ones (e.g., rape, robbery, arson, burglary). Premeditation means that the murder was planned in advance, and deliberation means that the murder was given considerable thought; it did not occur simply on impulse. Another condition of first-degree murder is *malice aforethought*, meaning that the offender intentionally — and with malice — took the life of another person. *Second-degree murder* is criminal homicide intended by the offender (thus malice is present), but generally without a measurable period of either premeditation or deliberation. Crimes of passion often fit into this category. In some states there is a category of "felony murder," which is similar to second-degree murder because premeditation is not present and includes killing(s) committed during the course of a felony *other* than specified in first-degree murder.

Any unlawful homicide without malice is called *manslaughter*. Manslaughter is usually divided into *voluntary* manslaughter, the killing occurring "in the heat of passion" or in a violent fight with provocation, and *involuntary* manslaughter, an unintended killing committed recklessly, in gross negligence, or during the commission of an unlawful act, such as when a driver under the influence of alcohol causes the death of another person due to intoxication.

Under the law, it is possible for a homicide to be classified as *justifiable homicide*. A police officer, who kills someone in a life-threatening situation, having no criminal intent and discharging his or her lawful responsibilities, would be "justified" in the homicide. Further clarification of innocent homicide takes place through consideration of excusable homicide. Basically, killings of this type involve self-defense against a threat from an attacker; no criminal intent is involved.

Patterns and Trends

Established in 1930 the FBI's *Uniform Crime Reports* (UCR) is the oldest official source of information on crime including homicide in the United States. Since the beginning of the UCR's annual publications in 1958, crime rates, particularly the homicide rates, have been reported annually as well as tracked and compared over several-year periods. Tracking homicide rates from 1960 (starting with a rate of 5 per 100,000 population) through the

1970s, we can note a steady and alarming incline during this period, which peaks in 1974 (with a rate of 10 per 100,000 population). The murder rate then seems to decline slightly in 1975 and for the remainder of the 1970s (hovering around 9 per 100,000). Then in a pendulum-like motion, the homicide rate goes up and down before it assumes a more stable motion. In 1980 we see another peak increase (10.2 per 100,000) followed by declines through 1987 (8.3 per 100,000) and then it again gradually increases through 1990 (9.4. per 100,000). It is not until 1997 (with a rate of 6.8 per 100,000) that we can chart significant declines extending to the most current reporting year (with a rate of 4.8 in 2010) (FBI, 1960; 1975; 1980; 1987; FBI, 2011, Table 1).

In 2010, the volume of reported homicides in the U. S. is 14,748. All crime trends are affected by certain phenomenon, including demographics of the population, economic conditions, geographic factors, and even meteorological conditions (e.g., Archer and Gartner, 1984). The UCR has in the past noted, for example, that homicide rates generally tend to be highest during the summer months (July and August) and lowest during the winter months such as February (FBI, 2005, p. 16); the FBI also cautions that climate is one of a number of variables that affect the volume and type of crime (FBI, 2011, Caution Against Ranking). Also, certain regions of the country seem to experience higher incidents of homicides than others. The South, historically, accounts for a disproportionately large number of homicides (43.8% of the murders in 2010 compared with 20.6% for the West, 19.9% for the Midwest, and 15.6% for the Northeast). Large metropolitan areas of the country report an average murder rate of 5.0 per 100,000 compared with an average rate of 3.6 per 100,000 for mid-size metropolitan areas and 3.2 per 100,000 for non-metropolitan counties (FBI, 2011, Tables 2 and 3). The influence of these various factors on crime in general, but especially homicide, is complicated and still generally not well understood, at least in terms of any predictability factors.

Characteristics of Offenders

Offenders arrested for murder tend to be young males. In 2010, 64 percent of all the homicide offenders are under 29 years of age with 15 percent of those arrested for murder between 12 and 18 years old (FBI, 2011, Table 38). Approximately 90 percent of all those arrested for murder in 2010 are males, indicating that murder is chiefly a male activity, as is most violent criminality (Table 33). About forty-nine percent (49.3%) of the total arrestees for murder are Caucasian and 48.7 percent are African-American, the remainder represent other ethnic/racial backgrounds (FBI, 2011, Table 43a).

Characteristics of Victims

According to the UCR 77.4 percent of homicide victims in 2010 are males; about 60 percent are between the ages of 17 and 34 years (Expanded Homicide Table 2). When race is known, 46.5 percent of homicide victims are white, 49.8 percent are black, and 3.7 percent represent other races or are unknown. Generally speaking, reported homicides are typically intra-racial, with 90 percent of black murder victims being slain by black offenders and about 84 percent of white murder victims being slain by white offenders (Expanded Homicide Table 6). Similarly, males are most often killed by men (85% in single-victim/single offender murder); however, nine out of ten women are killed by men.

In 2010, among all female murder victims, 37.5 percent were killed by husbands or boyfriends, suggesting that many homicides involve intimate partners; cases that law enforcement efforts have very little control over. Only 2.4 percent of the male victims are killed by their wives or girlfriends. Overall, in incidents of murder for which the relationships of murder victims and offenders are known, 53 percent of victims are killed by someone they knew (e.g., acquaintance, neighbor, friend) and 24.8 percent of victims are killed by family members. The relationship of murder victims and offenders is unknown in 44.0 percent of murder and manslaughter cases in 2010 (UCR, 2011, Expanded Homicide Tables 2, 10).

Circumstances of homicides, when known, indicate that 41.8 percent of victims are killed during arguments (including romantic triangles) in 2010. Homicides related to felony circumstances (e.g., rape, robbery, burglary) account for about 23 percent of all reported homicides. Circumstances are unknown for approximately 36 percent of all reported homicides in 2010 (Expanded Homicide Table 12). According to the UCR, 665 justifiable homicides have been reported in 2010; private individuals justifiably killed 278 people during the commission of a crime and law enforcement officers killed 387 felons (FBI, 2011, Expanded Homicide Tables 14 and 15).

Typologies

Since many murder offenders and victims are somehow related (by marriage or kinship) or are acquainted with the offender, criminologists have examined more closely the "murder transaction." Criminologist Marvin Wolfgang in his classic study of criminal homicide in Philadelphia coined the term, "victim precipitation," to refer to a particular type of homicide where the victim has been involved in his or her own demise. Victim-precipitated murders often occur when the victim strikes the first blow, pulls out a weapon, or otherwise threatens the other person. Wolfgang finds that of the 588 homicides examined, about 25 percent could be classified as victim precipitated, including factors such as intimate partner conflict/fights, presence of alcohol use, and victims with prior criminal convictions (1958; 1966). Levitov and Harper (2012) examine drug and revenge/retaliatory murder in New Orleans at the neighborhood level and report that many of these murders in the period from 2003 through 2005 (post-Hurricane Katrina) appear to occur as a form of dispute resolution or informal justice. According to the researchers, many of New Orleans "high murder" areas are run by their own informal justice system (p. 145).

David Luckenbill (1977) goes beyond the concept of victim precipitation by examining murder situations especially offender/victim interactions and argues that a "transaction" occurs between murder offenders and victims in a definite sequence of events. He refers to criminal homicide as a "social occasion" that represents the culmination of an intense interchange between an offender and a victim. There is, he notes, a consensus among both parties "that violence is a suitable if not required means for settling the contest" (p. 177). Luckenbill describes six stages:

Stage 1: The opening move in the transaction is an event performed by the victim and subsequently defined by the offender as an offense to face, i.e., the image of self that a person claims during a particular contact. In about 40 percent of the murders the offensive verbal expression is made by the victim and the offender takes offense. Another 34 percent of the murders involve the victim's refusal to co-operate or comply with requests of the offender.

Stage 2: In all cases leading to murder, the offender interprets the victim's actions as personally offensive. And in 60 percent of the cases the offender learns the meaning of the victim's move from inquires made of the victim or audience.

Stage 3: The offender engages in some sort of retaliation against the victim by either issuing as a verbal or physical challenge.

Stage 4: Unless the victim has been eliminated in the previous stage, he/she demonstrably stands up to the offender's challenge further acerbating the situation.

Stage 5: The offender attacks the victim who has been either killed or is dying. In about 36 percent of the cases, the offender carries a handgun or knife into the setting; but in the remainder of the cases, the offender either leaves the situation temporarily to secure a weapon or utilizes an existing object on the scene and uses it as a lethal weapon. The presence of weapons makes the murder possible.

Stage 6: Once the victim is killed, the transaction is terminated and in about 60 percent of the cases, the offender flees the scene (1977, pp. 179–185).

While most homicides involve single offenders and single victims, a great deal of attention has been given to *multicide* or multiple murders, which usually involves a single offender and multiple victims. Due to the sensationalism associated with multicide, the mass media often give extensive coverage to such cases. Indeed, the more victims, the greater the media coverage (Duwe, 2004), which often gives the public the impression that multicides are relatively common, when, in fact, they are relatively very rare events.

Accounts of multiple murders by the same individual are noted in cases dating back to the late 1700s and continuing through the twenty-first century. Historian Otto Rothert (1924) describes numerous cases of multicide (such as the case involving the brothers Micajah and Wiley Harpe, who in 1789–1799, murdered twenty to thirty-eight people in the frontier states of Kentucky and Tennessee, and the case of the Bender family, who ran a roadside house in southeastern Kansas and killed at least twelve travelers who made the unfortunate decision to stop at their house for the night). Other historians such as Richard Brown also document notorious cases of multicide (e.g., Herman Mudgett, aka H.H. Holmes of Englewood, Illinois, who confessed to killing twenty-seven people between 1890 and 1894 several of whom were lured in his castle-like house while they were attending the Chicago World's Fair of 1893) (Brown, 1969, p. 56).

It is not until the 1960s, however, that scientific research on the dynamics of multiple-murder or multicide began to appear. Part of this growing interest has been stimulated by two particularly heinous multiple murders. In Chicago, Richard Speck killed eight student nurses, one at a time within a short period. A month later, Charles Whitman ascended the University of Texas library tower with a small arsenal of weapons and systematically shot thirteen people to death and wounded thirty-one others. Also in the 1960s, the case of Albert DeSalvo, the Boston strangler, aroused the nation's fear of multiple-murder. Since the 1960s there have been numerous other multiple-murders documented in the United States as well as in other countries (Holmes and Holmes, 2000; Hickey, 2010).

Currently two other terms are frequently used to describe cases of multicide, serial murder and mass murder. Both terms refer to cases with multiple victims and a single perpetrator; both are subsets of multicide. *Serial murder* refers to the killing of several victims one at a time over an extended period (e.g., over several days, weeks, months, or years). A distinction is also made between the serial murder and the *murder spree*. A killer engaging in a murder spree selects victims by chance and kills victims, often three or more, over a relatively short period of time, hours or days, on impulse or mood (Hickey, 2010, p. 21). An example of a serial murderer would be Theodore Bundy, who systematically murdered thirty-three women between 1974 and 1978. Bundy was caught by sheer chance after he killed two sorority coeds on the campus of Florida State University in Tallahassee in 1978 (Michaud and Aynesworth, 1983). A recent example of a spree murder took place on September 6, 2011 in Carson City, Nevada were 32 year old Eduardo Sencion wielded an AK47 assault rifle and opened fire on a table of uniformed National Guard members having breakfast at an International House of Pancakes (IHOP) restaurant. Before entering the restaurant, the shooter pulled his blue minivan into the strip shopping center of retail stores and shops, got out of his minivan and shot a man on a motorcycle. After he left the IHOP, Sencion got back into his vehicle, drove around in circles shooting into nearby businesses. In total four people were killed, and eight others were wounded. He shot himself in the head and died later at a hospital (Chereb, 2011, p. B2).

Mass murder is generally reserved for the killing of several people in the same general area at basically one time usually in succession during a short period of time (Egger, 1984; Hickey, 2010). The case of Charles Whitman would fit the category of mass murder. Another mass murder incident is the school shooting at Columbine High School, where students Eric Harris and Dylan Klebold, dressed in black trench coats and armed with explosives and guns, went to their high school in Littleton, Colorado on April 20, 1999 and shot 12 of their fellow classmates and a teacher (Hickey, 2010, pp. 10–11).

According to Eric Hickey (2010), there are significant differences among mass, serial and spree murderers. Mass murderers usually appear to give little thought to their capture or death. These mass killers are often killed by the police. These killings have been discussed as possible cases of suicide-by-cop or they kill themselves or surrender to authorities (Lord, 2004). The exceptions to this pattern are those who kill their families (often called *family slayers* or *family annihilators*) who typically seem to plan in advance the killing of their family members along with committing suicide following the homicides (Harper and Voigt, 2007; 2012). Overall mass murderers are usually white, male, and encompass a wide age range; although family annihilators on average tend to be middle age. Almost exclusively, hand guns, rifles, and other semi-automatic guns are used to kill "suddenly and swiftly" (Hickey, 2010, p.13). Motives for mass murders have some common themes including but not limited to: (1) striking back at people because of "feelings of rejection, failure, and loss of autonomy;" (2) lashing out at "society" for perceived injustices (e.g., killing children at school); and (3) seeking to gain some form of "power and control" over their lives by wreaking vengeance (p. 17). While victims are often specifically targeted by mass murderers (e.g., family members, former employers, and people representing specific racial or ethnic groups), random people or bystanders are frequently killed in the attack (see Box 3.1).

Unlike mass murder, *serial murder* involves perpetrators that go to great lengths *not* to get caught, often killing over a long period (with some killing over many years) before getting caught or never getting caught (see Box 3.2). The serial killer generally "hunts" for his (or her) victims throughout his/her killing career, rather than making a final statement with a murderous "rampage" killing of multiple victims all at once (Hickey, 2010, pp. 19–21). Criminologists Ronald Holmes and James DeBurger (1988) delineate the central elements in serial murders, focusing chiefly on the traits of the perpetrators:

- The central element is repetitive homicide. The serial murderer kills again and again, and will continue to kill if not prevented.
- They are almost exclusively white men between the ages of 25 and 35, coming from all social classes.
- Their victims are usually white females ranging from the very young to the very old, although there are exceptions including some serial murderers who prey on young males.

Box 3.1 Anders Behring Breivik: Norway Mass Murderer

Source: Updated file image obtained from the Twitter page of Anders Behring Breivik, 32, who was arrested in connection with the twin attacks on a political youth camp on the island of Utoya and a government building in Oslo, Norway (AP Photo/Twitter).

It is alleged that on July 22, 2011, Anders Behring Breivik killed 69 people, mostly teenagers, in a mass shooting spree at the youth camp of the Workers Youth League of the Labor Party; eight people were killed in the bombing of a government building. Masquerading as a police officer, Breivik methodically shot youth attending the island youth camp, the youngest of his victims being 14 years old (Hewitt, 2011; Erlanger and Cowell, 2011).

Some reports suggest that he targeted the youth camp because former Norwegian prime minister Gro Harlem Brundtland, a Labor party member, spoke the day before the massacre to the participants. Based on early investigations of Breivik, his political leanings suggest a man on the far right political continuum, and "a Christian fundamentalist with a deep hatred of multiculturalism, of the left and of Muslims, who had written disparagingly of prominent Norwegian politicians" (Beaumont, 2001). Some of Breivik's ideology was posted online in a rambling manifesto which may give clues to his atrocities. Breivik is alleged to have used a front company, called Breivik Geofarm, founded in 2009 to legally purchase and stockpile fertilizer and other chemicals used to build a bomb (Jaccarino, 2011). Although court appointed psychiatrists indicate that he is a paranoid schizophrenic, other psychological diagnoses do not find Breivik to be psychotic. A Norwegian court on Friday January 13, 2012 ordered a new psychiatric evaluation of the confessed killer because of criticism from the initial diagnosis that he is "insane", suggesting that Breivik should be sent to a psychiatric facility instead of prison (Orange, 2012). On Friday, August 24, 2012, Breivik was judged sane by a Norwegian court and sentenced to 21 years in prison. Under Norwegian law, the sentence could be extended indefinitely if he is considered to be a danger to society (Smith-Spark, 2012).

- Serial murders are typically one-on-one involving the victim and the perpetrator.
- The relationship between victim and perpetrator is usually that of a stranger or slight acquaintance; serial murders seldom occurs among strongly affiliated persons.
- The serial murderer is motivated to kill; these are not crimes of passion in the conventional sense nor do they stem from any victim precipitation.
- Other apparent and clear-cut motives are typically lacking in most serial murders, due to the frequent stranger-perpetration of this crime. However, there are intrinsic motive systems—typically nonrational that seem to originate within the individual perpetrator's personality—which seem to govern and structure the serial killer's homicidal behavior. These motive systems ordinarily do not reflect passion or personal gain or profit tendencies (pp. 18–19).

Serial killers' apparent lack of motives and random stranger victimizations, coupled with life style factors that prevent public or familial notice of any suspicious behavior, make it particularly difficult to catch felons. Even after the establishment of the Violent Criminal Apprehension Program (VICAP), which was created in 1984 as part of the FBI's Behavioral Science Unit (BSU) to provide a nationwide clearinghouse on cases that appear to suggest

Box 3.2 California Zodiac Killer

Random and motiveless, they are the most difficult serial murder cases to solve. San Francisco endured a brief reign of terror in 1968 and 1969, during which time a ruthless killer slew five people and wounded two more. The killings were followed by detailed descriptions of the atrocities in letters to newspapers, signed by a cross placed on a circle; the symbol of the Zodiac. The first murders firmly attributed to the "Zodiac Killer" were of a student couple, aged 16 and 17, who were shot in a quiet lane near Vallejo, near San Francisco, in December 1968. The pair had apparently been fleeing from their car when gunned down, but there was no obvious motive for the crime.

A similar double shooting followed the next July. The gunman had driven up alongside a car and opened fire without warning, killing a 22-year old-girl and seriously injuring her 19-year-old boyfriend. Police were alerted to the crime by a call from a man, described as having a "gruff voice", who boasted: 'I also killed those kids last year.'

Following this attack, three newspapers received coded notes which, when matched and decoded, provided a weird message from 'Zodiac' in which he said, 'I like killing people' and added that 'when I die I will be reborn in paradise and those I have killed will become my slaves'.

'Zodiac' fell silent again until September 1969 when the gruff voice at the end of the phone line directed police to the shore of Lake Berryessa, in the Napa Valley, where two students, a girl of 22 and her boyfriend aged 20, had been killed in a frenzied attack. The assailant had daubed the zodiac sign on the side of the couple's white car, along with the dates of the previous murders. The girl, who had been stabbed with a foot-long bayonet 24 times, died in the hospital two days later; her boyfriend, with bayonet wounds in the back, survived. He described the attacker as wearing a black hood with slits for his mouth and eyes.

'Zodiac' moved onto the streets of San Francisco itself to strike again two weeks later, shooting a 29-year-old student and part-time taxi driver as he sat in a cab. The gunman, described by witnesses as short, in his 40s, with thick horn-rimmed glasses and crew-cut brown hair, fled into the side-streets pursued by two patrolmen and escaped in the wooded military reservation known as The Presidio. The shooting was followed by letters to newspapers, this time enclosing a shred of bloodstained shirt torn from the victim—and claiming, not the five slayings attributed to him, but eight murders so far.

The 'Zodiac Killer' next struck in march 1970 when a 23-year-old woman was traveling toward Petaluma, northeast of San Francisco, when another driver flagged her down, told her that one of her rear wheels was wobbling, and offered her a ride. Once in his car, he warned her: 'You know you're going to die—you know I'm going to kill you.' As he slowed, she leapt out and flagged down another car. Her description exactly fitted the taxi driver's killer.

Again, 'Zodiac' wrote to newspapers, acknowledging the kidnap attempt and upping his claimed victims to 37. The last letter was sent in April 1974. Since then, noting ... and the identity of the 'Zodiac Killer' has remained one of the greatest unsolved mysteries of modern crime.

Source: True Crimes: Serial Killers, 2009: 218–222.

characteristics of serial murders in the hope of increasing the clearance rate, due in part to its inability to effect any increase in the rate of offender arrests, the VICAP was closed down. Limited cooperation between local and state law enforcement agencies, funding cuts, and reorganization in the FBI also contributed to its closure. At this point in time, the FBI's BSU, which is now known as the Investigative Support Unit (ISU), a component of the Critical Incident Response Group at the FBI Academy in Quantico, Virginia, handles many of the same functions as VICAP (Hickey, 2010, p. 380).

Rape

Rape is a violent crime steeped in myth and misinformation. Until relatively recently rape was classified exclusively as a sexual crime. Historically theories of rape, going back to the early women's movement, however, have explained rape as a reflection of cultural patterns of aggression and power emanating from gender role socialization and sexual stratification and economic organization (Brownmiller, 1975; Rose, 1979; Largen, 1981, Schwendinger and Schwendinger, 1983). Currently, rape is predominately viewed sociologically to result from differential gender role socialization and stratification, i.e., males learn at an early age to be aggressors in encounters with females. This perceived dominance perpetuates stereotypes in which women are somehow defined as deserving of or wanting to be raped (e.g., Murnen, et al, 2002; Osman, 2003; Adams-Curtis, 2004; Locke and Mahalik, 2005; Loh, et al., 2007). Hence, it is argued that until the role of women is truly redefined from a subservient role to one of equal status with men, the conditions of rape will remain. While the act of rape in some situations continues to have sexual connotations, it is chiefly considered a violent crime found throughout the world.

The Law

It has been argued that historically rape laws have developed to protect the property rights of men rather than to protect women (Deming and Eppy, 1981, p. 359). As noted above, only recently have people come to legally understand rape as a crime of violence and power rather than a crime of sex and passion.

In most states, rape is generally defined as unlawful sexual intercourse with a female without her consent. It is not necessary for the defendant to achieve an emission. All that is required is that there is sexual penetration, however slight. Many states now encompass penetration of the anus, as well as the vagina, in their rape statues. The *Model Penal Code* also recognizes anal penetration as rape. Historically, under common law, the rape victim must be other than the defendant's wife (Russell, 1990). During the 1970s and 1980s most states either refined or eliminated marital exemption (Anderson, 2005; Emanuel, 2010, p. 149). Presently only the state of Kentucky retains the full marital rape exemption whereby a husband cannot be criminalized for forcibly having sex with his wife.

The precise meaning of "intercourse without consent" varies from state to state. Historically, most rape laws have made it a necessity that the woman physically resists (often to her "utmost"). Currently in most states it often suffices if a woman merely fails to give actual consent, especially in situations where physical resistance would endanger her life. Thus, rape may be committed without the use of actual force provided there is a meaningful threat of serious bodily injury. While most courts have amended the "utmost" resistance ruling out of their statutes, the requirement of "resistance" to some degree still remains. However, many states have overhauled their rape laws rewording their statutes to focus on the lack of consent rather than on the use of force, minimizing the level of resistance necessary to qualify the behavior as rape (Lyon, 2004; Anderson, 2005). Thus in most states, the threat to commit imminent serious bodily harm can be a substitute for the use of actual physical force. And, some states also recognize that a threat to engage in other kinds of acts not involving serious bodily harm such as a threat of kidnapping may suffice under the Model Penal Code (Emanual, 2010, p. 150).

Lack of consent also encompasses situations other than overt harm, including mental, emotional and/or physical incapacitation or trickery that might prohibit the woman from giving her consent. Some courts extend the requisite lack of consent to a victim who is, for example, drunk, drugged, or unconscious, irrespective of whether this altered state has been induced by the offender. This type of rape is often classified as simple rape (as opposed to forcible or aggravated rape where a woman fears for her life) and carries a less severe punishment. All states establish an age of consent, below which the law regards a female's consent as impossible. A person who has intercourse with a female below this age may be charged with *statutory rape*. Most states hold that even a reasonable belief by the offender that the female is over the age of consent is not a defense. It should be noted that a majority of states have amended their rape laws to be gender neutral, where homosexual rape is the same as heterosexual rape (Emanual, 2010, p.151). As we discussed in Chapter 2, the Uniform Crime Reports recently updated its 80 year old definition of rape from "the carnal knowledge of a female, forcibly against her will" to a much broader definition more in line with most state rape statutes.

During the 1970s, feminist groups lobbied for changes to broaden the concept of coercion to include psychological, economic, and vocational coercion. Changes in the law have generally occurred over the years such as efforts to lessen the requirement for corroboration (i.e., the legal requirement to provide evidence that a rape has occurred including force, penetration, and identity). Corroboration is not required except under unique circumstances, e.g., inability of the victim to understand the crime because of young age or previous sexual relationship with the perpetrator (Karmen, 1990).

Another change in the law involves the regulation of the use of the rape victim's sexual history. Historically, the crime of rape has placed suspicion and in many instances actual "blame" on the victim. Often this accusatory stance begins with the police investigation of the crime. Many horror stories exist of cross-examining defense attorneys, usually male, dredging up the sexual history of a rape victim and inferring that she either "wanted it" or fantasized about being raped and, therefore, "invited" the attack. Strong rape reform groups have forced all states and the District of Columbia to pass *rape shield* laws. These laws prohibit the introduction of opinion and reputation evidence about the victim. They also typically indicate that evidence of specific sexual conduct of the victim is irrelevant unless it represents direct evidence germane to the case (e.g., source of injury, semen, pregnancy, or disease) or it relates to specific conduct with the alleged offender. Some rape shield laws also prohibit information about the victim's manner of dress (National Center for Victims of Crime, 2011). However, under actual judicial conditions, almost all rape shield laws allow exceptions to the presumptive rule against admissibility of sexual history. For example, even the most stringent statutes allow for the history regarding sexual relations with the defendant. Many other exceptions exist either by judicial discretion or under evidential rules.

Legal reform groups, dissatisfied with changes in rape statutes in general, have sought major revision of the law to include rape as one component of sexual assault. In a number of states, rape is included under the category of "crimes of sexual assault." The purpose of such legislation is to lessen the special nature of the offense of rape and to treat it as another type of violent crime, thus reducing discriminatory treatment of rape cases. Comparisons of states that have instituted such model rape legislation with traditional rape laws generally reveal few differences in the handling of rape victims, plea bargaining, and convictions.

Patterns and Trends

Since rape is perhaps more than 50 percent unreported, we must examine both official and unofficial crime statistics to obtain a more accurate picture of the crime. However, given the nature of rape—a violent, interpersonal act that often causes irreparable psychological and physical harm to its victims—we still have only a skeletal representation of the volume and rate of this violent crime.

The Uniform Crime Reports' definition of rape is "the carnal knowledge of a female forcibly and against her will." (According to FBI Director, Robert S. Mueller III, the new definition will go into effect in spring of 2012.) Based on the definition above, the UCR statistics includes assaults or attempts to commit rape by force or threat of force. Statutory rape and other sex offenses are not included.

The total volume of rape as reported in the UCR for 2010 is 84,767 offenses, with a rate of 27.5 rapes per 100,000 population. However, the rate of forcible rapes is estimated at 54.2 per 100,000 *female* population; this is about a 4 percent decrease when compared with the estimated 2009 rate of 56.6. Rapes by force account for 93 percent of reported rape offenses in 2010, and attempts or assaults to commit rape account for 7.0 percent of reported rapes (FBI, 2011, Table 19). Over the past twenty years, the rate of rape (rapes per 100,000 population and rapes per 100,000 females) has been steadily decreasing, e.g., from a rate of 80 per 100,000 females in 1990 to about 60 per 100,000 females in reporting year 2010 (FBI, 1990–2004; FBI, 2010b). As we discussed in Chapter 2, the Uniform Crime Reports' recent revision of its 80 year old definition of rape in January 2012 represents a much broader definition more in line with most state rape statutes. The new definition (which includes sexual assault cases involving anal or oral penetration or penetration with an object, cases where victims are drugged or under the influence of alcohol, and male victims) is likely to lead to an increase in reporting.

Geographically, the southern region in the U. S., which is the region with the largest population, accounts for the highest proportion of reported rapes, standing at 37.7 percent in 2010. Following are the western region with 25.1 percent, the midwestern region with 24.6 percent, and the northeastern region with 12.7 percent. The nation's metropolitan statistical areas, including the largest cities, have the highest rates and rural counties have the lowest (FBI, 2011, Tables 2 and 3).

Characteristics of Offenders

Looking at both UCR and National Crime Victimization Survey (NCVS) data, we can obtain some general information about rape offenders. UCR figures indicate that in 2010, 42.7 percent of those arrested for rape are less than 25 years of age and about 30 percent of the total offenders arrested are less than 21 years of age (FBI, 2011, Table 53). About 66 percent of the total offenders arrested are white, 33 percent are black, and the remaining 2 percent represent other ethnic/racial groups (Table 43a).

The NCVS adds additional information about offenders. According to NCVS 2010 data about 75 percent of rapes are carried out by single offenders (NCVS, 2010, Table 37). About 40 percent of single offender rapists are between the ages of 15 and 20, and 35 percent are 30 years old or above. Rapists are generally younger when they act in groups than when they act alone. Most offenders are unarmed, with weapons being used in a small number of cases. Approximately 22 percent of rapes and attempted rapes are committed by strangers; the remainder or majority of incidents involves acquaintances or family members. Single-offender rapes are for the most part intra-racial, with about

75 percent of white offenders raping white victims, and about 75 percent of black offenders raping black victims (NCVS, 2010, Tables 27, 39, 42, 59, and 61).

Characteristics of Victims

According to results in the National Crime Victimization Survey (NCVS), based on random samples of households in the U.S., an estimated 188,380 rapes or sexual assaults have been experienced by individuals aged 12 and over in 2010 (Truman, 2011, Table 1). (It is interesting to note that this amount is more than double the amount reported by the UCR for the same year). NCVS estimates that in 2010, females experienced about 92 percent of all reported rapes and sexual assaults based on a total figure of 169,370 victimizations, with 73 percent of these crimes being committed by non-strangers, including intimate partners (17%), other relatives (8%), and friends and acquaintances (48%), 25 percent committed by strangers, and 2 percent unknown. Male victims of rape and sexual assault in 2010 also indicate that an estimated 78 percent were committed by non-strangers, friends and acquaintances; no information is provided on other relationships (Truman, 2011, Table 5). The NCVS definition of the crime of rape is forced sexual intercourse, including psychological coercion as well as physical force, and attempted rapes that probably accounts for the substantially larger estimate of the incidents of rape compared to the UCR, which has been traditionally based on a more narrow definition and only includes those offenses of rape that have been reported to the police, excluding statutory rapes. In the NCVS sexual assault covers a wide range of victimizations distinct from rape/attempted rape. Based on the NCVS between 1993 and 2008, the rate of rape or sexual assault against females has declined by 70 percent from 4.7 to 1.4 per 1,000 females aged 12 and above. The rate of rape or sexual assaults against females and males in 2008 is 1.4 and 0.3 per 1,000 persons, respectively, for victims aged 12 and over. Current reductions in the rates hold for the 2010 NCVS with rates for female victims being 1.3 and male victims being 0.1 (Catalano and Snyder, 2009; NCVS, 2010; Truman, 2011, Table 11).

From the current NCVS and earlier victimization data, detailed characteristics about the crime of rape have emerged. More than half of rapes and other sexual assaults occur at night, with the largest proportion occurring between 6:00 pm and midnight. While rape sites vary, about one-third of reported rapes occur in the home of the victim. The rest occur in a variety of locations including streets, commercial buildings, and schools (NCVS, 2010, Tables 59, 61).

Typologies

Aside from the legal definition of rape, the crime of rape can be classified in many different ways, e.g., by motive, by circumstances, and by offender or by victim profiles. For example, the well known work of psychologists Nicholas Groth and H. Jean Birnbaum (1979) illustrates a typology that categorizes rapists by their motives. Their typology is based on psychological theories including explanations tied to displaced aggression, compensation, and sexual diffusion. In displaced aggression, the goal of the rapist is to physically harm and degrade the victim; there is little thought of sexual gratification. In compensation, sexual excitation is the key component and aggression is generally minimized. Sexual diffusion explains the rapist's behavior in terms of attempts to fulfill sexual fantasies (sexual sadism is an extreme example of this phenomenon). Groth and Birnbaum classify the *anger rapist* as someone who uses displaced aggression, often after an argument or conflict with other individuals such as a wife or girlfriend. The *power rapist* basically wants to possess his victim sexually and he uses only minimal force to achieve this goal. This type of offender may be trying to assert his misplaced masculinity or perception of masculinity (compensation). Finally, the *sadistic rapist*, according to Groth and Birnbaum, gets extremely excited by such activities as tormenting and torturing the victim. He may be trying to destroy some female personal characteristics that he dislikes or is threatened by. This type of rapist, engaging in sexual diffusion, usually commits the most heinous of all acts of rape.

Classifications may be more broadly framed around certain fact patterns that may actually combine various theories or explanatory perspectives. For example, consider the following synopses describing several different types of rape:

Acquaintance/Date/Intimate Partner Rape: Some rapists deny wrongdoing interpreting their crimes as an extension of the male role and indicating that rape cannot occur among friends and acquaintances (Groth and Birnbaum, 1979; Katz and Mazur, 1979; Loh, et al., 2007). Some researchers suggest that in many ways acquaintance rape has only recently been taken seriously, because of findings of victimization studies suggesting that the majority of rapes are not perpetrated by strangers, but by someone known by the victim (Baum and Klaus, 2005; Fisher, Cullen, and Daigle, 2005; NCVS, 2010, Table 27).

These rationalizations are particularly prevalent among so-called "date" rapists, who assault women during the course of a regular date (Koss, 1989). For example, Bonnie Fisher and her colleagues (2000) have found that college campuses are especially vulnerable places where young women are at a greater risk of rape and other forms of sexual assault, than comparable aged women in the population at large. In their National College Women Sexual Victimization Survey (NCWSV) they estimated that for every 1,000 women attending a college or university, there are 35 incidents of rape each academic year. It has been found that in an overwhelming majority of cases, i.e., in about 9 out of 10 cases of completed and attempted rapes, offenders were known to the victim. In most of these cases, it was a boyfriend, ex-boyfriend, classmate, friend, acquaintance, or coworker who committed the offense. Alarmingly, Fisher and her research team's results suggest that many of the women who were raped typically do not characterize their victimizations as crimes. The most frequently stated reasons include: embarrassment, blaming themselves for the assault, not wanting to define someone they know as a rapist, or not clearly understanding the legal definition of rape (Fisher, Cullen and Turner, 2000).

Gang/Peer Group Rape: Rapes carried out by multiple offenders as a form of collective behavior typically occur in groups of males with some common bond (e.g., juvenile gangs, fraternities, athletic team members, and the military). Gang or peer group rapes usually involve a single victim during an event in which consecutive sex occurs by each member of the group (O'Sullivan, 1991). For instance, violent crimes such as rape may be carried out by organized gangs representing youths from different socio-economic income groups and occur in various areas of the city including the inner city as well as the suburban areas. Since the police often do not classify crimes, such as rape or murder, as gang-related (e.g., some cities even deny that they have gangs), we really do not have accurate statistics on gang rapes (National Gang Threat Assessment, 2009). A study by Sarah Ullman (1999) reports that gang rapes appear to be associated with more alcohol and drug use, less use of weapons, more attacks at night, less victim resistance, and greater physical violence compared to individual rapes. In another study, Ullman (2007) found that although gang rape victims are more likely to report their victimizations to the police or medical and mental health agencies than single offender victims, they also received more negative reactions.

In addition to juvenile neighborhood gang rapes, peer group rapes by middle and upper class college students in fraternities on college campus also occur. These are also notoriously underreported (Neumann, 2006, p. 401). Stephanie Neumann reviews the influence of peer support and alcohol use in fraternities on gang rapes and indicates that these two things "are powerful predictors of sexually aggressive behavior of males" in general. Other features of fraternities also tend to perpetuate sexual aggressive tendencies like peer rape including a fraternity's emphasis on the norm of masculinity, a pledging process that entails heavy alcohol use and pornographic entertainment, and an environment that fosters "rape myths" and the view of women as sexual objects (2006, p. 399).

Robbery

Although the crime of robbery is primarily profit motivated, the act itself—putting another person in fear of his or her life—serves to classify the crime as a violent one. The NCVS reports that from a total of 551,820 completed and attempted robbery victimizations in 2008, about 37 percent resulted in injury to the victim; interestingly completed robberies resulted in fewer victim injuries (26%) than attempted robberies (35%), possibly suggesting that physical injury occurs more often in robbery events where the victim resisted or possibly attempted to use other self protection (NCVS, 2010, Table 26). The logical conclusion here might be that in cases where victims usually obey the instructions of the armed robber and handover their money, jewelry, or other valuables, the robber quickly disappears from the scene of the crime in order to avoid attention or otherwise run the risk of being caught. Evidence from the NCVS is, however, subject to various interpretations. Early analyses of crime victimization data by some researchers suggest that victim resistance does not necessarily increase the risks of physical injury in violent crimes including robberies (Tark and Kleck, 2004). More recent data suggests that at least in some circumstances, using self protective measures by the victim may be harmful. For example, 49 percent of robbery victim respondents who used self protective measures indicated that it "made the offender angrier, more aggressive" and 42 percent reported that it "led to injury or greater injury" (NCVS, 2010, Table 74). (Please note that these results are based on very small samples of cases.) However, in cases where robbery victims "attacked an offender with a weapon," there were no differences in the victims being physically injured (4.3%) or not being physically injured (4.1%) (NCVS, 2010, Table 70). (Again, please note that these results are derived from small samples of cases.) Over the years researchers have examined the victim-offender relationships in armed robberies and have suggested numerous factors that may affect the nature of the relationships (e.g., type of weapon, single or group robbery, characteristics of the offender, characteristics of the victim, nature of the robbery [personal or commercial], drug related, and type of self protective and/or other defensive measures employed by victim) (Ziegenhagen and Brosnan, 1985; Cook, 1986; Kleck and Delone, 1998; and Southwick, 2000).

The Law

In most states, robbery is defined as larceny, the trespassory taking and carrying away of the personal property of another with intent to steal. Two additional elements include: (1) the property is taken from the person or presence of the owner and (2) the taking is carried out by force or by putting the owner in fear.

Common sense dictates what the law means by "person" (although there have been cases where the concept of "person" has been in question, e.g., a dead person). By "presence" the law looks at whether the victim could have prevented the taking of property if he or she were not intimidated or forcibly restrained.

In a robbery, the taking of property must be accompanied by use of violence or intimidation. Violence encompasses the offender struggling with the victim, hitting or striking the victim, using a weapon, or otherwise using substantial force to accomplish the theft. Such crimes as pick-pocketing and purse-snatching are generally not classified as robbery due to the lack of requisite use of force or violence. A "threat of harm" can suffice in lieu of overt violence. An offender who pulls a gun on a victim and demands money is engaging in an armed robbery. Violence and intimidation must occur either before or simultaneously with the taking of the property. Even if an offender uses a bar of soap that has been crafted to look like a gun — this can be considered to be a use of force or intimidation because the victim believing the bar of soap is a real weapon has been made fearful for his/her life.

Most states recognize several degrees of robbery. *Aggravated robbery* (armed robbery) usually requires the use of a weapon (such as a gun) to intimidate or commit violence against the victim. *Simple robbery*, on the other hand, involves theft while not armed with a dangerous weapon. This type of robbery carries a lighter punishment.

Patterns and Trends

According to official crime statistics robbery like most violent crimes in the U.S. has been decreasing substantially over the past two decades. With the above definition of robbery, the total volume of reported robberies in the UCR for 2010 is 367,832, a rate of 119.1 robberies per 100,000. Long-term trends (see Table 2.1 in Chapter 2) show that robbery rates have decreased substantially in the United States from 1990 (about 273 robberies per 100,000 population) to 2005 (about 145 robberies per 100,000 population) and, with the exception of some slight increases (e.g., in 2006 and 2007), robberies have been steadily declining. The robbery rate is down by 10.1 percent for reporting year 2010 compared to 2009, the largest decrease of all violent crimes. Robberies, as reported by the UCR are classified into six types: (1) street/highway robbery, (2) robbery of commercial houses (businesses), (3) robbery of gas or service stations, robbery of convenience stores, (4) robbery of residences, (5) bank robbery, and (6) miscellaneous robbery. In 2010 the distribution of robberies includes the following listed from the most frequent type: street/highway robberies (43.2 %), residence robberies (17.3%), miscellaneous robberies (16.6 %), commercial houses (13.2%), convenience stores (5.2 %), gas/service stations (2.3 %), and banks (2.2 %) (FBI, 2011, Table 1). Robberies in people's residences, often referred to as "home invasions" are particularly brutal, sometimes involving other crimes such as rape (Hurley, 1995).

The UCR data for 2010 show that regionally, the southern states register about 38.1 percent of all reported robberies, followed by the western states with 23.6 percent, the midwestern states with 19.6 percent, and the northeast with 18.7 percent. Most robberies occur in cities and suburbs. Since many suburban areas are experiencing greater growth than cities, this finding is not surprising (FBI, 2011, Tables 2 and 3). Shopping centers, suburban banks and other retail establishments where people shop and do business make good "hunting" grounds for both professional and occasional robbery offenders. The prevalence of ATM machines at banks and other businesses has over the years created an opportunity for robberies to take place at or near these machines as people withdraw money, although many offenders have found it easier to steal money from ATM machines by various ploys such as skimming devices placed on machines to read the information on bankcards (Robbery at Automated Teller Machines, 2006). In 2010 a total of 6,536 bank robberies have been recorded in the U.S. Violence has been used in about 26 percent of these robberies (FBI, 2011, Table 23).

Characteristics of Offenders

Like most violence-oriented crimes, robbery offenders are generally young males. According to the most recent UCR reports, 87.3 percent of robbery arrestees are males and 12.6 percent are females, representing a slight increase in arrests from reporting year 2009 (FBI, 2011, Table 42). UCR figures show that 33 percent of all robbery arrestees in 2010 are 18 years of age and under and about 43 percent are between the ages of 19–29 (Table 39). Similar figures on age are reported for females arrested for armed robbery. About 26 percent of females arrested for armed robberies are ages 18 and under and 42% are ages 19 to 29 (Table 40). Fifty-five percent of those arrested for robbery are black, 43.3 percent are white, and the remainder represents other racial/ethnic groups (FBI, 2011, Table 43). Guns are used in about 41.1 percent of the robberies for which the FBI received information in 2010. Strong arm tactics are used in 42 percent of robberies, knives and cutting instruments are used in 7.9 percent of robberies, and other dangerous weapons are used in 8.8 percent of robberies (Table 19).

According to the National Crime Victimization Survey, offenders display weapons in about 40 percent of all robberies (guns are used in about 24 percent of these cases). Firearms are used in about 30 percent of completed robberies (taking the property) (NCVS, 2010, Table 66). In about 23 percent of robbery victimizations, the victim perceived the offender to be under the influence of alcohol or drugs (Table 32). Evidence also suggests that as many as 40 percent of bank robbers today are under the influence of drugs when they commit their crimes (FBI, Bank Crime Statistics, 2010a).

Characteristics of Victims

According to the National Crime Victimization Survey, in 2009 there have been 533,790 robberies reported, which is about 11 percent less than in 2008. The NCVS does not include commercial robberies in its tabulations. Since 2000, the NCVS has noted a 35 percent decrease in robbery victimization rates per 1,000 persons age 12 or older, declining from 3.2 to 2.1. Victimization data indicate that males, blacks, and persons aged 24 or younger are victimized for robbery at higher rates than females, whites, and persons aged 25 or older. Hispanics are also victims of robbery at higher rates than non-Hispanics. About half of the total number of robberies reported has involved the use of weapons, 28% being firearms. Contrary to popular opinion, the elderly are the least likely to be robbed, although their victimizations (when they do occur) usually result in more psychological than physical damage. Robbery is a crime more likely to be reported to the police if: (1) anything of value is stolen, (2) injury occurs, and (3) a weapon is used in the robbery. On the basis of NCVS data, approximately 50 percent of robbery victimizations are reported to the police (Truman and Rand, 2010).

Typologies

Studies examining the nature of robbery indicate that armed robbery occurring in streets is a crime motivated primarily by economic need. While other crimes can obviously achieve the same results, street robbery has characteristics making it particularly attractive to certain types of offenders (Normandeau and Gabor, 1987; Willis, 2006). It is a simple crime that generally requires less sophistication and planning. It provides immediate cash, cutting out the need for a middleman (who gives cash for stolen property); there is an unlimited number of easy targets or victims who are generally much more vulnerable than persons in homes or businesses that may have alarm systems, guards, and other security devices; and finally, it can give its perpetrators, usually those lowest in education and social class, instant power and importance (e.g., Wright, et al., 2006). Many of these types of robberies occur in large cities in socially disadvantaged areas with low economic opportunities, ethnic diversity, low family incomes, and young offender pools (Miethe and Meier, 1994; Wright and Decker, 1997). However, robberies also occur in non-metropolitan communities as well (Bouffard and Muftic, 2006).

Several classical and contemporary studies have sought to classify robbery *offenders* (Conklin, 1972; Clinard and Quinney, 1973/1986; Matthews, 2002). For instance, John Conklin (1972) provides a typology (including the opportunistic robber, addict robber, alcoholic robber, and professional robber) based on interviews with a sample of convicted robbers in Massachusetts. The basis of his classification scheme is the motivation for the theft, the techniques used, and the degree of individual commitment to crime as a way of life.

Conklin (1972) reports that the *opportunist robber* is the most frequent type of robbery offender in the United States (this has been confirmed by more recent evidence, e.g., Willis, 2006). However, as has been the case in the past, close to half of all robberies take place "on the street" involving a stranger who strikes an unsuspecting victim. The opportunist robbers apparently act randomly, although they select victims who appear to be the most vulnerable. For example, William Thornton and Lydia Voigt note that in post-Katrina New Orleans there were increases in armed robberies of Latino laborers from Central and South America who had the reputation of keeping their hard-earned cash on their persons until such time that they could send it to their families. Being associated with carrying large amounts of cash or not trusting banks (or being unable to initially use banks) made many Latino migrant workers targets of armed robberies, including home invasions, and robbery/murders. In the local vernacular, these individuals have been referred to as "walking ATMs" (Thornton and Voigt, 2010, p. 45). Opportunist robbers are usually young (teens or early twenties); they are typically poor, black males seeking money and they are sometimes gang members. The *modus operandi* of some street robbers has been studied by criminologists. For example, James Wright and Scott Decker (1997) describe collaborative efforts where multiple offenders working together perpetrate their robberies, often employing strategies where they use a division of labor to accomplish the crime, e.g., one keeps watch, while others take the victims down an alley to relieve them of their valuables.

In striking contrast to the opportunistic robber is the *professional robber*. Relatively few professional robbers operate today. The professional robber is a person who plans the robbery and uses accomplices, who are each assigned to different roles during the crime. Large sums of money are sought and often guns are carried on the job. These robbers are usually white males in their mid-twenties and thirties. They come from working-class backgrounds and have a long-term commitment to crime as a major source of livelihood. Early research on professional robbers has emphasized the elaborate subcultural norms and rules that are believed to guide behavior, including illegal behavior (Einstadter, 1969). Early depictions of bank robbers fit the profile of professional robber; however, now bank robbers tend to have similar characteristics of opportunist robbers (i.e., they are more likely to be young, male recidivists, and slightly more likely to be black than white, who are probably unemployed at the time of the crime). Martin Gill's interviews with commercial robbers in England also finds that professional robbers, i.e., those committed to the crime as a way of life, generally tend to plan more before committing the crimes (2000).

Other types of robbers described by Conklin (1972) include the *addict robber*, who commits the crime chiefly to support a drug habit, and the *alcoholic robber*, who commits the crime, often on the spur of the moment, to obtain funds to cover expenses related to his/her excessive consumption of alcohol (e.g., Feeney, 1999). Both of these types of robbers generally have a low commitment to robbery as a special type of crime, but a high commitment to theft in general, which is seen as a way to get funds to pay for their drug or alcohol addictions. Physical force, rather than the use of a weapon, is more often used to take money from victims. Conklin (1972) also describes the *acquaintance robber*, who seeks targets that otherwise are in no position to report their victimizations to the authorities. The acquaintance robber robs people he knows, including family members, especially those involved in other criminal activities such as drug dealing or other illegal activities in which they may have acquired money, merchandise or drugs. Acquaintance robbery victims as opposed to victims of stranger-perpetrated robberies are less likely to report the victimization to the police for obvious reasons including fear of retaliation from the offender. In fact, some research suggests that acquaintance victims are harmed more often in robberies than victims of stranger-perpetrated robberies (Felson, Baumer, and Messner, 2000).

Increasing sophistication in law enforcement techniques along with advancements in surveillance and security technology has led to several emerging trends in the crime of robbery, e.g., carjacking robbery and home invasion robbery. *Carjacking robbery* is a newer form of robbery involving the stealing of a vehicle during the commission of the robbery in which the owner may also be abducted, sometimes resulting in a another crime such as rape. It is speculated that carjackings have probably increased as most new cars come equipped with alarms, making them more difficult to steal. For instance, one study based on victimization self-reports from the NCVS has revealed that from 1993 through 2002, an average of 38,000 carjacking offenses have occurred annually (Klaus, 2004). A weapon was used in 74 percent of these carjackings, with 45 percent of these carjackings committed using a gun. About 32 percent of victims of completed carjackings and about 17 percent of victims of attempted carjackings were injured. Approximately half of carjacking incidents occurred in an open area such as a street or near public transportation and 24 percent occurred in parking lots or garages or near commercial places such as stores, gas stations, restaurants and bars and other commercial facilities (Klaus, 2004).

Home invasion robbery, an evolving, and particularly brutal type of armed robbery, which first attracted attention in the 1990s, involves direct and strong-arm entry into a targeted residence, usually by multiple offenders. Entry in such cases is often gained by sheer force, e.g., kicking the door in, rushing inside the residence, confronting the victims and gaining immediate control by confrontation, threats, intimidation, and even torture. Some offenders develop well organized plans and have a division of labor among themselves. For instance, one or more of the offenders control the victims while others systematically ransack the residence looking for money, jewelry, and drugs. Unlike burglary, which is defined as breaking and entering with the intent to commit a felony (theft) and usually does not involve face-to-face encounters with victims, home invasion robbers typically target the residents, not the residence (Hurley, 1995). Home invasion groups may, according to some experts, be organized street gangs, but others are opportunistic armed robbers seeking easy targets (National Gang Threat Assessment, 2009, p. iii).

A rash of home invasion robberies in New Orleans in the summer of 2011 involved offenders who kicked in doors of homes, arm robbed the victim(s), sometimes engaging in assaults, including rape, and kidnappings where they forced the victim(s) to go with them to withdraw money from ATM machines (Urbazzewski, 2011, pp. B1–2). Thornton, Voigt, and Walsh's (2009) analysis, based on official police reports of crimes against Latino workers in the New Orleans metropolitan area for the years 2005–2008, suggests that the unique post-recovery environment in New Orleans with the influx of highly vulnerable Latino workers, coupled with the absence of capable guardianship, resulted in a new victim pool for armed robbers, including large numbers of home invasion robberies of Latino workers living in low rent housing units. Many of these crimes have been particularly brutal, committed by groups of young black males and in some instances inter-racial groups (Thornton, et al., 2009).

Assault

Assaults and batteries may be referred to as the "grocery store" variety of violent crimes. These crimes occur not only between strangers, but also largely between acquaintances, friends, and, tragically, between intimate partners and family members.

The Law

The crimes of assault and battery may occur anywhere and, therefore, exist in every jurisdiction. They usually are classified as statutory misdemeanors (punishable by a fine or prison time less than a year), although more serious types of battery (e.g., with weapons) are classified as felonies. A *battery* occurs when a person intentionally either causes bodily injury or offensively touches another in a reckless or criminally negligent manner. Offensive touching can include fondling or unwanted kissing. (The special case of *sexual battery* exists in many states; it involves the touching of the anus or genitals of a victim; this crime is usually not treated as a misdemeanor and it carries a harsh punishment, such as a long prison sentence.)

Simple battery, usually a misdemeanor, requires that a weapon has not been used to inflict injury to a victim or cause fear. However, battery may be regarded as aggravated if a deadly weapon such as a gun or knife is employed, even if serious bodily harm does not occur. Also, battery committed "with intent to kill" will usually be classified as *aggravated battery*. Aggravated batteries are felonies and carry harsh sanctions in most states.

The crime of *assault* occurs when a person (a) attempts to commit a battery and fails or (b) places another person in fear of imminent injury (Emanuel, 2010). An offender who fails in an attempt to commit a battery is guilty of assault. Most states recognize two grades of assault: (1) simple assault, committed without a dangerous weapon, and (2) aggravated assault, committed with a dangerous weapon.

Patterns and Trends

The *Uniform Crime Reports* utilize the term of *aggravated assault* to include "an unlawful attack by one person upon another for the purpose of inflicting severe or aggravated bodily injury" (FBI, 2011). Attempted assaults, usually involving a weapon, are also included. For the 2010 reporting year 777,901 aggravated assaults are tabulated with a rate of 252.3 per 100,000 inhabitants. Since 1990, according to UCR figures, the assault rates, with some fluctuation, have generally been decreasing. For example, a comparison of trend data from 2001 and 2010 shows that the rates of aggravated assaults have dropped by almost 21 percent (FBI, 2011, Tables 1 and 1a).

Geographic distribution figures indicate that in 2010, 45.6 percent of the assaultive crimes have occurred in the southern states, 22.8 percent in the western states, 18.8 percent in the midwestern states, and 14.8 percent in the northeastern states. Of the UCR reported assaults, 27.4 percent of aggravated assaults involve personal weapons such as hands, feet, and fists; 20.6 percent involve firearms; and 19 percent involve knives or other cutting instruments; the remaining 33.1 percent of aggravated assaults are committed with other weapons (Tables 3, 19).

The National Criminal Victimization Survey (NCVS) data base for 2010 reports 725,180 aggravated assault victimizations. According to the NCVS results, about 2.4 million simple assaults have occurred in the same time period, not all of which have been reported to the police. Typically, a higher number of aggravated assaults are reported to the police than simple assaults (Truman, 2011, p. 2; NCVS, 2010).

Characteristics of Offenders

The UCR supplies little information about assault offenders. Of the 317,435 persons arrested for aggravated assault in 2010, whites represent about 64.0 percent of the arrestees, blacks about 34 percent, and all other races the remaining 2 percent (Table 43a). Close to 77 percent of arrestees for aggravated assault are males and 23 percent are females (Table 42). Of the males arrested, 14 percent are age 18 and under, and about 38 percent are between the ages of 19 to 29 (FBI, 2011, Table 39). While no information is given about the socioeconomic status of assault offenders in the UCR, various studies have revealed an over-concentration of assaultive behavior among individuals representing lower income groups. Criminologist Marvin Wolfgang and his associates (1972) long ago noted that a disproportionate number of offenders of serious violent crimes, such as aggravated assault, are committed by young males in the lower range of socioeconomic status. Donna Hamparian and her associates (1978), in their *Dangerous Offender Project*, similarly conclude that most violent offenders come from lower social classes. More recent research results have reflected similar patterns (e.g., Greene, 1993; Miethe and Meier, 1994; Kubrin and Weitzer, 2003; Kane, 2005; Sampson, 2012). Additionally, various other types of information such as court data suggest that a large proportion of violent offenders, i.e., assault (and murder) suspects appearing before the courts, have prior arrest records and typically represent lower income brackets (Rainville and Reaves, 2003). Research results also suggest that factors such as family history of violence including child abuse and neglect (Widom and Maxfield, 2001; English, Widom, and Ford, 2004), multi-assaultive families (Hotaling, Straus, and Lincoln, 1989), and early anti-social behavior (Wasserman and Seracini, 2001; Wasserman, et al., 2003) are also found in assault offenders' backgrounds.

Explanations for assaultive behavior generally cover macro theoretical perspectives of violence, which include homicide, robbery, and rape. In reality, assault is often a component of these other crimes. Noting the connection between assault and social class, sociologists have considered the notion of a *subculture of violence* (referring to a way of life of a group of people whose backgrounds, experiences, and norms and values are related to violence, i.e., greater tolerance and acceptance of violence, making them culturally distinct from the rest of the society in which they live).

Historically different subcultures in the United Sates have been associated with violence, e.g., reference is frequently made to the inner-city, lower-class subculture and its reliance on violence as a way of life (Lee and Ousey, 2012). For instance, criminologists such as Walter Miller (1958) and Marvin Wolfgang and Franco Ferracuti (1967/1982) in their studies have found that lower class youths possess their own distinctive subcultural system focused on violence as a normal element of everyday life, which they argue is largely responsible for higher levels of violent crimes in some areas of the city. Elijah Anderson (1999) also describes a violence "code of the streets" and associated set of prescriptive behavioral expectations placed on inner city youths, which is enforced by neighborhood peer groups/gangs. Within these subsystems of norms and values, influenced by lack of opportunities and discrimination, assaultive behavior is a normative feature of daily interactions and acceptable ways of resolving disputes and problems. Indeed, violence and assaultive behavior are regarded as key to establishing and protecting ones reputation as well as maintaining status within the subcultural hierarchy (Stewart and Simons, 2006; Stewart and Simmons, 2010; Levitov and Harper, 2012; Patel and Wright, 2012).

Characteristics of Victims

The National Crime Victimization Survey (NCVS) provides the most comprehensive material on the victims of assault. The "typical" assault victim is a single male, black or white, between the ages of 16 and 24, from a low income family. Younger black female assault victims have somewhat higher assault rates than white females. The victimization rate for all assaults in 2009 is 14.5 per 1,000 persons; for aggravated assaults it is 3.2. The rate for males for all assaults is 15.6 per 1,000 (4.3 for aggravated assaults) compared with 13.5 for all assaults for females (2.3 for aggravated assaults) (Truman and Rand, 2010).

As is noted above, young poor males, black and white, have the highest victimization rates for assault. These characteristics of assault victims mirror, to some extent, the characteristics of assault perpetrators. It is not beyond the realm of possibility that some of the assault victims precipitated their victimizations. As is suggested in some of the research literature, these types of victimizations may be occurring in neighborhoods where violent behavior constitutes a collective and normative feature of daily living including carrying a weapon, fighting, asserting masculinity, and also by placing the victims themselves in situations where violence occurs. Usually victims of assaults with injuries are more likely to report their victimization to the police than assault victims without injuries, for obvious reasons (NCVS, 2010, Table 93).

Typologies

Assaultive behavior, which is the most common or frequent form of interpersonal violence has not drawn much attention by researchers in and of itself. What has attracted interest of researchers is its expression in certain institutional contexts. Most of us have an image of the "violent criminal" as a stranger lurking in an alley waiting to pounce on an unsuspecting victim either to do him or her bodily harm or to take money or property, or both. In actuality, the violent criminal often is someone the victim knows — mother, father, spouse, boyfriend, girlfriend, sibling, son or daughter, classmate in school, co-worker, or other some other acquaintance. Following is a brief overview of interpersonal violence in the institutional context; these areas will be discussed in further detail in Chapter 4, which focuses on institutional forms of violence.

Interpersonal Violence in Institutional Contexts

In considering the patterns of occurrence or explanations of the various forms of interpersonal violence (i.e., homicide, rape, robbery, and assault), it is helpful to examine the institutional context in which these forms of violence often take place such as the family, the school, the workplace, or the larger community.

Family Violence

Family violence can take many forms. The ultimate type — domestic homicide — has declined substantially in recent years, yet it remains a substantial portion of homicides in the U.S. each year. According to the 2010 UCR data, about 38 percent female murder victims, where relationships to the offender are known, were murdered by husbands or boyfriends (FBI, 2011, Expanded Homicide Data Tables 2 and 10). The incidence of homicide among intimate partners or family members, however, does not approach that of the large number of assaults and batteries that "loved ones" inflict upon one another each year. Violence that occurs in domestic or family settings includes intimate partner abuse, child abuse and neglect, and parental or grandparental abuse.

One of the problems in developing accurate statistical information on family or domestic violence in general is defining what is to be measured. For example, in cases involving the abuse of children, there is still disagreement over what is acceptable or what is unacceptable discipline. For instance, at what point does a spanking change from an act of discipline to an act of abuse (Coleman, Dodge, and Campbell, 2010)? Where does an intimate partner's abusive behavior toward other family members cross the line from un-desirable to criminal (Jaffee, Crooks, and Wolfe, 2003)?

Intimate Partner Abuse

The term *intimate partner violence* (IPV) has been used to describe any actual or threatened behavior in an intimate relationship, heterosexual or same-sex, that causes physical, sexual, psychological or emotional abuse by a current or former intimate partner, boyfriend or girlfriend, or dating partner (Thompson, et al., 2006, p. 151). Criminologists have previously used the term *domestic violence* generally referring to violence between spouses, particularly woman abuse and wife battering (Regehr and Roberts, 2010, p. 197). The exact number of these offenses is not known, since many go unreported; however, studies reveal that they are quite frequent in the United States and world-wide. Existing evidence does suggest that while IPV may occur on males and females, and between same sex partners, one of the most common forms of violence against women is carried out by a male, usually a husband or an intimate partner. NCVS reports that in 2010, out of 163,150 females victimized by non-strangers by aggravated assault, 71,640 or 24 percent are perpetrated by an intimae partner (current or former spouses, boyfriends or girlfriends). Out of 209,020 males victimized by non-strangers for the same offense, 29,290 or 7 percent are perpetrated by an intimate partner (Truman, 2011, p. 9). Continuous abuse in the same relationship is commonly referred to as "battering." Men are much more likely to be attacked by a stranger or acquaintance than by an intimate partner (Tjaden and Thoennes, 2006).

Intimate partner violence occurs in all countries of the world, irrespective of social, economic, religious or cultural group. There has been focused attention on violence against women as a criminal justice problem, a human rights issue, and a major public health concern for many years. As reported in the *2002 World Report on Violence and Health*, based on 48 country population surveys from around the world, "between 10 percent and 69 percent of women report being physically assaulted by an intimate male partner at some point in their lives." Estimates of the percentage of women assaulted by a partner within a 12-month period has varied from 3 percent or less in Australia, Canada, and the United States to over 27 percent of women in ongoing sexual partnerships in Leon, Nicaragua; 38 percent of currently married women in the Republic of Korea, and 52 percent of currently married Palestinian women in the West Bank and Gaza Strip. It has been noted that for large numbers of these women, physical assault is continuous and not an isolated incident (Krug, et al., 2002, p. 89). Data reported from a wide range of countries alarmingly reveals that IPV accounts for a significant number of murders among women. For example, studies from Australia, Canada, Israel, South Africa, and the United States show that 40–70 percent of female murder victims are killed by their boyfriends or husbands, usually within the context of an ongoing abusive relationship (Krug, et al., 2002, p. 93).

As noted earlier, in the United States, over one-third of female homicide victims reported in official police records are killed by an intimate partner such as a husband or boyfriend (see Harper and Voigt, 2012). Other research reported in the World Report on Violence and Health shows that physical abuse in intimate relationships often goes hand-in-hand with psychological abuse, and in one-third to over one-half of reported cases of sexual violence take place among intimate partners (Koss, et al., 1994; Yoshihama and Sorenson, 1994; Ellsberg, et al., 2000). More recent findings from the World Health Organization (WHO) including a landmark study on domestic violence in 2005 using population-based prevalence data from more than 90 countries reveal that IPV remains the most common form of violence in women's lives, substantially more so than assaults and rapes by strangers or non-intimate acquaintances (WHO, 2005). There is a growing body of evidence-based data demonstrating the wide range of negative health and development consequences of IPV including violence during pregnancy resulting in increased risk of miscarriage, premature delivery, and other negative consequences for children (Garcia-Moreno and Watts, 2011).

In addition to the obvious human costs of IPV, there are substantial economic costs, including the direct costs to health and medical care, legal, police, and other services to victims and families, which by even conservative estimates run into billions of dollars each year (National Center for Injury Prevention and Control, 2003). Broader and indirect social costs of IPV are many, including continued poverty for some women because of reduction in productive employment, undermining of efforts to have access to education, and negative impact on the welfare and education of children in the family (Garcia-Moreno and Watts, 2011).

Box 3.3 Intimate Partner Violence: I Ran Into the Door

Permission was granted to use this image and text in its entirety from Laura Ann Sminkey, Communications Officer, WHO (sminkey@who.int). This comes from the World Health Organization "Explaining Away Violence" poster series (http://www.who.int/violence_injury_prevention/publications/violence/explaining/en/).

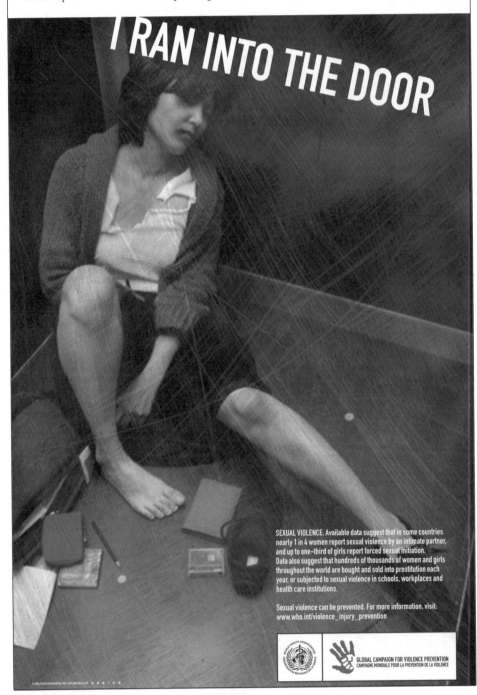

Child Abuse

Another area of public concern related to violence in the family is the battery, assault, maltreatment, and neglect of children (Finkelhor, et al., 2005). Criminal justice system personnel, advocates, laypeople, and researchers employ a variety of definitions of child abuse and neglect. Although abuse and neglect both fall under the more encompassing term *maltreatment,* they represent different phenomena. Each state has its own definition of child abuse and neglect based on minimum standards set by federal law, The Child Abuse Prevention and Treatment Act (CAPTA) (42 U.S.C.A. § 5106g) and as amended by the Keeping Children and Families Safe Act of 2003. Child abuse and neglect are defined as:

- Any recent act or failure on the part of a parent or caretaker, which results in death, serious physical or emotional harm, sexual abuse or exploitation; or

- An act or failure to act, which presents an imminent risk of serious harm.

Most states, within the standards of CAPTA, generally recognize four major types of maltreatment: *neglect, physical abuse, sexual abuse, and psychological maltreatment.* Statutory definitions also specify that any form of sexual exploitation, pornography, and prostitution involving minors constitutes a violation of child abuse laws. In 1999 the state of Minnesota expanded the legal definition of child abuse to include exposure to intimate partner violence; however, due to a substantial increase in reports to child protection agencies, which overwhelmed the system, the state repealed the law in 2000 (Taylor and Sorenson, 2007). The term neglect or deprivation of necessities is reserved for the failure by the caregiver to provide basic or essential needs for the child such as food, clothing, shelter, and medical treatment. Included in this category is fetal alcohol syndrome, prenatal substance abuse exposure, abandonment, or educational neglect (USDHHS, 2010, p. 113).

The physical abuse of children involves the intentional, rather than accidental, act of injury and ranges from parents losing their tempers and punishing a child too harshly to deliberate and sadistic offenses against a child including beating with belts and electric cords and burning. It can also include risk of physical abuse or threatened harm. Clinicians have developed terms such as the *shaken baby syndrome,* to describe shaking of an infant, either accidentally or intentionally, in such a manner as to cause severe intracranial trauma in the absence of signs of external head trauma (Burgess and Clements, 2010, pp. 131–132).

Child sexual abuse refers to contacts or interactions between a child and an adult when the child is being used for the sexual stimulation of the perpetrator or another person or financial benefit to the perpetrator and includes rape, molestation, fondling, prostitution, pornography, exposure, incest, or other sexually exploitative activities. Based on *Child Maltreatment, 2008,* a national study of child maltreatment derived from data collected by child protection agencies through the National Child Abuse and Neglect Data System (NCANDS), slightly less than 10 percent of children have been victims of reported sexual abuse (USDHHS, 2010, p. 27). Psychological or emotional maltreatment "refers to acts or omissions, other than physical abuse or sexual abuse that cause or could have caused, conduct, cognitive, affective or other mental disorders and includes emotional neglect, psychological abuse, and mental injury." Frequently this type of abuse occurs as verbal abuse or excessive demands on a child's performance; however, it can also put the child at risk for physical or sexual abuse, threatened harm, and/or domestic violence (p. 114).

According to the *Child Maltreatment, 2008,* there are an estimated 3.3 million referrals, involving the alleged maltreatment of about 6 million children, reported by child protection agencies across the U.S. Of these referrals, 772,000 children have been confirmed victims of abuse or neglect. The rate of victimization is 10.3 per 1,000 children in 2008. Reports

Box 3.4 Child Abuse and Neglect: I Fell Out of My Cradle

Permission was granted to use this image and text in its entirety from Laura Ann Sminkey, Communications Officer, WHO (sminkey@who.int). This comes from the World Health Organization "Explaining Away Violence" poster series (http://www.who.int/violence_injury_prevention/publications/violence/explaining/en/).

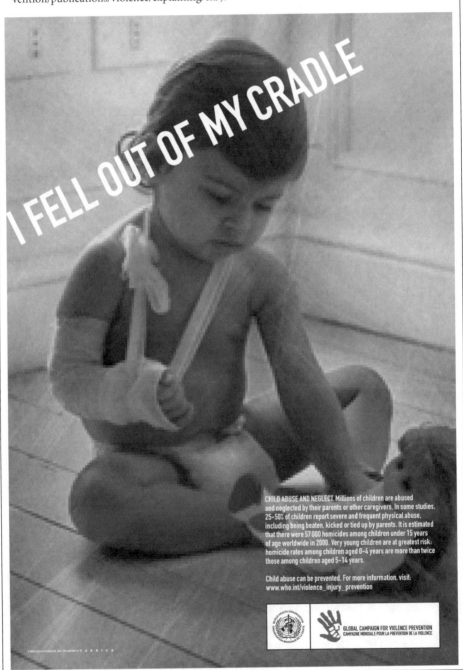

of maltreatment come from multiple sources with over half of the reported incidences (57.9%) coming from professionals (social services, medical and mental health professionals, and law enforcement officers). Child maltreatment takes many forms, and children may experience multiple forms. Since 1999, the majority of children confirmed to be victims of child treatment have experienced neglect (USDHHS, 2010).

Following is a list of various types of maltreatment and the percentages of children who have experienced these forms of maltreatment in 2008 (USDHHS, 2010, p. 27):

- Neglect (71.1%)
- Physical abuse (16.1%)
- Sexual abuse (9.1%)
- Other (9.0%)
- Psychological/emotional abuse (7.3%)
- Medical neglect (2.2%)
- Unknown or missing (0.3%)[1]

In a national study of 2,000 children, Finkelhor and his colleagues (2005) have found that emotional abuse (e.g., name calling or denigration by an adult) is the most frequent of the five types of maltreatment examined including emotional abuse, physical abuse, sexual abuse, neglect, and family abduction. Boys and girls are equally likely to suffer abuse and neglect. In 2008, 48.3 percent of child victims are male, and 51.3 percent are female. Victimization rates are highest among the youngest population of children, birth to 1 year at a rate of 21.8 per 1,000 male children and 21.3 per 1,000 female children. The victimization rate for children 4–7 years old is 10.9 per 1,000 for both boys and girls. Overall, the victimization rate has decreased for older groups (USDHHS, 2010, p. 26).

Despite controversies regarding semantics and issues of measurement, many experts on the family indicate that the home is a key training ground for learning how to be violent or not violent (Wasserman and Seracini, 2001; Ackerman, et al., 2003). In fact there is general consensus in the psychological and sociological literature that exposure of children to violence in the home can result in problem behavior, including violence during the child's early and adolescent years and beyond. This particularly holds true for children who are physically abused in the home (Herrenkohl, et al., 2003). According to the results of a study published by the Bureau of Justice Statistics in the Office of Justice Programs, it is estimated that a child has witnessed violence in 22 percent of intimate partner violence cases filed in state courts in 2002; in another 14 percent of intimate partner cases, a child has been present at the time of the incident, but did not directly witness the violence (Smith and Farole, 2009, p. 4).

Child-Parental Abuse

Another form of familial violence that evokes disbelief is the abuse of parents by their children, referred to as *child-parent violence* (CPV). Much like other types of family violence, parental abuse is grossly under-reported with the exception being *parricide*, the killing of a parent. Also, it is one area of family violence where there is a gap in research

---

1. The maltreatment percentages above total to more than 100% because children who were victims of more than one type of maltreatment have been counted for each incident of maltreatment (USDHHS, 2010, p. 27).

(Finkelhor and Pillemer, 1988; Cottrell and Monk, 2004). Historical studies by family researchers such as Richard Gelles and Claire Cornell suggest that child-to-parent violence may be a missing link in understanding the transmission of violence from families of orientation to families of procreation. For instance, they argue that "victims of childhood violence ... begin to express it where they learned it, in their families of orientation" (Gelles and Cornell, 1985, p. 8). In a sense then, such individuals begin familial violence often before they start their own families (Kitzmann, et al., 2003). Another study by Arina Ulman and Murray Straus (2003) supports this social learning aspect of family violence. The researchers have found that violence between parents, either by the husband or by the wife, or both, corporal punishment of children, and physical abuse of children is associated with a greater rate of CPV. Their study focusing exclusively on physical harm, defines violence "as an act carried out with the intention or perceived intention of causing another person to experience physical pain or injury" (p. 42). Other significant findings from their research show that mothers are more likely to be victims of CPV than fathers for both boys and girls; slightly more boys than girls at all ages abuse parents; and the younger the child was when abused, the greater the likelihood of CPV. A particularly interesting finding suggests that the highest rates of child-parent violence towards mothers come from families where mothers hit fathers, but where fathers do not hit the mothers in return. Ulman and Straus argue that contrary to the commonly accepted beliefs that fathers are the key role model for children learning to be violent, they argue that a child "witnessing a mother physically attacking a father may be a more powerful model for family violence than we realize" (2003, p. 52).

Other studies of parental abuse have examined violence against elderly parents (Finkelhor and Pillemer, 1988). The typical victim of such abuse is usually a woman 75 years old who has one or more serious medical problems. However, men are also abused, usually by their sons. Abuse falls into four categories: financial/material, psychological, physical, and neglect. Neglect can be of two types: *active neglect* (e.g., cases of deliberate withholding of food or medication) and *passive neglect* (e.g., cases of ignorance or inability of children to care for parents). Like other forms of family violence, a wide variety of factors have been linked to elderly parental abuse including: lack of financial resources, resentment of a disability, problems of responsibility, and antisocial behavior by elders. The abuse of the elderly is but one of the larger problems facing the elderly in the United States today. Many elderly, living on fixed incomes have found that the ravages of inflation, coupled with inadequate planning for old age, leave them severely economically restrained and deprived.

School Violence

In recent years, shooting incidents in the nation's schools and universities have attracted considerable media attention and subsequent public concern over perceptions that there has been an increase in such incidents in grade and high schools, and in colleges and universities. The Columbine High School mass shooting in 1999 by two students, Eric Harris and Dylan Klebold, who killed 12 fellow students and a teacher and wounded 24 others before killing themselves, has served as a warning for school administrators, stimulating greater emphasis on security and threat assessment in schools. As a result, the FBI National Center for the Analysis of Violent Crime (NCAVC) has spearheaded a special task force to develop, among other things, a procedure for evaluating a school threat and the person making the treat, in hopes of preventing a violent incident from occurring (O'Toole,

2000). Likewise, the Virginia Technical University mass shooting by student Seung Hui Cho in 2007, who killed over 30 people, has stimulated higher educational institutions to reexamine their ability to better monitor potentially dangerous people on campus and to efficiently and effectively warn a campus community when active shooting events take place (Fischman and Foster, 2007a; 2007b; Lipka, 2007).

Violence in Primary and Secondary Schools

According to experts, contrary to what most people think, school violence including shootings, assaults, injuries, and even deaths have not significantly increased in the past decade. In fact, most types of interpersonal school crimes, both violent and non-violent, have decreased since 1993 (Lawrence, 2007, p. xi). Crimes most often committed in schools include drug and alcohol use or distribution and property crimes such as theft and vandalism. Small numbers of students bring weapons to schools. However, activities such as bullying (including cyber-bullying), harassment, and teasing, while probably not increasing, have come to be recognized by school officials as serious problems in some schools and are believed to possibly escalate to more serious incidents such as school shootings (Lawrence, 2007, pp. xi–2). In reality, school shootings, especially those that result in the death of students, teachers, or staff are very rare events. However, when they do occur, they generate a great deal of attention from many groups ranging from parents and school administrators to law enforcement officials with calls for addressing the "problem."

The National Center for Educational Statistics along with the Bureau of Justice Statistics has for the past 13 years published *Indicators of School Crime and Safety* compiled from a number of statistical data sources funded by the federal government (e.g., Centers for Disease Control and Prevention, National Crime Victimization Survey, School Crime Supplement, and the Uniform Crime Reports). According to the 2010 edition, approximately 55.6 million students (including prekindergarten to 12th grade students) committed acts of crime (violent and non-violent) on school property during the 2008–2009 school years. The 2010 report also includes results from previous years and covers topics such as student and teacher injuries, school conditions, fights, weapons, drug and alcohol availability and use, and student perceptions of personal safety at school (Roberts, Zhang, and Truman, 2010). In 2008, for students 12–18 years old, there were about 1.2 million victims of nonfatal crimes at school including 619,000 thefts and 629,800 violent crimes (simple assault and *serious violent crimes* including rape, sexual assault, robbery, and aggravated assault). In reporting year 2009, some 8 percent of the respondents indicated that they were threatened or injured with a weapon, such as a gun or knife at school (Roberts, et al., 2010, p. iii). Select key finding from the 2010 report, *Indicators of School Crime and Safety*, include the following:

Violent Deaths

- Of the total 38 student, staff, and nonstudent school-associated deaths (i.e., occurring on a campus of a functioning elementary or secondary school or on the way to or returning from a regular session or while attending or traveling to and from an official school sponsored event) between July 1, 2008 and June 30, 2009, 24 were homicides and 14 were suicides; of these totals 15 homicides and 7 suicides involve school-age youth (ages 5–18) at school (p. iii).

- The percentage of youth homicides occurring at our nation's schools remains at less than 2% of the total number of youth homicides in the U.S. over all available survey years, 1992–2008. Since 1992, the highest number of school-related homicides in any given year is 34 (occurring in 1992 and 1997), and the lowest is 14 (occurring in 1999 and 2000) (pp. 6–7).

Nonfatal Student and Teacher Victimization

- The rates for serious violent crimes (e.g., rape, sexual assault, robbery, and aggravated assault) are generally lower at school than away from school. In 2008, students aged 12–18 were victims of 4 serious violent crimes per 1,000 students at school and 8 serious violent crimes per 1,000 away from school. Victimization rates for students including victimization due to violent and serious violent crimes has generally declined between 1992 and 2008 both at school and away from school (p. 10).
- Eight percent of all students in grades 9–12 have reported being threatened or injured with a weapon, such as a gun, knife, or club, on school property in 2009; 10 percent of male students in grades 9–12 have reported being threatened or injured with a weapon on school property, compared to 5 percent of female students (p. 16).
- During the 2007–08 school year, a greater percentage of teachers in city schools (10%) have reported being threatened with injury than teachers in town schools (7%) and suburban or rural schools (6% each). A greater percentage of teachers in city schools (5%) have reported being physically attacked compared to teachers in suburban schools (4%) and rural schools (4%) (p. 20).

School Environment

- In 2009, 31 percent of students in grades 9–12 have been in a physical fight at least one time during a 12-month period anywhere, and 11 percent have been in a fight on school property during the same timeframe. Generally a higher percentage of ninth-graders have been in fights anywhere or on school property (p. 50).
- Between 1993 and 2009, the percentage of students carrying a weapon at least one day *anywhere* during a 30-day period has declined from 22 to 17 percent; and the percentage carrying a weapon at least one day on school property has also declined from 12 percent to 6 percent (p. 54).
- In 2009, about 42 percent of students in grades 9–12 reported having at least one drink of alcohol anywhere in a 30-day period, while 4 percent had at least one drink on school property (p. 56).
- In 2009, 21 percent of students in grades 9–12 reported using marijuana anywhere in a 30-day timeframe, while 5 percent reported using marijuana on school property (p. 60).

Fear and Avoidance

- In 2009, approximately 5 percent of students ages 12–18 have indicated that they are fearful of attack or harm at school, while 3 percent have said that they are afraid of attack or harm away from school.

Safety and Security Measures

- Between the 1999–2000 and 2007–2008 school years, there has been an increase in the percentage of public schools reporting the use of the following safety and security measures: (1) controlled access to the building during school hours; (2) controlled access to the school grounds during school hours (from 34 percent to 43 percent); (3) the requirement that students wear uniforms; (4) students and faculty required to wear badges or picture IDs; (5) the use of one or more security cameras to monitor school; and (6) the provision of telephones in most classrooms (p. 76).

• During the 2007–08 school year, 43 percent of public schools have reported that they have an electronic notification system for a school-wide emergency, and 31 percent of public schools have reported that they have a structured, anonymous threat reporting system (p. 76).

Violence on College and University Campuses

Since 1990 with passage of the Jeanne Clery Disclosure of Campus Security Policy and Campus Crime Statistics Act (now known as the Clery Act), colleges and universities that dispense federal financial aid are required to maintain and report annual crime statistics, which occur on their campuses and immediate area, as well as report on their safety and security measures, crime prevention programs, and ability to offer timely warnings to the campus community of impending threats (20 USC § 1092 (f)). Since the law is tied to the federal student financial aid programs, it applies to most public as well as private institutions of higher learning and is strictly enforced by the U.S. Department of Education. The Act has been amended over the years to include affording victims of campus sexual assaults certain rights and provisions dealing with registered sex offender notification.

While it may appear that all "school" crime and violence are the same, there are some differences in colleges and universities, which merit comment. There are over 4,000 public and private colleges and universities including two year institutions in the United States (Chronicle of Higher Education, 1999). The size of these educational institutions varies ranging from a few hundred to many thousands of students, staff, and faculty. Many larger universities quite literally are like small towns or cities with respect to space usage and provision of many services. For example, large universities may include large residence facilities, food establishments, stores, banks, post offices, medical facilities, police departments, entertainment areas, galleries and museums, maintenance facilities, and, of course, a wide range of educational facilities. Both types, violent crimes and property crimes, routinely occur on college campuses; however, campuses vary considerably with respect to the volume or rate of occurrence based on any number of factors such as physical size and location of the campus, number of enrollments, demographics of the surrounding community, ratio of male to female students, accessibility of the campus to outside visitors, and level of campus security (e.g., FBI, 2011, Table 9).

The Department of Education annually provides an online list of Summary Crime Statistics for nine categories of institutions of higher education (e.g., public — 4 year or above, private non-profit — 4 year or above, public — 2 year, etc.). The information displayed below includes violent crimes (murder, negligent manslaughter, forcible sexual offenses, non-forcible sexual offenses, robbery, and aggravated assault). The most current statistics for reporting years 2007–2009 indicate the aggregated figures in Table 3.1.

As can be seen, there have been significant decreases in murders between 2007 and 2009 and minor decreases in other violent offenses during this time. It is important to note that the 2007 cases of mass murders on college campuses obviously inflated figures for that particular year (e.g., the mass shooting at Virginia Tech resulted in 32 deaths in 2007). In 2009, of the 17 murders occurring on various college campuses, 8 took place in a 4-year or above public college or university, 6 in a 4-year or above private non-profit college or university, 2 in a public 2-year institution, and 1 in a private for-profit, less than 2-year institution.

Table 3.1 Violent Criminal Offenses on College and University Campuses 2007–2009

	2007	2008	2009
Murder	45	13	17
Manslaughter	3	3	0
Forcible sex offenses	2736	2670	2590
Non-forcible sex offenses	42	36	72
Robbery	1932	1939	1865
Aggravated assault	2772	2689	2675

Source: http://www2.edu.gov/admin/lead/safety/criminaloffenses2007-2009.pdf.

Offenses in which the reporting location is on the campus premises including residence halls; some offenses not included in the table occur on non-campus property (owned or controlled by the respective school but off the campus) and public property (not owned by the school but near such structures as parking lots, sidewalks, etc.). The summary crime statistics found on this website represent alleged criminal offenses reported to campus security authorities and/or local law enforcement agencies. Because some statistics are provided by non-police authorities, the data are not directly comparable to data from the FBI's Uniform Crime Reporting System (http://ope.ed.gov/security/).

Fox and Savage (2009), who have examined cases of campus mass murders (i.e., involving multiple murder victims), suggest that with respect to "shooting rampages" at colleges and universities, as in cases at lower schools, they are still rare events. However, they argue that college mass murders are unique with respect to the pattern of events and motivation and ages of the shooters, thus calling for significantly different methods of prevention (p. 1465). They note that despite ubiquitous media accounts of mass shootings like Virginia Tech and Northern Illinois suggesting that college campus violence is rampant, "by any measure … the risk of serious violence on campus remains remarkably low, particularly in its extreme form" (p. 1466). Their examination of 76 homicides that have been reported on college campuses nationwide between 2001–2005, which focuses on undergraduate and graduate students (excluding faculty, staff, or other non students as victims), finds that there are 51 victims, averaging about 10 per year. They have found that the majority of these homicides are classified as acquaintance killings or drug deals gone bad, not rampage shootings (p. 1467). Fox and Savage further claim that while institutions of higher learning in the wake of major tragedies have instituted some very reasonable and needed safety and security measures, as recommended by expert reports (e.g., interoperable communication systems, risk and safety assessments, and educating faculty and university personnel to properly recognize and respond to signs of mental health issues and possible threats), many colleges have overreacted and instituted "knee-jerk campus safety measures of questionable effectiveness" (p. 1467).

Fox and Savage and others have found that the perpetrators of college and university mass shootings are often older, graduate students who become violent because of high levels of perceived stress and/or the inability to succeed or deal with failure (Vossekuil, et al., 2004; Fox and Savage, 2009, p. 1475). Interestingly, Fox and Savage (2009) show that of the 14 fatal multiple shootings since 1990 on U.S. campuses, 8 were done by current or former graduate, law, medical or nursing students; the others included 3 traditional undergraduate students and 3 outsiders coming on the campus (p. 1475). Likewise, the researchers indicate that certain security measures like the "active shooter" responses, for example, adopted by law enforcement agencies after the 1999 Columbine incident to respond to a random perpetrator on campus, is probably not suitable for college campuses. Many campuses are very large, making it difficult to lock down a campus. Additionally, college campuses, unlike, high schools, do not lend themselves to access control. By their very nature, colleges and universities are open, inviting students and other people from the community (p. 1471).

Workplace Violence

Since most people spend much of their time involved in making a living, it comes as no surprise that crime and violence take place routinely in the private or public "workplace." Workplace violence, including homicides, suicides, rapes, robberies, and assaults including sexual assaults, do occur routinely. According to reports by Bureau of Justice Statistics (BJS) covering the years from 1993 to 1999, an average 1.7 million people have been victims of violent crime while at work or on duty in the U.S. About 1.3 million (75%) of these incidents have been classified as simple assaults, while an additional 19 percent have been recorded as aggravated assaults as measured by the National Crime Victimization Survey (NCVS). Homicide, rape, robbery, and sexual assault account for a small percentage, i.e., 6 percent of all workplace violent crime during these years. Of the various occupations examined, law enforcement officers, corrections officers, and taxi drivers are victimized at the highest rates (Duhart, 2001). A more recent study based on NCVS data indicates that in 2009, there were 572,000 non-fatal violent crimes (rape/sexual assault, robbery, and aggravated and simple assaults) that took place against persons 16 or older in the workplace, accounting for about 24 percent of non-fatal violence against persons 16 or older. Non-fatal violence in the workplace is about 15 percent of all non-fatal violent crime against persons 16 or older in the U.S. population. In general, the rate of violent crime against employed persons in the above age category declined since 1993—from a rate of 16 to 4 violent crimes per 1,000 employed persons in 2009, a 75 percent decrease. Occupational groups from 2005–2009 with the highest average rates of work-related violent crimes included law enforcement (48 violent crimes per 1,000 employed persons), followed by mental health occupations (21 per 1,000 employed persons); among retail sales jobs, bartenders had the highest workplace violence rate (80 per 1,000) (Harrell, 2011, pp. 1–4).

The Bureau of Labor Statistics' Census of Fatal Occupational Injuries (CFOI), which tracks workplace homicide, reports that 13,309 workplace homicides have occurred between 1992 and 2008, averaging about 700 homicides per year; the largest number of homicides (1080) took place in 1994 and the lowest number (526) occurred in 2008 (Occupational Violence, n.d.). Over the past five years, 2004–2008, an average of 564 work-related homicides has occurred in the U.S. More recent data from BLS report 542 workplace homicides in 2009 and 506 in 2010 for persons aged 16 and older. Overall, work-related homicides decreased more than 50 percent from 1994 to 2010 (http://www.bls.gov/iif/oshfaq1.htm).

Four out of five work-related homicide victims are males. It is interesting to note that the type of assailants in these homicides differ for males and females. Robbers and other perpetrators make up 72 percent of assailants for men, and 51 percent of assailants for women. Personal acquaintances and family members account for only 4 percent of workplace homicide assailants for men, but 28 percent for women (Bureau of Labor Statistics, 2010). As a case in point, a recent shooting on July 12, 2010 in Albuquerque, New Mexico in which a man opened fire at a fiber optics manufacturing plant, killing five people and wounding four others before turning the gun on himself, was described as a "domestic violence" dispute by the police (Montoya, 2010). In their article, "Work-related homicides: The facts," researchers Eric Sygnatur and Guy Tuscano stress that, "while many may assume that most work-related homicides are crimes of passion or anger, committed by disgruntled co-workers, spouses, or acquaintances, this is not the case.... Most result from robberies" (2000, pp. 3, 6). A review of 8,654 occupational homicides by BLS between the years 1997–2010 reveals that about 75 percent were committed by robbers and other assailants, 18 percent were committed by work associates, and the remainder was committed by relatives or other acquaintances (Homicide: Occupational Homicides by Selected Characteristics, 1997–2010).

The Survey of Workplace Violence Prevention conducted in 2005 by the Bureau of Labor Statistics, for the National Institute for Occupational Safety and Health (NIOSH), which provides data representative of over 128 million workers employed in 7.4 million private industry and government establishments, includes current information about violent risks facing employees, employers' policies and training, and the prevalence of security features. Select findings include the following:

- Five percent of all commercial/industrial establishments, including state and local governments, have experienced at least one violent incident. Among these, the largest establishments in private industry, particularly the goods-producing industries, have reported the highest incidence of co-worker workplace violence; however, service-providing industries have reported the highest percentages of customer- and domestic-related incidents of violence.

- Seventy-two percent of establishments, employing 91 percent of the workers, had at least one form of security — either security staff, physical security (such as locked entries), or electronic security (such as metal detectors).

- Over 70 percent of U.S. workplaces *do not* have a formal program or policy that addresses workplace violence. Programs or policies related to workplace violence are more prevalent among larger private establishments and in government establishments.

- In establishments that report having a workplace violence program or policy, private industry most frequently reports addressing co-worker violence (82%). Customer or client violence is the next most frequent subject of private industry policies or programs (71%), followed by criminal violence (53%) and domestic violence (44%) (*Survey of Workplace Violence*, 2005).

Community Violence/Hate Crimes

Ordinary street violence and other crimes become *hate crimes* when perpetrators select and attack victims because of some characteristic such as race, gender, religion, ethnicity, disability, or homosexuality (McDevitt, et al., 2002). Crimes of hatred and prejudice have been in our country since its origins and include lynchings, cross burnings, vandalism of synagogues, and bombings of churches. While this is no doubt a sad commentary on our history, the actual term "hate crime" was not used regularly by criminologists until the 1980s when so called emerging groups such as the Skinheads caught the nations' attention with their bias-related crimes.

Hate crime is also referred to as bias crime. Although the Federal Bureau of Investigation (FBI) going as far back as World War I has been involved in investigating and responding to civil rights violations including the racist and anti-Semitic crimes committed by the

Ku Klux Klan, it was not until 1992 that the FBI commenced gathering data on hate crimes. This was a result of Congress passing the Hate Crime Statistics Act of 1990 that was amended in 1992, which, in part, reads:

> Under the authority of section 534 of title 28, United States Code, the Attorney General shall acquire data, for each calendar year, about crimes that manifest evidence of prejudice based on race, religion, disability, sexual orientation, or ethnicity, including where the appropriate crimes of murder, non-negligent manslaughter, forcible rape, aggravated assault, simple assault, intimidation, arson, and destruction and damage or vandalism of property (FBI, 2009, Hate Crimes Statistics Act).

In 2009, Congress again amended the Act by passing the Matthew Shepard and James Byrd, Jr. Prevention Act, adding the terms "gender and gender identity" after race (FBI, 2009, Hate Crime Statistics Act).

Currently, national data on hate crimes comes from two sources, the FBI's Uniform Crime Reporting Program (UCR) and the BJS's National Crime Victimization Survey (NCVS). Based on NCVS data for the years 2003–2009, there is an annual average of 195,000 hate crime victimizations each year reported by persons aged 12 or older. Approximately 3 percent of all violent crimes measured by the NCVS for these years are hate crimes; however, hate crime victimizations accounted for less than 1 percent of total victimizations during this seven year period (Langton and Planty, 2011). Other select results from the study indicate:

- In nearly 90 percent of hate crime victimizations occurring between 2003 and 2009, the victim suspected the offender was motivated by racial or ethnic prejudice or both.

- More than 4 in 5 hate crime victimizations involved violence; about 23 percent were serious violent crimes.

- In about 37 percent of violent hate crimes, the offender knew the victim; in violent non-hate crimes, half of all victims knew the offender.

- Police were notified of fewer than half (45%) of all hate crime victimizations.

- From 2004 to 2009, no differences were found between hate and nonhate crime in the percentage of violent victimizations involving a weapon or causing injury to the victim.

- The majority of violent hate crimes were interracial, while the majority of non hate violent crimes were intra-racial.

- Fewer than 1 in 10 hate crime victims stated that the offender left hate symbols at the crime scene; nearly all hate crime victims said that the offender used hate language (Langton and Planty, 2011, p. 1).

The FBI also collects data on hate crimes based on law enforcement reports nationwide. Reported motivations for hate crimes are similar for the NCVS victimizations reported to the police and the UCR. Race is the primary motivation for both, followed by ethnicity, bias against sexual orientation, and religious bias. Likewise, both the NCVS and UCR indicate that about 8 in 10 hate crimes are violent crimes, and the remaining 2 in 10 are property crimes. However, among violent hate crimes, the NCVS has found substantially higher percentages of aggravated assault reported to the police compared to the UCR (Harlow, 2005, pp. 9–10). The NCVS does not collect data on homicides; however, eight hate crime homicides (including murders and non-negligent manslaughters) occurred in reporting year 2009 (Langton and Planty, 2011, p. 1).

The Crime Victims with Disabilities Awareness Act (Public Law 105-301) has mandated that the National Crime Victimization Survey (NCVS) maintain statistics on crimes committed against people with disabilities (e.g., health conditions and other impairments causing disability). Based on the 2008 NCVS report, approximately 730,000 disabled individuals over aged 12, excluding those in institutions, have been victims of nonfatal violent crimes and 1.8 million of property crimes. About 37 percent of the violent crimes perpetrated against people with disabilities in the U.S. are serious violent crimes including: (1) rape or sexual assault (40,000); (2) robbery (116,000); and (3) aggravated assault (115,000). In addition, about 459,000 simple assaults have occurred against disabled persons. Crimes against disabled people are usually committed by "well known or casual acquaintances" similarly for males (40%) and females (36%) (Harrell and Rand, 2010).

Conclusion

Interpersonal criminal violence is what most people associate with the term violence. It is found in all areas of our lives, i.e., in our homes, schools, workplaces, and in our communities, often involving family members and acquaintances, as well as strangers. When references to "fear of crime" are made, violent crimes such as homicide, rape, robbery and assault usually come to mind. While these types of crime are relatively rare in terms of actual incidents in comparison to property and other types of white collar crimes, they nevertheless receive considerable attention in our society by the media and experts from the scientific community. These sources and others serve to construct a social reality of violent crime that most people have come to accept as real. The current dominant view of violence in the United States is the criminal justice perspective, which focuses on the incidence of violent crimes, examining perpetrators, victims, and other factors associated with the commission of these criminal events including prevention and control of such crimes, usually at the individual or personal level.

Although violent interpersonal crimes between individuals have been decreasing substantially in the United States over the years, at least those we know about, many people believe that it has been rising. In the typical responses to interpersonal violence, the public often does not consider the institutional and structural forces in our society that contribute to encouraging and reinforcing certain patterns of interpersonal violent crimes. We rarely ask questions about what structures our general understanding of violence or how specific acts of violence may be differentially interpreted based on the context of occurrence or who the perpetrators are and who the victims are.

As we continue our consideration of violence in society, in the next chapters we focus attention to how the institutional organization of society and the underpinning infrastructure of power and hierarchical socioeconomic structure affect our perceptions and understanding of violence.

References

Ackerman, B. P., Brown, E. and Izard, C.E. (2003). Continuity and change in levels of externalizing behavior in school children from economically disadvantaged families, *Child Development*, 74, 694–709.

Adams-Curtis, L.E. (2004). College Women's Experiences of Sexual Coercion: A Review of Cultural, Perpetrator, and Situational Variables. *Traumas, Violence and Abuse*, 5, 91–122.

Anderson, Elijah. (1999). *Code of the Streets*. NY: W.W. Norton.

Anderson, M.J. (2005). All-American Rape. *St. John's Law Review*, 79(1), 625–633.

Archer, D., and Gartner, R. (1984). *Violence and Crime in Cross National Perspective*. New Haven, CT: Yale University Press.

Baum, K., and Klaus, P. (2005). *Violent Victimizations of College Students, 1995–2002*. United States Department of Justice: Bureau of Justice Statistics (NCJ 206836).

Beaumont, P. (July 23, 2011). Anders Behring Breivik: Profile of a Mass Murderer. Retrieved from: http://www.guardina.co.uk/world/2011/jul/23/anders-behring-norway-attacks/print.

Bouffard, L.A., and Muftic, L.R. (2006). The "Rural Mystique": Social Disorganization and Violence beyond Urban Communities. *Western Criminology Review*, 7(3), 56–66.

Brown, R. M. (1969). *American Violence*. Englewood Cliffs, NJ: Prentice Hall.

Brownmiller, S. (1975). *Against Our Will: Men, Women and Rape*. New York: Simon and Schuster.

Burgess, A.W., and Clements, P.T. (2010). Child and Adolescent Victimization. In A.W. Burgess, C. Regehr, and A.R. Roberts (Eds.). *Victimology: Theories and Research*. Boston: Jones and Bartlette Publishers, 127–163.

Bureau of Labor Statistics (BLS). (July 14, 2010). Fact Sheet. Workplace Shootings. Retrieved from: http://www.bls.gov/iif/oshwc/cfoi/osar0014.htm.

CASA (2005). See The National Center on Addiction and Substance Abuse.

Catalano, S., and Snyder, H. (2009). *Female Victims of Violence*. Bureau of Justice Statistics (NCJ 228356).

Cherub, S. (2011). Gunman Dead after Killing Three at Diner. New Orleans: *The Times-Picayune*, B-2).

Chronicle of Higher Education. (1999). Retrieved from: http://chronicle.com/free/almanac/1999/nation/nation.htm.

Clinard, M.B., and Quinney, R. (1973). *Criminal Behavior Systems: A Typology*. New York: Holt, Rinehart and Winston (reissued by Cincinnati: Anderson, 1986).

Cloud, J. (2011). A Mind Unhinged. *Time*, January 24, 177(3), 32–35.

Coleman, D.C., Dodge, K.A., and Campbell, S.K. (2010). Where and How to Draw the Line Between Reasonable Corporal Punishment and Abuse. *Law and Contemporary Social Problems*, 7(2), 107–165.

Conklin, J. (1972). *Robbery and the Criminal Justice System*. Philadelphia: J.B. Lippincott.

Cook, P.J. (1986). The Relationship between Victim Resistance and Injury in Noncommercial Robbery. *Journal of Legal Studies*, 15, 405–16.

Cottrell, B., and Monk, P. (2004). Adolescent-to-Parent Abuse: A Qualitative Overview of Common Themes. *Journal of Family Issues*, 25(8), 1072–1095.

Deming, M., and Eppy, A. (1981). The Sociology of Rape. *Sociology and Social Research*, 65, July, 357–380.

Dewan, S., Saul, S., and Zezlma, K. (2010). For Professor, Fury Just Beneath the Surface. *The New York Times*. Retrieved from: http://nytimes.com/2010/02/21/us/21bishop.htm?pagewanted=all.

Duhart, D.T. (2001). Bureau of Justice Statistics Special Report. Violence in the Workplace, 1993–1999. Retrieved from: http://bjs/ojp.usdoj.gov/content/pub/pub/vw99.pdf.

Duwe, G. (2000). Body Count Journalism: The Presentation of Mass Murder in the News Media. *Homicide Studies*, 4, 365–379.

Erlanger, S., and Cowell, A. (July 25, 2011). Norway suspect hints he did not act alone. Retrieved from: http://www.nytimes.com/2011/07/we/world/europe/weoslo.html?hp.

Egger, S. A. (1984). A Working Definition of Serial Murder and the Reduction of Linkage Blindness. *Journal of Police Science and Administration*, 12, 348–357.

Einstadter, W.J. (1969). The Social Organization of Armed Robbery. *Social Problems*, 17, 64–83.

Ellsberg, M.C., et al. (2000). Candies in Hell: Women's Experience of Violence in Nicaragua. *Social Science and Medicine*. 51, 1595–1610.

Emanuel, S.L. (2010). *Criminal Law*. New York: Aspen Publishers.

English, D.J., Widom, C.S., and Ford, B. (2004). Another Look at the Effects of Child Abuse. *NIJ Journal*, 251, 23–24.

Federal Bureau of Investigation (FBI). *2009. Hate Crimes Statistics Act*. Retrieved from: http://www2.fbi.gov/ucr/hc2009/hatecrimestatistics.html.

Federal Bureau of Investigation (FBI). (2010a). *Bank Crime Statistics*. Washington, DC: Department of Justice.

Federal Bureau of Investigation (FBI). (2010b). *Crime in the United States, 2009*. Washington, DC: U.S. Department of Justice. Retrieved from: http://www2.fbi.gov/ucr/cius2009/index.html.

Federal Bureau of Investigation (FBI). (2011). *Crime in the United States, 2010*. Washington, DC: U.S. Department of Justice. Retrieved from: http://www2.fbi.gov/ucr/cius2009/offenses/violent_crime/murder_homicide.html.

Federal Bureau of Investigation. (1960, 1975, 1980, 1987, 1990–2005). *Crime in the United States*. Washington, DC: U.S. Government Printing Office (Please note each year represents a separate edition).

Feeney, F. (1999). Robbers as Decision Makers. In P. Cromwell (Ed.). *In Their Own Words: Criminals on Crime*. Los Angeles, CA: Roxbury Publishing Co., 119–129.

Felson, R., Baumer, E. and Messner, S. (2000). Acquaintance Robbery. *Journal of Research in Crime and Delinquency*, 37, 284–305.

Finkelhor, D., and Pillemer, K. (1988). Elder Abuse: It's Relationship to Other Forms of Domestic Violence. In G. Hotaling et al (Eds.). *Family Abuse and Its Consequences*. Beverly Hills, CA: Sage, 244–254.

Finkelhor, D., Ormrod, R., Turner, H. and Hamby, S.L. (2005). The Victimization of Children and Youth: A Comprehensive National Survey. *Child Maltreatment*, 10, 5–25.

Fischman, J., and Foster, A.L. (April 27, 2007a). New Phone Technologies Can Help Colleges Communicate Campus-wide in Emergencies. *The Chronicle of Higher Education*, LIII, 34, A16.

Fischman, J., and Foster, A.L. (April 27, 2007b). Campus Safety Gains Sharper Vision with New Breed of Surveillance Cameras. *Chronicle of Higher Education*, LIII, 34, A15.

Fisher, B.S., Cullen, F.T., and Daigle, L.E. (2005). The Discovery of Acquaintance Rape: The Salience of Methodological Innovation and Rigor. *Journal of Interpersonal Violence*, 20(4), 493–500.

Fisher, B.S., Cullen, F.T., and Turner, M.G. (2000). *The Sexual Victimization of College Women*: U.S. Department of Justice, Bureau of Justice Statistics, (NCJ 182369).

Fox, J.A., and Savage, J. (2009). Mass Murder Goes to College: An Examination of Changes on College Campuses Following Virginia Tech. *American Behavioral Scientist*, 52, 1465–1485.

Fox, J.A., Levin, J., and Quinet, K. (2011). *The Will to Kill: Making Sense of Senseless Murder*. New York, Pearson.

Garcia-Moreno, C., and Watts, C. (2011). *Violent Against Women: An Urgent Public Health Priority*, Bulletin of the World Health Organization, 2011. Retrieved from: http://www.who.int/bulletin/volumes/89/1/10-085217/en/.

Gelles, R.J., and Cornell, C.P. (1985). *Imitative Violence in Families*. Beverly Hills, CA: Sage.

Gill, M. (2000). *Commercial Robbery*. London: Blackstone Press.

Greene, M. (1993). Chronic Exposure to Violence and Poverty: Interventions that Work for Youth. *Crime and Delinquency*, 39, 106–124.

Groth, N., and Birnbaum, H.J. (1979). *Men Who Rape: The Psychology of the Offender*. New York: Plenum.

Hamparian, D.M., Schuster, R., Dinitz, S., and Conrad, J.P. (1978). *The Violent Few: A Study of Dangerous Offenders*. Lexington, MA: D.C. Heath.

Harlow, C.W. (2005). *Hate Crime Reported by Victims and Police*. Bureau of Justice Statistics Special Report, U.S. Dept of Justice, NCJ 209911.

Harper, D.W., and Voigt, L. (2007). Homicide Followed by Suicide: An Integrated Theoretical Perspective. *Homicide Studies*, 11, 275–318.

Harper, D.W., and Voigt, L. (2012). Intimate Partner Homicide Followed by Suicide. A Case of Gendered Violence. In D.W. Harper, L. Voigt, and W.E. Thornton (Eds.). *Violence: Do We Know It When We See It?* Durham. NC: Carolina Academic Press, 45–65.

Harrell, E. (March, 2011). *Workplace Violence, 1993–2009*. Bureau of Justice Statistics. U.S. Department of Justice, NCJ 233231.

Harrell, E., and Rand, M.R. (2010). *Crimes against People with Disabilities, 2008*. Bureau of Justice Statistics Report, U.S. Department of Justice, NCJ 233231.

Herrenkohl, T.L., Huang, B., Tajima, E.A., and Whitney, S.D. (2003). Examining the Link between Child Abuse and Youth Violence: An Analysis of Mediating Mechanisms. *Journal of Interpersonal Violence*, 18, 1189–1208.

Hewitt, G. (July 25, 2011). Norway Gunman has accomplices. Retrieved from: http://www.bbc.co.uk/news/world-europe-14280210.BBC.

Hickey, E. (2010). *Serial Murderers and Their Victims.* Belmont, CA: Wadsworth/Cengage.

Hoatling, G.T., Straus, M.R., and Lincoln, A.J. (1989). Intrafamily Violence, Crime and Violence Outside the Family, *Crime and Justice*, 11, 315–375.

Holmes, R.M., and J. DeBurger. (1988). *Serial Murder.* Newbery Park, CA: Sage.

Holmes, R.M., and Holmes, S.T. (2000). Mass Murder in the United States. Upper Saddle River, NJ: Prentice Hall.

Homicide: Occupational Homicides by Selected Characteristics, 1997–2010. Retrieved from: http://www.bls.gov/iif/oshwc/cfoi/work-hom.pdf.

Hurley, J.T. (1995). Violent Crime Hits Home: Home Invasion Robbery. Retrieved from: http://www.fbfl.us/index.aspx?NID=153.

Jaccarino, M. (July 23, 2011). Who is Anders Behring Breivik? Norway shooting suspect's profile emerges. Retrieved from: http://articles.nydailynews.com/2011-07-23/news/29822386_1_facebook-page-huffington-post-norway.

Jaffe, P., Crooks, C., and Wolfe, D. (2003). Legal and Policy Responses to Children Exposed to Domestic Violence: The Need to Evaluate Intended and Unintended Consequences. *Clinical Child and Family Psychology Review*, 6(3), 205–213.

Kane, R.J. (2005). Compromised Police Legitimacy as a Predictor of Violent Crime in Structurally Disadvantaged Communities, *Criminology*, 43, 469–499.

Karmen, A. (1990). *Crime Victims.* Pacific Grove, CA: Brooks Cole.

Katz, S., and Mazur, M. (1979). *Understanding the Rape Victim: A Synthesis of Research Findings.* New York: Wiley.

Kitzmann, K.M., Gaylord, M.K., Holt, A.R., and Kenny, E.D. (2003). Child Witness to Domestic Violence: A Meta Analytic Review, *Journal of Consulting and Clinical Psychology*, 71(2), 339–352.

Klaus, P. (2004). *Carjacking, 1993–2002.* U.S. Department of Justice, Bureau of Justice Statistics.

Kleck, G., and Delone, M.A. (1998). Victim Resistance and Offender Weapon Effects in Robbery. *Journal of Quantitative Criminology*, 9, 55–81.

Koss, M.P. (1989). Hidden Rape: Sexual Aggression and Victimization in a National Sample of Students in Higher Education. In M.A. Pinog-Good and J.E. Stets (Eds.), *Violence in Dating Relationships*, New York: Praeger, 145–168.

Koss, M.P., et.al. (1994). *No Safe Haven: Male Violence against Women at Home, at Work, and in the Community.* Washington, DC: American Psychological Association.

Krug, E.G., Dahlberg, J.A., Zwi, A.B., and Lozano, R.M. (2002). *World Report on Violence and Health*, Geneva: World Health Organization. Retrieved from: http://www.who.int/violence_injury_prevention/violence/world_report/en/.

Kubrin, C., and Weitzer, R. (2003). Retaliatory Homicide: Concentrated Disadvantage and Neighborhood Culture. *Social Problems*, 50, 157–180.

Langton, L., and Planty, M. (June 2011). *Hate Crime, 2003–2009.* Bureau of Justice Special Report, NCJ 234085. Retrieved from: http://www.bjs.gov/index.cfm?ty=pbdetail&iid=1760.

Largen, M.A. (1981). Grassroots Centers and National Task Forces: A History of the Anti-Rape Movement. *Ageis*, Summer, 46–52.

Lawrence, F.M. (1999). *Punishing Hate: Bias Crimes under American Law.* Cambridge, MA: Harvard University Press.

Lawrence, T. (2007). *School Crime and Juvenile Justice.* New York: Oxford University Press.

Lee, M.R., and Ousey, G.C. (2012). Southern Violence: A Contemporary Overview. In D.W. Harper, L. Voigt, and W.E. Thornton (Eds.). *Violence: Do We Know It When We See It?* Durham. NC: Carolina Academic Press, 115–125.

Levitov, J.J., and Harper, D.W. (2012). You Can't Do Crack on Credit: Drug and Retaliatory Murder. In D.W. Harper, L. Voigt, and W.E. Thornton (Eds.). *Violence: Do We Know It When We See It?* Durham. NC: Carolina Academic Press, 129–145.

Lipka, S. (April 27, 2007). Lessons from a Tragedy: Safety and Risk-Management Experts Debate Virginia Tech's Response. *Chronicle of Higher Education*, LIII, 34, A12–A13.

Locke, B.D., and Mahalik, J.R. (2005). Examining Masculinity Norms and Athletic Involvement as Predictors of Sexual Aggression in College Men. *Journal of Counseling Psychology,* 52(3), 279–283.

Loh, C., Orachowski, L.M., Gidyez, C.A., and Elizaga, R.A. (2007). Socialization and Sexual Aggression in College Men: The Role of Observational Influence in Detecting Risk Cues. *Psychology of Men and Masculinity*, 8(3), 129–144.

Lord, V. B. (2004). *Suicide by Cop: Inducing Officers to Shoot: Practical Direction for Recognition, Resolution, and Recovery.* Flushing, NY: Looseleaf Law Publications.

Luckenbill, D. (1977). Criminal homicide as a Situated Transaction. *Social Problems*, 25, 176–186.

Lyon, M.R. (2004). No means No? Withdrawal of Consent during Intercourse and the Continuing Evolution of the Definition of Rape. *The Journal of Criminal Law and Criminology*, 91(1), 277–314.

Matthews, R. (2002). *Armed Robbery.* Compton, Devon: Willan.

McDevitt, J., Levin, J., and Bennett, S. (2002). Hate Crime Offenders: An Expanded Typology. *Journal of Social Issues*, 58(2), 303–317.

Michaud, S.G., and Aynesworth, H. (1983). *The Only Living Witness.* NY: Simon & Schuster

Miethe, T., and Meier, R.F. (1994). *Crime and Its Social Context: Toward an Integrated Theory of Offenders, Victims, and Situations.* Albany, NY: State University of New York Press.

Miller, W.B. (1958). Lower Class Culture as a Generating milieu of Gang Delinquency. *Journal of Social Issues*, 14, 5–9.

Monahan, J. (1981). *Predicting Violent Behavior.* Beverly Hills, CA: Sage.

Montoya, S. (July 12, 2010). *Police: 6 Killed in Albuquerque Plant Shooting.* Retrieved from: http://www.manufacturing.net/News-Police-6-Killer_in_Albuquereque-Plant Shooting-07121.

Murnen, S.K., Wright, C. and Kaluzny, G. (2002). If "Boys will be Boys," then girls will be Victims? A meta-analytic review of the research that related masculine ideology to sexual aggression. *Sex Roles*, 46, 359–375.

National Center for Injury Prevention and Control. (2003). *Costs of Intimate Partner Violence against Women in the United States.* Atlanta (GA): Centers for Disease Control and Prevention.

National Center for Victims of Crime. (2011). *Rape Shield Laws*. Washington, DC: 2000 M. Street, N.W.

National Crime Victimization Survey (NCVS). (March 10, 2010). *Criminal Victimization in the United States, 2008. Statistical Tables*. U.S. Department of Justice, NCJ 231173.

National Gang Threat Assessment, 2009. Washington, DC: National Gang Intelligence Center. Retrieved from: http://www.justice.gov/ndic/pubs32/32146/32146p.pdf.

Neumann, S. (2006). Gang Rape: Examining Peer Support and Alcohol in Fraternities, in E.W. Hickey (Ed.). *Sex Crimes and Paraphilia*. Upper Saddle, NJ: Pearson, 397–408.

Normandeau, A., and Gabor, A. (1987). *Armed Robbery: Cops, Robbers and Victims*. Springfield, Ill: Charles C. Thomas.

Occupational Violence. (n.d.) Centers for Disease Control and Prevention, Retrieved from: http://www.cdc/nosh/topics/violence/.

Orange, R. (January 15, 2012). Anders Behring Breivik Psychiatric Report Reveals "Kindergarten" Prison Life. Retrieved from: http://www.telegraph.com.uk/news/worldnews/europe/norway/9016174/Anders-Behring-Breivik-psychiatric-report-reveals-kindergarten-prison-life.html.

Osman, S. (2003). Predicting Men's Rape Perceptions based on the Belief that No really means "Yes." *Journal of Applied Social Psychology, 33*, 683–692.

O'Sullivan, C.S. (1991). Acquaintance Gang Rape on Campus. In A. Parrot and L. Bechhofer (Eds.). *Acquaintance Rape: The Hidden Crime*. New York: Wiley and Sons, 140–156.

O'Tolle, M.E. (2000). *The School Shooter: A Threat Assessment Perspective*. Washington, DC: Dept. of Justice, Federal Bureau of Investigation.

Patel, A., and Wright, J.D. (2012). Rape and the Glorification of Guns and Violence in Inner City Youth Culture. In D.W. Harper, L. Voigt, and W.E. Thornton (Eds.), *Violence: Do We Know It When We See It?* Durham. NC: Carolina Academic Press, 223–245.

Rainville, G., and Reaves, B.A. (2003). Felony Defendants in Large Urban Counties, 2000. U.S. Department of Justice. Bureau of Justice Statistics. NCJ 202021. Retrieved from: http://bjs.ojp.usdoj.gov/content/pub/fd1u00.pdf.

Regehr, C., and Roberts, A.R. (2010). Intimate Partner Violence. In A.W. Burgess, C. Regehr, and A.R. Roberts (Eds.). *Victimology: Theories and Research*. Boston: Jones and Bartlette Publishers, 197–223.

Reiss, A., and Roth, J. (1993). *Understanding and Preventing Violence*. Washington, DC: National Academy Press.

Roberts, S., Zhang, J., and Truman, J. (2010). *Indicators of School Crime and Safety: 2010* (9NCES 2011-002/NCJ 2308 12). National Center for Education Statistics, U.S. Department of Education, and Bureau of Justice Statistics, Office of Justice Programs, U.S. Department of Justice. Washington, DC: Retrieved from: http://nces.ed.gov

Robbery at Automated Teller Machines, (August, 2006). U.S. Department of Justice Resources Information Center. Retrieved from: http://www.cops.usdoj.gov/ric/ResourceSearch.aspx.

Rose, V.M. (1979). Rape as a Social Problem: A by product of the Feminist Movement, *Social Problems, 25*, 75–88.

Russell, D.E. H. (1990). *Rape in Marriage*. New York: Macmillan Press.

Sampson, R.J. (2012). Great American City: Chicago and the Enduring Neighborhood Effect. Chicago: University of Chicago Press

Schwendinger H., and Schwendinger, J.S. (1980/1983). *Rape and Inequality.* Beverly Hills, California: Sage.

Smith, E.L., and Farole, Jr., D.J. (2009). *Profile of Intimate Partner Violence Cases in Large Urban Counties.* (NCJ 228193). Retrieved from: http://www.ojp.usdoj.gov/bjs/abstract/pipvcluc.htm.

Smith-Spark, L. (August 24, 2012). Norway killer Anders Breivik ruled sane, given a 21-year prison term. CNN. Retrieved from: www.cnn.com/2012/08/24/world/europe/norway-breivik-trial/index.html.

Southwick, L. (2000). Self-defense with guns. *Journal of Criminal Justice* 28, 5, 351–370.

Spitzberg, B.H., and M. Cadiz. (2002). The Media construction of Stalking Stereotypes. *Journal of Criminal Justice and Popular Culture*, 9(3), 128–149.

Stewart, E.A., and Simons, R.L. (2006). Structure and Culture in African American Adolescent Violence: A Partial Test of the 'Code of the Street' Thesis. *Justice Quarterly*, 23(1), 2–33.

Stewart, E.A., and Simons, R.L. (2010). Race, Code of the Street and Violent Delinquency: A Multilevel Investigation of Neighborhood Street Culture and Individual Norms of Violence. *Criminology*, 48(2), 569–606.

Surette, R. (2007). *Media, Crime and Criminal Justice: Images, Realities, and Policies.* Belmont, CA: Thomson Wadsworth.

Survey *of Workplace Violence, 2005.* (October 27, 2006). Washington, DC: United States Department of Labor, Bureau of Labor Statistics. Retrieved from: http://www.bls.gov/iif/home.htm.

Sygnatur, E.F., and Toscano, G.A. (2000). Work Related Homicides: The Facts. *Compensation and Working Conditions*, Spring, 3–8.

Tark, J., and Kleck, G. (2004). Resisting Crime: The Effects of Victim Action on the Outcomes of Crimes. *Criminology*, 42(4), 861–909.

Taylor, C., and Sorenson, S. (2007). Intervention on Behalf of Children Exposed to Intimate Partner Violence: Assessment of Support in A Diverse Community-Based Sample. *Child Abuse and Neglect*, 31, 1155–1111.

The National Center on Addiction and Substance Abuse at Columbia University (CASA). (2005). Family Matters: Substance abuse and the American family. New York: CASA.

Thompson, M.P., Basile, K.C., Hertz, and M.F., Sitterle. (2006). *Measuring Intimate Partner Violence Victimization and Perpetration: A Compendium of Assessment Tools.* Atlanta, GA: Centers for Disease Control and Prevention, National Center for Injury Prevention and Control.

Thornton, W.E., and Voigt, L. (2010). Disaster Phase Analysis and Crime Facilitation Patterns. In D.W. Harper and K. Frailing (Eds.). *Crime and Justice in Disaster.* Durham, NC: Carolina Academic Press, 27–59.

Thornton, W.E., Voigt, L., and Walsh, P.D. (2009). Migrant *Workers and Criminal Victimization in Post Katrina New Orleans.* Paper presented at Southern Sociological Society, New Orleans, LA.

Tjaden, P., and Thoennes, N. (2006). *Extent, Nature, and Consequences of Rape Victimization: Findings from the National Violence against Women Survey.* Washington, DC: U.S. Dept of Justice, National Institute of Justice, Office of Justice Programs.

Truman, J. L., and Rand, M.R. (2010). Criminal Victimization, 2009. National Crime Victimization Survey. U.S. Department of Justice. NCJ 231327.Retrieved from: http://bjs.ojp.usdoj.gov.

Truman, J.L. (September, 2011). *Criminal Victimization, 2010.* National Crime Victimization Survey. U.S. Department of Justice. NCJ 235509. Retrieved from: http://bjs.ojp.usdoj.gov/index.cfm?ty=pbdetail&iid=2224.

Ullman, S.E. (1999). Comparisons of Gang and Individual Rape Incidents. *Violence and Victims*, 14(2), 123–133.

Ullman, S.E. (2007). Comparing Gang and Individual Rapes in a Community Sample of Urban Women. *Violence and Victims*, 22(1), 43–51.

Ulman, A., and Straus, M.A. (2003). Violence by Children against Mothers in Relation to Violence between Parents and Corporal Punishment by Parents. *Journal of Comparative Studies*, 34, 41–63.

Urbaszewski, K. (2011). Another Home Invaded in N.O. New Orleans, LA: *The Times-Picayune*, September 11, 2011, B1–2.

U.S. Government Accounting Office (GA). (August, 2008). *Military Personnel: DOD's and the Coast Guard's Sexual Assault Prevention and Response Programs Face Implementation and Oversight Challenges.* Retrieved from: http://www.gao.gov/new.items/d08924.pdf.

U.S. Department of Health and Human Services (USDHHS), Administration for Children and Families, Administration on Children, Youth and Families, Children's Bureau. (2010). *Child Maltreatment 2008.* Retrieved from: http://www.acf.hhs.gov/programs/cb/stats_research/index.htm#can.

Vossekuil, B., Fein, R.A., Reddy, Borun, R, and Modzeleski, W. (2004). *The Final Report and Findings of the Safe School Initiative: Implications for the Prevention of School Attacks in the United States.* Washington, DC: U.S. Secret Service and U.S. Department of Education.

Wasserman, G.A., and Seracini, A.M. (2001). Family Risk Factors and Intervention. In R. Loeber and D. P. Farrington (Eds.). *Child delinquents: Development, Intervention, and Service Needs.* Thousand Oaks, CA: Sage.

Wasserman, G. A., et al (2003). Risk and Protective Factors of Child Delinquency. *Child Delinquency, Bulletin Series.* Washington, DC: U.S. Dept. of Justice, Office of Justice Programs, OJJDP.

Widom, C.S., and Maxfield, M.G. (2001). An Update on the "Cycle of violence." U.S. Department of Justice. National Institute of Justice. Retrieved from: https//www.ncjrs.gov/pdfiles1/NIJ/184894.pdf.

Widom, C.S. (2000). Childhood Victimization: Early Adversity, Later Psychopathy. *The National Institute of Justice Journal*, 3–9.

Willis, K. (2006). *Armed Robbery: Who Commits It and Why?* Canberra: Australian Institute of Criminology.

Wolfgang, M.E. (1958/1966). *Patterns of Criminal Homicide.* New York: Wiley.

Wolfgang, M.E., and Ferracuti, F. (1967/1982). *The Subculture of Violence: Toward an Integrated theory in Criminology*. Beverly Hills, CA: Sage

Wolfgang, M.E., Figlio, R.M., and Sellin, T. (1972). *Delinquency in a Birth Cohort*. Chicago: University of Chicago Press.

World Health Organization (WHO). 2005. *Landmark Study on Domestic Violence*. Retrieved from: http://www.who.int/mediacentre/news/releases/2005/pr62/en/index.html.

Wright, R., Brookman, F., and Bennett, T.H. (2006). The Foreground Dynamics of Street Robbery in Britain. *British Journal of Criminology*, 46(1), 1–15.

Wright, R., and Decker, S. (1997). *Armed Robbery in Action, Stickups, and Street Culture*. Boston: Northeastern University.

Yoshihama, M., and Sorenson, S.B. (1994). Physical, Sexual, and Emotional Abuse by Male Intimates: Experiences of women in Japan. *Violence and Victims*, 9, 63–77.

Ziegenhagen, E.A., and Brosnan, D. (1985). Victim Responses to Robbery and Crime Control Policy. *Criminology*, 23, 675–695.

Chapter 4

Institutional Violence

This chapter is divided into two parts. In Part 1, we briefly review the different types of institutional violence as introduced in Chapter 1, examining family violence, educational violence, religious violence, and political or state violence. In Part 2, Leo Barrile provides in-depth coverage of another type of institutional violence, economic violence—more specifically corporate violence. As you may recall, institutional violence refers to acts of violence that emanate in the context of definitions and patterns of interactions and relationships within the social milieu of the fundamental institutions of society (*institutions*

---

* Part 2 of this chapter has been contributed by Dr. Leo Barrile, Professor of Sociology, Bloomsburg University.

are enduring or permanent social structures within a society that meet basic human needs). Sociologists typically refer to five basic institutions including the family and familial organizations, educational organizations and schools, work and economic organizations, places of worship and religions organizations, and the state including the political/legal and public agencies or organizations. In order to operate and fulfill their respective functions in society, institutions evolve complex sets of norms, positions, roles, and statuses. "Violence takes place in an institutional context when those in positions within these organizations commit acts of violence as part of their position and role" (Iadicola, 2012, p. 13).

Much of our discussion thus far has focused on various forms of interpersonal violence, which as we have seen, is a serious problem both in the United States and other parts of the world. However, interpersonal violence occurs in the contexts of our basic social institutions, but the "motives" (e.g., *instrumental motives* such as stealing money or property and *expressive motives* such as anger and revenge) as well as "intent" are expressed primarily through the actions of individuals within various social groupings and social relationships. Archer and Gartner in their work on cross-national violence note that the term violence usually "conjures up the image of dangerous individuals," which often "obscures the very real violence committed by authorities in the pursuit of domestic social control or by governments in the pursuit of foreign war" (1984, p. 63). They go on to say that when we define violent acts and violent actors in concrete, personalized forms outside of the institutional context, we tend to miss the reality of serious violence, including homicide, being produced routinely in the course of law enforcement, criminal punishment and executions, crowd and riot control, political subversion and assassination and, of course, war (1984, p. 63).

As we shall see in Part 1, much violence occurs within the context of the fundamental institutions of society that contextually define the norms of interaction and determine our respective roles and structure our everyday lives. To this extent violence is a "normal" part of the patterns of our daily interactions and existence. To help illustrate the institutional dimension of violence, in Part 2 we will take a close look at the economic sphere, where victims of business and corporate violence may be the general public, other organizations, specific consumers, employees, or the environment. It is worth pointing out that the human and social harms and economic losses associated with corporate acts of violence, which result from decisions made in corporate suites by corporate executives/officials regarding the commission or omission of certain business practices, far exceed the human injuries, deaths, and property losses incurred from traditional street crimes and other interpersonal forms of violent crimes. These business decisions made by corporate officials/executives on behalf of their corporations are usually made with the intent to increase profits with the conscious disregard for human safety or the quality of life. Many of these "suite" crimes are extremely violent. Thousands of deaths result each year from corporate violence involving production/manufacture and distribution of unsafe products and harmful food and drugs as well as unsafe storage and disposal of contaminates and environmental pollution, resource depletion, and willful neglect of unsafe working conditions (Barrile, 1993; Voigt, et al., 1994, p. 358; Iadicola and Shupe, 2003; Barrile and Slone, 2005).

Part 1: General Description of Institutional Forms of Violence

Institutional violence refers to an implicitly conventional way of interacting, which may be accepted as part of a long-standing tradition that is not usually considered as violence or treated as illegitimate. Our social levels of tolerance for violence in certain institutional contexts, however, vary historically and culturally.

Family Violence

Within the institution of the family, there are many examples of acceptable/tolerable levels of violence that have been guided by cultural mores and laws, which are rooted in patriarchal and gender-biased perceptions. In the context of the institution of the family, which has undergone tremendous changes over time, the interactions between spouses or intimate partners as well as between parents or parental-type guardians and children may involve violence based on the cultural definitions of their relationships including the respective positions of individual family members within the family unit and the expectations for behavior that those roles carry.

Intimate Partner Violence (IPV)

Historically, in most parts of the world, spousal or intimate partner violence has been largely ignored officially (i.e., not recognized legally) under the assumption that the family is a private male-dominated domain, in which females have little rights or protections. It is only relatively recently that legal protections have been enacted to protect against intimate partner violence. For instance, forced intercourse in the context of marriage in the United States has not been historically regarded as a form of violence; it has only been since the 1970s that various state legislators have passed laws that extend rights to wives to bring formal charges of forced rape against husbands.

Domestic violence or intimate partner violence (IPV) presently refers to the physical, sexual, or psychological harm and other controlling behaviors by a current or former intimate partner or spouse. Acts of *physical aggression* include slapping, hitting and kicking. Acts of *sexual aggression* include forced intercourse and other forms of sexual coercion. Acts of *psychological abuse* include intimidation, constant belittling and humiliation, and other forms of controlling behavior such as isolating a person from family and friends, monitoring their movements (e.g., stalking), and restricting their access to assistance or information (Krug, et al., 2002, p. 89). Intimate partner violence may occur among heterosexual or same-sex couples.

Research evidence suggests that there are both individual and various community and cultural factors that impact the rate of intimate partner violence (e.g., Easteal, 2012). While the great bulk of studies to date have focused on intimate partner violence in North America, which may not be generalized to other parts of the world, a number of population-based studies conducted by the World Health Organization (WHO) over the last decade have begun to examine IPV in different countries, especially developing countries. Table 4.1 summarizes several key factors associated with a man's risk of abusing his partner as has been determined in the literature.

Table 4.1 Factors Associated with a Man's Risk for Abusing His Partner

Individual Factor	Relationship Factors	Community Factors	Societal Factors
• Young age • Heavy drinking • Depression • Personality disorders • Low academic achievement • Low income • Witnessing or experiencing violence as a child	• Marital conflict • Marital instability • Male dominance in family • Economic stress • Poor family functioning	• Weak community sanctions against domestic violence • Poverty • Low social capital	• Traditional gender norms • Social norms supportive of violence

Source: Krug, et al., 2002, p. 98.

As can be seen, individual factors associated with IPV include a number of demographic variables such as young age and low income, which have been consistently noted in most studies. Two other factors commonly associated with intimate partner abuse include witnessing or experiencing violence in ones family of orientation as a child. Heavy alcohol use, no doubt reducing inhibitions and judgment, is also linked to abuse as well as antisocial, aggressive and borderline personality disorders (Black, et al., 1999). Studies indicate that abusing males may also be more emotionally dependent and insecure and lacking in self esteem, and have problems with impulse control (e.g., Kantor, et al., 1998). Research results related to relationship factors and IPV, suggest that there may be a connection between marital conflict and physical violence, even after controlling for socioeconomic status and stress in the relationship (Black, et al., 1999).

Under community factors, poverty seems to increase the risk of violence for some men, and women, likely generating marital disagreements, stress, frustration, and feelings of inadequacy. However, just as important is how communities respond to IPV, which seems especially important in determining frequency. Societies that have lower levels of IPV have community sanctions against intimate partner violence in the form of strong laws as well as programs providing sanctuary or family support and counseling (Counts, et al., 1992). Researchers who have examined societal and cultural factors, which might explain IPV (particularly "partner beating"), have reported that it occurs in those societies where men have economic and decision-making power in the household, where females do not have ready access to divorce, and where adults generally resort to violence to solve conflicts (Levinson, 1989; Krug, et al., 2002, p. 100). Other possible cultural explanations of IPV point to structural inequalities between males and females, very traditional and rigid gender roles, and notions of masculinity tied to honor and aggression (Heise, 1998; Easteal, 2012). The concept of *honor related violence* (HRV) "referring to acts of violence predominantly against women who are perceived to have transgressed a religious-cultural divide, particularly in matters related to sexuality" has received attention in recent years (Idriss, 2011, p. 1). For instance, *honor killing*, the most extreme form of HRV, as practiced in some very conservative Muslim communities, involves the slaying of girls and women by their male relatives including brothers, husbands, and fathers for bringing "dishonor" on the family. Females can be targeted by their families for any number of perceived or alleged "immoral or shameful" acts, including talking to a man other than her husband or blood relative, marrying someone the family does not approve, or engaging in extramarital sex or even being a victim of rape. "Male relatives may beat, shoot, stab, or otherwise physically harm an accused woman, with the approval of both her family members and large sections of the general population" (Human Rights Watch, 2004, p. 1). For example, in Jordan, police rarely investigate honor murders, take little initiative to deter these crimes, and "typically treat the killers as vindicated men." Adding insult to injury, law enforcement officers routinely force threatened females to undergo painful and humiliating virginity examinations in order to determine if their hymens are intact. As noted by Human Rights Watch, "the perverse reality is that while many perpetrators of 'honor' crimes walk free, many would-be victims end up incarcerated" (2004, p. 1). Many women who have been interviewed by Human Rights Watch have spent up to ten years in prison and have been planning on remaining there until the family members that threatened them died or left the country (2004, p. 1). As a form of institutionalized violence, there is no law in the Hashemite Kingdom of Jordan that gives a male the legal right to murder a female relative who he perceives has dishonored the family. Honor killing, however, generally does not carry a sentence of more than one year incarceration. Under the Jordan Penal Code (Article 98), if the victim's family waives charges against the offender, the sentence may be reduced to six months. Although there have been efforts on the part of Jordanian women's rights groups to get laws that protect family honor killers reformed, these efforts have not for the most part been successful; "the courts still routinely accept a killer's excuse that he acted out of 'fury' and diminished capacity — even when the murder occurred weeks after the alleged offensive act — and are willing to consider the slightest gestures of female autonomy as provocations tainting family honor" (Human Rights Watch, 2004, p. 2).

Growing public awareness and concern over the serious impact of IPV and greater understanding of the causes of IPV have reinforced the necessity for establishing primary, secondary, and tertiary levels of prevention including increasing the availability of services to address the needs of victims who have been harmed by IPV as well as victims who are experiencing IPV. In addition, there has been increasing attention placed on IPV by organizations such as the World Health Organization (WHO) and Centers for Disease Control (CDC), which have focused on implementing strategies that have demonstrated success in prevention as well as initiating new evidence-based interventions (Thompson, et al., 2006). For instance, WHO has advocated on behalf of women in developing and developed countries, stressing the importance of legal and social support strategies "to empower women, financially and personally, and of challenging social norms that perpetuate violence." In addition, WHO has urged that laws and policies that promote and protect the human rights of women are a vital part of addressing violence against women (Garcia-Moreno and Watts, 2011).

Child Abuse and Neglect

The fine line between discipline and abuse of children is still largely subject to parental discretion. Throughout history adults have abused their children. For instance, the ancient Greeks practiced infanticide (the killing of newborns, particularly physically deformed newborns). The ancient Roman law held that fathers were endowed with the power of *patriae protestas* (i.e., the inalienable right of fathers to sell, kill, or allow their progeny to live). Originating in early English Common Law, courts have developed the general rule that parents cannot be held liable in a civil suit for excessive or brutal punishment of their children. "The courts reasoned that an orderly society depends on parents having discretion in disciplining within the home in order to maintain domestic harmony and family government" (Thomas, 1972, p. 304). Unless a case of abuse was considered particularly brutal and could be shown to be a "pressing danger to the child or to be of interest to the state" and received sufficient publicity, little court action took place (Fraser, 1976, p. 326). To some extent, this situation still exists.

Historically, in the United States child abuse was not recognized as a social problem until 1946 when John Caffey, a pediatric radiologist, published a study outlining some characteristic bone damage of mysterious origin prevalent in some of his young patients. While not accusing parents as the source of these injuries, Caffey did note that some parental explanations of various "accidents" were preposterous (Caffey, 1946). This discovery prompted several other researchers to conduct similar investigations. The first public incrimination of parents as intentional abusers of their offspring appeared in 1962. In a ground-breaking publication, Henry Kempe and his medical associates (1962) introduced the concept the *battered child syndrome*. Kempe applied the new terminology to "young children who have received serious physical abuse, generally from a parent or foster parent" (p. 17). This discovery launched a new movement uniting diverse professional groups and laypeople, which provided the impetus for nation-wide legislation in the U.S. outlawing child abuse.

The American Humane Association has a long history of conducting research on national child abuse and neglect trends. Established in 1990, one of the most reliable and extensive information sources on children who are abused and neglected is the *Child Maltreatment Report*, which is based on data collected by the National Child Abuse and Neglect Data System (NCANDS) from state child protection agencies (USDHHS, 2010).

The ultimate abuse of a child is murder by parents or caretakers. In *infanticide*, the infant is usually 1 year old or less (Fox, et al., 2012, pp. 81–87). The UCR reports that for reporting year 2010, there were 186 infants murdered less than one year old. There are probably other infants (and older babies) murdered by parents; however, the offense may go undetected because it is classified as an accident or as a case of SIDS (sudden infant death syndrome). The murder of older children is referred to as *filicide*; the UCR has reported 314 of these in 2010 (ages 1 to 4) (FBI, 2011, Expanded Homicide Data, Table 9). While this figure covers deaths known to be homicides, other reports estimate substantially higher figures of child fatalities as a consequence of maltreatment. The NCANDS estimates that 1,740 children died due to child abuse and neglect in 2008; the overall rate of child fatalities was 2.33 deaths per 100,000 children. About 80 percent of the children who died due to child abuse and neglect were younger than 4 years old, and most child fatalities (77%) happened at the hands of parents. The majority of perpetrators of child maltreatment, about 80 percent, were parents and another 6.5 percent were other relatives of the child. Females comprised a larger percentage of all offenders than men, 56.2 percent female compared to 42.6 percent male. Thirty-nine percent of victims were maltreated by their mother acting alone and about 18 percent of victims were abused by their father acting alone (p. 28). Slightly more than 75 percent of all perpetrators were younger than age 40. Perpetrators who were child daycare providers, 21.2 percent, committed sexual abuse (USDHHS, 2010, Summary).

Theoretical explanations for the existence of child abuse and neglect are categorized into several approaches including the psychiatric approach, the sociological approach, and the interaction approach. The psychiatric approach looks at the abuser and asks whether the person is suffering from some type of psychological malady that propels him or her to engage in abusive behavior. The sociological approach emphasizes the amount of challenges and stresses found within the family situation related to factors such as unemployment, female-headed family structure, social isolation, socioeconomic status, substance abuse, and lack of parenting skills. For instance, there is some evidence suggesting that family conflict is associated with child abuse (Kitzmann, et al., 2003). Recent research shows a possible link between physical child abuse and economic stress experienced in families struggling with unemployment and/or low wages as a result of a poor economy (Tanner, 2011). There is also evidence suggesting that parental/guardian substance abuse is a significant factor in child maltreatment. The National Center on Child Abuse and Substance Addiction at Columbia University (CASA) has estimated that substance abuse is a factor in at least 70 percent of reported cases of child abuse and neglect (2005, p. 20). The third approach based on the interaction model, focuses on the interplay between the caretaker and the child. This model is well grounded in the socialization literature and examines how a child's reaction to parents or stepparents or other caretakers affects subsequent parent-child interactions (Bronfenbrenner, 1973; Burgess and Youngblade, 1988; and Whitcomb, 2001). For example there is research pointing to a significant relationship between intimate partner and domestic violence in the family and child maltreatment (Edleson, 1999; Slep and O'Leary, 2005). The World Health Organization (WHO) in particular has examined global evidence, which shows that infant and early childhood experiences impact the likelihood of individuals becoming victims or perpetrators of IPV.

Overall research results indicate that child maltreatment has serious negative effects on every aspect of a child's well being—physical and mental health, social and cognitive development, and later life adjustment (Krug, et al., 2002, Chapter 3). For example, maltreatment causes stress that can disrupt early brain development as well as development of the nervous and immune systems (Morgan and Lilienfeld, 2000; National Scientific Council on the Developing Child, 2005). Abused and neglected children are at higher risk for health problems as adults including alcoholism, depression, drug abuse, eating disorders, obesity, high risk sexual behaviors, smoking, suicide, and certain types of chronic diseases (Felitti, et al., 1998; Raine, 2002; Runyan, et al., 2002). Also, research suggests that maltreated children are more likely to engage in delinquent behavior (Stouthamer-Lober, et al., 2001). Bartol and Bartol (2009) conclude that being a victim of childhood abuse and neglect increases the probability of future delinquency, substance abuse, and adult criminality and violence in boys by 40 percent (p. 42). Similarly, Widom (2000) finds that being maltreated as a child increases the chances of arrest as a juvenile by over 50 percent, as an adult by 38 percent, and arrest for a violent crime by 38 percent. Maltreatment during youth is also reported to increase the odds of becoming a gang member (Thompson and Braaten-Antrim, 1998).

Educational Violence

Institutional violence in educational institutions include such things as ignoring abusive treatment of students by school authorities or even medicating students to keep them compliant. Other examples can be failure to offer an adequate education to all students through discriminatory educational practices such as tracking students to succeed or fail and the use of corporal punishment.

Tracking

Tracking or student ability-grouping refers to the assignment of students to specific curriculum groups and subsequent courses based on such things as test results, past performance, and other criteria. Tracking began in the early 20th Century in America with the influx of large numbers of immigrant children into the public schools and efforts on the part of the schools to place children in appropriate classes/sections based on their respective levels of abilities. The practice continues today and begins in primary school and continues through high school. Tracking in high schools generally includes the practice of grouping students by ability into differentiated curriculums where students take high-, middle-, or low-level courses related to curricular tracks they have chosen or been assigned to (e.g., academic or college track, general educational track, and vocational or technical trade track) (Futrell and Gomez, 2008). Much research has addressed the question of how the practice of tracking in schools is related to social inequality. While this practice on the surface appears logical, in reality, students who are assigned to the higher-level tracks are exposed to more challenging and enriched course skills and content and students who are assigned to lower-level tracks are often given rote lessons, which focus on memorization (Ascher, 1992; Wheelock, 1992; Burns and Welner, 2005; Futrell and Gomez, 2008). The differences in the material and learning styles obviously have an impact on later life opportunities for careers, jobs, and income earning potential. A number of studies confirm that poor and minority students are arbitrarily selected for tracts on the basis of race and ethnicity or social class level rather than performance or ability and, thus, are "over-represented in the lower tracks and underrepresented in the higher tracks" (Burns and Welner, 2005; Wyner, Bridgeland, and Dilulio, 2007).Unfortunately, evidence suggests that tracking has allowed some student populations, such as the poor and minority students, to be left behind academically, a blatant form of discrimination (Futrell and Gomez, 2008). As noted by educational experts, Mary Futrell and Joel Gomez: "We cannot ignore the fact that for more than five decades, ability grouping has resulted in the separation of students by race, ethnicity, and socioeconomic status" (2008, online). Despite recent efforts such as recommendations from the *No Child Left Behind* (NCLB), legislation in 2002 that focused attention on more rigorous standards of education for the poor and minorities, serious problems still continue in terms of improved academic achievement (Lee, 2006).

Research suggests that students placed in lower tracks are well aware of the teaching and learning disparities that they encounter in their early educational careers. In a recent survey conducted with students in Alexandria, Virginia, surveyed students indicated that they knew that their school contained two tracks:

> An exclusive track, in which a small group of students are actively prepared for academic success, and a mainstream, unprivileged track, in which the majority of the students are not expected to excel and receive little support or opportunity to pursue their academic goals. Perhaps even more disconcerting is that the tracks are racially identifiable (Tamara, 2007, p. i).

Students also reported that their efforts to enhance their academic achievements were met with resistance. Many minority students who wanted to take advanced courses were thwarted by school guidance counselors and other adults in their schools who did not support their efforts. Surveys in other states have found similar results (Futrell and Gomez, 2008). These and other students like them are already part of the minority-majority population in the United States who are competing for jobs and careers in a struggling economy with classmates who are better educationally prepared. Increasingly educational experts urge that it is time to make significant changes to better serve low income and minority students in the nation's schools.

Corporal Punishment

A recent controversy in St. Augustine Catholic High School, a private school run by the Josephite Order of Catholic Priests in New Orleans, Louisiana, involved a decision by the school leadership and supported by the Archdiocese of New Orleans, to abolish the use of corporal punishment (via a wooden paddle), a practice used in the school for the past 60 years. Despite parents and alumni who rallied in support of the practice, thought to be part of character-building for students, and who argued that the school community should decide how to discipline children, corporal punishment was ended on June 11, 2011 (Russell, 2011). Archbishop Gregory Aymond is reported to have said that "corporal punishment institutionalizes violence and runs counter to both Catholic teaching and good educational practice. It also violates local archdiocesan school policy" (Nolan, 2011, p. 2). The Center for Effective Discipline, a national nonprofit advocacy organization against corporal punishment reported that St. Augustine is the lone outlier among Catholic schools still practicing corporal punishment. Robert Fathman, a clinical psychologist who helped found the center, indicated that there is a substantial amount of educational research rejecting corporal punishment. He noted: "The paddle is not a tool. The paddle is a weapon. It's designed to inflict pain.... Not a single developed country in the world but us allows a teacher to hit. Not in Europe, Mexico, China, Japan, Canada, all of Europe, Israel." (pp. 4–5). As of June, 2010, 117 countries prohibit corporal punishment in schools (*Discipline and the Law*, online).

According to estimates by the Department of Education, in 2005–2006, 233,190 children in the United States have been subjected to corporal punishment (*U.S. Corporal Punishment*, online). Evidence suggests that there has been a steady drop in school children submitted to physical punishment since the 1980s. Currently, there are nineteen states that have laws that still permit the use of corporal punishment in schools (Frosch, 2011).

Even though corporal punishment is widely recognized as a form of institutionalized violence against children in most of the nation's schools, proponents still make arguments for the continuation of the practice including: (1) it is necessary for teachers to control students; (2) the threat of it keeps many kids in line so that they can learn; (3) it builds character; and (4) it achieves high graduation rates (Frosch, 2011). While there is no supporting evidence for the positive effects suggested by the arguments above, there is evidence of the negative consequences of corporal punishments. Various studies indicate that corporal punishment sends a message to students that violence is an acceptable way to solve problems and that it promotes pro-violence attitudes. Corporal punishment does not result in long-term changes in children's behavior, and can also negatively impact social, psychological, and educational development in students (Andero and Stewart, 2002; Society for Adolescent Medicine, 2003; Owen, 2005). The American Academy of Pediatrics reported that "corporal punishment adversely affects a student's self-image and school achievement and it may contribute to disruptive and violent behavior" (2000, website).

Religious Violence

The French philosopher, Blaise Pascal, in his writing concerning violence and religion once commented: "Men never do evil so completely and cheerfully as when they do it from religious conviction" (cited in Evans, 1968, p. 201). Peter Iadicola and Anson Shupe (2003) observe that while religion is often seen as a source of goodwill and nonviolence, with positive beliefs and values, it can likewise "inflame passions of outrage and fear that motivate not just individual believers, but also, on occasion, entire societies to repress or eliminate "non-believers" (p. 176). Throughout history we have seen religious wars and crusades, persecution of heretics and non-believers, as well as missionaries who have engaged in or aided in the destruction of indigenous cultures and populations through genocidal violence, often followed by military conquest, and colonization (pp. 176–201). Contemporary forms of religious violence can be found in the Arab countries like Iran where fundamentalist Muslim leaders (e.g., Ayatollah Ruhollah Khomeini) persecuted, tortured, and annihilated non-Islamics (Baha'is) in the 1980s or in Afghanistan where extremist Muslims (e.g., Taliban regime) sponsored and harbored terrorists such as al-Qaida and Saudi Arabian Osama bin Laden, who lead the terrorist attack on New York's World Trade Towers on September 11, 2001 as well as a reign of terror until his death in 2011 (p. 175).

In the context of religious institutions, other violent acts include violations of clergy trust, abuse, and violence. Although there have been numerous examples of so-called "clergy violence" over the years where clergymen (and some clergy women) who abused their positions were charged with physical and sexual abuse of children and adults (Berry, 1992; Iadicola and Shupe, 2003, p. 189), perhaps the most widely known form of religious institutional violence has involved the sexual abuse of children by Catholic priests and deacons, which has taken place over the last sixty years. The John Jay College of Criminal Justice (2004, 2006) as well as the United States Conference of Catholic Bishops (2003–2010) has examined the nature and scope of the sexual abuse of minors by Catholic priests and deacons and estimated that during the years 1950 through 2010 approximately 14,000 victims have reported being sexually abused by priests and deacons (Vollman, 2012, p. 345; John Jay College, 2004; USCCB, 2003–2010). Although the last decade has brought to light what has been called the "child sexual abuse scandal" in the Catholic Church and exposed the magnitude of the problem to both the public and researchers, several high profile priest abuse cases in the 1980s and 1990s drew particular attention to the problem. For example, the former diocesan priest, John Geoghan, serving in the Archdiocese of Boston was accused of abusing over 130 young boys. The publicity surrounding the case precipitated the break of silence and flood of thousands of reports of hidden sexual abuse by priests from around the United States (Vollman, 2012, p. 345). Other cases of abuse by Catholic priests and sisters in Ireland, going back to the 1930s, similarly attracted national and international attention and added to the negative publicity including the views that "those charged with the task of modeling higher standards of behavior have been exposed as having engaged in behavior that is "vile" and abusive" (p. 347). In the spring of 2010, Pope Benedict XVI was accused of covering up allegations against a priest in his charge in 1980. As a result, media accounts have reported the problem of pedophile priests as "endemic" in the Catholic Church, and accused the church of a "long time cover-up of sexual abuse"(p. 347). Despite findings from the 2004 John Jay College study indicating "that only 4% of priests and deacons (approximately 4300) over five decades (1950–2002) had been formally charged, and that a majority (55%) of those accused had only one formal allegation" irreparable damage had been committed (John Jay College, 2004, p. 51; Vollman, 2012, p. 347).

Political or State Violence

Peter Iadicola claims that of all the various forms of institutional violence, "the violence of the police and military or state violence in general is the most easily recognized examples of institutional violence. The organizations of the state and those who have positions within are using violence to defend or extend the order" (2012, p. 13). Established power groups and recognized governments determine, to a large extent, which individuals are criminal, and in which circumstances violence is legitimate. They also consider which groups are considered terrorists, which acts are treasonous, and which citizens are insurgent threats, and which wars are just.

State violence is defined in an ideological context. Ideology refers to a body of doctrines, beliefs, or ideals that guide a group, class, or nation. An ideology represents the agreed upon conceptions of the "normal" or "ideal" social order (i.e., a presumed concept of justice). It presupposes a particular understanding of social existence, that is, how individuals socially construct their reality (Mannheim, 1936; Berger and Luckman, 1967). Ideology is used by powerful groups and nations to maintain their status, domination, and control, often by violent means, and may be used by less powerful groups, also by violent means, to attain a voice, equity, concession on issues, a place in the political decision-making process, or an edge or dominance over a rival group (Voigt, et al., 1994, pp. 378–379).

Protecting national security is a universal rationalization for state violence. For example, China referred to the Beijing students who demonstrated for democracy in 1989 in Tiananmen Square as counterrevolutionaries who, they claimed, were instigated by capitalist/imperialist agitators to overthrow the Chinese government. China summarily executed many of the leaders of the demonstration for treason. Other illustrations of governments acting against groups that they perceive to be threats to their national security can be found all over the world across all historical periods. For instance, the U. S. government has seen nothing wrong in sponsoring assassination attempts, coups, and violence against communist and socialist leaders and heads of state, in Latin America or against the Taliban regime or extremist Muslims in Afghanistan. All of these activities have been defined as serving the national security interests of the United States.

Iadicola and Shupe argue that there is really no way to comprehensively know the extent of state violence in the world today. It is sometimes difficult to differentiate legitimate or illegitimate forms of state violence. The most commonly referred to examples of extralegal forms of state violence or violence without justification or legitimization by the laws of a particular state include human rights violations in the form of torture and severe brutality, disappearances, genocide, and extrajudicial executions (2003, pp. 266–267). Even legitimate forms of state violence such as capital punishment executions, police use of deadly force, military actions, and covert counterintelligence operations are widely debated publically. We discuss this issue in greater detail when we consider the nature and forms of state and structural violence in Chapter 6.

Part 2: Corporate Violence: An In-Depth Analysis

Corporate violence may be defined as the preventable physical harm that is a consequence of the decisions made by legitimate organizations and their agents within the context of the organization's goals and operating culture. Anger, sexual jealousy, revenge, and reputational challenges, which are integral to so much conventional violence, are typically absent in corporate violence. Rather than being struck by the "heat of the moment," like many conventional violent law-breakers, corporate actors are consumed with "cold calculation" or unthinking conformity to their company's risky, sometimes dangerous, but nearly always accepted business practices. Financial goals are front and center for the company, specifically, cost cutting, profit making, time saving, and market competing. For company agents, job preserving, group conforming, life-style supporting or status climbing are motivations.

Harm and Blame in Corporate Violence

Despite the lack of direct physical contact with or emotional reaction to the victim, the physical harm caused by corporate violence can be as devastating as conventional crime, and is sometimes more widespread and insidiously enduring, as in cases where companies allow disease-provoking toxins to be released into the workplace, into the environment or into consumable products. The physical harm caused by corporate violence is as real as battering and can be quite consequential, even if it is often unseen or unknown at first. A case in point was documented by Jonathan Harr (1996) in his book, *A Civil Action*, which was later made into a movie. During the 1970s a cancer cluster occurred in Woburn, Massachusetts in which 28 children developed leukemia, which was the consequence of W.R. Grace & Co. and Beatrice Foods, Inc. illegally dumping chemical carcinogenic waste into abandoned wells that leached into the water supply. After a long civil trial, W.R. Grace settled with 8 plaintiffs in 1986 for $8 million, and both companies were ordered by the federal Environmental Protection Agency (EPA) to furnish money to its Superfund to clean up the sites. Two years later W.R. Grace pleaded guilty in criminal court to misleading the EPA and was fined $10,000 (Associated Press, 1988), a minuscule amount considering W.R. Grace has sales of over $2.5 billion and over 6,500 employees.

This was not the only contamination case involving W.R. Grace. The company operated a vermiculite mine and plant in Libby, Montana where 200 people died and hundreds were sickened by exposure to asbestos. In that case, W.R. Grace settled out of court for $1.75 billion, paying $250 million in 2008 and deferring payments of $1.5 billion from 2019 to 2033 (Reuters, 2008). In addition to the civil court charges, W.R. Grace and six of its executives were indicted by a Federal grand jury under the "knowing endangerment" provision of the Clean Water Act, but the defendants were either found not guilty or charges were dismissed, and the company agents avoided prison while the company avoided a large fine (Johnson, 2009; Reisch, 2009).

No doubt the slow death of a preventable cancer is a real and substantial physical harm whether it is criminalized or not, and corporate violence paints a broad stroke across society. While estimates vary, deaths in the U.S. workplace number over 4,000 while injuries and illnesses from work number around 4 million (Bureau of Labor Statistics, 2009); tainted, unsafe and harmful products in the marketplace number in tens of millions, 76 million for food contamination alone (Centers for Disease Control, 2009); and toxic pollution in the environment numbers in the billions of pounds of waste, some of it toxic, and some of it finding its way into public consumption (EPA, 2011).

Corporate Violence and Dangerous Consumer Products

Notwithstanding harm, pinning criminal blame on a company, particularly a multinational behemoth like W.R. Grace, is not straightforward or, in some cases, warranted. Many of the injuries and 4,350 fatal injuries in the workplace are accidental and not easily preventable. In the environment, some levels of burning, burying, and discharging of wastes and pollutants are permissible under the law. And some tainted or dangerous consumer products do slip into the marketplace without the knowledge of a company, and farther down the food processing chain, in restaurants and food handling activities (Tierno, 2004). Notwithstanding that possibility, "accident attribution" is rolled out often as a neutralization of blame by companies, largely because of the inherent issues involved in criminalizing corporately caused harm.

Consider the effects of the E-coli contamination of spinach that hit the U.S. in 2006. Many of the vegetables and fruit that are consumed, like meat products, are produced and packaged by a few large centralized companies. In this so called "vegetable-industrial complex" (Pollan, 2006), Natural Selection Foods LLC, with revenues over $400 million and over 1,000 employees, distributed, in 2006, over 26 million servings of packaged salad per week. Natural Selection Foods takes spinach (as well as other vegetables and fruits) from many fields—produce from 150 organic farmers in four states—and washes all of it together in water vats in a single plant, then packages it for distribution to supermarkets across the country and the world (Preston and Marshall, 2006). This centralization of production is efficient but it magnifies many times the effect of an E-coli contamination of just a few spinach heads. In 2006, that is exactly what happened in the United States. Contaminated spinach killed 3 people and sickened 200 others, several of whom had complications from kidney failure (Associated Press, 2007). Recently, in 2011, a similar bacterial contamination of vegetables in Europe killed 17 people and sickened many others.

The Centers for Disease Control and Prevention estimate that 5,000 people die, 300,000 are hospitalized and 76 million are sickened by food supply contamination every year (Pollan, 2006; Centers for Disease Control, 2009). The Emerging Pathogens Institute at the University of Florida estimates that food contamination costs the U.S. $14 billion in medical costs and lost earnings each year and that poultry contamination alone is responsible for an estimated 7,000 hospitalizations and for sickening 600,000 people (Zimmer, 2011).

There is certainly harm to consumers caused by food producing companies as there is harm to employees and the public from unsafe work sites and from toxins released into the environment. *The fundamental issue for considering this harm of violence and criminality is preventability.* Is the harm purely accidental, a mistake, an unusual error made in the process or is there provable blame, a pattern of behavior that is accepted by the organization, a punishable crime, caused by unrestricted carelessness, negligence, recklessness, knowledge or willfulness?

Certainly in the classic case of the Ford Pinto, prior knowledge of the dangers of the product was indisputable. The car was produced by the Ford Motor Co. and released for sale in September of 1970. It was prone to exploding in rear-end collisions at fairly low speeds, because a flaw in its design left the gas tank vulnerable to puncture. Ford engineers discovered the problem during the pretesting of the car, but Ford conspired to withhold the information from the public and refused to correct the problem, believing that civil suits from burn victims would be less than the cost of a recall. Essentially an economic decision trumped a moral one. Decision-makers in the company high and low were essentially reacting to the pressure placed on production by the company president, Lee Iacocca, who wanted a cheap subcompact car on the market (2,000 pounds at $2,000) as quickly as possible—25 months of production instead of the usual 43 months—to compete in the burgeoning subcompact car market. The managers were not about to contradict their president's time-frame even if it meant risking some customers' lives. Ford managers estimated that 180 persons would die and 180 would be seriously burned, and further estimated that civil suits would cost $50 million (a maximum of $200,000 per settlement) versus a recall that they believed would cost $137 million (Dowie, 1977, Table 2).

Ford's projections were far off the mark. Richard Grimshaw, who was badly burned and disfigured won a $128 million suit ($125 million in punitive damages), which Ford vigorously appealed. In addition, Ford fought the adoption of the fire safety standard in cars proposed by the National Highway Traffic Safety Administration (NHTSA). Eventually a recall was ordered of all 1971–1976 Ford Pintos and Mercury Bobcats in 1977, and Ford had its dealers make a relatively minor modification in each car to prevent explosions, which would have saved money and deaths if done years earlier (Dowie, 1977).

Ford was not out of the water yet. In 1978 it was the first multinational company to be indicted and charged in the U.S. with criminal negligence for the deaths of three teenagers in Elkhart County, Indiana. Ford's defense was able to get the judge to throw out critical evidence, including pictures of the girls who were burned to death in the accident. Ford was acquitted. While it would have faced a relatively small fine if convicted ($30,000) and while individual company agents avoided prosecution, it did signal the end of the perceived immunity of large corporations from criminal prosecution (Cullen, Maakestad, and Cavendar, 1987).

The Ford Pinto case points out the recurring issue of determining criminal blameworthiness in corporate violence cases even in those in which criminality appears obvious. This issue will be covered in more depth below, but first, let us lay out the ten most salient characteristics of corporate violence.

Ten Characteristics of Corporate Violence

Corporate violence contains these ten characteristics:

(1) Corporate violence causes physical harm and the threat of physical harm to persons in three major areas, consumer products, work conditions and the environment.

(2) Corporate violence is committed by company agents that have no direct physical contact or situational interaction with the victim.

(3) The victim of corporate violence is oftentimes unaware of the harm and its cause, as in cases where carcinogenic toxins, which are illegally disposed of by a company, affect the quality of air, the land and drinking water.

(4) The agents of corporate violence are typically not emotionally motivated to commit the crime. Their reasons are usually financially oriented, to ensure the company's profit and economic well-being by, for example, skirting safety and health measures, guidelines or laws. While the violence is committed to benefit

the company, individuals financially benefit from the success of the company; they keep their jobs or they move up the latter.

(5) The operative organizational culture of the company emphasizes profit over other values such as health and safety and thus facilitates, encourages or even coerces the problematical decision-making of corporate agents. The organizational culture is formed in interaction between the company and the political and economic environment in which it operates.

(6) Companies using modern technology can produce millions of pounds of toxic substances and millions of dangerous products, causing the scope of violent victimization to be far more widespread than in conventional street violence.

(7) Regulatory law and regulatory agencies are the main social control agents of corporate violence and thus sanctioning is more often in the form of administrative decisions such as consent decrees, compliance orders and civil actions, such as fines or monetary judgments, rather than criminal prosecution and prison.

(8) Determining individual criminal blameworthiness especially in large, complex, hierarchically organized companies, where there is a greater diffusion of responsibility and decision-making, is difficult. For significant criminal exposure, say misdemeanors or felonies, ordinarily there must exist some level of negligence or knowledge, some general intent. Evidence indicates that individuals who own and operate small companies are more likely to be criminally prosecuted and imprisoned. In large organizations, the company as a whole is more likely to be charged and sentenced to financial penalties, creating a structural bias in prosecution and punishment. For large companies, then, corporate violence, might be perceived as a "cost of doing business" that the company can bear.

(9) The importance of some corporations to the economic livelihood of a region can influence the charges and the severity of the punishment. Consider that a year after the most disastrous oil spills in the U.S., interest groups and many unemployed persons were clamoring for the restoration of oil drilling. The ban on deep water drilling was lifted and British Petroleum, which was responsible for the spill, quickly bid on well sites in the Gulf of Mexico, while oleaginous tar was still being cleaned up.

(10) The global nature of the economy and the transnational nature of large corporations lead some companies to exploit countries with less stringent regulatory systems. Corporate violence is more tolerated and less often punished in some countries abroad, allowing for the production and sale of dangerous products, (some banned in the U.S.), the existence of more unsafe worksites, and the disposal of greater quantities of toxic substances.

The Definition and Social Construction of Corporate Violence by Social Scientists

Social scientists trace the "discovery" of corporate crime to Edwin Sutherland, who was a trailblazer in defining the harmful acts of companies and their managerial class, the educated, respectable and trusted people of middle to high social status, as crime and

Box 4.1 The Most Dangerous Serial Corporate Killers

A poignant historical case of corporate violence is the Johns Manville Company's treatment of asbestos workers. From the 1930s to the 1970s thousands of workers in asbestos manufacturing and related jobs experienced the respiratory disease, asbestosis, which often led to lung cancer from years of breathing in irritating asbestos fibers without protective masks. The owners, managers and in-house scientists at Johns Manville Corporation knew for decades that their employees would suffer from work related illnesses that would significantly shorten their lives. Yet they did nothing to reduce the risks. They made a calculated decision to maintain their corporation's productivity, profit and competitiveness at the cost of their workers' well-being. The president of the company Lewis Brown and his brother and main attorney Vandiver Brown went further. They engaged in a cover up. As David Kotelchuck (1989) describes it, officials at Johns Manville either fired employees with work induced disabilities, usually older workers, replacing them with younger ones, or JM managers transferred them to "no dust" factory areas ("N.D." jobs as they were tagged in their files). JM officials sponsored their own medical research on asbestosis, and though they discovered, as had independent researchers during the same period, that asbestosis and lung cancers indeed existed at very high rates among asbestos workers, they criticized the independent studies, denied any linkage between asbestos and illness (arguing that diseases could have come from pre-existing conditions in workers) and prevented their employees' medical records from being used in epidemiological research until 1958. Lewis Brown is quoted as calling some managers, "a bunch of fools" for letting workers know they had asbestosis. And when asked if he seriously would rather see workers die than be notified of the dangers, he said, "We save a lot of money that way" (Kotelchuck, 1989, p. 202).

The intentionality of the Browns' decision making and the callousness of their opinions certainly are tied to the historical period. In the social context of the era, owners and corporate presidents operated as if companies were their fiefdoms, and workers were their subjects. They had little concern that their acts would be criminalized. Yet similar acts of corporate violence and subsequent denials of responsibility, mostly often without the openly callous statements about victims, repeat themselves in subsequent generations, often without criminalization. The most glaring case to follow asbestos was the cigarette menace to consumers.

Cigarettes, like asbestos, were linked to lung diseases and cancer. For asbestos the link was discovered in the 1930s, for cigarettes it was the 1950s. Like the asbestos companies, corporate cigarette makers thwarted civil suits, denied research findings, and resisted warning labels. Quite the contrary, the big manufacturers made cigarettes more addictive by increasing their nicotine content, and made them more attractive by deliberately marketing cigarettes to children, as in R.J. Reynolds', "Joe Camel" advertising campaign. Yet not one cigarette executive did any prison time for the increases in diseases and shortened lives in consumers. Rather, the companies paid civil judgments to cover the costs of medical care associated with lung diseases. The major tobacco companies Liggett Myers, R.J. Reynolds, Brown & Williamson, Lorillard, and Philip Morris, struck agreements with the states individually or in the the the Master Settlement Agreement (MSA) to establish a fund to pay medical costs incurred from smoking, but they received immunity from further action. Unfortunately, the litigation has failed to slow down the cigarette oligopolies from marketing and selling their products to millions of people in the global market. Over 400,000 people die from tobacco related illnesses in the U.S. alone (Brandt, 2009).

as a legitimate object of criminological research and theorizing. Sutherland called for explanations of crime that would include both white collar and street crime and that would be class neutral. He believed that two theories, differential association and social disorganization, could be applied to suite criminals as readily as to street criminals. From his presidential address to the American Sociological Society in 1939 Sutherland stated:

> Those who become white collar criminals generally start their careers in good
> neighborhoods and good homes, graduate from colleges with some idealism,
> and with little selection on their part, get into particular business situations in
> which criminality is practically a folkway, become inducted into that system of
> behavior just as into any other folkway.... Differential association culminates in
> crime because the community is not organized solidly against that behavior
> (Sutherland, 1940, p. 11).

Sutherland also argued that violations of administrative and regulatory laws such as those
covering restraint of trade, false advertising, and labor law violations were sufficient to
consider business acts as crimes (Sutherland, 1940; 1945; 1985). Some balked at Sutherland's
criminalization of legitimate businesses and his application of the notions of crime and
criminality to business acts because they saw them as "technical violations" of regulatory
law rather than, strictly speaking, criminal violations (Tappan, 1947). That resistance
continued decades later in a stinging rebuke by a sociologist, who referred to advocates
of criminalization of any number of harmful corporate acts as "moral entrepreneurs,"
and "corporate crusaders," who were more motivated by moral outrage and private
grievances than by social science (Shapiro, 1983).

At the diametrically opposite end, some social thinkers believed that Sutherland's
notion of crime was overly restrictive and that many other harmful, immoral, unethical
and dysfunctional acts of companies and their agents should be considered, at the very
least, "corporate deviance" (Clinard and Yeager, 1980; 1990; Ermann and Lundmann,
1982; Hills, 1987; Snider, 1993. For a discussion of this debate see Coleman, 1987; Green,
1991; Friedrichs, 2007). Notwithstanding the debate over how restrictive or how
expansionist the definition of white collar crime is, few if any social thinkers doubted
that some business decisions could cause serious harm to individuals, and that many of
those decisions were made with the knowledge, agency and approval of company agents,
and were thus not inadvertent mistakes or unpreventable accidents, whether or not they
broke specific criminal laws. Indeed Shapiro (1983), who earlier labeled some social
thinkers "corporate crusaders" for overreaching on corporate criminalization, conducted
extensive research on Wall Street stock scams, specifically Equity Funding Corporation,
describing the lying, cheating, white collar corporate swindlers as "wayward capitalists."
Apparently some have greater insight into when the criminalization shoe fits.

Subsequent generations of scholars delineated two types of white collar crime, individual
and organizational. Individual white collar crime is committed for personal benefit and is
oftentimes done at the expense of the company. Embezzlement is an example. Organizational
white collar crime is committed by agents to benefit the organization and, and fortuitously,
to benefit themselves. Organizational crime is usually consistent with the company's
ideology, operational practices and past actions (Clinard and Quinney, 1973, Clinard and
Yeager, 1980; Kramer, 1983). W.R. Grace's illegal disposal of chemical waste is a good
example. Schrager and Short (1978, pp. 411–412) define organizational crimes as:

> ... illegal acts of omission or commission of an individual or a group of individuals
> in a legitimate formal organization in accordance with the operative goals of the
> organization, which have serious physical or economic impact on employees,
> consumers or the general public.

Similar to Sutherland, Clinard and Yeager (1980; 1990) argued that definitions of corporate
crime should include administrative and civil cases because companies are more commonly
adjudicated for harmful acts in that manner rather than in criminal court. In this vein,
Stuart Hills (1987, p. vii) proffered a definition of corporate violence as the:

... actual harm and risk of harm inflicted on consumers, workers, and the general public as a result of decisions by corporate executives or mangers, from corporate negligence, the quest for profits at any cost, and willful violations of health, safety, and environmental laws.

In Hills's definition, notice the inclusion of regulatory laws and negligence as well as willful violations. A definition like this begs the question: When is corporate violence truly criminal? Since the violent acts of companies are usually done at a distance without the presence of malicious intent, they may be perceived as unpreventable accidents, technical violations or civilly actionable cases, but not crime. This is very evident in larger companies, where diffusion of responsibility and decision-making are common. In smaller companies malice is still absent, but identifying a culpable company agent is more clear-cut, and thus they may be subject to more frequent criminalization.

Social Construction of Corporate Violence in Law

Usually for an act to be considered a crime, harm is not sufficient; some form of blame, responsibility, or intent must also exist. Since corporate violence typically contains no "specific intent to harm," regulatory law addresses the issue of criminal blame by applying the legal notions of "general intent," "strict liability" and "vicarious liability" (Bucy, 1992; Androphy, 2007). The legal principle of general intent allows the state to charge and prosecute crimes against organizational agents and the company itself when negligent, reckless, knowing and willful decisions and acts lead to harm or death. Regulatory law also establishes strict liability offenses in which liability exists for any violations even if negligence, recklessness or knowledge is absent. Crimes can include failure to keep adequate records, failure to notify, and failure to follow a consent decree. Strict liability offenses are typically punished less severely. In addition regulatory law has long adopted the principle from civil law of vicarious liability, *respondeat superior,* i.e., an organization can be held liable for the actions of its employees. While corporations are not persons in the literal sense of the word they are persons under the law for certain rights and responsibilities. In environmental law the organization can be charged criminally not only for technical violations, but also for felonies that require a "person's" state of mind, such as knowledge, negligence, and knowing endangerment. For instance, under the Clean Water Act, knowing endangerment, placing a person in imminent danger of death or serious bodily injury, can elicit felony charges and severe sentences for both the individual and the company. The Clean Water Act also has a provision for identifying a "responsible corporate officer" who can be held criminally liable for harm caused. Individuals can receive imprisonment for up to 15 years, and companies can be sentenced to fines of up to $1 million per count. Companies can also be debarred, de-licensed, placed on organizational probation, ordered to clean up polluted areas, or ordered to publish negative publicity ads. Company agents, besides prison, can be sentenced to home confinement, probation, restitution, or to pay cleanup costs (Clean Water Act, 1992).

Philosophical arguments about whether or not a company is being overly anthropomorphized with human decision-making traits has not stopped the law from keeping pace with organizations, which, like societies and institutions, have an existence, culture and structure, created by but separate from any particular individuals, and which should be held responsible and subjected to appropriate interventionist strategies such as restructuring, deterrence, punishment, and prevention. The collective liability of organizations, particularly businesses, is virtually taken-for-granted in civil law, and is becoming more common in criminal law, through regulatory statutes. Criminologists have for decades considered organizations, particularly businesses, a cause of criminality, and we will discuss this shortly.

Much like general intent violations in conventional crime, such as involuntary manslaughter, a company's gross negligence, recklessness, or willing and knowing disregard of the risks that it imposes on others warrants criminal sanctioning both of the company and its agents (Barrile, 1993), even though some find that criminalization is encroaching into the territory of civil law and that civil penalties would suffice for actions that cause harm but have slippery blameworthiness at best (Coffee, 1992; Mann 1992; Dimento, 1993). Still, proving corporate criminality in court is not as straightforward as experiencing corporate violence. The townspeople of Libby, Montana disappointedly discovered that fact in the trial outcome of W.R. Grace.

Vital to successful criminal prosecutions is technical expertise in investigating and preparing a corporate crime case and also overcoming the jurisdictional boundaries among federal, state, and local agencies to induce communication and cooperation to police, identify, report, and prosecute corporate violence (Benson and Cullen, 1998). Larger companies get a break because of the difficulty in identifying a culprit and because they can readily negotiate with regulators, paying for recalls, cleanups, or expensive compliance requirements, most often averting a criminal trial. Smaller companies are likely to receive more typical criminal prosecution. Differential treatment of companies based on size and economic status indicates a class or structural bias in prosecuting corporate violence (Goff and Reasons, 1978; Hagan and Parker, 1985; Yeager, 1987).

Given such bias, one wonders whether the term corporate violence is itself somewhat of a misnomer. Most companies are small. In the U.S. there are over 27 million companies, about 6 million have employees, 89% of them have fewer than 20 employees, and 79% have fewer than 10 employees. Most firms are owner-operated, though middle to large firms (500 or more employees) employ 51% of all workers (U.S. Census Bureau, 2011). The overwhelming odds are that small companies will be charged and prosecuted merely from their prevalence in the economy. And the evidence does show that smaller companies are charged more severely (Goff and Reasons, 1978; Hagan and Parker, 1985; Yeager, 1987) and that there is a much higher percentage of upper status employees sentenced for corporate crime than lower status (Wheeler, Weisburd, and Bode, 1982; Barrile and Slone 2005; Barrile and Slone, 2012). However, the truth is that smaller firms are not only more numerous but they relinquish blameworthy culprits more readily than firms insulated by layers of bureaucracy. There are few or no employees to whom to diffuse responsibility and no "vice presidents for going to prison." Thus, much of the social control of corporate violence by regulatory agencies and prosecutors is of small companies, of owner/operators and individuals, the petit-bourgeoisie. When the moral hammer of the criminal law swings it often misses the bigs and comes down harder on the smalls. Nevertheless, there is an established statutory underpinning for criminalizing corporate violence. Organizations cannot avoid criminal blame. And the bias in sentencing is due more to legal technicalities than to preferential treatment.

Social Construction of Corporate Violence in the Mass Media and the Public

The public has no difficulty perceiving corporate misdeeds as serious as street crime (Cullen, Maakesstad, and Cavender, 1987). Across the board in surveys, white collar crimes, such as embezzlement, credit card fraud, and contract fraud are rated higher in seriousness by respondents than motor vehicle theft (NWCCC, 2006). Corporate violence is ranked similarly by the public. From the National White Collar Crime Center's (NWCCC) survey, when asked to compare two scenarios, one in which a store owner sells a package of meat that is known to be bad, causing a serious illness in a customer, to a scenario in which an armed robber causes a serious injury during a holdup, 69% of the sample rated the business violence as more serious or as serious as armed robbery, only 36% rated the armed robbery as more serious (Rebovich and Layne, 2000, p. 6; Piquero, Carmichael, and Piquero, 2008).

Given the recent misdeeds of organizations, such as the recent mortgage origination fraud financial disaster, Bernard Madoff's billion dollar Ponzi scheme, BP's explosion and oil discharge in the Gulf of Mexico, and Chinese companies' tainted baby formula and pet food, the U.S. public would have little difficulty in interpreting harmful corporate acts as crime. Outside of his family, it is doubtful that anyone shed a tear for Madoff when he was thrown in prison.

The news media serve as a major source of information for crime and their amount and type of coverage can frame the discourse on crime. The mass media can play the role of a claims-maker (a person or entity that defines or constructs an "issue" or "social problem" from an otherwise random set of brute facts, incidents of harm or tragedy). The news media plays this role either "secondarily" by streaming the prevailing views of officials such as criminal justice system personnel, politicians and "experts" on causes of crime, or they can play the role "primarily" by how they spin the story of the case, what interpretations they weave together and what they emphasize as important (Best, 1991). Mass media can thus help to create a "moral panic," or a huge public concern about an issue that they make claims about, such as drug or serial killer "epidemics" (Jenkins, 1994). Entertainment media can play a similar role in their character portrayals of criminals and crime fighters and in their underlying themes of crime in fictional movies and television programs (Jenkins, 1994; Rafter, 2000). George Gerbner and his associates claimed to have found a "cultivation effect" of violent entertainment media on television viewers; i.e., a mainstreaming and cultivation of a "mean world syndrome" in which heavy viewers of television and violent films would exaggerate their risk of violence and favor more law and order protection from the state (Gerbner and Gross, 1976; Gerbner, et al., 2002).

Thus it is with corporate violence. The mass media can socially construct acts of corporately caused harm as violence and crime, or neither, by its descriptions, explanations and interpretations of cases, real or fictional. In "describing" cases the media set the agenda on what is important to cover — which cases, which details, which role players. In "explaining" cases, they identify the consequences and causes of the incidents. And in "interpreting" cases they try to show the societal significance of the incidents and which policies would prevent or deter the behavior from occurring (Best, 1991).

Whether or not the media speak with a unified voice is debatable and certainly the content is affected by the business of media as much as by the expertise, values and political leanings, right or left, of writers and journalists (Gans, 1979). It is debatable how much the mass media influence the public's perception of corporate violence and on policy-makers' treatment of it. The empirical research is mixed on the relationship between conventional violent media and behavior and attitudes. Research show little to no relationship between media content and violent behavior (Freedman, 2002) and shows a qualified relationship between media and fear of crime (Gerbner and Gross, 1976; Gerbner, et al., 2002) that may actually be related to self-selective uses and individually relevant interpretations of media content (Barrile 1984; Chiricos, Paget, and Gertz, 2000).

Unfortunately much of the "study" of media and crime is dominated by speculation about what audiences perceive. Media critics too often perform subjective and ideological content analyses claiming that mass media is a conduit for the corporate state, stigmatizing powerless law-breakers while letting the corporation and the state off of the hook. This conclusion flies in the face of surveys of public attitudes, which clearly show a growing public enmity towards corporate misdeeds. The conclusion also weakened by recent research showing the increase of news coverage of corporate crime over the last few decades (Maguire, 2002). Even methodologically sound studies, producing a wealth of information have trouble avoiding ideologically tinged conclusions. The analysis of the media coverage of the Imperial Food Products fire is a case in point. The company is an emblematic example of corporate violent crime in the workplace, but it is also an example of how criminologists can come to different conclusions on a case, one blaming the media and the other the state.

Corporate Violence in the Workplace, the Fire at Imperial Food Products, Inc.

On September 3, 1991 in the rural town of Hamlet, North Carolina a chicken processing plant, Imperial Food Products Inc., caught on fire killing 25 and injuring 55 company employees. A faulty hydraulic line, which was filled with flammable fluid, was rigged-up by workers trying to temporarily fix it while keeping up the pace of production that was demanded by the owner. The fix did not hold. It burst, leaking fluid that quickly vaporized and caught fire from gas burners below, which were heating a vat of bubbling oil used for cooking chicken parts that caught on fire as well. Thick smoke spewed throughout the plant and sent workers blindly scrambling for their lives. Many of the workers were trapped inside the plant, largely because the company's owner and operator, Emmett Roe, ordered his son and a plant manager to padlock one main set of exit doors to prevent employee thefts and unapproved breaks. Other doors were either locked or blocked that day. While some workers were able to break through the locked doors, other workers huddled together in the walk-in freezer to try to escape the flames, but most of those workers were asphyxiated by smoke inhalation. Workers could be heard screaming and pounding on doors by a witness that day. Investigators found scratch marks on the inside of the doors. Prior to the fire, the plant was in miserable condition. It had no windows, no plant sprinkler system, no escape plan and no safety inspection done on it for many years. The forced pace of production, the poor condition of the plant, and the inherent dangerousness of large vats of hot cooking oil were a perfect storm for a fire. As if a harbinger of the disaster to come, there were several prior small fires at the plant, some before it was owned by Roe. In 1983, after one such fire, the local fire department required Roe to install a carbon dioxide driven extinguisher above the vats. During the fire that day, the extinguisher delayed the oil being set ablaze, allowing time for most of the 200 workers to escape death (Smothers, 1991a; Smothers, 1991b; Aulette and Michalowski, 1993/1995; Wright, Cullen and Blankenship, 2001; Wright, 2007).

Before the fatal fire, North Carolina's Occupational Safety and Health Administration struck an agreement with the federal OSHA to perform its own state run safety inspections, a task made more difficult because of state budget cutbacks, inspector layoffs that were responsible for inspections across the 150,000 worksites in North Carolina. Inspectors claim they performed 2,000 inspections per year, but that they did not have the staff to do more (Smothers, 1991a).

The owner/operator, Emmett Roe, pleaded guilty to two counts of involuntary manslaughter, saving his son Brad and his plant manager John Hair from prosecution. Roe received one of the highest criminal sentences for corporate violence, 19 years of prison. However, because the judge issued a sentence of just under 20 years, Roe was eligible for parole in 3 years and served only 4 years of the sentence before he was released (Wright, 2007). Roe was also fined over $800,000, and insurance was to pay $16 million to the families.

Researching the media coverage of the tragedy, Wright, Cullen, and Blankenship (2001) performed a content analysis of 10 national newspapers, and found that, unlike conventional crime, few of the news stories, which covered the Imperial Food case, described the tragedy as criminal until after the government began pursuing it. The news stories emphasized the harm experienced by the workers, their families, and the community. The stories also tended to blame the regulatory agencies for the fire, stating that they did not do their job. But the papers initially steered away from considering the criminality of the owner.

The authors identified three main periods of news coverage. In the first period, the first week of the crime, only one line per news story mentioned a crime compared to 7 lines for regulatory agencies and 11 lines for worker harm. During the second period, after the first week, the mentions of crime increased to 3 lines per story, but the number of stories covering the case decreased by about 70%. Finally in the last period, immediately after the criminal conviction, 5 lines per news story were devoted the criminality of the owner, but by this time the number of stories covering the case had decreased by 82%. While the case led to very serious criminal charges, 25 counts of involuntary manslaughter, and one of the most punitive prison sentences ever for corporate violence, the newspapers, they argue, showed little interest in covering the conviction and sentence. The authors aver that once the reporters developed their "hook," their theme of regulatory breakdown as a cause, other issues as well as interest waned. The authors say the media, "showed little consciousness that corporate violence might be seen as a crime" (p. 32). Indeed the story faded in the newspapers the longer it progressed.

The authors focus on national media reports, however, underestimated the media attention by selecting newspapers for their sample, by availability and convenience, thus failing to include the local news near Hamlet, North Carolina, for which the crime would have paramount relevance and importance. Was this really a case of the news media ignoring the criminality of corporate violence or rather that the appropriate media were not sampled?

The authors accuse the news media of steering away from the violent and criminal nature of the tragedy, inferring that they did so because they are biased in favor of the powerful business class and against the powerless conventional criminal class, which is stigmatized relentlessly. The media's role may be more complex than what the authors' explanation may first suggest.

Organizational Culture as a Cause of Corporate Violence

As we mentioned above, organizations may sometimes seem overly anthropomorphized or reified. Do they really have a personality? Do they really act or decide anything apart from individuals? But the power of the organization, like the power of any social institution or society itself, is evident in its effects on the groups and individuals that comprise it, and their effect on it.

Companies can possess a "criminogenic organizational culture," a set of norms that lead to crime. While no legitimate company will state publicly in its policies and procedures that occasional violations of regulatory statutes are tolerated or rewarded if they meet the

Box 4.2 Organizational Causes of Corporate Violence: Another Look at the Imperial Fire

Social scientists have argued for an integrated approach to explain corporate crime, one that combines three levels of analysis, the "social structure"—for instance the political economy, competition in the economic sector, the influence of the state, the social environment of the organization; the "meso-structure"—for instance the organizational structure, culture and processes, its values and goals, its diffusion of responsibility, its criminogenic characteristics; and "individual or interpersonal" characteristics—for instance how individuals interpret organizational goals, make day-to-day decisions and circumscribe their thinking to the bounded rationality of the organization (Needleman and Needleman, 1979; Coleman, 1987; Braithwaite, 1989; Vaughan, 1999; Friedrichs, 2007).

The social structure is a key to the "state-corporate crime theory," which has been used to explain the Imperial Food Products fire. The theory assumes that the economic and political interests of the state and corporations are compatible, and the state, while appearing to keep businesses honest with its regulatory regime, is ultimately concerned about economic productivity. Sectors of the economy, and companies competing within it, which are perceived as crucial to jobs, products, energy and revenue production, may be more protected when they violate the rules than are conventional law-breakers. As a result, the theory contends, the state might either help companies commit violations of law, *state initiated corporate crime*, or it might aid them by deliberate inaction, by failing to furnish statutory safeguards, by failing to financially support regulatory agencies or by purposely withholding resources from them, *state facilitated corporate crime* (Aulette and Michalowski, 1993; Kramer, Michalowski and Kauzlarich, 2002, pp. 271–272). In state facilitated corporate crime "agency capture" often occurs, that is a regulatory agency, under-supported by the state, is influenced by the economic interests and leverage of the company, and if large, by its bureaucratic and legal complexity. There is pressure on the regulatory agency from the political system to negotiate with or, worse, tolerate a company's technical violations of regulations.

Judy Aulette and Raymond Michalowski (1993) claim that this is exactly what occurred in the case of Imperial Food Products, which was a main employer in Hamlet, and part of an economic sector, the chicken-processing business, that was the number one industry in North Carolina, exceeding even the tobacco industry. Applying the theory to the Imperial fire, the authors maintain that the state of North Carolina significantly contributed to the crime because of its antiunion, antiregulatory political ideology and policies, which promoted a laissez-faire approach to businesses. The state politics, for the most part, rejected interventionism on health and safety issues considering it deleterious for business and an impediment of economic growth. Consistent with this ideology, the state substantially slashed the budget and personnel of state regulatory agencies, and stabbed deeper when it signed an agreement with the federal Occupational Safety and Health Administration to do its own inspections, such as they were, even returning money to OSHA for inspections it did not perform. This "hands-off" approach to business practices, allowed Imperial's owner/operator, Emmett Roe, not only to flout existing safety laws but also to repudiate even the most marginal commonsense notions of what comprised a dangerous, unhealthy worksite.

Roe could be blatantly unethical as well as criminal. In essence, he was able to treat his workers as if they were 19th Century prisoners hired out to a work boss. The conditions of employment to him were irrelevant because detection and punishment were nonexistent, unless of course a tragedy occurred, as it did.

Aulette & Michalowski focus on the political environment, the social structure, implicating many agencies that simply abandoned their obligations to worker safety, including the governor, the state legislature, the state OSHA, the county inspectors, the local fire department, federal OSHA and the US Department of Agriculture, which, incidentally, knew of the problematical locked exits at Imperial through a regional inspector, who did nothing because he believed he lacked jurisdictional authority to intervene. Each of the agencies, they contend, turned a blind eye to the conditions that existed at Imperial and other businesses across the state, effectively privileging capital over labor, and business interests over the safety of workers, the public and the environment. The authors argue that these agencies facilitated the tragedy by "omission," by not performing their expected roles as social control agents and protectors of health and safety.

For Aulette and Michalowsi (1993/1995) the state was as culpable in the Imperial Food Products fire as the company owner. In their words:

> In the case of the Hamlet disaster, the critical intersections were between a private business, Imperial Food, and several government agencies at the federal level (US-OSHA and the USDA), at the state level (NC-OSHA, the office of the governor, and the state legislature), and at the local level (the county building inspectors and the city of Hamlet fire department). For a variety of reasons each of these agencies, by omission — that is, by failing to perform the control functions assigned to them — made possible the continuation of the hazardous conditions at the Imperial plant in Hamlet that led to the deaths of 25 workers (pp. 181–182).

Their conclusion is remarkably close to what the national media reported about the Imperial Food fire, though the media was much narrower in its focus and criticism. What Emmet Roe did was, by the reckoning of the courts, criminologists and the public, "criminal," even if the national media was cautious about calling it a crime. The more important issue, especially given the authors' analysis, is that there were many Emmett Roes in North Carolina, and in states with similar political policies, demonstrating that corporate violence will be common if the state relinquishes its obligation to protect and punish health and safety violations.

Besides the political environment, and with an eye toward an integrated theoretical approach, the Imperial Food Products case is amenable to the strain, opportunity, and rational choice theories. In a billion dollar industry, the chicken-processing sector is highly competitive, creating the financial strain motivating the crime. The criminal opportunity for the owner to cut costs by pushing production and skirting safety rules, his "innovation" as Robert Merton (1938) would say was readily available. Workers from Hamlet depended on Imperial Food for their livelihood and were unlikely to contradict the owner's orders to hurriedly patch the fluid line, and to lock the exit doors, particularly considering that their complaints fell on the regulators' deaf ears. Roe was thus able to pass the risk of unsafe work conditions onto his employees and benefit from the savings. Finally, with the low level of regulatory supervision, the infinitesimally low level of punishment of company violators in the state, and the payoff in profits from saving money on safety, the owner evidently "rationally" rated the benefits of his rule-breaking above the costs of punishment. He miscalculated. And miscalculations are a common feature in corporate violence cases. They are part of the organizational characteristics and cognitive decision making of organizational employees the other aspects of an integrated explanation.

---

ultimate goal of capital accumulation, decision-making that breaks the law develops informally, interpersonally, occupationally, and often routinely as part of an operating organizational culture.

Gilbert Geis (1967/1977) found exactly this phenomenon in his study of the restraint of trade scandal in the heavy electrical equipment sector in 1961. The managers and vice presidents of General Electric and Westinghouse along with other companies conspired to fix prices and rig bids on contracts so as to stabilize any uncertainties in the market — the immediate economic environment of the company. They took turns rotating the "lowest" bids among themselves, naming the process, the "phases of the moon." Fictitious names and codes were used among them as well. Their stealth was eventually uncovered and four vice presidents, two division managers and one sales manager served short jail sentences while nearly $2 million in fines were issued.

Geis found four major elements as causes of the crime. First, the employees perceived an unpredictable, competitive market and believed that the company would approve of their strategy to control the market for the company's sake. Secondly, the employees believed that they would be rewarded for improving the company's bottom line. Thirdly, the employees had a set of rationalizations and neutralizations for their actions, including: "All we did was recover costs." "I thought it was part of my duty to do so." "If I didn't do it I thought someone else would." "Illegal? Yes, but not criminal." All of which minimized their sense of doing deviance. Fourthly, the employees assessed that there was little regulatory or criminal justice system intervention in such activities. They counted on the usual agency capture to cover for them.

Geis tapped the crux of organizational culture and its contribution to corporate wrong-doing. As illegal practices were initiated by employees from top to bottom over time to deal with the vagaries of the market, the company tolerated decisions and practices that worked, despite their deviations from regulation and law, and they became part of the informal values and operating norms of the company, the ways of conducting work and business, the organizational culture, complete with neutralizations of blame.

Thus, performance pressures in organizations and the perceived benefits of deviance can affect the decision-making of employees who may consider rule-breaking as acceptable, especially when the payoff is clear and the regulators are nowhere to be seen. In the Imperial Food case, there undoubtedly was such an organizational culture developed by the owner and his two closest mangers that tolerated extremely risky decisions and behavior, such as blocked exits and hastily patched pipes, which aided the pace of production, but seriously compromised the workers' safety.

Is There a Subculture of Corporate Violence?

No doubt group dynamics affect violence and criminality. In his classic study, Marvin Wolfgang discovered a "subculture of violence" among a cohort of chronic violent lawbreakers in Philadelphia, who learned to accept alternative norms regarding the use of violence and who perceived violent threats and challenges in others to a much greater extent than the rest of society. They did not feel guilty about using violence and did not perceive it as deviant in certain contexts. They were responsible for the bulk of the robberies and homicides in the city (Wolfgang, 1958; Wolfgang and Ferracuti, 1967; Wolfgang, Figlio, and Sellin, 1987). While the subculture of violence has its critics, revisionists and adapters, and this is certainly not the venue to debate it, the theory is roughly paralleled in legitimate organizations in which the violent consequences of employees' decisions are "normalized" or "routinized," such that deviation from societal rules is not perceived as deviant. Like the subculture of violence, in some organizations, cheating in competition, lying to regulators and accepting risks of harm to others are subcultural norms that achieve societally accepted monetary goals and status illegitimately. The organizational subculture embraces materialism without morality, productivity without ethics, and operating procedures without a principled concern for the harmful consequences to others.

Recent High Profile Cases of Corporate Violence

Some organizational cultivation of a subculture of corporate violence particularly when it serves the ultimate survival goals of the company, is not adequately controlled by the society, and is perceived as relatively "normal" operating procedures in the field. A president's commission alluded to these points in 1986 regarding the Challenger Space Shuttle disaster; Diane Vaughan (1997) confirmed them in her research a few years later.

The Challenger and Columbia Disasters

On January 28, 1986 the Challenger with seven crew members aboard, including for the first time a schoolteacher, Christa McAuliffe, was launched, but shattered into pieces a little over a minute after lift-off, killing all aboard. The tragedy grounded the space program for nearly two years. The Presidential Commission on the Space Shuttle Challenger Accident (the Rogers Commission) stated that the O-rings on the right solid rocket booster failed to seal hot gases, because cold weather that day compromised them, and that managers from NASA and the Marshall Space Flight Center approved of the launch despite reservations raised by some of the engineers at Morton Thiokol, a main subcontractor, whose managers conceded to the managers at NASA, waiving launch delays for the Challenger as they had for previous flights related to checks on the O-rings. More damning, managers at Marshall knew of the issues with the O-rings for years, but since previous flights were successful, they did not even officially write-up waivers of launch constrains for the O-rings, which were considered a "criticality 1" issue, the highest level of concern. NASA's Flight Readiness Review system did not record the oral waivers on 6 previous occasions. In the commissioners' words Marshall allowed:

> … six consecutive launch constraint waivers prior to 51-L, permitting it to fly without any record of a waiver, or even of an explicit constraint. Tracking and continuing only anomalies that are "outside the data base" of prior flight allowed major problems to be removed from and lost by the reporting system. (The Presidential Commission on the Space Shuttle Challenger Accident, 1986, Chapter 6, p. 148).

Adding to the pressure to launch, NASA had planned to increase the number of shuttle flights from nine in 1985, which was itself a strain on resources and parts replacement, to 14 in 1986 and projected 24 by 1990. The commission believed this to be unsupportable. One of the commissioners referred to the risk-acceptance attitude of the managers as playing "Russian roulette." NASA and Thiokol accepted escalating risk apparently because they "got away with it last time" (The Presidential Commission on the Space Shuttle Challenger Accident, 1986, chapter 6, p. 148).

In her analysis Vaughan (1996; 1997) finds that the commission's explanation of the Challenger disaster unfairly heaped most of the blame onto middle managers from Marshall Space Flight Center, as if they were solely responsible for creating the organizational culture underlying the risky decision-making. Vaughan contends that three main elements affect risky, disaster producing decisions in organizations: (1) the broader political economic environment; (2) the bureaucratic structure and processes of the organization; and (3) the technical culture (the occupational ideology and individual cognitive processes of the company agents) (Vaughan, 1996; 1997; 1999).

First, on the political economic environment, NASA was dependent on Congress and the president for continued funding and over time politicians had come to see the space program as less experimental and more operational, creating a resource strain. It was NASA higher-ups not middle managers that wanted to routinize shuttle flights to appeal to Congress and businesses by taking civilians on board and furnishing transportation for private business equipment. Second, NASA is hierarchically organized with more than 16,000 employees and several times more subcontractor employees. Because of its federal funding and the intrinsic dangers of the operation, it is intensely procedure- and rule-oriented to the extent that Vaughan calls it "bureaupathological," that is, rules often interfere with reasonable decision-making. Rules often impede common sense hunches about safety and become an obstacle to professionals and skilled employees. Third, middle managers and engineers were not "macho risk takers." They were concerned during every take-off, but the pressures from higher-ups to launch and the technological intricacies involved in the job, influenced their assessments of risk and danger. What was the standard for O-ring performance? If damage occurred to O-rings on previous flights, but the flights succeeded did that indicate an acceptable condition? Once the shuttle was considered "operational," money for testing was withheld unless a significant danger to safety could be proved, making it more difficult to justify launch delays.

It appears that the commercialization of NASA affected the organizational culture such that mistakes in judgment on safety became more common; risk and danger were redefined, bounded by organizational goals and, to those on the inside, risk acceptance appeared rational. In Vaughan's words (1997, p. 16):

> In terms of individual accountability, middle managers were, of course, responsible. But their isolation in the spotlight deflected attention from the responsibility of top decision makers who made political bargains, established goals, allocated resources, and made other key decisions that altered both the structure and culture of the agency.... The emphasis on middle managers also obscured from the public the truly experimental nature of the technology, its unpredictability under even the best of circumstances, and the logical possibility of another failure.

For Vaughan the structural and cultural elements affecting NASA exist in most organizations, the political economy, and bureaucratic structure and occupational decision-making, and can lead to the toleration of high levels of risk, mistakes and misconduct as long as the organizational goals are satisfied. Vaughan calls this the "dark side of organizations," we call it here the subculture of corporate violence. And her projection above that the experimental and unpredictable nature of the technology could lead to another disaster was prophetic because the subculture resiliently reseeded itself 17 years later, even after the implementation of an "independent" safety committee in NASA, when the Columbia Space Shuttle disintegrated upon reentry on January 28, 2003.

As if the Challenger disaster déjà vu, employees minimized or ignored risks of obvious dangers, obvious at least retrospectively. This time it was pieces of foam insulation that broke from the external tank on take-off and hit Columbia's wing. Columbia had 28 previous successful flights, and since tiles broke free in earlier flights and employees simply replaced them, organizational agents were able to trivialize both the danger and established safety rules, and routinize the practice of mending and sending Columbia back into space, using the successful flights as evidence that their risky assessments were appropriate. Again as with Challenger, all seven of the crew members died. Again the shuttle was put on hold, but now the program would end with Atlantis in 2011. Again, there was an investigation, and this time it pointed directly to the risk acceptance attitude in the organizational culture that circumvented obvious safety issues. Again, an accident investigation zeroed in on middle managers. In the words of the investigators from the Columbia Accident Investigation Board (CAIB) (2003, p. 181):

The Columbia accident is an unfortunate illustration of how NASA's strong cultural bias and its optimistic organizational thinking undermined effective decision-making. Over the course of 22 years, foam strikes were normalized to the point where they were simply a "maintenance" issue—a concern that did not threaten a mission's success. This oversimplification of the threat posed by foam debris rendered the issue a low-level concern in the minds of Shuttle managers.... Even after it was clear from the launch videos that foam had struck the Orbiter in a manner never before seen, Space Shuttle Program managers were not unduly alarmed.... More importantly, learned attitudes about foam strikes diminished management's wariness of their danger. The Shuttle Program turned 'the experience of failure into the memory of success.'

The CAIB pointedly implicated the deviant "learned attitudes" in NASA's organizational culture, particularly the acceptance of safety risks, which affected the decisions of employees attitudes about which regulations to follow loosely or strictly and which dangers to deny or trivialize. But like the investigation of the Challenger, the influence of the political economy, and the organizational structure, process, goals and rules, directed as it was by the executive level management, took a back seat to the focus on the culture and decision-making of middle to lower level employees. Evidently, the larger and more complex the organization is, the greater the diffusion of responsibility, or more accurately "consolidation of responsibility" in the middle, where disaster can be attributed to an "accident" caused by the mistakes of an entrenched, enculturated cadre of employees.[1]

The BP Disaster: Employee Safety and Environmental Destruction

The same "accident attribution" occurred in the British Petroleum disaster in the Gulf of Mexico in which 11 workers died and 17 were injured, and thousands of square miles of the Gulf were polluted. It was an incident remarkably similar in nature to the space shuttle disaster. A presidential commission (National Commission on the BP Deepwater Horizon Oil Spill and Offshore Drilling, 2011) found that employees of three companies BP, Halliburton and Transocean, made excessively risky decisions largely because of company pressures to cut costs and promote production. And further that there was agency capture in the deep-water oil-drilling sector because the U.S. had underfunded the regulatory regime.

The state was duplicitous in the mind of the commissioners. It espoused environmental protection in some areas (the EPA is one of the most interventionistic agencies) but promoted a policy of energy independence by allowing rampant oil extraction in other areas, such as the Gulf, with a practically inert regulator, the Minerals Management Service. The state supported businesses in the oil extraction sector with tax write-offs, economic incentives, and weak enforcement, which contributed to the high risk acceptance in their organizational cultures. In the Commission's words (Chapter. 3, p. 56):

Any revenue increases dependent on moving drilling further offshore and into much deeper waters came with a corresponding increase in the safety and environmental risks of such drilling. Those increased risks, however, were not matched by greater, more sophisticated regulatory oversight. Industry regularly and

1. Karp and Yoels (1976) coined the term "consolidation of responsibility" to describe how college students typically rely on a few talkers to carry the classroom discussion.

intensely resisted such oversight, and neither Congress nor any of a series of presidential administrations mustered the political support necessary to overcome that opposition. Nor, despite their assurances to the contrary, did the oil and gas industry take the initiative to match its massive investments in oil and gas development and production with comparable investments in drilling safety and oil-spill containment technology and contingency response planning in case of an accident.

The stakes were high for the government not only in energy policy but in money. From 2005 to 2010 the federal government received about $50 billion in lease money from extraction businesses and, with revenues from royalties; the MMS was processing $20 billion per year in revenues. The commission called it a "culture of revenue maximization in the government." As exploration increased, the diligence of MMS's inspections waned from its peak of over 7,000 in 1994 to under 5,000 in 2009, and its unannounced inspections plummeted from a peak of 45% of all inspections in 1990 to less than 3% in 2009. For decades, the MMS had no director with any expertise or training in petroleum engineering, petroleum geology or drilling safety (National Commission, 2011, Chapter 3, pp. 64–76). Intentional or not, the state kept the agency weak.

It would seem that the BP case is textbook example of state-corporate crime, where the interests of the state and the corporation are intertwined and the organizational culture of the companies is allowed to embrace risky decisions in a mundane manner. But the state is but one contributing factor. There are numerous technological difficulties in drilling for oil three miles below sea level. It can take a full day or more simply to lower tools or casings to the bottom of the well, and thus upper management's constant push for saving time can place strain on company agents. Science, engineering, logistics, and cooperation from several subcontractors complicate the decisions that have to be made on a daily basis by engineers and managers in the field. In the BP disaster there were several difficult events, including: (1) too few centralizer subs (a type of casing) of the correct type available from subcontractors; (2) not enough sealing mud because engineers wanted to maximize oil flow; (3) sealing cement that was inadequate for the application; (4) the use of leftover fluids to flush the well instead of water so they could avoid paying to dump the fluid onshore; (5) misreading the pressure tests within the well; and (6) being distracted by other jobs such as mud testing and disposal (National Commission, 2011, Chapter 4).

Putting the decisions of the mangers and engineers in context, and similar to the Challenger and Columbia disasters, employees had hunches that certain technological fixes would work, those hunches became part of their occupational culture, their norms, and they relied on innovating in the field, though this time their hunches turned out to be a series of tragic mistakes and miscalculations. Similar to the Challenger and Columbia disasters, the risk acceptance was affected by the political economy, performance demands, deadlines, and the need to conserve or compete for resources. But also the risk acceptance was affected by the "trained incapacity" to seriously consider health and safety conditions and rules, the organizationally "bounded rationality" that favored performance and the approval of other agents in the organization above what the larger society would consider reasonable, ethical, or moral behavior (Fisse, 1991; Fisse and Braithwaite, 1993; Vaughan, 1999, Paternoster and Simpson, 1993). Additionally, in the BP case, like the Imperial Food case, the disaster was aided by a state that encouraged production while neglecting adequate regulation.

Unlike the Imperial Food Products case, no individual employee high or low was criminally charged for the deaths caused by the BP and NASA cases, as was Emmett Roe, who actually served prison time, albeit short. Herein lays the great divide between "accident attribution" and criminalization. Deaths from unsafe, unhealthy worksites and consumer products are usually attributed to accidents not crimes, regardless of how seriously individuals are harmed directly. Emmett Roe is an anomaly.

Harming the Environment—
The Most Criminalized Corporate Violence

Environmental legislation over the years, particularly at the federal level, specifies crimes and criminal penalties for the company and/or the individual for state-of-mind violations that range from technical and negligence related violations to the knowing and knowingly endangering of individuals. Following the state-of-mind degrees, punishments run the continuum from fines and clean up to probation and imprisonment. As mentioned previously, in federal environmental law, individuals, for knowing endangerment violations where substantial harm occurs, can be sentenced to prison for up to 15 years while a company can be fined up to $1 million per count.

Environmental violations are frequently criminalized. In 2010 the federal EPA investigated 346 criminal cases, referring 277 of them to U.S. courts which successfully prosecuted and sentenced the convicted to $41 million in fines, $18 million in environmental projects and 72 years of prison. The EPA also refers civil cases to the courts in which 200 companies in 2010 were assessed civil penalties of $70.2 million (EPA, 2011). The state and county courts have also increased their numbers of prosecutions over the years (Benson, Cullen, and Maakestad, 1993; Rebovich and Nixon, 1994).

Using a sample of 1,081 EPA criminal referrals to the courts from 1983 to 2005, Barrile and Slone (2011) found that in the 859 cases in which individuals were convicted, in 46% of those cases individuals were sentenced to prison for an average (median) of 12 months per case, and in 84% of the cases individuals were sentenced to probation for an average (median) of 36 months per case. Nearly two thirds of those sentenced to prison were owner/operators of companies. In the 506 cases in which companies were convicted nearly all were sentenced to economic penalties, but in 54% of the convictions, companies were sentenced to organizational probation for an average (median) of 36 months per case.

The EPA is the most proactive regulatory agency dealing with corporate violence. Unfortunately, there is no comparable criminalization in the areas of worker and consumer health safety. For instance, while the EPA was referring 277 cases for criminal prosecution in 2010, the Occupational Safety and Health Administration (OSHA) referred merely 14. The EPA has benefitted over the years by punitive enhancements in its environmental statutes (particularly the Clean Water Act, Clean Air Act, and Resource Conservation and Recovery Act) including federal support for 200 EPA criminal investigators across the country, who have arrest powers. It collaborates regularly with state and federal enforcement and regulatory agencies, particularly the Department of Justice (DOJ), which has an Environmental Crimes Section (ECS) dedicated to prosecuting violators of environmental and wildlife laws. Ironically, the EPA is also one of the major vehicles for the federal courts to prosecute worker safety cases. The EPA regularly investigates and refers cases in which workplace pollutants affect both the environment and workers.

In 2005 the Environmental Crimes Section of the DOJ began the Worker Endangerment Initiative to prosecute companies and individuals for cases in which environmental violations led to serious worker injury or death. The Initiative also trains regulatory agents, particularly at OSHA and the Department of Labor to recognize and report cases in which employers were acting criminally. Environmental and criminal laws have had to be implemented to prosecute worker injuries because of the virtual absence of criminalization in the Occupational Safety and Health Act, 1970, the main federal worker safety law (Cruden, 2010). In his testimony before Congress, John Cruden, the deputy assistant attorney general in the Environment and Natural Resources Division of the Department of Justice, pointed out the disparities between the environmental and worker safety laws, and implored the U.S. Congress to increase the criminal penalties of worker safety laws to make them more compatible with environmental and other criminal laws. Cruden (2010, p. 15), summarizing his proposal to Congress, said:

> In sum adding felony provisions to the OSHA Act, as proposed, would provide important tools to prosecute those employers who expose their workers to the risk of death or serious injury, whether charged in conjunction with environmental crimes or charged alone. The Department of Justice supports the strengthening of OSHA's criminal penalties to make [them] more consistent with other criminal statutes and further the goal of improving worker safety.

Cruden reaffirms that, as written, health and safety laws are inadequate for an appropriate criminalization of preventable injuries and deaths in the workplace. And social scientists could take a stronger stance in calling for the definition of these behaviors as violent crime and the inclusion of them in official data collections of crime, such as the National Crime Victimization Survey (NCVS) and the Uniform Crime Reports (UCR). Critics have pointed out that workplace injuries and deaths are perceived largely as accidents, and this accident attribution minimizes the likelihood of defining even egregious acts as crimes, of applying deterrent strategies, and of developing criminological explanations to worker safety crimes (Tombs, 2007).

Preventing Corporate Violence

There are two main types of strategies that can be taken to address corporate violence, compliance and enforcement oriented strategies. Both have merits and can be applied to companies and company agents. Compliance strategies attempt to encourage companies to adhere to safe, ethical best practices and standards for conducting their business. The regulator in this model would serve as a teacher, counselor, information and plan provider, encouraging and cajoling companies to conform by, for example, promoting the establishment of active internal health and safety committees.

Compliance strategies have two basic premises. First, most companies and company agents want to be responsible citizens and see the value in establishing and maintaining an honorable reputation. For John Scholz (1984a, p. 80), corporate agents are: *"willing to obey legitimate laws, and therefore [the cooperative strategy] stresses the need for reasonable enforcement rather than coercion."* Second, most companies respond to positive reinforcement at both informal and formal levels and become defensive and recalcitrant when threatened with punishment (Braithwaite, 1982; Kagan and Sholz, 1983; Scholz, 1984a, 1984b, Paternoster and Simpson, 1993). Compliance advocates contend that companies and individuals benefit from a more reintegrative approach, i.e., companies should be required to take accountability for their violations (as in negative publicity ads or shaming from regulators) and show how they will be good citizens in the future (encouragement from regulators and positive publicity for compliers) but also accepted back as good corporate citizens if "repentant" and allowed to establish self regulation restructuring of their organizations (Braithwaite, 1982; Scholz, 1984a, 1984b; Fisse and Braithwaite, 1993; Makkai and Braithwaite, 1994).

Some compliance advocates believe that guilt makes the corporate world go "round." Makkai and Braithwaite (1994) developed a "guilt score" to measure the relationship of self-sanctioning versus deterrence strategies on nursing home managers' compliance with regulations in Australia. They found that guilt and shame were more effective than formal and other informal social controls in eliciting compliance, though the coefficient was fairly low, explaining a small amount of the variation. In the long run, compliance advocates point out that the U.S. is the single largest enforcer of criminal laws against companies with little to show for it in prevention. Further they argue that obtaining cooperation from companies is far more utilitarian as well as cost effective.

By contrast, enforcement strategies promote the use of civil and criminal penalties in the attempt to punish, incapacitate, or deter the violator. Deterrence advocates point out that criminalization of corporate violence confirms the seriousness of the acts in the mind of the public and reaffirms its moral code (Ball and Friedman, 1965). Criminalization of corporate violence levels the inequities between the criminal justice system's treatment of interpersonal violence and corporate violence (Goff and Reasons, 1978). Criminalization is deserved in proportion to the harm caused and the state-of-mind of the decision-makers (Barrile, 1993). Imprisoning responsible corporate agents, particularly if they run a small firm, effectively incapacitates the company and the person from reoffending. This approach is favored by regulators who believe that some small owner/operators do not possess the resources to comply with regulations. It is the hope of enforcement advocates that significant penalties will deter both specifically and generally, and that, for instance, being thrown into prison or stuck with an enormous fine might raise the costs of noncompliance over the benefits of committing the crime, not only in the minds of the punished but also in their compatriots, who might perceive that the justice system takes corporate violence seriously (Schlegal, 1990; Abrams, 1991). A benefit of such punishments is to reward those companies that have spent resources on compliance and may have placed themselves in a competitive disadvantage with non-complying companies in their economic sector (Cruden, 2010). A salubrious effect of the threat of criminal punishment is to make civil judgments more effective at deterrence (Block, Nold, and Sidak, 1981). Even died-in-the-wool compliance advocates admit that criminal enforcement is necessary for the most egregious cases and also acts as leverage in making compliance strategies more effective (Fisse and Braithwaite, 1993; Makkai and Braithwaite, 1994).

One of the main issues with enforcement strategies is fairness, particularly differential sentencing for large and small companies (Yeager, 1987). Large companies are far more likely to receive an economic sentence rather than imprisonment for a corporate agent as is the case with smaller companies. Whether or not this occurs because of an intrinsic bias or the difficulties in finding a criminally blameworthy individual in a large firm (or ever finding a criminally responsible executive), the most severe penalties tilt against owner/operators of small firms. Also, assessing high fines to large companies might backfire as firms pass on the costs to consumers, stockholders and taxpayers, minimizing any deterrent effects to the company. As a result, some social thinkers advocate identifying a responsible corporate agent so that collateral punishment is minimized (Barnett, 1993; Coffee, 2007). Yet, on the other hand, some argue that targeting certain corporate agents for criminal blame is a recipe for large companies to consolidate responsibility for safety compliance to specific "managers for going to jail," and that holding companies accountable is preferable to targeting individuals (Fisse and Braithwaite, 1993).

Invariably there is a need to apply both compliance and punishment strategies. When horrific harm is caused by companies with knowledge and indifference to the safety risks they have unleashed, the full force of criminalization is necessary even if only to morally reaffirm the society's norms and take a public stand against such behavior. However, it is also productive in the vast majority of the cases that exist to use compliance strategies, to resocialize or restructure companies, and to light the path toward moral as well as business decision-making.

Conclusion

In Part 1, we discussed illustrations of violence that occur in the context of the fundamental institutions of society such as the family, education, government or polity, religion, and the economy. Violence committed by individuals in institutional contexts is often considered normal, not illegitimate or criminal, and sometimes exists on a more or less unconscious or taken-for-granted level. Violence in the institutional context is usually the result of collective definitions of relationships and certain role-expectations and folkways that serve to maintain the basic organization of society and which fluctuate culturally and historically. Discussion of social problems related to intimate partner violence and child maltreatment as a reflection of the patriarchal structures of society, school tracking programs that serve to assign some students to failure and others to succeed, recent concern over clergy abuses, and political malfeasance serve to exemplify the expressions of violence in various institutions.

Part 2 provides an in-depth analysis of economic violence or corporate violence, which is defined as the preventable physical harm caused by the decisions of legitimate organizations and their agents that are consistent with the organization's main monetary or political goals and established organizational culture. Corporate violence rises to the level of crime, from a legal perspective, when statutes containing criminal offenses are violated. Some criminologists are cautious about when to define organizationally caused harm as corporate crime, circumscribing it to higher intent levels, particularly when the organization is furnishing a legitimate service, product or employment to the society. By contrast, other criminologists would expand the notion of corporate crime, or at least corporate deviance, to include corporately caused harm that originates in immoral, unethical, or consistently overly risky decision-making.

There is little doubt that corporate violence can and has caused serious injuries, illnesses and deaths to consumers, workers and the public by creating unsafe workplaces, dangerous products, and environmental pollution. The cases of Imperial Food Products, W.R. Grace, BP, and the Space Shuttle disasters painfully demonstrate the harmful consequences of corporate decision-making. And public opinion surveys confirm that the majority of the population perceives corporately caused harm as equally or more serious than conventional violence.

Yet the issue of harm has been tempered by the notion of intent and proving some level of criminal blameworthiness. Regulatory laws, specifically federal environmental statutes, facilitate corporate criminalization by implementing general intent as the basis for felonies and misdemeanors, such that negligence and knowing endangerment can elicit criminal charges and severe penalties such as prison or corporate probation or debarment.

The motives for corporate violence are typically instrumental rather than expressive as they are in cases of interpersonal violence. The underlying causes of corporate violence can be social structural stemming from the political economy, the competition in the economic sector, and the influence of the state and regulatory agencies. The causes can be meso-structural; e.g., the organization's culture and structure, its dominant goals, its performance pressures, operating ideology, and its rules and values that can routinize risky decision-making and the propensity to make mistakes and miscalculations. Or the causes can be individualistic and interpersonal, and rationalistic (bounded by organizational, financial, and status enhancement concerns).

The economic and political importance and leverage of corporations will always pose a challenge to criminalizing corporate violence, but it is a necessity if we wish to reduce it.

Because the environmental law contains serious criminal sections, the federal EPA implements an entire range of prevention strategies from compliance to deterrence. And while it criminalizes only a few hundred cases per year, it refers more cases of corporate violence for criminal prosecution than all of the other federal regulatory agencies combined; the same is true for state environmental prosecutions. Some social thinkers advocate using the federal environmental law as a model for expanding the criminalization of the corporate harm done to workers and consumers, which now are rarely criminalized.

References

Abrams, R. (1991). The Maturing-Discipline of Environmental Prosecution, *Columbia Journal of Environmental Law*, 16, 279–291.

American Academy of Pediatrics (2000). Committee on School Health, Corporal Punishment in Schools, *Pediatrics*, 106 (2), 343. Retrieved from: http://aapolicy.aappublications.org/egi/content/full/pediatrics;106/2/343.

Androphy, J. M. (1992). *White Collar Crime*. New York: Sheppard/McGraw-Hill, Inc.

Andero, A.A., and Stewart, A. (2002). Issues of Corporal Punishment: Re-Examined. *Journal of Instructional Psychology*, 29, 90–96.

Archer, D., and Gartner, R. (1984). *Violence and Crime in Cross National Perspective*. New Haven, Conn: Yale University Press.

Ascher, C. (1992). Successful Detracking in Middle and Senior High Schools (ERIC/CUE Digest No. 82). New York: ERIC Clearinghouse on Urban Education. Retrieved from: http://ericae.net/edo/ED351426.htm.

Associated Press. (1988). Guilty Plea from W. R. Grace in a Case of Water Pollution. Published in *New York Times*: June 1, 1988. Retrieved from: http://www.nytimes.com/1988/06/01/us/guilty-plea-from-w-r-grace-in-a-case-of-water-pollution.html?scp=2&sq=wr%20grace%20woburn&st=cse.

Associated Press. (2007). Spinach Recalled After Positive Test for Salmonella. Published in *New York Times* August 30, 2007. Retrieved from: http://www.nytimes.com/2007/08/30/us/30spinach.html?scp=7&sq=spinach%20contamination&st=cse.

Aulette, J. R., and Michalowski, R. (1993/1995). Fire in Hamlet: A Case Study of State-Corporate Crime. Pp. 166–190 in G. Geis, R.F. Meier, and L.M. Salinger (Eds.), *White Collar Crime: Classic and Contemporary Views 3rd Ed*. NY: Free Press.

Ball, H., and Friedman, L.M. (1965). The Use of Criminal Sanctions in the Enforcement of Economic Legislation: A Sociological View, *Stanford Law Review*, 17, 197–213.

Barnett, H.C. (1993). Crimes against the Environment: Superfund Enforcement at Last, *Annals of the American Association of Political and Social Sciences*, 525, 119–133.

Barrile, L. G. (1984). Television and Attitudes about Crime: Do Heavy Viewers Distort Criminality and Support Retributive Justice. In R. Surette (Ed.). *Justice and the Media: Issues and Research*, Springfield, IL: C.C. Thomas, 141–158.

Barrile, L.G. (1993). A Soul to Damn and a Body to Kick: Imprisoning Corporate Criminals. *Humanity and Society*, 17, 176–196.

Barrile, L.G., and Slone, N. (2005). Punishing Environmental Criminals: Extra Legal Factors and the Sentencing Guidelines. Paper presented at the national meeting of the Academy of Criminal Justice Sciences.

Barrile, L.G., and Slone, N. (2012). Corporate Violence: The EPA's Criminalization and Control of Environmental Destruction. In D.W. Harper, L. Voigt and W.E Thornton (Eds.). *Violence: Do We Know It When We See It?* Durham, NC: Carolina Academic Press, 323–340.

Bartol, C.R., and Bartol, A.M. (2005). *Criminal Behavior: A Psychosocial Approach*. Upper Saddle River, NJ: Prentice Hall.

Bartol, C.R. and Bartol, C.R. (2009). *Juvenile Delinquency and Antisocial Behavior: A Developmental Perspective*. Columbus, Ohio: Pearson/Prentice Hall.

Benson, M. L., and F. T. Cullen; F.T. (1998). *Combating Corporate Crime: Local Prosecutors at Work*. Boston, MA: Northeastern University.

Benson, M. L., Cullen, F.T., and Maakestad, W.J. (1993). Local Prosecutors and Corporate Crime. *National Institute of Justice*. Washington, DC: U.S. Department of Justice.

Berger, P., and Luckmann, T. (1967). *The Social Construction of Reality*. New York: Doubleday.

Berry, J. 1992. *Lead us not into Temptation: Catholic Priests and the Sexual Abuse of Children*. New York: Double Day.

Best, J. (1991). 'Road Warriors' on 'Hair-Trigger Highways': Cultural Resources and the Media's Construction of the 1987 Freeway Shootings Problem. *Sociological Inquiry*, 61, 327–345.

Black, D.A., et al. (1999). *Partner, Child Abuse Risk Factors Literature Review*. National Network of Family Resiliency, National Network for Health. Retrieved from: http://www.nnh.org/risk.

Block, M. K., Nold, F.C., and Sidak, J.G. (1981). The Deterrent Effect of Antitrust Enforcement. *Journal of Political Economy*, 89, 429–445.

Braithwaite, J. (1982). Enforced Self Regulation: A New Strategy for Corporate Crime Control. *Michigan Law Review*, 80, 1466–507.

Braithwaite, J. (1989). Criminological Theory and Organizational Crime. *Justice Quarterly*, 6, 333–358.

Brandt, A. M. (2009). *The Cigarette Century: The Rise, Fall, and Deadly Persistence of the Product That Defined America*. NY: Basic Books.

Bucy, P. H. (1992). *White Collar Crime: Cases and Materials*. St. Paul, MN: West Publishing.

Bureau of Labor Statistics. (2009). *Fatal Occupational Injuries by Event or Exposure*. U.S. Department of Labor. Retrieved from: http://www.bls.gov/news.release/cfoi.t01.htm.

Bronfenbrenner, U. (1973). *Two Worlds of Childhood: U.S. and U.S.S.R.* New York: Basic Books.

Burgess, R. L., and Youngblade, L.M. (1988). Social Incompetence and the Intergenerational Transmission of Abusive Parental Practices. In G. Hotaling, D. Finkelhor, J. Kirkpatrick, and M. Straus (Eds.). *Family Abuse and its Consequences*. Beverly Hills, CA: Sage, 38–61.

Burns, C., and Welner, K. (2005). Closing the Achievement Gap by Detracking. *Phi Delta Kappan*, 86(8), 594–598.

Caffey, J. (1946). Multiple Fractures in the Long Bones of Children Suffering from Chromic Subdural Hematoma. *American Journal of Roentgenology*, 56, 30–41.

Centers for Disease Control. (2009). Surveillance for Foodborne Disease Outbreaks: United States, 2006. *Morbidity and Mortality*, June 12, 58(22), 609–615. Retrieved from: http://www.cdc.gov/mmwr/preview/mmwrhtml/mm5822a1.htm.

Chiricos, T., Pagent, K., and Gertz, M. (2000). Fear, TV News, and the Reality of Crime. *Criminology*, 38, 755–785.

Clean Water Act. 1992. 33 USC 1319 (c) (3) Retrieved from: http://www.epa.gov/npdes/pubs/cwatxt.txt.

Clinard, M. B. (1983). Corporate *Ethics and Crime: The Role of Middle Management*. Beverly Hills: Sage.

Clinard, M. B., and Quinney, R. (1973). *Criminal Behavior Systems: A Typology (2nd Ed.)*. NY: Holt, Rinehart & Winston.

Clinard, M. B., and Yeager, P.C. (1980). *Corporate Crime*. New York: Macmillan.

Clinard, M. B., and Peter, C.Y. (1990). *Corporate Corruption: The Abuse of Power*. NY: Prager.

Coffee, J. C. Jr. (1992). Paradigm Lost: The Blurring of the Criminal and Civil Law Models—And What Can Be Done About It. *The Yale Law Journal*, 101, 1875–1893.

Coffee, J. C. Jr. (2007). Law and the Market: The Impact of Enforcement. Working paper No. 304. *The Center for Law an Economic Studies, Columbia University School of Law*. Retrieved from: http://papers.ssrn.com/paper.taf?abstreact_id=967482.

Coleman, J. W. (1987). Toward an Integrated Theory of White-Collar Crime. *American Journal of Sociology*, 93, 406–439.

Columbia Accident Investigation Board (CAIB). (2003). *Columbia Accident Investigation Board Report. Volume 1*. Columbia Accident Investigation Board. Retrieved from: http://caib.nasa.gov/news/report/pdf/vol1/full/caib_report_volume1.pdf.

Counts, D.A., Brown, J., and Campbell, J. (1992). *Sanctions and Sanctuary: Cultural Perspectives on the Beating of Wives*. CO: Westview Press.

Cruden, J. C. (March 16, 2010). Possible Modifications to the Criminal Penalty Provisions of the Occupational Safety and Health Act. *Testimony presented to the U.S. House of Representatives, Committee on Education and Labor, Subcommittee on Workforce Protections*, published by the U.S. Department of Justice. Retrieved from: http://www.justice.gov/ola/testimony/111-2/2010-03-16-enrd-cruden-occupational.pdf.

Cullen, F. T., Maakestad, W.J., and Cavender, G. (1987). *Corporate Crime under Attack: The Ford Pinto Case and Beyond*. Cincinnati, OH: Anderson.

Discipline and the Law. (n.d.). The Center for Effective Discipline. Retrieved from: http://www.stophitting.com/index.php?page=laws-main.

DiMento, J. (1993). Criminal Enforcement of Environmental Law. *The Annals of the Academy of American Political and Social Sciences,* 525, 134–146.

Dowie, M. (1977). Pinto Madness. *Mother Jones.* September/October, 1977.

Easteal, P. (2012). Violence against Women: Colliding "Realities." In D.W. Harper, L. Voigt and W.E Thornton (Eds.). *Violence: Do We Know It When We See It?* Durham, NC: Carolina Academic Press, 27–40.

Edleson, J.L. (1999). The Overlap between child Maltreatment and Woman Battering. *Violence against Women,* 3, 134–154.

EPA. (1998). Summary of Criminal Prosecutions: Louisiana Pacific, Corp. 1998. U.S. Environmental Protection Agency, Office of Compliance and Enforcement.

EPA. (2011). National Enforcement Trends (NET) Report. *U.S. EPA Office of Enforcement and Compliance Assurance (OECA).* Retrieved from: http://www.epa.gov/compliance/data/results/nets.html.

Ermann, M. D., and Lundman, R.J. (1982). *Corporate Deviance.* NY: Holt, Rinehart and Winston.

Evans, B. 1968. *Dictionary of Quotations.* New York: Delacorte Press.

Federal Bureau of Investigation (FBI). (2011). Crime in the United States, 2010. Washington, DC: U.S. Department of Justice. Retrieved from: http://www.fbi.gov.

Felitti, V.J., Ande, R.F., Nordenberg, D., Williamson, M.S., Spiz, A.M., Edwards, V., Koss, M.P., and Marks, J.S. (1998). Relationship of childhood abuse and household dysfunction to many of the leading causes of adults in adults. *American Journal of Preventive Medicine,* 14(3), 245–258.

Fisse, B. (1991). Corporate Criminal Responsibility. *Criminal Law Journal,* 15, 166–174.

Fisse, B., and Braithwaite, J. (1993). *Corporations, Crime and Accountability.* Cambridge, UK: Cambridge University Press.

Fox, J.A., Levin, J., and Quintet, K. (2012). *The Will to Kill: Making Sense of Senseless Murder.* New York: Pearson.

Freedman, J. L. (2002). *Media Violence and its Effect on Aggression: Assessing the Scientific Evidence.* Toronto, Canada: University of Toronto Press.

Friedrichs, D. O. (2007). *Trusted Criminals: White Collar Crime in Contemporary Society.* Belmont, CA. Wadsworth.

Frasher, B.G. (1976). The Child and His Parents: A Delicate Balance of Rights. In R. Helfer and H. Kempe (Eds.). *Child Abuse and Neglect: The Family and the Community.* Cambridge, Mass: Ballinger, 315–331.

Frosch, D. (March 29, 2011). Schools under Pressure to Spare the Rod Forever. *The New York Times Reprints.* Available at: http://www.nytimes.com/2011/03/28/education/30paddle.html?_r=1&pagewanted+print.

Futrell, M. H., and Gomez, J. (2008). How Tracking Creates Poverty of Learning. *Educational Leadership,* 65(8), 74–78. Retrieved from: http://www.ascd.org/publicaitons/educational-leadership/may08/vol65/num08/How-Tracking-Creates-a-Poverty-of-Learning.

Gans, H. J. (1980). *Deciding What's News: A Study of CBS Evening News, NBC Nightly News, Newsweek and Time.* NY: Random House, 1979.

Garcia-Moreno, C., and Watts, C. (2011). Violence against Women: An Urgent Public Health Priority, *Bulletin of the World Health Organization*, 2011. Retrieved from: http://www.who.int/bulletin/volumes/89/1/10-085217/en/.

Geis, G. (1967/1977). The Heavy Electrical Equipment Antitrust Cases of 1961. Pp. 117–132 in Geis and Meier (1977) originally pp. 139–150 in Marshall Clinard and Richard Quinney (Eds.), 1967, *Criminal Behavior Systems*. NY: Holt, Rinehart and Winston.

Gerbner, G., and Gross, L. (1976). Living with television: The violence profile. *Journal of Communication*, 26, 172–199.

Gerbner, G., Larry, G., Morgan, M., Signorielli, N. and Shanahan, J. (2002). Growing Up With Television: Cultivation Processes. In J. Bryant and D. Zillmann (Eds.). *Media Effects: Advances in Theory and Research*. Mahwah, NJ: Lawrence Erlbaum, 43–67.

Goff, C., and Reasons, C. (1978). *Corporate Crime in Canada*. Scarborough Ontario: Prentice-Hall.

Green, G.S. (1991). *Occupational Crime*. Chicago, IL: Nelson-Hall.

Hagan, J., and Parker, P. (1985). White-Collar Crime and Punishment: Class Structure and Legal Sanctioning of Securities Violations. *American Sociological Review*, 50, 302–316.

Harr, J. (1995). *A Civil Action*. NY: Random House.

Harry, J. (1996). A *Civil Action*. NY: Vintage.

Heise, I. (1998). Violence against Women: An Integrated and Ecological Framework. *Violence against Women*, 4, 262–290.

Hills, S. L.(Ed.) (1987). *Corporate Violence: Injury and Death for Profit*. Savage, MD: Rowan & Littlefield.

Human Rights Watch. (2004). Honoring the Killers: Justice Denied for "Honor" Crimes in Jordan. 16 (1) (E), New York: Human Rights Watch. Retrieved from: http://www.hrw.org/reports/2004/04/19/honoring-the-killers-0.

Iadicola, P., and Shupe, A. (2003). *Violence, Inequality, and Human Freedom*. New York: Rowman & Littlefield Publishers.

Iadicola, P. (2012). Violence; Definition, Spheres, and Principles. In D.W. Harper, L. Voigt & W.E. Thornton (Eds.). *Violence: Do We Know It When We See It?* Durham, NC.: Carolina Academic Press, 7–25.

Idriss, M. M., and Abbas, T. (2011). Honour, Violence and Islam — An Introduction. In Mohammad Mazur Idriss and Tahir Abbas (Eds.). *Honour, Violence, Women and Islam*. London: Taylor & Francis Group, 1–15.

Jenkins, P. (1994). *Using Murder: The Social Construction of Serial Homicide*. NY: Aldine, Transaction Books.

Jenkins, P. (1999). Synthetic *Panics: The Symbolic Politics of Designer Drugs*. NY: NYU Press.

John Jay College of Criminal Justice (2004). *The Nature and Scope of the Problem of Sexual Abuse of Minors by Catholic Priests and Deacons in the United States*. Washington, DC.: The United States Conference of Catholic Bishops. Retrieved from: http://www.usccb.org/nrb/johnjaystudy/.

John Jay College of Criminal Justice. (2006). *Supplementary Report of the Nature and Scope of the Problem of Sexual Abuse of Minors by Catholic Priests and Deacons in the*

United States. Washington, DC: The United States Conference of Catholic Bishops. Retrieved from: http://www.usccb.org/ocyp/JohnJayReport.pdf.

Johnson, K. (2009). Chemical Company is acquitted in Asbestos Case. *New York Times:* May 9, 2009, p. A10. Retrieved from: file:///F:/PAPERS/Papers/ ACJS%2005%20epa%201983-2005/WR%20Grace%20asbestos%20Libby%20MT.html.

Kagan, R. A., and Scholz, J.T. (1983). The Criminology of the Corporation and Regulatory Enforcement Strategies, In K. Hawkins and J.M. Thomas (Eds.). *Enforcing Regulation*, Boston: Kluwer Nijhoff, 67–95.

Kantor, G.K., and Jasinski, J.I. (1998). Dynamics and Risk Factors in Partner Violence. In Jasinski, J.L. and Williams, I.M. (Eds.). *Partner Violence: A Comprehensive Review of 20 Years of Research*. Thousand Oaks, CA: Sage

Karp, D.A., and Yoels, W.C. (1976). The college classroom: Some observations on the meaning of student participation. *Sociology and Social Research*, 60, 421–439.

Kempe, H., et al. (1962). *The Battered Child Syndrome*. Chicago: American Medical Association.

Kitzmann, K.M., Gaylord, M.K., Holt, A.R., and Kenny, E.D. (2003). Child Witness to Domestic Violence: A Meta Analytic Review, *Journal of Consulting and Clinical Psychology*, 71(2), 339–352.

Kotelchuck, D. (1989). Asbestos: 'The Funeral Dress of Kings'—and Others. In David Rosner and Gerald Markowitz, (Eds.). *Dying for Work: Workers' Safety and Health in Twentieth-Century America*. Bloomington, Indiana: Indiana University, 192–207.

Kramer, R. (1983). A Prolegomenon to the Study of Corporate Violence. *Humanity and Society*, 7, 149–178.

Kramer, R C., Michalowski, R. J., and Kauzlarich, D. (2002). The Origins and Development of the Concept and Theory of State-Corporate Crime. *Crime and Delinquency*, 48, 263–282.

Krug, E.G., Dahlberg, L.L., Mercy, J.A., Zwi, A.B. and Lozano, R. (2002). *World Health Report on Violence and Health*. Geneva, World Health Organization.

Lee, J. (2006). *Tracking Achievement Gaps and Assessing the Impact of NCLB on the Gaps*. Cambridge, MA: Civil Rights Project at Harvard University.

Levinson, D. (1989). *Family Violence in Cross Cultural Perspective*. Thousand Oaks, CA: Sage.

Maguire, B. (2002). Television Network News Coverage of Corporate Crime from 1970–2000. *Western Criminology* Review, 3(2). Retrieved from: http://wcr.sonoma.edu/v3n2/maguire.html.

Makkai, T., and Braithwaite, J. (1994). Reintegrative Shaming and Compliance with Regulatory Standards. *Criminology*, 32, 361–385.

Mann, K. (1992). Punitive Civil Sanctions: The Middleground between Criminal and Civil Law. *Yale Law Journal*, 101, 1795–1802.

Mannheim, K. (1936). *Ideology and Utopia*. New York: Harcourt Brace.

Merton, R. (1938). Social Structure and Anomie. *American Sociological Review*, 3, 672–682.

Mokhiber, R. (2011). Top 100 Corporate Criminals of the Decade. *Corporate Predators.Org*. Retrieved from: http://www.corporatepredators.org/top100.html.

Morgan, A.B., and. Lilienfeld, S.O. (2000). A meta-analytic review of the relation between antisocial behavior and neuropsychological measures of executive function. *Clinical Psychology Review,* 20(1), 113–136.

National Commission on the BP Deepwater Horizon Oil Spill and Offshore Drilling. (2011). Deep *Water: The Gulf Oil Disaster and the Future of Offshore Drilling. (Report to the President).* Retrieved from: http://www.oilspillcommission.gov/final-report.

National Scientific Council on the Developing Child (2005). *Excessive Stress Disrupts the Architecture of the Developing Child. NSCDC Working Paper No. 3.* Waltham, Mass.: National Scientific Council on the Developing Child, Brandeis University.

National White Collar Crime Center (NWCCC). (2006). The 2005 National Public Survey on White Collar Crime. Morgantown, WV: *National White Collar Crime Center.*

Needleman, M. L., and Needleman, C. (1979). Organizational Crime: Two Models of Criminogenesis. *Sociological Quarterly,* 20, 517–528.

Nolan, B. (March 6, 2011). St. Augustine High School Corporal Punishment Debate is About More Than the Paddle. New Orleans: *The Times-Picayune.* Retrieved from: http://www.nola.com/education/index.ssf/2011/03/st_augustine_high_school_corpo.html.

Owen, S.S. (2005). The Relationship between Social Capital and Corporal Punishment in Schools: A Theoretical Inquiry, *Youth and Society,* 37, 85–112.

Paternoster, R., and Simpson, S. (1993). A Rational Choice Theory of Corporate Crime. In R.V. Clarke and M. Felson (Eds.). *Routine Activity and Rational Choice: Advances in Criminological Theory Vol. 5,* New Brunswick NJ: Transaction, 37–58.

Pearce, F. (1991). *Corporate Structure and Corporate Crime.* Paper presented at the annual meetings of the American Society of Criminology, San Francisco.

Pearce, F., and Tombs, S. (1990). Ideology, Hegemony, and Empiricism: Compliance Theories of Regulation. *British Journal of Criminology,* 30, 423–443.

Pearce, F., and Snider, L. (1995). Regulating Capitalism. In F. Pearce and L. Snider (Eds.), *Corporate Crime: Contemporary Debates.* Toronto: University of Toronto, 19–47.

Piquero, N. L., Carmichael, S. and Piquero, A.R. (2008). Research Note: Assessing the Perceived Seriousness of White-Collar and Street Crimes. *Crime & Delinquency,* 54, 291–312.

Pollan, M. (2006). The Vegetable-Industrial Complex. *New York Time Sunday Magazine* October 15. Retrieved from: http://www.nytimes.com/2006/10/15/magazine/15wwln_lede.html?scp=4&sq=2006%20spinach%20contamination&st=cse.

Preston, J., and Marshall, C. (2006). Tainted Spinach Sickens 100 in U.S. *Americas-International Herald Tribune.* Retrieved from: http://www.nytimes.com/2006/09/17/world/americas/17iht-spinach.2836288.html?scp=1&sq=spinach%20contamination&st=cse.

Rafter, N. (2000). *Shots in the Mirror: Crime Films and Society.* New York: Oxford University.

Raine, A. (2002). Biosocial studies of antisocial and violent behavior in children and adults: A review. *Journal of Abnormal Child Psychology,* 30, 311–326.

Reasons, C. L., Ross, L., and C. Patterson. (1982). Your Money and Your Life: Workers' Health in Canada. *Crime and Social Justice,* 17, 55–60.

Rebovich, D., and Nixon, R. T. (1994). Environmental Crime Prosecution: A Comprehensive Analysis of District Attorneys' Efforts in This Emerging Area of Criminal Enforcement.

Washington, DC: The American Prosecutors Research Institute of the National District Attorneys Association under a grant from the National Institute of Justice—NCJ 150043.

Rebovich, D. J., and Layne, J. (2000). *The National Public Survey on White Collar Crime, 1999*. Morgantown, WV: National White Collar Crime Center. Retrieved from: http://www.nw3c.org/research/visitor_form_val.cfm.

Reisch, M. C. (2009). *Chemical & Engineering News*. May 18, 2009, p. 7. Retrieved from: http://pubs.acs.org/cen/news/87/i20/8720news3.html.

Reuters. (2008). Grace Will Settle Asbestos Claims. *New York Times:* April 8, 2008. Retrieved from: http://www.nytimes.com/2008/04/08/business/08grace.html?ref=wrgraceand-company.

Runyan, D.K. (1998). Prevalence, risk, sensitivity, and specificity: a commentary on the epidemiology of child sexual abuse and the development of a research agenda. *Child Abuse and Neglect,* 22, 493–498.

Runyan, D.K., Wattam, A. Ikeda, F. Hassan, and L. Ramiro. (2002). Child Abuse and Neglect by Parents and other Caretakers. In E. Krug, L. Dahlberg, J. Mercy, A. Zwi, and R. Lorenso (Eds). *World Report on Violence and Health*. Geneva, World Health Organization, 59–86.

Russell, G. (2011). Religious Order Vows End to Paddling at New Orleans School. Retrieved from: http://blog.beliefnet.com/news/2011/06/religious-order-vows-to-end-paddling-at-new-orleans-school.html.

Schlegal, K. (1990). *Just Deserts for Corporate Criminals*. Boston: Northeastern University Press.

Scholz, J. T. (1984a). Cooperation, Deterrence, and the Ecology of Regulatory Enforcement, *Law & Society Review,* 18, 179–224.

Scholz, J. T. (1984b). Voluntary Compliance and Regulatory Enforcement. *Law and Policy,* 6, 385–404.

Schrager, L. S., and J. F. Short, Jr. (1978). Toward a Sociology of Organizational Crime. *Social Problems,* 25, 407–419.

Shapiro, S. P. (1983). The New Moral Entrepreneurs: Corporate Crime Crusaders. *American Sociological Review,* 12, 304–307.

Slep, A.M., and O'Leary, S.G. (2005). Parent and Partner Violence in Families with Young Children: Rates, Patterns, and Connections. *Journal of Consulting and Clinical Psychology,* 73, 435–444.

Smothers, R., (1991a). 25 Die, Many Reported Trapped, as Blaze Engulfs Carolina Plant. *New York Times* September 4, 1991. Retrieved from: http://www.nytimes.com/1991/09/04/us/25-die-many-reported-trapped-as-blaze-engulfs-carolina-plant.html?scp=3&sq=Imperial+Foods+Fire&st=cse&pagewanted=all.

Smothers, R. (1991b). North Carolina Examines Inspection Lapses in Fire. *New York Times* September 5, 1991. Retrieved from: http://www.nytimes.com/1991/09/05/us/north-carolina-examines-inspection-lapses-in-fire.html?scp=8&sq=Imperial%20Foods%20Fire&st=cse.

Society for Adolescent Medicine, Ad Hoc Corporal Punishment Committee (2003). Corporal Punishment in Schools: Position Paper of the Society for Adolescent Medicine. *Journal of Adolescent Health* 32, 385–393.

Stouthamer-Loeber, M., Loeber, R., Homish, D.L. and Wei. E. (2001). Maltreatment of Boys and the Development of Disruptive and Delinquent Behavior. *Development and Psychopathy*, 13, 941–955.

Snider, L. (1993). *Bad Business: Corporate Crime in Canada*, Toronto, Canada: Nelson.

Sutherland, E. H. (1940). White-Collar Criminality. *American Sociological Review*, 5, 1–12.

Sutherland, E. H. (1945). Is White-Collar Crime Crime? *American Sociological Review*, 10, 132–139.

Sutherland, E. H. (1985). White *Collar Crime: The Uncut Version with and Introduction by Gilbert Geis and Colin Goff.* New Haven, CT: Yale University.

Tamara, T.R. (2007). Obstacles to Opportunity: Alexandria, Virginia Students Speak Out. Alexandria, VA: Alexandria United Teens, George Mason University. Retrieved from: www.advancementproject.org.pdfs/Obstacles2Opportunity-final.pdf.

Tanner, L. (September 19, 2011). Child Abuse Rises in recession, research says. New Orleans, LA: *The Times-Picayune*, A 1, 8.

Tappan, P. (1947). Who is the Criminal? *American Sociological Review*, 12, 96–102.

The National Center on Addiction and Substance Abuse at Columbia University (CASA). (2005). *Family Matters: Substance Abuse and the American Family*. New York: CASA.

The Presidential Commission on the Space Shuttle Challenger Accident. (1986). Report *of the Presidential Commission on the Space Shuttle Challenger Accident.* Retrieved from: http://science.ksc.nasa.gov/shuttle/missions/51-l/docs/rogers-commission/table-of-contents.html.

Thomas, M. (1972). Child Abuse and Neglect. Part 1. *North Carolina Law Review*, 30.

Thompson, K.M., and Braaten-Aaten, R. (1998). Youth Maltreatment and Gang Involvement. *Journal of Interpersonal Violence*, 13, 328–345.

Thompson, M.P., Basile, K.C., Hert, M.F., and Sitterle, D. (2006). *Measuring Intimate Partner Violence Victimization and Perpetration: A Compendium of Assessment Tools.* Atlanta, GA: Centers for Disease Control and Prevention, National Center for Injury Prevention and Control.

Tierno, P. M. (2004). *The Secret Lives of Germs: What they are, Why We Need them and How We Can Protect Ourselves against Them.* NY: Atria Books.

Tombs, S. (2007). 'Violence', Safety Crimes and Criminology. *British Journal of Criminology*, 47, 531–550.

U.S. Census Bureau. 2011. Statistics of U.S. Businesses, 2008. *U.S. Census Bureau.* Retrieved from: http://www.census.gov/econ/smallbus.html.

U.S. Corporal Punishment and Paddling Statistics by State and Race. The Center for Effective Discipline. (n.d.). Retrieved from: http://www.stophitting.com/index.php?page=statesbanning.

U.S. v. Louisiana Pacific 106 F. 3rd 345, 1997.

U.S. Department of Health and Human Services (USDHHS), Administration for Children and Families, Administration on Children, Youth and Families, Children's Bureau. (2010). *Child Maltreatment 2008.* Retrieved from: http://www.acf.hhs.gov/programs/cb/stats_research/index.htm#can.

U.S. Department of Health and Human Services, Administration on Children, Youth, and Families. (2007). *Child Maltreatment 2005*, Washington, DC: U.S. Government Printing Office.

U.S. Department of Health and Human Services, Children's Bureau. (2003). *Child welfare information gateway: A bulletin for professionals*. Washington, DC: U.S. Government Printing Office.

U.S. Department of Health and Human Services, National Center on Child Abuse and Neglect. (1996). Third national incidence study of child abuse and neglect (NIS-3). Washington, DC: Government Printing Office.

(USCCB). United States Conference of Catholic Bishops. (2003–2010). Annual Report of the diocesan/eparchial compliance with the bishops' Charter for the Protection of Children and Young People Formation. Washington, DC: Office of Child and Youth Protection.

Vaughan, D. (1996). *The Challenger Launch Decision: Risky Technology, Culture, and Deviance at NASA*. Chicago, IL. University of Chicago.

Vaughan, D. (1997). The Trickle-Down Effect: Policy Decisions, Risky Work and the Challenger Tragedy. *California Management Review,* 39(2), 80–102.

Vaughan, D. (1999). The Dark Side of Organizations: Mistake, Misconduct, and Disaster. *Annual Review of Sociology,* 25, 271–305.

Voigt, L., Thornton, W.E., Barrile, L., and Seaman, J.M. (1994). *Criminology and Justice.* New York: McGraw Hill.

Vollman, B. (2012). Pedophilia and the U.S. Catholic Church: Victimization and its Effects. In D.W. Harper, L. Voigt and W.E. Thornton (Eds.). *Violence: Do We Know It When We See It?* Durham, NC: Carolina Academic Press, 345–361.

Wheeler, S., Weisburd, D., and Bode, N. (1982). Sentencing the White-Collar Offender: Rhetoric and Reality. *American Sociological Review,* 47, 641–659.

Wheelock, A. (1992). *Crossing the Tracks.* New York: New Press.

Widom, C.S. (January, 2000). Childhood Victimization: Early Adversity, Later Psychopathology. *The National Institute of Justice Journal,* 3–9.

Whitcomb, D. (2001). Child Victimization. In G. Coleman, M. Gaboury, M. Murray, and A. Seymour (Eds.). *National Victim Assistance Academy*. Washington, DC: U.S. Department of Justice

Wolfgang, M. E. (1958). *Patterns in Criminal Homicide.* Philadelphia, PA: University of Pennsylvania Press.

Wolfgang, M. E., and Franco, F. (1967). *The Subculture of Violence: Towards an Integrated Theory in Criminology.* London: Tavistock.

Wolfgang, M. E., Figlio, R.M., and Sellin, T. (1987). *Delinquency in a Birth Cohort* Chicago, IL: University of Chicago.

Wright, J. (2007). Imperial Food Plant Fire. In J. Gerber and E. L. Jensen, *Encyclopedia of White Collar Crime.* Westport, CT: Greenwood Press, 137–139.

Wright, J. P., Cullen, F.T., and Blakenship, M.B. (2001). The Social Construction of Corporate Violence: Media Coverage of the Imperial Food Products Fire. *Crime and Delinquency,* 41, 20–36.

Wyner, J.S., Bridgeland, J.M. and Dilulio, J.J. (2007). *Achievement Trap: How America is Failing Millions of High-Achieving Students from Lower Income-Families.* Lansdowne, VA: Jack Kent Cooke Foundation.

Yeager, P. C. (1987). Structural Bias in Regulatory Law Enforcement: The Case of the U.S. Environmental Protection Agency. *Social Problems,* 34, 330–344.

Zimmer, C. (2011). Rise of the Superbacteria. *Newsweek,* July 13, 2011, 11–12.

Chapter 5

Collective and Group Violence

Ralph Turner and Lewis Killian argue that collective violence typically occurs when usual conventions are suspended and participants begin to collectively develop new norms of behavior in response to an emerging situation (Turner and Killian, 1988; 1993). These emergent norms may involve and condone violence, as well as a "mob mentality" where behaviors not usually considered by individuals take place. As a recent example, in what began as a peaceful demonstration over the killing of a man shot by the police in northern London on August 6, 2011 turned into several days of rioting resulting in deaths and widespread looting and burning of hundreds of stores in London, Manchester, Birmingham, and other British cities (Thornburgh, August 22, 2011, p. 30). While some people suggested that organized gangs were the cause of the riots, as well as general disaffection with the London Police, others claim that there were a lot of young people swept up in the violent activities including looting and burning, and "the only generalization that is credible is that on the whole they were young and poor" (De Castella, August 16, 2011). Worth noting, is that the unemployment rate among the young, ages 16 to 24, in Great Britain is at an all time high rate, about 20%, and some of the boroughs looted and burned had the highest rates of unemployment, suggesting that at some level the rioting was a result of shared concern over the lack of economic and social opportunities for a large underclass in the UK. According to The Organization for Economic Co-operation and Development, "the UK has the worst social mobility of the developed nations: those born to a certain social class tend to stay there" (Thornburgh, 2011, pp. 30–31). In the wake of the riots, law-abiding crowds of hundreds of citizens, coordinated by a Twitter campaign, #riotcleanup, gathered in riot-affected areas and began citizen clean-up activities (De Castella, August 10, 2011).

Sociologists make a distinction between *collective behavior*, i.e., "voluntary, often spontaneous activity that is engaged in by a large number of people and typically violates dominant-group norms and values," and other more structured types of behavior such as *organizational* behavior and *institutional* behavior (Kendall, 2006, p. 514). In contrast with organizational behavior found in corporations, collective behavior does not have an official division of labor, hierarchy of authority, and formal rules and procedures. Also differing from institutional behavior (e.g., as found in political, economic, educational, religious institutions) collective behavior does not have institutional norms, i.e., rules and laws specifying appropriate or inappropriate behavior, to govern behavior.

Various forms of collective groupings that may involve violence have been referred to as crowds, mobs, riots, panics, social movements, protests, demonstrations, strikes, rebellions, mutinies, insurrections, and revolutions, to name a few. The French journalist, Gustav Le Bon, in his book, *The Crowd* (1896), which was written in response to the French Revolution when France was in a period of rapid social change, describes crowds as temporary gatherings of individuals who have some common interest and share a focus of attention and who are a threat to organized social order. He further describes crowds as "pathological, violent, hateful, bizarre and threatening" and notes that their destructive powers come from the "law of the mental unity of the crowd" whereby "the conscious personalities of its members are leveled and replaced by a collective mind" (Perry and Pugh, 1978, p. 26). Despite Le Bon's negative view of crowds, he describes several characteristics or elements of crowd behavior that underpin some modern interpretations of this form of collective behavior, good and bad, including such things as: (1) the collective mind of the crowd, (2) feeling of power or invincibility of people in a crowd, (3) disavowal of personal responsibility within a crowd, (4) heightened suggestibility of the crowd, and (5) contagion effect of ideas and behaviors within a crowd (Perry and Pugh, 1978, pp.

26–27). Crowds are considered a prototype of collective behavior and as studied by sociologists may assume several different forms:

- *Conventional crowds:* gatherings of people who happened to be in the same place at the same time for events such as religious services, concerts, lectures, or other social events.

- *Expressive crowds:* gatherings of people who come together to express some form of heightened emotion such as grief, joy, or excitement; examples of such gatherings may include mourning the death of a loved national leader; New Year's Eve celebration; or the Jazz Fest in New Orleans.

- *Acting crowds:* gatherings of individuals who may have started out as conventional or expressive crowds but who become so intensely focused and highly charged that they exhibit high levels of emotion such as anger that may erupt into destructive and violent behavior.

Types of Active Crowds

There are many different types of active crowds that have from time to time been connected with violence. Acting crowds are often pejoratively referred to as mobs, riots, or panics:

Mobs

A *mob* is defined as a highly emotional crowd that generally pursues a specific target — a person, a category of people, or property — and attacks it violently, and then retreats or fades away (Kendall, 2006, pp. 518–20). Mobs often arise in revolutionary situations. A classic example may be taken from the American Revolution where mobs of patriots engaged in anti-tax revolts resulting in the Boston Tea Party in 1770 as well as other revolutionary groups using violence aimed at intimidating the Tories (i.e., British sympathizers) living in seaport cities and other towns (Brown, 1989, pp. 24–25). Likewise, other types of mob violence can unfortunately be found in American history including lynch mobs who engaged in vigilante justice in the western frontier, and white assaults on blacks particularly between 1880 and 1930 (with reports of over 5000 African Americans murdered by lynch mobs in the South during this time span) (Franklin, 1967; Raper, 1970; Lindsey and Beach, 2000, p. 608).

Since passage of the 1990 Hate Crime Statistics Act, hate crimes data (focusing on offenders who choose a victim because of some characteristic such as race, ethnicity, religion, or disability) are collected by the FBI and NCVS and include data not only related to interpersonal violent crimes, but also offenses committed by violent groups. Some research has suggested that the motive for group hate crimes, e.g., attacks by teens and young adults, is more likely to occur in a group setting when the perpetrators perceive that their immediate environment, e.g., neighborhood, workplace, or school, is being intruded upon by "out-group" members, and the perpetrators are engaging in a "defensive" attack. On the other hand, retaliatory hate crimes, where the offender is "getting even" for a real or imagined hate attack, more likely involves a sole offender perpetrating his or her attack outside of his/her own turf (McDevitt, Levin, and Benett, 2002, pp. 310–11).

Riots

A *riot* is a type of acting crowd that is fairly spontaneous, noisy, and involves violent outbursts of disorder by a large number of people (Barkan and Snowden, 2001, p. 29). Differing from mobs, people caught up in riots often focus their anger and hostility on multiple and shifting targets in an unpredictable manner engaging in any number of aggressive tactics. So called race riots often come to mind in our nations' major cities particularly in the 20th Century, e.g., the Watts riots in Los Angeles in the summer of 1965 and other cities such as Detroit and Newark later in the 1960s. During the 1960s at least 239 riots took place between 1964 and 1968 involving more than 150,000 black participants, with over 50,000 arrested. Many of these riots were precipitated by allegations of police brutality and other unfair treatment against African Americans. Other riots, such as the one in Los Angeles in 1992 after the acquittal of a police officer for the beating of Rodney King, took place well past the 1960s era (Barkan and Snowden, 2001, p. 34). When considering isolated events it is important to historically contextualize them, e.g., it is important to remember that in earlier periods in U.S. history, e.g., after the Civil War and through the early 1900s, there were a number of *pogroms*—one sided and violent attacks on urban blacks by whites, which took place in cities such as Wilmington, N.C. (1898) and Atlanta, Georgia (1906) (Brown, 1989, p. 44).

Evidence indicates that despite the assumptions made by people about the types of individuals involved in race riots, often referred to as the "riff raff theory," suggesting that most participants are criminals, research results show that there is a fairly broad based cross-section of the community that typically participates in large scale race riots (National Advisory Commission on Civil Disorders, 1968; Obserschall, 1973; Lindsey and Beach, 2000, p. 608). Despite the loss of lives and property damage connected with race riots, such events have a latent effect of drawing attention to deep rooted discrimination and poor living conditions of minority lower classes. It is important to underscore that often participants involved in race riots do not characterize their collective behavior in terms of a "riot" (a term that has negative connotations), but rather they choose to define their behavior as a "rebellion" or "insurrection" (Jacobs, 1996).

Another common reference associated with riots is in connection with prison uprisings. For instance, during the Santé Fe, New Mexico, prison riot of 1980, rampaging inmates used acetylene torches to torture, disfigure, and kill other inmates. Within a day of the riot, thirty-three prisoners had been killed by fellow inmates. In the Attica, New York, prison riot of 1971, forty-two persons were killed by state police, corrections officers, and national guardsmen during the retaking of the prison. While prison riots are usually described as being fairly spontaneous, they are often preceded by numerous pleas or communications expressing basic needs of prisoners. For example, key points raised by inmate rioters at Attica Prison included: humane treatment, religious expression and freedom, rehabilitation, education, no censorship, parole reform, better recreation, and inmate representation. In addition, quite often there is also a precipitating factor that ignites the riot, such as the killing of an inmate by a correctional officer, or a punitive lockup or strip search in the prison (Voigt, et al., 1994, pp. 543–44).

Riots may also take place within the context of seemingly normal events such as recreational sports, which suddenly turn violent, such as riots occurring at British soccer matches, which are notorious for their violence during and after the event (Dunning, 2003; Collins, 2008, p. 315). Spectator and other forms of violence at sporting events can take several forms and usually involve large crowd disturbances: (1) fans can invade the field; (2) fans fight with one another; (3) fans fight with the police (Adang, 2011); (4) players and fans fight with one another; and (5) players fight with each other. Large numbers of people are injured or killed at soccer, hockey, football, and other sporting events around the globe each year. The spontaneous violence is often carried outside the sports stadium or arena into the streets resulting in what Collins refers to as "celebration and defeat riots," which can turn into full-scale riots resulting in significant property damage and physical violence (Collins, 2008, pp. 307–311).

Panics

A *panic* is another form of crowd behavior, which can occur when a large number of people respond to a real or perceived threat that can elicit self destructive behavior or possible violence to others, often through mass flight to safety or other actions to secure safety and security. Historical and contemporary examples of individuals in life threatening situations trampling one another and fighting to get out of sports stadiums (e.g., soccer game stampedes) and burning buildings can be found (Cohen, 2003). However, there are also other instances where people do not panic but rather help one another and act in a calm, rational and orderly fashion (Canter, 1980). For example, a deadly Memorial Day fire at the Beverly Hills Supper Club in a suburb of Cincinnati in 1977, where 165 people died, revealed from interviews with survivors that the initial response of the victims was one of order and assistance and while some people were instructed to slow down, most survivors did not panic (Drabek, 2010, p. 45).

Social Movements

A *social movement* generally refers to a relatively large and wide-spread group of people, that is somewhat organized and goal directed seeking to bring about or resist change through collective efforts such as protest demonstrations, strikes, marches, sit-ins, and other forms of collective expression. Some social movements may include unconventional or uninstitutionalized methods (Lindsey and Beach, 2000, p. 614). In some instances, these collective efforts/gatherings may be facilitated by social media (e.g., *Twitter* or *Facebook*) and they may sometimes involve or lead to conflict and different types of violence used by the participants and/or resistance against them such as police intervention. Although social movements are typically classified as a form of collective behavior, some scholars argue that since social movements differ somewhat from other types of collective behavior such as riots or panics, which occur spontaneously and often dissipate as quickly, they represent a special category of collective behavior. Unlike other forms of collective behavior, social movements, which as mentioned above are by comparison usually of longer duration, exhibit some organizational structure and agreed upon goals, may also result in significant social change (e.g., civil rights, women's rights, children's rights, gay rights, and environmental rights) (McAdam, McCarthy, and Zald, 1988). Many social movements serve to stimulate the development of more lasting, formal organizations, which take on the goals of the original social movement. These social movement organizations (SMOS)

Box 5.1 Occupy Wall Street

A protestor against Wall Street photographs a national flag he made with corporate logos instead of stars at the city's financial district in New York on October 5, 2011. The demonstration dubbed "Occupy Wall Street," chanting economic inequality spread across the United States. (The Yomiuri Shimburn via AP Images).

develop formal professional leadership, infrastructure, division of labor, resources, and are often able to exert political influence to bring about the initial changes originally sought by the social movement, e.g., National Association for the Advancement of Colored People (NAACP) and National Organization of Women (NOW). Many of these formal organizations have become formally institutionalized and operate globally seeking social changes on a large scale across nations (e.g., enacting international legislation/sanctions against human rights violations) that may have been initiated in a specific country. Occasionally some forms of violence may accompany some phase of a particular movement (e.g., Greenpeace in efforts to prevent the harvesting of whales responded by harassing Japanese commercial whaling vessels) (Greenpeace International, 2010).

Social scientists have attempted to classify social movements into differ types, based on such things as their goals, the degree of change they seek, the type of change they seek (progressive or regressive), the speed of the social change, and the target of the change, e.g., individuals, organizations, or entire societies, and level of violence employed (Blumer, 1974; Turner and Killian, 1993; Rucht, 2003). Beginning in the 1970s and 1980s, the term *new social movements* (NSM) came to the forefront initially in Western Europe, using the adjective "new" to focus on issues such as "peace and disarmament, democracy and participation, human and civil rights, the Third World, equal rights for women, the protection of minorities, ecology and urban renewal." The thrust of the new social movements, as opposed to "old," social movement theory was less of a focus on change through revolution and violence, but rather "more or less on radical reforms" (Rucht, 2003, p. 370). Three types of social movements, each seeking different types of social change include *reform movements, revolutionary movements*, and *reactionary movements*.

Reform Movements

Reform movements, which usually seek specialized types of social change to an existing social structure or institution, generally work within the existing political and economic infrastructure. Minimal types of violence may be employed on the part of the participants in connections with mass demonstrations, sit-ins, boycotts, and other forms of protest. Although it must be pointed out that when violence occurs, it is often in response to violence used against the people involved in the movements as history has shown repeatedly in the United States. Examples of reform efforts include workers and labor rights, war protests, civil rights, women's rights, gay rights, and environmental rights. Maxwell Brown provides a comprehensive history of violence used in the American experience in various reform (and revolutionary) social movements including, for example, the labor reform movement depicting violence used by and against workers striking in the automobile, steel, rubber, maritime, timber, and other industries seeking unionization and collective bargaining rights (Brown 1989, p. 47). Brown suggests that there have certainly been negative aspects of violence in America since its origins but that "violence has [also] formed a seamless web with some of the most positive events of U.S. history" (p. 48).

Revolutionary Movements

Revolutionary movements seek a radical or fundamental change usually in a political or economic institution within a society and quite often employ violent means, although that may not always be the case. Revolutions may seek to change just the political structure of a society, a leader or form of government, or the entire social structure such as the Russian Revolutions of 1917 and 1989 (Skocpol, 1979; Lindsey and Beach, 2000, p. 618). The American Revolution of 1776, which sought to resist the British by any means after it was evident that there could be no reconciliation with the British, would most likely be considered a political revolution, but according to Brown, "from the very beginning to the very end, the meanest and most squalid sort of violence was put to the service of revolutionary ideals and objectives. The operational philosophy that the end justifies the means became the keynote of revolutionary violence" (Brown, 1989, pp. 25–26).

More recently major youth-inspired revolutionary demonstrations have occurred in the Arab countries of Tunisia, Egypt, Libya, Syria, Yemen, Bahrain, Algeria, Iraq, Jordan, Morocco and lesser civil discord in countries such as Kuwait, Lebanon, Saudi Arabia, and the Sudan, and have been referred to in the media as the "Arab Spring." Whether all these uprisings can be classified as full-fledged social revolutions is perhaps debatable, but there is no doubt that significant political changes appear to be taking place en masse in the Arab world. As of September 2011, these upheavals have led to the overthrow of three heads of state. In January, Tunisian President Zine El Abidine Ben Ali fled the country after revolutionary protests. In February, Egyptian President Hosni Mubarak resigned after 30 years in office in the face of weeks of major demonstrations. And, in Libya, in August, a violent revolution leading to an eight month civil war between his supporters and rebels forced dictator Moammar al-Gadhafi to abandon his office after his compound in Tripoli was attacked and ransacked (Schemm and Al-Shalchi, 2011, p. A-12). Since then, after weeks of bloodshed, Gadhafi was killed on October 20, 2011 after found hiding in a large drainpipe (Nossiter and Gladstone, 2011, p. A4). Whether the Transitional National Council in charge of the interim government can unify the anti-Gadhafi fighters and move the country to hold elections and guarantee rights for women and religious minorities remains to be seen.

More recently, on September 11, 2012, the eleventh anniversary of 9/11, the death of U.S. Ambassador Chris Stevens and three other Americans at the U.S. Consulate in Benghazi suggests that the region is still fraught with intertribal violence and strong Islamist extremist groups, including Al-Qaeda, which have taken advantage of a central government run by Lybia's President Mohamed el Magariaf having little or no control (e.g., Gosh, 2012: 28-33).

Protests and demonstrations have also caused the resignations of several other heads of states. While many have been celebrating their victories over repressive regimes, it is still early to predict the outcomes. Whether the seemingly ubiquitous Arab Spring revolutions will purge the region of dictators and other repressive regimes and bring about major political and institutional changes including basic freedoms and due process obviously depends on a number of factors subject to change.

Reactionary Social Movements

Reactionary social movements seek to maintain the status quo or otherwise retard or reverse social change to some earlier period of time, perceived to be better. Quite often, as certain categories of people formerly oppressed and discriminated against in society gain equality, often through their own reform efforts, and advance into previously dominant-group held jobs and occupations and other social institutions formally closed to them, they are seen as a threat to others. Those feeling threatened by changes may join together into reactionary groups with accompanying ideologies, which seek to return to previous definitions of reality. For example, in the U.S. the once relatively powerful groups such as the Ku Klux Klan, which harkens back to Reconstruction times in the South, originally arose to intimidate through violence and threats the freeing of slaves and to advocate for the renewed rule of southern whites. The Klan went through several phases including intimidation and denunciation of Catholics, Jews, Blacks and other groups who opposed their Anglo-Saxon, Protestant, and racist views. The Klan made resurgence in the 1950s, and not just in the South, and is best known for its incredible violence against the civil rights movement and desegregation in the South (Brown, 1989, p. 42). The Klan spawned a host of other relatively recent violent oriented reactionary groups motivated by racial, ethnic, and religious malice such as the Aryan Nation, a white supremacist coalition, which seeks to create a racially pure decentralized state (Ferber, 1998; Blee, 2008). For instance, some survivalist, militia-based movements advocating white supremacy and overthrow of the government are extremely violent and often operate from armed compounds, where they stockpile weapons and ammunition and train for an impending "revolution of the people" (Mulloy, 2004).

Other reactionary groups across the U. S., such as the "pro-life" movement that seeks to overturn the legalization of abortion, which occurred as a result of the Row V. Wade Supreme Court decision in 1973, have engaged in violent acts to bring back more restrictive laws. Many of these coalitions engage in violent activities including picketing abortion clinics and other medical facilities, harassing and even murdering doctors who perform abortions (Rohde, 1998; Tumulty, 2009; Parker, 2010).

In the Arab world, the Al Qaeda terrorist acts may be an illustration of a reactionary movement. Indeed, some experts suggest that the revolutions and civil strife throughout the Arab nations are not necessarily an Islamic uprising, but rather reflect a shift in Muslim attitudes from fundamentalism to modernization within the context of their own culture and religion. For example, public opinion polls administered in major Muslim countries such as the Pew Global Attitudes Project report substantial declines in support for Al

Qaeda. According to the Pew survey substantially more people identified with modernizers than fundamentalists (Wright, 2011, p. 112). This may be in part due to the demographics suggesting that in Arab countries the population is young and comprise a decisive majority. In Egypt, the median age is 24 and in Pakistan, Iraq, Jordan, Sudan and Syria, it is 22 or younger. In Yemen and Gaza, it is 18. In fact, about a third of the population (one hundred million Arabs) in 22 Arab countries is between the ages of 15 and 29. These young people are generally better educated than their parents, are technologically more sophisticated; and they want jobs and careers and a political voice (Wright, 2011, pp. 112–113). Traditional means of civil remedy tactics such as demonstrations, strikes, sit-ins, rallies, and marches have been employed. Many people have been wounded or killed in these activities by the opposition in the form of pro-government militias, private police, the military, and counter-demonstrators. In addition, the use of the social media, e.g., *Twitter*, *Skype*, *YouTube*, *Facebook*, etc., perhaps more so than in any point in history, has been used to organize, communicate, monitor, and raise social awareness in many of these events. Various governmental regimes have attempted to block these social communication efforts through internet censorship, but they have not been successful in preventing social networking and communication (Kirkpatrick and Sanger, 2011; Timeline: Egypt's Revolution, 2011). This new generation realizes that Al Qaeda cannot provide the job opportunities and quality of life that they want (Wright, 2011, p. 113).

Terrorism

Everyday news is saturated with stories of political violence, of a government's repression of its citizenry, of various incidence of terrorist group violence against public figures or innocent bystanders, and of various groups seeking to prevent others from achieving certain civil or human rights. For average U.S. citizens it is easy to attribute the atrocities of terrorist groups such as Al Qaeda (which is infamous for its September 11, 2001 [simply referred to as 9/11] hijacking of commercial airplanes and steering them into the World Trade Center in New York City and the Pentagon in Washington, D.C. and also for countless acts of violence that have followed over the last decade or so) to the actions of dangerous criminals or mad men. Likewise, political leaders such as President George W. Bush have labeled Al Qaeda and its former leader, Osama bin Laden, as the epitome of evil itself (e.g., Brown, 2012).

While on the surface the definition of terrorism may appear self-evident, in reality there is considerable debate on the subject among experts (Laqueur, 1999; 2001; Cooper, 2001; Reinares, 2003; Combs, 2003). As noted by criminologist, Austin Turk: "Terror is organized violence, but the nature of the organization cannot be specified in defining terror" (1990, p. 215). One working definition of terrorism proposed by political scientist, Ted Gurr (1989, pp. 202–203) refers to "the use of unexpected violence to intimidate or coerce people in the pursuit of political or social objectives." His definition, like many others (e.g., Schmid and de Graff, 1982; Gibbs, 1989; Combs, 2003; Hoffman, 2006) suggests that terrorist acts such as 9/11 are not "terrorism" unless there are statements from the perpetrators or "sustained campaigns" that have a political message for a larger audience or group. Gurr further suggests that there are four distinctive types of terrorism (1989, pp. 204–205):

(1) *Vigilante terrorism* — initiated by private groups but aimed at other private groups in resistance to threatening social change (e.g., Ku Klux Klan and other right wing extremist groups seeking to preserve the status quo — anti-Catholic, anti-Jew, anti-immigrant, etc.). This form of terrorism, as noted earlier, fits within the category of reactionary social movements and has been frequent in America's

Box 5.2 Arab Spring and American Fall

Some people have made comparisons between the Occupy Wall Street demonstrations and what has been referred to as the Arab Spring. On November 17, 2011 hundreds of Wall Street protestors marched through New York's financial district toward the stock exchange to emphasize economic inequality in American. This demonstration came two days after New York police evicted hundreds of the protestors who were camping in Zuccotti Park in lower Manhattan. The movement spawned other solidarity protests and occupation of public places throughout the country. These demonstrations were also met by police intervention, such as in Oakland, California where the police employed tear gas and stun grenades to disperse the crowds. However, most of the protests were met with much milder actions on the part of authorities. Many of the protestors were not unemployed but included professionals and other working people who were angry about the billions of dollars that were used to bail out the banks while many Americans were experiencing high unemployment rates on top of a recession and a struggling economy. Among their concerns was the fact that the top 1 percent of wage earners in the United States should pay a larger share of taxes. A recent report by Sentier Research, a Maryland-based research group, confirmed the beliefs of many of the Wall Street protestors, but found that there is significant variation geographically in terms of what it takes for a household income to be among the 1 percent, e.g., in Connecticut it is a family income of $651,000 but in West Virginia, it is $265,000. The report also confirmed that although much of the nation has no doubt experienced severe economic circumstances, there have been "selected pockets of income growth and prosperity" (Alpert, 2012, p. A1).The ubiquitous government breakup of the non-violent Occupy Wall Street protestors across the country in the Fall, rather than being seen as a healthy sign of social unrest and expression of dissatisfaction with political leaders and government and financial elites, has been seen by some as the American Fall, signifying political apathy more than anything else (e.g., Garrison, 2011; Mohyeldin, 2011). Many Americans either did not understand or otherwise support the intent of the Occupy Wall Street protests.

Arab Spring protests and demonstrations, starting in December, 2010 in the Arab world such as Cairo, Egypt, during January and February 2011, like Occupy Wall Street, involved a large number of young people who occupied Cairo's Tahrir Square and were angry and felt marginalized by the political system perceived to be run by an elite class. Unlike American protestors, in Egypt the political system is undemocratic and no doubt ruled by an elite class significantly different than in America. Arab Spring protestors were also angry about the state of the Egyptian economy, which has been rebounding in recent years, perhaps suggesting to the rest of the world their economy was improving, but the young protestors railed that there were few jobs, no trickle down of income to the average citizens, and that a small wealthy elite class reaped the benefits of any changes in the economy. As noted by Ayman Mohyeldin, Middle East Time reporter, both sets of protesters shared a common goal that social justice must be at the core of any reform that occurs (2011). Mohyeldin likewise sees similarities between the two protests, noting that no particular political group stimulated either movement, rather momentum and support for the movements came from the ground up and neither protest had formalized leadership. Additionally, the social media rather than traditional media gave birth to the protests, sustained them, and aided in getting the information out to the rest of the world.

Key differences in the movements involved the treatment of the protestors by their respective governments. In Egypt young protestors no doubt feared the very real reprisals by the brutal regime of Dictator Hosni Mubarak, but through their efforts, he was forced to resign from power on February 11, 2011. The Mubarak regime used violence against the protestors and also shut down the internet and cell phone networks, which eventually crippled the country but did not keep the dictator in power (Mohyeldin, 2011). While there were arrests and some mild violence used against the Occupy Wall Street protestors, this was by no means the norm despite complaints from some city mayors and opponents to the protests. Since the deposing of Hosni Mubarak, a year later a military council that took the dictators place has used security forces to control new protestors, many of whom were at Tahrir Square, and who are concerned about the future Egypt as presidential elections loom (Giglio, 2012).

history directed at racial, ethnic and religious minorities (see Barkan and Snowden, 2001, pp. 67–68).

(2) *Insurgent terrorism*—directed by private groups against public authorities and aimed at bringing about radical political change (e.g., social revolutionist movements such as Irish Republic Army (IRA), Palestine Liberation Organization [PLO]; China's [People's Revolutionary Army], etc.) seeking to overthrow a government in power and making radical political, economic, and social changes.

(3) *Transnational terrorism*—distinct not in purposes but by its international implications whose objectives, targets, or the terrorists themselves originate in a country other than the one in which the terrorist incidents occur (e.g., Al Qaeda, Hezbollah, Islamic Jihad, etc.).

(4) *State terrorism*—used by authorities to intimidate private citizens or groups such as the often cited illustrations in Maoist China, Stalinist Russia, Apartheid South Africa, Nazi Germany, and other historical cases all over the world including in the United States (e.g., genocide of Native Americans, labor movement violence, and civil rights violence) as well as countless contemporary occurrences across the globe.

What is important in Gurr's definition of terrorism, and others, is the fact that the motives of terrorism, also frequently referred to as a political crime, reflect group interest rather than individual interest. Terrorist violence is essentially politically-oriented in nature, whether used at a group level or a state level. Violence in this context is employed to create, maintain or enhance the power, interests, or ideology of a particular group, organization, or institution to the detriment or destruction of rival groups, often causing fear and victimization of innocent people. Examples of terrorist violence are murder and assassination, torture, enslavement, deprivation of rights to assembly and speech, furnishing arms or economic support to destabilize a government, domestic and foreign spying, bombings, kidnappings, and hostage taking. When violence is committed by powerful institutions or the state, we generally refer to these acts as political crimes of domination and oppression or state crime. When they are committed by non-state affiliated or relatively powerless groups against an oppressive social system, we typically refer to them as politically-oriented crimes of rebellion, insurgency, or terrorism.

By suggesting that there exists an imbalance in the definition of terrorism, we do not mean to underestimate or trivialize the dangerousness of certain terrorist groups. Certainly the legacy in the United States of white supremacist groups and other vigilante groups attest to both the potential and realization of large-scale violence and viciousness of such politically-oriented groups. It is equally difficult to erase the memory of Islamic terrorists killing innocent Americans in 9/11 and preceding earlier attack on the World Trade Center in 1993.

It is important to note, however, that while the political crimes of sovereign nations often have the same devastating effects as those of terrorist groups, the rationalizations of established governments for their own acts assume a greater legitimacy; and, moreover, they rarely evoke reaction from their respective justice system. This is to say that the actions of government usually are above the reach of domestic law. Non-state terrorists, on the other hand, are usually treated as murderous fanatics and their rationalizations are considered wholly illegitimate by the respective justice system. So the question arises: When is an act considered to be criminal or "illegitimate" and when is it considered to be a "legitimate" use of force to defend one's country and preserve law and order?

The social response or interpretation of a terrorist act of violence or crime—more than in any other type of violence or crime—depends on what group it is associated with. Group affiliation or membership determines the perception or definition of an act as being either politically justifiable or condemnably criminal. Truly, one group's treasonous terrorism is another groups' patriotic heroism.

While variations in political sentiment produce different perceptions of terrorism, in reality those groups that have the power to enforce order are usually able to punish less powerful groups for acts that differ little in nature and consequences from their own. Power, position and accompanying perceptions of legitimacy have been historically instrumental in determining what constitutes terrorism and in defining terrorist acts as "illegitimate" or criminal in a particular country and at a particular time.

Organized Crime and Violence

When most people hear the term organized crime, they think of the Italian and Sicilian Mafioso popularized by countless books, television programs, and movies (e.g., "The Godfather") where the Mafia boss (or "Don") who, from a dimly lighted office directs a multitude of criminal enterprises through a complex and secretive network of subordinates, middlemen, and retainers. Chief among these criminal enterprises are those involving the supply of very profitable illegal goods to the general public. Vestiges of this type of organized crime, La Cosa Nostra, still exist and have a long history in the United States, but as the FBI describes the current state of organized crime on their website, "It's not just the Mafia anymore," indicating that in recent years, the very face of organized crime has changed substantially and now has extended to every corner of the world into national and international syndicates. As the FBI note, organized crime now includes:

- Russian mobsters who fled to the U.S. in the wake of the Soviet Union's collapse;

- Groups from African countries like Nigeria;

- Chinese tongs, Japanese Boryokudan, and other Asian crime rings; and

- Enterprises based in Eastern European nations like Hungary and Romania.

These and many other groups, including Mexican and South American drug cartels and major national gangs such as the Bloods and Crips, have a presence in the United States supplying illegal products and services, some from the Internet and other technologies, and have literally "become partners in crime, realizing they have more to gain from co-operating than competing" with one another "(FBI, Organized Crime, n.d.). Criminal activities that organized crime groups engage in continue to expand and include traditional crimes such as illegal drug importation and distribution, which spawn violence in our cities through extortion, murder, intimidation, and corruption. In addition, prostitution and human-trafficking—"the acquisition of people, including children, by means such as force, fraud, or deception, with the aim of exploiting them" including the performance of labor or commercial sex acts—is an international problem with unimaginable violence and harm to the victims (FBI, Organized Crime, n.d.; UNODC, 2009a). Organized crime groups also "manipulate and monopolize financial markets, traditional institutions like labor unions, and legitimate industries like construction, trash hauling" as well as waste and toxic waste disposal. It is conservatively estimated that the economic impact of all these illicit enterprises from global organized crime involves as much as $1 trillion annually

(FBI, Organized Crime, n.d.) and incalculable harm to victims as a result of violence done in the course of doing business.

Definition and Nature of Organized Crime

Definitions that capture the nature of organized crime as a unique type of criminal activity are difficult to derive, and are among the most debated issues. Definitions vary from country to country, from federal to state levels, from state to state, and from agency to agency (Mallory, 2012). The FBI defines "organized crime as any group having some manner of a formalized structure and whose primary objective is to obtain money through illegal activities. Such groups maintain their position through the use of actual or threatened violence, corrupt public officials, graft, or extortion, and generally have a significant impact on the people in their locales, region, or the country as a whole" (FBI, Organized Crime, n.d.).

The term *criminal enterprise* is also used by the FBI and others to describe a group of individuals who have some type of hierarchy or organizational structure and are engaged in significant criminal activities. Criminal enterprise and organized crime are similar and often used synonymously, but there are specific federal criminal laws that define those elements of a criminal enterprise that must be met for conviction. For example, the Racketeer Influenced and Corrupt Organizations (RICO) statute or Title 18 of the United States Code, Section 1961(4) defines an enterprise as "any individual, partnership, corporation, association, or other legal entity, and any union or group of individuals associated in fact although not a legal entity." The Continuing Criminal Enterprise statute, or Title 21 of the United States Code, is more precise and specifies that a criminal enterprise is any group of six or more people, one of whom occupies a supervisory or management position over the others, and which generates substantial income or resources, and is engaged in narcotics producing or distribution such as organized crime (FBI, Organized Crime, n.d.; Mallory, 2012, p. 6). Under RICO, so called *racketeering crime* (Title 18 of the United States Code, Section 1961 (1) includes these federal crimes, and certain state crimes, many of which include violence:

- Bribery
- Sports Bribery
- Counterfeiting
- Embezzlement of Union Funds
- Mail Fraud
- Money Laundering
- Obstruction of Justice
- Murder for Hire
- Drug Trafficking
- Prostitution
- Sexual Exploitation of Children
- Alien Smuggling
- Trafficking in Counterfeit Goods
- Theft from Interstate Shipment

- Interstate Transportation of Stolen Property, and
- State crimes of Murder, Kidnapping, Gambling, Arson, Robbery, Bribery, Extortion, and Drugs (FBI, Organized Crime, n.d.).

Other definitions of organized crime, such as the 1986 President's Commission on Organized Crime, gives more detailed characteristics of both the criminal group as well as its activities. In their definition, the criminal group, in its various manifestations, *cartel, corporation, family, gumi, triad*, etc., is a continuing structured collectivity of defined members utilizing criminality, including violence, to gain and maintain profit and power. The six characteristics of the criminal group are continuity, structure, defined membership, criminality, violence, and power as its goal (President's Commission on Organized Crime, 1986).

Stephen Mallory (2012) presents a very useful synthesis of common characteristics/attributes of organized crime derived from scholarly works as well as various governmental reports from the U.S. and other countries, which have studied organized crime. These include the following:

- Has non-ideological motives
- Exhibits continuity over long periods of time; is perpetual in nature
- Uses tactical and strategic or long-term planning to reach the goals of organized crime
- Governed by rules and codes of secrecy
- Seeks to monopolize products and services
- Has an organized hierarchy
- Uses force and intimidation
- Restricts membership
- Provides illegal goods and services as demanded by the public
- Obtains enormous profits by criminal means
- Employs corruption for immunity and control
- Creates a division of labor with job specialization
- Engages in money laundering
- Invests profits in legal enterprises and seeks to control these businesses
- Exhibits an ability to adapt to changes in supply and demand, law enforcement, and competition
- Operates internationally
- Engages in more than one illicit activity (diversity in business)
- Uses legal businesses as fronts for illegal activities (pp. 9–10).

History of Organized Crime in the United States

Organized crime in various forms has always flourished in America. In the colonial period organized crime was especially prevalent in the port cities of New York and Boston, where groups of criminals systematically pilfered cargos from ships and warehouses and provided sailors with prostitutes, gambling, and contraband liquor. Evidence suggests that some of our famous founding fathers, in fact, made fortunes from smuggling and illegal trade under British rule. Perhaps the best known was the Hancock family, led by Thomas and his son John (who would later affix his signature to the *Declaration of Independence*). The Hancocks had fleets of merchant ships sailing between Holland, Spain, London, and the Caribbean, smuggling in the colonies, violating British law, and evading taxation (Lupsha, 1986, p. 41).

Following the American Revolution, organized criminal activities that had flourished under British rule continued (e.g., organized vice, smuggling, cargo theft). However, with the opening of new unclaimed lands, another pattern of criminality emerged—land fraud. Perhaps the most famous of the early schemes was the Yazoo land fraud of 1795 "which surpassed many modern organized crime capers in the prominence, ambition, and shrewdness of the men involved" (Lupsha, 1986, p. 41). This fraud involved the bribing of almost the entire Georgia state legislature to obtain ownership of some 35 million acres of land for a mere half cent per acre. This scam netted a profit of more than $4 million. The conspirators included four members of the United States Congress, three high court appellate judges (one from the U.S. Supreme Court), and several prominent bankers and financiers, all of whom ultimately escaped conviction despite widespread public outcry.

Other major figures in the post-revolutionary period, the so-called robber barons— all men of relatively poor white Anglo-Saxon families—made their fortunes through bribery, extortion, fraud, usury, and violence. This included such luminaries as John Jacob Astor, Cornelius Vanderbilt, James Fisk, Jr., Jay Gould, Russell Sage, Leland Stanford, John D. Rockefeller, J.P. Morgan, Andrew Carnegie, and the DuPont family. Howard Abadinsky (1990, p. 60) notes that these "financial pirates" of the nineteenth century were divorced from the moral and ethical imperatives of the Protestant work ethic and were guided only by the desire for wealth and power obtained by whatever means were most efficient. He also made an especially relevant point, that "it was these Robber Barons who helped enrich the fertile soil necessary for the growth of organized crime in the United States and whose spiritual legacy lives on in twenty-first century corporate crime" (Abadinsky, 2010, p. 41). These examples are also important because they show the absurdity of linking the origins of organized crime in America to the arrival of the foreign immigrants who followed in later years; these men were the trailblazers and role models for the foreign immigrants who followed.

Historically, foreign immigrants began to increase in America in the 1830s with a large influx of Irish and Germans. Immigrant populations peaked in early 1900s with immigrants from southern and eastern Europe, most notably Italians and eastern Europeans. While many of these immigrants were from rural backgrounds, most settled in the larger urban areas of the Northeast, Midwest, and South. Poverty and discrimination closed off many legitimate career opportunities; many sought to achieve wealth and power through organized crime (Ianni, 1974; Lupsha, 1986).

In many major cities such as Boston, New York, and Chicago, a strong system of patronage, however, existed between the political bosses and the vice operators (e.g., gambling, prostitution, drugs, and alcohol) regardless of their ethnicity. In exchange for protection from law enforcement, ethnic gangs provided the political bosses with "financial and electoral support" (Abadinsky, 2010).

White Anglo-Saxon Protestant alarm over the vices of foreign immigrants helped fuel the political and legal reforms of the Progressive Era in the first three decades of the twentieth century. Included among the new measures to control immigrant vices were the *Mann Act of 1910* (outlawing the transportation of females across state lines for illegal purposes), the *Harrison Tax Act of 1914* (regulating the importation, manufacture, distribution, and sale of opiates), and the *Volstead Act of 1919* (ultimately becoming the Eighteenth Amendment and resulting in the nationwide ban on alcoholic beverages in January 1920).

Of all these measures, the Volstead Act of 1919 was by far the most significant because it changed the scope and character of organized crime by creating an instant national market for illegal spirits. It served as the stimulus for creating large-scale criminal enterprises, i.e., transforming disparate organized crime groups operating on local levels into nationally organized crime networks. Prohibition provided the opportunity to make organized crime into big business operating in interstate and international commerce and requiring an infrastructure for the manufacture and distribution of alcohol and the coordination of a variety of specialized activities to ensure smooth operations. This national network to supply illegal liquor would later after the repeal of the Volstead Act be used to supply illegal narcotics and other drugs.

The transition to a national level operation was, however, not a smooth one. The newly developed market in illegal liquor set off a torrent of "cutthroat" competition marked by bloody gang violence in which Italian syndicates first battled Irish syndicates for control of the market; then they went to war with each other. For example, in Chicago Al Capone's organizational struggle with competitors came to an end with the infamous "St. Valentine's Day massacre" of 1929, leaving Capone and his successor firmly in control of the Midwestern market and the importation of liquor from Canada. In New York City, the famous "Castellammarese War" of 1931 resulted in the elimination of the older Sicilian bosses whose reluctance to cooperate with other ethnic groups in the liquor business stifled the creation of an efficient importation and distribution syndicate that younger Italian gangsters (those borne or raised in America) were eager to develop and capitalize on. Crime boss Charles "Lucky" Luciano (whose associates included Jewish gangster Meyer Lansky) is widely believed to have been the mastermind behind the liquidation of the older Mafiosi, assuring the men of the Luciano group dominant positions (Kelly, 1992). Under Luciano's influence, the ways and means of organized crime were infused with modern management techniques that included, among other things, a willingness to negotiate and cooperate with other ethnic groups whenever that course served to maximize profit. The current internationalization of organized crime indicates that Luciano was, in some ways, very progressive in his thinking about expanding the markets of organized crime.

When it became clear that popular sentiment would soon bring Prohibition to an end, Italian and Jewish syndicates began to plan the enterprises they would venture into in the post-Prohibition era. Some simply resolved to use their vast fortunes to purchase controlling interests in legitimate liquor and other businesses and retire from the rackets altogether. Others made plans to syndicate gambling on a national basis or to use the organizational liquor networks and infrastructure already in place to supply consumers with illegal narcotics. Still others resolved to return to some of the older rackets, including labor racketeering, cargo hijacking, fencing of stolen property, loan sharking, and prostitution.

The *Task Force Report: Organized Crime*, which came out of President Lyndon B. Johnson's Commission on Law Enforcement and the Administration of Justice (1967) described the Italian-American crime families (called "La Cosa Nostra"), who gained nationwide control following Prohibition, as a rigid and highly bureaucratized organizational command structure. At the top of this hierarchy is the boss who directs and manages a host of criminal networks through "family" members of lesser rank (e.g., an "underboss" and a group of "lieutenants" and their "soldiers"). The soldiers at the bottom of the hierarchy are the front-line managers of the family businesses; they are the ones who corrupt police and other public officials, enforce discipline over members and non-members on orders from above, and recruit nonmembers to operate criminal enterprises at the points of direct contact with consumers (Cressey, 1969).

This view of Italian-American dominance in the post-Prohibition era, however, is controversial. In the first place, it does not give adequate attention to the role of other ethnic groups such as the Jewish gangs who worked in close association with some of the Italian groups and who were heavily involved in gambling, narcotics trafficking, loan sharking, and the "contract killer business (Kelly, 1992; Rogovin and Martens, 1992). Nor does it do justice to the variety of autonomous ethnic and racial groups who were involved in illegal enterprises during this period (Woolston, 1969; Chin, 1990). Research on the heroin business in the Southwest in the mid-1960s revealed that this activity was controlled almost exclusively by Hispanics rather than Italians (Redlinger, 1969). Other data suggest that independent African-American, Hispanic, and Asian syndicates controlled gambling, narcotics, and prostitution in the Northeast, Midwest, and Far West (Abadinsky, 1990). A second criticism is that the evidence in support of a national Italian-American monopoly is based on very fragmentary data—mostly sensational and poorly substantiated news stories, transcripts of vague telephone conversations obtained from wiretaps, and the congressional testimony of some lower-level Italian syndicate members (e.g., Joseph Valachi) during the 1950s and 1960s (Block, 1978; Bell, 1988; Kelly, 1992). The Italian-American monopoly over organized criminal activities after Prohibition was not evident by the late 1960s when the theory of Italian dominance gained widespread acceptance among politicians, law enforcement personnel, and the general public. It is curious that the federal government continued to promulgate the view of an omnipresent Italian-American mafia as late as 1980, and did so at the very time when most criminologists believed that other groups had displaced the Italians in many of the more lucrative rackets. Only after 1980 did the federal government finally concede that Italian-Americans were no longer in monopoly control. However, it is still too soon to write the final obituary of the traditional Italian-American mafia. While La Cosa Nostra (LCN) may no longer possess the national presence and influence it once had, it remains a significant threat in major metropolitan areas such as New York City, Boston, Philadelphia, Chicago, and Detroit (FBI, Mafia Takedown, n.d.).

We may accurately conclude that since the 1970s, the variety of ethnic, racial, and national crime groups has been growing. Some of these have waxed and waned over time, and been replaced by new crime groups, some well organized and others loosely structured. These groups have included: outlaw motorcycle gangs that deal in prostitution, synthetic drugs, and organized theft and fencing rings; the Mexican Connection, also known as Nuestra Cosa, who were involved initially in heroin trafficking; the Columbia Connection, leading suppliers of marijuana and cocaine; Jamaican gangs that specialize in marijuana, cocaine and contraband weapons; Dominican gangs selling crack, cocaine, and heroin in New York and other cities; Asian gangs on the West Coast who deal in illegal immigration, drugs, and prostitution; Black gangs, including the Black Guerrillas, Gangster Disciples, and others who controlled much of gambling, prostitution, and drug businesses in inner-cities; and the Russian immigrant "mafia" in Brighton Beach, New York, and in the Tri-State area (New York, New Jersey and Pennsylvania) who have engaged in drug trafficking, extortion, and fencing stolen products.

Box 5.3 New York's Five Families

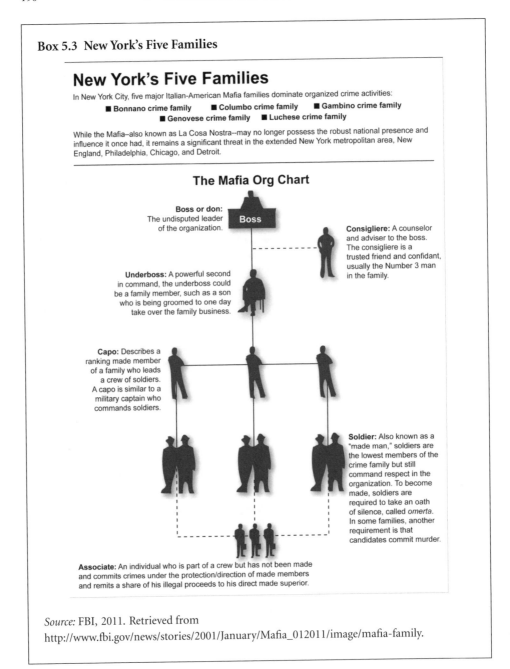

New York's Five Families

In New York City, five major Italian-American Mafia families dominate organized crime activities:

■ Bonnano crime family   ■ Columbo crime family   ■ Gambino crime family
■ Genovese crime family   ■ Luchese crime family

While the Mafia–also known as La Cosa Nostra--may no longer possess the robust national presence and influence it once had, it remains a significant threat in the extended New York metropolitan area, New England, Philadelphia, Chicago, and Detroit.

The Mafia Org Chart

Boss or don: The undisputed leader of the organization.

Boss

Consigliere: A counselor and adviser to the boss. The consigliere is a trusted friend and confidant, usually the Number 3 man in the family.

Underboss: A powerful second in command, the underboss could be a family member, such as a son who is being groomed to one day take over the family business.

Capo: Describes a ranking made member of a family who leads a crew of soldiers. A capo is similar to a military captain who commands soldiers.

Soldier: Also known as a "made man," soldiers are the lowest members of the crime family but still command respect in the organization. To become made, soldiers are required to take an oath of silence, called *omerta*. In some families, another requirement is that candidates commit murder.

Associate: An individual who is part of a crew but has not been made and commits crimes under the protection/direction of made members and remits a share of his illegal proceeds to his direct made superior.

Source: FBI, 2011. Retrieved from
http://www.fbi.gov/news/stories/2001/January/Mafia_012011/image/mafia-family.

Contemporary Transnational Organized Crime Networks

The "internationalization" of organized crime and an unprecedented degree of cooperation among different ethic and national groups are among the most current developments in what is commonly referred to as *transnational organized crime* (TOC).

Beginning in the final decade of the 20th Century, so called "cross border" crime became a major security issue for law enforcement agencies in Europe and the United States (Williams, 2001; Felsen and Kalaitzidis, 2005). These organized crime operations operating out of Asia, Eastern Europe, and North, South and Latin America have become the supplier of illegal goods and services throughout the world (van Duyne, et al., 2010).

Antonio Maria Cosa, executive director of the United Nations Office on Drugs and Crime, aptly notes in the 2010 report, *The Globalization of Crime: A Transnational Organized Crime Threat Assessment*: since the end of the cold war "global governance has failed to keep pace with economic globalization ... as unprecedented openness in trade, finance, travel and communication has created economic growth and well being, it has also given rise to massive opportunities for criminals to make their business prosper" (UNODC, 2010, preface). In a sense, organized crime has both diversified and gone global and reached macro-economic levels with illicit goods produced in one continent, trafficked across another, and marketed in another. Organized crime has become a true transnational problem, including a threat to countries' security, especially third world countries, fueling violence and corruption, infiltrating businesses, politics, and hindering development (UNODC, 2010).

There are at least two competing definitions of transnational organized crime (TOC). One definition focuses on particular *groups* of people, e.g., multi-crime groups of professional criminals, and another focuses on particular *types of crime*, which rely on illicit markets. Both definitions have some utility in understanding TOC, but neither is sufficient to understand and/or control global crime. Most of the attention to date has been given to TOC groups, focusing on law enforcement efforts such as arrest and seizure. This traditional approach certainly has benefits, apprehending specific offenders engaging in illegal activities, much of them violent, but these people may be replaced, and little is done to halt the illicit market. However, there is recent evidence from several international organizations that have studied TOC, which indicates that, while there are both highly structured and loosely structured criminal groups or organizations involved in transnational organized crime, in recent years "traditional hierarchical organized crime groups have developed a "cell structure" similar to that seen in terrorist groups, with small networks doing the work formerly performed by more rigid structures" (UNOCD, 2010, p. 3; United States Dept. of Justice, 2008; Europol, 2006). Each cell and its controller operate anonymously from other cells and if one of the cells is lost, e.g., apprehended by law enforcement, the criminal organization continues and the cell is subsequently replaced (Abadinsky, 2010, pp. 10–11). Some experts suggest that there are some similarities between organized crime groups and terrorist groups; in fact there is even evidence of cooperation among them and mutually beneficial relationships (Shelley and Picarelli, 2005; Shelly and Melzer, 2008).

The types of transnational organized crime activities are many, including human trafficking, migrant smuggling, cocaine and heroin trafficking, firearms trafficking, counterfeit goods trafficking, maritime piracy, environmental resources trafficking, and cybercrime. It is important to realize that the very nature of transnational organized crime is constantly changing, often depending on supply and demand patterns of certain goods and services as well as issues pertaining to business interruption by law enforcement agencies. It is also important to note that all forms usually involve more or less violence in the transactions.

Trafficking in Persons

Trafficking in persons is a global phenomenon involving "the use of violence, threats or deception to create a pliant and exploitable work force" (UNODC, 2010, p. 39). There are two major categories of human trafficking: trafficking for the purposes of sexual exploitation and labor exploitation, both types includes children. According to UNDOC's *Global Report on Trafficking in Persons* (2009a) based on reports from 137 countries, estimates suggest that approximately two thirds of the victims are women and 79% are sexually exploited. An estimate on global trafficking from the International Labor Organization(ILO) reports at least 2,450,000 persons currently being exploited with costs suffered by all victims of forced labor at 12 billion U.S. dollars in 2009 (ILO, 2005; UNDOC, 2009a). It is important to note that many counties do not have legislation making human trafficking a crime, or have just passed such laws; and, of course, there are a large number of undetected and unreported victims.

Human trafficking for commercial sexual exploitation is generally seen as a larger problem than victims of other labor exploitation. Immediately after the Cold War a large number of laborers of all types moved from Eastern to Western Europe and some of these were "sex" workers, many involuntary (UNODC, 2010, pp. 45–46). In 2005–2006 about half of human trafficking victims in Europe came from the Balkans or the former Soviet Union, in particular Romania, Bulgaria, Ukraine, the Russian Federation, and the Republic of Moldova. According to information gathered on human trafficking groups, each criminal trafficking group employs its own modus operandi for selection, recruitment, transportation, and exploitation of victims (Surtees, 2008). In the Balkans, for example, promises of employment, modeling opportunities, participation in beauty contests, affordable vacations, study abroad opportunities, or lucrative marriage services are used to entice recruits (Denisova, 2004; Surtees, 2008). Victims are also recruited through acquaintances, friends, relatives, even husbands. Although some victims are recruited knowingly into prostitution, they usually end up being exploited, violently harmed, and generally deceived about the bad conditions of their "work" (UNODC, 2010, pp. 45–46; Glowers, 2007).

Smuggling of Migrants

Many individuals in poorer countries and developing nations who are unable to legally immigrate to other more affluent countries for work and a better life will employ organized criminals to "broker" deals for them at great financial and personal costs. An estimated 80% of the current illegal immigrant population in the U.S. comes from Latin America. Most of the migrants are smuggled in boats or trucks and they may be held in "stash houses" either before or after they are brought into the U.S. to ensure that the smugglers receive payment. About 3 million people are smuggled illegally across the southern border of the U.S. each year and the income for smugglers is around 7 billion dollars per year. Similar smuggling occurs from other countries, especially from Africa to Europe through smuggling routes by land and water to European Islands. Many of the migrants are subjected to gross exploitation and violent treatment throughout their journey (UNODC, 2010, pp. 4–5; UNODC, 2009c; Vayrynen, 2003).

Cocaine and Heroin Trafficking

The operation of the two major drug cartels (Medellin and Calli) in Columbia before their dismantling in the early 1990s marked some of the most violent organized crime activities in recent history, perhaps the exception now being the "drug war" in Mexico with estimates of over 40,000 people murdered since 2006 (Grillo, 2011; Thompson, 2011, p. A7). Prior to their dismantling, these drug cartels were part of multinational operations that rivaled many legitimate multinational corporations with respect to structure and volume of profits from goods and services and that "became a model for multinational crime" including a top down organizational structure with a CEO, chief of operations, production, distribution, security, and financial divisions (Mallory, 2010, pp. 54–57). Although the big Columbian drug cartels have been dismantled, the international trafficking of cocaine remains the most "organized" and largest in scale compared to the trafficking of other drugs including heroin. This is measured by international law enforcement efforts in terms of the size of cocaine shipments, at least 10 to 20 times larger than average heroin seizures; multi-ton seizures are made every year (UNODC, 2009b). This yield indicates the work of well resourced criminal organizations including close cooperation between smaller organized crime groups, which is no surprise since modern global cocaine trafficking goes back at least 40 years. Although cocaine use has been declining in the U.S. since the 1980s, and particularly since 2006, America remains the largest national cocaine market in the world and as noted by the 2009 U.S. Drug Threat Assessment, "Cocaine trafficking is the leading drug threat to the United States" (National Drug Intelligence Center, 2009). The flow of cocaine today originates from the Andean countries to North America (usually through Central America) and to Europe (often through West Africa), although recently it has been coming through the Southern Cone of South America. Now, cocaine is usually transported from Columbia to Mexico or Central America by sea and then by land to the U.S. and Canada, usually by Mexican groups. Transnational organized crime direct cocaine shipments from Columbia to Mexico and have shown incredible ingenuity with a variety of marine craft in recent years including "cocaine" submarines or submersibles capable of transporting anywhere from 2 to 9 tons of cocaine. Most of the seizures have been made in the Pacific Ocean, but some have occurred in the Atlantic (UNODC, 2010, pp. 87–88).

Currently about 90% of the world's heroin comes from opium poppy grown in Afghanistan. The majority of this is consumed in Europe, the Russian Federation, and countries in route to these destinations. The Taliban virtually stopped cultivation of the drug in 2001 and today poppy farming is primarily done in the south, in the province of Hilmand, where the processing is also done (UNODC, 2010, p. 109). Out of an international market of about $55 billion in U.S. money for Afghan heroin, only about $2.3 billion actually goes to the farmers and traders in Afghanistan. This amount of money, however, is vital to the local economy, a problem found in trying to wean the locals off of the poppy crop to other less profitable conventional crops. The largest market share of profits goes to the heroin traffickers, followed by the retailers in destination countries (p. 111). In Afghanistan, heroin trafficking to Central Asia is dominated by five key Afghan drug networks comprised of organized crime groups, officials, and warlords. These groups work with local village-based networks and ethnic relations on both sides of the border, Afghanistan and Tajikistan, in particular. There is also evidence that there are larger organized crime groups operating in Tajikistan and Uzbekistan who share the market with numerous opportunistic smaller groups built around ethic lines. In the Russian Federation, the Russian Ministry of Internal Affairs estimates that as many as 450 criminal organizations are involved in the heroin trade. These organized crime groups are involved in many other criminal activities including smuggling of human beings, cigarettes, fuel, precursor chemicals, and weapons (p. 123).

Box 5.4 El Narco — Inside Mexico's Criminal Insurgency

The world has watched stunned at the bloodshed in Mexico. More than forty thousand civilians and drug traffickers have been murdered since 2006. Journalist Ioan Grillo spent a decade in Mexico covering the "drug war" and attempting to make sense of the carnage from firsthand information including testimonials from drug cartel members, police, and politicians. His book, El Narco, provides a fascinating and scary glimpse into the immense criminal network of drug smugglers who have literally taken over the country in recent years with their own militia armed with military weapons such as fully automatic AK-47s and .50 caliber guns set up with rocket-propelled grenades.

According to Grillo, "Drug cartel members have killed more than 2500 public servants, including 2200 policemen, 200 soldiers, judges, mayors, a leading gubernatorial candidate, the leader of a state legislature, and dozens of federal officials. Such a murder rate compares to the most lethal insurgent forces in the world, certainly more deadly to government than Hamas, ETA, or the Irish Republic Army in its entire three decades of armed struggle. It represents a huge threat to the Mexican state. The nature of the attacks is even more intimidating. Mexican thugs regularly shower police stations with bullets and rocket-propelled grenades: They carry out mass kidnappings of officers and leave their mutilated bodies on public display; and they even kidnapped one mayor, tied him up, and stoned him to death on a main street" (Grillo, 2011, p. 11).

"In Mexico, traffickers are described collectively by the Spanish word El Narco, using a singular proper noun. The term, which is shouted loudly in news reports and whispered quietly in cantinas, provokes the image of an enormous ghostlike form leering over society. Its capos are shadowy billionaires from ramshackle mountain villages, known from grainy, twenty-year-old photos and the verses of popular ballards. Its warriors are armies of ragged, mustachioed men who are thrust before the press like a wraith under the noses of thousands of police and soldiers patrolling city streets, and the vast majority of its murders are never solved. This ghost makes an estimated $30 billion every year smuggling cocaine, marijuana, heroin, and crystal meth into the United States. But the cash disappears like comic mist into the global economy" (pp. 7–8).

In short, according to Grillo, "El Narco is the eight-hundred-pound gorilla in the room. But most people can't put much of a face on that gorilla. On the street where El Narco reigns, being in the drug underworld is referred to as being in the "movement." That word gives a sense of the broad meaning of organized crime on the ground; it is a whole way of life for a segment of society. Gangsters have even begotten their own genre of music, *narcocorridos*, lead their own fashion style, *buchones*, and nurture their own religious sects. These songs, styles, and sermons all build up an image of the drug lords as iconic heroes, celebrated by dwellers of Mexico's cinder-block barrios as rebels who have the guts to beat back the army and the DEA. El Narco has entrenched itself in these communities over a century. By following its development as a movement — rather than just sketching the police stories of the drug kingpins — we can get much closer to understanding the threat and figuring out how to deal with it" (Grillo, 2011, pp. 7–8).

El Narco has become so entrenched into the Mexican culture that in some areas, local cartels are the largest businesses and employers. One of the largest and most violent cartels, the Zetas even post want ads and actively recruit new members, especially if they are ex-military. According to Grillo, the Zetas are former special-forces soldiers who turned the "war on drugs" to a "drug war" in Mexico (p. 94).

Grillo asks the question," But what prize is El Narco fighting for? If gangsters simply want the right to smuggle drugs, observers argue, it doesn't pose such a destructive insurgent threat to society. However, as the Mexican Drug War has escalated, gangsters have got increasingly ambitious. Certain cartels now extort every business in sight. Moreover, they have muscled into industries traditionally shaken down by the Mexican government. The Zetas dominate the east of Mexico, where the oil industry is the strongest. They "tax" as much as they can from it, both by extorting the union and stealing gas to sell off as contraband. Over in Michoacán, La Familia [another drug cartel] shakes down both the mining industry and illegal logging — both assets the government used to benefit from. Such activities vary from gang to gang. The Sinaloa Cartel is largely limited to the traditional traffic of drugs. Meanwhile, the criminal groups that have branched out most are the very same that attack federal forces the hardest. When gangs can 'tax" industry, there is a serious weakening of the state. When cartels are the strongest, their power seeps from politics into the private sector and media. In Juarez, business leaders argued that if they have to pay protection money to the mafia, they shouldn't have to cough up taxes to the federal government. It was a telling argument. The city's main newspaper, El Diario de Juarez, made the point even harder following the mafia murder of a twenty-one-year-old photographer on his lunch break. In a front-page editorial entitled "What Do You Want from US?" El Diario addressed the cartels directly—and touched nerves in the Calderon government" (pp. 207–208).

Ioan Grillo concedes that Mexican society has been traumatized by the violence during the past several years but offers no immediate solutions to the problem. He says, "Unfortunately, no superman or messiahs are going to zap away the Mexican Drug War. No magic wands will make it all better. The solution is in flawed, greedy, evasive, confused, deceitful human beings. It is in the same humans who have created the problem in the first place, made El Narco grow slowly but surely by buying its drugs, selling it guns, laundering its money, taking its bribes, paying its ransoms. And it is in the pushed policies that don't work, left kids stuck in a corner with no hope, and let killers get away with murder. The way out doesn't involve one improved policy in one country, but a group of improved policies in Mexico, the United States, and beyond. Even though El Narco is a criminal insurgency, soldiers are only a small part of the solution. America and Europe have to wake up and confront the drug money and guns we spew out. The debate cannot conveniently be tucked away any longer. Estimated Mexican drug profits over the last decade total more than a quarter of a trillion dollars. Giving psychopathic cartels another quarter of a trillion dollars in the next decade should not be acceptable. Would we accept foreigners throwing such money at insurgent militias in our countries" (p. 275)?

Source: Grillo, I. (2011). *El Narco—Inside Mexico's Criminal Insurgency.* New York: Bloomsbury Press.

Counterfeit Products

A common form of Transnational Organized Crime (TOC) is product counterfeiting, which involves manufacturing or producing or outsourcing the production of unauthorized products, which are based on the same or similar designs, often making them indistinguishable from the original. The counterfeit goods can then be sold either through parallel markets or even in regular commercial markets. Anyone who has visited a major city in China is often bombarded by street vendors selling knockoff products such as designer handbags or Rolex watches, literally for a few dollars. These counterfeit goods are relatively cheap because they are produced and/or distributed with low overheads and often employ sweatshop labor. While there are different grades of counterfeit goods, some of the products are plagued by shoddy workmanship and/or substandard materials. Product counterfeiting is globally pervasive, but exact estimates of how much of these illegal products are traded internationally are hard to determine. One estimate derived by The International Chamber of Commerce estimates that "Counterfeiting accounts for between 5–7%, worth an estimated $600 billion U.S.D. a year" (UNOCD, 2010, p. 173). In many parts of the developing world, counterfeit products have essentially replaced the original high quality products that have been priced out of the market. Many counterfeit products can be dangerous, if not deadly in some instances. Without a brand to protect, counterfeiters have no incentive, legal or otherwise, to produce quality goods. Thus, knockoff toymakers do not have to worry about choking hazards or lead paint toxicity.

Counterfeit auto parts, are not subject to safety testing, counterfeit batteries and cigarette lighters are prone to explode, and counterfeit medicines may not contain any active ingredients at all, or may contain substandard doses, causing the target microbes to develop resistance to the disease (p. 173). Pharmaceutical counterfeiting has been described as a form of health fraud that essentially amounts to mass "manslaughter" (p. 184). A common drug that is counterfeited is artesunate, an anti-malarial drug produced in China and used extensively in South East Asia and Africa (Newton, et al., 2008). While China has taken extensive measures to control the manufacture of counterfeit products, according to the World Customs Organization, the U.S. Government and the European Commission, the great bulk of the world's counterfeit goods can be traced back to China (p. 177). There is recent concern that in addition to organized transnational criminals being heavily involved in counterfeit drug production and trafficking that some terrorists groups such as al Qaeda may be involved in, pharmaceutical counterfeiting is a way to replace revenues lost from counterterrorism efforts since 9/11 (Finlay, 2011).

Maritime Piracy

Maritime piracy is a violent acquisitive crime occurring on a ship, which "is considered a sovereign terrority of the nation whose flag she flies" (UNODC, 2010, p. 193). It is considered a transnational organized crime (TOC) because of the extensive planning, coordination, and expertise required to carry out the act of piracy. One of the largest problems with piracy in recent years is found off the coast of Somalia, particularly in the Gulf of Aden. Maritime piracy does occur in other areas such as the Gulf of Guinea in West Africa, and the waters along Bangladesh and the South China Sea. However, more than half of the international piracy crimes in 2009 were carried out by Somali pirates (p. 193). Somalia ship piracy generally involves kidnapping for ransom, as opposed to robbery or hijacking of the vessel or its cargo.

Modern piracy is said to have arisen through vigilante efforts on the part of local fisherman to protect their coastal waters from the depletion of their fishing grounds from foreign boats from Europe as well as toxic waste dumping in their waters. In these cases reparations were secured by the fisherman holding the vessels and their cargo until compensation was paid and over time, seizing vessels through piracy became an illicit business in much the same manner that it operates today. Currently, Somali pirates operate at vast distances from the Somali coast. They have developed very well organized techniques to pirate vessels using motherships as a base of operation with alleged electronic based intelligence via GPS and satellite phones to select their targets, which suggest that an international criminal network is at work (pp. 197–198).

Environmental Resource Trafficking

Another type of transnational organized crime (TOC) involves "the theft and smuggling of a country's natural resource assets, and environmental crime" (UNODC, 2010, p. 149). Natural resources not only include such things as oil, diamonds, ore, gold, and other precious metals and minerals, but also biological resources such as endangered wildlife, plants, and trees as well as their illegal misappropriation and trafficking. Environmental crimes, also referred to as "green crimes" are universal, but especially occur in third world or underdeveloped countries where enforcement is relatively lax or non-existent and government officials are often a part of the problem. Two broad categories of environmental crimes include offenses related to pollution, particularly hazardous and toxic waste dumping and the trade in ozone-depleting substances such as chlorofluocarbons (CFCs). These crimes are by nature harmful to the entire world and our global environmental heritage. Control of these crimes is beyond the scope of any one nation. Although there have been international conservation agreements over the years including the Convention on International Trade in Endangered Species of Wild Fauna and Flora (known as CITES), adopted in 1973 by the International Union for Conservation of Nature (IUCN), compliance has not been enforced (p. 149).

The UNODC Globalization of Crime report examines in detail TOC environmental resource trafficking of wildlife from Africa and South-East Asia to other parts of Asia and the trafficking of timber to China and Europe. In particular, long sought in Asia for its purported aphrodisiac and medicinal value, the illicit rhino-horn trade that was once mainly involved small time South African poachers killing one or two animals for their horns is now part of a global network of criminal syndicates, often relying on organized poaching gangs. By weight, rhino horn, often ground up, is now worth more than gold, fetching tens of thousands of dollars per kilogram in China or Vietnam (Beech and Perry, 2011, pp. 42–43). With the growth of China's economy has come a huge consumer demand for all kinds of endangered wildlife and wildlife products, especially illicit elephant ivory (UNODC, 2010, p. 156). In addition to the illegal transportation of wildlife, the importation of illegally harvested timber, including raw timber and wood-based products, are imported into the European Union and Asia, China in particular. The primary source of the illegal logging or trafficking of timber is Indonesia. Illegal logging gangs operating in the source countries, often with assistance from corrupt government officials and business entrepreneurs help perpetuate the crime (Human Rights Watch, 2010).

Cybercrime

Cybercrime encompasses a broad range of offenses. However, crimes such as identity theft and transnational trafficking in child pornography are vastly increasing in scope and are attracting the attention of organized crime groups both nationally and internationally. Presently, these offenses seem to favor lone or small groups of perpetrators (Beech, et al., 2008), as opposed to organized criminal groups or organizations, although some do exist (Flowers, 2007). With respect to identify theft, when organized crime groups exist, they tend to be both smaller, and more loosely structured (Brenner, 2002; Choo, 2008). Nigeria, followed by Ghana and Malaysia are countries, for example, with reports of repeated online frauds (UNODC, 2010, p. 208). A large Nigerian identity theft ring discovered in New York in 2008 has resulted in the indictment of 48 people who were part of a network purported to have over $12 million in profits (*Times Newsweekly*, 2009). However, two thirds of Internet crimes reported to the U.S. National Internet Crime Complaint Center in 2008 has been based in the United States. It is estimated that in 2006, 10 million people in the U.S. lost approximately $15.6 billion to identity theft (UNODC, 2010, p. 208).

In the past, the production and acquisition of child pornography was a risky activity and dissemination was limited to social networks and was difficult to obtain. Since internet child pornography is prolific and continues to increase and since child pornography now approaches the profitability of adult cyber pornography, organized crime groups have become involved. This has led to greater levels of victimization including the abduction/trafficking of children for purposes of producing pornographic materials. A problem with the criminal control of child pornography relates to differences in the criminal laws of various countries. Countries such as the U. S. and United Kingdom criminalize the possession, production, and distribution of child pornography; however, there is significant variability in the laws in other countries. Some countries like Japan, Russia, Thailand, and Korea only criminalize the production or distribution of child pornography, but allow personal possession without the intent to distribute (Akdeniz, 2008). Because of these difficulties, the current focus on international control of child pornography from a TOC perspective examines the *networks* that distribute these images. These networks involve groups that have been operating for some time and are committing many criminal offenses. "The acquisition of new images represents a form of 'material benefit', so even networks engaged in bartering could be considered organized crime groups under the United Nations Convention against Transnational Organized Crime"; the same is true of identity theft (UNODC, 2010, p. 218).

Control of Transnational Organized Crime

The United Nations Office of Drugs and Crime report, *The Globalization of Crime*, suggests several things to consider in combating TOC:

1. Since crime has gone global, purely national responses are inadequate; they displace the problem from one country to another;

2. States have to look beyond borders to protect their sovereignty. In the contemporary globalized world, this approach makes states more rather than less vulnerable. Trans-border intelligence—sharing information and law enforcement cooperation are essential;

3. Since transnational organized crime is driven by market forces, countermeasures must disrupt those markets, and not just the criminal groups that exploit them;

4. Since traffickers follow the paths of least resistance—characterized by corruption, instability and underdevelopment—it is essential to strengthen security and the rule of law;

5. Since criminals are motivated by profit, the key is to go after the money. This means strengthening integrity by implementing the United Nations Convention against Corruption. It also means stopping informal money transfers, offshore banking, and recycling through real estate that make it possible to launder money; and

6. Greater vigilance is needed to keep illicit goods out of the supply chain; prevent the diversion of licit products into the black market; strengthen anti-corruption measures; profile suspicious container and air traffic; and crack down on cybercrime and exercise due diligence (UNODC, 2010, preface; U.S. Department of Justice, 2008).

Comparison of Organized Crime Groups and Terrorist Groups

Criminologists have examined the linkage between organized crime, especially transnational organized crime, and terrorism. The two groups, as we noted, have some similarities in organizational structure such as compartmentalization or the use of cells in conducting criminal activities. Both groups engage in similar logistical activities in moving people, money, materials, and weapons across borders (Abadinsky, 2010, p. 5). Organized crime and terrorist groups also engage in a number of similar criminal and violent activities including assassination, hijacking, kidnappings, drug trafficking, arms trafficking, human trafficking, money laundering, armed robbery, fraud, and counterfeiting. Even though there are many similarities, differences between the two groups, however, do exist, e.g., in the motivations for the commission of crimes.

Organized crime groups' are mainly profit-oriented. Their involvement in criminal activities is mainly instrumental. They are centrally focused on maximizing making money and profits from their various criminal enterprises. As a result they follow demand and supply and when demand shifts, they change course as well. Moreover, organized crime groups do not typically seek change in society. Rather than seeking to destroy an existing governmental entity, they tend to choose to work within it; they often collude with, or otherwise bribe and corrupt governmental officials. Generally, if profits are coming in, they tend to support the status quo (including working to elect their preferred political candidates). Organized crime groups rarely publicize their activities. In fact, today they are much more subtle in their activities, particularly acts of violence, than their counterparts in the past so as not to bring undue public attention, which may get in the way of business/profits (in other words, violence may be bad for their "business").

Terrorist groups' involvement in criminal activity is primarily to further their cause. Many of the acts of violence are expressive, although terrorist groups may also use the resources from crime to finance their activities that serve to further their political/religious goals or to create, maintain, or enhance their power, interests, or ideology. Terrorist organizations often seek change through annihilation of an opposing government. They use different criminal tactics as a means of gaining power or destroying their rival governmental opponents or causing fear in and victimization of innocent people, which is designed to weaken the opposition. Terrorist groups frequently seek publicity for their activities, through symbolic bombings, beheadings, and the like, e.g., consider Al-Qaeda's publicity related to their brutal activities over the years (Adbadinsky, 2010).

Despite these significant differences, there is evidence suggesting that terrorist organizations such as Al-Qaeda, Hezbollah, and Hamas have found that criminal activities such as those engaged in by organized crime groups can help support their goals especially when there are diminished finances from other sources such as state sponsorship. In recent years some terrorist organizations have been expanding into a wide range of organized enterprise crimes. In fact terrorist groups have actually formed working partnerships with organized crime groups (Mallory, 2012, p. 258; Curtis and Karacan, 2002; Sheptycki, 2003).

Gangs and Violence

Criminologists have studied gangs in America for close to 100 years trying to understand why they form, their structure, how they evolve over time, and how to control the crimes that they perpetrate, which include violent crimes. Studies consistently show that gang members commit property, weapons, drug, and violent crimes including murders at substantially higher rates than individuals not involved in gangs (Huff, 1989; Thornberry, et al., 2003). Despite much research done on gangs, there is no single, universally accepted definition of a "gang." Even though criminologists who study gangs and law enforcement officials who deal with gang violence are not in agreement as to the precise definition of a gang, there is general agreement that much crime and delinquency is of a collective nature, which means it is committed by juveniles and/or adults in the company of peers in group settings. Over the years there have been many causal explanations proffered regarding the existence of gangs as well as their attributes including membership and structure (Howell and Moore, 2010).

Classical gang researcher, Frederick Thrasher (1927), who studied over 1300 gangs in Chicago during the 1920s, believed gangs were formed naturally during adolescence from spontaneous play groups. According to Thrasher groups of youths are transformed into gang members as a result of conflict with other groups of youths or with common enemies such as the police. Conflict functions to integrate gang members and stimulates the development of "traditions, unreflective internal structure, esprit de corps, solidarity, morale, group awareness, and attachment to a local territory" (p. 46). He also noted that gangs may be characterized by several types of behaviors including certain types of communication and face-to-face interactions, milling, movement through space as a unit, and planning. Despite certain characteristics of gangs, Thrasher argued that "No two gangs are just alike" (p. 36), some are marginally "organized," lacking permanence, solidarity, or permanent leadership, and not all gangs are "criminal types," involved in habitual crime. Many gangs are focused on conventional activities such as sports and recreation. Thrasher's definition and characteristics of gangs laid the foundations for theorizing about gangs for many years to follow (Cohen, 1955; Cloward and Ohlin, 1960; Short and Strodtbeck, 1965; Klein, 1969; Cartwright, et al., 1975; Miller, 1958; 1975; Haskell and Yablonsky, 1978).

Walter Miller's early multicity gang surveys (1975, 1982, 1990, and 1992) found that nationally the growth of gangs in the 1970s continued though the early 1990s, dropping dramatically in 1995. According to some experts, growth in street gangs and gang violence from the mid-1980s to the early 1990s may be explained by the crack cocaine epidemic during that time (Klein, 1995). Miller points to several other factors that might explain the growth of gangs and their violence during that time, which include: (1) population growth and movement aided by expansion of cars and highways; (2) gangs moving into new suburban and rural areas; (3) family migration leading to spread of gang culture (Maxson, 1998); and (4) court-mandated busing (Hagedorn, 1988; Huff, 1989; National Gang Center, FAQ). Due to the paucity of major national gang studies in the country, Miller, a leader in the field, has recommended that a federal center be established for the tracking and monitoring of gangs and their activities in the country; this happened with the creation of the National Youth Gang Center in 1995.

Definition of Gangs

According to the National Gang Center, the following criteria appear to be commonly accepted by gang researchers today for classifying groups as gangs:

- The group has three or more members, generally aged 12–24.
- Members share an identity, typically linked to a name, and often other symbols.
- Members view themselves as a gang, and they are recognized by others as a gang.
- The group has some permanence and a degree of organization.
- The group is involved in an elevated level of criminal activity (National Gang Center, FAQ).

The term "street gang" or "criminal street gang" is often used in the same context as a youth gang, and suggests that the group has a street presence, sometimes reflected in the name of the gang (e.g., the 18th Street Gang in Los Angeles), and that the gang primarily engages in "street crimes"(e.g., aggravated assault, robbery, rape, gun crimes, drug crimes, and murder), the types of crimes that the police, citizens, and policy makers are most concerned about and seek to control. Most street gangs are commonly thought to be "loosely structured, with transient leadership and membership, easily transcended codes of loyalty, and informal rather than formal roles for the members" (Klein, 2004, p. 59). This aspect of many youth gangs, despite the older ages of some members, does not, according to some criminologists, meet the criteria of "organized crime," which includes an infrastructure and organization, although many street gangs in the U.S. and other countries make huge sums of money from drug trafficking and other criminal enterprises (Taylor, 1990; Decker, et al., 1998; Weisel, 2002; Ribando, 2005). Klein notes that "to remain in business, organized crime groups such as drug cartels must have strong leadership, codes of loyalty, severe sanctions for failure to abide by these codes, and a level of entre-preneurial expertise that enables them to accumulate and invest proceeds from drug sales (2004, p. 58). Some gangs have transformed themselves from street gangs into formidable organized criminal organizations such as the Black Gangster Disciples Nation in Chicago, which is involved in national drug trafficking, murder, and a variety of other criminal enterprises (Spergel, 1995).

Demographic Characteristics of Gang Members

The National Gang Center (NGC) has been tracking and measuring the presence, char-acteristics, and behaviors of local gangs, including violent crimes such as homicides, in jurisdictions in the U.S. since 1996. The National Youth Gang Survey (NYGS) is based on a nationally representative sample of law enforcement agencies in major cities, suburban counties, smaller cities, and rural counties (National Gang Center, 2009). Their latest trend analysis, 14-year gang prevalence from 1996–2009, found that gang activity in the United States remains a widespread problem. There was a peak in reported gang activity in 1996, and then a sharp decline nationwide throughout the late 1990s. A substantial increase in the number of gangs beginning in 2001 continued until 2005, and while seemingly having leveled off somewhat thereafter, both the number of gangs and number of localities increased by more than 20 percent from 2002 to 2009. The most current figures from the 2009 survey report suggest that there are approximately 28,100 gangs and 731,000 gang members throughout the 3,500 jurisdictions nationwide (Egley and Howell, 2011). As in the past, gang problems are most prevalent in the nation's largest cities, with populations of 100,000 or more reporting multiple years of gang problems. Survey results offer the following information regarding the age, gender, and race/ethnicity of gang members:

Age

Contrary to the popular association of juveniles with gang membership, in almost every survey year, the NYGS has reported a greater percentage of adult (18 and over) gang members than juvenile gang members (under 18). The most recent figures indicate that adult-aged gang members make up about two-thirds of gang member recorded by law enforcement agencies. Some variation is found across jurisdictions. Larger cities and suburban counties report more adult-aged gang members; smaller cities and rural counties, report less frequent gang problems and greater proportions of juvenile aged members (National Gang Center, 2009).

Gender

Based on law enforcement agency reports, the NYGS indicates "overwhelmingly" a greater percentage of male gang members than female gang members. Despite concerns over females joining gangs, there has been little change over the 14 years of surveys. However, about 15 percent of larger cities, 13 percent of suburban counties, 18 percent of smaller cities, and 12 percent of rural counties reported that more than half of the gangs *have* female members (National Gang Center, 2009).

Race/Ethnicity

Across all jurisdictions, from larger cities on down, NYGS results report that African-American/black and/or Hispanic/Latino predominate among documented gang members. The most current national statistics suggest that 49 percent of gang members are Hispanic/Latino, 35 percent are African-American, 9 percent are white, and 7 percent are of unknown race/ethnicity. Across all jurisdictions, from larger cities on down, NYGS results indicate that African-American and/or Hispanic/Latino members predominate among documented gang members. Prevalence rates for white gang membership are lowest in cities, but are twice as high in rural areas (National Gang Center, 2009).

Types of Gangs

Although gangs vary in terms of any number of factors such as membership, structure, age, ethnicity, and gender, criminal activities, and the like, three basic types of gangs have been identified by gang investigators: (1) street gangs, (2) outlaw motorcycle gangs, and (3) prison gangs (National Gang Threat Assessment, 2009, p. 6).

Street Gangs

A large variety of street gangs can be found in most areas in the United States and their criminal activities can include drug trafficking as well as various forms of violent crimes; and they may operate with local, regional, national and in some instances international influences (see Howell and Moore, 2010, for a good historical view of street gangs). Obviously gangs that have national and international threads, especially those that develop associations with drug trafficking organizations (DTO), as some street gangs have with Mexico, Central America and Canada, pose the greatest threats. As reported by local, state, and national law enforcement agencies, there are currently (i.e., as of 2009), 11 national-level gangs identified in the United States that have "associates or members" otherwise identified or linked to foreign countries. These national gangs may have several hundred to several thousand members nationwide who operate in multiple regions of the U.S. and with some having cells in foreign countries who assist the U.S. based-gangs.

Box 5.5 U.S. Based Street Gangs (Regional and National)

18th Street (National)

Formed in Los Angeles, 18th Street is a group of loosely associated sets or cliques, each led by an influential member. Membership is estimated at 30,000 to 50,000. In California approximately 80 percent of the gang's members are illegal aliens from Mexico and Central America. The gang is active in 44 cities in 20 states. Its main source of income is street-level distribution of cocaine and marijuana and, to a lesser extent, heroin and methamphetamine. Gang members also commit assault, auto theft, carjacking, drive-by-shootings, extortion, homicide, identification fraud, and robbery.

Almighty Latin King and Queen Nation (National)

The Latin Kings street gang was formed in Chicago in the 1960s and consisted predominantly of Mexican and Puerto Rican males. Originally created with the philosophy of overcoming racial prejudice and creating an organization of "Kings," the Latin Kings evolved into a criminal enterprise operating throughout the United States under two umbrella factions—Motherland, also known as KMC (King Motherland Chicago), and Bloodline (New York). All members of the gang refer to themselves as Latin Kings and, currently, individuals of any nationality are allowed to become members. Latin Kings associating with the Motherland faction also identify themselves as "Almighty Latin Kin Nation (ALKN)," and make up more than 160 structured chapters operating in 158 cities in 31 states. The membership of Latin Kings following KMC is estimated to be 20,000 to 35,000. The Bloodline was founded by Luis Felipe in the New York State correctional system in 1986. Latin Kings associating with Bloodline also identify themselves as the "Almighty Latin King and Queen Nation (ALKQN)." Membership is estimated to be 2,200 to 7,500, divided among several dozen chapters operating in 15 cities in 5 states. Bloodline Latin Kings share a common culture and structure with KMC and respect them as Motherland, but all chapters do not report to the Chicago leadership hierarchy. The gang's primary source of income is the street-level distribution of power cocaine, crack cocaine, heroin, and marijuana. Latin Kings continue to portray themselves as a community organization while engaging in a wide variety of criminal activities, including assault, burglary, homicide, identity theft, and money laundering.

Asian Boyz (National)

Asian Boyz is one of the largest Asian street gangs operating in the United States. Formed in southern California in the early 1970s, the gang is estimated to have 1,300 to 2,000 members operating in at least 28 cities in 14 states. Members primarily are Vietnamese or Cambodian males. Members of Asian Boyz are involved in producing, transporting, and distributing methamphetamine as well as distributing MDMA and marijuana. In addition, gang members are involved in other criminal activities, including assault, burglary, drive-by shootings, and homicide.

Black P. Stone Nation (National)

Black P. Stone Nation, one of the largest and most violent associations of street gangs in the United States consists of seven highly structured street gangs with a single leader and a common culture. It has an estimated 6,000 to 8,000 members, most of whom are African American males from the Chicago metropolitan area. The gang's main source of income is the street-level distribution of cocaine, heroin, marijuana, and, to a lesser extent, methamphetamine. Members are also involved in many other types of criminal activity, including assault, auto theft, burglary, carjacking, drive-by shootings, extortion, homicide, and robbery.

Bloods (National)

Bloods is an association of structured and unstructured gangs that have adopted a single-gang culture. The original Bloods were formed in the early 1970s to provide protection from the Crips street gang in Los Angeles, California. Large, national-level Bloods gangs include

Bounty Hunter Bloods and Crenshaw Mafia Gangsters. Bloods membership is estimated to be 7,000 to 30,000 nationwide; most members are African American males. Bloods gangs are active in 123 cities and in 33 states. The main source of income for Bloods gangs is street-level distribution of cocaine and marijuana. Bloods members also are involved in transporting and distributing methamphetamine, heroin, and PCP (phencyclidine), but to a much lesser extent. The gangs also are involved in other criminal activity including assault, auto theft, burglary, carjacking, drive-by shootings, extortion, homicide, identity fraud, and robbery.

Crips (National)

Crips is a collection of structured and unstructured gangs that have adopted a common gang culture. Crips membership is estimated at 30,000 to 35,000; most members are African American males from the Los Angeles metropolitan area. Large, national-level Crips gangs include 107 Hoover Crips, Insane Gangster Crips, and Rolling 60s Crips. Crips gangs operate in 221 cities in 41 states. The main source of income for Crips gangs is the street-level distribution of powder cocaine, crack cocaine, marijuana, and PCP. The gangs also are involved in other criminal activity such as assault, auto theft, burglary, and homicide.

Florencia 13 (Regional)

Florencia 13 (F 13 or FX 13) originated in Los Angeles in the early 1960s; gang membership is estimated at more than 3,000 members. The gang operates primarily in California and increasingly in Arkansas, Missouri, New Mexico, and Utah. Florencia 13 is subordinate to the Mexican Mafia (La Eme) prison gang and claims Surenos (Sur 13) affiliation. A primary source of income for gang members is the trafficking of cocaine and methamphetamine. Gang members smuggle multikilogram quantities of powder cocaine and methamphetamine obtained from supply sources in Mexico into the United States for distribution. Also, gang members produce large quantities of methamphetamine in southern California for local distribution. Florencia members are involved in other criminal activities, including assault, drive-by shootings, and homicide.

Fresno Bulldogs (Regional)

Fresno Bulldogs is a street gang that originated in Fresno, California, in the late 1960s. Bulldogs is the largest Hispanic gang operating in central California, with membership estimated at 5,000 to 6,000. Bulldogs is one of the few Hispanic gangs in California that claim neither Surenos (Southern) nor Nortenos (Northern) affiliation. However, gang members associate with Nuestra Familia (NF) members, particularly when trafficking drugs. The street-level distribution for methamphetamine, marijuana, and heroin is a primary source of income for gang members. In addition, members are involved in other criminal activity, including assault, burglary, homicide, and robbery.

Gangster Disciples (National)

The Gangster Disciples street gang was formed in Chicago, Illinois, in the mid-1960s. It is structured like a corporation and is led by a chairman of the board. Gang membership is estimated at 25,000 to 50,000; most members are African American males from the Chicago metropolitan area. The gang is active in 110 cities in 31 states. The gang is also involved in other criminal activity, including assault, auto theft, firearms violations, fraud, homicide, the operation of prostitution rings, and money laundering.

Latin Disciples (Regional)

Latin Disciples, also known as Maniac Latin Disciplines and Young Latino Organization, originated in Chicago in the late 1960s. The gang is composed of at least 10 structured and unstructured factions with an estimated 1,500 to 2,000 members and associate members. Most members are Puerto Rican males. Maniac Latin Disciples is the largest Hispanic gang in the Folk Nation Alliance. The gang is most active in the Great Lakes and southwestern regions of the United States. The street-level distribution of powder cocaine, heroin, marijuana, and PCP is a primary source of income for the gang. Members also are involved in other criminal activity, including assault, auto theft, carjacking, drive-by shootings, home invasion, homicide, money laundering, and weapons trafficking.

Mara Salvatrucha (National)

Mara Salvatrucha, also known as MS 13, is one of the largest Hispanic street gangs in the United States. Traditionally, the gang consisted of loosely affiliated groups known as cliques; however, law enforcement officials have reported increased coordination of criminal activity among Mara Salvatrucha cliques in the Atlanta, Dallas, Los Angeles, Washington, D.C., and New York metropolitan areas. The gang is estimated to have 30,000 to 50,000 members and associate members worldwide, 8,000 to 10,000 of whom reside in the United States. Members smuggle illicit drugs, primarily power cocaine and marijuana, into the United States and transport and distribute the drugs throughout the country. Some members also are involved in alien smuggling, assault, drive-by shootings, homicide, identity theft, prostitution operations, robbery, and weapons trafficking.

Suenos and Nortenos (National)

As individual Hispanic street gang members enter prison systems, they put aside former rivalries with other Hispanic street gangs and unite under the name Surenos or Nortenos. The original Mexican Mafia members, most of whom were from southern California, considered Mexicans from the rural, agricultural areas of northern California weak and viewed them with contempt. To distinguish themselves from the agricultural workers or farmers from northern California, members of Mexican Mafia began to refer to the Hispanic gang members who worked for them as Suenos (Southerners). Inmates from northern California became known as Nortenos (Northerners) and are affiliated with Neustra Familia. Because of its size and strength, Fresno Bulldogs is the only Hispanic gang in the California Department of Corrections (CD) that does not fall under Suenos or Nortenos but remains independent. Suenos gang members' main sources of income are retail-level distribution of cocaine, heroin, marijuana, and methamphetamine within prison systems and in the community as well as extortion of drug distributors on the street. Some members have direct links to Mexican DTOs and broker deals for Mexican Mafia as well as their own gang. Suenos have direct links to Mexican DTOs and broker deals with Mexican Mafia as well as their own gang. Suenos gangs also are involved in other criminal activities such as assault, carjacking, home invasion, homicide, and robbery. Nortenos gang members' main sources of income are the retail-level distribution of cocaine, heroin, marijuana, methamphetamines, and PCP within prison systems and in the community as well as extortion of drug distributors on the streets. Nortenos gangs also are involved in other criminal activities such as assault, carjacking, home invasion, homicide, and robbery.

Tango Blast (Regional)

Tango Blast is one of the largest prison/street criminal gangs operating in Texas. Tango Blast's criminal activities include drug trafficking, extortion, kidnapping, sexual assault, and murder. In the late 1990s, Hispanic men incarcerated in federal, state, and local prisons founded Tango Blast for personal protection against violence from traditional prison gangs such as the Aryan Brotherhood, Texas Syndicate, and Texas Mexican Mafia. Tango Blast originally had four city-based chapters: Houstone, Houston, Texas; ATX or La Capricha, Austin, Texas; D-Town, Dallas, Texas; and Foros or Foritios, Fort Worth, Texas. These founding four chapters are collectively known as Puro Tango Blast or the four Horsemen. From the original four chapters, former Texas inmates established new chapters in El Paso, San Antonio, Corpus Christi, and the Rio Grande Valley. In June 2008 the Houston Police Department (HPD) estimated that more than 14,000 Tango Blast members were incarcerated in Texas. Tango Blast is difficult to monitor. The gang does not conform to either traditional prison/street gang hierarchical organization or gang rules. Tango Blast is laterally organized, and leaders are elected sporadically to represent the gang in prisons and to lead street gang cells. The significance of

Tango Blast is exemplified by corrections officials reporting that rival traditional prison gangs are now forming alliances to defend themselves against Tango Blast's growing presence.

Tiny Rascal Gangsters (National)

Tiny Rascal Gangsters is one of the largest and most violent Asian street gang associates in the United States. It is composed of at least 60 structured and unstructured gangs, commonly referred to as sets, with an estimated 5,000 to 10,000 members and associates who have adopted a common gang culture. Most members are Asian American males. The sets are most active in the southwestern, Pacific, and New England regions of the United States. The street-level distribution of powder cocaine, marijuana, MDMA, and methamphetamine is a primary source of income for the sets. Members also are involved in other criminal activity, including assault, drive-by shootings, extortion, home invasion, homicide, robbery and theft.

United Blood Nation (Regional)

Bloods is a universal term that is used to identify both West Coast Bloods and United Blood Nation (UBN). While these groups are traditionally distinct entities, both identify themselves by "Blood," often making it hard for law enforcement to distinguish between them. United Blood Nation (NBN) started in 1993 in Rikers Island GMDC (George Mochen Detention Center) to form protection from the threat posed by Latin Kings and Netas, who dominated the prison. United Blood Nation (UBN) is a loose confederation of street gangs, or sets, that once were predominantly African American. Membership is estimated to be between 7,000 and 15,000 along the U.S. eastern corridor. UBN derives its income from street-level distribution of cocaine, heroin, and marijuana; robbery; auto theft; and smuggling drugs to prison inmates. UBN members also engage in arson, carjacking, credit card fraud, extortion, homicide, identity theft, intimidation, prostitution operations and weapons distribution.

Vice Lord Nation (National)

Vice Lord Nation, based in Chicago, is a collection of structured gangs located in 74 cities in 28 states, primarily in the Great Lakes Region. Led by a national board, the various gangs have an estimated 30,000 to 35,000 members, most of whom are African American males. The main source of income is street-level distribution of cocaine, heroin, and marijuana. Members also engage in other criminal activity such as assault, burglary, homicide, identity theft, and money laundering.

Source: National Gang Threat Assessment, 2009: 23–27.

National gangs operating in the U.S. include the Crips, the Bloods, and the Latin Kings. The Crips who range from structured to non-structured groups composed of black males have their origins from the high schools in the Compton areas of Los Angeles in the late 1960s and early 1970s. Current national Crips gangs include the 107 Hoover Crips and the Insane Gangster Crips operating in 41 states. Criminal activities of these gangs encompass the distribution of power cocaine, crack cocaine, marijuana and PCP (phencyclidine), and other crimes such as assault, homicide, burglary, and motor vehicle theft.

The Bloods likewise have their roots in Los Angeles in the early 1970s and originated to provide protection from the Crips; they too are composed of black males with active gangs in 33 states. Blood gangs include the Bounty Hunter Bloods and Crenshaw Mafia Gangsters. The Bloods engage in street level distribution of cocaine and marijuana and they also are involved in the distribution of methamphetamine, heroin, and PCP. Other criminal activities include assault, auto theft, carjacking, drive-by shootings, extortion, homicide, identity fraud, and robbery.

The Latin Kings street gang was created in Chicago in the 1960s, and consists chiefly of Mexican and Puerto Rican males, although any nationality can become a member.

The organization of "Kings" was originally conceived to overcome racial and ethnic prejudice, but evolved into the Latin Kings criminal enterprise throughout the United States under two different factions—Motherland, also known as KMC (King Motherland Chicago) and Bloodline (New York). Those Latin Kings associating with the KMC faction also identify themselves as Almighty Latin King Nation (ALKN) and now operate in 158 cities and 31 states. Latin Kings linking themselves with the Bloodline faction, also referred to as the Almighty Latin King and Queen Nation (ALKQN), operates in 15 cities in 5 states. The gangs' main sources of income come from street level dealing of power cocaine, crack cocaine, heroin, and marijuana; and they also engage in many other criminal activities such as homicide, assault, identity theft, burglary, and money laundering (National Gang Threat Assessment, 2009, pp. 23–24).

Regional level street gangs are numerous but there are several significant ones that are organized and have a few hundred to several thousand members. These gangs distribute drugs wholesale at the street level and some are tied to drug trafficking organizations (DTOs) or other criminal organizations. Five well known regional gangs are the Florencia 13, Fresno Bulldogs, Latin Disciples, Tango Blast, and United Blood Nation.

Local street gangs are likewise numerous and often are nothing more than neighborhood based gangs that operate in single locations, yet they are often very violent and pose a serious problem to local law enforcement. These gangs engage in violence in conjunction with traditional crimes including retail-level drug dealing, but usually have no ties to DTOs although more recently it has been discovered that some gangs along the U.S.-Mexican border have dual membership with counterpart gangs in Mexico (National Gang Threat Assessment, 2009, p. 7).

Prison Gangs

Beginning in the 1960s, prisons showed evidence of being undermined by highly organized gangs of inmates with well established rules and codes of conduct. Prison gang allegiances fall mainly along racial and ethnic lines, and no one in prison is safe from gang intimidation and other forms of violence. Prison gangs currently operate in major state and federal prisons. Young inmates basically have no choice but to join a prison gang for their own protection. Many prison gangs are considered to be national level gangs and exert considerable control over local and regional street gangs. Released prison gang members often go back to their home street gangs and serve as links to the prison gangs. Many prison gangs control drug distribution both within the correctional facilities they are in as well as in their respective communities. In particular, prison gangs in the southwest region of the U.S. and in southern California heavily influence mid-level and retail-level drug dealing. These activities are facilitated through connections with Mexican drug trafficking organizations. For example the California based Mexican Mafia prison gang, formerly organized to protect Hispanic prisoners from racial violence in the prisons, is currently responsible for most of the narcotics trafficking within some prisons as well as on the streets. Through fear and intimidation, The Mexican Mafia (La Eme) controls Hispanic street gang members in prison and in many communities in California. Other prison gangs such as the Aryan Brotherhood (AB), established in the 1960s to allegedly protect white inmates from black prison gangs, is highly structured, and composed chiefly of Caucasian males. The gang is active in the southwestern and Pacific regions of the U.S. and, in addition, is known to be notoriously violent and involved in murder-for-hire enterprises; its main revenues come from dealing drugs (cocaine, heroin, marijuana, and methamphetamine) within the correctional system and on the streets. More recently, the AB has aligned itself with the Mexican Mafia and other Mexican DTOs (National Gang Threat Assessment, 2009, pp. 7, 28).

Outlaw Motorcycle Gangs

Outlaw motorcycle gangs (OMGs) are generally highly structured criminal organizations with centralized leadership and rules regulating membership and conduct. The gangs are particularly violent, engaging in any number of crimes including weapons and drug trafficking and many other violent crimes including assault, alien smuggling, drive-by shootings, extortion, home invasion robberies, and homicide. Other criminal activities include identity theft, insurance fraud, mortgage fraud, and the operation of prostitution rings. It is estimated by local and state law enforcement that between 280 and 520 OMGs operate at the local, regional, and national levels and include hundreds of chapters. Regional level chapters have anywhere from 50 to several hundred members. The Hells Angels Motorcycle Club is one of the most widely known OMG with over 250 chapters in the U.S. and foreign countries with up to 2,500 members. The Hells Angels are heavily involved in the drug trade and produce, transport and distribute most illegal drugs as well as diverted pharmaceuticals. Their other stock and trade is violence including assault, extortion, and homicide. Other OMGs include the Bandidos, the Outlaws, and the Mongols (National Gang Threat Assessment, 2009, p. 30).

Homicides and Gangs

Gang related homicides, including inter-gang conflict and other gang crimes, are thought to be a major indicator of gang-related problems in cities and other areas, but current trend research conducted by researchers for the National Gang Center suggest that gang homicides are heavily concentrated geographically in the U.S. Most cities report having few or no gang-related homicides (Howell, et al., 2011). According to the most recent National Youth Gang Survey, gang-related homicides, as in previous years, have continued to be highly concentrated in the most populated areas, with larger cities and suburban counties accounting for over 96 percent of all gang-related homicides in 2009. These homicides are, however, episodic, occurring in spurts depending on level of gang conflict and other factors. Out of the 167 cities that had populations over 100,000 for which homicide data has been provided, 57 (34%) had no gang-related homicides and the remainder, 110 (66%), had a total of 1,017 gang-related homicides in 2009; this total represents a 2 percent increase from 2002. In fact, there has been an overall steady increase of homicides, including a 7 percent increase from 2005 to 2009, and an 11 percent increase from 2008 to 2009. (Egley and Howell, 2011: 1–3; National Gang Center, 2009). About three quarters of larger cities reported a total of 10 or more gang-related homicides between 2002 and 2009. Between 2002 and 2009, the largest cities reported anywhere from 1,000 to 1,300 gang-related homicides in the NYGS survey. In fact, two cities, Los Angeles and Chicago, accounted for close to one-third of the aggregate total of annual gang-related homicides (National Gang Center, 2009).

Conflicts between gangs as well as local gang violence are consistently reported in the NYGS and other gang studies. Gang-related homicides, and other violence, have been linked to several factors and circumstances including:

- Maintenance of set space (i.e., protecting gang territory)
- Interpersonal "beefs" among members
- Surprise assaults
- Drug related factors including drug turf disputes
- Defending one's gang identity
- Defense of the gang's honor and reputation
- Gang revenge or retaliation
- Return of gang members after prison confinement
- Gang member migration from within the United States
- Gang member migration from outside the United States (Egley and Howell, 2011, p. 3).

Other Gang-Related Violence

Gangs are responsible for other types of violent crime in cities and other areas in our country (Harrell, 2005). Some of the violent crime is connected to drugs, drug use, and drug distribution; however, as noted by some researchers, "the association between gangs, drugs, and violence remains a complex issue" (Egley and Howell, 2011, p. 3). According to results of the National Youth Gang Survey, in 2009 about half of the law enforcement agencies list "drug-related" factors, along with inter-gang conflict, and prison inmates returning to the gang as the major factors affecting gang violence. However, factoring out the affects of drugs from other causal variables is difficult, at least from the use of law enforcement driven data; 6 in 10 departments reporting gang activity in their areas did not link drug crimes as gang influenced.

The 2009 National Drug Threat Survey found that 58% of law enforcement agencies in the U.S. report that gangs are involved in drug distribution, compared with 45% in 2004, and that the primary drugs dispersed by gangs are marijuana, followed by powder cocaine, crack cocaine, MDMA, (aka ecstasy), methamphetamine, and heroin. Gangs also engage in many other types of criminal activities including motor vehicle thefts, assaults, burglary, drive by shootings, extortion, alien smuggling, firearm offenses, weapons trafficking, home invasion robberies, identity theft, insurance fraud, and operating prostitution rings (National Drug Intelligence Center, 2009).

Gang violence rates have continued at exceptional levels over the past decade (2000–2009) despite the remarkable overall crime drop in the nation. Gang violence that is rather commonplace in very large cities seems largely unaffected by, if not independent from, other crime trends—with the possible exceptions of drug trafficking and firearm availability (Howell, et al., 2011).

The Future of Gangs

What is particularly interesting is that many of the major gangs that currently present serious problems to communities have operated for several generations (some go back to the 1960s or earlier) and have literally become "institutionalized" within their respective communities. While some of these gangs were originally founded to provide protection for their ethnic members (e.g., Latin Kings initially organized to protect Latinos in the community or in prisons), many of them evolved into violent criminal organizations, some more structured and organized than others, but nevertheless very violent and dangerous. The shift of single location gangs to regional, national, and, in some cases international levels, has been fueled mostly by the illegal drug trade, which served to expand their criminal networks and which no doubt will continue into the foreseeable future (Hagedorn, 2005). Gangs in the United States currently exist in most major cities and have migrated over the past 40 or so years into suburban and rural locations. Gangs are also reported to be operating in U.S. domestic and international military bases. The thought of gang members that are well-trained in weapons, explosives, and combat tactics poses a significant threat to law enforcement efforts to abate gang violence and other criminal activities.

Many gangs now use internet-based methods such as social networking sites, encrypted e-mail, and the internet to communicate with one another and to conduct "business" with customers (e.g., drug clientele). Gangs use social networking sites such as *MySpace*, *YouTube*, and *Facebook*, and personal Web pages to advertise their gangs and their exploits and to even recruit members (National Gang Threat Assessment, 2009, 10–11). By all indications gangs will operate in the future and will continue to pose challenges for communities and law enforcement.

Conclusion

This chapter examines several forms of collective violence, i.e., violence carried out by individuals in groups or other collective/crowd formations where they generally come together for specific purposes, which may include seeking social, political, or economic change or, as in the case of organized crime groups and gangs, to carry out criminal activities. Collective behavior associated with seeking social change, including resisting social change, in the form of acting crowds such as protests and social movements, may involve violence, which often emerges spontaneously as people get caught up in a particular event where emotions are high or in some cases may be in response to law enforcement use of violence. For instance the manifest function of some collective events was to bring attention to such issues as inequality, discrimination, and police brutality against African Americans. In these cases the participants saw themselves and were perceived by many as freedom fighters or civil rights activists. However, among the latent functions of the protests included destruction of life and property, which resulted in others perceiving participating individuals as rioters and law violators. As sociologist Howard Becker (1963) has suggested, violence like any form of deviance is often in the eye of the beholder. One person's freedom fighter may be another person's terrorist. This is an important observation to keep in mind when studying collective behavior that results in violence contemporaneously or historically. Recent rioters in Great Britain have been perceived by many as young hooligans out of control; and, yet from the perspective of others, they were seen as an oppressed group of social protestors who were demonstrating against the rigid social class system and dire economic conditions in Great Britain.

In this chapter we also discuss organized crime, which typically refers to collective behavior in the context of criminal networks comprised of groups that exhibit formalized structures and whose primary goals are to make money through any number of illegal activities that may involve violence. Although most people think of organized crime as originating during the Prohibition and Post Prohibition era of the 1930s in America, run by mobsters like Al Capone and the Italian Mafia, organized crime is literally as old as the country itself, originating literally with the birth of the country during pre-revolutionary times. Organized crime activities can be documented as far back as the colonial period where groups of criminals systematically stole cargos from ships and warehouses and provided illegal goods, e.g., contraband liquor and services such as prostitution and gambling.

Over the decades, organized crime in America has encompassed a diverse spectrum of ethnic and racial groups that have adapted their "business model" to every manner of illegal activities (e.g., drugs, alcohol, gambling, loans, murder, and disposal of hazardous or toxic wastes). More recently, since the end of the cold war, organized crime has become a true global enterprise, referred to as transnational organized crime (TOC), which has diversified and has been spread out all over the world encompassing developed nations as well as Third World countries yet continuing to operate through violence and corruption in many of their illegal activities. As has been noted by several scholars, "regardless of the degree of maturity or sophistication enjoyed by an organized crime group, violence will always be regarded as a pragmatic resource, which is never gratuitous, but a last resort when other intimidation proves inadequate" (Hobbs, 2003, p. 680; Falcone, 1993, p. 7; Gambetta, 1993, p. 2).

The TOC's diversified and expanded criminal activities and global markets have gone far beyond the traditional illicit activities of global drug production, transportation and distribution to include trafficking in persons for labor and sex, counterfeit products, maritime piracy, natural resource trafficking and environmental crimes, and cybercrime. More recently, to everyone's horror, there appears to be a linkage between some TOC groups and terrorist groups involving collusion and cooperation in certain criminal activities.

Collective violence also occurs in the context of gangs that range in organizational structure from highly structured to loosely structured groups, whose primary motives involve the commission of criminal activities, often involving extreme covert as well as overt violence, for power and/or illegal profit. Although most people when they hear the term "gang" think of juvenile gangs, in reality there are many types of gangs, street gangs, prison gangs, and outlaw biker gangs, whose membership and criminal activities may be highly specialized. Many gangs have national or regional status with large memberships of mostly adults who are involved in extensive criminal activities that often revolve around drug production, transportation and distribution as well as other violent criminal pursuits such as extortion, homicide, assault, murder for hire, home invasion robberies, and weapons trafficking. Many of these gangs have connections and ties to drug trafficking organizations (DTOs) and other criminal organizations (global organized crime networks) including gang members who have dual membership with counterpart gangs in other countries around the world.

Contemporary gang research suggests that gangs remain appealing to juveniles as well as younger adults. In fact one aspect of gangs today is the phenomenon of older members remaining in gangs. A reason for this is that gangs like other social groups provide many fundamental needs including companionship, training, activities, protection, self-esteem, a sense of belonging, and, in many instances, livelihoods and income through the commission of crime. Some gangs, especially those involved in the drug trade, approach organized/corporate crime status in terms of their organizational structure and lethality in retaliating against competitors (Blumstein, 2003). Many gangs now, as in the past, reflect racial, ethic, and cultural identity confirmation as well as geographical delineation and demarcation, a factor that often precipitates violence among gang members over drug turf and other symbolic territorial imperatives.

References

Abadinsky, H. (1985/1990). *Organized Crime*. Chicago: Nelson Hall.

Abadinsky, H. (2010). *Organized Crime*. Belmont, CA: Wadsworth Cengage Learning.

Adang, O.M. (2011). Imitation and Escalation of Collective Violence: An Observational Study. In T.D. Madensen and J. Knutsson (Eds.). *Preventing Crowd Violence*. London: Lynne Rienner, 47–67.

Akdeniz, U. (2008). *Internet Child Pornography and the Law: National and International Responses*. Burlington, VT: Asgate Publishing Co.

Alpert, B. (2012). Who is the 1 Percent? Location is Everything. New Orleans, LA: *The Times-Picayune*, February 03, 2012, A1–7.

Barkan, S.E., and Snowden, L.L. (2001). *Collective Violence*. Boston: Allyn and Bacon.

Becker, H. (1963). *Outsiders: Studies in the Sociology of Deviance*. New York: Free Press.

Beech, H., and Perry, A. (June 13, 2011). Killing Fields. *Time*, June 13, 2011.

Beech, A., Elliott, I., Birgden, A., and Findlater, D. (2008). The Internet and Child Sexual Offending: A Criminological Review. *Aggression and Violent Behavior*, 13, 217–228.

Bell, D. (1988). *The End of Ideology*. Cambridge, Mass: Harvard University Press.

Blee, K. (1991). *Women of the Klan: Racism and Gender in the 1920s*. Los Angeles: University of California Press.

Blee, K. (2008). White Supremacy as Extreme Deviance. In E. Goode and D. Vail. *Extreme Deviance*. Los Angeles, CA: Pine Forge, 108–117.

Block, A. (1978). History and Study of Organized Crime. *Urban Life*, 6, 455–474.

Blumer, H. (1974). Social Movements. In R. S. Denisoff (Ed.). *The Sociology of Dissent*. New York: Harcourt Brace Jovanovich, 74–90.

Blumstein, 2003. Youth Violence and Guns. In W. Heitmeyer and H. Hagan (Eds.). *International Handbook of Violence Research*. Boston: Kluwer Academic Publications, 657–677.

Brenner, S.W. (2002). Organized Cybercrime: How Cyberspace May Affect the Structure of Criminal Relationships. *North Carolina Journal of Law and Technology*, 4(1), 27.

Brown, B. (2012). As Terrifying as Terrorism Is ... Are We Safer? A Survey of the State of "Homeland Security." In D.W. Harper, L. Voigt, and W. Thornton (Eds.). *Violence: Do We Know It When We See It?* Durham, NC: Carolina Academic Press, 147–159.

Brown, R.M. (1989). The History of Protest, Rebellion, and Reform in America: An Overview. In T.R. Gurr (Ed.). *Violence in America: Protest, Violence and Reform, Volume 2*. Newbury Park, CA: Sage, 23–61.

Canter, D. 1980. *Fires and Human Behavior*. Chichester: John Wiley and Sons.

Cartwright, D.S., Tomson, B. and Schwartz, H. (1975). *Gang Delinquency*. Monterey, CA: Brooks/Cole Publishers.

Chin, K. (1990). *Chinese Subculture and Criminality: Non Traditional Crime Groups in America*. Westport, CT: Greenwood Press.

Choo, K.K.R. (2008). Organized Crime Groups in Cyberspace: A typology. *Trends in Organized Crime*, 11(3), 270–295.

Cloward, R., and Ohlin, L. (1960). *Delinquency and Opportunity: A Theory of Delinquent Gangs*. New York: Free Press

Cohen, S. (Feb. 18, 2003). Spray Used to Quell Fight Sparks Chaos at Chicago Nightspot. *Rocky Mountain News*, pp. 20A, 27A.

Cohen, A.C. (1955). *Delinquent Boys: The Culture of the Gang*. Glencoe, Ill.: Free Press.

Collins, R. (2008). *Violence: A Micro-Sociological Theory*. Princeton, NJ: Princeton University Press.

Commission of the European Communities. (2001). *Towards a European Strategy for Preventing Organized Crime: Joint report from Commission Services and Europol*. Brussels: European Commission, p. 8.

Combs, C. (2003). *Terrorism in the Twenty-First Century*. Upper Saddle River, N.J.: Prentice Hall.

Cooper, H.H.A. (2001). Terrorism: The Problem of Definition Revisited. *American Behavioral Scientist*, 44, 891–893.

Cressey, D. 1969. *Theft of a Nation: The Structure and Operations of Organized Crime in America*. New York: Harper.

Curtis, G. (October, 2002). *Involvement of Russian Organized Crime Syndicates, Criminal elements in the Russian Military, and Regional Terrorist Groups in Narcotics Trafficking in Central Asia, the Caucus, and Chechnya*. Washington, DC: Federal Research Division, Library of Congress.

Curtis, G., and Karacan, T. (December, 2002). *The Nexus among Terrorists, Narcotics Traffickers, Weapons Proliferations, and Organized Crime Networks in Western Europe*. Washington, D.C.: Federal Research Division, Library of Congress.

De Castella, T. (August 10, 2011). England Riots: Are Brooms the Symbol of the Resistance. *BBC News Magazine*. Retrieved from: http://www.bbc.co.uk/news/magazine-14475741.

De Castella, T. (August 16, 2011). England Riots: What's the Evidence Gangs were behind the Riots. *BBC News*. Retrieved from: http://www.bbc.co.uk/news/magazine-14540796.

Decker, S.H., Bynum, T.S., and Weisel, D.L. (1998). Gangs as Organized Crime Groups: A Tale of Two Cities. *Justice Quarterly*, 15, 395–423.

Denisova, T.A. (2004). *Trafficking in Women and Children for Purposes of Sexual Exploitation*. Zaporizhie State University.

Drabek, T.E. (2010). *The Human Side of Disaster*. New York: CRC Press.

Dunning, E. (2003). Violence and Sport. In W. Heitmeyer and J. Hagan (Eds.). *International Handbook of Violence Research*. Boston: Kluwer Academic Publishers, 903–920.

Egley, A.E., Jr., and Howell, J.C. (June 2011). Highlights of the 2009 National Youth Gang Survey. *Juvenile Justice Fact Sheet*. U.S. Department of Justice, Office of

Juvenile Justice and Delinquency Prevention. Retrieved from: http://www.ncjrs.gov/app/publications/alphalist.aspx.

Europol. (2006). *Organized Crime Threat Assessment 2006*. The Hague, Europol, p. 7.

Fagan, J. (1989). The Social Organization of Drug Use and Drug Dealing Among Urban Gangs. *Criminology*, 27, 633–669.

Falcone, G. (1993). *Men of Honour: The Truth about the Mafia*. London: Warner.

Felsen, D., and Kalaitzidis, A. (2005). A Historical Overview of Transnational Crime. In P. Reichel (Ed.). *Handbook of Transnational Crime and Justice*. London: Sage Publications, 3–19.

Ferber, A.I. (1998). *White Man Falling: Race, Gender and White Supremacy*. Lanham, MD: Rowman and Littlefield.

Federal Bureau of Investigation (FBI). Organized Crime. Retrieved from: http://www.fbi.gov/about-us/investigate/organizedcrime.

Federal Bureau of Investigation (FBI). Mafia Takedown Largest Coordinate Arrest in FBI History. Retrieved from: http://www.fbi.gov/news/stories/2011/january/mafia_012011/mafia_012011.

Finlay, B.D. (2011). *Counterfeit Drugs and National Security*. New York: The Stimson Center. Retrieved from: www.stimson.org.

Flowers, R.B. (2007). The Sex Trade Industry's Wordwide Exploitation of Children. In R. L. Callaway and J. Harrelson-Stephens (Eds.). *Exploring International Human Rights*. London. Lynne Rienner Publishers, 222–227.

Franklin, J.H. (1967). *From Slavery to Freedom: A History of Negro Americans*. New York, Vintage.

Gambetta, D. (1993). *The Sicilian Mafia: The Business of Private Protection*. Cambridge: Harvard University Press.

Garrison, J. (November 30, 2011). Arab Spring, American Fall. Huff Post Politics. Retrieved from: http://www.huffingtonpost.com/jim-garrison/arab-spring-american-fall_b_1120902.html.

Ghosh, B. (September 24, 2012). Flash Point. *Time*. 180(13), 28–33.

Gibbs, J.P. (1989). Conceptualization of Terrorism. *American Sociological Review*, 54, 329–340.

Giglo, M. (February 6, 2012). Crowd Sourcing. *Newsweek*, p. 18

Glowers, R.B. (2007). The Sex Trade Industry's Worldwide Exploitation of Children. In R. L. Callaway and J. Harrelson-Stephens (Eds.). Exploring *International Human Rights*. London: Lynne Rienner Publishers, 222–227.

Greenpeace International. (Sept. 6, 2010). *Unjust Sentence for Japanese Anti-Whaling Activities*. Retrieved from: http://www.greenpeace.org/international/en/news/features/unjust-sentence-for-tokoyo-two/.

Grillo, I. (2011): *El Narco. Inside Mexico's Criminal Insurgency*. New York: Bloomsbury Press.

Gurr, T. (1989). Political Terrorism: Historical Antecedents and Contemporary Trends. In T. Gurr (Ed.). *Violence in America: Protest, Rebellion, Reform*. Newbury Park: Sage, 201–230.

Hagedorn, J.M. (1988). *People and Folks: Gangs and the Underclass in a Rustbelt City*. Chicago, Illinois: Lakeview Press.

Hagedorn, J.M. (2005). The Global Impact of Gangs. *Journal of Contemporary Justice*, 21 (2), 153–169.

Harrell, E. (June, 2005). *Violence by Gang Members, 1993–2003*. Bureau of Justice Statistics Crime Date Brief, NCJ 208875.

Haskell, M.R., and Yablonsky, L. (1978). *Juvenile Delinquency*. Chicago: Rand McNally.

Hobbs, D. (2003). Organized Crime and Violence. In W. Heitmeyer and J. Hagan (Eds.). *International Handbook of Violence Research*. Boston: Kluwer Academic Publishers, 679–699.

Hoffman, B. (2006). *Inside Terrorism*. Columbia University Press.

Howell, J.C., Egley, A., Tita, G.E., and Griffiths, E. (May, 2011). *U.S. Gang Problem Trends and Seriousness, 1996–2009*. National Gang Center Bulletin (No. 6), Bureau of Justice Statistics, Office of Juvenile Justice and Delinquency Prevention.

Howell, J.C., and Moore, J.P. (May 2010). *History of Street Gangs in the United States*. National Gang Center Bulletin (No. 4). Bureau of Justice Statistics, Office of Juvenile Justice and Delinquency Prevention.

Huff, C.R. (1989). Youth Gangs and Public Policy. *Crime and Delinquency*, 35, 524–537.

Human Rights Watch. 2010. Unkept Promise Failure to End Military Business Activity in Indonesia. Jan. 11, p.7. Retrieved from: http://www.hrw.org/en/reports/2010/01/12/unkept-promise-0.

Ianni, F. A. (1974). *Black Mafia: Ethnic Succession in Organized Crime*. New York: Simon and Schuster.

International Labor Organization (ILO). (2005). *A Global Alliance against Forced Labor*. Geneva.

Jacobs, R.N. (1996). Civil Society and Crisis: Culture, Discourse, and the Rodney King Beating. *American Journal of Sociology*, 101(5), 1238–1272.

Kelly, R.J. (1992). Trapped in the Folds of Discourse: Theorizing about the Underworld. *Journal of Contemporary Criminal Justice*, 8, 11–35.

Kendall, D. (2006). *Sociology in Our Times*. Independence, KY: Thomson/ Wadsworth.

Kirkpatrick, D.D., and Sanger, D.E. (Feb. 13, 2011). A Tunisian-Egyptian Link that Shook Arab History. *The New York Times (Middle East)*. Retrieved from: http://www.nytimes.com/2011/02/14/world/middleeast/14egypt-tunisia-protests.html?pagewanted=all.

Klein, M.W. (1969). Violence in American Juvenile Gangs. In D. Mulvihill and M. Tumin (Eds.). *Crimes of Violence* (National Commission on the Causes and Prevention of Violence). Washington, DC: U.S. Government Printing Office.

Klein, M. W. (1995). *The American Street Gangs: Its Nature, Prevalence, and Control*. New York: Oxford University Press.

Klein, M. W. (2004). *Gang Cop: The Words and Ways of Officer Paco Domingo*, Walnut Creek, CA: Alta Mira Press.

Laqueur, W. (2001). *A History of Terrorism*. New Brunswick: Transaction Books.

Laqueur, W. (1999). *The New Terrorism: Fanaticism and the Arms of Mass Destruction*. New York: Oxford University Press.

LeBon, G. (1960/1896). *The Crowd: A Study of the Popular Mind.* New York: Viking, Originally published in 1896.

Lindsey, L.L., and Beach, S. (2000). *Sociology: Social Life and Issues.* Upper Saddle River, N.J.: Prentice Hall.

Lupsha, P.A. (1986). Organized Crime in the United States. In R. Kelly (Ed.). *Organized Crime: A Global Perspective.* Totowa, NJ: Rowman and Littlefield, 32–57.

Mallory, S.L. (2012). *Understanding Organized Crime.* Sudsbury, MA: Jones & Bartlett.

Maxson, C.L. (1998). *Gang Members on the Move.* Bulletin. Youth Gang Series. Washington, DC: U.S. Department of Justice, Office of Juvenile Justice and Delinquency Prevention.

McAdam, D., McCarthy, J.D., and Zald, M.N. (1988). Social Movements. In Neil J. Smelser (Ed.). *Handbook of Sociology*, Newbury Park, CA: Sage, 695–737.

McDevitt, J., Levin, J., and Bennett, S. (2002). Hate Crime Offenders: An Expanded Typology. *Journal of Social Issues*, 58(2), 303–317.

Miller, W.B. (1958). Lower Class culture as a generating milieu of gang delinquency. *Journal of Social Issues,* 15, 5–19.

Miller, W.B. (1975). *Violence by Youth Gangs and Youth Groups as a Crime Problem in Major American Cities.* Washington, DC: U.S. Dept of Justice, Office of Juvenile Justice and Delinquency Prevention.

Miller, W.B. (1982/1992). *Crime by Youth Gangs and Groups in the United States.* Washington, DC: U.S. Department of Justice, Office of Juvenile Justice and Delinquency Prevention.

Miller, W. B. (1990). Why the United States has failed to solve its Youth Gang Problem. In C.R. Huff (Ed.). *Gangs in America.* Newbury Park, CA: Sage Publications, 263–287.

Mohyeldin, A. (October 12, 2011). From the Arab Spring to the American Fall? Retrieved from: http://ideas.time.com/2011/10/12/from-the-arab-to-the-american-fall/.

Mulloy, D. (2004). *American Extremism: History, Politics and the Militia Movement.* London: Routledge.

National Advisory Commission on Civil Disorders. (1968). *Report of the National Advisory Commission on Civil Disorders.* New York: Bantam.

National Drug Intelligence Center. (2009). *National Drug Threat Assessment,* 2009. Washington, DC.

National Gang Center. (n.d.). Frequently Asked Questions About Gangs (FAQ). Retrieved from: http://www.nationalgangcenter.gov/about/FAQ.

National Gang Center. 2009. National Youth Gang Survey Analysis. Retrieved from: http://www.nationalgangcenter.gov/Survey-Analysis.

National Gang Threat Assessment, (2009). Jonestown, PA: National Gang Intelligence Center. January, 2009.

Newton, P., Proux, S., Green, M., Smituis, F., Rozendeal, J., et al. (2008). A Collaborative Epidemiological Investigation into the Criminal Artesunate Trade in South East Asia, *PLoS Medicine,* 5, 2.

Nossiter, A., and Gladstone, R. (Oct. 25, 2011). *Libya's Interim Leaders to Investigate Quadafi's Killing. The New York Times,* International, A-4.

Oberschall, A. (1973). *Social Conflict and Social Movements.* Englewood Cliffs, N.J.: Prentice Hall.

Organized Crime Control Act of 1970 (Pub. L. 91-452, Stat.922)

Parker, B. (Feb. 10, 2010). *Antiabortion demonstration picket Brookline clinic opening. The Boston Globe,* Retrieved from: http://www.boston.com/news/local/massachusetts/ articles/2010/02/10/antiabortion_demonstrations-picket_brookline_clinic_opening/.

Perry, J.B., and Pugh, M.D. (1978). *Collective Behavior: Response to Social Stress.* St. Paul: West Publishing.

President's Commission on Organized Crime. (1986). *The Impact: Organized Crime Today.* Washington, DC: U.S. Government Printing Office.

President's Commission on Law Enforcement and Administration of Justice. (1967). *Task Force Report: Organized Crime.* Washington, DC: U.S. Government Printing Office.

Reinares, F. 2003. Terrorism. In W. Heitmeyer and J. Hagan (Eds.). *International Handbook of Violence Research.* Boston: Kluwer Academic Publishers, 309–321.

Raper, A.F. (1970). *The Tragedy of Lynching.* New York: Dover.

Redlinger, L. (1969). *Dealing in Dope: Market Mechanisms and Distribution Patterns of Illicit Narcotics.* Ph.D. dissertation, Northwestern University. Ann Arbor, Mich: University Microfilms.

Reinares, F. (2003). Terrorism. In W. Heimeyer and J. Hagan (Eds.). *International Handbook of Violence Research.* Netherlands: Kluwer Academic Publishers, 309–321.

Ribando, C. (2005). *Gangs in Central America.* Washington, DC: Congressional Research Service, Library of Congress.

Rogovin, C.H., and Martens, F.T. (1992). The Evil That Men Do. *Journal of Contemporary Criminal Justice,* 8, 62–77.

Rohde, D. (Oct. 29, 1998). Sniper Attacks on Doctors Create Climate of Fear in Canada. *The New York Times,* Retrieved from: http://www.nytimes.com/1998/10/29/nyregion/sniper-attacks-on-doctors-create-climate-of-fear-in-canada.html2pagewanted=all&src=pm.

Rucht, D. (2003). Violence and New Social Movements. In W. Heitmeyer and J. Hagan (Eds.). *International Handbook of Violence Research.* Boston: Kluwer Academic Publishers, 369–382.

Sheptycki, J. (2003). Global Law Enforcement as a Protection Racket. In A. Edwards and P. Gill (Eds.). *Transnational Organized Crime.* London: Routledge.

Schemm, P., and Al-Shalchi, H. (August 26, 2011). Fight 'the rats" Gadhafi Implores as Rebel Leaders Push on in Libya. New Orleans, LA: *The Times-Picayune,* A-12.

Schmid, A.P., and de Graff, J. (1982). *Violence as Communication: Insurgent Terrorism and the Western News Media.* Beverly Hills, CA: Sage.

Shelly, L.I., and Picarelli, J.T. (2005). Methods and Motives: Exploring Links between Transnational Organized Crime and International Terrorism. *Trends in Organized Crime,* 9, 52–67.

Shelley, L.I., and Melzer, S. (2008). The Nexus of Organized Crime and Terrorism: Two Case Studies in Cigarette Smuggling. *International Journal of Comparative and Applied Criminal Justice,* 32, 44–62.

Short, J., and Strodtbeck, F. (1965). *Group Process and Gang Delinquency.* Chicago: Aldine de Gruyter.

Skocpol, T. 1979. *States and Social Revolution: A Comparative Analysis of France, Russia, and China.* New York: Cambridge University Press.

Spergel, I.A. (1995). *The Youth Gang Problem*. New York, NY: Oxford University Press.

Surtees, R. T. (2008). Traffickers and Trafficking in Southern and Eastern Europe. *European Journal of Criminology*, 5(1), 39–68.

Taylor, K. (1990). *Dangerous Society*. Detroit: Michigan State University Press.

Thompson, G. (2011). U.S. Infiltrating Criminal Groups across Mexico. *The New York Times*, Oct. 25, A1, 7.

Thornberry, T.P., Krohn, M.D., Lizotte, A.J., Smith, C.A., and Tobin, K. (2003). *Gangs and Delinquency in Developmental Perspective*. New York, NY: Cambridge University Press.

Thornburgh, N. (August 22, 2011). London's Long Burn. *Time*, pp. 28–31.

Timeline: Egypt's Revolution. (Feb. 14, 2011). Retrieved from: http://english.aljazeera.net/news/middleeast/2011/01/201112515334871490.html.

Times Newsweekly. (May 2009). Fraud Ring Smashers, Indictment Names 48, p.21.

Thrasher, F.M. (1927). *The Gang: A Study of 1,313 Gangs in Chicago*. Chicago: University of Chicago Press, 1966. (Originally published in 1927).

Tumulty, K. (May 32, 2009). George Tiller Murdered. *Time Swampland*. Retrieved from: http://swampland.time.com/2009/05/31/george-tiller-murdered/.

Turk, A. T. (1990). Social Dynamics of Terrorism. In N.A. Weiner, M.A. Zahn, and R. J. Sagi (Eds.). *Violence: Patterns, Causes, Public Policy*. New York: Harcourt Brace Jovanovich, 212–218.

Turner, R. H., and Killian, L.M. (1993). *Collective Behavior*. Upper Saddle River, NJ: Prentice Hall.

United Nations Office on Drugs and Crime (UNODC). (February 2009c).UNODC on Human Trafficking and Migrant Smuggling. Retrieved from: http://ww.unocd.org/unodc/en/human-trafficking/index.html?ref=menuside.

United Nations Office of Drugs and Crime (UNODC). (2009a). *Global Report on Trafficking in Persons*. Vienna: UNODC.

United Nations Office of Drugs and Crime (UNODC). (2009b). *World Drug Reports*. Vienna: UNODC.

United Nations Office on Drugs and Crime (UNODC). (2010). *The Globalization of Crime: A Transnational Organized Crime Threat Assessment*. Vienna.

United States Department of Justice. (April 2008). *Overview of the Law Enforcement Strategy to Combat International Organized Crime*. Retrieved from: http://www.fbi.gov/news/pressrel/press-releases/department-of-justice-launches-new-law-enforcement-strategy-to-combat-increasing-threat-of-international-organized-crime.

Van Duyne, P.C., Antonopoulos, G., Maljevic, A., Vander Beken, T., and von Lampe, K. (Eds.). (2010). *Cross-border Crime Inroads on Integrity in Europe*. Nijmegen: Wolf Legal Publishers.

Vayrynen, R. (2003). *Illegal Immigration, Human Trafficking, and Organized Crime*. United Nations University and World Institute for Development Economics Research. Helsinki, Finland.

Voigt, L., Thornton, W.E., Barrile, L., and Seaman, J.M. (1994). *Criminology and Justice*, New York: McGraw Hill.

Weisel, D.L. (2002). The Evolution of Street Gangs: An Examination of Form and Variation. In W. Reed and S. Decker (Eds.). *Responding to Gangs: Evaluation and Research.* Washington D.C.: U.S Department of Justice, National Institute of Justice, 25–65. Retrieved from: http://www.ncjrs.gov/profiles1/nij/190351.

Williams, P. (2001). Organizing Transnational Crime: Networks, Markets, and Hierarchies. In P. Williams and D. Vlassis (Eds.). *Combating Transnational Crime. Concepts, Activities and Responses.* London: Fran Cass, 57–87.

Woolston, H.B. (1969). *Prostitution in the United States.* New York: Patterson Smith.

Wright, R. (September, 2011). The Struggle within Islam. *Smithsonian.* 43(5), 104–114.

Chapter 6

State Violence

In this chapter, we examine violence at the macro sociological level of analysis. One rather simple definition of state violence sees it as an institutionalized form of collective violence that follows a script or the edict of a ruler or that it is codified in the law. This, no doubt, is too simplistic a definition. However, any definition of state violence presupposes agreement on what we mean by the term "state." Generally speaking, those who study state violence tend to "equate state with government" (e.g., Iadicola and Shupe, 2003). Sociologist Max Weber (1958) in his political work, *Politics as a Vocation*, in answer to the question: What is a 'state'? says that "ultimately, one can define the modern state sociologically only in terms of the specific means peculiar to it, as to every political association, namely, the use of physical force" (pp. 77–78). He goes on to say "if no social institutions existed which knew the use of violence, then the concept of 'state' would be eliminated, and a condition would emerge that could be designated as 'anarchy,' in the specific sense of the word" (p. 78). Weber cautions that force is not the only means that states have but "the relation between the state and violence is an especially intimate one" (p. 78). While historically the use of physical force, he notes, was probably more accepted and normal, even in present society "we have to say that a state is a human community that (successfully) claims the *monopoly of the legitimate use of physical force* within a given territory" (p. 78). (Weber sees territory as one of the characteristics of the state). And while the right to use physical force can be delegated to other institutions or individuals, it can so only "to the extent to which the state permits it. The state is considered the sole source of the 'right' to use violence" (p. 78). In essence, Weber sees the state composed of three elements: territoriality, legitimacy, and violence (Iadicola and Shupe, 2003, p. 261). More to our point, Weber discusses the rise of the modern state in relation to the legitimation of authority and power within a specific geographic locale. He indicates that power can only be legitimized rationally by the state, which can use violence to keep its own people in check or to protect the state and its interests from perceived outside threats (Weber, 1978; Iadicola, 2012, p. 16).

State sponsored violence is almost always motivated by a specific ideology. Ideology refers to a body of doctrines, beliefs, or ideals that guide a group, class, or society. An ideology represents the agreed upon conceptions of the "normal" or "ideal" social order (i.e., a presumed concept of justice). It presupposes a particular understanding of social existence including how individuals socially construct their reality (Mannheim, 1931/1936; Berger and Luckman, 1967). State violence, legitimate and "illegitimate" (also referred to as extra legal violence), is always defined in an ideological context. As noted by Iadicola and Shupe (2003, p. 262), given "that the state is in a monopoly position of power to define the legal status of the violence ... most of the acts within the broader domain of violence ... are those acts that threaten the state." Moreover, they pose the question: "If the state is unlikely to define its own acts of violence as illegitimate, then who is left to do so?" Ideology is used by powerful groups and nations to maintain their status, domination, and control, and is used by less powerful groups to attain a voice, equity, concession on issues, a place in the political decision-making process, or an advantage or dominance over a rival group. Clearly, then, there is a general dichotomy in political crime and violence, with the state and "legitimate" powerful interest groups on one side and non-state, non-legitimate, less powerful groups on the other. Unfortunately, even established and recognized democratic governments like the United States, can abuse legitimate authority including the circumstances when violent force is perceived as necessary to control individuals and groups in its own jurisdiction or other individuals, groups or governments who are perceived to be hostile or pose a threat. When is an act considered a "crime", and when is it a legitimate use of force to defend one's country, preserve law and order, or protect one's group? In any discussion of state violence, perhaps more than any other type of crime, one's group membership can completely determine the perception and definition of an act as either politically justifiable or condemnably criminal. Truly, one group's treasonous terrorism is another group's patriotic heroism. Historically in America, anticommunist ideology, and more recently "war on terror" ideology, for some, justifies illegal and violent acts in the name of the state (e.g., Guantanamo Bay abusive interrogation techniques, sending detainees to third countries or their own countries for torture, and racial and ethnic profiling (see Kalb, 2012). While variations in political sentiment produce the relativity in the perception of state crime, in reality, those groups able to enforce order are usually able to punish less powerful groups for violent acts that differ little in consequences from their own. Criminologists have long known that power, position, and legitimacy possess an instrumental role in defining crime, including state crimes.

State Power and Legality

Established power groups and recognized governments determine, to a large extent, which individuals are criminals, which acts are criminal, and in which circumstances force is legitimate. They also determine which groups are considered terrorists, which acts are treasonous, which citizens are insurgent threats, and which wars are just.

Operation Iraq Freedom in which the U.S. started a war with Iraq and invaded the country on March 20th 2003 under the administration of George W. Bush is a prime example. The impetus behind the war was the concern for Weapons of Mass Destruction (WMD), which never actually materialized (see Brown, 2012). Nine years later, the United States is withdrawing its military (December 17, 2011) leaving a country transformed by the removal of Saddam Hussein and also by U.S. military occupation and the bitter ethnic and sectarian fighting that followed. Minority Sunnis who were in power under Hussein perceive that a majority Shi'ite-led government will further marginalize them (Markey, 2011). According to the defense department, 4,487 service members were killed in the war, and more than 30,000 were wounded (Basu, 2011).

Over the years, the U.S. government has seen nothing wrong in sponsoring assassination attempts, coups, and other forms of violence against communist, socialist and terrorist group/government leaders and heads of state. Protecting national security is a universal rationalization for state violence, e.g., suspension of rights for Japanese Americans during World War II. More recently, in response to 9/11 the U.S. launched a global war against terrorism, both within and outside its own country. Under the new cabinet department of the U.S. government, The Department of Homeland Security (DHS) has grown into a massive organization with almost one million people having top-secret security clearances working in different capacities on counter terrorism, homeland security and intelligence, surveilling and monitoring many of its own citizens on a daily basis (Priest and Atkins, 2010).

Governments, justifiably or not, have an advantage over protesting groups. They can and do arrest, adjudicate, and imprison individuals who are perceived to be threats to the established rule of law for acts that may or may not be criminal. However, while the crimes of sovereign nations often have the same devastating effects as those of terrorist groups, the rationalizations of established governments for their acts assume a greater legitimacy and, moreover, evoke little or no reaction from their own justice systems. This is to say that the actions of government usually are above the reach of domestic law. Non-state terrorists, on the other hand, are usually treated as murderous fanatics and their rationalizations for use of violent force are often considered crazy and they are held wholly illegitimate by the justice system.

A Typology of State Violence

Acts of authorized violence committed by a sovereign state and its legitimate institutions to protect and promote their interests are many. Conflict criminologists and other international watchdog groups such as the United Nations, Amnesty International, and the International Criminal Court (ratification blocked by the United States for many years) have monitored state violence for many crimes of domination and oppression "including genocide, crimes against humanity including rape, murder, enslavement, and various war crimes including torture, and attacking civilians" (Iadicola and Shupe, 2003, pp. 262–263). As previously noted, state violence can be directed internally, at its own people or externally, to protect the state from threats or perceived threats outside its borders. *Endogenous violence* (in this context referring to acts of state violence within a national state including against its own citizenry) can be subtle, such as control of citizens/residents through the use of propaganda, racial and ethnic profiling, and human rights violations of immigrant populations; or it can be severe, such as control of

Table 6.1 Crimes of Domination and Oppression Generated by Sovereign State and Their Legitimate Institutions to Protect and Promote their Interests

(1) State violence against other countries include:
- Assassination
- Wars and "conflicts"
- Military intervention
- Genocide
- Torture
- Counterterrorism
- Support for insurgency and terrorism in those countries
- Embargoes or blockades of other countries' export commodities

(2) General illustrations of state, governmental and institutional violence against the citizenry include:
- Domestic spying (illegal surveillance)
- Human rights violations (no elections or freedom of speech)
- Discrimination (groups eliminated from the mainstream, including unfair restrictions placed on them, often called violation of civil rights)
- Kidnapping
- Imprisonment (including false imprisonment)
- Torture, rape
- Execution (including false execution)
- Police use of deadly force
- Genocide
- Accepting lobbyists' money for special concessions
- Illegally restricting labor through harassment, complicity with business, and violence
- Fraud, deception and endangerment

populations through legal institutions, which are empowered to punish certain transgressions of the law by imprisonment or death. *Exogenous violence* (referring to acts of violence against outsiders or other nation states) typically takes the form of war, genocide, torture and/or various sanctions that are designed to eliminate the enemy and/or economically cripple the enemy and force them to conform to the will of the state imposing the sanctions. The two forms of violence are by no means mutually exclusive and may be used in some instances against a state's own constituents or its outside enemies.

Select Forms of State Violence

Isaiah Berlin, a British social and political theorist, described the 20th century as the worst century that has ever been in terms of sheer numbers of civilians and soldiers killed in wartime and deaths resulting from genocides and political oppression (1998). The advent of a new century apparently has not brought the deaths to an end. Since 2000, there have been terrorist attacks on civilian populations, ethnic cleansing, genocides and now with the "war on terror," ongoing and incessant conflict.

We begin by examining state or structural violence from an historical perspective including both its exogenous and endogenous forms. As we consider the various forms of exogenous and endogenous state (structural) violence, keep in mind Peter Iadicola and

Box 6.1 International Criminal Court (ICC)

Confirmation of charges hearing in The Prosecutor v. Jean-Pierre Bemba Gombo case (copyright ICC-CPI/Michael Kooren) (permission granted).

The International Criminal Court (ICC), governed by the Rome Statute, "is the first permanent, treaty based, international court established to help end impunity for the perpetrators of the most serious crimes of concern to the international community" (ICC website, About the Court). The Rome Statute was adopted by the international community on July 17, 1998 at which time 120 countries outlined the legal guidelines for the eventual establishment of the International Criminal Court, which began its operation on July 1, 2002 under Article 1 (Rome Statute, 2011, p. 2). The ICC is not part of the United Nations, rather it exists as an independent international organization chiefly receiving funds from member states and other voluntary contributions. The Court does, however, maintain a cooperative relationship with the U.N. Currently the ICC is based in The Hague, Netherlands; however, it holds proceedings in other countries. Crimes within the jurisdiction of the ICC, as outlined in Articles 5–8 of the Rome Statute include the prosecution for genocide, crimes against humanity, war crimes (including grave breaches of the Geneva Conventions of 1949), and crimes of aggression (including manifest violations of the Charter of the United Nations General Assembly (Rome Statute, 2011: 3–12). Since its creation in 2002, cases brought before the court come from Uganda, the Democratic Republic of the Congo, Central African Republic, Darfur, Sudan, Libya, and most recently in Kenya (The Prosecutor v. Laurent Gbagbo for four counts of crimes against humanity, November, 2011) (ICC website, Situations and Cases).

Anson Shupe's (2003, p. 261) observation that "as we move from the interpersonal to institutional to structural forms of violence, the scale and scope of violence increases."

Exogenous State Violence

As noted, exogenous violence includes war, assassination, genocide, torture and various sanctions designed to inflict economic damage on an enemy and otherwise defend national interests. Thomas Hobbes, an English philosopher (1588–1679), lays out in his classic work *Leviathan* (1651/1957), the need for the foundation of states and accompanying legitimate governments who have a monopoly on power and the ability to enforce the law and sanction aggressors. Without the Leviathan, Hobbs suggests that human beings would revert into some form of a "natural state" and there would be a "war of all against all."

The kind of violence perpetrated by the "state" has, no doubt, evolved historically, and today has the potential of killing people more efficiently than in previous historical eras. However, according to some experts, such as Jonathan Pinker (2011) in his book, *The Better Angels of Our Nature: Why Violence Has Declined*, claims that compared to the past where various non-state societies have existed, such as traditional bands and tribes, Leviathan or centralized state societies have actually been less violent in many ways including deaths from wars (and homicides) (also see Muchembled, 2012). He argues that even though the modern state has a greater potential for killing people as a result of modern technology, that in fact there has been less violence due to various socio-legal controls on expressions of violence. For example, Pinker argues that "Modern Western countries, even in their most war-torn centuries, suffered no more than around a quarter of the average death rate of non-state societies, and less than a tenth of that for the most violent ones" (p. 52). Pinker bases his findings, among other things, on samples of non-state and state societies historically and through modern times in terms of percentage of deaths and death rates in warfare (pp. 47–56). Pinker does not infer that non-state societies have not been deadly serious about wars including their tactics and armaments and use of chemical, biological and antipersonnel weapons, e.g., arrowheads coated with toxins from venomous animals or putrefied tissue that causes a wound to fester (p. 44) (see Box 6.2). Irrespective of the rise of the state and its potential for possibly controlling violence within its own borders, and outside its borders with other states, horrible types of violence in the forms of war and other civil conflicts encompassing acts such as genocide and torture continue to be ubiquitous.

Genocide

The term "genocide" is relatively new; it did not come into common use until 1944. The word has been coined by the Polish Jewish lawyer Raphael Lemkin, who combines the Greek word for race or tribe, *genos*, with the Latin word for killing, *cide*. His objective in using this term was to describe a policy of systematic annihilation of a group of people of a particular ethnicity or nationality (USHMM, 2010).

While the term is relatively new, the act itself is not. Ben Kiernan (2007), a noted expert on the history of genocide, argues that the impulse to genocide is as ancient as human society. There is some archeological evidence that early modern humankind (Cro-Magnon) probably exterminated their more primitive competitor, Neanderthal. According to Kiernan (2007), there are many references in the Old Testament to extreme violence over land and against competing ethic groups. The book of Deuteronomy is full of passages that refer to hatred and violence: "But thou shalt utterly destroy them—the Hittites, Amorites, Canaanites, Perizzites, Hivites and Jebusites—as the Lord your God has commanded you" (20:17). Listing these same ethnic groups, the book of Exodus adds: "I will wipe them out" (23:23). Again in Deuteronomy, we read: "[T]hou shalt smite them, and utterly destroy them; thou shalt make no covenant with them, nor show mercy unto them.... Thou shalt consume all the people which the Lord thy God shall deliver thee; thine eye shall have no pity upon them" (7:2, 16).

In the 20th Century, at least 30 million people have perished in genocides across the globe. Probably the single largest genocide in terms of the number of lives lost is the artificial famine/genocide instigated by Soviet leader Joseph Stalin and his henchman Lazar Kaganovich that resulted in the death of seven to 10 million mostly ethnic Ukrainians in the northern Caucasus and the lower Volga River region in 1932–33. The reason for

---

Box 6.2 Prehistoric Evidence of Violence

There has been much speculation about how violent our ancestors actually were. Larry Keeley in his book *War before Civilization: The Myth of the Peaceful Savage* suggests that violence was ubiquitous in prehistoric times. Prehistory probably accounts for 98 percent of human existence; in fact prehistory ended in some parts of the world less than 50 years ago. It is highly speculative to think that human beings only became violent in the last 5,000 years. Most of the ancient oral and literary traditions almost exclusively recount wars and the military exploits of various heroes and kings. It is not likely that the people of ancient civilizations were the creators of violence either. We know little about prehistoric violence because it has not been seriously studied until recently. Some scholars believe that this is the result of a bias in the anthropological community toward a peaceful Neolithic age where warfare and murder did not exist (Keeley, 1996). Recent evidence seems to reflect the contrary. The archeological record, while scant in certain regions of the world, provides clear evidence of homicide whenever modern humans appear. There are several sites in central and western Europe dating from 24,000 to 34,000 years ago that contain the remains of people who were victims of homicide including a child's skeleton with a projectile point embedded in its spine found at Grimaldi in Italy. Evidence of violence also comes from upper Paleolithic cemeteries of the former Czechoslovakia, dating between 24,000 and 35,000 years ago, in which are buried dozens of men, women and children with direct evidence of weapons trauma (Keeley, 1996, p. 37).

Indications of conflict and violent death are pervasive during the Neolithic period in Western Europe (ca. 7,000 to 4,000 years ago). Two notable sites of mass killings have been found at Talheim in Germany and Roaix in France. In Teleim, 34 people, 16 of them children, were thrown into a pit; the intact skulls indicated that they had been killed by blows to the head with at least six different axes. The Roaix site in France contained more than 100 persons of all ages and both sexes with arrow tips imbedded in their bones (Keeley, 1996, p. 38). The simultaneous burial of victims at the Roaix site suggests that a whole village may have been annihilated.

There is evidence during the same period of time of fortifications being built consisting of palisades with ditches dug in front of them. There is also evidence in several of these enclosures that have been excavated in Britain that people had been attacked and burned by interlopers (Keeley, 1996, p. 38). Peace may have been rarer for bands, tribes and chiefdoms than for the average citizen of a civilized state.

---

this barbarity was to break the renaissance of Ukrainian culture in this region, which Moscow perceived as a threat to Russo-Centric rule (Ukes, 2010). In the Soviet Union, Stalin's regime of terror rose and fell incrementally over nearly three decades, before and after the famine/genocide of 1932–33. After the Cold War and the authoritarianism of the Soviet Union ended in 1989, Yugoslavia, and Czechoslovakia collapsed and ethnic divisions emerged.

Genocide can be sudden or concentrated outbursts of mass murder, like those committed by the Young Turks in 1915, the Nazis in the Second World War,[1] and the Khmer Rouge in Cambodia in 1975–79. The Tutsi genocide in Rwanda by the Hutu regime was carried out in just three months in 1994. Other genocides have been more gradual and prolonged. Various enemies, including the Japanese and the Maoists subjected China to intermittent cycles of deadly violence from the 1920s to the 1970s. This violence peaked in the Great Leap Forward, the mismanagement of agriculture that resulted in

---

1. A discussion of the Holocaust is included in the section of this chapter on World War II.

a regime-made famine that killed between 12 and 26 million people in the late 1950s. Third-world populations have suffered under smaller, but equally relentless killer regimes like that of Kim Il Sung in North Korea, and that of his son, Kim Jong Il, who died on December 18, 2011, who have tacitly used starvation to control certain areas of the country (Haggard and Noland, 2007).

After a United States-sponsored coup in Guatemala in 1954, a murderous political repression persisted in the country until 1996; this repression included an intense genocidal phase lasting from 1981 to 1983. Extermination in East Timor began with the Indonesian invasion of 1975, reached its zenith between 1978 and 1980 and continued sporadically until Jakarta's violent withdrawal in 1999. The Islamic regime in Sudan has been responsible for the deaths of as many as 2 million people between 1982 and the present, first Christians and animists, then black Muslims in the Darfur region. Armed territorial secessions occurred in other large multi-ethnic states such as Indonesia and the Congo. After the 1994 genocide in Rwanda, ethnic violence spread to Burundi and to the Congo where genocide was used extensively. Ethnic cleansing campaigns in the Caucasus region and Chechnya cleared ground for new conflicts that seem to resist solution (Shelton, 2005).

One of the most troubling issues about genocide is how policy makers in the United States have been able to ignore genocides while they are occurring and justify inaction by claiming that intervention is not appropriate because it does not serve the national interest (Power, 2002). The problem of genocide, as described by Samantha Power (2002) in her book titled, *A Problem from Hell*, is a thorough rebuke of the United States past failures by ignoring and not promptly intervening in episodes of genocide. The book chronicles a century of almost continuous genocide somewhere in the world with a lack of practical response particularly on the part of the United States.

Torture

While torture is often associated with medieval Europe, it is considerably more ancient and continues to the present. The Roman practice of crucifixion can hardly be viewed as anything less than torture (Bucher, 2000). Torture has been used for a variety of reasons: extraction of confessions, public humiliation as punishment, and production of intense pain and ultimately death. Ironically, in some instances where a confession was to be extracted and the victim refused and died as a result of the torture, they were deemed innocent. In other instances where the victim was exposed to a mild form of torture designed to extract a confession and none was forthcoming, the torturer would move on to a form of torture designed ultimately to kill.

During the administration of George W. Bush, torture (water boarding, sleep deprivation, electric shock, and humiliation) was used on so-called enemy combatants, those accused of terroristic acts, in direct opposition to Article 1 of the United Nations Convention against Torture (1975). The article reads:

> For the purposes of this Convention, torture means any act by which severe pain or suffering, whether physical or mental, is intentionally inflicted on a person for such purposes as obtaining from him or a third person information or a confession, punishing him for an act he or a third person has committed or is suspected of having committed, or intimidating or coercing him or a third person, or for any reason based on discrimination of any kind, when such pain or suffering is inflicted by or at the instigation of or with the consent or acquiescence of a

public official or other person acting in an official capacity. It does not include pain or suffering arising only from, inherent in or incidental to lawful sanctions (United Nations, 1984, online).

Also, it would appear that the Bush administration violated Article 3, Part 1 of the Third Geneva Convention (1949) relating to the treatment of prisoners in armed conflict. This article states:

Persons taking no active part in the hostilities, including members of armed forces who have laid down their arms and those placed hors de combat by sickness, wounds, detention, or any other cause, shall in all circumstances be treated humanely, without any adverse distinction founded on race, colour, religion or faith, sex, birth or wealth, or any other similar criteria. To this end the following acts are and shall remain prohibited at any time and in any place whatsoever with respect to the above-mentioned persons:

(a) violence to life and person, in particular murder of all kinds, mutilation, cruel treatment and torture;

(b) taking of hostages;

(c) outrages upon personal dignity, in particular, humiliating and degrading treatment;

(d) the passing of sentences and the carrying out of executions without previous judgment pronounced by a regularly constituted court affording all the judicial guarantees which are recognized as indispensable by civilized peoples (ICRC, 2005, online)

John Yoo, an attorney working in the United States Department of Justice's Office of Legal Counsel from 2001 to 2003 played a crucial role in crafting the legal opinion that provided justification for the Bush Administration's policy in the war on terror. He argued that prisoner of war status is not available to "enemy combatants" captured in Afghanistan and held at Guantanamo Bay. His opinion enhanced presidential authority to authorize water boarding and other "enhanced interrogation techniques," which are viewed as torture by most international standards. He further asserted that the President is not bound by the War Crimes Act (1996) and could conduct a warrantless wiretapping program with impunity (Yoo's torture memoranda was almost immediately retracted by Jack Goldsmith when he assumed the duties of chief of the Office of Legal Counsel in the Department of Justice in October, 2003).[2]

In spite of the rejection of torture by several international treaties including the ones mentioned above, torture is still in use even among so-called civilized nations. The recent use of torture by the Bush Administration euphemistically referred to, according to former editor at large of *Newsweek*, Evan Thomas (2006) as "aggressive interrogation measures" includes: (1) induced hypothermia, (2) long periods of forced standing, (3) sleep deprivation, (4) the "attention grab," forcefully seizing the suspect's shirt, (5) the "attention slap," (6) the "belly slap," and (7) sound and light manipulation. These procedures, including water boarding (i.e., forcing an individual to inhale water to the point of asphyxiation), have been used on "high value targets," those captives who are alleged to be top al Qaeda operatives. The Bush Administration claimed that the use of harsh interrogation techniques was necessary to foil terrorist plots and save lives. But did they?

---

2. In one sense Yoo was correct in asserting that the President is not bound by the War Crimes Act because neither the President nor wiretapping is mentioned in the Act.

According to Thomas (2006), U.S. intelligence officers say they have little, if any, evidence that useful intelligence has been obtained using techniques generally understood to be torture. This begs the question of why torture is ever used.

The rationale for torture by the Bush administration has been called "The Terrorist and the Ticking Bomb" (Stanford, 2008). Consider the scenario: A bomb has been planted with a timing device and when it goes off, the bomb will likely kill thousands. The police have a terrorist in custody and through other intelligence, know that the attack is imminent. The terrorist refuses to talk and time is slipping away. The police believe that if torture is used, there is a reasonable chance that he will talk. Under this scenario, torture might seem to be justifiable. Given this context at least, the illegality of torture alone may not render it impermissible.

War and International Conflict

The apotheosis of state violence is war. The history of humankind can be chronicled by the dates of interstate warfare. One of the more familiar wars of the ancient world is the Battle of Megiddo (1457 B.C.). We know about this battle because a scribe named Tjaneni recorded it in hieroglyphs in the Halls of Annals at the Temple of Amun. The event that led to the battle was a rebellion against Egyptian rule in an area that the Romans would later refer to as Palestine. Encouraged by the King of Kadesh and allied with the kingdoms of Mitanni and Megiddo, the Canaanites sought to achieve their independence. They were crushed by Pharaoh Thutmose III and an Egyptian army of approximately 10,000.

The size of this army and the logistical support it would require suggests that the Egyptians and other ancient kingdoms possessed the knowledge and material to conduct large scale military maneuvers perhaps at a much earlier date than the Battle of Megiddo, which was fought nearly 3,460 years ago. We also know that strategy and tactics at that time were sophisticated enough for Thutmose III to go against his advisors and take a route to Megiddo by approaching the enemy through the Aruna valley, a narrow ravine that could have led to easy defeat and the destruction of his army. Instead, Thutmose III emerged from the ravine and made camp near Megiddo. The next day, he attacked, drove the enemy from the field of battle and subsequently, crushed the rebellion (AEO, 2008).

Warfare as a form of human interaction has ancient roots on every continent. An early Chinese commander, Sun Tzu, wrote a military treatise called the *Art of War* in the 6th century B.C. that focused on strategy and tactics in warfare (Giles, 1910). Translations of the book remain influential in military circles even today. Niccolo Machiavelli, perhaps better known for his work, *The Prince* (2005), also published a book entitled, *The Seven Books on the Art of War*, in 1520. Perhaps the most influential military theorist even today is Carl von Clausewitz. His manuscript, *On War* (1873), still remains quite influential, as attested to by a 2005 conference on Clausewitz at Oxford University and the titles of some of the presentations such as "Clausewitz and the War on Terror," "Clausewitz and the Nonlinear Nature of Warfare," and "Clausewitz and Information Age Warfare" (Strachan and Herberg-Roth, 2007).

Why do nations go to war? Clark Wissler, curator of anthropology at the American Museum of Natural History in New York has devised what he called the "universal culture pattern" (1923). He identifies war as one of his universal cultural patterns. He argues that group violence, both offensive and defensive, can to be found in every society with an ethnographic record of that time. His position has stirred a great deal of controversy. More recently, drawing on archeology and fieldwork on primitive bands from around the world, Douglas Fry (2007) works to debunk the ideas that war is a universal culture pattern or that conflict is ancient and inevitable or that humans possess an instinct for aggression. Fry shows that warfare appears quite recently and is an apparent corollary of the rise of states. Anthropological evidence across different studies shows a correlation between increasing social complexity and the likelihood of war. What this means is that the simplest type of society, i.e., nomadic hunter gatherer bands, tends to be relatively unwarlike and as social complexity increases into kingdoms and chiefdoms, the chance of warfare increases. Moreover, Fry's argument that war is a relatively recent phenomenon implies that war is unnecessary and that it detracts from real conflict resolution on an international scale. Fry also points out that although war is present in our times, the vast majority of us live peaceful, nonviolent lives. Fry asserts that we are therefore not as warlike as it might seem and if we learn anything from our ancestors, we may be able to move beyond war altogether.

Unfortunately, the historic record provides ample evidence that the United States has what appears to be an insatiable appetite for warfare. American colonists and United States citizens have officially participated in 26 wars, six before the American Revolution, nine before the close of the 19th Century and another 11 beginning with World War I in 1914 until the present. The longest period in history without a war has been from 1865 and the Spanish American War in 1898 (AHT, 2010). This 33 year interregnum was perhaps the result of the memory of the amount of blood spilled during the Civil War. The Civil War produced more American fatalities (618,000 perished—204,000 died in battle and 414,000 died from diseases) than all the wars the United States has been involved in combined (Veterans Affairs, n.d.). While the actual numbers are in dispute, the 20th Century has produced more worldwide, deliberate, politically motivated killing than any other period in human history, with the death toll estimated at 167,000,000 to 175,000,000 (Brzezinski, 1993)!

World War I, the "war to end all wars," was the first major war of the 20th Century. Ten million died, 21 million were wounded and 7.7 million were missing or imprisoned. The war, essentially fought to a standstill, was probably ended by the lethal effect of the 1918 influenza pandemic. The armistice was signed on November 11, 1918. The events and issues leading up to the war were quite complex and its conclusion brought to an end the struggle between Germany and the Allied powers. The Treaty of Versailles, signed on June 28, 1919, is thought to have laid the groundwork for the rise of Nazi Germany and, ultimately World War II. The parts of the treaty that fanned the resurgence of German nationalism were the call to disarm, to make territorial concessions, and to pay substantial reparations, i.e., 132 billion marks, a sum deemed by many economists as excessive because it would have taken Germany until 1988 to pay it off (Levack, et al., 2007, p. 806).

By the time Hitler assumed power on January 30, 1933, the Treaty of Versailles for all intents and purposes had been ignored (Viault, 1990, p. 471). By March of 1933, the Reichstag passed the Enabling Act, which essentially allowed Hitler to assume dictatorial power. Before the end of the year, the Nazi party was declared the official party of Germany with all other political parties banned. Germany withdrew from the Disarmament Conference at Geneva, Switzerland and Chancellor Adolf Hitler withdrew Germany from the League of Nations (WWIInet, 2006a).

In 1934, with the death of German President von Hindenburg, Hitler assumed the office, combined it with Chancellor and changed the title to Fuhrer. The following year, Hitler denounced the disarmament clauses of the Versailles Treaty. He announced that Germany would introduce compulsory military service, thereby creating an army of 36 divisions. Germany also announced the existence of the Luftwaffe, an air force that was explicitly forbidden by the Versailles Treaty. In 1936, Hitler denounced the Rhineland

Image 1 **The machine gun effectively put an end to cavalry charges in World War I.** File from Wikipedia commons. Commons is a freely licensed media file repository (http://upload.wikimedia.org/wikipedia/commons/7/7f/U.S._Hotchkiss_Machine_Gun.jpg).

provisions of the Treaty of Versailles and the Locarno Treaty. German troops marched in to re-occupy the Rhineland. At the same time, German representatives informed foreign ministers and ambassadors of a German peace plan with all countries bordering Germany. In spite of this peace posturing, Hitler and his staff were planning the occupation of Austria and an aggressive war with Czechoslovakia.

In September of 1938, following a two day conference between Hitler, Italy's Benito Mussolini, Britain's Neville Chamberlain, and France's Edouard Daladier, an agreement was reached to allow Germany to annex a portion of Czechoslovakia known as the Sudetenland. Chamberlain was famously quoted as saying: "This is the second time that there has come back from Germany to Downing Street peace with honour. I believe it is peace for our time." But appeasement was not a strategy that would work with Hitler. In the same month, Nazi brown shirts carried out a nationwide pogrom against the Jews in Germany and Austria. Jewish homes, businesses, and synagogues were looted and burned. Ninety-one Jews were killed and 20,000 were taken to concentration camps. This became known as *Kristallnacht*, the Night of Broken Glass (WWIInet, 2006a). This event signaled the beginning of what became the official policy of the Third Reich: the annihilation of the Jewish population of Europe.

During the Nazi regime, the annihilation of the Jews was most comprehensive, particularly in Eastern Europe, with Poland alone accounting for three million deaths. By the end of World War II, the Jewish population of Europe was reduced by 5,933,900 or 67 percent (Dawidowicz, 1986, p. 403)!

September 1, 1939 signaled the real beginning of World War II in Europe with the German invasion of Poland. After Germany rejected the British and French ultimatum of September 1st, which called for the withdrawal of all German forces from Poland,

Image 2 Infamous entrance building to the Auschwitz II (Birkenau) death camp in Oswiecim. Factbook photos—obtained from a wide variety of sources—are in the public domain and are copyright free (https://www.cia.gov/library/publications/the-world-factbook/photo_gallery/pl/photo_gallery_B1_pl_29.html).

Image 3 Jewish Neighborhood of Paris: Infants murdered by the Nazis with the complicity of the Vichy government. Personal photo from Dr. Dee Harper.

France declared war on Germany. For the next 69 months, war raged throughout Europe, with the heaviest fighting occurring on the eastern front. Russia sustained the highest numbers of casualties and death rates. It was not until D-Day, June 6, 1944, that the focus of the war shifted to Western Europe. Realizing defeat was eminent, Hitler along with his new wife Eva Braun, committed suicide in 1945.

When Japan signed the tripartite pact with Germany and Italy on September 27, 1940, the effect from the perspective of the United States was that Japan was siding with the aggressors. The following year, Germany urged Japan to enter the war by attacking Russia. Even though the United States and the United Kingdom froze all Japanese assets, Japan reciprocated the freeze and began to move in the direction of war with the United States and its allies. Despite a last minute appeal for peace by President Franklin Roosevelt to Emperor Hirohito of Japan, Japanese naval forces launched a surprise aerial attack on military installations in Hawaii on December 7, 1941; a date which President Roosevelt famously said would "live in infamy."

The following day, the United States declared war on Japan and the conflict raged for nearly four years. After fighting what appeared to be a strategy of never surrendering (e.g., 20,000 Japanese soldiers were killed and only 216 captured on Iwo Jima island alone) and having their navy effectively destroyed in the three day battle of Leyte Gulf in October, 1944, mainland Japan was now within range of United States' heavy B-29 bombers. Following the destruction of the Kawasaki aircraft factory near Kobe, Japan, United States bombers began to systematically firebomb major Japanese cities. Tokyo was bombed continuously for 10 days with an estimated loss of civilian life exceeding 100,000. On August 6, 1945, the world entered a new era as the United States B-29 bomber Enola Gay dropped an atomic bomb on Hiroshima, Japan, killing an estimated 140,000 people and completely wiping out a 10 square kilometer area of the city. On August 9, a second atomic bomb was dropped on Nagasaki, killing 113,000 of the city's 250,000 inhabitants. Six days later, the Japanese cabinet decided to surrender to the Allies. At the time, the official casualty figures for the main island of Japan from air raids including the atomic bombs were 260,000 killed (likely underestimated by 100,000), 412,000 injured and 9.2 million homeless, along with 44 cities being completely wiped out (WWIInet, 2006b).

Before the end of the 20th Century, the United States would be involved in two more major wars in the Pacific region, in Korea from 1950 to 1953 and in Vietnam beginning in earnest in 1964 and lasting until 1973. The Vietnam War left 3 to 4 million Vietnamese, 1.5 to 2 million Laotians and Cambodians, and 58,226 American soldiers dead (Vietnam War Casualties, 2009). Because the Vietnam War was the first war essentially carried live on television in the United States, it fundamentally changed the way most Americans responded to war and military loss of life. Beginning in 1973, the United States converted to an all-volunteer or professional military. Eighteen year olds are still required to register with the Selective Service but there is no requirement to enlist. While the United States remains in many ways the most powerful military force in the world today, it has been challenged by new ways of conducting warfare, so-called asymmetrical conflict or warfare.

The Rise of Asymmetrical Warfare and Terrorism[3]

Terrorism is an elusive concept — one person's or group's terrorist is another's freedom fighter. The term terrorist is applied liberally to a variety of behaviors, individuals and

---

3. This section is adapted from *Crime and Criminal Justice in Disaster* (Harper & Frailing, 2010).

groups. As pointed out by Bruce Hoffman (2006), the term can include such "disparate acts as the bombing of a building, the assassination of a head of state, the massacre of civilians by a military unit, the poisoning of produce on supermarket shelves, or the deliberate contamination of over-the-counter medication in a drugstore" (p. 1). Most recently, in the debt ceiling debates some congress persons allied with the so-called Tea Party were referred to as "jihadists" because of their unwillingness to compromise on anything. These varied examples of the use of the term reflect on the history of the concept to some degree. Contemporarily, its usage has become more focused on a covert or surrogate form of warfare promoted by otherwise weaker states confronting more powerful states with minimal risk of retribution (Hoffman, 2006, p. 17). Hoffman finally defines terrorism as:

> the deliberate creation and exploitation of fear through violence or the threat of violence in pursuit of political change.... Terrorism is specifically designed to have far-reaching psychological effects.... It is meant to instill fear within, and thereby intimidate a wider "target audience" that might include a rival ethnic or religious group, an entire country, a national government or political party, or public opinion in general. Terrorism is designed to create power where there is none or to consolidate power where there is very little. Through the publicity generated by their violence, terrorists seek to obtain leverage, influence, and power they otherwise lack to effect political change ... (2006, p. 41).

On September 11, 2001,[4] the United States suffered the first large scale terrorist attack on its soil. This attack is commonly said to have changed everything. On that day, four airplanes were hijacked and flown into pre-selected targets that symbolized the American economy and government. American Airlines flight 11 left Boston for Los Angeles at 7:59 am. The last routine transmission was made 15 minutes later. The plane got as far west as upstate New York before turning south toward New York City. Piloted by Mohammed Atta and with four other hijackers on board, it crashed into the North Tower of the World Trade Center at 8:46 am. A short time later, United Airlines flight 175 left Boston for Los Angeles, taking off at 8:14 am. The last routine transmission was made about a half hour after takeoff. The plane got as far south as the border between Pennsylvania and New Jersey before turning north toward New York City. Piloted by Marwan al Shehhi and with four other hijackers on board, it crashed into the South Tower of the World Trade Center at 9:03 am. Both towers later collapsed as a result of being struck. Meanwhile, American Airlines flight 77 departed Washington, D.C. for Los Angeles. It took off at 8:20 am, with the last routine transmission occurring about a half hour later. The plane got as far west as eastern Ohio before turning east and heading toward Washington, D.C. Piloted by Hani Hanjour and with four other hijackers on board, it crashed into the Pentagon at 9:37 am. Finally, United Airlines flight 93 left Newark for San Francisco, taking off at 8:42 am. The last routine transmission was made about 45 minutes later. The plane made it as far west as Ohio before turning back east toward Washington and its target, the White House. It is estimated that the famous passenger revolt began at 9:57 am. The revolt caused pilot Ziad Jarrah, one of four hijackers on board, to crash the plane into an empty field in Shanksville, Pennsylvania at 10:03 am (9/11 Commission, 2004, pp. 32–33, 238–239). Nearly 3,000 people were killed in these three attacks.

---

4. The literature on September 11 is extensive. Among some of the most important books, in addition to *The 9/11 Commission Report* (2004), are: *Out of the Blue* by Richard Bernstein (2002), *Why America Slept* by Gerald Posner (2004), and *Ghost Wars* by Steve Coll (2004).

Though the terrorists took steps to avoid detection as they prepared for their attacks, such as selecting hijackers who could travel without detection, there were instances in which the terrorists' behavior could have brought them to the attention of the authorities. In addition to the strange behavior exhibited during their flight school training, two of the pilots, Atta and Shehhi, had difficulty reentering the United States after trips overseas.

The man deemed responsible for the 9/11 attacks, Osama bin Laden, was never brought to justice but was killed at his compound in Abbottabad, Pakistan on May 2, 2011 by a U.S. team of Navy SEALS ordered by President Barrack Obama and under the direction of the Central Intelligence Agency (CIA). Operation Neptune Spear, as the raid was named, was launched from Afghanistan. Bin Laden has been on the United States' radar since 1993, but at that time, only as a financier of terrorist acts. It was not until 1996 that he was understood to be an inspirer and organizer of these acts, as well. By early 1998, as he and al Qaeda became better known to various government agencies, each developed a strategy for dealing with him. The Central Intelligence Agency (CIA) planned to capture and remove him from Afghanistan, the Justice Department planned to indict him and the State Department was focused more on Indian/Pakistani relations than on bin Laden. Reports of a 2001 planned attack instigated by bin Laden began in May, 2001, culminating in the now infamous August 6, 2001 memo entitled "Bin Laden Determined to Strike in U.S." Among the highlights of this memo were that bin Laden had been wanting to attack inside the U.S. since 1997, that failure of previous plots was no deterrent and that he had been planning over the course of several years (9/11 Commission, 2004, pp. 255–262).

The 9/11 attacks revealed failures in four areas, the first of which was imagination. Before 9/11, an attack from a stateless terrorist organization on American soil using aircraft as weapons was inconceivable. The second failure area was policy. A pre-9/11 response to al Qaeda was formed in response to the embassy bombings of 1998. The tragedy of those attacks provided an opportunity for the U.S. to examine the full threat that bin Laden posed, but this opportunity was not taken. The third failure area was capability. Though al Qaeda was probably the most dangerous threat to the United States, at no time before 9/11 did the Department of Defense engage in a comprehensive effort to mitigate the danger. Finally, the fourth failure area was management. The inability to effectively share information was especially symptomatic of the government's broader inability to adapt to changing threats (pp. 339–353). With all that said about what went wrong and what could have been done better, the 9/11 Commission made 28 detailed recommendations on what to do to prevent another attack and to shore up the United States' standing in the world. It made 13 equally detailed recommendations on how to implement them and in so doing, reorganize the government (pp. 361–428). Among the principal changes that followed 9/11 was the creation of the Department of Homeland Security (DHS). DHS was supposed to bring about improved interagency information sharing (see Brown, 2010).

Endogenous State Violence

As noted, endogenous violence refers to state violence aimed at the citizens of the state and can include such acts as any cruel and unusual punishment (e.g., the death penalty), domestic spying, disruption of political and other groups, state propaganda campaigns, police use of deadly force, imprisonment, ethnic cleansing, and various types of political oppression or human rights violations against indigenous and ethnic minority populations.

The sheer scale of violence committed by governments, democratic and otherwise, is far greater than interpersonal acts of criminal violence.

Why would the state direct violence against its own people? Mainly because individuals or in some cases groups are alleged to violate rules and threaten the very existence of the state or at least threaten the public order. The state's monopoly on violence, coupled with a system of social control, namely the police, courts, and corrections, allows it to direct the ultimate form of violence—execution—against some of its own citizenry (with the other citizens either completely terrorized into inaction or supporting it). Many other types of states' sanctioned violence have been condoned (see Table 6.1) and have been perpetrated against citizens and non-citizens within their own national borders. Following is a select sample of these various forms of endogenous state violence. We begin with state sanctioned executions.

State Executions

State violence in the form of execution is nothing new. The Code of Hammurabi in 1800 B.C. identified 25 crimes that were punishable by death. Not to be outdone, the Draconian Code of Athens in the 7th century B.C. prescribed the death penalty for every crime committed. The Romans handed down death sentences for a variety of offenses that, depending on whether the offender was patrician, plebian or slave, could include such things as committing libel by publishing an insulting song, cheating a client, or committing perjury (Laurence, 1960).

England has a long history of executing on its soil and its colonies, influenced by British law and culture, which legitimized execution. As early as 450 B.C., the condemned was thrown into a quagmire (quicksand). By the 10th century, hanging from gallows was the most frequent form of execution mentioned in the historic record. During this period and later in the Middle Ages, executions were preceded by torture. Regional rulers (barons) had gallows and a drowning pit and used these, often for minor offenses. Henry VIII was probably the most prolific user of death as punishment. In addition to having some of his wives executed, it is believed that he put an estimated 72,000 of his subjects to death. Approved in 1531, boiling to death was another form of the death penalty. People were apparently placed in the pot before the water came to a boil and it could take as long as two hours before they died. Capital offenses continued to grow in number until there were 222 crimes punishable by death. Many of the offenses were quite trivial, so much so that juries would not convict. As a result, laws were passed during the 1800s that began to exempt many crimes from resulting in an execution.

The first recorded execution in the English American colonies was in 1608 when officials executed George Kendall of Virginia for allegedly plotting to betray the British to the Spanish. In 1622, the first legal execution of a criminal, Daniel Frank, occurred in Virginia for the crime of theft (Bedau, 1982). By 1776 the colonies, with some exceptions, had roughly comparable death statutes, which covered arson, piracy, treason, murder, sodomy, burglary, robbery, rape, horse-stealing, slave rebellion, and counterfeiting. Hanging was the usual sentence for these crimes. In the early years of the republic, one of the more severe states when it came to meting out the death penalty was North Carolina. In 1837 North Carolina required death for the crimes of murder, rape, statutory rape, slave-stealing, stealing bank notes, highway robbery, burglary, arson, castration, buggery, sodomy, bestiality, dueling where death occurs, hiding a slave with intent to free him, taking a free Negro out of state to sell him, bigamy, inciting slaves to rebel, circulating seditious literature among slaves, accessory to murder, robbery, burglary, arson, and mayhem (Bedau, 1982).

Reforms aimed at doing away with the death penalty, however, occurred quite early in the United States. Thomas Jefferson proposed to the Virginia legislature that the death penalty only be used for treason and murder. The reforms did not pass, but the seeds of change were planted (Mackey, 1976). Thomas Jefferson was probably influenced in his thinking by the 1767 English translation of the Italian jurist Cesare Beccaria's book, *On Crimes and Punishment*, which advocated for the abolition of capital punishment. Beccaria asserted that the state had no justification for the taking of life of a citizen. He also said that the death penalty was "a war of a whole nation against a citizen, whose destruction they consider as necessary or useful to the general good" (p. 103). Beccaria conceded that the death was necessary when only the death could ensure the security of a nation, which would be rare, and only in cases of absolute anarchy or when a nation was on the verge of losing its liberty. Beccaria claimed that the history of punishment by death has demonstrated that it has not deterred determined individuals from injuring society and that death was only a "momentary spectacle, and therefore a less efficacious method of deterring others" (p. 103).

The death penalty is still available in 34 states and in the federal courts of the United States (DPIC, 2011). In 2011, 43 executions were carried out in the U.S., 13 in Texas alone (See Table 6.2). As of 2011, 3,751 inmates were on death row. The number of new death sentences dropped substantially in 2011, "falling below 100 for the first time in the modern era of capital punishment." Also executions continued to decline (DPIC, 2011, p. 1). As of October 16, 2012, there have been 32 executions in the U.S. (DPIC: Facts, 2012, p. 1). This system of punishment is incredibly expensive. A study in California reported that the state has spent over $4 billion since 1978 "including such things as pre-trial and trial costs, costs of automatic appeals and state habeas corpus petitions, costs of federal habeas corpus appeals, and costs of incarceration on death row" (p. 4). Florida has spent $51 million a year enforcing the death penalty. Based on 44 executions carried out in the state from 1976 through 2000 the cost of each execution in Florida was $24 million. Maryland's bill for the death penalty is over $186 million, with an average death penalty case resulting in death a sentence cost of about $3 million (p. 4). New York and New Jersey have spent over $100 million on a system that has produced no executions, and both states have abandoned the death penalty.

Doing away with the death penalty in the United States is a politically difficult problem. In the face of all the reasons for not having it (e.g., its arbitrary nature as well as evidence of racial bias, its barbarity, and its related high social and economic costs), legislators have exhibited little political will to deal with it for fear of being accused of "being soft on crime." It has been claimed that one reason why the United States persists with the death penalty is our relatively high murder rate. As in the past, the death penalty is a political device, an ideological tool that allows the public to think that definitive steps are being taken to solve the crime problem, when in fact the system that creates poverty and fatalism in the population generates the crime problem to begin with.

The death penalty is a dramatic and symbolic punishment. It is the only penalty for violent crime in which proportionality (punishment fitting or resembling the crime) and *lex talionis* ("a life for a life") is supposed to be manifested. Through the 19th and 20th centuries, more and more capital punishments were abolished in countries of the world (Laurence, 1960). Amnesty International's (AI) research shows that globally countries that still carry out executions are the exception currently rather than the rule (AI, 2012). The number of executions in China is still a state secret but AI suspects the number is in the thousands each

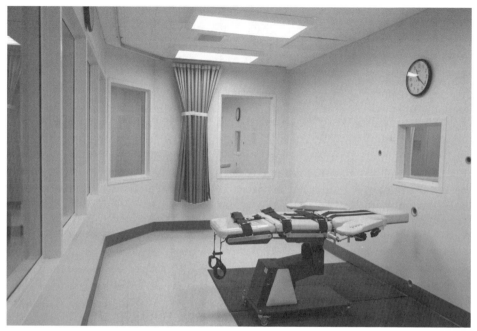

Image 4 Lethal Injection Gurney. The death chamber of the new lethal injection facility at San Quentin State prison in San Quentin, California, September 21, 2010 (AP Photo/Eric Risberg).

year. In addition to China, the worst offending nations in 2011 were Iran with at least 360 executions, Iraq with at least 68, Saudi Arabia with at least 82 and the United States with 43 (p. 7). The year 2011 saw capital punishment applied extensively to send political messages, to silence opponents, or to promote political agendas in China, Iran and Sudan.

Amnesty International reports also address the discriminatory way the death penalty has been applied in 2011, often after grossly unfair trials, and its disproportionate use against the poor, minorities or members of racial, ethnic and religious communities. The report shows that the world continues to move toward abolition in 2011. For instance in 2011, 175 of the 193 United Nations member states were execution free (p. 5). In 2011 Belarus and Russia were the only countries in Europe to conduct executions (p. 30). Across the Americas, the United States is the only country to carry out executions in 2011 (p. 10).

Five methods of execution are presently available for use in the United States: lethal injection (34 states and the federal government[5]), electrocution (10 states), lethal gas (4 states), firing squad (3 states), and hanging (3 states). The death penalty in the United States is hotly debated. For those favoring the death penalty emphasis is placed on *retribution* (specific deterrence) or *individual incapacitation* (general deterrence). For those against the death penalty, emphasis is placed on its selectivity and arbitrary nature, irreversibility, and cruelty and inhumanity.

---

5. Lethal injection is the general method pursuant to 28 CFR, Part 26. However, under the Violent Crime Control Act of 1994, the method is that of the state in which the conviction took place, pursuant to 18 U.S.C. 3596.

Karamouzis and Harper (2008) point out, that the arguments against the death penalty in the United States for the most part have centered on problems with due process and fairness. Since the death penalty is so rarely rendered and subsequently applied, it appears on the surface to be arbitrary. Applying Artificial Neural Networks (ANNs) (i.e., a computer program that mimics how the brain works to make decisions and classify information), the researchers attempted to predict death penalty outcomes. Using this tool they investigated the potential of determining whether or not a death row inmate is actually executed by reconstructing the profiles of 1,366 death row inmates, utilizing variables that are independent of the substantive characteristics of the crime for which they had been convicted. The ANNs successfully predicted who was executed and who was not with above 92 percent accuracy. The arbitrary nature of the application of the death penalty was demonstrated by focusing only on characteristics of the condemned that had nothing to do with the specifics of the crime that placed them on death row. These results have serious implications concerning the fairness of the death penalty.

Experimentation on Human Populations

When we hear of people being used as "guinea pigs" for various forms of "scientific" experimentation, our thoughts usually conjure up visions of Nazi Germany where death camps such as Buchenwald were used for horrible types of human experimentation conducted by medical doctors such as Joseph Mengele. However, it may surprise some people to discover that in our own country, people have been used for various types of experimentation, some for medical purposes, and some for military, and other nefarious purposes. One of the earlier "medical" studies conducted between 1932 and 1972 was the Tuskegee Syphilis Experiment in which the U.S. Public Health Service ran an experiment on 399 black men in the late stages of syphilis, with a control group of 201 black men without the disease. Most of the men were poor and illiterate sharecroppers from Marion County Alabama who did not even know what type of disease they had. The men assumed that they were receiving medical care but in reality received only token doses of medicine and all eventually received only aspirin; the purpose of the study being to discern how syphilis affected blacks as compared to whites. None of the men were informed of their disease or knew they were involved in a medical experiment. Although the study continued for forty years, during which time penicillin was discovered in the 1940s, which would have cured the men, none of them received the drug. When the experiment ended, 28 of the men had died from syphilis, 100 died of related complications, 40 of their wives had acquired the disease, and 19 of their children were born with congenital syphilis (Brunner, n.d., online). James Jones, author of the book, *Bad Blood: The Tuskegee Syphilis Experiment*, noted that this was "the longest nontherapeutic experiment on human beings in medical history" (1993, p. 91). Since the disclosure of the experiment in 1972, "it has come to symbolize racism in medicine, ethical misconduct in human research, paternalism by physicians, and government abuse of vulnerable people" (Final Report of the Tuskegee Syphilis Study, 1996).

The United States has been involved in nuclear bomb testing both in the United States and outside of the country. The government exploded sixty-seven atomic and hydrogen bombs between 1946 and 1958 in the Marshall Islands in the Pacific Ocean. Code named Bravo; the largest of the bombs, 15 megatons—more than 1,000 times the size of the Hiroshima bomb—spread lethal radioactive fallout over thousands of Rongelap atoll islanders unaware of what was going on. They were evacuated two days after the bomb

Table 6.2 Executions in the United States: Total and by State

Total Executions Since 1976	1309
Executions to Date	
Executions in 2012*	32
Executions in 2011	43
Executions in 2010	46
Executions in 2009	52

State	Executions by State				
	Total Executions	Executions in 2012*	Executions in 2011	Executions in 2010	Executions in 2009
Texas	487	10	13	17	24
Virginia	109		1	3	3
Oklahoma	100	4	2	3	3
Florida	73	2	2	1	2
Missouri	68		1		1
Alabama	55		6	5	6
Georgia	52		4	2	3
Ohio	48	2	5	8	5
North Carolina	43				
South Carolina	43		1		2
Louisiana	28			1	
Arizona	33	5	4	1	
Arkansas	27				
Indiana	20				1
Delaware	16	1	1		
California	13				
Mississippi	21	6	2	3	
Illinois**	12				
Nevada	12				
Utah	7			1	
Tennessee	6				2
Maryland	5				
Washington	5			1	
Nebraska	3				
Montana	3				
Pennsylvania	3				
U.S. Federal Government	3				
Kentucky	3				
Oregon	2				
Colorado	1				
Connecticut	1				
Idaho	3	1	1		
New Mexico	1				
South Dakota	2	1			
Wyoming	1				

Source: 2011 Death Penalty Information Center.
*Executions in 2012 as of October 16, 2012.
**Illinois abolished the death penalty in January, 2011.

exploded. The Atomic Energy Commission's Advisory Committee expressed interest in studying the genetic effects of the radiation on the islanders, and data is still being collected on the "subjects" today. It has been noted that this was a near-perfect longitudinal human subject radiation experiment (Ensign and Alcalay, 1994, pp. 5–10).

Closer to home, there is evidence of deliberate atmospheric radiation releases endangering both military personnel and civilians from bomb tests at the Atomic Energy Commission's Los Alamos, New Mexico. The government sought to develop a radiation weapon that would send clouds of radioactive fallout including strontium and uranium to be used on enemies. In one of these experiments at Los Alamos on March 24, 1950, scientists exploded a conventional bomb containing large concentrations of nuclear materials in which radioactive fallout was discovered 70 miles away. As many as 250 of these tests may have occurred over the years. All the tests released from several hundred to several thousand curies, concentrations of radiation. To date there has been no official accounting of the total radiation doses that local residents received as the clouds passed over from radioactivity contamination in their air, water, and food (Schneider, 1993; Ensign and Alcalay, 1994; First Atomic Bomb, 1997). Another similar test ran in 1949 at the AEC Green Run site at the Hanford (Washington) Nuclear Reservation released thousands of curies of radioactive iodine-131, several times the amount released from the 1979 Three Mile Island disaster, into the atmosphere which passed over Spokane and reached as far as the California-Oregon Border. The Green Run test irradiated thousands of people and contaminated large amounts of dairy land and cattle (Ensign and Alcalay, 1994).

From the early 1950s until as late as the mid-1970s, the Central Intelligence Agency (CIA) and the U.S. Army experimented with drugs, particularly hallucinogens, as biological weapons against spies, insurgents, and enemies. The subjects were usually unwitting citizens, mental patients, prisoners, CIA operatives, street people, soldiers, and Vietnamese soldiers. The CIA's project to investigate mind control drugs was rationalized by the cold-war anti-communistic ideology. The CIA funded investigations in particular hallucinogens such as LSD-25 (lysergic acid diethylamide) and super hallucinogen BZ (quinuclidinyl benzilate). At first the search was for a truth serum to be administered to spies and POWs. The idea then expanded to use drugs to destabilize socialistic government leaders, and citizens as well as to use them as a pacifier of insurgent populations in foreign nations and of radical black and New Left groups at home (Lee and Shalin, 1985).

The army also experimented with LSD, administering it at Fort Bragg, North Carolina, to troops performing war games. By the 1960s the Army's Chemical Corps had administered LSD to nearly 1,500 soldiers who were coerced into volunteering. The Army wanted "to see what would happen in subways, for example, when a cloud was laid down on a city" (p. 40). With the cooperation of Johns Hopkins University researchers, the Army also administered a super hallucinogen, BZ, to 2,800 soldiers from 1959 to 1975. BZ is an incapacitator as well as a hallucinogen. It disrupts signals to nerves, causing difficulty standing, disorientation, and hallucination; its main effects can last three days. BZ was developed because LSD could not be transformed into airborne mists. BZ was placed in cluster bombs, grenades, and other shells and used in Vietnam experimentally as a counterinsurgency weapon (p. 43).

While the Army was investigating hallucinogens as tactical weapons against enemies of the state and exploiting soldiers as guinea pigs, the CIA was looking for an arsenal for its covert operations and experimenting on CIA operatives and researchers as well as civilians. In 1953, the CIA began Operation MK-Ultra at the behest of Richard Helms, a long-time intelligence officer who would later, under President Richard Nixon, become the director of the CIA. Dr. Sydney Gottlieb began testing LSD on unsuspecting scientists and agencies' operatives in the Technical Services Staff of the agency. Typically, a drink was randomly laced with the drug at a gathering of CIA personnel. Frank Olsen, an army scientist who unwittingly ingested the drug, became extremely depressed and psychotic. After several weeks of seeing a CIA research physician in New York City, it was decided he should be sent to a mental institution. The evening before he was to be admitted, he jumped to his death from the tenth-floor hotel room in New York City. Many other victims of MK-Ultra's research were to follow. With the cooperation of the Federal Bureau of Narcotics (now the DEA), MK-Ultra established "safehouses" in New York City and San Francisco to experiment on unsuspecting citizens. The safehouses were false bordellos to which prostitutes lured men, and then slipped them an LSD-laced drink. Through a two-way mirror the actions of the men could be observed. The prostitutes were paid $100 per night by the CIA (pp. 27–32).

The cooperation of many doctors and medical researchers in the LSD experiments is alarming. The researchers treated patients with serious psychological difficulties as little more than experimental rats. For the CIA, the politics of the Cold War superseded constitutional safeguards. For the doctors, one can only guess that the politics of scientific funding from the federal government superseded the rights and mental health of their patients. CIA-funded LSD experiments were performed with dispatch by Dr. Paul Hoch on psychiatric patients in New York, by Dr. Ewen Cameron in Montreal at McGill University's Allain Memorial Institute on diagnosed schizophrenics, by Dr. Robert Heath at Tulane University in New Orleans, and by Dr. Harris Isbell at the Addiction Research Center in Lexington, Kentucky, on mostly black inmates. Many of the experiments were ghoulish. Hoch removed pieces of the brain from patients who received LSD. Cameron used massive electroshocks and LSD along with long periods of sleep deprivation to "psychically drive" schizophrenics. Heath used electric brain stimulation with LSD. And Isbell administered increasingly large doses of LSD for more than seventy-five days in a row to inmates with drug problems (Lee and Shalin, 1985, pp. 20–25, 38).

The MK-Ultra program and the Army's investigation of hallucinogens are concrete cases of state crimes against the public. Ostensibly the reason is to find a way to combat communism and foreign enemies of the state. Yet one cannot help but see that the rights of citizens are trivial to those of agents of the government. Anthony Giddens'(1987) thesis, still very much viable today, that the modern state spies on its population and attempts control to the extent of its ideas appears quite explanatory in light of the Patriot and Homeland Security Acts, making public and private surveillance more secretive and pervasive than ever imagined (Monahan, 2006).

Anti-Communist Attacks

The history of owner-labor relations in the United States is a prickly reminder of political crimes of domination and the position of the state in class conflict. There is little doubt, from the historical record, that the U.S. government saw labor unrest as precariously close to revolution, an attack on the social order itself. During the nineteenth and early twentieth centuries, the owners of factories, mines, railroads, and other companies were allowed by, and in some cases asked by, government in breaking strikes. Companies forced laborers to work 12 hour shifts at subsistence wages, and in some cases owned company towns, charging workers exorbitant rents and food prices that were deducted from their pay. Owners arbitrarily attacked strikers with hired guards and armed security. If their private army was not adequate to squelch strikes, owners could count on the local police, militia, state guardsmen or even federal troops. Hence the enormous attacks against anarchists, who were seen as manipulating the labor movement to bring about disorder — a new socialist order. The owners jumped at any chance to associate unionists and strikers with anarchists. Owners always managed to pull the strings of the state and court system with this ploy. After the Russian Revolution, efforts mushroomed to rid the United States of anarchists. Many were jailed and deported after 1919.

Perhaps the most discussed case of political oppression was the trial and execution of Nicola Sacco and Bartolomeo Vanzetti, Italian immigrants who professed anarchist ideologies. In 1920 Sacco and Vanzetti were arrested for a robbery and murder that took place in Braintree, Massachusetts. The major pieces of "evidence" were a car, owned by an Italian, which they had at one time used and which was purportedly used in the crime; and a witness for the prosecution, who did not recognize Sacco a few days after the crime at the grand jury hearing but identified him one year later at the trial. Defense witnesses placed Sacco and Vanzetti in other cities but Judge Webster Thayer deliberately attempted to discredit these witnesses, deviating from the expected impartiality of a trial judge. The prosecutor brought up their ethnicity, their political views, and their antiwar stance in the trial, fanning this irrelevant but charged information to the jury, while Thayer threw out ballistics and witness affidavits relevant to the trial and to their defense. The trial was a circus of "red baiting." Many believe that the guilty verdict, the loss in the appellate court, and the eventual execution of Sacco and Vanzetti in 1927 were prompted by the anti-communism and anti-immigrant sentiment of the period.

A similar distrust for political thought and expression that leans towards socialism surfaced with a vengeance after World War II in a virulently anti-communist period known as the Cold War. The Taft-Hartley Act of 1947 outlawed union shops (nullifying the requirement that all workers represented by a union be members of that union) and required union leaders to file affidavits swearing of any connection with communism. During the 1950s, under the tutelage of Senator Joseph McCarthy and with the illegal and secret help of J. Edgar Hoover, director of the FBI, the House Un-American Activities Committee (HUAC) and the Senate Internal Security Subcommittee (SISS) hunted for spies and communists. Some people made their careers by "commie baiting"; two eventually became president. Richard Nixon worked with McCarthy. Nixon was an avid red baiter, attacking or persecuting a person or group as communist, socialist, or anarchist, and falsely smeared the reputation of many, including Helen Douglas against whom he ran for Congress. Ronald Regan, president of the Screen Actors Guild, was a spy for the government, turning in names of actors, writers, and directors whom he suspected of communist leanings. McCarthy's real and imaginary list grew. It included those who merely belonged to radical left organizations during the Depression, or who subscribed to the Daily Worker, a communist newspaper published in New York City, or the New Masses, an American Marxist publication. Anyone who ever expressed a socialist idea in word or deed was considered suspect. The attorney general published a list of subversives. Loyalty oaths were required for government-affiliated jobs. People were arrested; many were "blacklisted" (they were placed on a no-hire list). The damage done to the lives of blacklisted people is inestimable.

The conflict between the former Soviet Union and the United States became a rationalization for the state to wage war against most forms of dissent during the 1950s and 1960s. Anti-communism was the major rationalization for the FBI's domestic surveillance of the 1960s civil rights movement, the anti-Vietnam war movement, the black power movement, and the Socialist Workers Party. Under Hoover's watchful eye, a counterintelligence program (COINTELPRO) began what some have called the "secret war on political freedom" (Blackstock, 1976).

Domestic Spying and Disruption of Political Groups

During the 1960s the FBI spent little of its time and personnel combating organized crime and foreign espionage from the former Soviet Union. President John F. Kenney and FBI Director J. Edgar Hoover had concluded that a bigger threat came from domestic groups with revolutionary ideology (i.e., ideologies that were considered challenging to elite civil rights, namely, black equality, world peace, and a more evenly distributed economy). The FBI surveilled and disrupted organizations with agents, wiretaps, microphone "bugs," mail openings, office break-ins, paid informants, violent provocateurs, blackmail, and fabricated information. For instance, in the 1970s both the House and Senate Select Committees on Intelligence found that Hoover, with the approval of Attorney General Robert Kennedy, had civil rights leader Martin Luther King, Jr., head of the Southern Christian Leadership Conference (SCKC) and recipient of the Nobel Peace Prize in 1964, followed, wiretapped, and electronically bugged from 1963 to 1968. When an extramarital affair was recorded in a hotel, Hoover sent a tape to Coretta Scott King, his wife, with a note to Dr. King encouraging him to commit suicide. Hoover collected a 500–600 page file on King. Before then, FBI agents stood by and allowed black and white civil rights demonstrators to be beaten by mobs and the police, and even harassed some of them through threatening letters and the filing of false complaints (Chomsky, 1976, p. 7; Theoharris and Cox, 1988, p. 338).

FBI tactics were sometimes violent. Provocateurs, hired by the FBI or FBI agents, infiltrated protest groups and urged members to destroy property and to strike at police, or initiated such action, to justify police retaliation. They tried to incite gang warfare between rival black power groups—the Panthers and the Rangers in Chicago—and helped organize and arm right-wing groups to attack dissenters (Chomsky, 1976, pp. 11–12).

The most heinous state crimes of the COINTELPRO were the planned assassinations of Black Panther leaders. The FBI considered black radicalism, particularly the Black Panther Party, as the most serious revolutionary threat to the social order. Thus, in 1969 the FBI plotted to eliminate Fred Hampton, a rising star in the Black Panther Party. It hired an informant, William O'Neal, who became Hampton's bodyguard. O'Neal furnished his FBI contact, Roy Mitchell, with detailed information on Hampton's activities, habits, and apartment. In the raid, police claimed they heard gunshots, panicked, and fired back, killing Hampton and another Panther, Mark Clark. However, Hampton was killed in bed, likely drugged by O'Neal, and all of the police bullets were directed at the bedroom where they knew he would be.

There were five major goals that COINTELPRO was to achieve with regard to Black Nationalist groups. These were established in a March 4, 1968, Hoover memo:

1. Prevent the coalition of militant Black Nationalist groups.

2. Prevent the rise of a "messiah" who could unify, and electrify, the militant Black Nationalist movement [Malcolm X or Dr. Martin Luther King, Jr.].

3. Prevent violence on the part of Black Nationalist groups.... Through counterintelligence it should be possible to pinpoint potential troublemakers and neutralize them before they exercise their potential for violence.

4. Prevent militant Black Nationalist groups and leaders from gaining respectability, by discrediting them to ... the responsible Negro community ... to the white community ...

5. A final goal should be to prevent the long range growth of militant black nationalistic organizations, especially among youth. Specific tactics to prevent these groups from converting young people must be developed (Blackstock, 1976, pp. 31–32).

While this memo might sound like a paranoid conspiracy theory, rumors still remain about what role the FBI might have played in the assassination of Martin Luther King (he was assassinated one month after this memo was released) and Malcolm X and the deaths of students in protests in Kent State University in Ohio and Jackson State University in Mississippi. After the assassination of Dr. King in 1968 there was an even greater fear of urban dissent, stoked by riots in many large cities. Military intelligence began collection of its own "files" on civilians. The Pentagon, under the "Directorate for Civil Disturbance Planning and Operation," developed plans for deploying a quarter of a million troops in cases of serious domestic protest and riots. Army intelligence surveilled various organizations such as Americans for Democratic Action, the Urban League, and the American Civil Liberties Union. It infiltrated moratorium marches against the Vietnam War and against poverty. It monitored Black Studies classes at colleges and universities and it monitored the Chicago Democratic Convention in 1968 posing as journalists. It held a computerized file at Fort Holabird, Maryland that had nearly a quarter of a million "subversives" listed (Halperin, et al., 1976, pp. 164–166).

During the same period, Hoover's FBI and the Nixon administration identified the "New Left," a varied collection of countercultural and political groups, as a main enemy of the state. An FBI agent, George Demmerle, was the bodyguard of Yippie leader Abbie Hoffman, and Bob Pierson, a Chicago police officer, was the bodyguard of Yippie leader Jerry Rubin. Both participated as provocateurs in the eventual police riots that took place at the 1968 Democratic Convention (Rubin, 1971). Both violently incited police retaliation and later testified against the protest leaders, dubbed the "Chicago Eight," who were convicted but vindicated on appeal.

Richard Nixon, the consummate red baiter of the 1950s, renewed his attack on domestic groups during his presidency. He not only met with Hoover about domestic spying on the New Left and other Nixon's enemies, but also encouraged CIA director under Operation Chaos. Also, Nixon cooperated closely with Hoover in an attempt to reconstruct the federal judiciary by replacing "liberal" judges with conservatives. Nixon's political criminality eventually backfired with the Watergate scandal. Members of the Committee to Reelect the President, appropriately acronymed CREEP, staged a burglary and theft of materials at the Democratic presidential campaign headquarters at the Watergate Building in Washington, D.C. The congressional investigation incriminated top advisors to the president, former CIA agents, and anti-Castro Cuban nationals, and the president himself. Nixon's own tapes implicated him. Under threat of impeachment, Nixon resigned, the only president to do so in the twentieth century, clearly contradicting his most famous Watergate phrase, "I am not a crook."

Crimes of Intergroup Conflict

The conflict among nations and between insurgent groups and regimes is replicated on a microcosmic scale in the conflict between competing groups in society. Race, national origin, gender, age, class fractioning, status differences, and even neighborhood origin de facto make people members of groups. Such memberships inevitably draw people into clashes, outgroup discrimination, and victimization.

The United States has a history of institutional racism, at many times directly tied to policies of the national government. Native Americans, black slavery, exclusion of Chinese, segregated schools, prison camps, confiscation of homes and businesses from Japanese Americans during World War II, exclusion of Jews fleeing Nazi Germany, and various discriminatory immigration practices are salient reminders of the officially and legally prescribed discrimination that our government adopted and some within it embraced.

Discrimination at both national, state, and community levels functions to serve the economic interests and the political position of a group. Perhaps the most common kind of political crime against another group is the deliberate discrimination in employment with respect to hiring, assignments, wages, and promotion. This kind of discrimination violates the Civil Rights Act of 1965 and its subsequent revisions. As with so much corporate crime (see Chapter 4), the adjudication of these violations is usually handled in civil court rather than criminal court. The Justice Department and the Civil Rights Commission are designated the major federal advocates of civil rights. However, during certain times in our history, such as the 1980s, particularly under the Regan Administration and continuing in the George Bush, Sr., Administration, affirmative action policies were suspended. More recently we see similar instances; some began under the administration of G.W. Bush, Jr., that facilitated human rights violations of certain groups (Walsh, Thornton, and Voigt, 2010). After 9/11 the Bush Administration established policies where thousands of immigrants were questioned and wrongly detained; large numbers were deported. More recently in 2010, Governor Jan Brewer signed a new anti-immigration law in Arizona, which required the police to question individuals about their immigration status during everyday police encounters if they have "reasonable suspicion" to believe the person is in the country illegally (ACLU, 2010). Currently there is a civil rights investigation against the Maricopa County Sheriff's Office (MCSO) in Arizona under the leadership of Sheriff Joseph M. Arpaio. The investigation by the Department of Justice alleges "a practice of unconstitutional conduct and/or violations of federal law" in several areas against Latinos including:

- Discriminatory policing practices including unlawful stops, detentions and arrests
- Stopping Latinos on the basis of their appearance
- Use of excessive force
- Discriminatory jail practices against Latino inmates with limited English proficiency by punishing hem and denying them critical services
- Police practices that have the effect of significantly compromising MCSO's ability to adequately protect Latino residents
- Failure to adequately investigate allegations of sexual assaults (U.S. Department of Justice, 2011).

Violations against immigrant groups, particularly Latinos, remain a serious problem in other parts of the United States.

Government Facilitation of Human Rights Violations of Migrant Workers

After the Katrina Disaster, literally tens of billions of dollars in federal and private contracts were awarded to companies by the Federal Emergency Management

Administration (FWMA), the Army Corps of Engineers, and other federal agencies, the largest going to companies like Bechtel, Halliburton, and its then sub-subsidiary Kellogg, Brown and Root.[6] The obvious intent of the infusion of capital into the area was to stimulate the cleanup, renewal and rebuilding of New Orleans, which most people did honestly. However, in the aftermath of Katrina, with very little higher level oversight of reconstruction employers from the Department of Labor, and with relaxation of rules designed to protect employees, many employers became more concerned with making huge profits at the expense of workers. As one person put it, "They became predators in a lawless environment" engaging in wage theft (withholding wages, paying partial wages, and not paying overtime), employee intimidation, toxic and hazardous working conditions, immigrant abuse, human trafficking, and exploitation and monetary extortion (Beutler, 2007, pp. 1–2). Since the vast majority of the cleanup and rebuilding activities was funded through large government contracts, "taxpayer dollars [were literally] going to businesses that routinely violated basic labor and employment law" (Working on Faith, 2006, p. 5).

Many Latino immigrant workers who were recruited by contractors to come to New Orleans and the Gulf Coast were often at the mercy of the contractors for a place to live (often they had to pay exorbitant rents for substandard housing typically in the very places where they worked or in "tent cities"). The laborers performed a variety of dangerous jobs ranging from cleaning up toxic storm debris and tearing down moldy sheetrock and asbestos from gutted buildings, to clearing out contaminated medical wastes, and in some cases human remains, from buildings such as hospitals, usually without proper protective gear. The rebuilding of New Orleans and other areas in the region would have been impossible without the hard labor of Latino migrant workers. Despite their sacrifices and hard work, it has become abundantly clear that a disproportionate number of these workers had wage theft violations as well as many other human rights violations perpetrated against them. What has come to light in post-Katrina New Orleans is that this practice was more a norm than an exception!

As described by Catherine Ruckelshaus, Litigation Director of the National Employment Law Project, in testimony before the U.S. Congress Subcommittee on "Hearing on Adequacy of Labor Law Enforcement in New Orleans, chaired by Representative, Dennis Kucinich, a series of executive orders designed to aid in the cleanup and rehabilitation of New Orleans worked together to create a climate for job injustices and clear humans rights violations, at a degree and level that is unprecedented in modern America. These executive orders included the following:

- President Bush suspended parts of the prevailing wage law, requiring government contractors to pay wages at rates that are customary for a particular job and to keep records of hours and pay.

- U.S. Occupational Safety & Health Administration (OSHA) suspended enforcement of worksite health and safety rules.

- U.S. Department of Homeland Security suspended immigration law's "employer sanctions," permitting employers to hire workers without checking for work authorization.

---

6. The following section is adapted from Walsh, P., Thornton, W.E., and Voigt. L. (2010). "Post-Hurricane Katrina and Human Rights Violations in New Orleans, Louisiana." In M. Boersma and H. Nelen (Eds.) *Corruption and Human Rights: Interdisciplinary Perspectives*, Cambridge: Intersentia, pp. 144–148.

- U.S. Department of Labor (DOL) suspended affirmation action requirements by the Office of Contract Compliance Programs (OFCCP) (Testimony of Katherine Ruckelshaus, 2007, p. 3).

To illustrate, on September 8, 2005, President Bush temporarily suspended the Davis-Bacon Act of 1931 in the hurricane damaged areas of Alabama, Florida, Louisiana, and Mississippi. This Act is a United States federal law, which established a minimum pay scale for workers on federal contracts by mandating that contractors pay the prevailing or average pay in the region. The rational for the suspension was to expedite the reconstruction of the region by allowing contractors, many of whom got FEMA and other federal contracts for Katrina related work on schools, hospitals, and thousands of public works projects, to save taxpayers money by hiring employees at the lowest wages the depressed local conditions would bear. However, the suspension of the Davis-Bacon Act did not require contractors to pass on savings they accrued as a result of cheap hiring. In fact, the result of the suspension of the Act ensured that local native workers were forced into receiving lower wages than before Katrina, affecting their ability to rebound from the disaster. New Latino immigrant migrant workers, many who could not speak the language and were unaware of standard pay scales, became, according to many, virtual slave laborers, "routinely cheated out of their earnings and denied basic health and safety protections" (Southern Poverty Law Center, p. 4). The prevailing wage in Louisiana for laborers was already relatively low by U. S. standards, i.e., $9.26 per hour; however, even that rate was no longer the minimum standard. Contractors were free to pay the federal minimum wage of $5.15 per hour and lower if they so choose, while engaging in wage theft with no limits on profit-taking (Working on Faith, 2006, p. 9). "In addition, contractors were no longer required to maintain records on wage rates paid for specific work, thereby facilitating wage discrimination and fraud" (Browne-Dianis, et al., 2006, p. 33).

While the federal government did not require contractors to demand documentation from their workers, at their own request hundreds of Immigration & Customs Enforcement (ICE) agents were sent to New Orleans in 2006 and 2007 with the authority to deport undocumented workers. Contractors took advantage of this situation especially on paydays when migrant workers were seeking cash payments for their work. The contractors "often called in ICE causing frightened workers to either scatter without pay or face deportation to their home countries." According to Saket Soni, an organizer with the New Orleans Workers Center for Racial Justice, "this ... was a routine practice" (Beutler, 2007).

Likewise, due to suspensions of regular enforcement of Occupational, Safety, and Health Administration (OSHA) requirements in an effort to increase their own profits, many contractors did not supply their workers with proper health and safety equipment (e.g., masks and contamination suits), which resulted in significant health problems for workers, especially Latino workers (Aguilar, 2006). The majority of the migrant workers had no access to medical care and could not afford services that were available to them in the local area.

Moreover, the suspension of affirmative action requirements by the Office of Contract Requirements of the U.S. Department of Labor (DOL), which dropped requirements for federal contractors to develop and implement anti-discrimination plans in their bids, resulted in cutting out many minority companies from participating in the huge federal grants. Ostensibly to cut down on paperwork and to expedite the bid process to get cleanup and reconstruction projects going, the anti-discrimination exemption no doubt resulted in blatant racism in the contract awards. Reports show that "as of October 4, 2005, only 1.5 percent of the $1.6 billion in Hurricane Katrina — and Hurricane Rita — related contracts led by FEMA had gone to minority businesses, well below the low goal of 5 percent required to meet federal standards" (Working on Faith, 2006, p. 9).

Evidence abounds of the unprecedented opportunities for the violation of human rights related to the Katrina Disaster, especially the abuses of Latino migrant workers. A survey of more than 500 immigrant Latinos conducted by the Southern Poverty Law Center in post-Katrina New Orleans reveals:

- Eighty percent of Latinos interviewed in New Orleans reported that they had not been paid for work they performed.

- Almost half of those surveyed (47 percent) had been injured on the job, and a large majority of those (70 percent) said they were not treated appropriately (i.e., they received no medical treatment, lost wages, and/or were fired) after the injury.

- New Orleans was the location where Latinos were least likely to have heard of the Department of Labor or know how to contact it. Only 37 percent said they had heard of the department, and only 14 percent said they knew how to contact it.

- Most had received no health and safety training at all, and few (only 23 percent) had even heard of the Occupational Safety and Health Administration (Southern Poverty Law Center, 2009, p. 43).

In another survey, the organization named Interfaith Worker Justice interviewed 218 workers in New Orleans in 2006 and found that workers of all major racial groups in the area experienced abuses of human rights, including wage theft and non-payment of overtime, exposure to toxins without proper safety training or equipment, workplace injuries without workers' compensation and, discrimination in the workplace (Working on Faith, 2006, p. 5).

Currently, there are no specific federal or state criminal statutes that address the issue of labor wage theft or other human rights violations. Wronged workers are able to file civil suits against employers, but they often have to overcome certain obstacles due to their immigration status. Also, when a case is brought against an employer, the limited penalties imposed against the defendant in wage theft may do more to encourage than discourage the practices. "Settlements are usually awarded for back wages only, with no interest or penalties paid. Employers can steal wages and overtime pay and at worst be made to pay back what they should have paid in the first place" (Testimony by Ted Smukler, 2007). As has been documented repeatedly, the Department of Labor (DOL), which through its Work and Hour Division (WHD) is in charge of the supervision of settlement payouts to workers, has been notoriously ineffective in getting payouts to migrant workers. Many workers are still waiting to obtain checks for unpaid wages (Testimony of Jennifer Roesnbaum, 2007).

The purpose of the DOL is to monitor and protect the basic rights of all workers in the United States. Through its WHD, it is responsible for enforcing the Fair Labor Standards Act (FLSA) including enforcing minimum wages (or prevailing wages for federally-funded contracts), the right to be paid for all of the hours of work at a rate stipulated before work has started, and overtime pay regulations. The DOL's Occupational Safety and Health Administration (OSHA), has jurisdiction over regulations to protect against unsafe conditions in the work environment, including enforcement of requirements that employers provide safety training and equipment for employees. The DOL's Office of Federal Contract Compliance Programs (OFCCP) ensures that affirmative action reporting requirements are met by federal contractors and that there is compliance with all federal affirmative action and anti-discrimination laws. At a time when the strongest message to employers was needed that labor law abuses will not be tolerated, a message that could only be delivered by targeted investigations and substantial penalties, the DOL proved ineffective at best (Working on Faith, 2006, p. 12).

Conclusion

In this chapter, we have examined examples of the many ways in which states have inflicted violence on others, including their own citizens, often with impunity and in some instances, claiming justification in the name of state or national interests or the interests of particular groups. The modern state and its various institutions, according to theorists such as Max Weber, has the only legitimate power and authority to use violence to keep its own people in check or to protect itself from outside threats. Unfortunately those in control of government or major institutions of the state may attempt to eliminate dissent and challenges to their rigid authoritarian hold on decision making for a variety of reasons. Techniques such as illegal domestic spying, intimidation, harassment, and even assassination are used. During the turbulent 1960s, an era of civil rights and antiwar activism, agencies of the federal government such as the FBI and CIA excused much illegal surveillance activity as well as violent activities against some citizens as being in the national interest. The Cold War was justification enough for the CIA to test LSD on other hallucinogenic drugs on unsuspecting citizens, prisoners, and mental patients. Likewise, countries that are considered strategic to the national interest or economic interests of a state may be manipulated by economic pressure, support for counterterrorism, assassination, and military conflict and war. The United States has long justified support for such activities in its fight against communism and more recently terrorism.

Global nuclear warfare concerns have shifted away from a preoccupation with mutual self destruction between the superpowers to a concern with nuclear weapons in the hands of so-called "rogue states" (North Korea and Iran) and in some cases, allies who either deny having the weapons (Israel) or who have the weapons but whose government appears precarious at best (Pakistan). The fear, of course, is that the weapons might be used in attacks on neighboring states or fall into the hands of terrorists and be used in the advancement of their cause. Neither fear is unreasonable.

State violence may never be completely eliminated. There may always be a struggle for power, within countries and between countries. However, the role of economic and political inequality in nations and the global economy, and the class conflict and corporate capitalism that power it, are major elements in generating state violence. In this context addressing inequality would go far in reducing it. Moreover, defending the human rights of all human beings and potential victims of state violence and its accompanying harms must be a guiding principle if we are serious about the issue.

References

9/11 Commission. (2004). *The 9/11 Commission Report: Final Report of the National Commission on Terrorist Attacks Upon the United States*. Washington, DC: U.S. Government Printing Office.

American Civil Liberties Union. (April 23, 2010). Arizona Immigration Law Threatens Civil Rights and Public Safety, Says ACLU. Retrieved from: http://www.aclu.org/immigrants-rights/arizona-immigration-law-threatens-civil-rights-and-public-safety-says-aclu.

AEO. (2008). Thutmose III. Retrieved from: http://www.ancient-egypt-online.com/thut-mose.html.

Aguilar, T. (2006). *Risk and Recovery: Occupational Health and Safety of Latino Immigration Workers in the Aftermath of the Gulf Coast Hurricanes*, UCLA Labor Occupational Safety and Health Program and National Day Laborers Network, June, 2006, 1–25.

AHT. (2010). *American history timeline: American involvement in wars from colonial times to the present.* Retrieved from: http://americanhistory.about.com/library/timelines/bltimelineuswars.htm.

AI. (2012). *Death Penalty in 2011.* Amnesty International. Retrieved from: http://www.amnesty.org/en/death-penalty.

Basu, M. (Dec. 17, 2011). *Deadly Iraq War Ends With Exit of Last U.S. Troops.* Retrieved from: http://www.wdsu.com/news/30022411/detail.html.

Beccaria, C. (1767, reprinted in 1963). *On Crimes and Punishment.* Trans. H. Paolucci. Indianapolis, IN: Bobbs-Merrill.

Bedau, H. A. (1982). *The Death Penalty in America.* New York: Oxford University Press.

Berger, P., and Luckmann, T. (1967). *The Social Construction of Reality.* New York, NY: Doubleday

Berlin, I. (1998). *The Proper Study of Mankind.* New York: Farrar, Straus and Giroux.

Bernstein, R. (2002). *Out of the Blue: A Narrative of September 11, 2001.* New York: Times Books.

Beutler, B. (2007). *Post-Katrina Aftermath: In Absence of Oversight, Reconstruction Workers Became another Casualty.* Retrieved from: http://www.motherjones.com/politics/2007/07/post-katrina-aftermath-absence-oversight-re.html.

Blackstock, N. (1976). *COINTELPRO: The FBI's Secret War on Political Freedom.* New York: Vintage/Random House.

Brown, B.L. (2012). As Terrifying as Terror Is … Are We Safer? A Survey of the State of Homeland Security." In D.W. Harper, L. Voigt, and W.E. Thornton (Eds). *Violence: Do We Know It When We See It?* Durham, NC: Carolina Academic Press, 147–160.

Browne-Dianis, Lai, J.J., Hincapic, M., and Soni, A. (2006). *And Injustice for All: Workers' Lives in the Reconstruction of New Orleans*, 2006, 33. Retrieved from: http://www.advancementproject.org/reports/workersreport.pdf.

Brunner, B. The Tuskegee Syphilis Experiment. Retrieved from: http://www.infoplease.com/spot/bhmtuskegee1.html.

Brzezinski, Z. (1993). *Out of Control: Global Turmoil on the Eve of the Twenty-First Century.* New York: Scribner.

Bucher, R. P. (2000). *Crucifixion in the ancient world.* Retrieved from: http://www.orlutheran.com/html/crucify.html.

BJS. (2007). Capital punishment 2007—Statistical tables. Bureau of Justice Statistics, United States Department of Justice. Retrieved from: http://bjs.ojp.usdol.gov/content/pub/html/cp/2007/tables/cp07st11.cfm.

Chomsky, N. (1976). Introduction to COINTELPRO. In N. Blackstock and T. Nelson (Eds). *COINTELPRO: The FBI's Secret War on Political Freedom.* New York: Vintage? Random House, 3–26.

Clausewitz, C. (1873). *On War.* Trans. J. J. Graham. London: N. Trubner.

Coll, S. (2004). *Ghost Wars: The secret history of the CIA, Afghanistan, and bin Laden, from the Soviet Invasion to September 10, 2001.* New York: Penguin Putnam.

Dawidowicz, L. (1986). *The War against the Jews.* New York: Bantam.

Death Penalty Information Center. (2009). The Death Penalty in 2009: Yearend report. Death Penalty Information Center. Retrieved from: http://www.deathpenaltyinfo.org/documents/2009YearEndReport.pdf.

Death Penalty Information Center. (2011). *The Death Penalty in 2011.* Retrieved from: http://www.deathpenaltyinfo.org/documents/2011-year-end.pdf

Death Penalty Information Center. (2012). Facts about the Death Penalty. Retrieved from: http://www.deathpenaltyinfo.org/documents/factsheet.pdf

Ensign, T., and Alcalay, G. (1994). Duck and Cover(up): U.S. Radiation Testing on Humans. *Covert Action Quarterly*, 28–35. Retrieved from: http://www.netti.fi/~makako/mind/radiatio.htm.

Final Report of the Tuskegee Syphilis Study Legacy Committee (May 20, 1996). Retrieved from: http://hsl.virginia.edu/historical_history/bad_blood/report.cfm.

Ford, H. (1922). *The International Jew: The World's Foremost Problem. Being a Reprint of a Series of Articles Appearing in the Dearborn Independent from May 22, 1920 to January 14, 1922.* Dearborn, MI. Dearborn Publishing Company.

Fry, D. (2007). *Beyond War.* New York: Oxford University Press.

First Atomic Bomb Test Exposed New Mexico Residents to Radiation. (2007). Retrieved from: http://www.science20.com/news/first_atomic_bomb_test_exposed_new_mexico_residents_to_radiation.

Gerth, H.H., and Mills, C.W. (1946). *From Max Weber: Essays in Sociology.* New York: Oxford University Press.

Giddens, A. (1987). *The Nation State and Violence.* Berkeley: University of California Press.

Giles, L. (1910). *The Art of War by Sun Tzu.* Retrieved from: http://www.chinapage.com/sunzi-e.html.

Haggard, S., and Noland, M. (2007). *Famine in North Korea: Markets Aid and Reform.* New York: Columbia University Press).

Halperin, M.H., Berman, J.J., Borosage, R.L., and Marwick, C.M. (1976). *The Lawless State: The Crimes of the U.S. Intelligence Agencies.* New York: Penguin Books.

Hamm, M. S. (2007). *Terrorism as Crime: From Oklahoma City to Al-Qaeda and Beyond.* New York: New York University Press.

Halperin, M.H., Berman, J.J., Borosage, R.L., and Marwick, C.M. (1976). *The Lawless State: The Crimes of the U.S. Intelligence Agencies.* New York: Penguin Books.

Halsall, P. (1998). The Black Death and the Jews 1348–1349 CE. *Jewish History Sourcebook.* Retrieved from: http://www.fordham.edu/halsall/jewish/1348-jewsblackdeath.html.

Harper, D. W., and Frailing, K. (Eds.). (2010). *Crime and Criminal Justice in Disaster.* Durham, NC: Carolina Academic Press.

Hitler, A. (1925). *Mein Kampf.* Munich: Eher Verlag.

Hobbes, T. (1651/1957). *Leviathan.* New York: Oxford University Press.

Hoffman, B. (2006). *Inside Terrorism.* New York: Columbia University Press.

HRP. (2009). *The Protocols of the Elders of Zion.* Retrieved from: http://www.holocaus-tresearchproject.org/holoprelude/protocols.html.

Iadicola, P., and Shupe, A. (2003). *Violence, Inequality, and Human Freedom.* Boulder, CO: Rowman & Littlefield Publishers.

Iadicola, P. (2012). Violence: Definition, Spheres, and Principles. In D.W. Harper, L. Voigt, and W.E. Thornton (Eds). *Violence: Do We Know It When We See It?* Durham, NC: Carolina Academic Press, 7–25.

International Criminal Court (ICC). Retrieved from: www.icc-cpi.int.

ICRC. International Committee of the Red Cross. (2005). Convention (III) related to the treatment of Prisoners of War. Geneva, 12 August, 1949. Retrieved from: http://www.icrc.org/ihl.nsf/WebART/375-590006.

Joly, M. (1864). *The Dialogue in Hell between Machiavelli and Montesquieu.* Brussels: A. Mertens and Son.

Jones, J.H. (1993). *Bad Blood: The Tuskegee Syphilis Experiment,* New York: The Free Press.

Kalb, J. (2012). Guantanamo Continued. In D.W. Harper, L. Voigt, and W.E. Thornton (Eds). *Violence: Do We Know It When We See It?* Durham, NC: Carolina Academic Press, 289–304.

Karamouzis, S., and Harper, D. W. (2008). An artificial intelligence system suggests arbitrariness of death penalty. *International Journal of Law and Information Technology, 16,* 1–7.

Keeley, L.H. (1996). *War before Civilization: The Myth of the Peaceful Savage.* Oxford, UK: Oxford University Press.

Kiernan, B. (2007). *Blood and Soil: A World History of Genocide and Extermination from Sparta to Darfur.* New Haven: Yale University Press.

Laurence, J. (1960). *A History of Capital Punishment.* New York: The Citadel Press.

Lee, M.A., and Shalin, B. (1985). *Acid Dreams: The CIA, LSD and the Sixties Rebellion.* New York: Grove Press.

Levack, B. P., Muir, E., Veldman, M., and Maas, M. (2007). *The West: Encounters and Transformations.* Vol. II. New York: Pearson Education, Inc.

Machiavelli, N. (1520). *The Seven Books on the Art of War.* Retrieved from: http://www.gutenberg.org/files/15772/15772-h/15772-h.htm.

Machiavelli, N. (2005). *The Prince.* Trans. P. Sonnino. New York: Oxford University Press.

Mackey, P. E. (1976). *Voices against Death: American Opposition to Capital Punishment, 1787–1975.* New York: Burt Franklin & Co., Inc.

Malinowski, B. (1926, 1985). *Crime and Custom in Savage Society.* Totowa, NJ: Littlefield, Adams and Co.

Mannheim, K. (1931/1936). "The Sociology of Knowledge." In K. Mannheim, *Ideology and Utopia.* New York: Harcourt, Brace and World, 264–311.

Markey, P. (Dec. 16, 2011). *U.S. Withdrawal in Iraq rolls into final act.* Retrieved from: http://www.reuters.com/article/2011/12/16.us-iraq-withdrawal-idUSTRE7BF1N62011216.

Monahan, T. (2006). Questioning Surveillance and Security. In T. Monahan (Ed). *Surveillance and Security.* New York: Routledge, 1–23.

Muchembled, R. (2012). *A History of Violence.* New Jersey: Wiley

NAACP. (2010). *Death Row USA*, Fall, 2009. NAACP Legal Defense and Education Fund.

Pilbeam, D. (1972). *The Ascent of Man. An Introduction to Human Evolution.* New York: Macmillan.

Pinker, S. (2011). *The Better Angels of our Nature: Why Violence Has Declined.* New York: Viking:

Posner, G. (2004). *Why America Slept: The Failure to Prevent 9/11.* New York: Ballantine Books.

Power, S. (2002). *A problem from hell: America and the age of genocide.* New York: Basic Books.

Priest, D., and Atkins, W.M. (2010). *Top Secret America: A Washington Post Investigation.* Retrieved from: http://projects.washingtonpost.com/top-secret-america/.

Radelet, M. L., and Bedau, H. A. (1998). The execution of the innocent. *Law and Contemporary Problems, 61*(4), 105–124.

Richter, P. (2010). Senate panel puts off vote on arms treaty with Russia. *Los Angeles Times*, August 3.

Rome Statute of the International Criminal Court. (2011). The Hague: The Netherlands: International Criminal Court. Retrieved from: www.icc-cpi.int.

Rubin, J. (1971). *We Are Everywhere.* New York: Harper and Row.

Schneider, K. (1993). Trying to Build Secret Weapons, U.S. Spread Radiation in 1950s. *New York Time Archives.* Retrieved from: http://www.nytimes.com/1993/12/16/us/trying-to-build-secret-weapons-us-spread-radiation-in-1950-s.html.

Shelton, D. L (Ed). (2005). *Encyclopedia of Genocide and Crimes against Humanity.* New York: MacMillan Reference.

Southern Poverty Law Center (SPLC). (2009). *Under Siege: Life for Low-Income Latinos in the South.* Montgomery, Alabama, 2009, 4. Retrieved from: www.splcenter.org.

Strachan, H., and Herberg-Rothe, A. (Eds). (2007). *Clausewitz in the Twenty-First Century.* New York: Oxford University Press.

Stanford. (2008). Torture, *Stanford Encyclopedia of Philosophy.* Retrieved from: www.plato.stanford.edu/entries/torture/.

Testimony of Catherine K. Ruckelshaus. (2007). Hearing before the United States Congress House of Representatives Committee on Oversight and Government Reform, Adequacy of Labor Enforcement in New Orleans, June 26, 2006, 3. Retrieved from: http://domesticpolicy.oversight.house.gov/documents/2007070312162.pdf.

Testimony by Ted Smukler. (2007). Hearing on Adequacy of Labor Law Enforcement in New Orleans Domestic Policy Subcommittee of the House Committee on Oversight and Government Reform, U.S. House of Representatives, June 26, 2007. Retrieved from: http://www.iwj.org/template/page.cfm?id=130.

Testimony of Jennifer F. Rosenbaum. (2007). Hearing on Labor Law Enforcement in New Orleans Domestic Policy Subcommittee on Oversight and Government Reform, U.S. House of Representatives, Adequacy of Labor Enforcement in New Orleans, June 26, 2007, 10. Retrieved from: http://domesticpolicy.oversight.hous.gov.

Theoharris, N.G., and Cox, J.S. (1988). *Boss: J. Edgar Hoover and the Great American Inquisition.* Philadelphia: Temple University Press.

Thomas, E. (2006). "24" versus the real world: Does torture really work? Most intelligence experts say no. *Newsweek,* September 20.

Ukes. (2010). *The artificial famine/genocide (Holodomor) in Ukraine 1932–33.* Retrieved from: http://www.infoukes.com/history/famine/.

United Nations. (December 10, 1984). *Convention against Torture and Other Cruel, Inhuman or Degrading Treatment or Punishment.* Retrieved from: http://wwwlun.org/documents/ga/res/39/a39r046.htm.

United Stated Department of Justice. (December 15, 2011). Department of Justice *Releases Investigative Findings on The Maricopa County Sheriff's Office.* Retrieved from: http://www.justice.gov/opa/pr/2011/December/11-crt-1645.html.

USHMM. (2010). *What is genocide? United States Holocaust Memorial Museum.* Retrieved from: http://www.ushmm.org/genocide/take_action/genocide.

Van den Haag, E. (1975). *Punishing Criminals: Concerning a Very Old and Painful Question.* New York: Basic Books.

Veterans Affairs. (n.d.). United States Department of Veterans Affairs American War Casualty Lists and Statistics. Official Records of the Union and Confederate Armies. Library of Congress: National Park Service.

Viault, B. S. (1990). *Schaum's Outline of Modern European History.* New York: McGraw-Hill Professional.

Vietnam War Casualties. (2009). Vietnam War Casualties. Retrieved from: http://www.vietnam-war.info/casualties/.

Walsh, P.D., Thornton, W.E., and Voigt, L. (2010). Post-Hurricane Katrina and Human Rights Violations in New Orleans, Louisiana. In M. Boersma and H. Nelen (Eds.). *Corruption and Human Rights: Interdisciplinary Perspectives.* Cambridge, Intersentia

War Crimes Act. (1996). War Crimes Act of 1996, Title 18: I Chapter 118 § 244. War Crimes.

Weber, M. (1958). Politics as Vocation. In H.H. Gerth and C.W. Mills (Eds). *From Max Weber: Essays in Sociology.* New York: Oxford University Press, 77–83.

Weber, M. (1978). *Economy and Society.* Berkley: University of California Press.

Weldes, J. (1999). *Constructing National Interests: The United States and the Cuban Missile Crisis.* Minneapolis, MN: University of Minnesota Press.

Wissler, C. (1923). *Man and Culture.* Oxford: Crowell.

Working on Faith: A Faithful Response to Worker Abuse in New Orleans. (2006). Chicago, Illinois: Interfaith Workers Justice, 5. Retrieved from: www.iwj.org.

WWIInet. (2006a). *Prelude to war.* Retrieved from: http://www.worldwar-2.net/prelude-to-war/prelude-to-war-index.htm.

WWIInet. (2006b). *Pacific islands.* Retrieved from: http://worldwar-2.net/timelines/asia-and-the-pacific/pacific-islands/pacific-islands-index-1945.htm.

Zimring, F.E., and Laurence, M. (n.d.). Death penalty. *Crime File Study Guide.* Washington, DC: National Institute of Justice.

Chapter 7

Who Are the
Victims of Violence?[*]

In a society plagued by a morbid curiosity for violence and media that grossly over represents violent content (Surette, 2011), victims of violence are all too often either blamed for their own victimization (Ryan, 1971), marginalized by a system designed to bring justice by focusing on offenders (Green and Roberts, 2008), or they are forgotten altogether (Benedict, 1992).

The notion of victim blame is not a new concept, nor is it unique to crime victimization. Indeed, blaming the victim has been common practice since social problems have been addressed, and includes every type of social and personal ill from poverty and poor health,

---

[*] This Chapter has been contributed by Dr. Shauna Rae Taylor, assistant professor in the Criminal Justice Department at Loyola University New Orleans.

to oppression and murder (Ryan, 1971). It does appear, however, that crime victims, females in particular, tend to be most harshly blamed for their victimizations (Benedict, 1992; Berns, 2004; Taylor, 2009).

This chapter seeks to provide an overview of victimization, with discussions regarding specific types of violent crimes not covered in depth in other chapters, such as hate crime, sexual assault, and workplace violence, as well as brief overviews of victimizations often overlooked as being non-violent or indeed non-criminal, including human rights violations, financial-related violence, underserved populations as victims of the state, and environmental degradation. In addition, historical and current legal rights for victims and crisis intervention strategies are discussed. The focus of the chapter is on the *victim*, with special attention to the consequences these violent crimes have, the rights and services available for victims of violence, and the areas of victimization and structural responses in need of further attention and improvement.

Legal Rights of Violent Crime Victims

The justice system was historically a private endeavor controlled largely by those crime victims who had the money and influence to pursue prosecution. It then became a public, government controlled entity when the constitution granted rights to defendants, unfortunately marginalizing victims in the process to the point where they had few rights and little to no input in the process. In fact, the only role victims played was that of witnesses for the state until the mid-twentieth century (Howley and Dorris, 2007; Tobolowsky, Gaboury, Jackson, and Blackburn, 2010). The 1960s marked a turning point with an increase in academic and political interest in victimology and in the criminal justice system's response to victimization (Tobolowsky, et al., 2010), as well as with the momentum of the victim rights movement, providing the catalyst for a variety of victim-centered legislation over the next few decades (Howley and Dorris, 2007).

Among the first legislative responses to the new interest in victim rights was the establishment of crime victim compensation programs, first enacted by California in 1965, with most of the others states following suit throughout the next several years (McCormack, 2000; Tobolowsky, et al., 2010). Advocates for victims' rights began to organize and, throughout the 1970s, numerous groups emerged, such as the National Coalition against Domestic Violence and the National Organization for Victim Assistance, furthering the movement to give a voice to crime victims and to encourage legislative and social recognition and response to the plight of crime victims (Tobolowsky, et al., 2010).

In 1982, President Reagan assembled the President's Task Force on Victims of Crime, which marked a major turning point in the history of victims' rights. The group issued a comprehensive report in December of 1982 based on their findings from nationwide hearings with professionals involved with victim services and informed by their review of the scholarly literature on crime victimization. Included in the report were dozens of recommendations for all state and federal branches of government, all criminal justice system agencies, and for professionals in the victim services field. Although it took many years following the release of the Task Force's report, legal rights and social services for crime victims have increased and are included in the legal statutes for every U.S. state and the federal government (McCormack, 2000; Howley and Dorris, 2007; Tobolowsky, et al., 2010).

Over the years since the Task Force's report, the federal and state governments have passed numerous pieces of legislation, including enacting constitutional amendments in 32 states and granting a variety of victim rights and services, such as: allowing victim impact statements to be made prior to sentencing, reinstating restitution as a part of sentencing for crimes, formalizing witness protection and fair treatment for victims, allocating funds for crime victim compensation and a variety of other victim services, and guaranteeing the victim's right to notification and participation in criminal justice system process (Tobolowsky, et al., 2010). In addition, the noteworthy Victims of Crime Act of 1984 led to the creation of the Office for Victims of Crime within the federal government (McCormack, 2000).

Although great strides have been made in legislating victims' rights, these rights and services are not necessarily afforded to all victims, but vary by state according to crime and the definition of a victim (Howley and Dorris, 2007). Stemming from the Crime Victims Assistance Act of 1998, the general list of victim rights granted at the state and federal levels include: (1) the right to notice; (2) the right to be present at criminal justice proceedings; (3) the right to be heard; (4) the right to protection; (5) the right to a speedy trial; (6) the right to restitution; and (7) the right to privacy/confidentiality (Howley and Dorris, 2007; Green and Roberts, 2008; Swanson, 2008; Tobolowsky, et al., 2010).

The Right to Notice

The right to notice refers to the right for victims to be made aware of their legal rights, to be notified of criminal justice proceedings and outcomes, the right to information about the case, including the status of the offender, referrals for contact for criminal justice-related concerns, and referrals to social and victim services, including victim compensation (Howley and Dorris, 2007; Tobolowsky, et al., 2010).

The Right to Be Present

This refers to the right to attend proceedings pertaining to the criminal case. There are restrictions to this right, particularly as it relates to infringement on defendants' rights (Howley and Dorris, 2007; Tobolowsky, et al., 2010).[1]

The Right to Be Heard

The right to be heard refers to two areas of input victims have with regard to their cases. They are (a) The right to consult with key criminal justice officials before certain decisions are made, such as pretrial diversion of the defendant or a plea agreement, and (b) The right to address or submit a written statement to the court or other authority at various proceedings, including release proceedings or sentencing (Howley and Dorris, 2007, p. 302; Green and Roberts, 2008).

As with all areas of legal rights for victims, the right to be heard varies from state to state. In some states, this right merely refers to the victim of the crime being notified of

---

1. For a listing of victim rights and constitutional provisions by state, see Tobolowsky, et al., 2010.

the intentions of the prosecutor in the case, whereas crime victims in other areas may play a more integral role, such as participating in the decision making process (Howley and Dorris, 2007; Tobolowsky, et al., 2010).

The right for crime victims to issue a victim impact statement was one of the recommendations of the President's Task Force Final Report as a way to provide more balance between the rights of defendants and victims, and was reiterated in the Victims' Rights Clarification Act of 1997 (Green and Roberts, 2008). Although they are widely used, there is a great deal of controversy surrounding the appropriateness of victim impact statements (Johnson and Morgan, 2008). Proponents argue that the statements have a positive effect on the outcome of a case, particularly in sentencing, by informing the court of the extent to which the crime(s) impacted the victim, and they allow victims to be heard and feel that they are important in the criminal justice process. Opponents of victim impact statements, however, argue that the effect of these statements is inappropriate in that they are emotionally, not legally driven, and that the inclusion of victim impact statements may slow down the criminal justice process (Johnson and Morgan, 2008, p. 128).

The Right to Protection

In response to victim intimidation and fear of retaliation by their offender, the right to protection may include issuing no contact orders at the time of pretrial release, providing crime victims with information about resources available to them if they are in fear or if they are experiencing intimidation by the defendant in the case, and providing separate waiting spaces in court to avoid contact with the defendant (Howley and Dorris, 2007; Tobolowsky, et al., 2010).

The Right to a Speedy Trial

In response to the often slow pace at which the criminal justice system processes criminal cases, this right involves the consideration of the impact of continuances on the victim in the case and encourages a speedy process for disposition of the case (Howley and Dorris, 2007; Tobolowsky, et al., 2010).

The Right to Restitution

Victims of crime may suffer in many ways as a result of their victimization, including financial loss related to physical and emotional health treatment, loss of wages associated with missing work or losing a job, and damage to or loss of property. The financial impact of the crime may also be considered in regards to court costs, victim compensation, and insurance. The right to restitution addresses the need for victims to be reimbursed for their financial losses (Howley and Dorris, 2007; Tobolowsky, et al., 2010).

The Right to Privacy and Confidentiality

The right to protect a crime victim's privacy is exercised in a number of ways, such as excluding victim's home or work contact information in court testimony and in official records, keeping records confidential related to victim compensation and other requests, and in some states, offering confidential address programs where victims can have mail sent to an alternate address and forwarded to them (often through the state attorney general's office) (Howley and Dorris, 2007; Tobolowsky, et al., 2010).

It is important to reiterate that, while victims' rights have evolved and improved measurably throughout history, and are now recognized at the federal level and in every state in the U.S., not all of the rights discussed are a part of every state. There is still great variation among the states with respect to the extent to which each right is exercised. Further, despite the gains made by the victims' rights movement, many victims of crime continue to report a sense of "revictimization" by the system, including violations of legal rights and general feelings of frustration, fear, and uncertainty with regard to the justice system (Bennett, Goodman, and Dutton, 1999; Howley and Dorris, 2007). Given that very few states have any measures in place to address the violation of victims' rights (Howley and Dorris, 2007; Tobolowsky, et al., 2010), these fears may be well-founded.

Howley and Dorris explain that the advocacy for constitutional ratification is based on the notion that constitutional protection would provide permanence for victims' rights, would strengthen victims' rights provisions, and would given them "implied enforceability" (2007, p. 310). However, the recommendation by the President's Task Force Final Report to ratify the 6th amendment of the U.S. Constitution to include the rights of victims along with the existing constitutional rights guaranteed explicitly to defendants has yet to materialize (Tobolowsky, et al., 2010). This, too, is a source of revictimization for victims, as there are over 15 federal constitutionally amended rights and none for victims (Green and Roberts, 2008).

Crisis Intervention for Violent Crime Victims

The chapters in this book provide ample evidence that violent crime is among the leading social problems in the U.S. as well as other parts of the world. In addition to the many potential physical injuries (including death) that violent crime victims may suffer, their experiences often result in emotional and psychological trauma, including shock, fear, confusion, guilt, shame, anxiety, depression, hostility, rage, post traumatic stress disorder (PTSD), suicidal ideation, and many others, and these effects may continue for months and years after the victimization (Norris and Kaniasty, 1994; Green and Roberts, 2008). In addition to the physical and psychological elements of violent victimizations, it has been noted that victims have "suffered in varying degrees a violation of self (or extension of self in the case of property) as well as a violation of their senses of trust and autonomy" (Kennedy, 1983, p. 219).

Crisis as a response and an experience is common for violent crime victims (Green and Roberts, 2008). Informed by the work of numerous experts in crisis intervention, Puleo and McGlothlin define a crisis as one containing the following three elements: (1) a precipitating event, (2) a perception of the event that leads to subjective distress, and (3) diminished functioning when the distress is not alleviated by customary coping resources (2010, p. 1). There are numerous models of crisis intervention, all with essentially the same underlying goals of offering safety, stabilization, empowerment, and facilitating other necessary victim services. Experts warn that early intervention is necessary to minimize the damage from the many effects suffered by those in crisis, particularly for those, such as rape victims, shown to suffer most significantly as a result of their victimization (Green and Roberts, 2008).

Crisis theory is a common theoretical framework for intervention programming design and evaluation, as well as empirical understanding of the plight of victims (Corcoran and Allen, 2005; Green and Roberts, 2008). According to crisis theory, "intervention at the crucial period of crisis helps individuals with almost overwhelming stress to eventually return to their previous level of functioning" (Corcoran and Allen, 2005, p. 41). Similarly, Green and Roberts note "crisis intervention can lead to early resolution of acute stress disorders or crisis episodes, while providing a turning point so that the individual is strengthened by the experience" (2008, p. 61). Crisis intervention may reduce lethality and other imminent risk, and provides critical resources to meet other needs crime victims may have (Roberts and Green, 2007).

In their 1994 longitudinal comparison study of non-victims, victims of property crime, and victims of violent crime, Norris and Kaniasty (1994) found that, controlling for pre-crime circumstances, crime victims still presented "pervasive symptomatology across diverse domains, including depression, anxiety, somatization, hostility, and fear" three months post-crime, and that violent crime victims were "clearly the most distressed" (p. 120). They found the symptoms declined over the following six months, that after nine months, the victims were unlikely to improve from any residual symptoms, and that after 15 months, violent crime victims still suffered more than the other two groups. Although the study did not compare those victims who sought crisis intervention and subsequent victim services to those who did not, the impact of their victimization and the lasting effects the crisis had on the participants underscores the need for immediate intervention to optimize recovery.

In addition to immediate intervention in acute crisis situations, victims of violent crime may also utilize a number of other immediate and long-term victim services, which are far more prevalent since the victim rights movement, the President's Task Force Final Report, and subsequent legislative funding. These include, for example, domestic violence shelters (Roberts, 2005), rape crisis centers (Decker and Naugle, 2009), state and national hotlines (Finn and Hughes, 2008), and others noted previously, such as crime victim compensation programs. Crisis intervention and other victim services are vital to the safety, security, and healing of violent crime victims, (Roberts and Green, 2007).

Hate Crime

Since the passage of the Hate Crime Statistics Act in 1990, data have been collected to establish the prevalence of hate-related crime (also referred to as bias crime) (Barnes and Ephross, 1994; Lauritsen, 2005). In 2008, the FBI reported 7,783 incidents of hate-motivated crime in the U.S., with 9,691 victims. However, researchers note that there is a shortage of empirical data on the true nature and extent of hate crime victimization in the U.S. (Messner, McHugh, and Felson, 2005; Stohr, Vazquez, and Kleppinger, 2006), particularly since official figures do not include the many hate crimes that go unreported each year. This research challenge is not unique to the U.S. For example, Chakraborti and Garland (2009) report that there is significantly less data collection, academic research, and legislation in England than in the U.S.

The FBI considers hate crime to be those crimes involving perpetration on the basis of race, religion, sexual orientation, ethnicity/national origin, and disability. The FBI does not include gender-based crime in hate crime statistics. Hate crimes include harassment and intimidation, vandalism and destruction of property, and both lethal and non-lethal physical assaults (Barnes and Ephross, 1994; McDevitt and Balboni, 2003; Chakraborti and Garland, 2009). Experts note that hate crime is particularly insidious due to the purposeful targeting of the victim, enduring negative effects on both victims and the entire community to which the victim belongs, and also is especially conducive to retaliation on the part of victims (Perry, 2001; Herek, Cogan, and Gillis, 2002; McDevitt and Balboni, 2003; Stohr, Vazquez, and Kleppinger, 2006; Chakraborti and Garland, 2009).

It is the group nature of hate-motivated crime that distinguishes it from other types of interpersonal violence. In fact, hate crime does not necessarily involve hatred toward the victim, per se, but rather, it constitutes violence stemming from prejudice against the group to which the victim belongs, providing the motive for the violence (Chakraborti and Garland, 2009). The actual victim is somewhat irrelevant, as a suitable target could potentially be any member of the group (McDevitt and Balboni, 2003; Chakraborti and Garland, 2009). In addition, the context of a structural social and political power differential that exists between the perpetrator and the victim (and the victim's group) in this type of victimization distinguishes it from other types of violent crime (Chakraborti and Garland, 2009). For instance, Chakraborti and Garland (2009) claim that hate crime is "an extension of the types of prejudice, marginalization, and oppression experienced by minority groups within the structure of everyday society" (p. 5).

Racially-Motivated Hate Crime

Racial bias is the basis for the majority of hate crime (Perry, 2001; McDevitt, Farrell, Rousseau, and Wolff, 2007; Chakraborti and Garland, 2009), constituting 51.3 percent of the 7,783 incidents of hate crimes reported to the FBI in 2008 (3,992 incidents/4,934 victims), with 11.5 percent resulting from ethnic/nationality bias (FBI, 2008). African-Americans are the most common target (Perry, 2001; Stohr, Vazquez, and Kleppinger, 2006); although some other researchers have found that members of other racial minorities are just as likely to become victims as blacks when compared to the risk of whites (Messner, McHugh, and Felson, 2004). According to the FBI (2008), 72.6 percent of racially motivated hate crimes in 2008 were motivated by anti-black bias, compared to 17.3 percent as anti-white bias. Research specifically addressing the effects of racially-motivated hate crime on victims is scarce, particularly involving a comparison of bias and non-bias crimes (Messner, McHugh, and Felson, 2004).

In their study using data from the National Incident Based Reporting System (NIBRS), comparing racially motivated hate crimes to those based on religion, ethnicity, or sexual orientation, Messner, McHugh, and Felson (2004) found that victims of racially-biased violent crime were more likely to belong to a minority group, to be male, to suffer serious injuries in the attack, and to be attacked by a stranger. Further, they found that the perpetrators of racially-motivated hate crime were "versatile offenders," as opposed to offenders who were "specialists" (2004, p. 607). That is, the offenders were likely to commit other types of crime as well, as impulsively as non-bias offenders, and that their actions were motivated more by criminality than by hatred for the victim or the group. They explain that the bias motivated violent offender is indeed prejudiced, but that this bigotry affects the selection of the target more than affecting the decision of whether or not to take advantage of an opportunity to commit the crime. Their model was not tested with regard to the other types of hate crime.

Religious-Based Hate Crime

The FBI reports that in 2008, 19.5 percent of all hate crime was religious-based (1,519 incidents/1,732 victims), with 65.7 percent involving anti-Jewish incidents, 13.2 percent as "anti-other religion," 7.7 percent anti-Islamic, and less than 5 percent each for anti-Catholic, anti-multiple religions, anti-Protestant, and anti-Atheism/Agnosticism (FBI, 2008). While individuals and groups of people are victimized directly by violence, the majority of anti-religious crimes are targeted at symbols of the religion, such as religious buildings (i.e. synagogues, churches, mosques), likely due to difficulty in identifying an individual as belonging to one religious group or another (Levin and McDevitt, 1993). McDevitt and colleagues (2007) note that hate crimes perpetuated at Arabs and/or Muslims resulted in a 1,554 percent increase (from 34 in 2000 to 546 in 2001), following the terrorist attacks in the U.S. on September 11, 2001 (p. 102). Further, they note that national origin-based hate crime in general resulted in a 308 percent increase during the same time period (from 429 in 2000 to 1,752 in 2001) (p. 102).

Sexually-Oriented Hate Crime

Bias crimes based on sexual orientation constituted 16.7 percent of all hate crime reported to the FBI in 2008 (1,287 incidents/1,706 victims) (FBI, 2008). Of these, 58.6 percent were anti-male homosexual bias, 25.7 percent general anti-homosexual bias, 12 percent anti-lesbian bias, and about 3 percent anti-heterosexual or anti-bisexual. Research findings from Herek, Gillis, and Cogan (1999) suggest that lesbians and gay men suffer particularly harsh effects from hate crime violence compared to lesbian and gay victims of non-bias crimes in a number of ways. In their study of 2,259 women and men of both bias and non-bias attacks, they found that gay men and lesbian women experienced significantly greater psychological distress than those suffering from non-bias victimization, and for extended periods of time post-victimization, including depression, traumatic stress, anxiety, and anger. In addition, they were more likely "to view the world as unsafe, to view people as malevolent, to exhibit a relatively low sense of personal mastery, and [attributed] their personal setbacks to sexual prejudice," indicating that the victim linked the negative effects they felt with their sexual orientation (p. 949).

To explain the exacerbated effects suffered by gay, lesbian, and bisexual victims, Herek and colleagues (1999) explain that, first, because of the existing social and legal acceptance of some degree of sexual prejudice and discrimination in society, hate-related violence targeting lesbian, gay, and bisexuals victims may be accepted by society, indicating that they deserved what they experienced. Those with a negative sense of self with regard to their sexuality may be particularly prone to believe this assertion, worsening the effects of the experience. Next, due to the social stigma historically attached to homosexuality, those affected may not have adequate social support and skills to cope with the effects of their victimization (p. 945). After experiencing a hate-related victimization, they are more likely to attribute all their negative life experiences to sexual prejudice (Herek, et al., 1999).

Although victims of this type of hate crime experience attacks mostly in public places, and by multiple offenders, usually white males who are strangers to the victim, they also experience bias-based violence in all other social settings including in their homes, schools, and workplaces, and by acquaintances, coworkers, and family members (Herek, Cogan, and Gllis, 2002). Though these characteristics may mirror violent crime generally, interviews with 450 gay and bisexual women and men revealed their attackers used anti-gay language during the crime and the crimes took place in a context where their sexuality was explicit or suggested (Herek, Cogan, and Gllis, 2002).

Disability-Based Hate Crime

Disability bias hate crimes accounted for 1 percent of reported hate crime in 2008 (78 incidents/85 victims) (FBI, 2008). However, the special characteristics of disability-related hate crimes indicate that rates are likely much higher than official statistics suggest (McDevitt, et al., 2007). Specifically, unlike other forms of hate crime where victims are usually attacked by strangers, disabled victims usually know their perpetrators, and their victimizations are often obscured since they occur in private settings more frequently than other hate crimes (McMahon, et al., 2004; McDevitt, et al., 2007). Further, anti-disability bias as a motivation for hate crime was only relatively recently included in federal hate crime legislation, with many states still offering no provisions for disability as a hate crime (McMahon, et al., 2004).

In their analysis of five years of FBI data on hate crime, McMahon, et al. (2004) found that the degree of risk for hate crime was about the same for mentally and physically disabled persons. However, those with physical disabilities were more likely to be victimized by intimidation whereas those with mental disabilities were more likely to experience assault. While this study offers some understanding of the nature of this particular type of hate crime, generally there is a severe shortage of research literature dedicated to the study of disability bias victimization (McDevitt, et al., 2007).

Consequences of Hate Crime Victimization

Relatively few studies have addressed the consequences of hate crime on victims (McDevitt and Balboni, 2003); most studies involve small samples and do not compare victims of hate-related violence to victims of violence in general. Barnes and Ephross (1994) found in their focus group study (n = 59 participants) that physical and verbal assault and threats were the most common type of victimization, with over half their sample experiencing multiple attacks (these consisted of incidents reported to police). Contrary to previous research where victims of hate crimes suffered much more severe injuries compared to victims of non-bias crimes (Levin and McDevitt, 1993; Messner, McHugh, and Felson, 2004), most of the participants in the Barnes and Ephross (1994) study did not suffer severe injury from the attacks. However, there were numerous psychological effects, including anger, fear, sadness, and behavioral changes such as moving, decreasing social interaction, purchasing a gun and/or taking other security measures to prevent or respond to future attacks. The Barnes and Ephross study, however, did not include a comparison group of victims of non-bias crime.

McDevitt and Balboni (2003) compared violent assault victimizations of bias and non-bias victims in reported cases, though plagued by low response rates for both groups

(23% and 11%, respectively, resulting in sample sizes of 91 and 45). They found that, compared to victims of non-bias violent assaults, victims of bias crimes were more likely to be attacked in places familiar to them, including their homes and other places they frequented, more likely to be attacked by a group, more likely to be attacked by a stranger than an acquaintance, less likely to have felt they provoked the attack, less likely to feel they had any power to prevent future attacks, and were more likely to have spoken to a family member or friend before contacting police after the attack. While the behavioral changes reported between the two groups were not significantly different, victims of bias crimes experienced more negative consequences and for longer periods of time than non-bias victims. These included nervousness, depression, lack of concentration, persistent thoughts of the incident, and suicidal ideation.

Researchers must work to identify more accurate prevalence rates of hate crime generally and of the specific types, as official numbers are plagued by underreporting by victims (Herek, Cogan, and Gillis, 2002), suggesting actual rates are much higher. We know that victims of anti-gay violence are reluctant to report due to fear of police bias and general public discourse (Herek, Cogan, and Gillis, 2002). It stands to reason that victims of the other types of hate crime would also fear judgment by police and the criminal justice system, as well as within their own social networks and communities.

Studies using data from other sources typically rely on small samples and often lack a comparison of non-bias victimizations (McDevitt and Balboni, 2003). To better understand hate crime victimization, we must increase our empirical investigations into the various types, and must address the methodological challenges presented in existing studies. An additional problem concerning the understanding of the nature and extent of hate crime stems from the possibility that many victims may reject the "hate crime" label, feeling that it is disempowering, when victims of these crimes already struggle with social stigmas and the residual negative effects of their victimization (Herek, Cogan, and Gllis, 2002).

Violent Sexual Assault Victimization

In 2009, there were 125,910 incidents of rape in the U.S., representing a rate of 0.5 percent, and down 38.7 percent from 2008, according to data from the National Crime Victimization Survey (Truman and Rand, 2010). According to the same report, only about 55 percent of these were reported to police and reflected in the Uniform Crime Reports. Experts warn that while official figures are certainly gross underestimates for rape, even self-report surveys can produce inaccurate figures due to the way the questions are framed (Alvarez and Bachman, 2008). In fact, the National Violence against Women and Men Surveys estimated over 900,000 women and men over the age of 18 were victims of rape each year, and this disparity in findings is likely due to the wording of questions. Questions asking about specific behaviors, rather than questions such as "Have you been raped?" or "Have you been forced to have sex?" are likely to get more accurate answers, revealing higher estimates of sexual violence (Alvarez and Bachman, 2008).

Belknap (2007) contends that the media are responsible for perpetuating certain rape myths, including the notion that the typical rape victim is a white female attacked by a black male while out late; however, she points out that empirical evidence suggests "all women [are] at risk, regardless of age, race, or class," and that "anyone can be a victim" (p. 273). Though women experience much greater incidence of rape, males can be victims as well. National Crime Victimization Survey results for 2009 reveal that 19,820 men and 106,100 women were victims of rape. Men were victims of a friend or acquaintance in 26 percent of these cases, and women were victims of an intimate partner, other relative, or friend/acquaintance in 79 percent of these cases (Truman and Rand, 2010).

Although risk and victimization for rape transcends sociodemographic lines (Belknap, 2007; Alvarez and Bachman, 2008), researchers have identified those who have an increased risk for rape victimization. With regard to age, younger people tend to have a higher risk (Alvarez and Bachman, 2008; Campbell and Townsend, 2011). In fact, college women may be particularly vulnerable to rape (Belknap, 2007; Alvarez and Bachman, 2008; von Wormer and Bartollas, 2011), with about 25 percent of college women reporting attempted or completed rape, the vast majority of which are acquaintance rape (Belknap, 2007; von Wormer and Bartollas, 2011). A disturbingly large number of sexual victimizations are suffered by children. The National Violence against Women Survey revealed that 29 percent of the rapes among respondents occurred before the age of 11, with 32 percent occurring between 11 and 17 years of age (Tjaden and Thonnes, 2000). African Americans have higher rates than whites (Alvarez and Bachman, 2008). Those never married (correlated with age), and those from lower income families have higher rates (Alvarez and Bachman, 2008). In addition, in comparison to women in many other countries such as Germany, Japan, and England, for example, women in the U.S. are at a much higher risk for rape (Alvarez and Bachman, 2008).

Victims of sexual victimization are reluctant to report to police or to seek help from others for support for a number of reasons, and rape is the least reported of the eight index crimes (Belknap, 2007). According to Alvarez and Bachman, "fewer than one in 10 women who meet the legal criteria of being raped on college campuses and fewer than one in four victims in the general population is willing to report their victimization to police" (2008, pp. 206–207). Generally, victims of rape may fear retaliation by the perpetrator if they report, they suffer from self-blame, shame, and humiliation due to the ever-present social context which tends to hold women responsible for their own victimization, they may not trust the police or courts to protect and support them, and they may expect negative treatment from the media (Belknap, 2007; Alvarez and Bachman, 2008; von Wormer and Bartollas, 2011). With acquaintance rapes (including intimate partners), which are more difficult to prove than stranger-perpetrated rapes, victims may feel responsible in some way, or may not feel the rape is a "real rape," particularly if the victim has at some point had a consensual sexual relationship with their attacker, including being married to him (Belknap, 2007; Campbell and Townsend, 2011). Similarly, victims who were raped in a context other than stranger-perpetrated, vaginal rape, may believe their cases will not be taken as seriously, that the incident is not a "real rape," and is not serious enough to report, fears which are fueled by perpetual rape myths and judgment of victims (Belknap, 2007; Melton, 2010). Rapes involving children are often not reported due to a child's physical, emotional, and financial vulnerability since the attacker is a relative or acquaintance, their lack of knowledge regarding their rights, or even the lack of realization that they have been sexually victimized, and other reasons such as guilt, shame, and being blamed for the rape (Belknap, 2007).

The impact of rape on victims consists of many negative psychological and physical effects, both immediately following the attack, and continuing for prolonged periods of time (Norris and Kaniasty, 1994). A review of studies reveal that psychological effects may include shock, fear, anger, anxiety, confusion, depression, social withdrawal, post-traumatic stress disorder, and suicidal ideation/attempts (Koss, Woodruff, and Koss, 1990; Siegel, Golding, Stein, Burnam, and Sorenson, 1990; Norris and Kaniasty, 1994; Tjaden and Thonnes, 2000; Melton, 2010; Campbell and Townsend, 2011; von Wormer and Bartollas, 2011). For example, Kilpatrick and associates (2007) found PTSD in about 1/3 of rape cases. Physical effects of rape may include insomnia, gastrointestinal problems, back and other muscular/skeletal pain, cardiopulmonary symptoms, neurological symptoms, chronic pelvic pain and other gynecological problems, negative effects on sexual health, substance abuse, and pregnancy (Melton, 2010; Campbell and Townsend, 2011; von Wormer and Bartollas, 2011). Not only do victims of rape suffer from many effects following their victimization, they tend to suffer more severely than victims of other violent and non-violent crimes, and for more prolonged periods of time (Norris and Kaniasty, 1994).

In addition to the myriad psychological and physical consequences of rape on women, Melton (2010) notes the pervasiveness of rape myths and stereotypes, further revictimizing survivors, and contributing to a victim-blaming society with regard to violence against women. These myths include: "Good girls don't get raped, women provoke rape by what they wear, rapists are strangers who jump out of the bushes, rape is an act of sex [as opposed to an act of power and control], women cry rape when they have been rejected or engaged in consensual sex that they later regret, and any healthy woman should be able to resist rape," and others (Melton, 2010, p. 116).

An additional hardship on survivors of rape is the particularly harsh judgment and blame they receive in society (von Wormer and Bartollas, 2011). This explains the common reluctance for rape victims to report their victimization and feelings of shame in discussing it with others (Belknap, 2007; Alvarez and Bachman, 2008; von Wormer and Bartollas, 2011). Von Wormer and Bartollas (2011) point out the necessity for survivors of rape to get the appropriate treatment and counseling for mental and physical healing, and highlight the benefits of survivor support groups in providing an empathetic and supportive environment, since society neglects to provide such an environment for victims of rape.

Victims of Workplace Violence

According to the most recent Bureau of Justice Statistics report on violence in the workplace, about 572,000 violent victimizations occur each year in this context, with about 521 work-related homicides (Harrell, 2011). Included in their non-lethal measures of workplace violence were rape and sexual assault, robbery, and aggravated and simple assault (as measured in the National Crime Victimization Survey), with the majority of incidents as simple assault (80% of all violent victimizations in the workplace). According to the report, the majority of workplace violence victims were male (except for rape and sexual assault), white, between 20 and 34 years of age, and were most likely to be single (either never married or divorced/separated). Police officers suffer the highest percentage of workplace violence (19%). Retail workers experience 13 percent of workplace violence, with mental health and medical professionals experiencing a combination of 14 percent (3.9% and 10.2%, respectively) (Harrell, 2011). One of the most notable findings in recent research on workplace violence is the drop in prevalence. From 2002 to 2009, non-fatal workplace violence declined by 35 percent, with a 62 percent rate decrease from 1993 to 2002. Lethal workplace violence has consistently decreased over the years, with a 51 percent decrease between 2003 and 2009 (Harrell, 2011).

Santana and Fisher (2010) highlight important gender differences in workplace violence victimizations. First, females suffer more rape, sexual assault, intimate partner violence,

Image 1 Jerry Sandusky. Former Penn State assistant football coach Jerry Sandusky, leaves the office of Centre County District Justice Danile A. Hoffman under escort by Pennsylvania State Police and Attorney General's Office officials in Bellefonte, Pa. on Thursday, December 7, 2011. Sandusky was convicted June 23, 2012 on 45 of 48 counts of sexual assault of young boys. On October 9, 2012 a judge sentenced him 30 to 60 years in prison, essentially a life sentence for the 68 year old Sandusky. (AP Photo/The Patriot-News, Andy Colwell).

and stalking, while males experience higher rates of robbery, assault, and homicide in the workplace than do females. Further, female victims are more likely than males to be victimized by someone they know in the workplace, including incidents involving the current or former intimate partner of the woman targeting her in her workplace.

Researchers have extended the definition of workplace violence beyond exclusively physical acts to include threats and other forms of verbal aggression, various forms of harassment, and bullying, all of which create an environment of fear and severe stress (Callender Knefel and Bryant, 2004; Mayhew and Chappell, 2007; Barling, Dupre, and Kelloway, 2009). A recent national study found that 6 percent of U.S. workers had been victims of physical workplace violence during the previous year, and that 41.4 percent had experienced non-physical forms of workplace aggression (Schat, Frone, and Kelloway, 2006). The evidence from studies globally suggests that risk for workplace violence is increasing (Mayhew and Chappell, 2007).

The effects of workplace physical violence and bullying on victims are vast and potentially severe (to include death), including minor and severe physical injuries from assaults, as well as many emotional and psychological effects including stress, anxiety, depression, and fear, and can even lead to post traumatic stress disorder (i.e., Mayhew and Chappell, 2007 Kaplan, 2010; Vickers, 2010). Mayhew and Chappell (2007) point out that the severity of consequences on the health and well-being of victims of workplace violence are not dependent on the severity of the incident. In fact, they found in their review of research that bullying resulted in the most severe effects on victims, even beyond physical violence. Moreover, even those coworkers who witness workplace violence, including witnessing bullying, suffer similar effects from the experience and the ongoing stressful environment (Rhodes, et al., 2010; Vickers, 2010). In addition to the many harmful effects of workplace violence on victims, witnesses, and bystanders, workplace violence costs employers billions of dollars every year due to such things as the loss of productivity and legal costs (Kaplan, 2010).

Underserved Populations as Victims of Institutional and State Violence

Despite the advances in victims' rights and the increases in social and criminal justice responses to victims of violent crime over the past several years, a diverse and large subgroup of people remain marginalized and underserved within the system. This unique group suffers not only from the effects of victimization, but from a lack of resources afforded to more "mainstream" crime victims (Muscat and Walsh, 2007).

A number of conditions may contribute to a person falling among the underserved, including poverty and homelessness (Muscat and Walsh, 2007; Swick, 2008; Wright and Donley, 2011); being elderly (Jones and Powell, 2006); sex trafficking, legal and/or illegal prostitution-related victimization (Holman, 2008); physical and/or mental disability (Muscat and Walsh, 2007); immigrant and/or non-English speaking status (Chavez and Griffiths, 2009; Jargowsky, 2009; Muscat and Walsh, 2007); geographic isolation (Websdale and Johnson, 1997; Websdale, 1998; Logan, et al., 2003; Grossman, Hinkley, Kawalski, and Margrave, 2005; Muscat and Walsh, 2007); racial/ethnic minority status (Williams and Becker, 1994), including American Indians (Norton and Manson, 1995; Perry, 2002; Hart and Lowther, 2008); sexual minority status (Muscat and Walsh, 2007); offenders under criminal justice supervision, such as probation, and particularly in urban areas (Hammett, Gaiter, and Crawford, 1998), and the incarcerated (Covington, 2007; Ristad, 2008). While there are other characteristics or conditions that result in a group being underserved, these areas represent the more prominent in the literature.

Much of the research concerning the underserved pertains to disparate medical care (Weitz, Freund, and Wright, 2004; Jones and Powell, 2006), and within the violence literature, a significant amount of work has focused on underserved victims of domestic violence (Williams and Becker, 1994; Zweig, Schlichter, and Burt, 2002), indicating a paucity of literature on the broader issue of lack of service to these populations when they become victims of crime. It is important to note that the populations of underserved crime victims largely mirror the nature of the marginalized within society in a more general sense. In addition, a combination of these conditions (i.e., being poor and disabled, or poor and of minority status) can compound the effects of marginalization, including for underserved victims of crime (Covington, 2007; Weitz, Freund, and Wright, 2004; Covington, 2007).

Homelessness and Crime Victimization

The problem of homelessness provides a meaningful example of structural marginalization of human beings, as well as of the compound effect that perpetuates the plight of homeless individuals that occurs both generally and in the context of violent crime victimization.

Image 2 Protestors seek recognition for bias crimes against the homeless and better protection for this vulnerable population (Preblestreet.org by permission).

According to Swick (2007), the homeless are more likely to be at an increased risk for violent victimization compared to the general population; "violence is one of the most prevalent elements in the lives of homeless families with young children" (p. 208). In fact, homeless families are the most rapidly growing subgroup within the homeless population (Wright and Donley, 2011). This increased homelessness among families is due largely to the prevalence of domestic violence, and this subgroup is comprised mostly of women and children who have escaped violent homes (Muscat and Walsh, 2007; Jasinski, et al, 2010; Wright and Donley, 2011). Roschelle (2008) adds that welfare oppression adds another dimension to the plight of abused women who become homeless.

A recent study revealed that 63 percent of homeless women in Orlando, Florida reported being victims of violence, with the vast majority (nearly 75%) including being "beaten up, choked, slapped, kicked, shot at, stabbed, and the like," 63 percent were victimized by an intimate partner, and more than half had experienced at least one rape (Wright and Donley, 2011, p. 144). These figures mirror more general findings with homeless women in the U.S. (Jasinski, et al., 2010).

In addition to the frequent context of domestic violence in the lives of homeless women, the homeless experience much more violent crime that the general population (Fitzpatrick, et al., 1993). Homeless shelters are crime ridden, though theft of property is more common than violence, and residents report feeling safer in shelters than on the street (Wright and Donley, 2011). In their extensive studies on the homeless in Florida, Wright and Donley (2011) identified a number of interesting patterns regarding the behaviors of the homeless to avoid victimization. For example, they avoid certain areas to reduce the likelihood of violence; they try not to "look homeless"; and they do not carry their belongings with them, in order to avoid being prey to would-be offenders looking for easy targets. Others avoid utilizing shelter services for fear that they are too dangerous, opting for homeless "camps" instead (Wright and Donley, 2011).

A particularly troubling area of victimization that has increased among the homeless is hate crime (Wright and Donley, 2011), which Muscat and Walsh refer to as "brutality against the homeless for sport" (2007, p. 317). The nationwide occurrence of these brutal, unprovoked attacks on homeless women, men, and children is growing, sometimes resulting in death (Muscat and Walsh, 2007; Wright and Donley, 2011). The National Coalition for the Homeless report 472 incidents of hate-related violence perpetrated against the homeless in the U.S. from 1999–2005, 169 of which have resulted in death (Wright and Donley, 2011). Although these acts represent more extreme forms of violence against the homeless, they do represent clearly the most detrimental effects that marginalization can have on a group.

Environmental Degradation as Violence

Environmental degradation is an area of victimization often not framed as inherently criminal, yet, when categorized in the area of corporate and governmental crime, very likely accounts for more victimization than the violent crimes we typically think of first (Croall, 2007). While much of the focus in criminological research and policy, as well as the fear on the part of citizens stems from interpersonal violence, Donohoe (2003) asserts that "the greatest effects on the health of individuals and populations results from environmental degradation and social injustice" (2003, p. 573). He goes onto to list causes such as: overpopulation, air and water pollution, deforestation, global warming, unsustainable agricultural and fishing practices, overconsumption, maldistribution of wealth, the rise of the corporation, the Third World debt crisis, and militarization and wars (2003, pp. 573–580), which have far reaching consequences including poverty, overcrowding, famine, weather extremes, species loss, acute and chronic medical illnesses, war and human rights abuses, and an unstable global situation" (2003, p. 578). Experts warn that environmental degradation has now reached unprecedented levels in history (Adeola, 2001).

Homer-Dixon (1994) studied the question of whether the severity of environmental scarcities, including degradation, depletion of environmental resources, population growth, and unequal distribution of resources would lead to violence, both domestically and internationally. His research showed that such scarcities are indeed already contributing to violent conflicts in many parts of the developing world, which he predicts will only get worse, particularly for the poorest societies. "Social movement, economic decline, and the weakening of states" are the specific impacts he cites that will continue to contribute to violence (1994, p. 36). Additionally, Homer-Dixon (1994) predicts that a major source of violent conflict for several decades will be agricultural degradation and depletion of forests, water, and fish and will contribute more to social turmoil in coming decades than will climate change or ozone depletion.

The right to a safe environment has been deemed a fundamental human right (Nickel, 1993; Adeola, 2001). The issues associated with environmental degradation victimization have increasingly received attention by scholars for the past couple of decades (Nickel, 1993; Johnston, 1994; Nickel and Viola, 1994; Dias, 1999; Adeola, 2001). The human rights-environmental degradation relationship is reciprocal. As Adeola explains: "In most cases, environmental degradation leads to human rights transgressions and quite often, human rights abuse involves serious ecological disruptions" (p. 39), with examples

Image 3 Deep Horizon oil rig burning. In this April 21, 2010 file aerial photo taken in the Gulf of Mexico more than 50 miles southeast of Venice on Louisiana's tip, the Deepwater Horizon oil rig is seen burning. A federal probe has found that a trapped piece of drill pipe prevented a blowout preventer from properly sealing the well to stop the massive Gulf oil spill. The explosion killed 11 and resulted in the most disastrous oil spill in U.S. history (AP Photo/Gerald Herbert by permission).

including toxic waste dumping, natural resource exploitation, land acquisition, and economic development (2001).

It is clear from the research in this area that the costs of environmental degradation are felt most significantly by those who are already the most disadvantaged and marginalized in the world, underscoring the classification of this type of victimization as a human rights issue (Adeola, 2001). However, environmental degradation is but one of the ways in which people can suffer violations of their human rights.

Human Rights Violations and Corruption as Violence

Following the Nuremberg Trials after World War II when Nazi leaders were tried for crimes against humanity, the Universal Declaration of Human Rights was adopted by the General Assembly of the United Nations on December 10, 1948 to outline the fundamental rights afforded to human beings (von Wormer and Bartollas, 2011). The declaration includes a preamble of statements, beginning with "Whereas recognition of the inherent dignity and of the equal and inalienable rights of all members of the human family is the foundation of freedom, justice and peace in the world…," followed by thirty separate articles, and concluding with the proclamation that the Declaration is to be a universal standard afforded to every individual in the world. The thirty articles in the Declaration cover political and civil rights as well as economic, social, and cultural rights (von Wormer and Bartollas, 2011). Examples include freedom and equality regardless of race/ethnicity, sex, or religion; freedom from oppression such as slavery, servitude, or cruel and inhumane punishment/torture; equal protection under the law; freedom from arbitrary arrest, detention, or exile, and right to a fair public trial; and the right to an adequate standard of living with regard to health and well-being (United Nations Department of Public Information, 2011).[2]

Human rights are often superseded by religious and cultural beliefs and customs, which has resulted in sanctioned violations of women's rights far beyond the passage of the Universal Declaration of Human Rights and ratifications of various international conventions since then (von Wormer and Bartollas 2011). Acts such as female genital mutilation (where young girls are typically the victims), infanticide of females, sex and labor trafficking of women, bride burnings, dowry murders, honor killings, sexual assault, and domestic violence, which are present in the U.S. and around the world, are emphasized in the literature pertaining to "women's rights as human rights" (von Wormer and Bartollas, 2011). Strides have been made by feminist and other activist groups to gain international support for the abolition of these types of gender-based acts of oppression, which has resulted in more vigilant work on the part of Amnesty International and other watch groups to identify and condemn those countries who still tolerate these kinds of acts, In fact, due largely to the work of the activists on behalf of women's rights, the United Nations adopted the Convention on the Elimination of All Forms of Discrimination against Women in 1979, which was signed by then President Jimmy Carter (von Wormer and Bartollas, 2011). However, the U.S. has the unfortunate distinction of being the only Western nation to fail to ratify this and other international human rights treaties (Putnam, 2010; von Wormer and Bartollas, 2011). Putnam (2010) notes the curious nature of the historical U.S. resistance to ratifying international human rights treaties while yet maintaining that the U.S. epitomizes the values idealized in the treaties. She warns, however, that U.S. involvement in such treaties does not guarantee the improvement of human rights practices and policies, and that such claims should be empirically supported.

Intertwined with human rights violations is corruption, where actions taken by some to gain advantage, power, and authority, include acts such as: bribery, extortion, fraud, and embezzlement that disproportionately affect those who are poor and powerless (Pilapitiya, 2004). According to UN legal program analyst Thusitha Pilapitiya, "Corruption hinders economic development, reduces social services, and diverts investments in infrastructure, institutions, and social services," and may be petty, or need-based, or grand (based on greed) (2004, p. 9).

Access to equal and fair justice, outlined clearly in the Universal Declaration of Human Rights, is an area particularly susceptible to corruption globally. This includes access to equality and fairness in the criminal justice system, from police to the courts to corrections, as well as in the civil justice system, within civil organizations, and equal vigilance from watchdog institutions (e.g., Amnesty International, Human Rights Watch) (Pilapitiya, 2004). The United Nations has held that large-scale corruption should be considered a crime against humanity and a violation of the Universal Declaration of Human Rights. However, in terms of international conventions, anti-corruption efforts and human rights efforts are often treated separately without regard for the correlation (International Council

---

2. See http://www.ohchr.org/EN/UDHR/Documents/UDHR_Translations/eng.pdf for full document.

on Human Rights Policy, 2009). In a 2009 report titled "Corruption and Human Rights: Making the Connection," the International Council on Human Rights Policy outlined the ways in which a variety of acts of corruption around the world directly translate into a number of human rights, and how certain groups are particularly vulnerable to such violations through corruption, including women, children, impoverished people, and indigenous and minority people (International Council on Human Rights Policy, 2009).[3]

Financial Victimization as Violence

In 2008, a financial recession hit the U.S. with resounding global effects (Aalbers, 2009). This credit crisis, due largely to the bursting of the "housing bubble" where homes had been financed for far more than they were worth, commonly by predatory lenders, left many Americans with mortgages they could not pay, for homes worth less than they owed for them. In addition, lending institutions were stuck with foreclosures and defaulted mortgages on subprime loans, credit was negatively affected across the board, and unemployment continued to worsen as the economy was deteriorating (Aalbers, 2009; Rochon and Rossi, 2010; Treas, 2010). Rochon and Rossi (2010) note that it is difficult to identify the precise cause of the crisis, but that deregulation, predatory lending, and fraudulent investment banking were a part of the overall housing bubble and led to clearly detrimental effects on both macro and micro levels across the globe, with households bearing the brunt. Treas claims that, "For many Americans, the recession is a bewildering tragedy that has pushed them to the brink of economic despair and tested their faith in our social institutions" (2010, p. 13). Further, many victims were from low income areas and minority populations, and thus considered targets for the subprime predatory lending (Aalbers, 2009; Treas, 2010).

The case of the Bernie Madoff ponzi scheme offers another timely example of financial victimization. Madoff was arrested in December of 2008 for fraudulent investment advising involving thousands of victims and billions of dollars. In a content analysis of 167 victim impact statements submitted in Madoff's case before his plea and sentencing, Lewis (2010) identified a diverse group of victims and consequences. Victims included working class to wealthy individuals and families, organizations, domestic and international financial institutions and banks. The effects included a loss of intergenerational wealth affecting families' abilities to care for elderly parents, children, and grandchildren, trust fund and college fund depletions, partial to complete loss of all savings and retirement, loss of homes and other material possessions, loss of financial independence and security, and bankruptcy. In addition, some were forced to place elderly parents in nursing homes due to loss of money to care for them or due to the elderly losing their homes, many were facing financial ruin since they had retired and were too old to work, and many victims reported a number of stress-related physical and psychological health problems, as well as relationship problems resulting from their victimization (Lewis, 2010).

Victims of interpersonal violent crime make for more sensationalized and, thus, newsworthy stories, but financial-related victimizations are not perceived as being as disturbing so more attention is given to the perpetrators and the scope of their crimes (Lewis, 2010). Treas (2010) identified a disturbing trend in relation to financial crimes, where victims

---

3. See http://www.ichrp.org/files/reports/40/131_web.pdf for full document.

of the recession were accused of being opportunistic, frivolous spenders. She points out that recession victims' heavy use of credit cards were often to cover medical expenses and other bills, and that they have indeed endured serious hardships to keep themselves out of bankruptcy and to hold onto their homes.

While the social and media focus of financial crises is typically on a more macroeconomic level and without regard for the individuals whose lives are affected, the aforementioned effects on individuals who suffer from economic crisis can be devastating in a number of ways, similar to those faced by victims of violent interpersonal crime. In addition to bankruptcy and foreclosures as financial catastrophes, long-term financial stress, and employment struggles present chronic emotional and physiological stress (Bennett, Scharoun-Lee, and Tucker-Seeley, 2009). These events and the corresponding stress can leave victims in a state of acute and also long-term crisis, which can increase risk for serious health consequences. Furthermore, the lack of money may also lead to lack of medical care, lack of access to prescriptions, and so on (Bennett, Scharoun-Lee, and Tucker-Seeley, 2009).

Conclusion

The chapter began with a discussion of victim rights and the evolution of our criminal justice as a private institution for those with the resources to access it, to a defendant-centered system, to the current state, where various legislative acts have served to grant victims a number of important rights. These rights generally include: The right to notice, the right to be present at criminal justice proceedings, the right to be heard, the right to protection, the right to a speedy trial, the right to restitution, and the right to privacy/confidentiality. Although 32 states have ratified victims' rights in their constitutions, the federal government has yet to ratify such an amendment, despite over a dozen ratified for defendants at the federal level.

Victims of violence commonly experience crisis as a result of their victimization. Crisis intervention is an important component of the response, as experts have determined that early intervention in dealing with the myriad deleterious effects of victimization is crucial in helping victims recover These effects may be physical, emotional, and/or financial, and may continue for extensive periods of time following an event.

Hate crimes are perpetrated against victims on the basis race, religion, sexual orientation, ethnicity/national origin, and disability, and include harassment and intimidation, vandalism and destruction of property, and both lethal and non-lethal physical assaults. Hate crime affects the victim(s) targeted as well as the larger community of people associated with the victim.

Violent sexual assault, on the other hand, tends to be a highly targeted violent crime, affecting hundreds of thousands of victims annually in the U.S., with precise figures difficult to estimate due to underreporting and measurement issues. Despite pervasive media myths about the nature of rape, it affects not only women and men of all sociodemographic classifications, but also those who are younger (including children and adolescents) as well as those who are older and those who are in minority positions in society disproportionately; e.g., it affects those never married (correlated with age) and those from lower income families. Finally, American women appear to be at a much higher risk for rape compared to women in other industrialized nations (Green and

Roberts, 2008). Victims of rape tend to suffer even more severe negative effects, and for longer periods of time, than other victims of violence.

Victims of workplace violence suffer a range of crimes from sexual assault, robbery, simple and aggravated assault, stalking, and homicide in the workplace, and these incidents occur hundreds of thousands of times times a year in the U.S. Recently, scholars have begun to include verbal aggression, including threats of violence, harassment, and bullying into the research on workplace violence, since these acts also contribute to a fearful and stressful environment in the workplace. The acts affect the victims in a variety of negative ways, while also costing billions of dollars a year in loss of productivity and legal costs.

Underserved victims of violence closely resemble the marginalized populations within society generally. Underserved victims may be: poor and/or homelessness; victims of certain crimes such as sex trafficking, legal and/or illegal prostitution-related; suffer from physical and/or mental disability; be an immigrant and/or non-English speaking person; reside in a rural or otherwise isolated area; be of a racial/ethnic minority status, including American Indians; be of a sexual minority status; and/or be offenders under criminal justice supervision. Special discussion was provided regarding the homeless; experts report that the homeless experience an increased risk for violent victimization compared to the general population, and compared to others within the underserved community.

Overpopulation, air and water pollution, deforestation, global warming, unsustainable agricultural and fishing practices, overconsumption, mal-distribution of wealth, the rise of the corporation, the Third World debt crisis, militarization, and wars make up a list of environmental degradation practices and social injustices that experts believe have the harshest effects on victims. Environmental degradation has reached unprecedented levels, and has been the cause of violence both in the U.S. and abroad, which experts warn will only worsen.

While environmental degradation is a form of human rights violation, there are numerous others. The Universal Declaration of Human Rights was adopted by the General Assembly of the United Nations in 1948 to outline the fundamental human rights, including political and civil rights as well as economic, social, and cultural rights. Religious and cultural beliefs often take precedence over human rights, particularly in acts of violence against women such as female genital mutilation, infanticide of females, sex and labor trafficking of women, bride burnings, dowry murders, honor killings, sexual assault, and domestic violence. In addition to human rights, acts of corruption to gain advantage, power, and authority such as bribery, extortion, fraud, and embezzlement, affect many people around the globe, particularly those who are poor and powerless.

While financial crises and crimes may occur in many forms, two prominent and timely examples were discussed: the 2008 start of the U.S. recession caused in large part by the bursting of the "housing bubble," and the 2008 arrest of Bernie Madoff for his multibillion dollar ponzi scheme. While victims of financial crimes are not generally given the same "victim status" as those suffering from interpersonal violence victimizations, researchers have identified numerous devastating consequences that victims of these crimes suffer, including financial difficulties to absolute financial ruin, along with the same types of psychological and physiological effects suffered by victims of violence.

Along with victims of financial crimes, victims of environmental degradation and human rights violations are not always regarded as victims of violence, if regarded as victims of crime at all. In three brief sections, an overview was given of how victims of these phenomenon do in fact suffer in the same ways as victims of more explicit violence, if not even more severely, and how these crimes tend to target those members of society who are already plagued by the effects of marginalized social status. In his seminal work, *Categorically Unequal*, sociologist Douglas Massey explains that, although societies have evolved over time, from agrarian to industrial, to the current post-industrial structures found in the U.S. and many other societies, the tendency for people to be categorized (i.e., stratified) and therefore, granted differential access to a variety of resources, has not evolved much. He explains, "all stratification processes boil down to a combination of two simple but powerful mechanisms: the allocation of people to social categories and the institutionalization of practices that allocate resources unequally across these categories" (2007, pp. 5–6). It is clear from the discussions of the various victimizations types in this chapter that those in the lower strata of society, indeed on a global level, are most commonly and severely affected by violence.

A disturbing pattern regarding violence victimization is that, for a number of reasons, much of this crime is never reported to police, so estimates of prevalence are underestimates, and the majority of victims do not get the justice they are afforded through their basic human rights. Many victims report negative experiences with the criminal justice system, which leads to reluctance to cooperate and hesitance to involve the police in future victimizations. Davies asserts that "the greatest amount of victimization that people experience in society takes place outside the scope or view of the criminal justice system and some of the most vulnerable and neglected victims and forms of victimization in society remain invisible to the agencies of the criminal justice system" (2007, p. 253).

What we can take away from a focus on victims is that the crimes they suffer are diverse, prevalent, and, although people of all walks suffer from violent victimizations, those in the margins of society suffer more often and from harsher consequences as a result. Victims' rights and services have certainly evolved and helped tremendously to minimize the detrimental impact of a violent victimization, but further legislation, greater resources, and more formal recognition of victims' rights is warranted. Furthermore, these rights and services need to be extended more fairly to reach those who are underserved and oppressed, such as the homeless and those ostracized because of their sexual orientation or because their crimes were committed by a family member or intimate partner.

References

Adeola, F.O. (2001). Environmental injustice, and human rights abuse: The states, MNC's, and repression of minority groups in the world system. *Human Ecology Review*, 8(1), 39–59.

Aalbers, M. (2009). Geographies of the financial crisis. *Area*, 41(1), 34–42.

Alvarez, A., and Bachman, R. (2008). *Violence: The enduring problem*. Thousand Oaks, CA: Sage Publications.

Barling, J., Dupre, K.E., and Kelloway, E.K. (2009). Predicting workplace aggression and violence. *Annual Review of Psychology*, 60, 671–692.

Barnes, A., and Ephross, P.H. (1994). The impact of hate violence on victims: Emotional and behavioral responses to attacks. *Social Work*, May, 247–251.

Bennett, L., Goodman, L., and Dutton, M.A. (1999). Systematic obstacles to the criminal prosecution of a battering partner. *Journal of Interpersonal Violence*, 14(7), 761–772.

Bennett, G.G., Scharoun-Lee, M., and Tucker-Seeley, R. (2009). Will the public's health fall victim to the home foreclosure epidemic? *PLoS Med*, 6(6), e1000087.

Belknap, J. (2007). *The invisible woman: Gender, crime, and justice*, 3rd Ed. Thomson Wadsworth.

Benedict, H. (1992). *Virgin or vamp: How the press covers sex crimes*. New York: Oxford University Press.

Berns, N. (2004). *Framing the victim: Domestic violence, media and social problems*. Hawthorne, NY: Aldine de Gruyter.

Callender Knefel, A.M., and Bryant, C.D. (2004). Workplace as combat zone: Reconceptualizing occupational and organizational violence. *Deviant Behavior*, 25, 521–601.

Campbell, R., and Townsend, S.M. (2011). Defining the scope of sexual violence against women. In C.M. Renzetti, J.L. Edleson, & Bergen, R.K. *Sourcebook on violence against women*, 2nd Ed., 95–110.

Chakraborti, N., and Garland, J. (2009) *Hate crime: Impact, causes, and responses*. Sage Publications.

Chavez, J.M., and Griffiths, E. (2009). Neighborhood dynamics of urban violence: Understanding the immigration connection. *Homicide Studies, 13*(3), 261–273.

Corcoran, J., and Allen, S. (2005). The effects of a police/victim assistance crisis team approach to domestic violence. *Journal of Family Violence*, 20(1), 39–45.

Covington, S. (2007). Women and the criminal justice system. *Women's Health Issues*, 17(4). Retrieved from: http://www.centerforgenderandjustice.org.

Croall, H. (2007). Victims of white collar and corporate crime. In P. Davies, P. Francis, and C. Greer (Eds.). *Victims, Crime, and Society*. Sage Publications, 78–108.

Davies, P. (2007). Criminal (In)justice for victims? In P. Davies, P. Francis, and C. Greer (Eds.). *Victims, Crime, and Society*. Sage Publications, 251–278.

Decker, S.E., and Naugle, A.E. (2009). Immediate intervention for sexual assault: review with recommendations and implications for practitioners. *Journal of Aggression, Maltreatment, & Trauma*, 18, 419–441.

Dias, C.J. (1999). Human rights, development, and environment. In Y. Daniel, E. Stamatopoulou and C.J. Dias (Eds.). *The Universal Declaration of Human Rights: Fifty-Years and Beyond*. New York: Baywood Publishing Co., 395–401.

Donohoe, M. (2003). Causes and health consequences of environmental degradation and social injustice. *Social Science & Medicine*, 56, 573–587.

FBI. (2008). Hate crime incident reports. Retrived from: http://www2.fbi.gov/ucr/hc2008/incidents.html.

Finn, J., and Hughes, P. (2008). Evaluation of the RAINN national sexual assault online hotline. *Journal of Technology in Human Services*, 26(2/4), 203–222.

Fitzpatrick, K.M., LaGory, M.E., and Ritchey, F.J. (1993). Criminal victimization among the homeless. *Justice Quarterly*, 10(3), 353–368.

Green, D. L., and Roberts, A.R. (2008). *Helping victims of violent crime: Assessment, treatment, and evidence-based practice*. New York, NY: Springer.

Grossman, S.F., Hinkely, S., Kawasiski, A., and Margrave, C. (2005). Rural versus urban victims of violence: the interplay of race and region. *Journal of Family Violence*, 20(2), 71–81.

Hammett, T.M., Gaiter, J.L., and Crawford, C. (1998). Reaching seriously at-risk populations: health interventions in criminal justice settings. *Health, Education, & Behavior, 25*(1), 99–120.

Harrell, E. (2011). Workplace violence, 1993–2009. U.S. Department of Justice, Bureau of Justice Statistics. Retrieved from: http://www.bjs.gov/index.cfm?ty=pbdetail &iid=2377.

Hart, R.A., and Lowther, M.A. (2008). Honoring sovereignty: Aiding tribal efforts to protect Native American women from domestic violence. *California Law Review*, 96, 185–233.

Herek, G.M., Cogan, J.C. and Gillis, J.R. (2002). Victim experiences in hate crimes based on sexual orientation. *Journal of Social Issues, 58*(2), 319–339.

Herek, G.M., Gillis, J.R., and Cogan, J.C. (1999). Psychological sequelae of hate-crime victimization among lesbian, gay, and bisexual adults. *Journal of Consulting and Clinical Psychology.* 67, 945–951.

Holman, M. (2008). The modern-day slave trade: How the United States should alter the Victims of Trafficking and Violence Protection Act in order to combat international sex trafficking more effectively. *Texas International Law Journal*, 44(99), 99–121.

Homer-Dixon, T.F. (1994). Environmental scarcities and violent conflict: Evidence from cases. *International Security*, 19(1), 5–40.

Howley, S., and Dorris, C. (2007). Legal rights for crime victims in the criminal justice system. In R. Davis, A.J. Lurigio, and S. Herman, S. (Eds.). *Victims of crime*, 3rd. ed. Sage Publications, 255–297.

Jargowsky, P.A. (2009). Immigrants and neighborhoods of concentrated poverty: Assimilation or stagnation? *Journal of Ethnic and Migration Studies*, 35(7), 1129–1151.

Jasinski, J., Wesley, J.K., Wright, J.D., and Mustaine, E.E. (2010). *Hard lives, mean streets: Violence in the lives of homeless women.* Northeastern.

Jones, H., and Powell, J.L. (2006). Old age, vulnerability and sexual violence: Implications for knowledge and practice. *International Nursing Review*, 53, 211–216.

Johnson, I.M., and Morgan, E.F. (2008). Victim impact statements — fairness to defendants? In L.J. Moriarty (Ed.). *Controversies in Victimology*, 2nd Ed. Anderson Publishing, 115–132.

Johnston, B.R. (1994). Environmental degradation and human rights abuse. In Johnston, B.R. (Ed.). *Who pays the Price? The Sociocultural Context of Environmental Crisis*, Covelo, CA: Island Press, 7–15.

Kaplan, J.F. (2010). Help is on the way: A recent case sheds light on workplace bullying. *Houston law Review*, 47(1), 141–173.

Kennedy, D. B. (1983). Implications of the victimization syndrome for clinical intervention with crime victims. *The Personnel and Guidance Journal*, December, pp. 19–222.

Kilpatrick, D., Amstadter, A., Resnick, H., and Ruggiero, K. (2007). Rape-related PTSD: Issues and interventions. *Psychiatric Times*, 24(7), 50–52.

Koss, M.P., Woodriff, W.S., and Koss, P.G. (1990). Relation of criminal victimization to health perceptions among women medical patients. *Journal of Consulting Psychology*, 58(2), 147–182.

Knefel, C., Koss, M., Woodruff, W., and Koss, P. (1990). Relation of criminal victimization to health perceptions among women medical patients. *Journal of Consulting and Psychology*, 58, 147–152.

Lauritsen, J.L. (2005). Social and scientific influences on the measurement of criminal victimization. *Journal of Quantitative Criminology*, 21(3), 245–266.

Leadership Conference on Civil Rights. (1996). Hate crime statistics. Retrieved from: http://www.civilrights.org/lcef/hcpc/stats/table1.htm.

Levin, J., and McDevitt, J. (1993). *Hate crime: The rising tide of bigotry and bloodshed*. New York: Plenum.

Lewis, L.S. (2010). Madoff's victims and their day in court. *Culture and Society 47*, 439–450.

Logan, T.K., Walker, R., Cole, J., Ratliff, S., and Leukefeld, C. (2003). Qualitative differences among rural and urban intimate violence victimization experiences and consequences: A pilot study. *Journal of Family Violence*, 18(2), 83–92.

Massey, D.S. (2007). *Categorically unequal: The American stratification system*. Russell Sage Foundation: New York.

Mayhew, C., and Chappell, D. (2007). Workplace violence: An overview of patterns of risk and the emotional/stress consequences on targets. *International Journal of Law and Psychiatry*, 30, 327–339.

McCormack, R.J. (2000). United States crime victim assistance: History, organization, and evaluation. In P.M. Tobolowsky (Ed.). *Understanding Victimology*. Cincinnati, OH: Anderson Publishing Company, 247–260.

McDevitt, J., and Balboni, J. (2003). Hate crime victimization: A comparison of bias- and nonbias-motivated assaults. In J.M. Sgarzi, and J. McDevitt (Eds.). *Victimology: A Study of crime victims and their roles*. Upper Saddle River: Prentice Hall, 189–204.

McDevitt, J., Farrell, A., Rousseau, D., and Wolff, R. (2007). Hate crimes: Characteristics of incidents, victims, and offenders. In R. Davis, A.J. Lurigio, and S. Herman (Eds.). *Victims of crime, 3rd Ed*. Thousand Oaks, CA: Sage Publications.

McMahon, B.T., West, S.L., Lewis, A.N., Armstrong, A.J., and Conway, J.P. (2004). Hate crimes and disability in America. *Rehabilitation Counseling Bulletin*, 47, 66–75.

Messner, S.F., McHugh, S., and Felson, R.B. (2004). Distinctive characteristics of assaults motivated by bias. *Criminology, 42*(3), 585–618.

Melton, H.C. (2010). Rape myths: Impacts on victims of rape. In V. Garcia, and J.E. Clifford (Eds.). *Female victims of crime: Reality reconsidered*. Prentice Hall, 113–127.

Muscat, B. T., and Walsh, J.A. (2007). Reaching underserved victim populations: Special challenges relating to homeless victims, rural populations, ethnic/racial minorities, and victims with disabilities. In Davis, R.C., Lurigio, A.J., and Herman, S. (Eds.). *Victims of Crime*, 3rd Ed. Thousand Oaks, CA: Sage Publications, 315–336.

Nickel, J.W. (1993). The human right to a safe environment: Philosophical perspectives on its scope and justification. *The Yale Journal of International Law*, (18), 281–295.

Nickel, J.W., and Viola, E. (1994). Integrating environmentalism and human rights. *Environmental Ethics* (16), 265–273.

Norris, F.H., and Kaniasty, K. (1994). Psychological distress following criminal victimization in the general population: Cross-sectional, longitudinal, and prospective analyses. *Journal of Consulting and Clinical Psychology*, 62(1), 111–123.

Norton, I.M., and Manson, S.M. (1995). A silent minority: Battered American Indian women. *Journal of Family Violence*, 10(3), 307–318.

Perry, B. (2002). From ethnocide to ethnoviolence: Layers of Native American victimization. *Contemporary Justice Review*, 5(3), 231–247.

Perry, B. (2001). *In the name of hate: Understanding hate rimes.* New York: Routledge.

Pilapitiya, T. (2004). The impact of corruption on the human rights based approach to development. United Nations Development Programme-Oslo Governance Centre. Retrieved from: http://www.hrw.org; www.amnesty.org.

Puleo, S., and McGlothlin. (2010). Overview of crisis intervention. In L.R. Jackson-Cherry, and B.T. Erford (Eds.). *Crisis intervention and prevention.* Pearson, 1–24.

Putnam, T.L. (2010). Disregard or disposition? Assessing human rights practices in the United States. *Contemporary Sociology*, 39(6), 668–671.

Rhodes, C, Pullen, A., Vickers, M.H., Clegg, S.R., and Pitsis, A. (2010). Violence and workplace bullying: What are an organization's ethical responsibilities? *Administrative Theory and Praxis*, 32(1), 96–115.

Ristad, R.N. (2008). A stark examination of prison culture and prison ministry. Dialog: *A Journal of Theology*, 47(3), 292–303.

Rochon, L., and Rossi, S. (2010). Has it happened again? *International Journal of Political Economy*, 39(2), 5–9.

Roschelle, A.R. (2008). Welfare indignities: Homeless women, domestic violence, and welfare reform in San Francisco. *Gender Issues*, 25, 193–209.

Roberts, A.R. (2005). Bridging the past and present to the future of crisis intervention and crisis management. In A.R. Roberts (Ed.). *Crisis intervention handbook: Assessment, treatment and research*, 3rd Ed. New York: Oxford University Press, 3–35.

Roberts, A.R. and Green, D. (2007). Crisis Intervention with victims of violent crimes. In Davis, R.C., Lurigio, A.J., and Herman, S. (Eds.). *Victims of Crime*, 3rd Ed. Thousand Oaks, CA: Sage Publications, 255–265.

Ryan, W. (1971). *Blaming the victim.* New York: Pantheon Books.

Santana, S. A., and Fisher, B.S. (2010). Workplace violence: Identifying gender differences and similarities. In V. Garcia and J.E. Clifford (Eds.). *Female victims of crime: Reality reconsidered.* Upper Saddle River, NJ: Prentice Hall, 145–161.

Schat, A.C.H., Frone, M., and Kelloway, E.K. (2006). Prevalence of workplace aggression in the U.S. workforce: Findings from a national study. In E.K. Kelloway, J. Barling, and J.J. Hurrell (Eds.). *Handbook of workplace violence.* Thousand Oaks, CA: Sage Publications, 47–90.

Siegel, J., Golding, J., Stein, J., Burnam, M., and Sorenson, S. (1990). Reactions to sexual assault: A community study. *Journal of Interpersonal Violence*, 5, 229–246.

Stohr, M.K., Vazquez, S.P., and Kleppinger, S. (2006). It is not paranoia if people really are out to get you: The nature and the extent of hate crime victimization in Idaho. *Journal of Ethnicity in Criminal Justice, 4*(1/2), 65–91.

Surette, R. (2011). Media, crime, and criminal justice: *Images, realities, and policies, 4th Ed.* Wadsworth.

Swanson, C. (2008). Should victims have the right to meet with their offenders? In L. Moriarty (Ed.). *Controversies in victimology*, 2nd Ed. Anderson Publishing, 73–90.

Swick, K.J. (2008). The dynamics of violence and homelessness among young families. *Early Childhood Education Journal*, 36, 81–85.

Taylor, R. (2009). Slain and slandered: A content analysis of the portrayal of femicide in crime news. *Homicide Studies, 13*(1), 21–49.

Tjaden, P., and Thoennes, N. (2000). *Full report of the prevalence, incidence, and consequences of violence against women.* Washington, DC: National Institute of Justice.

Tobolowsky, P.M., Gaboury, M. T., Jackson, A. L., and Blackburn, A.G. (2010). *Crime victim rights and remedies, 2nd Ed.* Durham, NC: Carolina Academic Press.

Treas, J. (2010). The great American recession: Sociological insights on blame and pain. *Sociological Perspectives, 53*(1), 3–17.

Truman, J., and Rand, M. (2010). *Criminal Victimization, 2009.* Bureau of Justice Statistics Bulletin, October, 2010. Retrieved from http://bjs.ojp.usdoj.gov/content/pub/pdf/cv09.pdf.

United Nations Department of Public Information, 2011. Retrieved from: http://www.ohchr.org/EN/UDHR/Documents/UDHR_Translations/eng.pdf.

Von Wormer, K.S., and Bartollas, C. (2011). *Women and the criminal justice system*, 3rd Ed. Prentice Hall.

Vickers, M.H. (2010). Introduction—bullying, mobbing, and violence in public service workplaces: The shifting sands of "acceptable violence." *Administrative Theory and Praxis, 32*(1), 7–24.

Websdale, N.S. (1998). *Rural Woman Battering and the Justice System: An Ethnography.* Thousand Oaks, CA: Sage Publications.

Websdale, N.S., and Johnson, B. (1997). The policing of domestic violence in rural an urban areas: The voices of battered women in Kentucky. *Policing and Society*, 6, 297–317.

Weitz, T.A., Freund, K.M., and Wright, L. (2004). Identifying and caring for underserved populations: Experience of the National Centers of Excellence in Women's Health. *Journal of Women's Health & Gender-Based Medicine*, 10(10), 937–952.

Williams, O., and Becker, L.R. (1994). Domestic partner abuse treatment programs and cultural competence: The results of a national survey. *Violence and Victims*, 9(3), 287–296.

Wright, J.W., and Donley, A.M. (2011). *Poor and homeless in the sunshine state: Down and out in theme park nation.* New Brunswick, NJ: Transaction Publishers.

Zweig, J.M., Schlichter, K.A., and Burt, M.R. (2002). Assisting women victims of violence who experience multiple barriers to service. *Violence Against Women*, 8(2), 162–180.

Chapter 8

Individual Predictors of Violence and Dangerousness: Biological, Psychological/ Psychiatric, and Integrated Life-Course Theories

---

When we are confronted with what appears to be an inexplicable act of violence, we often ask rhetorically, "What made the individual act violently?" or "Is there something wrong with the perpetrator?" The typical range of attributions for the act of violence suggests that there is something inherently wrong with the perpetrators and, therefore, that the reasons for their violence lie within them. The idea that the individual exhibiting violent behavior is somehow defective has led to the emergence of a substantial literature suggesting a biological, hereditary or some other inherent basis for criminal or deviant behavior. Similarly, several psychodynamic theories of violence have concurrently developed, addressing whether the psychic development, emotional condition, and/or personality structure of people who commit violent acts differ significantly from those who do not. Interestingly, categorizing biological and psychological determinants of violent behavior is often difficult, especially when certain physiological conditions have psychological and behavioral manifestations. In this chapter, we will explore the antecedents of the biological and psychological theoretical perspectives, as well as contemporary biosocial, sociobiological, and psychological research and theories of crime and deviance specifically as they relate to violent behavior.

We also review developmental and life-course theories that offer more integrated explanations of violent behavior bringing together biological, psychological, and sociological factors. These integrative studies of human behavior take into account the ongoing interaction between human beings and their social environments over time and social space.

Biological/Hereditary Theories of Crime

The belief that biology is destiny has been around for quite some time (e.g., Lange, 1929; Niehoff, 1999; Barash, 2001). The idea that criminals might somehow be biologically different in a defective and abnormal way has also been a persistent proposition that is familiar to most of us.

Historical Overview

The idea of being born dangerous, particularly in the scientific context, may be attributed to Cesare Lombroso (1835–1909), an Italian physician and a pioneer figure in criminology. The ideas in Lombroso's book, *L'Uomo Delinquente (The Criminal Man)*, which was published in 1876, appear to have been influenced by Charles Darwin's seminal work, *Descent of Man*, which was published in 1871. Lombroso's theory is based on the assertion that certain physical stigmata indicate an atavistic type of human being or throwback to a primitive earlier man or born criminal. His research offers an extensive list of stigmata that he uncovered while dissecting cadavers in the prisons and asylums of Pavia, Italy, many of which focused on primitive or ape-like features such as ears, nose, chin, hair, facial wrinkles, and excessive arm length. Lomborso's notion of atavism, however, has not been supported with empirical evidence and has remained unsubstantiated or undocumented; in other words there is no evidence that suggests that prehistoric or even contemporary primitives are biologically prone to criminal or violent conduct.[1]

In his later research, Lombroso compared Italian criminals and non-criminal Italian soldiers and concluded that a very small proportion of criminals, perhaps a third, could

---

1. One of the better discussions of Lombroso's ideas and his contribution to the development of criminology can be found in the work of George Vold and Tom Bernard, *Theoretical Criminology* (1986).

be categorized as atavistic. Lombroso added to his typology what he described as a "criminoloid" type, a description resembling what we refer to now as an antisocial personality (compulsive law breakers with no sense of right or wrong or empathy for others). While criminoloids did not exhibit the stigmata of the atavistic type, they seemed to exhibit the same antisocial and vicious behavior (Vold and Bernard, 1986).

With Guglielmo Ferrero, Lombroso also wrote *Criminal Woman, the Prostitute, and the Normal Woman*, which was originally published in 1893. In this book, the first to address female criminality, he and his co-author argue that female deviations are usually sexual in nature often expressed through prostitution. In instances when women are involved in the crimes or acts of violence that are more typically male behaviors, the female perpetrator will likely have distinctly masculine traits. They also contend that women are not typically criminal because they are less intelligent and also because their jealous and cruel temperaments are mitigated by their maternal instincts. This notion of women being less criminal because they are less intelligent than males seems to run counter to the atavistic criminal proposition in Lombroso's earlier work where the atavistic criminal is assumed to be less intelligent. Contradictory statements and lack of sufficient evidence to support his view led to much scientific criticism of Lombroso's research.

In fact, his atavistic theory of violence as well as his theory of female criminality has been widely criticized by scholars across the world. Responding to a great deal of criticism, Lombroso modified many of his views and in his book, *Crime: Its Causes and Remedies* (1911), he acknowledges that there are many other factors related to crime ranging from climate and the economy to sex and marriage customs. Atavism was relegated to a single chapter at the end of the book. This work, however, was not published until after his death in 1909.

Lombroso's followers took up a substantially modified version of his theory, yet were still committed to the notion of a biological basis for criminal behavior. For example, Raffaele Garofalo (1914) emphasized psychological factors and argued that criminals lacked proper development of "altruistic sensibility," which had a physical basis. Lombroso's contemporary, Enrico Ferri, in his 1917 book, *Criminal Sociology*, argued that Lombroso gave too much weight to skull measurement and measurements of other parts of the body and should have given greater weight to social, political, and economic factors. Ferri proposed five types of criminals: criminal lunatics, born criminals (incorrigibles), habitual criminals, occasional criminals and emotional criminals. In spite of the implication in the typology of distinctiveness for each type, Ferri concluded that all criminals are abnormal and possess aberrant organic and psychological characteristics.

During most of the 20th Century, interest in the biological basis or constitutional correlates of crime remained a valid area of research, even though most criminologists did not support biological determinism. However, Arthur Fink's *Causes of Crime: Biological Theories in the United States, 1800–1915* found that some anthropologists and prison physicians who studied criminals maintained a strong interest in criminal physiology (1938). One among this group was a Harvard anthropologist, Ernest Hooten, who argued in his 1931 book, *Crime and the Man*, that criminals are organically inferior and that the inferiority is genetically inheritable. Hooten claimed that in order to solve the problem of crime and violence, a program of eugenics (sterilization of criminals or persons who are thought to have violent or criminal potential) is necessary. Based on measurements of more than 17,000 people from all walks of life, he concluded that 19 of 35 measurements showed significant differences between offenders and non-offenders. Hooten's research results suggested that criminals had low foreheads, high pinched nasal roots, crooked noses, compressed faces, narrow jaws, small ears, long necks, and stooped shoulders. He

---

Box 8.1 Governor Apologizes for Forced Sterilization: Virginia Eugenics Law Was One of 30 in U.S.

In Charlottesville, Virginia, "Governor Mark Warner apologized Thursday for Virginia's forced sterilization of thousands of people from 1924 to 1979, calling it "a shameful effort" that must not be repeated. Virginia conducted about 7,450 sterilizations under the banner of eugenics, or selective human breeding and social engineering. Virginia became the first of the 30 states that conducted sterilizations to apologize. There were more than 60,000 eugenics victims nationwide."

"Warner's apology coincides with the 75th anniversary of the U.S. Supreme Court's Buck v. Bell decision upholding Virginia's eugenics law, which became a model for other states. The law targeted almost any human shortcoming that was believed to be hereditary, including mental illness, mental retardation, epilepsy, alcoholism and criminal behavior."

In 2001, the "General Assembly passed a resolution expressing "profound regret" for the state's role in eugenics, but it stopped short of a formal apology. Some legislators expressed concern that an apology could make the state vulnerable to lawsuits. But Warner spokeswoman Ellen Qualls said Thursday that the governor, after consulting with Attorney General Jerry Kilgore, "felt comfortable that there would be no legal repercussions from issuing an apology" (Baskervill, 2002: A-1).

At least one state, North Carolina, that practiced forced sterilization of often poor and black young females, some raped, recently recommended in January, 2012 that victims, going back as far as forty four years ago, receive $50,000 compensation for the physical and mental harm caused by their involuntary sterilization (Zucchino, 2012: A-7).

---

believed physical inferiority is linked to mental inferiority, making the problem of crime all the more serious.

While scientists' interest in eugenics in the U.S. began to wane particularly after Hooton's work was severely critiqued both methodologically (inadequate controls and sampling bias) and conceptually (failing to link physical deviations with criminality in a causal way), politicians' interest in eugenics continued. For example, as many as thirty states in the U.S. between 1929 and 1974 sterilized thousands of young, poor, and often black females (and males) using state Eugenics Boards to protect the states' populations by "weeding out the mentally ill, diseased, feebleminded, and others deemed undesirable" on the assumption that they carried criminal tendencies (Zucchino, 2012, p. A-7). Thus even with wide-spread criticism of Hooten's work and other research of this type and lack of adequate scientific evidence, the link between physical traits and criminality would not go away.

William Sheldon's 1949 study of delinquency entitled: *Varieties of Delinquent Youth*, represents another type of biological research, which links physical and psychological traits with criminal or delinquent behavior. Sheldon borrowed and quantified Ernst Kretschmer's (1925) typology of body types and associated personality traits and renamed them *ectomorphs* (thin body types); *mesomorphs* (athletic body types), and *endomorphs* (heavy or obese body types). Sheldon devised a quantitative scale based on one used to grade poultry and dogs to classify people into the three types.

Sheldon argued that a specific personality type or temperament accompanied each body type. Ectomorphs, according to Sheldon, are "cerebrotonic" (restrained, self-conscious, and hypersensitive); endomorphs are "viscerotonic" (relaxed, food-oriented, and even-tempered); and mesomorphs are "somatotonic" (dominating, assertive, competitive, and unrestrained). While temperament alone is not viewed as criminal, Sheldon felt that physique in combination with corresponding temperament and certain other social factors could be criminogenic.

To test his theory, Sheldon compared 200 delinquent boys with a control group of 200 non-delinquents. From extensive measurements taken from photographs of each youth, Sheldon concluded that boys classified as mesomorphs possessed the physical and psychological characteristics most suitable for delinquency. Sheldon's research came under intense criticism by Edwin Sutherland, an eminent criminologist of the time. Sutherland (1951) took issue with Sheldon's operational definition of delinquency or method of classification of delinquents, his sampling design, and the methodology of somatotypical classification. In spite of these criticisms, Sheldon continued to work on this project until his death in 1977. Within the "delinquent" group, 60 percent were categorized as mesomorphic in the original study; however, only 7 percent were subsequently classified as adult criminals in follow-up studies (Hartl, Monnelly, and Elderkind, 1982).

In spite of scathing criticisms leveled at Sheldon's research and his somatotype theory of delinquency (i.e., the connection between body type/personality and criminality), two criminologists, the husband and wife team of Sheldon and Eleanor Glueck, embarked on a massive study comparing 500 delinquent boys with a control group of 500 non-delinquent boys. Even though the Gluecks used different (improved) methods to test Sheldon's hypothesis, they also found a similar significant difference (i.e., 60 percent of their delinquent sample was mesomorphic compared to 31 percent of the control group), thus offering support for Sheldon's thesis. Rather than making causal claims, however, the Gluecks merely viewed body type as a predisposing factor for delinquency (1956). In a later work, the Gluecks argued that delinquency begins long before children become adolescents. They claimed that signs are often visible by the time children are between three and six, and almost always before they are 11 years old. For instance, they noted: "The onset of persistent misbehavior tendencies was at the early age of seven years or younger among 48 percent of our delinquents, and from eight to ten in an additional 39 percent; thus a total of almost nine-tenths of the entire group showed clear delinquent tendencies before the time when boys generally become members of organized boys' gangs" (1964, p. 285). Despite considerable scientific gravitas provided by the Gluecks' long association with the Harvard Law School, their research received little support from other criminologists. Critics continued to note serious methodological flaws in the physiological study of crime and delinquency (Clinard, 1974).

Contemporary Perspectives

Today most criminological researchers are not likely to claim that crime or violence is solely a product of biological forces. In fact most scientists acknowledge the interplay of nature and nurture and the possibility that certain internal and physical characteristics interacting with environmental (social and economic) conditions may predispose individuals to respond violently or to refrain from violence. New scientific advancements, particularly the discoveries associated with the Human Genome Project, neural networks, and neural plasticity, have led to a resurgence of interest in biologically-oriented investigation and the rekindling of the "nature vs. nurture" debate (Barash, 2001; Pinker, 2002). The underlying biological basis for criminal behavior remains with us especially in popular culture. For example, the television series, *Criminal Minds*, and the 2009 Academy Award for Best Foreign Film winner, *El Secreto de Sus Ojos* (*The Secret in Their Eyes*), place the blame for violence behavior within the nature of the individual actors.

Some geneticists, psychiatrists, and other behavioral scientists have expressed reluctance in pursing genetic predictors of crime and violence warning that this may lead to the establishment of frightening policies based on biological determinism and other consequences of biology as destiny. It is feared that if we move in this direction, we may see control of criminals ultimately in terms of "medication" or correction of the problem through genetic engineering, which is another term for eugenics. There have been concerns expressed regarding the possibility of returning to a period in the history of the United States when morally and ethically challenged pseudo-scientists argued for a program of eugenics, which resulted in the implementation of policies that encouraged people with "exemplary" traits to have more children and legalized the sterilization of those with less than exemplary traits or histories of mental illness or feeblemindedness (Sagarin and Sanchez, 1988). For example, Charles McCaghy's (1976) research uncovered over 70,000 cases of sterilization between 1907 and 1937, the height of the eugenics movement in the U.S.

Genetics and Crime

To what extent can genetics explain human violent behavior or suggest correlates and risk factors of violence? Unraveling the complexities that are associated with this question is very difficult and suggests many challenges. For example, presently, there are no genetic studies with qualitative evidence that identify any genetic markers or genetic syndromes, which are linked with violence or criminal behavior. Similar to most other inherited types of behavior or predispositions, a genetic connection with violence involves many genes and a wide range of environmental influences.

Another challenge related to untangling the complexities due to multiple effects or influences associated with explaining violence is distinguishing the causes of violence from the correlates of violence and also determining to what extent a genetic predisposition for violence is associated with other behavior, such as mental illness. For instance, we often use labels such as psychopathic, sociopathic, and asocial for people who have committed acts of violence, as if the fate of some individuals were given to them at birth. It is interesting to note that according to the definition offered by the American Psychiatric Association, antisocial personality disorder (APD) is characterized by, among other things, persistent lying and stealing, apparent lack of remorse and empathy, recurring difficulties with the law, substance abuse, and aggressive and violent behavior (American Psychiatric Association, 2000). Under certain circumstances, many of these behaviors may constitute legal violations, but many do not. The issue here is whether or not there is a single underlying genetic basis for the disorder. Furthermore, still unresolved is the question of whether the genetic predisposition for mental illness is associated with a genetic propensity for violence? Research results in this area continue to suggest that while there appears to be a relationship between violent crime and mental illness in some cases, "the main problem in discussing any relationship between criminal behavior and mental disorder is that the two concepts are largely unrelated" (Gunn, 1977, p. 318).

A major challenge associated with establishing a causal relationship has been the control and the factoring out of social learning, social labeling, and genetic influences. When parents manifest disturbed or violent behavior themselves, it is difficult to ascertain from the usual family studies how much of the offspring's violent behavior is attributed to social forces and how much to inheritance. Two types of research strategies attempt to control for the methodological drawbacks of family studies (in which it is difficult to separate out genetic and environmental effects): twin and adoption studies (see Mednick and Christiansen, 1977; Van Dusen, et al., 1983; Gabrielli and Mednick, 1984; Rowe and Osgood, 1984). The key concept of such studies is the *concordance rate*, which refers to the similarity of behavioral outcomes among the pairs of individuals. When the individuals are dissimilar, they are *discordant*. The difference in the concordant rate between identical twins (monozygotic) and fraternal twins (dizygotic) is assumed to demonstrate the influence of inheritance (Shoemaker 1990, p. 21). The other side of the question is approached by adoption or separation studies in which concordance and discordance is tracked not only for the twins or siblings, but also for parents.

Glenn Walters (1992) analyzed the relationship presumed to exist between genetic inheritance and criminal conduct utilizing a meta-analysis technique. This approach allows for the collection of data from a series of research reports, which are converted to a common scale and reanalyzed (Lipsey and Wilson, 2001). Walters' meta-analysis is based on the examination of 38 family, twin, and adoption studies that focused on the gene-crime connection. His findings suggest that studies using the family method are not able to untangle the influences of heredity and environmental influences. He concludes that the effects reported in the various studies should be viewed in terms of a continuum of genetic influence ranging from zero to an "upper limit" estimate of genetic influence. He places the family studies close to zero. (Walters, 1992, p. 606). According to Walters the twin studies yield no better results, even though they more effectively controlled for environmental influences. Finally, the adoptive study model, while yielding the most accurate test of the gene-crime hypothesis, produced the lowest concordance rates or inheritability estimates. Walters concludes that it is unlikely that a direct genetic link to crime exists and that future research in this area should look at other characteristics that might bridge the modest gene-crime association reported in his meta-analysis.

Fear Conditioning and Crime

Another branch of research, which seeks to uncover biological influences of criminal (violent) behavior, looks at the conditioning and crime relationship. Studies on the relationship between variable levels of conditioning or learning by association and criminality, were promoted by the British criminologist Hans Eysenck. While in his work he acknowledges the mitigating influences of the environment, his theory rests on the assertion that the ability to learn by association and reinforcement is genetically and physiologically determined. The development of a conscience, which involves a long period of conditioning, compels the person to behave in moral and socially acceptable ways. If this conditioning process fails, it is likely to be a prominent cause of a person violating the law or more generally breaking social rules (Eysenck, 1964, p. 120). It might therefore be possible to suppress the genetic predisposition for adult crime in a young antisocial child by changing the behavior of the antisocial (or criminal) parents of the child.

Phillip Sterzer (2010) summarizes the body of research over several decades, which focuses on poor fear conditioning or inability to be conditioned as a predisposing factor of antisocial behavior. Most of these studies suggest that deficient amygdala functioning in the brain reduces individuals' ability to recognize threat, making them relatively fearless, less sensitive to negative consequences of their behavior, and more ready to engage in antisocial behavior. In the framework of a large birth cohort study, Gao and associates (2010) have tested fear conditioning in children at age three. In a 20 year follow-up study, they examined the association of poor fear conditioning in early childhood with adult criminal behavior. Comparing 137 individuals who had been convicted of a crime by age 23 with a matched sample of non-convicted individuals from the same age cohort, the researchers report that the skin response to a conditioned stimulus is almost nonexistent among the criminal group. According to the researchers, this points to the central brain (amygdala) structure, which underlies fear conditioning or the perception of threat in a person's environment, indicating that deficient amygdala functioning reduces individuals' level of fear and ability to recognize any threats and thus enabling antisocial behavior.

Brain Dysfunctions and Crime

Other brain dysfunctions have also been found to influence violent behavior, in particular those of the cortex and autonomic nervous system (ANS) that, depending on environmental and developmental factors, may give rise to criminality and/or antisocial behavior. Evidently drawing on the earlier work of Eysenck (1964), Raine and Dunkin (1990) suggest that it is possible that the genetic predisposition for criminality may be based in under arousal of the ANS and the central nervous system (CNS); psychophysiological measures of arousal have been shown to have a hereditary basis (Zahn and McBride, 1998). Although many studies have looked at the psychophysiological bases for criminality (see Hare 1999; Martens, 2000), few have devised explicit measures of how antisocial behavior and criminality are expressed. In a longitudinal study by Raine, Venables, and Williams (1990), the relationship between CNS and ANS measures of arousal at age 15 and criminality at age 24 have been studied. Using three independent measures of arousal, the authors correctly classified 74.7 percent of all subjects as criminal or noncriminal, a rate significantly greater than chance. The authors claim that all their arousal measures independently and correctly predicted criminality and antisocial behavior and that their results indicate strong support for the under arousal theory of antisocial behavior. Moreover, differences in social class, academic ability, and residence did not mediate the link between under arousal and anti-social behavior.

The idea of localization of brain function has laid the groundwork for investigations into brain anatomy relevant to the expression of violence (Macmillan, 2000). These studies attempt to find associations between structural brain damage and behavioral patterns. While there is no "violence center" in the brain, the limbic system and the frontal lobes are areas thought to be involved in the expression of violence. The limbic system is the anatomic substrate for emotion and the system's structure most often implicated in violent behavior is the amygdala; violence has been observed in those with abnormal electrical activity in this region (Miller, Collins, and Kent, 2008). The frontal lobes are regarded as the location of the cognitive and intellectual functions of the brain. In particular, the orbitofrontal cortices allow for the inhibition of aggression. Individuals with injury to this area have displayed antisocial traits, including disinhibition, impulsivity and lack of empathy and some are at increased risk of violent behavior (Miller, Collins, and Kent, 2008). Without injury, there is a balance between the potential for impulsive aggression mediated by the limbic brain and the control exerted by the orbitofrontal regions (Siever, 2008).

Another area of brain research is the neurochemistry of violence. A wide variety of hormones and neurotransmitters have attracted interest. Testosterone has received a great deal of attention because of a much higher incidence of violent behavior among males than females. However, evidence to support an association between testosterone and violence in humans is weak at best. The neurotransmitters acetylcholine, dopamine and gamma aminobutyric acid have received attention in violence/aggression research as well, with data on the role of serotonin and norepinephrine being the most convincing. Serotonin is an inhibitor of impulsive aggression and norepinephrine is a facilitator. The "low serotonin syndrome" has received substantial support in explaining impulsive aggression and there is evidence linking aggression with increased activity of norepinephrine (Filley, et al., 2001).

In 2006, genetic researchers in New Zealand discovered a genetic basis linked to risk-taking, aggression and criminality among the Maori, the indigenous people of New Zealand and the south Pacific, who historically have been characterized as warlike and adventuresome. The specific gene in question affects monoamine oxidases (MAOs), which are the enzymes responsible for breaking down neurotransmitters, including serotonin, dopamine and adrenaline, thereby affecting mood (Lea and Chambers, 2007). The authors go on to assert that individuals respond differently to environmental exposures based partly on different genetic make-ups. They further assert that behavioral characteristics grounded in genetics only confer potential. They do not establish an inescapable fate.

On a much larger scale, The Human Genome Initiative, generally referred to as the Human Genome Project, was initiated in 1988. The project's goal was to map and sequence the 100,000 plus genes of human DNA and, among other things learn how to read DNA in order to gain insight into the defects in genes leading to various diseases. Early in this project there was much speculation regarding the practical applications of research results from the project and questions whether the results will help clarify the long sought link between genetics and dangerous or violent behavior (e.g., Friedland, 1997; McInerney, 1999). Now, over twenty years later, many breakthroughs have been made identifying genes and suites of genes that contribute to diseases such as cancer, heart disease, diabetes, and other genetic defects, but none in the realm of predicting violent behaviors (see Than, 2010).

In recent years, sociobiology has inspired a great deal of interest and debate. The many conceptual, methodological, and theoretical problems associated with the phenomenon of crime and violence make the research findings in the area very tentative. The sociobiological perspective has generated more questions than answers. The interactive relationship between the internal and external environments of the individual is extremely complex. No single set of variables explains deviance or criminality adequately. Studies attempting to factor out the influence of heredity or physiology and social experiences have produced conflicting results.

Psychological and Psychiatric Perspectives on Criminality

We now turn to the questions: Does the psychic development, emotional condition, or personality structure of criminals differ significantly from non-criminals? Simply asking this question raises some serious methodological issues linking psychological profiles to crime. A crime is a legal construction that may or may not have a corresponding personality predisposition. Is there a personality profile for embezzlement (independent of opportunity), insider trading, misprision of a felony, aggravated crime against nature, or moonshining? Probably not. The issue is further complicated because most of the research looking at the personality traits that are predictive of crime and violence to date has been based on captured offenders and not the ones that got away, which leads us to presume that the research samples may be made up of the most frequent law violators or the dumbest of the "criminal class."

Box 8.2 The Nature-Nurture Debate, Redux

Genetic research finally makes its way into the thinking of sociologists.

If sociologists ignore genes, will other academics—and the wider world—ignore sociology?

Some in the discipline are telling their peers just that. With study after study finding that all sorts of personal characteristics are heritable—along with behaviors shaped by those characteristics—a see-no-gene perspective is obsolete.

Nor, these scholars argue, is it reasonable to concede that genes play some role but then to loftily assert that geneticists and the media overstate that role and to go on conducting studies as if genes did not exist. How, exactly, do genes shape human lives, interact with environmental forces, or get overpowered by those forces? "We do ourselves a disservice if we don't engage in those arguments," say Jason Schnittker, an associate professor of sociology at the University of Pennsylvania. "If we stay on the ropes, people from a different perspective, with a more extreme view, will be making them."

Schnittker is among the contributors to a special issue of the American Journal of Sociology, the field's flagship publication, devoted to "Genetics and Social Structure"—evidence that at least some sociologists are attempting to reckon with the genetic revolution. And not just in the AJS. Other top sociology journals, too, are publishing work incorporating genetic perspectives. The American Sociological Review in August [2008] published a much-discussed article on genes and delinquency by Guang Guo, of the University of North Carolina. (A couple of years ago, in an early foray on this front, Guo co-edited a special section of anther top journal, Social Forces, title "The Linking of Sociology and Biology.")

To concede that some people are genetically encoded to have shorter fuses than others or are more likely to gain weight if granted unlimited access to Oreos is hardly to embrace a give of humans as lumbering robots ruled by genes, contributors to the AJS issue argue. Admitting as much is just the first step in a rich inquiry into the biological and social forces shaping human lives—an inquiry that sociologists, like few others, are equipped to make.

But even the most gung-ho genetically minded sociologists will say that their first baby steps toward consilience, E.O. Wilson's term for the uniting of the biological and social sciences, don't match that lofty rhetoric. In general the genetic sociological work is highly statistical, often involving relatively new multivariable techniques. It is devoid of the narrative description that sociologists who immerse themselves in their subjects' lives can offer.

The idea that social theorists must account for genes sounds commonsensical. But those doing the work, of course, labor under some dark shadows. Social science has a history of misguide, or worse, attempts to link genes to crime, or to deviance, or to IQ; racial differences have often been either a subtext of this work or the researchers' main interest. Take our pick of flare-ups over the past 30 years; the reception of Crime and Human Nature (1985), written by UCLA political scientists James Q. Wilson and the late Harvard psychologist Richard Herrnstein; comments, in 1992, by a National Institute of Health official comparing inner cities to jungles and arguing that the breakdown of "social controls" in ghettos allowed genetic impulses to run free; a conference on crime and genes scheduled for 1992 and canceled after an uproar. (It was finally held in 1995.) Then, of course, there was the furor over The Bell Curve, in which Richard Herrnstein and the political scientist Charles A. Murray, of the American Enterprise Institute, attributed social problems among racial minorities in part to low intelligence.

Sociologists spoke up during those controversies, but they have also criticized less obviously combustible genetic studies. Just two years ago, in his presidential address to the American Sociological Association, Troy Duster, an eminent sociologist at New York University, went so far as to suggest that any sociologist who embraced genetic approaches was a traitor to the discipline. Two of the biggest problems facing sociology, he argued, were the "increasing authority of reductionist science" and "the attendant expansion of data bases on markers and processes 'inside the body.'" If anything defined sociology, Duster said, it was its role as "century-long counterpoint" to such efforts to connect the root of social problems to biology.

Jeremy Freese, of Northwestern University, frames his contribution to the AJS special issue as a direct rebuttal of Duster. An oppositional stance makes sense "for some highly charged areas," Freese grants, but it can't be the whole agenda. He brandishes a list of 52 characteristics that have been found to be partially heritable: cognitive ability, extroversion, aggressiveness, likeliness to marry, age at first sexual intercourse, support for the death penalty, and on and on. Indeed, by now one should assume that "genetic differences are partial causes of the overwhelming majority of outcomes" that sociologists study. Nevertheless, he says, social scientists still engage in "tacit collusion" to ignore the role of genetic differences.

Source: Excerpts from Shea, Christopher (January 9, 2009). The Nature-Nurture Debate, Redux, *The Chronicle of Higher Education*, pp. B6–B9.

While psychology and psychiatry are not focused on legality of behavior, they do intersect with the law. Both psychiatric and psychological theories of criminal behavior, especially insights and research results related to risk factors of violence and predictors of dangerousness, are recognized in the courtroom and play a role in the court's determination of criminal culpability.

Competence, Criminal Culpability, and the Insanity Defense

In a meaningful way, the presence of a psychiatrist in a criminal proceeding is to mitigate harshness of punishment. From this perspective, determining whether the defendant deserves punishment is synonymous with determining whether the defendant is criminally responsible (Szasz, 1970, p. 134). The role of a psychiatrist is to influence the decision of the court regarding the defendant's level of culpability and the appropriate disposition or sentencing; if for example the defendant is deemed not culpable, the question then focuses on whether the defendant should be treated in a mental hospital. Typically, mental hospitals, like prisons, are maximum security facilities that exercise total control over their inmates. Thus, the difference in our treatment of the insane and the criminal, as Erving Goffman (1961) has pointed out, is more symbolic than real.

The role of the psychiatrist in the adjudicative process is complicated by the issue of what criteria are used to determine competency to stand trial, culpability, insanity, and criminality. In 1989, the American Bar Association's Criminal Justice Mental Health Standards determined that:

(a) No defendant shall be tried while mentally incompetent to stand trial. (b) The test for determining mental competence to stand trial should be whether the defendant has sufficient present ability to consult with defendant's lawyer with a reasonable degree of rational understanding and otherwise to assist in the defense, and whether the defendant has a rational as well as factual understanding of the proceedings. (c) The terms *competence* and *incompetence* as used with Part IV of this chapter refer to mental competence or mental incompetence. A finding of mental incompetence to stand trial may arise from mental illness, physical illness, or disability; mental retardation or other developmental disability; or other etiology so long as it results in a defendant's inability to consult with defense counsel or to understand the proceedings (American Bar Association, Part IV: Competence to Stand Trial, Standard 7-4.1., online).

As reported in the MacArthur Adjudicative Competence Study (2004), the American Bar Association's Criminal Justice Mental Health Standards notes that "the issue of present mental incompetence, quantitatively speaking, is the single most important issue in the criminal mental health field." The number of forensic evaluations of criminal defendants' competency to stand trial ranges between 24,000 and 60,000 per year in the United States.[2] Ninety percent of criminal cases in the United States are resolved by guilty pleas and there is no firmly established specific empirical basis for the clinical assessment of competence, which indicates a serious problem in the administration of justice. The recognition of this issue led to the aforementioned MacArthur Adjudicative Competency Study. The goal of the study was to develop measures to provide clinicians and policy makers with the tools to address questions about the adjudicative competence of criminal defendants (Bonnie, et al., 1997).

Following the design of a research instrument to measure essential adjudicative competence, the MacArthur project conducted an epidemiological survey of the prevalence of impairments of decision making competence in a population of criminal defendants. The study includes 366 adult male and 106 adult female defendants recruited from Florida and Virginia. The sample is made up of pre-trial detainees, defendants currently in mental health intervention while in jail, and defendants recently admitted to state forensic hospitals for restoration of competence.

The study shows that 10 percent of all criminal defendants are perceived by their attorneys to be impaired. Nonetheless, defendants of dubious competence are usually not referred by their attorneys for a formal mental health evaluation. A defendant may be impaired in several different areas, such as the capacities to make choices, to understand information, to think rationally about alternative courses of action and to appreciate one's situation as a criminal defendant. Assessing only one of the above capacities is insufficient to determine adjudicative competence; a defendant with a mental disorder may not have an impairment on a singly assessed capacity, even though other capacities required for adjudicative competence may be impaired.

A person who lacks competence to accept or refuse treatment does not necessarily lack competence for adjudicating his or her criminal case. Put another way, a person may be competent for one legal purpose and incompetent for another. While no clinical diagnosis by itself indicates incompetence, competence impairments are strongly associated with symptoms of severe mental disorder, particularly with a diagnosis of schizophrenia. Nevertheless, many defendants with severe mental disorder can be competent to proceed with adjudication (Hoge et al., 1997a). Among defendants hospitalized for restoration of competence, significant improvement in decision making abilities was observed upon re-test for those treated and referred back to court as having been restored to competence (Hoge, et al., 1997b; Otto, et al., 1998; Edens, et al., 1999).

There is the perception on the part of the public that the insanity defense is a strategy the guilty use to try to escape the consequences of their criminal act. The insanity defense,

---

2. The standard for competence was enunciated by the United States Supreme Court in 1960 (*Dusky v. United States*, 362 U.S.402): "the test will be whether [the defendant] has sufficient present ability to consult with his lawyer with a reasonable degree of rational understanding and whether he has a rational as well as factual understanding of the proceedings against him" (p. 402). The focus in *Dusky* is on "present ability" to proceed to adjudication and is not retrospective, i.e. competence at the time of the offense.

in fact, is only used in one percent of cases and is only successful in 25 percent of those cases (Janofsky, et al., 1996). The defense is difficult to use with success because the defendant has the burden of proof of establishing that at the time of the offense, a preponderance of evidence supports the defendant's contention that he or she was insane (Louisiana Criminal Law Title XXI, Chapter 2, Art. 652). Marshalling a preponderance of evidence[3] is no easy task.

M'Naghten Rule

While a claim of irresponsibility for criminal acts is ancient, it did not become a part of codified law until the case of Daniel M'Naghten in 1843. M'Naghten was tried for the murder of the secretary to the Prime Minister Sir Robert Peel. M'Naghten wanted to assassinate Peel because he felt that Peel was directly responsible for a myriad of misfortunes that had befallen him. The court found M'Naghten to be not guilty by reason of insanity and the finding was later codified into what is now called the *M'Naghten* rule: "that to establish a defence on the grounds of insanity, it must be clearly proved that, at the time of committing the act, the party accused was labouring under such a defect of reason, from disease of the mind, as not to know the nature and quality of the act he was doing; or, if he did know it, that he did not know what he was doing was wrong" (Walker, 1968, p. 100). The principal criticism of the rule at the time of its codification was that it did not include any mention of irresistible impulse (1968, p. 105).

Irresistible Impulse

The *M'Naghten* rule was adopted in the United States without modification until the middle of the 20th Century. However, in 1887, the Alabama Supreme Court ruled in the case *Parsons v. State of Alabama* that under the duress of a mental disease, the defendant lost the power to choose between right and wrong and the alleged crime was so connected to the mental disease to be a product of it. So, even if the defendant could distinguish between right and wrong, he could not control the irresistible impulse to commit the wrongful act.

The Durham Rule

Monte Durham was convicted of housebreaking. His only defense at the trial was that he was of unsound mind when he committed the offense. His counsel argued that the existing test, knowing right from wrong and irresistible impulse, is not adequate for determining criminal responsibility. In *Durham v. United States* 214 F.2d 862 (1954), the U.S. Court of Appeals for the District of Columbia ruled that a defendant could not be found criminally responsible "if his unlawful act was the product of mental disease or mental defect." The decision marked the replacement of moral considerations with more neutral scientific determinations that reflected psychiatric and psychological research. The *Durham* rule proved vague, however. There was confusion over whether "mental disease or defect" should be interpreted to mean only psychosis or should also include the many other disorders identified by expert witnesses. There was confusion over whether a defendant's actions were a "product" of his disease and whether this is a question for the jury or for expert psychiatric witnesses? Under this ruling, the prosecution was required

---

3. One of three standards for conviction, a preponderance of evidence means the proposition is more likely true than not.

to prove beyond reasonable doubt that the defendant was sane at the time he broke the law. The Durham rule is currently used only in New Hampshire (Dix, 2010, p. 98).

Diminished Capacity

There are three court cases of note that deal with the legal issues surrounding diminished capacity, *United States v. Brawner* 471 F.2d 969 (1972), *Jones v. United States* 463 U.S. 354 (1983) and *Foucha v. Louisiana* 504 U.S. 71 (1992). The defendant is not made innocent by reason of insanity. They are still guilty, but because they lack the mental capacity to form intent, they are guilty of a lesser crime. For example, the crime of first degree murder may be reduced to negligent homicide when the defendant is incapable of forming the intent necessary to commit first degree murder as defined by law. In some states, this defense is referred to as "guilty but mentally ill." Indirectly related to this issue is *Foucha v. Louisiana*. The U.S. Supreme court ruled that an individual found not guilty by reason of insanity and not mentally ill could not remain involuntarily confined on the justification that he was potentially dangerous (Foucha was diagnosed with AntiSocial Personality Disorder, which is untreatable and, therefore, not considered a mental illness). The court ruled that potential dangerousness alone was not a justification for keeping the person in a mental hospital if no mental illness is present. There have been other cases that provide a legal basis for confinement on the basis of the potential for future dangerousness (see especially *Kansas v. Hendricks* 521 U.S. 346 [1997] and *Allen v. Illinois* 478 U.S. 364 [1986]).

Substantial Capacity Test

The acquittal of John Hinckley Jr. for the attempted assassination of President Ronald Reagan on March 30, 1981 so outraged the public that Congress began to formulate legislation either to abolish or reform the insanity defense. At the time of Hinckley's trial, all but one jurisdiction in the United States had adopted the American Law Institute's Model Penal Code (1962) that argued that a defendant was not criminally responsible if he or she lacked substantial capacity to appreciate that his conduct was wrongful or lacked substantial capacity to conform his conduct to the law. In the Insanity Defense Reform Act of 1984, the Model Penal Code's substantial capacity rule was essentially discarded in favor of requiring the defendant to prove with clear and convincing evidence that he/she were insane at the time of the crime. Clear and convincing evidence is a higher standard of proof than even preponderance of the evidence. Before Hinckley, the burden of proof that the defendant was not insane rested with the prosecution in a majority of jurisdictions (Appelbaum, 1994).

Assessing Dangerousness

In this section, we will look at how scientists make assessments concerning the potential dangerousness of people. This is a critical process in the legal context because a false positive decision, for example, could result in an otherwise harmless person being incarcerated because he or she is thought to be potentially violent and a risk to the public.

Clinical Predictions

Can propensity for violence be predicted? This issue typically surfaces in the criminal justice system when an offender who has been imprisoned for violent offending is about to be released. Our decisions in this instance require a balancing act between the civil liberties of the offender, the safety of the offender, and the safety of the community. Historically, decisions have been based on the offenders' criminal history and his/her behavior during incarceration. Common sense would suggest that the past predicts the future (Quinsey, 1980). Even now, anamnestic decisions like this are commonplace and are often viewed as correct if the decision maker has the proper credentials (judges or qualified experts with M.D. or Ph.D.). So long as the offender does not commit another violent act that becomes public, the expert is secure in his or her decision.

Considerable research evidence from social psychology has shaken confidence in the reliability of clinical judgments of dangerousness. The phenomena referred to as the *illusion of validity* means in practical terms people are willing to make more extreme judgments than warranted because they have more confidence than the data before them justifies. Human beings are, paradoxically, more confident when making extreme judgments (Einhorn and Hogarth, 1978, p. 395).

However, those in the community who will have contact with and may be responsible for managing ex-offenders with histories of serious aggressive behaviors do not have the luxury of disinterested clinical judgment. Literature on the topic of managing seriously aggressive ex-offenders makes it clear that neither treatment nor supervision has much effect on re-offending (Quinsey, 2004). Thus, from a clinical perspective, it is unclear what should be done with and for the violent offender. It should be noted however, that seriously dangerous offenders are easily identified clinically because the offenders have been convicted of violent crimes and the records are there for all to behold.

Actuarial Models

Actuarial predictive models are based on statistical techniques using multivariate analyses of individual characteristics and behaviors derived from data using large samples. Gardner, Lidz, Mulvey, and Shaw (1996) argue that actuarial prediction of violence in a population of mental patients far outperform clinical assessment accuracy. At present two actuarial instruments are used for the prediction of violent recidivism, the first of which is the Violent Risk Appraisal Guide (VRAG), which is used for the prediction of violent recidivism in three subpopulations-fire setters, sex offenders, and men who are assaultive in institutional settings. The variables that make up the VRAG are derived from the Revised Psychopathy Checklist Score (Hare, 1991). Hare takes the position, which is reflected in the checklist (see below), that psychopaths are fundamentally different from non-psychopaths, but their personality characteristics should be thought of as discrete and not continuous dimensions of personality. The checklist simply measures the extent to which the subject matches the prototype psychopath with the maximum score being closest to the prototype. The VRAG checklist includes the following items:

1. Elementary school maladjustment score (-1 to +5) (-1 equals no problems in school; +2 equals slight or moderate attendance and discipline problem; 3 and 4 suggesting increasing problems; and +5 equals severe behavior and attendance problems).

2. Meets *DSM III* criteria for any personality disorder (No = -2, Yes = +3).

3. Age at index offense (most recent birthday) (≥39 = -5, 34–38 = -2, 28–33 = -1, 27 = 0, ≤26 = +2).

4. Separation from either biological parent by age 16 (except for death of parent). Score *no* if offender did not live continuously with both biological parents until 16. In the case of a death of a parent score as *yes* (Yes = -2. No = +3).

5. Failure on prior conditional release, also includes bail violations and new charges, including the index offense (No = 0, Yes = +3).

6. Criminal history score for nonviolent offenses (using Cormier-Lang system) (0 = -2, 1 or 2 = 0, 3 or above = +3).

7. Marriage (Never married = +1, Ever married (including common law) = -2).

8. Meets *DSM III* criteria for schizophrenia (Yes = -3, No = +1).

9. Victim injury (Index offense only; most serious injury is scored) (Death = -2, Hospitalized = 0, Treated and released = +1, none or slight = +2).

10. Alcohol problems score. The score for this variable is determined by allotting one point for each of the following: alcohol abuse in biological parent, teenage alcohol problem, adult alcohol problem, alcohol involved in prior offense and alcohol involved in the index offense (0 points = -1, 1 or 2 points = 0, 3 points = +1, 4 to 5 points = +2).

11. Female victim (Yes = -1, No (includes no victim) = +1).

By using variable weights, the authors argue that the VRAG is user friendly for non-statisticians and does not require much computation on the part of users. The VRAG has been used in a study of 347 male forensic patients who were scored on the guide before release (Harris, Rice, and Cormier, 2002). The accuracy of the VRAG in predicting violent recidivism corresponded to relative operating characteristics (ROC) area of .80 over a five year follow up. There were no statistical differences between the VRAG norms and the results of this study, which is considered to validate the VARAG. Moreover, the results of the VRAG predictions were significantly more accurate than clinical assessments made on the same population prior to release and the superiority of the VRAG was demonstrated over a short-term follow-up of six months.

One of the problems with using the VRAG is its predictive accuracy in assessing an individual case. "The accuracy of an actuarial instrument (or any decision-making system) needs to be considered in combination with the *base rate* of the outcome to be predicted" (Quinsey, et al., 2006, p. 170). If violent recidivism is low, then the optimal decision would be to release everyone. However, an important consideration in the real world is the cost of a false positive (detaining a non-dangerous person) or a false negative (releasing someone who is, in fact, dangerous). The cost of either of these decisions depends on who is asked. Inmates and victims of violent crime are likely to see this differently. Ultimately, decisions about releasing and not releasing are constitutional questions (e.g., see *Kansas v. Hendricks* 521 U.S. 346 [1997]; *Allen v. Illinois* 478 U.S. 364 [1986] and *Foucha v. Louisiana* 504 U.S. 71 [1992]) or reflect political decisions on how much money to spend on secure custody beds in state forensic institutions.

The second actuarial instrument currently in use is the Sex Offenders Risk Appraisal Guide (SORAG). SORAG was developed by the same research team that developed the VRAG but reflects a greater concern for predicting recidivism among child molesters and rapists. This guide includes 10 of the elements of the VRAG plus four additional variables: Number of convictions for previous sex offenses, criminal history score for convictions and charges for violent offenses prior to the index offense, history of sex offenses against girls under 14 only, and a phallometric test. These variables are scored as follows:

1. Number of convictions for previous sex offenses (offenses prior to the index offense) and counts of any sexual offenses including, for example, indecent exposure (0 = -1, 1 or 2 = +1, ≥3 = +5).

2. Violent offenses (0 = -1, 2 = 0, ≥3 = +6).

3. Sex offenses against girls under 14 (if offender is less than 5 years older, always score +4) (yes = 0, no = +4).

4. Phallometric test results (all indicate nondeviant sexual preferences = -1; any test indicates deviant sexual preferences = +1).

While the SORAG contains some variables in common with the VRAG, it has been shown that at the very least it is equal in accuracy and sometimes better. In one study utilizing SORAG (Harris, et al., 2003), researchers have been able to predict the speed, severity, and frequency of recidivism. Hanson and Morton-Bouorgon (2004) report that phallometric test results indicating deviant sexual preferences are strong predictors of sexual recidivism. They argue that sexual deviance is central to explaining sexual aggression. Moreover, measures of antisocial personality or psychopathy are also strong predictors of sexual re-cidivism. This observation seems to run counter to Susan Brownmiller's (1975) thesis, widely accepted by social scientists, that rape is a violent expression of dominance by men over women, unnatural behavior that has little to do with sex. From a policy perspective, actuarial assessments can perhaps be used to identify some, but not all dangerous sex offenders (Quinsey, et al., 2006, p. 177). However, the SORAG or any other actuarial instrument cannot identify all dangerous sex offenders without a risk of a false positive predictions (identifying individuals as sex offenders when, in fact, they are not) or the risk of false negative predictions (failing to identify someone who turns out to be a sex offender).

Mental Illness and Violent Crime

In this section, we will examine what is known about the linkage between mental illness and violent behavior or dangerousness. In the *New England Journal of Medicine,* Richard Friedman (2006) offers a review of the relationship between mental illness and violent behavior. He begins by citing the results of the National Crime Victimization Survey for 1993–1999, which reports that the average annual rate of nonfatal, job-related violent crime is 12.6 per 1,000 workers in all occupations. However, among psychiatrists and mental health professionals, the rate is 68.2 per 1,000; for mental health custodial workers, the rate is slightly higher, 69.0 per 1,000. On the surface these data suggest that the risk of violence is substantially greater among those who are officially diagnosed as being mentally ill. But this conclusion seems to beg the question, "which psychiatric illnesses are associated with violence and what is the magnitude of the increase in risk?" (2006, p. 2064).

In an epidemiological study, Swanson (1994) identifies 7,000 mentally ill subjects who have committed violent acts. In this study violence is operationalized in terms of evidence of using a weapon such as a knife or a gun in a fight or becoming involved in a physical fight with someone other than a spouse or partner. The study shows that patients with serious mental illnesses, e.g., those with schizophrenia, major depression, or bipolar disorder, are two to three times more likely to be assaultive than people without such illnesses. In absolute terms, the lifetime prevalence of violence among people with serious mental illnesses is 16 percent, as compared with 7 percent among people without mental illnesses.

Of course, not all people with mental illnesses are assaultive nor does their rate of violence contribute much to the overall prevalence of violence in society. Nevertheless, mental illness appears to explain an estimated 3 to 5 percent of violent behavior in the population (Friedman, 2006, p. 2065). Friedman suggests that danger of violence is more likely to be a function of psychiatric symptoms rather than the illness itself. He claims that symptoms such as having paranoid thoughts or hearing voices that command a person with mental illness to hurt someone (command auditory hallucinations) are more likely to be violent than people with other mental illness symptoms. These conclusions raise a public policy question, namely, how should society respond to the potentially dangerous mentally ill (see Markowitz, 2011)?

On January 3, 1999, Kendra Ann Webdale, a 32 year old photographer/journalist, was pushed into an oncoming subway train in New York by a diagnosed schizophrenic, Andrew Goldstein. This event led to public outcry over the treatment of the chronically mentally ill and led to reform of New York's mental hygiene laws, in particular, Article 9 Hospitalization of the Mentally Ill, now referred to as Kendra's Law (2005).

Article 9 allows those with mental illness to be ordered to obtain Assisted Outpatient Treatment (AOT) if the court finds that:

> The patient is eighteen years of age or older; and the patient is suffering from a mental illness; and the patient is unlikely to survive safely in the community without supervision, based on a clinical determination; and the patient has a history of lack of compliance with treatment for mental illness that has: at least twice within the last thirty-six months been a significant factor in necessitating hospitalization in a hospital, or receipt of services in a forensic or other mental health unit of a correctional facility or a local correctional facility, not including any period during which the person was hospitalized or incarcerated immediately preceding the filing of the petition or; resulted in one or more acts of serious violent behavior toward self or others or threats of, or attempts at, serious physical harm to self or others within the last forty-eight months, not including any period in which the person was hospitalized or incarcerated immediately preceding the filing of the petition; and the patient is, as a result of his or her mental illness, unlikely to voluntarily participate in the recommended treatment pursuant to the treatment plan; and in view of the patient's treatment history and current behavior, the patient is in need of assisted outpatient treatment in order to prevent a relapse or deterioration which would be likely to result in serious harm to the patient or others as defined in section 9.01 of this article (Cohen, 2001, Treatment Advocacy Center online).

Currently 44 states permit court-ordered AOT of the mentally ill (Treatment Advocacy Center, 2012, online). New York's Kendra Law was one of the most stringent statutes and it and other AOT laws appear to have wide support in the mental health community. Some research suggests that AOT laws can be effective in reducing victimization and certain violent behavior. For example, a 2010 study conducted by the Columbia University's School of Public Health found that AOT recipients in New York City, when compared with a control group of other mentally ill patients, despite having more violent histories, were four times less likely to commit serious violence after mental health treatment (Phelan, et al, 2010; see also, Swanson, et al., 2001; Treatment Advocacy Center, 2012). However, until a violent incident occurs involving a mentally ill person, little is done.

For example, Bernal Johnson, described by his family as a paranoid schizophrenic with violent tendencies, had wandered the streets of New Orleans homeless for years. On January 28, 2008, 24 year old New Orleans Police Department Officer Nicola Cotton approached a man sitting in the parking lot of a small strip mall who fit the description of a man wanted for sexual assault. When Officer Cotton attempted to handcuff Johnson, he pounced on her and in the ensuing struggle (caught on surveillance cameras) Johnson got control of her service pistol and fired, hitting Officer Cotton. According to a police spokesperson, when Officer Cotton was on the ground wounded, Johnson stood over her and fired again, unloading her service weapon of all 15 of its rounds. Officer Nicola Cotton was pronounced dead minutes later at nearby University Hospital (McCarthy, Maggi and Sparacello, 2008). According to his family, Johnson suffered delusions and had tried to kill himself several times by overdosing on pills and on one occasion, shot himself in the chest. The family reported that their many efforts to have him institutionalized had failed and that they had been advised by social workers and attorneys alike that they could do nothing unless he hurt somebody. According to Johnson's brother, when he was institutionalized he would not stay for long because "He knows the system, and he knows what to say to get out" (McCarthy, Maggi and Sparacello, 2008). Johnson was subsequently indicted for first degree murder and if found guilty, will face either death by lethal injection or life in prison without parole (Filosa, 2008).[4]

The case of Amy Bishop is another instance of little attention given to earlier signs of mental illness. While undiagnosed with a mental illness, Amy Anderson (Amy Bishop), a 44 year old female biology professor, who shot six of the 12 individuals attending a routine biology department faculty meeting on the University of Alabama Huntsville (UAH) campus on February 12, 2010, had been reported to have at minimum some anger management issues (see Torrey, 2008). Allegedly, her attempt to kill additional faculty members failed because her gun "either jammed or ran out of ammunition" (Roebuck and Murty, 2010, p. 193). Roebuck and Murty (2010), however, report evidence of a history of undocumented violence. Hired as an assistant professor in 2003, Bishop was denied tenure and was serving the beginning of her last semester at UAH. A native of Braintree, Massachusetts, with a Ph.D. from Harvard University, she had demonstrated violent behavior on at least three previous occasions. First, in 1986 at the age of 19, she killed her 16 year old brother with a shot gun. This shooting was deemed an accident by the police and charges were not filed. Ironically, police reports of this crime were lost and did not resurface until Bishop was arrested in the UAH murders. Second, she along with her husband, James Anderson, were prime suspects and were questioned in a 1993 pipe bomb that was directed via mail to Dr. Paul Rosenberg, her then professor and lab supervisor at Children's Hospital in Boston. Shortly afterwards, she resigned from her position at the hospital. She was on the verge of a nervous breakdown and told a colleague prior to the attempted bombing that she wanted to "shoot, stab, or strangle Rosenberg" (2010, p. 193). She and her husband denied threatening Rosenberg and the case was subsequently closed. Third, she was charged with and pled guilty to misdemeanor assault and disorderly conduct in 2002, for punching a woman who refused to give up the last booster seat at an International House of Pancakes in Peabody, Massachusetts. For this, she received probation and despite the prosecution's stipulation that she attend anger management classes, she never attended any. Further, several of her colleagues at UAH noted what they called her "strange, erratic and bizarre behavior" (2010, p. 194) throughout her teaching career there. For example, she interrupted meetings abruptly, she reacted in an inappropriate, upset manner and demonstrated that she was "out of touch with reality" (2010, p. 194). As the sole suspect in the incident, Bishop has been charged with

---

4. *Ford v. Wainwright*, 477 U.S. 399 (1986) In this case the United States Supreme Court ruled and upheld the common law that the insane cannot be executed and is entitled to be evaluated including a hearing in court on the question of competency to be executed.

one count of capital murder and three counts of attempted murder. She is currently in jail still awaiting trial.

From time to time, we are stunned when we hear about grisly acts of violence that are connected with a mental illness of the perpetrator. For instance, in 2001 Andrea Yates systematically drowned her five children in her home, saying she believed that Satan was inside her and she was trying to save the children from hell. Her attorneys said she was suffering from postpartum psychosis (puerperal psychosis) and Yates was found not guilty by reason of insanity in 2006 (Suri, et al., 1998). In 2004, Dena Schlosser killed her 10 month old by slicing off the baby's arms. She testified that she killed the baby because she wanted to give her to God. She was found not guilty by reason of insanity. In a particularly grisly case, a mother dismembered her baby boy. She chewed off three tiny toes, tore his face away, severed his head and ripped out his brain. The mother told officers that the devil made her do it. This slaying occurred a week after the father had left. At the time of the incident, the police were investigating whether the mother had any significant mental health history (James and Brown, 2009).

Fred Markowitz (2011) addresses trends and associated policies connected with what is referred to as the "deinstitutionalization" of the mentally ill. He notes that until the 1960s the majority of people with mental illnesses were confined and treated in large, public and county hospitals. However, by 2005 there were relatively few of these facilities available to house psychiatric patients. The reasons for this include: (1) medications were developed to control the symptoms of severe mental disorders such as schizophrenia; (2) there was an ideological shift toward adopting stricter legal standards for involuntary psychiatric commitment; (3) a change in fiscal policy including substantial budget cuts and underfunding of community mental health services; and (4) shifting the costs for mental health care from the state to the federal government (i.e., Medicare, Medicaid, and Social Security Disability Income). The result of all this has been that our "capacity for maintaining and treating America's mentally ill, especially the most severely impaired and economically disadvantaged patients, has been substantially diminished" (p.37). Many of these people are literally on the streets, unable to care for themselves, and some of their behavior may be threatening or appear to be threatening to the police and public.

Even though the sample of cases described above represents very rare cases, they are the type of cases that people usually cite as illustrations of the linkage between mental disorder and violence. Despite the rarity of occurrence, the connection of mental illness with violent crime is popularly accepted. In fact the more bizarre the case, the more likely it will be reported by the media, which sometimes leads to the false impression that such cases are very common. It is worth noting again that most mentally ill people are not violent. Mental illness is estimated to contribute to approximately 3 to 5 percent of cases with serious instances of physical assault. The problem is that while mental illness and violence are largely unrelated, they are not completely unrelated (Monahan and Steadman, 1984).

Personality Disorders and Crime

According to the Diagnostic and Statistical Manual (DSM) of the American Psychiatric Association, "[a] personality disorder is an enduring pattern of inner experience and behavior that deviates markedly from the expectations of the individual's culture, is pervasive and inflexible, has an onset in adolescence or early adulthood, is stable over time, and leads to distress or impairment" (DSM-IV-TR, 2000, p. 685). Precursors of certain personality disorders often appear in childhood and adolescence. For example, child conduct disorder is a precursor of antisocial personality disorder.[5] Child Conduct Disorder (CCD) includes persistent, repetitive violation of rules and a disregard for the rights of others. Juveniles whose behavior falls under this disorder may manifest poor impulse control, lack of empathy, hostility, disobedience, and physical and verbal aggression. However, many adolescents who are diagnosed with CCD with certain accompanying symptoms and engage in deviant behavior may do so as "an adaptive response to an adverse environment. For example, a girl who has been sexually victimized by her stepfather may very well meet [CCD] criteria by running away from home, by lying repeatedly to her parents, and by staying out past her curfew" (McNally, 2011, p. 76)

It is possible for a person to exhibit more than one type of disturbed personality functioning, thus being afflicted by more than one disorder. The *DSM* groups personality disorders into three clusters. The first, Cluster A, includes Paranoid, Schizoid, and Schizotypical Personality disorders. Cluster B includes Antisocial, Borderline, Histrionic, and Narcissistic disorders. Dramatic, emotional and erratic behavior is characteristic of persons with these disorders. Cluster C includes Avoidant, Dependant, and Obsessive-Compulsive personality disorders. A fourth, residual category is "personality disorder not otherwise specified." Personality disorder not otherwise specified refers to those exhibiting mixed conditions that do not fit within a single specific personality disorder category (pp. 685–686).

Johnson and associates (2000) found that personality disorder symptoms proved to be even stronger predictors of violence than did an overall diagnosis. In fact, increased symptoms of Cluster A or Cluster B personality disorders correspond with a greater likelihood of violence in the community during adolescence and early adulthood. Paranoid, narcissistic, and passive aggressive personality disorder symptoms correlate significantly with violence.

In particular, the antisocial personality is characterized by a pervasive pattern of failure to conform to social norms and to repeatedly perform antisocial acts that are grounds for arrest. Such acts as domestic violence, destroying property, reckless driving, and a general lack of concern for the wellbeing of others are common symptoms of the disorder. When antisocial personality and other Cluster B disorders are coupled with drug and/or alcohol dependence, they become risk factors in suicide (Dumais, et al., 2005).

Psychiatric and psychological theories explaining violent behavior have become widely absorbed into our popular culture and are often taken for granted. Frequently, when we consider the greatest relevance of psychiatric or psychological theories of crime, it is in connection with evaluating or predicting the dangerousness of offenders. After reviewing the numerous studies using various measures of dangerousness, John Monahan (1987) concludes that irrespective what methods are used "violence is vastly overpredicted." The problem mainly stems from the fact that the *base rate* of occurrence of violent behavior is so low that any predictor tends to classify large numbers of nonviolent people as potentially violent. The base rate of behavior may be defined in terms of its relative frequency of occurrence in the population. Statistically, unless the base rate is close to 50 percent or better, the practical usefulness of a predictor is severely questionable. Behaviors that constitute rare events generate a large probability of error or false predictions for the

---

5. The DSM first published in 1952 is literally the bible of mental illness and despite many criticisms over the years, it serves as the major psychological classifications schemes in the country. The new edition, the DSM 5, scheduled to be released soon, will be the first revision since 2000, and is purported to include changes in the definitions of disorders such as autism, depression, and schizophrenia.

extremely small number of correct predictions that are possible. Because false positive predictions may lead to certain social consequences such as mandatory treatment, loss of liberty (incarceration) or even execution, the problem of misclassification poses serious social, moral, and ethical challenges. Dangerousness, as we have noted, is typically equated with violence, along with the further implication that the behavior is a manifestation of mental illness or mental instability. Even though no satisfactory legal, medical, or scientific methods of identification or predictions of dangerousness are available, and despite our inability to adequately separate the mentally ill from the "normal" population including the criminal population, the psychiatric and psychological perspectives have found their way into the daily decision making and routine operation of the criminal justice system ranging from the psychological assessment and classification of offenders to sentencing decisions.

Integrated Developmental and Life-Course Theories of Violent Behavior

Over the years a number of scholars have sought to bring a more integrated understanding of the developmental factors that explain the onset as well as continuation of criminal behavior, including violent behavior (e.g., Moffitt, 1993; Simmons, Johnson, Conger, and Elder, 1998; Loeber and Farrington, 2000; Sampson and Laub, 2000). Developmental and life-course theorists claim that since criminality is multidimensional and has multiple roots, the emphasis must be on the intertwining nature of personal/individual factors, cognitive factors, socialization factors, situational factors, and broader social factors.[6] For example, Ronald Simmons and his associates (1998) define the life-course perspective as follows: "Criminologists, who employ a life-course perspective, are concerned with identifying the processes whereby childhood disruptive behavior escalates to delinquency and crime, and with discovering the factors that enable some anti-social children to assume a more conventional lifestyle during adolescence" (p. 221).

Robert Sampson and John Laub are among the first to offer life-course explanations of criminal behavior. Their theory integrates biological, psychological, and sociological processes through time, and includes consideration of individual biography and history. By emphasizing the continuities and discontinuities in criminal behavior and noting the social influences on age-graded transitions including the most important life events, Sampson and Laub (2001) suggest we can better understand the fluctuations of criminal behavior over different stages of life. In other words, they study the patterns of causal influences that may shape offending behavior over time. They particularly focus on any systematic changes, noting how various types of behavior affect certain processes that can alter future outcomes; they especially underscore the cumulative effects of disadvantage on life outcomes. For example, they propose that certain "turning points" in life that are associated with maturity, such as getting married or getting a steady job, which provide

---

6. Both clinical and research knowledge on offenders with intellectual and developmental cognitive disabilities has expanded over the past few decades. Much of the attention has focused on juvenile and adult offenders with Intellectual Disabilities (ID) especially in terms of their trajectories in criminal careers (See Lindsey, W.R. (2012). Predicting the Risk of Violence in Offenders with Intellectual and Developmental Disabilities. In D.W. Harper, L. Voigt, and W.E. Thornton (Eds.). *Violence: Do We Know It When We See It?* Durham, NC: Carolina Academic Press, 71-83).

important social bonding, may account for the discontinuance of delinquency of most youth as they mature into adulthood. Sampson and Laub claim that "the cumulative continuity of disadvantage" across the life cycle may, be associated with "a dynamic processes whereby childhood antisocial behavior and adolescence foster adult crime through the severance of adult social bonds" (2001, p. 155).

Along similar lines David Farrington (2003) using data collected over a 20-year period concludes that the interplay of personal and social factors control the onset and stability of criminal careers. In his work he addresses three questions related to: "the development of offending and antisocial behavior, risk factors at different ages, and the effects of life events on the course of development" (p. 221). He arrives at ten observations (pp. 223–224):

1) The prevalence of offending peaks in the late teenage years—between 15 and 19.

2) The peak age of onset of offending is between 8 and 14, and the peak age of desistance from offending is between 20 and 29.

3) An early age of onset predicts relatively long criminal career duration and the commission of relatively many offenses.

4) There is marked continuity in offending and antisocial behavior from childhood to teenage years and to adulthood.

5) A small fraction of the population commits a large fraction of all crimes.

6) Offending is versatile rather specialized.

7) The types of acts defined as offenses are elements of a larger syndrome of antisocial behavior.

8) Most offenses up to the late teenage years are committed with others, whereas most offenses from age 20 onwards are committed alone.

9) The reasons for offending up to the late teenage years are quite variable [e.g., for excitement, enjoyment, or expression of anger].... In contrast from age 20 onwards utilitarian motives become increasingly dominant.

10) Different types of offenses tend to be first committed at distinctively different ages.

Loeber and Farrington (2000) offer an elaboration on the Problem Behavior Syndrome (PBS): Criminal behavior is one of many antisocial behaviors that cluster together and usually include family dysfunction, sexual and physical abuse, and substance abuse. More generalized PBS factors include:

• Unemployment

• Educational underachievement

• School misconduct

• Residing in a high crime areas

• Exposure to racism and poverty

• Personal problems such as suicide attempts, sensation seeking, early parenthood, accident proneness, medical problems, mental disease, anxiety, and eating disorders.

Terrie Moffitt (1993) offers a two part theory including explanations of 'adolescence-limited" antisocial behavior and "life-course-persistent" antisocial behavior. In adolescence-limited expressions of antisocial behavior, "a contemporary maturity gap" or some transient event may give rise to the antisocial behavior; the expression of which is typically within a relatively normal range of behavior, generally temporary, situational in nature, and less extreme (i.e., less likely to involve violence). Adolescence-limited behavior is generally influenced by peers. Moreover, adolescence-limited individuals usually quickly outgrow their delinquency. In contrast, life-course-persistent delinquents differ qualitatively from those who begin in their teenage years. Individuals who have behavioral problems as children and begin their delinquency at a relatively early age are more likely to persist with their criminality as adults. She suggests that the risk signs of childhood antisocial behavior and persistence into adulthood include: low verbal ability, hyperactivity, and impulsive personality. Peer group influences actually play a minimal role in life-course-persistent delinquency. Moffitt (1993) also suggest that this group is more likely to exhibit more serious patterns of offending, including violent behavior.

Taken together the development and life-course theories offer a more integrated approach to explaining antisocial behavior including violent behavior. They more than many of the ad hoc theories taken piecemeal provide a dynamic, holistic view of antisocial behavior through the integration of biological, psychological, and sociological processes across social space and time. This approach, however, is not intended to be used in a predictive model. Michael Benson (2002) perhaps expresses this point best:

> Theoretically the assumption that adult behavior can be predicted in early childhood flows against the central premises of the life course approach. The life course approach is based on the premises that development is an ongoing process that unfolds over the entire life span, and development involves interactions between the individual and the environment.... Predicting the life course of an individual based only on factors present at an early age ignores all of the causal factors that come into play later" (p. 14).

Critical Comment and Conclusion

Many books and research articles have been written on topics related to uncovering the underlying individual factors and predictors of violence or correlates of dangerousness. However, to date there has not been conclusive evidence produced to support any of the associated hypotheses. Early biological and psychological perspectives on violence have focused on various predisposing physiological factors, inheritance and genetic makeup, as well as individual body types and personality "traits" that have been correlated with criminal violence, usually excluding the interplay of environmental and cultural, socio-structural influences, such as inequality, racism, and poverty.

For example central to both historical and contemporary biological explanations of crime and violence is the notion that biological characteristics, such as morphology, physiology, and genetic disorders, either cause or contribute to criminal and antisocial behaviors. Early biological proponents stress what they considered the unchanging nature of these aspects of the offender. Contemporary biological researchers see potential for altering or controlling deviant behaviors through various means such as medication. Over the years, relatively few American criminologists have been serious adherents of biological theories. Early methodological inadequacies, lack of consistency among different lists of physical traits that correlate with criminality, inability to specify exactly what inheritable matter affects crime and violence, and association of these theories with genetic engineering, World War II Nazi experiments and exterminations, and other racist ideologies have produced an unfavorable climate for the biological study of crime and violence in this country. Some of these theories have been proven to be baseless (atavism, for example) while other seem more promising (neuroscience and brain chemistry, for example). What is clear is that much more research needs to be conducted before we can understand the nature—nurture relationship.

The relationship between insanity and criminality has had a long and intertwined history. Despite the fact that psychiatric and psychological theories actually explain a very small proportion of cases of violent behavior in our society, these theories remain very popular and they continue to inform polices and approaches used in the criminal justice system. To this day, psychiatrists and psychologists have distinct roles to play in criminal justice decision making and treatment. The role of the clinician in the criminal justice system has been the subject of much controversy. Particularly problematic are the definition of such concepts or labels as "mental illness" and "dangerousness." Because dangerous events, dangerous offenders, and mentally ill offenders (however these are defined) constitute only rare or aberrant cases, attempts to predict dangerousness or to identify violence-prone or mentally ill offenders have been notoriously problematic.

The difficulty associated with finding practical predictors or tests along with contradictory research results, has been linked to a low base rate of the incidence of violence in society (in other words violent crimes are relatively low in occurrence in comparison with other crimes). No matter how flawed the predictors, however, public demand for forecasts of dangerousness have been increasing. Since assessments of potential violence are often connected with more intrusive and severe handling of the cases in question, accuracy of prediction is very controversial, especially in light of the charge that "violence is grossly overpredicted."

Attempting to integrate the biological, psychological, and sociological dimensions of criminality, developmental and life-course theories have inspired investigation of the paths through which individuals travel during their life span examining how events that occur in early life can mitigate against antisocial outcomes. The questions that developmental and life-course theorists focus on include:

- Why do people commit antisocial acts? Why do some people commit violent acts?
- Why do some people stop or desist, while others continue or persist?
- Why do some people escalate the severity of their criminality, e.g., why do some go from shoplifting to drug dealing to armed robbery—while others deescalate and grow out of offending as they mature?

There are no simple answers to these questions. To date no one theory has proven to be superior in explaining crime or violence. Each brand of theory has its relative strengths and weaknesses. Taken together, however, the various theories help give us insights into the complexities of human nature and human society.

References

Allen v. Illinois 478 U.S. 364 (1986).

American Bar Association. (1989). Part IV Competence to Stand Trial. Criminal Justice Mental Health Standards. Retrieved from: http://www.abanet.org/crimjust/standards/mentalhealth.pdf.

American Law Institute. (1962). Model Penal Code.

American Psychiatric Association. (1987). *Diagnostic and Statistical Manual of Mental Disorders (DSM-III-R)* (3rd ed. revised). Washington, DC: Author.

American Psychiatric Association. (2000). *Diagnostic and Statistical Manual of Mental Disorders (DSM-IV-TR)* (4th Ed.). Washington, DC: APA.

Appelbaum, P. (1994). *Almost a Revolution: Mental Health Law and the Limits of Change.* Oxford: Oxford University Press.

Barash, D. (2001). *Understanding Violence.* Boston, MA: Allyn and Bacon.

Baskervill, B. (2002). Governor Apologizes for Forced Sterilization: Virginian Eugenics Law was one of 30 in U.S. New Orleans, Louisiana: *The Times-Picayune*, May 3, A-15.

Benson, M. (2002). *Crime and the Life-Course: An Introduction.* Los Angeles, CA: Roxbury Press.

Bonnie, R., Hoge, S., Monahan, J., Poythress, N., Eisenberg, M., and Feucht-Haviar, T. (1997). The MacArthur Adjudicative Competence Study: A comparison of criteria for assessing the competence of criminal defendants. *Journal of the American Academy of Psychiatry and the Law, 25,* 1–11.

Brownmiller, S. (1975). *Against our Will: Men, Women and Rape.* New York: Simon and Schuster.

Clinard, M. B. (1974). *Sociology of Deviant Behavior* (4th Ed.). New York: Holt, Rinehart and Winston.

Cohen, F., (July/August, 2001). *Assisted Outpatient Treatment Review of New York Case Law and Beyond.* Retrieved from: http://www.treatmentadvocacycenter.org/component/content/article/356.

Darwin, C. (1871). *Descent of Man and Selection in Relation to Sex.* London: John Murray.

Dix, G.E. (2010). *Criminal Law.* Chicago: Thomson/West.

Dumais, A., Lesage, A. D., Alda, M., Rouleau, G., Dumont, M., Chawky, N., Roy, M., Mann, J. J., Benkelfat, C., and Turecki, G. (2005). Risk factors for suicide completion in major depression: A case-control study of impulsive and aggressive behaviors in men. *American Journal of Psychiatry, 162,* 2116–2124.

Durham v. United States 214 F.2d 862 (1954).

Dusky v. United States 362 U.S. 402 (1960).

Edens, J. F., Poythress, N. G., Otto, R. K., and Nicholson, R. A. (1999). Effects of state organizational structure and forensic examiner training on pre-trial competence assessments. *Journal of Behavioral Health Services & Research, 26,* 140–150.

Einhorn, H. J., and Hogarth, R. M. (1978). Confidence in judgment: Persistence of the illusion of validity. *Psychological Review, 85,* 395–416.

Eysenck, H. (1964). *Crime and Personality.* London: Routledge and Kegan Paul.

Farrington, D. (2003). Development and life-course criminology: Key theoretical and empirical Issues. The 2002 Sutherland Award Address. *Criminology, 41*(2), 221–255.

Ferri, E. (1917). *Criminal Sociology.* Trans. J. Kellet and J. Lisle. Boston, Little Brown.

Filosa, G. (2008). Man indicted in NOPD officer's killing. New Orleans, LA: *The Times-Picayune*, February 14.

Filley, C. M., Price, B. H., Nell, V., Antoinette, T., Morgan, A. S., Bresnahan, J. F., Pincus, J. H., Gelbort, M. M., Weissberg, M., and Kelly, J. P. (2001). Toward an understanding of violence: Neurobehavioral aspects of unwarranted interpersonal aggression. Aspen Neurobehavioral Conference consensus statement. *Neuropsychiatry, Neuropsychology and Behavioral Neurology, 14*, 1–14.

Fink, A. (1938). *Causes of Crime: Biological Theories in the United States, 1800–1915.* Philadelphia: University of Pennsylvania Press.

Ford v. Wainwright, 477 U.S. 399 (1986).

Foucha v. Louisiana 504 U.S. 71 (1992).

Friedland, S.I. (1997). A Vision of the Future. FRONTLINE. Retrieved from: http://www.pbs.org/wgbh/pages/frontline/shows/case/revolution/reimaging.html.

Friedland, S.I. (1997). The Criminal Law Implications of the Human Genome Project: Reimaging a Genetically Oriented Criminal Justice system, *Kentucky Law Journal*, 86, 303–366.

Friedman, R. A. (2006). Violence and mental illness — How strong is the link? *New England Journal of Medicine, 355*, 2064–2066.

Gabrielli, W., and Mednick, S.A. (1984). Urban environment, genetics and crime. *Criminology, 22*, 645–652.

Gao, Y., Raine, A, Venables, P. H., Dawson, M. E., and Mednick, S. A. (2010). Association of poor childhood fear conditioning and adult crime. *American Journal of Psychiatry, 167*, 56–60.

Gardner, W., Lidz, C. W., Mulvey, E. P., and Shaw, E. C. (1996). Clinical versus actuarial predictions of violence in patients with mental illness. *Journal of Consulting and Clinical Psychology, 64*, 602–609.

Garofalo, R. (1914). *Criminology.* Trans. R. Wyness. Boston: Little Brown.

Glueck, S., and Glueck, E. (1956). *Physique and Delinquency.* New York: Harper and Row.

Glueck, S. and Glueck, E. (1964). *Ventures in Criminology: Collected Recent Papers.* London: Tavistock Publications.

Goffman, E. (1961). *Asylums: Essays on the Social Situation of Mental Patients and Other Inmates.* New York: Doubleday.

Gunn, J. (1977). "Criminal behavior and mental disorder." *British Journal of Psychiatry*, 130, pp. 317–329.

Guo, G. (2006). The Linking of Sociology and Biology. *Social Forces, 85*(1), 145–149.

Hanson, R. K., and Morton-Bourgon, K. (2004). Predictors of sexual recidivism: An updated meta-analysis. Ottawa, Ontario: Public Safety and Emergency Preparedness.

Hare, R. D. (1991). *The Revised Psychopathy Checklist.* Toronto, Ontario: Multi-Health Systems.

Hare, R. D. (1999). *Without Conscience.* New York: The Guilford Press.

Harlow, J. M. (1848). Passage of an iron rod through the head. *Boston Medical and Surgical Journal, 39*, 389–393.

Harris, G. T., Rice, M. E., and Quinsey, V. L. (1993). Violent recidivism of mentally disordered offenders: The development of a statistical prediction instrument. *Criminal Justice and Behavior, 20*, 315–335.

Harris, G. T., Rice, M. E., and Cormier, C. A. (2002). Prospective replication of the Violent Risk Appraisal Guide in predicting violent recidivism among forensic patients. *Law and Human Behavior, 26*, 377–394.

Harris, G. T., Rice, M. E., Quinsey, V. L., Lalumiere, M. L., Boer, D., and Lang, C. (2003). A multi-site comparison of actuarial risk instruments for sex offenders. *Psychological Assessment: A Journal of Consulting and Clinical Psychology, 15*, 413–425.

Hartl, E.M., Monnelly, E.P., and Elderkind, R.D. (1982). *Physique and Delinquent Behavior*. New York: Academic Press.

Herrnstein, R. and Murray, C. (1994). *The Bell Curve*. NY: Free Press

Hoge, S., Poythress, N., Bonnie, R., Monahan, J., Eisenberg, M., and Feucht-Haviar. (1997a). The MacArthur Adjudicative Competence Study: Diagnosis, psychopathology, and adjudicative competence-related abilities. *Behavioral Sciences and the Law, 15*, 329–345.

Hoge, S., Poythress, N., Bonnie, R., Monahan, J., Eisenberg, M., and Feucht-Haviar. (1997b). The MacArthur Adjudicative Competence Study: Development and validation of a research instrument. *Law and Human Behavior, 21*, 141–179.

Hooten, E. (1931) *Crime and the Man*. Cambridge, MA: Harvard University Press.

James, S. and Brown, A. (2009). Decapitated baby stuns Texas investigators. *The Associated Press*, July 28.

Janofsky, J. S., Dunn, M. H., Roskes, E. J., Briskin, J. K., & Rudolph, M. S. (1996). Insanity defense pleas in Baltimore city: An analysis of outcome. *American Journal of Psychiatry, 153*(11), 1464–1468.

Johnson, J. G., Cohen, P., Smailes, E., Kasen, S., Oldham, J. M., Skodol, A. E., and Brook, J. S. (2000). Adolescent personality disorders associated with violence and criminal behavior during adolescence and early adulthood. *American Journal of Psychiatry, 157*, 1406–1412.

Jones v. United States 463 U.S. 354 (1983).

Kansas v. Hendricks 521 U.S. 346 (1997).

Kendra's Law. (2005). An explanation of Kendra's Law. Retrieved from: http://www.omh.state.ny.us/omhweb/kendra_web/Ksummary.htm.

Kretschmer, E. (1925). *Physique and Character*. London: Kegan Paul.

Lange, J. (1929). *Crime as Destiny (Verbrechen als Scchicksal)*. Leipzig: Georg Thieme Verlag.

Laub, J. (2004). The life-course of criminology. The 2003 presidential Address. *Criminology, 42*(1), 1–26.

Lea, R. & Chambers, G. (2007). Monoamine oxidase, addiction, and the "warrior" gene hypothesis. *Journal of the New Zealand Medical Association, 120*(1250). Retrieved from: http://www.nzma.org.nz/journal/120-1250/2441/.

Lindsey, W.R. (2012). Predicting the Risk of Violence in Offenders with Intellectual and Developmental Disabilities. In D.W. Harper, L. Voigt, and W.E. Thornton, (Eds).

Violence: Do We Know It When We See It? Durham, NC: Carolina Academic Press., 71-88.

Lipsey, M. and Wilson, D. B. (2001). *Practical Meta-Analysis.* Thousand Oaks, CA: Sage Publications.

Loeber, R., and Farrington, D. (2000). Young children who commit crime: Epidemiology, developmental origins, risk factors, early interventions, and policy implications. *Development and Psychopathology, 12,* 737–762.

Lombroso, C. (1876, reprinted in 2006). *The Criminal Man (L'Uomo delinquente).* Trans. M. Gibson and N. Hahn Rafter. Durham, NC: Duke University Press.

Lombroso, C. (1911). *Crime: Its Causes and Remedies.* Trans. H. P. Horton. Boston: Little Brown.

Lombroso, C., and Ferrero, G. (1893, reprinted in 2004). *Criminal Woman, the Prostitute, and the Normal Woman.* Trans. N. Hahn Rafter and M. Gibson. Durham, NC: Duke University Press.

Louisiana Criminal Law Title XXI, Chapter 2, Article 652.

MacArthur Adjudicative Competence Study. (2004). Executive Summary. Retrieved from: http://www.macarthur.virginia.edu/adjudicate.html.

Macmillan, M. (2000). *An Odd Kind of Fame: Stories of Phineas Gage.* Cambridge, MA: MIT Press.

Markowitz, F.E. (2011). Mental Illness, Crime, and Violence: Risk, Context, and Social Control. *Aggression and Violent Behavior* 16, 36–44.

Martens, W. H. J. (2000). Antisocial and psychopathic personality disorders: Causes, course and remission—A review article. *International Journal of Offender Therapy and Comparative Criminology, 44*(4), 406–430.

McCaghy, C. (1976). *Deviant Behavior: Crime, Conflict, and Interest Groups.* New York: Macmillan.

McCarthy, B., Maggi, L., and Sparacello, M. (2008). N.O. cop killed with own gun. New Orleans, LA: *The Times-Picayune,* January 28.

McInerney, J.D. (1999). Genes and Behavior: A Complex Relationship. *Judicature,* 83(3). Retrieved from: http://www.ornl.gov/sci/techresources/Human_Genome/publicat/judicature/article4.html.

McNally, R.J. (2011). *What is Mental Illness?* Cambridge, MA: Belknap Press.

Mednick, S.A., and Christiansen, K.O. (1977). *Biosocial Bases of Criminal Behavior.* New York: Gardner Press.

Miller, L. A., Collins, R. L., and Kent, T. A. (2008). Language and the modulation of impulsive aggression. *The Journal of Neuropsychiatry and Clinical Neurosciences, 20,* 261–273.

Monahan, J. (1987). "The prediction of violent criminal behavior: a methodological critique and prospectus." In National Research Council (Ed.), *Deterrence and Incapacitation: Examining the Effects of Criminal Sanctions on Crime Rates.* Washington, DC: National Academy of Science.

Moffitt, T. (1993). Adolescence-limited and life-course-persistent antisocial behavior: A developmental taxonomy. *Psychological Review, 100,* 674–701.

Monahan, J., and Steadman, H. J. (1984). *Crime and Mental Disorder*. Washington, DC: National Institute of Justice, September.

Niehoff, D. (1999). *The Biology of Violence*. New York: Free Press.

Otto, R. K., Poythress, N. G., Nicholson, R. A., Edens, J. F., Monahan, J., Bonnie, R. J., Hoge, S. K., and Eisenberg, M. (1998). Psychometric properties of the MacArthur Competence Assessment Tool-Criminal Adjudication (MacCAT-CA). *Psychological Assessment, 10*, 435–443.

Parsons v. State of Alabama, 81 Ala. 577, 2 So. 854 (1887).

Phelan, J.C., Sinkewicz, M., Castille, D., Huz, S., and Link, B.C. (2010). Effectiveness and Outcome of Assisted Outpatient Treatment in New York State. *Psychiatric Services*, 61, 137–143.

Pinker, S. (2002). *The Blank Slate: The Modern Denial of Human Nature*. New York: Penguin Books.

Quinsey, V. L. (1980). The bases rate problem and the prediction of dangerousness: A reappraisal. *Journal of Psychiatry and the Law, 8*, 329–340.

Quinsey, V. L. (2004). Risk assessment and management in community settings. In W. Lindsey, J. Taylor, & P. Sturmey (Eds.). *Offenders with Developmental Disabilities*. New York: Wiley, 131–141.

Quinsey, V. L., Harris, G. T., Rice M. E., and Cormier, C. A. (2006). *Violent Offenders: Appraising and Managing Risk* (2nd Ed.). Washington, DC: American Psychological Association.

Raine, A. & Duncan, J. J. (1990). The genetic and psychophysiological basis of antisocial behavior: Implications for counseling and therapy. *Journal of Counseling and Development, 68*(6), 637–644.

Raine A., Venables, P. H., and Williams, M. (1990). Autonomic orienting response in 15 year old male subjects and criminal behavior at age 24. *American Journal of Psychiatry, 147*, 933–937.

Roebuck, J. and Murty, K. (2010). *A Social Psychological Typology of Deviant Professors and Administrators in American Higher Education*. Bloomington, IL: iUniverse Inc.

Rowe, D.C., and Osgood, W. (1984). Heredity and sociological theories of delinquency. *American Sociological Review*, 49, 526–540.

Sampson, R., and Laub, J. (2001). A life-course theory of cumulative disadvantage and the stability of delinquency. In A. Piquero and P. Mazerolle (Eds.), *Live-Course Criminology and Classic Readings*. Belmont, CA: Wadsworth.

Sagarin, E., and Sanchez, J. (1988). Ideology and deviance: The case of the debate over the biological factor. *Deviant Behavior*, 9, 87–99.

Sheldon, W. (1949). *Varieties of Delinquent Youth: An Introduction to Constitutional Psychiatry*. New York: Harper.

Shoemaker, D. (1990). *Theories of Delinquency*. New York: Oxford University Press

Siever, L. J. (2008) Neurobiology of aggression and violence. *American Journal of Psychiatry, 165*, 429–442.

Simmons, R., Johnson, C., Conger, R., and Elder, G. (1998). A Test of Latent Trait versus Life-course Perspectives on the Stability of Adolescent antisocial Behavior, *Criminology*, 36, 217–244.

Sterzer, P. (2010). Born to be Criminal? What to make of early biological risk factors for criminal behavior. *American Journal of Psychiatry, 167*, 1–3.

Sutherland, E. (1951). Critique of Sheldon's *Varieties of Delinquent Youth. American Sociological Review, 16*, 10–14.

Suri, R. A., Altshuler, L. L., Burt, V. K., and Hendrick, V. C. (1998). Managing psychiatric medications in the breast-feeding woman. *Medscape General Medicine, 1*(3). Retrieved from: http://www.medscape.com/viewarticle/722316.

Swanson, J. W. (1994). Mental disorder, substance abuse, and community violence: An epidemiological approach. In J. Monahan and H. J. Steadman (Eds.). *Violence and Mental Disorder: Developments in Risk Assessment.* Chicago: University of Chicago Press, 101–136.

Swanson, J. W., Borum, R., Swartz, M.S., Hiday, V. A., Ryan, W. H., Wagner, H. R., and Burns, B. J. (2001). Can Involuntary Outpatient Commitment Reduce Arrests Among Persons with Severe Mental Illness? *Criminal Justice and Behavior, 28*, 156–189.

Szasz, T. (1970). *The Manufacture of Madness.* New York: Harper and Row.

Than, K. (March 31, 2010). Human Genome at Ten: 5 Breakthroughs, 5 Predictions. *National Geographic News.* Retrieved from: http://news.nationalgeographic.com/news/human-genome-project-tenth-anniversaty/.

Torrey, E. Fuller (2008). *The Insanity Offense: How America's failure to treat the seriously mentally ill endangers its citizens.* New York: W. W. Norton.

Treatment Advocacy Center (January, 2012). *Assisted Outpatient Treatment Laws.* Retrieved from: http://www.treatmentadvocacycenter.org/solution/assisted-outpatient-treatment-laws.

United States v. Brawner 471 F.2d 969 (1972).

Van Dusen, K., Mednick, S.A., Gabrielli, W.F., and Hutchings, B. (1983). Social class and crime in an adoption cohort. *Journal of Criminal Law and Criminology, 74*, 249–269.

Vold, G. B. and Bernard, T. J. (1986). *Theoretical Criminology.* New York: Oxford University Press.

Walker, N. (1968). *Crime and Insanity in England, Vol. I.* Edinburgh: Edinburgh University Press.

Walters, G. D. (1992). A meta-analysis of the gene-crime relationship. *Criminology, 30*(4), 595–613.

Wilson, J.Q. and Herrnstein, R. (1985). *Crime and Human Nature.* New York: Simon and Schuster.

Zahn, W. C. and McBride, A. (1998). Current perspectives on social and emotional development. In J.G. Adair, D. Belanger, and K.L. Dion (Eds.). *Advances in Psychological Science, Vol. 1: Social, Cultural and Personal Aspects.* Hove, UK: Psychology Press/Erlbaum, 513–546.

Zucchino, D. (2012). Sterilized by the state, she felt raped once more. New Orleans, LA: *The Times-Picayune*, January 29: A-7.

Chapter 9

Social Predictors of Violence and Dangerousness: Sociological and Humanistic/Critical Theories

---

The complexities associated with violence have not lent themselves to an unambiguous and cogent understanding of the problem. On the contrary, the study of violence has evolved into multidisciplinary, multiparadigmatic approaches with contributions coming from many fields such as biology, psychology, sociology, and criminology, each representing multiple perspectives. The bulk of theories typically stem from studies that consider questions of deviance or crime in general; relatively few theories address violence or particular forms of violence. Moreover, most theories of violence tend to be one-dimensional often based on ad hoc theoretical models with limited explanatory power (Barak, 2003). The previous chapter focused on biological and psychological theories, which offer micro-level analyses of individual factors that predict aggressive behavior largely emphasizing some defective or innate qualities in human beings that have been linked with violent behavior. Theories focusing on individual causes help us understand the motivational and other individual factors that are associated with interpersonal cases of aggression or violence. These types of theories are not designed to explain variable rates of violence across social space or institutional and structural patterns.

While it would be impossible to describe the full range of sociological and humanist/critical schools of thought related to violence in a single chapter, this chapter surveys a sample of theories that attempt to identify the main social causative factors and processes as well as structural covariates that are implicated in predicting the prevalence or rates of violence in society. The chapter also considers the social defining processes that underlie our perceptions of what is considered legal and illegal violence. A critique of violence theories is also offered along the way noting some of the relative strengths and weaknesses of various explanations and calling for the development of comprehensive, integrative theoretical models that capture the interplay among the interpersonal, institutional, and structural dynamics associated with violence.

Historical Accounts of Varying Patterns and Rates of Violence

Adolphe Quetelet, trained as an astronomer and mathematician, has been called the father of social statistics (Sellin and Wolfgang, 1964, p. 9). Quetelet's *social physics* (1869) literally meant applying the methods and techniques that had been so successfully used in the physical sciences to study social phenomena. In his book, *Research on the Propensity for Crime at Different Ages* (1831/1984), Quetelet analyzed French national crime statistics (property and violent offenses) for several years and then predicted the rates of crimes for succeeding years, controlling for variables such as the age, sex, race, social class, level of education, and residence. His statistical analysis of crime patterns controlling for various population characteristics is the forerunner to the *Uniform Crime Reports*. Quetelet was careful in making predictions based on crime rates (the number of crimes per standard unit of the population); he did not attempt the impossible task of predicting individual crimes. In trying to explain differences in the rates of various types of crimes, he suggested that each type (e.g., murder, rape, robbery) has a unique etiology or set of causes. He derived lists of associative factors of crime such as variations in customs (p. 38), amount of alcohol consumption patterns in certain areas (p. 67), degree of industrialization (p. 39), population size (p. 40), and types of occupations or professions as indicators of social class (p. 66). He found, for example, that alcohol consumption patterns were significantly related to higher levels of interpersonal offenses such as homicide. After concluding that men are overwhelmingly represented in all crime statistics, including violent crimes, he refined his conclusions by pointing out that men typically appear to enter crime at an earlier age and remain longer than women (p. 45). The best general predictor of crime rates in certain areas according to Quetelet is the average age of the population. He noted that crime sharply declines after the age of 25; and, as a result, areas with larger proportions of young males will have relatively higher crime rates (p. 64).

Crime analyst, Andre Guerry, a contemporary of Quetelet, was probably the first to use the cartographic approach, which has continued in popularity into the 21st Century; particularly in the U. S. Guerry (1833) employed official crime statistics to generate shaded ecological maps indicating high and low crime rates in various regions of France. Both he and Quetelet noted that crime rates are unevenly distributed throughout the city.

Guerry, like Quetelet, warned that crime statistics, while offering a powerful tool, must be carefully used so as not to breed distrust because "soon figures overturn that which figures had established" (Guerry, 1984/1831, p. 71).

Emile Durkheim, the renowned French sociologist and criminologist, employed many of Guerry and Quetelet's statistical methods; however, he went further than descriptive analyses of data by testing hypotheses, interpreting data, and offering elaborate explanatory models and theories of the underlying social factors affecting variable crime rates across social space and cultural contexts and among different groups. His concept of *anomie* (normlessness), for example, was used to explain many of the correlates of suicide and crime that he, like Quetelet, uncovered by analyzing demographic information in connection with official records of crime and suicide. Durkheim observed that suicide rates as well as crime rates rise when social norms change too rapidly, creating what he referred to as a state of anomie or social chaos. For instance, he attributed Europe's historic rise in crime rates at the turn of the 20th Century on the unprecedented changes and dislocating effects associated with the processes of industrialization and urbanization (Durkheim, 1895/1966).

Durkheim was also interested in the constraining affects of society, particularly the affects of institutional and group affiliation or bonding on normative patterns (e.g., the effects of living in a rural versus and urban communities as well the influence of relationships with family, peer groups, schools, religious organizations, and work groups in the prevention of suicide or crime). Rather than only addressing the question of what causes deviance, his works suggested what prevents deviances such as intrapersonal (suicide) or interpersonal (homicide) violence. Durkheim analyzed suicide rates and crime rates in the context of all sorts of structural and demographic combinations extrapolating the commonalities of various patterns in order to explain the variability of rates across different times, locations, group characteristics, and cultural norms. In this way, Durkheim (1893/1960; 1895/1966; 1897/1951) converted statistical information, such as crime rates, into indicators of social integration, social solidarity, and social change.

Another contemporary of Durkheim, Gabriel Tarde, also focused on the social roots affecting human behavior, especially learning factors associated with crime and violence. Tarde argued that criminal including violent behavior is learned and subject to the same learning processes connected with conventional behavior. His book, *Laws of Imitation* (1890/1903), proposes that learning through association with offenders or criminal groups results in the development of certain skills and values conducive to crime as well as a propensity to commit criminal or violent acts.

The contributions of Quetelet, Guerry, Durkheim, and Tarde drew attention away from studying defects within individuals or offenders and they challenged the presumption of the absolute nature of crime or violence. While they noted that from time to time there was general social consensus over legitimate/illegitimate action, these investigators treated crime or violence as a relative phenomenon dependent on the sociocultural context. However, they typically did not raise issue with the hierarchical order of society.

Early 20th Century American criminologists such as Edwin Sutherland (1939; 1978), Frederic Thrasher (1927; 1966), Clifford Shaw and Henry McKay (1931; 1969), and Robert Merton (1938) combined some of the theoretical contributions of Durkheim and Tarde with techniques suggested by Quetelet and Guerry (i.e., plotting crime incidents on maps and examining various crime rates in relation to urban characteristics such as substandard and overcrowded housing, poverty levels, migration patterns, unemployment rates, and minority status of residents in an attempt to explain high and low crime rates in certain urban areas). As a consequence of the broader implications of the social ecology of crime and violence in society, sociologists, economists, and other social scientists have become attracted to explaining varying patterns of crime and violence in society. Questions regarding the social process of learning, social change, and the function of crime, norms, laws, and social control that this rich legacy of theorists brought to the forefront continue to interest scholars and researchers today.

Along another trajectory of theory development, influential social thinkers such as Karl Marx (1848/1964) and Max Weber (1958) inspired humanistic/critical analyses of human behavior, social action, power relationships, and the social defining structures in society. The humanistic/critical paradigm also referred to as the conflict approach rests on the assumption that the hierarchical order of power in society determines the social order including the legal definitions of violence, the nature and enforcement of law, and the social responses to protect against the resistance of order. The definition of violence and the mechanisms of control are shaped in the interest of the elite who use the criminal justice system and the national defense system to suppress any actions (internal and external) that threaten their relative power and the status quo.

As a critic of the political economy, Marx (1848/1964) exposed the blinding effects of capitalist ideology. He also warned that the foundations of knowledge including theoretical and scientific works represented reductionistic portrayals of human behavior and social action, thereby sensitizing theoreticians to the underlying power relationships that affect the expert's vision of reality. While not pointing to sociologists or criminologists directly, Marx implied that theories of crime represented bourgeois interests and he claimed that the control of criminals or the criminal justice system was the main tool of the capitalists for maintaining the capitalist order and inherent inequalities.

Weber (1958) developed one of the most recognized conceptualizations of law. He noted: "An order will be called law if it is externally guaranteed by the probability that coercion (physical or psychological) to bring about conformity or avenge violation will be applied by a staff of people holding themselves specially ready for that purpose" (p. 5). Weber also raised issue with theories and typologies based on reductionistic and deterministic methods of science and urged social thinkers/scientific researchers (sociologists) to pose questions regarding the relationship between law, social control, and social conflict.

Both Marx and Weber and others that have followed their lines of thought suggest that the correlations associated with violence and such demographic characteristics as gender, age, race, and poverty have nothing to do with these characteristics, but rather reflect the relative positions of individuals in the hierarchical structure of the social order, thus demonstrating the way people are marginalized and criminalized by the powerful groups in society.

The humanistic/critical approach has produced a wide array of theories as well as a general critique of the knowledge-base associated with crime and violence and the taken-for-granted world. For example, Thorsten Sellin's (1938) work focusing on pluralist conflict to explain patterns of crime among immigrants, Edwin Sutherland's (1940, 1945, and 1949) work on white collar crime, George Vold's (1958) theory of group conflict particularly as applied to gangs and organized crime, Austin Turk's (1969) work on authorities and subjects, and Richard Quinney's (1977) work on the social reality of crime all have contributed to an impressive legacy of theories and research that continue to inspire current theorists/researchers.

Mainstream Sociological Theories of Violence

Mainstream sociological theories generally presume that basic social agreement or consensus can be reached over matters of right and wrong, good or bad in society. The social order (including the laws of the land), while not perfect is assumed to be in the public interest and therefore must be preserved. Crimes that defy the social order must be controlled and their rate of occurrence reduced. Accompanying the consensual view of society is the idea that positivism or science will uncover the objective roots or causes of social problems such as criminal violence and will point to objective solutions, which may be expressed in the form of policies or some prevention programs.

Demographic and Ecological Patterns Associated with Varying Rates of Violence

In the early part of the 20th Century in the U.S., the nature and rapidity of changes having to do with industrialization and urbanization and the rapid growth of crime rates, captured the attention of many criminologists. Sociologists of the so-called Chicago School were convinced that the ecology of place shaped in many ways the social life of the people in that area for good or bad (Shaw and McKay, 1931; 1942; 1969). Their focus on the roles of neighborhood and neighborhood organization on crime is referred to as the theory of social disorganization. Borrowing from social ecologists/urban sociologists Park and Burgess' concentric zone hypothesis (1925), Shaw and McKay observed fairly stable and high levels of juvenile crime in transitional zones (areas of land use available to poor immigrants) over several decades between 1900 and 1960. These invariable high levels of juvenile crime were found in the same social areas, even though they were inhabited by different immigrant groups. Shaw and McKay's explanation based on this information represented "a type of place" theory rather than "a type of people" theory. Their perspective was referred to as the social disorganization theory of crime.

Although social disorganization as an explanation of crime and violence has provided the theoretical underpinning for numerous studies; it has been significantly expanded to include the influence of social networks, social capital, and collective efficacy (Bursik, 2004, p. 96). Many of these studies have been conducted at the neighborhood level of analysis, which has turned out to be more efficacious because the main process linking social environments and violence depends, to some degree, on interaction with contiguous others (Sampson, 1986). Poverty, measured variously as unemployment, low income or percent below the federal poverty line, is among the most frequent components of the model of social disorganization used to explain variation in the incidents of homicide across neighborhoods. As a correlate of homicide, poverty is usually found to be significant by criminologists, i.e., the poorer the neighborhood, the higher the incidence of homicide (Sampson, 1986). Robert Sampson's recent work, *Great American City*, a comprehensive study of Chicago, reports that violence such as homicide and robbery while decreasing in some Chicago communities during the period of 1995–2000, as occurred nationwide, nevertheless retained their places in relative rankings of violence despite significant drops in violent crimes. Similarly, poverty and inequality in these communities also remained problematic. In fact, he noted that "communities can be said to inherit their positional inequality" (pp. 110–112). However, some studies have noted that the linkage is not direct; for instance, there are other intervening variables that appear to contribute to high rates of neighborhood-level distribution of homicide including community efficacy and cultural factors conducive to violence (Harper, Voigt, and Thornton, 2004).

An extensive body of research has been produced on social disorganization describing how demographic and socioeconomic characteristics of neighborhoods may create conditions favorable to crime and violence by limiting the ability of communities to self-regulate and solve common problems (e.g., Shaw and McKay 1969/1942; Sampson and Groves 1989; Sampson 2001; Kubrin and Weitzer 2003; Bursik, 2004). Studies of socially disorganized communities also suggest that these communities tend to be socially and culturally isolated from the larger urban system and experience "concentrated effects" in the form of multiple types of disadvantage (e.g., Wilson, 1987; Anderson 1999), which help explain varied patterns of crime and violence across cities. The link between poverty and violence is often discussed in terms of the *culture of poverty*. For example, William Julius Wilson (1987) argues that social isolation (concentrated poverty and concentrated race/ethnicity) influences cultural orientation—an orientation that is shaped by the lack of opportunity and a scarcity of conventional role models. These conditions affect the way people respond to their circumstances as well as how they are treated by officials.

Macro-analysis of ecological and geographic patterns of violence with consideration of structural characteristics, and historical and cultural features of various social spaces has received a resurgence of attention by social scientists over the last several decades (e.g., Blau and Blau, 1982; Skogan, 1986, 1990; Sampson, 1987; Sampson and Groves, 1989; LaFree, Drass, and O'Day, 1992; Bursik and Grasmick, 1993; Wilson, 1987, 1996; Kubrin and Herting, 2003; Peterson and Krivo, 2005; Hipp, 2007). Researchers have specifically tried to unravel the mystery of the ecological concentration of violence by studying the various spatial and temporal dynamics of nations, regions, cities, and neighborhoods and their connection with the official records of violence (such as the *Uniform Crime Reports'* data on homicide, rape, robbery, and assault).

Taken together, ecological studies of the clustering of violent crimes (particularly the pattern of homicides, which often serves as a proxy for violence) over time and space appear to point to the significance of characteristics of certain places, especially areas where there are high concentrations of poverty and racial and ethnic segregation. Even though some of these results have been noted over and over, many inconsistencies continue to fuel further investigation. For instance, researchers focusing on routine activities/opportunity argue that the convergence of motivated offenders, suitable targets, and a lack of capable guardians in time and space may explain the nonrandom distribution of crime and violence (Cohen and Felson, 1979; Wilcox, Land, and Hunt, 2003; Felson, 2004). Some integrated models incorporate aspects of socioeconomic structure, opportunity, and criminal facilitators (e.g., guns, drugs, alcohol) to explain changes in crime rate trends (Clarke, 1995). There is some work on how change in the homicide rate manifests over both time and across space in urban areas (Cohen and Tita, 1999; Cork, 1999; Messner, et al., 1999). Specific factors considered responsible for changes in the rate of homicide over time include: escalating handgun use, the emergence of crack cocaine markets in many cities in the mid-1980s and their subsequent decline in the 1990s, demographic changes in the population age structure, transformation of policing practices, and implementation of determinate/mandatory sentencing (LaFree, 1999; Cook and Moore, 1999; Blumstein and Wallman, 2000; Wintemute, 2000). Studies have also focused on how violence itself may be a cause of violence in traditionally nonviolent zones due to the process of diffusion across space (Cohen and Tita, 1999; Cork, 1999; Messner, et al., 1999).

Kenneth Land, Patricia McCall, and Lawrence Cohen (1990) have conducted a review of twenty-one studies with 11 overlapping structural covariates that are typically hypothesized to be related to the ecological clustering of homicides. The typical list of covariates include population size, population density, percent of population age 15–29, percent of male population 15 years and older, percent of minority population, percent of children under the age of 18 years not living with both parents, median family income, percentage of families living below the official poverty line, the GINI index of family income inequality, percent of unemployment, and in some cases a variable indicating southern/non-southern location of cities, metropolitan areas or states. The authors claim that while this list does not represent an exhaustive list of the structural covariates of homicide research, it does provide a reasonable profile of the literature mainly using U.S. data on inter-unit variation of rates homicide as the research problem (Land, McCall, and Cohen, 1990).

What is most striking about their findings of research that focuses on the covariates of homicide over time is that no covariates exhibit consistent statistically significant estimates across all studies. For example, three frequently tested covariates (i.e., population size, population density, and population heterogeneity as indexed by the percent black or white or non-white populations) fail to exhibit significant positive relationships with homicide rates across studies. Similarly, age structure indices also fail to consistently predict homicide rates (p. 931). The variables measuring a southern culture of violence fare no better. The same can be said of the GINI index of income inequality even when the percent poverty is significant. For example, median family income often displays a negative relationship suggesting that it moves in the opposite direction of the poverty and income inequality indicators (Land, McCall, and Cohen, 1990, p. 932). Moreover, not much can be gained by limiting the comparisons to specific time periods.

These results raise serious doubt about developing a general theory of variation in homicide rates that is more than context specific limiting the prospect for developing a general theory of homicide rate variation particularly across time and social space (Land, McCall, and Cohen 1990, p. 933). It is possible that these inconsistencies in the results of these various studies may stem from differences in research design and approaches to data analysis or issues of statistical inference.

Social Strain Theories

In his widely read article on social structure and anomie, Robert K. Merton (1938) argues that a general state of *anomie* (normlessness) prevails in American society because contradictions (disjunctions) exist between cultural goals (e.g., having lots of money, a nice home, fancy automobile, and other typical cultural markers of success) and the institutional means to achieve these goals (e.g., good education, good a paying job). These cultural goals are widely accepted along with an ideology that everyone has an equal opportunity to reach these goals. The fact, according to Merton, is that opportunities (means of achievement) are not evenly distributed. The main avenues toward success, education, and employment are not equally accessible. The quality of education and employment opportunities and rewards vary by social class.

Under these circumstances, according to Merton's strain theory, American society promotes a belief that everyone must strive for success because it is equally available, failure is just a temporary detour on the way to success and the real failure is the person who gives up his/her pursuit of success. How do people react to the very real disjunction between the cultural goals of success and the unequal distribution of institutional means to achieving them? Merton proposes that people adapt to *anomie* (i.e., disjunction between goals and means) by way of one of five different reactions: conformity, innovation, ritualism, retreatism and rebellion.

Robert Merton's *Social Structure and Anomie* (1938)

Mode of adaptation	goals	means
Conformity	+	+
Innovation	+	−
Ritualism	−	+
Retreatism	−	−
Rebellion	(−/+)	(−/+)

Conformity represents the most common adaptation. The person who works hard in school, graduates in order to get a good job and then works hard to afford the material markers of success is conforming to society's expectations and values.

Innovation characterizes individuals/groups that accept the cultural goals of success but embrace unconventional ways or means of achieving them. Urban youth who deal drugs in order to purchase expensive clothes and luxury automobiles would be an example of this adaptive mode. Another example may be organized crime groups who operate illicit "businesses" to reap profits.

Ritualism occurs when individuals are blocked from achieving success goals, they may adjust by abandoning them. For example, the context of the Oscar Lewis' "culture of poverty" (1966) people may simply give up on the American dream and no longer strive for the success symbols of society; however they continue to be law abiding and surviving as best they can.

Retreatism involves the rejection of both goals and means to achieve them. For example, some people/groups adapt by dropping out of conventional society, e.g., by becoming members of cults or drug subculture or other deviant subcultures.

Rebellion involves the rejection of existing goals and means and the substitution of both new goals and new means. Individuals/groups choosing this form of adaptation may seek to effect peaceful counter-cultural movements; others may seek to depose or destroy the existing social order and supplant a new order or even return to an older form (e.g., terrorist groups).

Elaborating on Merton's observations Robert Agnew (1992) offers three categories of stress-strain to specifically explain criminal behavior. Each category refers to a different type of negative relationships with others: (1) preventing achievement of positively valued goals such as wealth, status, or autonomy), (2) removing or threatening to remove positively valued stimuli such as love or nurturing, and (3) threatening to present noxious or negatively valued stimuli such as verbal or physical abuse, rejection or abandonment, or arrest. In his book, *Pressured into Crime: An Overview of General Strain Theory* (2006), he treats the question of whether strain theory can explain varying community/societal patterns of crime including the patterns typically associated with gender, class, and race/ethnic variations of crime rates. For example, he argues that inhabitants in truly disadvantaged neighborhoods are more likely to be limited or blocked from attaining social goals, especially economic and status (respect) goals because they have less access to the necessary paths of success (i.e., education, jobs, and social support/networks necessary for success) (p. 55). Moreover, residents (and their families and friends) of disadvantaged neighborhoods also run greater risks of victimization by crime and violence (p. 159), which not only affects the strain levels of individuals, but also of the people that they associate with.

While Agnew (1992) treats the three types of strain as mutually exclusive categories, there may be instances where they may overlap and, therefore, may increase the probability of a more serious range of emotional responses of aggression, including extreme outbursts of anger or rage as well as violent lethal attacks. For example, Dee Harper and Lydia Voigt (2007) reported several cases involving intimate/domestic lethal violence followed by suicide suggesting the expression of multiple strains during the different phases of the event. For example, the homicide-suicide event may have been triggered by one partner's attempt to leave, thereby challenging the power of the other through abandonment or rejection in the first phase of the homicide-suicide event; and then the killing of the partner leads to the next phase of the event by threatening the stability of the unit and introducing other strains (e.g., blocked goals/needs) thus resulting in self-demise. Perhaps because of the dual nature of cases of homicide followed by suicide, multiple sources of strain must be experienced for homicide-suicide to occur. It may be that any one element alone may be connected with either a homicide or a suicide, but not both. Obviously this is a difficult proposition to measure. Yet it is noteworthy that more than one of the elements of the different types of strain are evident across many of the cases included in the Harper and Voigt (2007) study (see also Harper and Voigt, 2012).

Agnew further claims that while general strain theory (GST) has been originated to explain U.S. patterns of crime and their relationship with cultural inhibitors of success, GST has been successfully applied in other countries such as China (Bao, et al, 2004) and Israel (Landau, 1998) (Agnew, 2006, p. 163). He does admit that the ability of GST to explain varying crime rates is not simple. It is still not clear why certain strain-producing situations, events, and conditions are conducive to crime for some individuals, neighborhoods, or societies, but not in others.

Focused more on the institutional level of anomie the book, *Crime and the American Dream* by Steven Messner and Richard Rosenfeld (2007), revisits Merton's thesis. In so doing, the authors set much of the blame of high crime in the United States on our inordinate cultural emphasis on wealth particularly obtaining material wealth by *any* means necessary. But this, they argue, is not the sole explanation. Economic preoccupations are so dominant that they overpower the mediating role that family, schools, church, and other institutions might play in mitigating criminal behavior including criminal violence.

Social Learning Theories

Psychological analysis of *learning* or *acquiring* patterns of violent behavior usually considers the role of the faulty learner or faulty teacher, i.e., someone with a character disorder or a mental illness or someone who is unable to learn society's rules or believes that the rules do not apply to him/her (see Chapter 8 in this volume). The learning process itself may also be faulty, suggesting a breakdown in the communication of expectations of society or improper inculcation of the norms (faulty teacher). Sociological analysis learning, however, does not necessarily assume a breakdown in communication or personal insufficiency on the part of the learner.

For instance, Edwin Sutherland (1939) views crime and delinquency as learned behavior. He argues that individuals must be taught how to commit criminal including violent acts either directly or vicariously. Additionally, individuals must learn or acquire the necessary attitudes, motives, and rationalizations conducive to the violation of legal norms. This is the underlying basis of his *differential association theory* of criminal behavior.

Sutherland's theory claims that the acquisition of skills and techniques of commitment, supporting motives, and rationalizations depends on the degree to which a person is immersed in differential associations with conventional versus nonconventional role models, behaviors, and attitudes. Differential association theory mainly focuses on associations with attitudes, values, and definitions that are connected with pro-criminal role models and types of behavior, suggesting that criminality is influenced by an "excess" of exposure to pro-criminal role models and types of behavior over neutral or anti-criminal ones (Sutherland and Cressey, 1978).

Over the decades a number of criticisms have been leveled against the theory of differential association. While Sutherland did not specially address why certain acts are regarded as criminal and others are not (Jeffrey, 1959) in the specific context of his differential association theory, he did treat this question in his work on white collar and corporate crime suggesting that those with power are in the position to affect legislation to protect their own particular interests and those with less power are treated more harshly (see Sutherland, 1940, 1945, and 1949). Travis Hirschi and David Rudisill (1976) have raised the question of which comes first—differential association or criminality. In the search for causes of crime, Sutherland may be credited for drawing attention to the general nature and extent of an offender's interpersonal interaction. However, while he has offered some insights into the general pattern of such interactions, he has neglected the particular interactions between the offender and victim.

Even though critics have raised important issues, the theory of differential association continues to be of interest to criminologists. For example, Robert Burgess and Ronald Akers (1968) have expanded the theory of differential association by adding the concept of *differential reinforcement*. Borrowing the idea that behavior that is rewarded will tend to be repeated from behavioral psychology, Burgess and Akers concede that while most criminal behavior is learned in association with others, some may be learned in nonsocial settings as long as the learner is rewarded or reinforced. In other words, the criminal act itself may be rewarding. They argue that criminal behavior will become part of an individual's behavioral repertoire only to the degree to which the individual has received ample positive reinforcement.

Ronald Akers and Adam Silverman (2004) have applied the social learning model "to all acts of illegitimate violence, use of force, physical aggression, assault, homicide, rape, and property destruction in which injury or death is expected or ignored" (p. 19). They summarize their theory as it applies to violence in the following statement:

> The probability that persons will commit acts of violence is increased when they differentially associate directly or indirectly with others who commit violent behavior and espouse definitions favorable to it (differential association), are relatively more exposed in-person or symbolically through media to *salient models of violence* (imitation), *define it as desirable or justified* (definitions) in a situation *discriminative* for the behavior, and have received in the past and/or anticipate in the current or future situation relatively *greater reward* (either through positive achievement of desired outcomes or avoidance of undesired outcomes) and *less punishment* (either directly or indirectly) for the behavior (differential reinforcement) (p. 24).

The empirical evidence in support of the various components of social learning (i.e., differential association, definitions favorable and unfavorable to offending, differential reinforcement, and imitation/ modeling) related to crime and violence is abundant (e.g., see review by Akers and Silverman, 2004; and Akers and Sellers, 2004). Evidence supporting the theory also exists in specific contexts such as peer groups or gangs (Thornberry, Lizotte, Krohn, Fransworth, and Jang, 1994; Warr, 2002). Experiences within the family particularly children witnessing abuse or being victims of abuse have been included among the high risk factors associated with adult abusive behavior later in life such as spouse abuse risk factors (Straus and Gelles, 1980; Black, et al., 1999; Wasserman and Seracina, 2001; Krug, et al., 2002, p. 98; Herrenkohol, et al., 2003; Adams, 2009; Smith and Farole, 2009; Regehr and Roberts, 2010).

Theories related to certain ecological patterns, anomie or strain, and learning of unconventional adaptations, which emphasize the lessening of social constraints with rapid cultural changes, have considered social disorganizations, unequal opportunities, contradictory value patterns respectively among the causes of increasing crime rates.

Social Control Theories

Social control theories, which are also interested in the constraining effects of society, focus mainly on human relationships and interaction in the context of institutions (e.g., within families, schools, places of worship, and workplaces) and on the effects of significant others in the prevention of crime (e.g., Reiss, 1951; Sykes and Matza, 1957; Hirschi, 1969; Reckless and Dinitz, 1972). Rather than asking what causes crime rates to increase, they address the question of how can crimes be prevented. For example, Travis Hirschi's (1969) *social bond* theory, which is primarily based on studies of juvenile delinquency, is perhaps among the most commonly cited theories associated with the social control perspective. Hirschi's concept of social bond refers to (1) the connection between the individual and social institutions (e.g., family and school); and (2) the connections between the individual and society. He describes four elements of social bond: *attachment* (respect and affection for one's family members); *commitment* (respect for socially defined age-appropriate activities/behaviors); *involvement* (time spent on conventional activities); and *belief* (respect for morality and authority of the law and social order). The theory suggests that individuals who have not developed respect for themselves, for their families, for others, and for the conventional order and values of their society are prime candidates for engaging in criminal activities. Social control theories claim that criminal behavior can be reduced or prevented by increasing the effectiveness of those institutions that have the greatest influence over socialization and control of people—family, school, places of worship, formal voluntary associations, media, and legal system.

Routine Activities Theories

The routine activities theory is based on the assumption that regularities or patterns in behavior exist and that behavior is repetitive and predictable. Inspired by Shaw and McKay's (1969) *Juvenile Delinquency in Urban Areas* and Hawley's (1950) *Human Ecology: A Theory Community Structure*, Lawrence Cohen and Marcus Felson (1979), in their article "Social Change and Crime Rate Trends" argue that the urban environment and social context will affect the relationship between certain types of activities and certain types of criminal victimizations. The routine activities approach to crime rate analysis rests on the observation that the association of high crime rates with modern society is largely due to the expansion and growth of illegal opportunities as well as increases in the probability of interaction between victim and offenders. Felson (1987) claims that the theory accomplishes these three things:

1.   It specifies three elements of crime: a likely offender, a suitable target, and the absence of a capable guardian against crime.

2.   It considers how everyday life assembles these three elements in space and time.

3.   It shows that a proliferation of lightweight, durable goods (e.g., televisions stereos, etc.) and a dispersion of activities away from family and household could account quite well for the crime wave in the U.S. in the 1960s and 1970s without fancier explanations (p. 911).

The theory suggests that offenders seek quick and easy risks and that they follow obvious routes (Cohen, Felson, and Land, 1980). It also assumes that daily movement and general mobility can either increase or diminish potential victimization. Moreover, it presupposes that offending may be deterred, displaced, or even encouraged depending on certain environmental and social conditions. While the routine activities theory has been criticized for mainly applying to property crime and less to violent crimes (Miethe, Stafford, and Long, 1987), there is evidence suggesting that certain life styles and routines (e.g., abusive family relations) may actually promote conflict situations and increase the exposure of certain victims to violence and also provide greater opportunities for conflict (Kennedy and Forde, 1990).

Rational Choice Theory

The rational choice theory views criminal behavior as a product of decisions and choices. By analyzing displacement resulting from opportunity-reducing measures or crime prevention, Derek Cornish and Ronald Clarke (1987) develop the concept of "choice-structuring properties" (i.e., relative opportunities, costs, and benefits attached to a specific crime and spatial relations). The theorists assert that particular crimes are selected and committed for some reasons and that "the readiness with which the offender will be prepared to substitute one offense for another will depend on the extent to which the alternative offenses share characteristics which the offender considers salient to his or her goals and abilities" (p. 935).

General Theory of Crime

In their book, *A General Theory of Crime* (1990), Michael Gottfredson and Travis Hirschi combine elements of routine activity, rational choice, "self control" theories and thereby bring together psychoanalytical and sociological control factors and personality trait theories of crime.

Gottfredson and Hirschi begin by distinguishing *crime* from *criminality*. Crime is defined as illegal acts of force or fraud carried out by individuals who are "motivated by the self-interest pursuit of pleasure and the avoidance of pain" (Hirschi and Gottfredson, 1987, p. 957). Criminality refers to "the [tendencies] of individuals to purse short-term gratification in the most direct way with little consideration for the long-term consequences of their acts" (1987, p. 959). Furthermore, they argue that while environmental conditions ultimately affect criminal opportunities (e.g., a crowded bar where people consume great quantities of alcohol is more likely to be the scene of arguments and fights than a church), people vary in their propensity to act on criminal opportunities. Individuals with low self-control are more likely to take advantage of a criminal opportunity than an individual with high self-control (Gottfredson and Hirschi, 1990).

Richard Felson and Wayne Osgood (2008) discuss the application of the general theory of crime to violent crimes. For example, they note:

> Those who are more punitive and concerned with showing toughness are more likely to use violence, whereas empathy and moral attitudes act as inhibitors. Self-control may play a greater role in dispute-related violence, but thrill seeking may play a greater role in predatory violence (p. 171).

Gottfredson and Hirschi's general theory of crime has been both praised and slammed by critics (Goode, 2008). It like other theories we have discussed represents an integrated model, which brings together several lines of thought. By stating the propositions in the context of a more general framework and conceptual vocabulary and by allowing for a wide range of testing or applications even in cross-cultural designs, integrative theories offer far more possibilities of new insights as well as new challenges for theorists.

Humanistic/Critical Theories of Violence

The humanistic/critical paradigm within criminology derives from a critical branch of social philosophy that has raised issue with theories and typologies based on the reductionistic and deterministic methods of science. This approach is critically opposed to studies of human behavior and social influences that are conducted apart from the historical and cultural context. Humanistic/critical theories of crime and violence also referred to as conflict theories rest on the assumption that conflict more than consensus is fundamental to an understanding of the nature of society and human relationships. Accordingly the existence of competing norms, values, interests, and social expectations in society are believed to affect the definitions of legitimate and illegitimate behavior including violence, as well as the social responses to it. One of the primary contributions of the humanistic/critical perspective has been to debunk the facts and findings accompanying the widely held views of the public and mainstream criminologists. This critique suggests that most people in society have been duped into rationalizing a system in which "the rich get richer and the poor get prison" (Reiman, 1984).

Within criminology this approach has been referred to by many different titles. Taken together in the most general form, the different approaches may be grouped under discussions of the *defining structures* involved in determining what is legitimate and illegitimate forms of crime and violence and *analyses of the political economy* and associated conflict and power relationships implicated in the structural patterns of inequities and false consciousness in society.

Defining Legitimate and Illegitimate Violence

Criminologists studying the defining structures that determine what behavior is legitimate and illegitimate and how social labels are discriminately applied consider the content, context, and source of beliefs, values, and actions associated with criminal law, criminal justice as they are reflected in political, public, and criminological treatment.

These theorists draw special attention to the disparity in societal perceptions, application of definitions, and treatment of the behavior of individuals representing different social characteristics. They argue that public awareness of crime and violence as well as the criminal justice processes reflects the social relationships (especially conflict relationships) within a particular culture. Various theorists point to conflicts arising from social class and power to explain the disparate patterns of crime and violence related to social economic status, age, gender, and race and ethnicity (e.g., Chambliss, 1973; Quinney, 1977; Schwendinger and Schwendinger, 1985; Messerschmidt, 1986; Barak and Bohm, 1989; Gillespie, 1989; Hagan, 1989; Lynch and Groves, 1989).

The Political Economy and Violence

To account for the disproportionate variability in the incidence and rates of violence, humanistic/critical theories point to the influence of dominate economic and power structures on the production of crime and violence in society. For example, Michael Lynch (2004) observes that the bulk of criminological research primarily looks at street violence, which is reflected in the official counts of violence (e.g., *UCR* counts of homicide, rape, robbery and assault) typically excluding violence associated with political corruption, corporate practices or white collar offenses. He goes on to note that when criminologists identify the correlates (e.g., class, gender, and race and ethnicity) associated with patterns of criminal violence, these findings are usually crime-specific and not universal mainly applying to street violence (p. 105). Among the important contributions to the research on violence have been studies related to corporate and environmental violence (e.g., Lynch, Michalowski, and Grove, 2000; Burns and Lynch, 2004; Barrile and Slone, 2012), which demonstrate the widespread harm caused by "toxic crimes" (such as negative health consequences, e.g., increases in rates of disease, illness, cancer, and death).

Rather than focusing on a *description of what is*, this perspective *questions what is* (i.e., the status quo) and seeks to demystify and debunk widely held perceptions. Instead of positing the question of *what is truth*, which is the hallmark of positivism or science, it asks *what is good* for human beings. Solutions are weighed in terms of freedom, equality, and social justice. As a unique perspective in criminology it "combines a theoretical concern with deviance and social control as interrelated aspects of human struggle for power in history with a practical concern for the realization of social justice" (Pfohl, 1985, p. 333).

Violence and the Reproduction of Power Control

While the great bulk of humanistic/critical theories address the overall societal nature of the patterns of violence particularly the fundamental or underpinning roots of violence, some theorists have shown how the structural social patterns of dominance and violence as a form of power control are reproduced on the institutional and interpersonal levels. For instance, John Hagan (1989) notes that that while "theories often imply that crime is a product of power relationships" in society, the research "methodologies conventionally ignore this premise" (p. 2). Hagan calls for the development of a research base dealing with the question of power and dominance in the context of the fundamental institutions of society (e.g., family and work) and the criminal justice system (e.g., judicial processing and sentencing). For example, he argues that the family reflects the power relations of society and as such is the seedbed for the linkage between the family and patterns of intimate partner or familial abuse as well as patterns of delinquency. Hagan finds that "the social organization of work and family relations influence the social distribution of delinquency through the gender stratification of domestic social control (1989, p. 200). He claims that the question of how general gender-specific authority relations affect parental and adolescent relations, especially in single-headed households, is particularly relevant for understanding discriminatory practices in court processing and sentencing. Hagan asserts that in order for us to understand the problem of crime including the problem of violence, we must understand the interplay among class, family, and gender in the context of our changing society.

James Messerschmidt, in his book, *Capitalism, Patriarchy and Crime: Toward a Socialist Feminist Criminology* (1986), argues that crime as well as violence is rooted in power that includes both gender (patriarchal) and class (capitalistic) dimensions. "Crime of both the powerless (working class and women) and powerful (capitalist class and men) is created by interaction of patriarchy and capitalism" (p. 157). Lower-class men (particularly young minority men) are portrayed as criminal, which functions to keep many out of economic and political competition. Lower-class families, especially those run by females, are assumed to be inferior and the breeding ground of criminals and thus subject to state intervention through the courts.

Power control theory of male dominance and the history of violence have served as the context to explain intimate partner violence (e.g., Dobash and Dobash, 1992; Daly and Wilson, 1988). For instance, women are most vulnerable to be victimized or killed by intimate partners when they attempt to leave relationships thereby challenging the power dominance relationships (Allen, 1983).

The Social Geometry of Conflict and Intensity of Violence

Donald Black (2004) claims that "most violence is explicitly or implicitly a form of justice—punishment, retaliation, resistance, or revenge" (p. 146). According to Black the problem with individualistic theories of violence or collective theories of violence is that no individuals or collectivities express violence in all of their conflicts. Black's work on the *social geometry of conflict* situations (reminiscent of Georg Simmel's [1908/1956] hypotheses related to conflict intensity) focuses on factors such as the social distance, the degree of attachment or responsibility, and the social status or the social direction of grievance (inequality) between parties to explain the variability of the resulting type or intensity of violence. Black argues that these factors may determine the particular form of violence employed, whether a weapon is used, and the degree of brutality inflicted. He notes that the greater the emotional involvement of the parties to a conflict, the greater the intensity of violence. For instance, violence escalates in situations: (1) where the parties to a conflict are closer in relationship, (2) where there is greater dependency/responsibility between the parties, (3) where the parties are more unequal (especially in the context of male and female status or role), (4) where there is greater previous hostilities, and (5) where there is previous jealousy between the parties. In addition Black claims that the structure of violence intensity also includes precipitating crises or trigger events such as threats of separation/loss or destruction or financial decline. For Black violence represents "both crime and social control at once" (2004, p. 146). For example, he writes that "Violence not only resembles law in its moralistic nature but also in the highly precise manner of its application" (p. 147).

Structural Production of Violence and the Cycle of Violence, Suppression of Freedom, and Inequality

In an attempt to reconcile the apparent disconnect between the mainstream consensus approach and the humanistic/critical approach, Peter Iadicola and Anson Shupe (2003) show the interconnection among the structural, institutional, and interpersonal relationships. They argue that the structural foundation of society (i.e., the global political economy and power relationships) are reproduced in the institutional and interpersonal realms of society and are expressed through the cycle of violence that reflects the social patterns of inequality and denial of freedom in society. Iadicola and Shupe hold that as violence increases, inequality increases, and consequently freedom decreases for all those who are in dominated positions (2003, p. 379). Conversely as inequality increases and freedom diminishes, violence increases. Accordingly populations that are repressed become most vulnerable to being controlled by violence, which further works to diminish their personal freedoms and equal participation in society as well as the freedom of response to inequitable treatment.

Iadicola and Shupe (2003) offer some illustrations of the cycle of violence, diminishment of freedom, and increases in inequality. For instance, a battered wife whose activities are monitored and who is isolated from the support of family and friends by an abusive partner becomes more vulnerable to increases of violence and further repression. Similarly laborers with relatively few job options become more vulnerable to workplace abuses including unsafe working conditions. Globally, the populations that are most repressed by governments are limited with respect to opportunities to prosper and in their expression of freedom, which makes them more vulnerable to violence and increasing subjugation leading to greater inequities.

Iadicola and Shupe (2003) write: "As violence in a society increases, freedom is increasingly denied for those who are most dominated and systems of inequity are extended" (p. 380).

According to Iadicola and Shupe, the policy implication of this is that the problem of violence cannot be solved with violence. Responding to violence with violence only serves to perpetuate more violence. Moreover, economic policies that lead to increasing inequality within society and diminishing freedom will ultimately result in increasing violence on all levels (2003, p. 381). The authors conclude that all forms of violence are connected and reflective of the cycle:

> The violence that we experience in our inner cities is linked to the international structural violence and institutional violence experienced in remote areas of the world. As people are victimized in countries on the periphery of the world system, they create an economic and political disadvantage for those dominated in the center counties (p. 389).

Conclusion

In this chapter, we have examined a sample of historical and contemporary theories that attempt to identify and examine social factors and processes and structural covariates used to predict and explain violence in society. The theories we examine include interpersonal as well as institutional and structural explanations. Both mainstream sociological and humanist/critical schools of thought are reviewed. Most mainstream theories generally presume that basic social agreement or consensus is reached over matters of right and wrong as is delineated in criminal law. Underlying the consensual view of society is the belief that positivism or use of the scientific method will help to discover the causes of violence and the development of solutions and subsequent social policies to prevent or control violence. Humanistic/critical criminological theories raise questions pertaining to this consensual view and set of assumptions. These theories take the position that violence is often a product of unequal power relations and clashing interests among different groups in society. Some groups have control—specifically, economic and political control—over others. Those groups with the most power are able to determine existing definitions of violence and enforce adherence to such definitions. Scholars working in this tradition look for hidden agendas and latent consequences; they look for evidence of nationalism, partisanism, classism, racism, gender bias, and discrimination of any kind. Unfortunately, many of the classical and contemporary criminological theories—consensual and humanistic/critical alike—that are used to explain the broadest category of crime in society have not been focused on violence per se, except in relatively few applications of theories that consider interpersonal criminal violence such as murder, rape, robbery, and assault. (This also holds true for the biological and psychological paradigms, discussed in Chapter 8.) Most of these theories have not, however, been applied to violence beyond the more traditional definitions of interpersonal criminal violence.

As noted in Chapter 1, definitions of violence are subject to numerous interpretations and perhaps aside from the limited official definitions of criminal violence, no single definition of violence has been proffered that meets with broad agreement or acceptance. No definition successfully captures the complexities of its many forms and contexts. While there are some specific categories of institutional violence such as intimate partner violence and domestic violence (Chapters 3 and 4) that have theoretical orientations focused specifically on these types of violence (e.g., critical feminist theory [Schwendinger and Schwendinger, 1983; Hagan, 1989]), this is not the case for many other types of violence (Zahn, Brownstein, and Jackson, 2004). This criticism of theories of violence has been made by several criminologists over the years (e.g., see Voigt, et al., 1994) and more recently by Margaret Zahn and her associates (2004) who argue that most theories of violence in existence still see violence as a subset of criminal or deviant behavior as opposed to a specific phenomenon to be studied based on its own merits. They suggest that the study of violent behavior as part of overall criminal or deviant behavior has some inherent problems. Most studies of violence, for example, imply that the behavior in question is not normative, whereas in reality violent behavior is, in many instances, part and parcel of given subcultures and cultures and is not always against the law (take for example, on the institutional-level parental spanking of children or abuse of women or state sanctioned capital punishment). Likewise, there is an inability of traditional general theories of crime and deviance to differentiate adequately between interpersonal, institutional, and structural forms of violence within single theories (Barak, 2003; Iadicola and Shupe, 2003).

Increasingly, theoretical efforts in the field of criminology appear to be moving in the direction of theory integration (Zahn, et al., 2004, pp. 254–255). This, in some instances, has held promise in efforts to focus attention on the multi-sided nature of theories of violence that have gone beyond the narrow scope of past theories. For example, rather than looking narrowly at intimate partner violence or inner-city youth violence as exclusively interpersonal forms of violence, we can expand the linkages of processes across levels of analysis and combine several different theoretical lines of thought into more "general" theories of violence. This more integrative approach can help resolve earlier attempts to explain violence within more restrictive traditional "criminological" theories.

The future of the study of violence no doubt hinges on the ability of criminologists and other social scientists to develop more comprehensive "theories of violence." The theoretical and methodological issues are many including but not limited to: (1) issues related to levels of analysis—interpersonal, institutional, and structural; (2) issues of conceptual definitions of violence; (3) issues of the measurement of violence; (4) issues of explaining individual and collective violence; and (5) issues of distinguishing legal and extralegal forms violence. With relatively few specific theories of violence outside the realm of criminal violence in existence, it is not surprising that scholars have been calling for more theoretical attention and research on violence. Zahn and her colleagues (2004), conclude: "In a society now at war against terror, where homicide rates are far higher than in other developed nations, and where violence against women remains a pressing problem, the need to advance violence theory with a coherent foundation of evidence could not be greater" (p. 261).

References

Adams, D. (2009). Predisposing childhood factors for men who kill their intimate partners. *Journal of Victims and Offenders, 4*(3), 215–229.

Agnew, R. (1990). The origins of delinquent events: An examination of offender accounts. *Journal of Research in Crime and Delinquency, 27,* 267–294.

Agnew, R. (1992). Foundation for a general strain theory of crime and delinquency. *Criminology. 30,* 47–87.

Agnew, R. (2004). A general strain theory approach to violence. In M. Zahn, H. Brownstein, and S. Jackson (Eds.). *Violence: From Theory to Research.* Cincinnati, OH: Anderson, 37–54.

Agnew, R. (2006). *Pressured into Crime: An Overview of General Strain Theory.* Los Angeles: Roxbury Publishing Company.

Akers, Ronald L., and Sellers, Christine S. (2009). *Criminological Theories: Introduction, Evaluation, and Application.* New York, NY: Oxford University Press.

Akers, R. L., and Sellers, C. S. (2004). *Criminological Theories: Introduction, Evaluation, and Application,* Los Angeles, CA: Roxbury Publishers.

Akers, R., and Silverman, A.L. (2004). "Toward a social learning model of violence and terrorism." In Zahn, M. A., Brownstein, H.H., and Jackson, S.L. *Violence: From Theory to Research.* LexisNexis Group: Anderson Publishing.

Allen, N.H. (1983). Homicide followed by suicide: Los Angeles, 1970–1979. *Suicide and Life-Threatening Behavior, 13,* 155–165.

Anderson, E. (1994). The code of the streets. *Atlantic Magazine*, May.

Anderson, E. (1999). *Code of the Street: Decency, Violence and the Moral Life of the Inner City.* New York: Norton.

Bao, W., Haas, A., and Pi, Y. (2004). Life Strain, Negative Emotions, and Delinquency: An Empirical Test of General Strain Theory in the People's Republic of China. *International Journal of Offender Therapy and Comparative Criminology*, 48, 281–297.

Barak, G. (2003). *Violence and Nonviolence: Pathways to Understanding.* Thousands Oaks, CA: Sage.

Barak, G., and Bohm, R. H. (1989). Crime of the Homeless or the Crime of Homelessness: A Self Reflective, Neo-Marxist Analysis of Crime and Social Control. Paper presented at American Society of Criminology, Montreal, Canada.

Barrile, L., and Slone, N. (2012). Corporate Violence: The EPA's Criminalization and Control of Environmental Destruction. In D.W. Harper, L. Voigt, and W.E. Thornton (Eds.). *Violence: Do We Know It When We See It?* Durham, NC: Carolina Academic Press, 323–340.

Black, D.A., et al. (1999). Partner, Child Abuse Risk Factors Literature Review. *National Network of Family Resiliency.* Retrieved from: http://www.nnh.org/risk.

Black, D. (2004). Violent Structures. In M.A. Zahn, H.H. Brownstein, and S.L. Jackson. *Violence: From Theory to Research.* New Providence, NJ: LexisNexis/Anderson Publishing, 145–158.

Blau, J., and Blau, P. (1982). The cost of Inequality: Metropolitan Structure and Violent Crime. *American Sociological Review*, 47, 114–129.

Blumstein, A., and Wallman, J. (2000). (Eds.). *The Crime Drop in America.* Cambridge University Press, 45–96.

Bottcher, J. (2001). Social practices of gender: How gender relates to delinquency in the everyday lives of high risk youths. *Criminology, 39*(4), 893–932.

Burgess, R. L., and Akers, R. L. (1968). Differential association-reinforcement theory of criminal behavior. *Social Problems, 14*, 128–147.

Burns, R.G., and Lynch, M.J. (2004). *Environmental Crime: A Sourcebook.* New York: LFB Scholarly.

Bursik, R.J. (1984). Urban Dynamics and Ecological Studies of Delinquency, *Social Forces* 63, 393–413.

Bursik, R.J., and Grasmick, H.G. (1993). *Neighborhoods and Crime.* New York: Lexington.

Burski, R.J. (2004). Social Disorganization and Violence. In M.A. Zahn, H.B. Brownstein, and S. L. Jackson (Eds.). *Violence: From Theory to Research*, Anderson Publishing, 91–120.

Chamblis, W. (1973). The Saints and the Roughnecks. *Society* 11, 24–31.

Chesney-Lind, M., and Pasko, L. (2004). *The Female Offender: Girls, Women, and Crime.* Thousand Oaks, CA: Sage.

Clarke, R.V. (1995). Situational Crime Prevention: Achievements and Challenges. In M. Tonry and D.P. Farrington (Eds.). *Building a Safer Society: Strategic Approaches to Crime Prevention, Crime and Justice: A Review of Research*, 19. Chicago: University of Chicago Press.

Cloward, R., and Ohlin, L. (1960). *Delinquency and Opportunity: A Theory of Delinquent Gangs.* New York: Free Press.

Cohen, A. K. (1955). *Delinquent Boys: The Culture of the Gang.* Glencoe, IL: Free Press.

Cohen, J., and Tita, G. (1999). Spatial Diffusion in Homicide: Exploring a General Methods of Detecting Spatial Diffusion Processes. *Journal of Quantitative Criminology,* 15(4), 451–493.

Cohen, L.E., and Felson, M. (1979). Social Change and Crime Rate Trends: A Routine Activity Approach. *American Sociological Review,* 44, 588–608.

Cohen, L.E., Felson, M., and Land, K.C. (1980). Property Crime Rates in the United States: A Macrodynamic Analysis 1947–77 with Ex Ante Forecasts in the Mid-1980s. *American Journal of Sociology,* 86, 90–118.

Comstock, G., and Scharrer, E. (1999). *Television, What's On, Who's Watching and What It Means.* San Diego, CA: Academic Press.

Cork, D. (1999). Examining Space Time Interactions in City-Level Homicide Data: Crack Markets and the Diffusion of Guns among Youth. *Journal of Quantitative Criminology,* 15, 379–405.

Cook, P.J., and Moore, M.H. (1999). Guns, Gun Control and Homicide. In M. D. Smith and M.A. Zahn (Eds.). *Studying and Prevention Homicide: Issues and Challenges.* Thousand Oaks, CA: Sage Publications.

Cornish, D., and Clarke, R. (1987). Understanding Crime Displacement: An Explanation of Rational Choice Theory. *Criminology,* 25(4), 933–949.

Dabbs, Jr., J. M., and Morris, R. (1990) Testosterone, social class and antisocial behavior in a sample of 4,462 men. *Psychological Science,* 1(3), 209–211.

Daly, M., and Wilson, M. (1988). *Homicide.* New York: Aldine de Gruyder.

Dobash, R.E., and Dobash, R.P. (1992). *Women, Violence and Social Change.* New York: Routledge.

Durkheim, E. (1893, reprinted in 1960). *The Division of Labor in Society.* Trans. G. Simpson. New York: Free Press.

Durkheim, E. (1895, reprinted in 1966). *The Rules of the Sociological Method.* (8th ed.). Chicago: University of Chicago Press.

Durkheim, E. (1897, reprinted in 1951). *Suicide.* Trans. J. R. Spaulding & G. Simpson. New York: Free Press.

Easteal, P. (1994). Homicide-suicides between sexual intimates: An Australian study. *Suicide and Life-Threatening Behavior, 24,* 140–151.

Felson, L. (1987). Routine Activities and Crime Prevention in the Developing Metropolis. *Criminology,* 25(4), 911–932.

Felson, M. (2004). The Basic Routine Activity Approach to Crime Analysis. In M.A. Zahn, H.B. Brownstein, and S. L. Jackson (Eds.). *Violence: From Theory to Research,* Anderson Publishing, 121–130.

Felson, R. B., Deane, G., and Armstrong. D. P. (2008). Do theories of crime or violence explain race differences in delinquency? *Social Science Research, 37*(2), 624–641.

Felson, R.B., and Osgood, W. (2008). Violent Crime. In E. Goode (Ed.). *Out of Control: Assessing the General Theory of Crime.* Stanford, California: Stanford University Press, 160–172.

Ferri, E. (1917). *Criminal Sociology*. Trans J. Kellet and J. Lisle. Boston: Little Brown.

Freese, J., Li, J. C. A., and Wade, L. D. (2003). The potential relevance of biology to social inquiry. *Annual Review of Sociology, 29*, 233–256.

Gelsthorpe. L. (2004) Back to basics in crime control: weaving in women. *Critical Review of International Social and Political Philosophy*. 7(2), 76–103.

Gillespie, C.K. (1989). *Justifiable Homicide: Battered Women, Self-Defense and the Law*. Columbus: Ohio State University.

Glueck, S., and Glueck, E. (1930). *Five Hundred Criminal Careers*. New York: Knopf.

Glueck, S., and Glueck, E. (1964). *Ventures in Criminology: Collected Recent Papers*. London: Tavistock Publications.

Cohen, J., and Tita, G. (1999). Diffusion in Homicide: Exploring a General Method for Detecting Spatial Diffusion. *Journal of Quantitative Criminology, 15*, 451–493.

Goode, E. (Ed.). (2008). *Out of Control: Assessing the General Theory of Crime*. Stanford, CA: Stanford University Press.

Goode, E. (2008). "Out of control? An introduction to the general theory of crime." In E. Goode (Ed.), Out *of Control: Assessing the General Theory of Crime*. Stanford, CA: Stanford University Press.

Gottfredson, M., and Hirschi, T. (1990). *A General Theory of Crime*. Stanford, CA: Stanford University Press.

Guerry, A. (1833). Essai sur la statistique morale. Paris.

Guerry, A. (1831). Letter to Quetelet, September 11, 1831. In A. Quetelet, *Research on the Propensity for Crime at Different Ages*, 1984. Cincinnati: Anderson.

Hagan, J. (1989). *Structural Criminology*. New Brunswick, NJ: Rutgers University Press.

Hagan, J., McCarthy, B., and Foster, H. (2002). A gendered theory of delinquency and despair in the life course. *Acta Sociologica, 45*, 37–46.

Harper, D. W., Voigt, L., and Thornton, W. E. (2004). Murder in the city: Do we have a witness? American Society of Criminology presentation in Nashville, TN.

Harper, D. W., and Voigt, L. (2007). Homicide followed by suicide: An integrated theoretical perspective. *Homicide Studies, 11*(4), 295–318.

Harper, D.W., and Voigt, L. (2012). Intimate Partner Homicide Followed by Suicide: A Case of Gendered Violence. In D.W. Harper, L. Voigt, and W.E. Thornton (Eds.). *Violence: Do We Know It When We See It?* Durham, NC: Carolina Academic Press, 45–65.

Hawkins, D. (1990). Explaining the black homicide rate. *Journal of Interpersonal Violence, 5*, 151–163.

Hawley, A.H. (1950). *Human Ecology*. New York: Ronald Press

Heimer, K., and De Coster, S. (1999). The gendering of violent delinquency. *Criminology, 37*(2), 277–317.

Herrenkohol, T.L., Huang, B., Tajima, E.A., and Whitney, S.D. (2003). Examining the Link between Child Abuse and Youth Violence: An Analysis of Mediating Mechanisms. *Journal of Interpersonal Violence*, 18, 1189–1208.

Hirschi, T. (1969). *The Causes of Delinquency*. Berkeley: University of California Press

Hirschi, T., and Gottfredson, M. 1987. *Causes of White Collar Crime*. Criminology 25(4), 949–974.

Hirschi, T., and Rudisill, D. (1976). The Great American Search: Causes of Crime, 1876–1976. *Annals of the American Academy of Political and Social Sciences*, 423(1), 14–22.

Hipp, J.R. (2007). Income Inequality, Race and Place: Does the Distribution of Race and Class in Neighborhoods Affect Crime Rates? *Criminology*, 45(3), 645–697.

Hood-Williams, J. (2001). Gender, masculinities and crime: From structures to psyches. *Theoretical Criminology*, 5(1), 37–60.

Iadicola, P., and Shupe, A. (2003). *Violence, Inequality, and Human Freedom*. Boulder, CO: Rowman & Littlefield Publishers.

Jefferson, T. (1996). Introduction. *British Journal of Criminology Special Issue, Masculinities and Crime, 33*(6), 337–347.

Jeffery, C.R. (1959). An Integrated Theory of Crime and Criminal Behavior. *Journal of Criminal Law, Criminology and Police Science*, 49, 533–552.

Katz, J. (1988). *Seductions of Crime*. New York: Basic Books.

Kennedy, L.W., and Forde, D.R. (1990). Routine Activities and Crime: An Analysis of Victimization in Canada. *Criminology*, 28(1), 137–152.

Kubrin, C.E., and Herting, J.R. (2003). Neighborhood Correlates of Homicide Trends: An Analysis using Growth-Curve modeling. *The Sociological Quarterly, 43*(3), 329–350.

Kubrin, C.E., and Weitzer, R. (2003). New Directions in Social Disorganization Theory. *Journal of Research in Crime and Delinquency, 40*(4), 374–402.

Krug, E.G., Dahlberg, L.L., Mercy, J.A., Zwi, A.B., and Lozano, R. (2002). *World Health Report on Violence and Health*. Geneva: World Health Organization.

LaFree, G., Dass, K.A., and O'Day, P. (1992). Race and Crime in Postwar America: Determinants of African-American and White Rates, 1957–1988. *Criminology*, 30, 158–185.

LaFree, G. (1999). Declining Violent Crime Rates in the 1990s: Predicting Crime Booms and Busts. *Annual Review of Sociology*, 25, 145–168.

Land, K., McCall, P., and Cohen, L. (1990). Structural Covariates of Homicide Rates: Are there any Variances across Time and Social Space? *American Journal of Sociology*, 95(4), 922–963.

Landau, S.F. (1998). Crime, Subjective Social Stress and Support Indicators, and Ethnic Origin. The Israeli Experience. *Justice Quarterly*, 15, 243–272.

Lewis, O. (1966). *The Culture of Poverty*. Scientific American, October

Lynch, M.J., and Groves, W.B. (1989). *A Primer in Radical Criminology*. New York: Harrow and Heston.

Lynch, M.J., Michalowski, R.J., and Groves, W.B. (2000). *The New Primer in Radical Criminology: Critical Perspectives on Crime, Power and Identity*. Monsey, NY: Criminal Justice Press.

Lynch, M.J. (2004). Toward A Radical Ecology of Urban Violence. In M.A. Zahn, H.B. Brownstein, and S. L. Jackson (Eds.). *Violence: From Theory to Research*, Anderson Publishing, 103–120.

Marx, K. (1848/1864). Theories of Surplus Value. In T. B. Bottomore and M. Rubel (Eds.). *Karl Marx: Selected Writings in Sociology and Social Philosophy*. New York: McGraw Hill.

Mazerolle, P., Piquero, R., and Capowich, G. (2003). Explaining the links between strain, situational and dispositional anger, and crime. *Youth and Society, 35*, 131–157.

Merton, R. K. (1938). Social structure and anomie. *American Sociological Review, 3*, 672–682.

Messerschmidt, J.W. (1986). *Capitalism, Patriarchy and Crime: Toward a Socialist Feminist Criminology*. Totowa, NJ: Rowman and Littlefield.

Messerschmidt, J. W. (1993). *Masculinities and Crime: Critique and Reconceptualization of Theory*. Lanham, MD: Rowman and Littlefield.

Messerschmidt, J. W. (1997). *Crime as Structured Action: Gender, Race, Class, and Crime in the Making*. Thousand Oaks, CA: Sage.

Messerschmidt, J.W. (2000). *Nine Lives: Adolescent Masculinities, the Body, and Violence*. Boulder, CO: Westview Press.

Messerschmidt, J. W. (2004). *Flesh and Blood: Adolescent Gender Diversity and Violence*. Lanham, MD: Rowman and Littlefield.

Messner, S. F. and Rosenfeld, R. (1997). *Crime and the American Dream*. Belmont CA: Wadsworth.

Messner, S.F. (1983). Regional and Racial Effects on the Urban Homicide Rate: The Subculture of Violence Revisited. *The American Journal of Sociology*, 88(5), 997–1007.

Messner, S.F., Anselin, L., Baller, R.D., Hawkins, D.F., Deane, G., and Tolnay, S.E. (1999). Spatial Patterning of County Homicide Rates: An Application of Exploratory Spatial Data Analysis. *Journal of Quantitative Criminology*, 15, 423–450.

Miller, J. (2002). The strengths and limits of "doing gender" for understanding street crime. *Theoretical Criminology*, 6(4), 433–460.

Miethe, T.D., Stafford, M.C., and Long, J.S. (1987). Social Differentiation in Criminal Victimization: A Test of Routine Activities/Lifestyle theories. *American Sociological Review*, 52, 189–194.

Newburn, T., and Stanko, E. A. (Eds.). (1994). *Just Boys Doing Business? Men, Masculinities and Crime*. London: Routledge.

Park, R.E., and Burgess, E.W. (1925). *The City*. Chicago: University of Chicago Press.

Peterson, R.D., and Krivo, L.J. (2005). Macrostructural Analyses of Race, Ethnicity, and Violent Crime: Recent Lessons and New Directions for Research. *Annual Review of Sociology*, 31, 331–56.

Pfohl, S.J. (1985). *Images of Deviance and Social Control: A Sociological History*. New York: McGraw Hill.

Quetelet, A. (1831/1984). *Research on the Propensity for Crime at Different Ages*. Trans. By S.F. Sylvester, Cincinnati: Anderson.

Quinney, R. (1977). *Class, State and Crime*. New York: David McKay.

Reckless, W., and Dinitz, S. (1972). *The Prevention of Juvenile Delinquency*. Columbus, OH: Ohio State University Press.

Regehr, C., and Roberts, A.R. (2010). Intimate Partner Violence. In A.W. Burgess, C. Regehr and A.R. Roberts (Eds.). *Victimology: Theories and Applications*, Boston: Jones and Bartlett Publishers, 197–223.

Reiman, J.H. (1984). *The Rich Get Richer and the Poor Get Prison: Ideology, Class and Criminal Justice*. New York: Wiley.

Reiss, A. J. (1951). "Delinquency as the failure of personal and social controls." *American Sociological Review,* 16, 196–207.

Sampson, R. J. (2012). *Great American City: Chicago and the Enduring Neighborhood Effect.* Chicago: The University of Chicago Press.

Sampson, R. J. (1986). Crime in cities: The effects of formal and informal social control. *Crime and Justice, Volume. 8: Communities and Crime.* Chicago: University of Chicago Press, 271–311.

Sampson, R.J. (1987). Urban Black Violence: The Effects of Male Joblessness and Family Disruption. *American Journal of Sociology,* 93(2), 348–382.

Sampson, R. J. (2001). Crime and Public Safety: Insights from Community-Level Perspectives on Social Capital. In S. Saegert, J.P. Thompson and M.R. Warren (Eds.). *Social Capital and Poor Communities.* New York: Russell Sage Foundation.

Sampson, R.J., and Groves, W.B. (1989), Community Structure and Crime: Testing Social Disorganization Theory. *American Journal of Sociology,* 94, 774–802.

Schwendinger, H., and Schwendinger, J.S. (1985). *Adolescent Subcultures and Delinquency.* New York: Praeger.

Sellin, T., and Wolfgang, M. (1964). *The Measurement of Delinquency.* New York: Wiley.

Shaw, C. R., and McKay, H. D. (1931). *Social Factors in Delinquency.* Chicago: University of Chicago Press.

Shaw, C. R., and McKay, H. D. (1942/1969). *Juvenile Delinquency in Urban Areas.* Chicago: University of Chicago Press.

Sheldon, W. (1949). *Varieties of Delinquent Youth: An Introduction to Constitutional Psychiatry.* New York: Harper.

Skogan, W. (1986). Fear of Crime and Neighborhood Change. In A. Reiss and M. Tonry (Eds.) *Communities and Crime.* Chicago: University of Chicago Press, 191–232.

Skogan, W. (1990). Disorder *and Decline: Crime and the Spiral of Decay in American Neighborhoods.* New York: Free Press, 15–35.

Smith, E.L., and Farole, Jr., D.J. (2009). *Profile of Intimate Partner Violence Cases in Large Urban Counties.* Bureau of Justice Statistics, NCJ 228356.

Straus, M., and Gelles, R. (1980). *Behind Closed Doors: Violence in the American Family.* Garden City, NJ: Anchor/Doubleday.

Sutherland, E.H. (1939). Mental Deficiency and Crime. In K. Young (Ed.). *Social Attitudes.* New York: Henry Holt.

Sutherland, E.H. (1940). White Collar Criminality. *American Sociological Review,* 5, February, 1–12.

Sutherland, E. H. (1945). Is 'White Collar Crime' Crime? *American Sociological Review,* 10, 132–139.

Sutherland, E.H. (1949). *White Collar Crime.* New York: Holt, Rinehart and Winston.

Sutherland, E. H., and Cressey, D. R. (1978). *Fundamentals of Criminology.* Philadelphia: J. B. Lippincott.

Sykes, G.M., and Matza, D. (1952). "Techniques of neutralization: A theory of delinquency." *American Sociological Review,* 22, 664–670.

Tarde, G. (1890, reprinted in 1903). *The Laws of Imitation (Les lois de l'imitation).* Trans E.C. Parsons. New York: Holt.

Tedeschi, J., and Felson, R. B. (1994), *Violence, Aggression, and Coercive Actions.* Washington, DC: American Psychological Association.

Thornhill, R., and Palmer, C. T. (2000). *The Natural History of Rape: Biological Bases of Sexual Coercion.* Cambridge, MA: MIT Press.

Toennies, F. (1887, reprinted in 1957). *Community and Society.* Trans. C. P. Loomis (Ed.). East Lansing MI: Michigan State University.

Thornberry, T. P., Lizotte, A. J., Krohn, N. D., Fransworth, M., and Jang, S. J. (1994). Delinquent peers, beliefs, and delinquent behavior: A longitudinal test of interaction theory. *Criminology,* 32: 47–84.

Thrasher, F.M. (1927/1966). *The Gang: A Study of 1,213 Gangs in Chicago.* 2nd. Abridged ed. Chicago: University of Chicago Press. (Originally published in 1927).

Turk, A. (1969). *Criminality and the Legal Order.* Chicago: Rand McNally.

Udry, J. R. (1995). Sociology and biology: What biology do sociologists need to know? *Social Forces, 73*(4), 1267–1278.

U.S. Census Bureau. (2010). *Annual estimates of the resident population by sex, race, and Hispanic origin for the United States,* April 1, 2000 to July 1, 2009.

Vold, G. (1958/1979). *Theoretical Criminology.* New York: Oxford University Press.

Warr, M. (2002). *Companions in Crime: The Social Aspects of Criminal Conduct.* Cambridge, UK: Cambridge University Press.

Wasserman, G.A., and Seracini, A.M. (2001). Family Risk Factors and Intervention. In R. Loeber and D.P. Farrington, (Eds.). *Child Delinquents: Development, Intervention, and Service Needs.* Thousand Oaks, CA: Sage.

Weber, M. (1958). *The Protestant Ethic and the Spirit of Capitalism.* (Originally published 1904–05). New York: Charles Scribner Sons.

Wilcox, P., Land, K.C., and Hunt, S.A. (2003). *Criminal Circumstances: A Dynamic Multicontextual Criminal Opportunity Theory.* New York: Aldine de Gruyter.

Wilson, W. J. (1987). *The Truly Disadvantaged: The Inner City, the Underclass and Public Policy.* Chicago: University of Chicago Press.

Wilson, W. J. (1996). *When Work Disappears: The World of the New Urban Poor.* New York: Knopf.

Winlow, S. (2001). *Badfellas: Crime, Tradition and New Masculinities.* New York: Berg.

Wintemute, G.J. (2000). Guns and Gun Violence. In A. Blumstein and J. Wallman. (Eds.). *The Crime Drop in America.* Cambridge University Press, 45–96.

Wolfgang, M., and Ferracuti, F. (1967). *The Subculture of Violence: Toward an Integrated Theory of Criminology.* London: Tavistock.

Wright, J. D., and Rossi, P. H. (1986). *Armed and Considered Dangerous: A Survey of Felons and Their Firearms.* New York: Aldine de Gruyter.

Zahn, M.A., Brownstein, H.H., and Jackson, S.L. (2004). *Violence: From Theory to Research.* New Providence, NJ: Lexis Nexis/Anderson.

Chapter 10

Is Peace Possible?

History appears to be replete with images of violence, e.g., prehistoric evidence of homicide, tribal feuds, as well as ancient and contemporary evidence of warfare and genocide. It seems a little presumptuous to think that a solution to the problem of violence might be available. In John Lennon's song, *Imagine*, he conjures up a world where there is "nothing to kill or die for ... all the people living life in peace." In his lyrics he ponders over why peace in the world remains a wishful ideal and not a reality.

Yet as we know, violence is not as pervasive either historically or presently across social space and among individuals as many of us may have been led to believe (Pinker, 2011; Muchembled, 2011). For example, whole civilizations that were once considered notoriously violent are now regarded to be among the most peaceful on earth.[1] Many countries of the world have eschewed warfare for centuries. War is uniformly denounced and condemned. All major world religions shun at least non-provoked violence and embrace pacifism in principle. Pacifism is institutionalized in all major religious groups as is conscientious objection to war (even though, historically, in actual wartime being an objector has not been without danger of imprisonment). Other forms of state-sanctioned violence also appears to have declined (e.g., according to Amnesty International most nations of the world no longer practice or accept capital punishment).

Many cities worldwide have exceptionally low murder rates and even in countries and cities with high rates of murder, the trends suggest that the rates are not distributed evenly across all social spaces but represent isolated cases. At an individual level nonviolence as

---

1. E.g., the Viking expansion or the so-called Viking Age, between 780 and 1070, was associated with both destructive and positively impressive consequences (Jones, 1968); the realms of the Vikings included Norway, Sweden and Denmark, which are currently among the most peaceful nations on earth (Sawyer, 1982, p. 6). What ended Viking violence? Sawyer suggests that the culture that supported raiding and plundering was changed by both endogenous and exogenous forces.

a way of life is possible and is practiced. Most people even without a pacifist's commitment to nonviolence live out their lives nonviolently. Police officers, who are armed, sometimes spend their whole career without drawing their weapon or discharging it in the line of duty. Clearly there must be something within these instances of nonviolence that suggest some promising resolutions and opportunities for peace.

Is peace a possibility? We believe that a more peaceful and less violent world is possible. A peaceful world, however, depends on our ability to recognize human rights and address the needs of human beings as well as on our willingness to respect and trust one another and commit to nonviolent resolutions to problems. This chapter serves as a concluding comment to our book. It begins with a summary of some of the key observations regarding the problem of violence treated in the preceding chapters and ends with a consideration of some promising pathways to nonviolence. We close our book by highlighting altruistic humanism, resilience, mutualism, and communitarianism, which are all predicated on restorative justice processes including conflict resolution and the affirmation and practice of human rights principles.

Violence as Sanctioned and Unsanctioned Harm

The most commonly recognized definitions of violence and corresponding system of classification and measurement of violence, i.e., criminal violence, usually ignore institutional and structural forms of violence and their consequent harms, which are part and parcel of the way in which societies past and present have been organized and stratified both locally and globally. For example, when mediated attention is focused almost exclusively on interpersonal acts of violence of the relatively powerless (such as in street criminal violence) and drawn away from the acts of violence of the relatively powerful (such as corporate safety violations or environmental degradation or state-sanctioned violence), a picture of violence emerges that is relatively incomplete! It is important to consider the reality that even if all of the different official measures and statistics related to violence are brought together, they would not begin to capture the human tragedy that has come from institutional and structural harm to human beings either nationally or world-wide. To emphasize, classifications of violence that we are all too familiar with does not provide much insight into the causes of violence or the ways they can be prevented, nor does it shed light on the connection between the visible and invisible forms of harms—interpersonal, institutional, and global. In short, recognition of violence as *harm* to human existence calls for an alternative vantage point that must include both the visible and invisible, the sanctioned and unsanctioned forms of harm across all levels!

The Need for a Holistic Understanding of Violence and Harm

A holistic understanding of violence as harm means that we acknowledge harm perpetrated at all levels: interpersonal, institutional, and structural (Iadicola and Shupe,

2003; Barak 2007). On the interpersonal level the focus is on what happens between people acting in their private lives without particular regard given to any occupational roles or associations with any formal institutions (e.g., homicide, rape and sexual assault, robbery, assault, corporal punishment, and verbal abuse, threat, and intimidation).

The institutional level focuses on what happens within an institutional context vis-à-vis the actions of institutional agents and others. For instance institutional harms include: familial harm—such as child abuse, elder abuse, sibling abuse, intimate partner abuse (it could be physical, sexual, psychological, or as a result of neglect); economic harm—corporate and workplace, such as distributing defective products or unhealthy work conditions or denying loans to poor people or not insuring some people; school-related harms—everything from hazing new students to administrative arbitrary "labeling" of success/failure, to administering drugs to misbehaving students, to warehousing students and failing to teach basic literacy skills; religious institutional harms or abuse in the name of religion—everything from religion-based terrorism to abuse of individuals, to misuse of people's life savings in the form of donations; military related harms—ranging from petty hazing of recruits to war crimes (violation of human rights); and state/government harms—ranging from abuse by authority of fundamental human rights to discrimination based on class, ethnicity/race, gender, and age in arrests, imprisonment, and executions.

The structural level (the underlying generative cause of interpersonal and institutional harms) focuses on what happens in the context of establishing, maintaining, extending, and/or resisting the hierarchical structures of privilege and inequality in society including direct and indirect harms committed in order to maintain the status quo/social order and to enforce social inequalities and hierarchies of privilege, which are carried out by authorities across the society. To enforce the social order, harms are created directly or indirectly by laws, policies and procedures that favor some people while disadvantaging others and ultimately fail to protect the human rights of people particularly of those who are the most vulnerable.

The available evidence on patterns of violence suggests that there is a connection between violence and social inequality (Iadicola and Shupe, 2003; Barak 2007). The more unequal the social order, the more violence will function to maintain the status quo. The national defense system as well as the criminal justice system ultimately protects the interests of the most powerful in society. The definitions of enemies or criminals alike function to socially dehumanize and demoralize human beings. Theories of war and crime are designed to distract attention from the harmful activities of the most powerful and draw attention to the most poor by portraying them as the cause of all problems.

One of the great challenges that we face in realizing a more peaceful world is that people are generally more conscious of the political scripts and rhetorical references associated with solving "violence with violence" or finding "peace through war" rather than working for peace through cooperation or compromise or conflict resolution or ensuring "peace through meeting the needs of people." Ironically, the development of peaceful conflict resolution has gone hand-in-hand with technology for exercising violence (Heitmeyer and Hagan, 2003). In this modern age with our democratic and rational institutions and unprecedented wealth, we have created the possibility for the realization of global basic human rights and nonviolent existence and, at the same time, we have magnified our potential for violence through the use of new technologies, increases in social distance and deepened inequality of members of society, and the development of a science of human repression and control!

Yet, future peace both globally and locally ultimately depends not on "peace through violence," but on our individual and collective courage to stand up for justice. Some hopeful signs for our future include renewed interest in restorative justice processes, increased emphasis and use of conflict resolution on individual, national and international levels in an effort to find a more lasting peace, and growing affirmation of human rights principles.

While the list of courageous human beings over time who have stood for peace would be much too long to reconstruct here, two individuals whose lives, deeds, and words continue to inspire people around the world to believe that peace is possible are: Mohandas Gandhi and Martin Luther King, Jr. They are both particularly known for their commitment to nonviolence as an instrument of social change (see Box 10.1 and Box 10.2 for brief overviews of their respective life stories and contributions).

Pathways to Peace

The pathways to peace begin with human qualities and abilities that support peace such as altruistic humanism, mutualism, communitarianism, and resilience. Aaron Beck (1999) in his book, *Prisoners of Hate: The Cognitive Basis of Anger, Hostility, and Violence* argues that altruism exists on a continuum ranging from demonstrating a kind gesture or providing a basic service to sacrificing or risking one's life for the sake of another. He claims that altruistic humanism or the human qualities of empathy, cooperation, and reason, which are intrinsic to human nature, can supply the building blocks for pro-social structures such as restorative justice. He suggests that there is evidence of a brighter side to human nature that can be gleamed from countless surveys, interviews, and studies showing that human beings have altruistic qualities that are routinely expressed in acts of selflessness and cooperation that can override any hostile tendencies. Nonviolence necessitates practicing *mutual rituals* (e.g., empathy, cooperation, caring, nurturing, and loving) as opposed to *adversarial rituals* (e.g., extreme individualism, competition for the sake of competition, and survival of the fittest or domination mentality that is engendered by combat or war, trials, ordeals, and punishments) that inhibit freedom. *Communitarianism*, which is rooted in a strong sense of community, is derived through strong social ties and bonding that provides a balance between needs of individuals and concerns of civil liberties and a strong connection to community with respect and trust of community members. Communitarianism does not rely on the adversarial processes as a first resort to resolve conflicts; rather, it is built on a bottom-up or grassroots justice such as restorative justice not a top-down approach justice such as criminal justice (Etzioni, 1992). *Resilience* or strength in terms of self-reliance or self-help and commitment to improvement is critical to reversing a sense of powerlessness. Victor LaCerva's "Pathways to Peace" (1996) lists ten important steps or protective factors (which spell out *Peacemaker*):

- Practice positive discipline
- Expand emotional fluency
- Approach conflict with a win-win attitude
- Create connections
- Emphasize essential values

Box 10.1 Mohandas Gandhi

"I am prepared to die, but there is no cause for which I am prepared to kill." Mohandas Karamchand Gandhi (1869–1948) was born into a wealthy Hindu family over a decade after the Indian sub-continent had become a British crown colony in 1857. After finishing high school Gandhi moved to London and received his law degree and after a brief return to India, in 1893 he took a position with a group of wealthy Mohammedan merchants in South Africa. The racially hostile climate of that country toward the Indian minority transformed him into an advocate for civil rights of the South African community. Here he introduced his principle of non-violent resistance, *Satyagraha*, which roughly translates as truth or firmness. His agitation was successful in getting South Africa to reform their anti-Indian legislation (Settel, 1995, p. 8). Impressed by Gandhi's success in South Africa, the Indian Parliament asked him to return to India and develop plans for their own self government. Over the years Gandhi conducted a number of satyagraha campaigns that got him jailed by the British authorities. Due largely to Gandhi's pacifist strategy in resisting British rule, independence finally came. Gandhi retreated to the peace and isolation of his ashram (commune). As a result of his efforts to promote Hindu-Muslim friendship he invoked the wrath of Hindu extremists who viewed the Muslims as enemies. Gandhi was assassinated in 1948 by a Hindu fanatic (Settel, p. 9).

The following two passages capture Gandhi's faith in the power of non-violence:

"Nonviolence is the greatest force at the disposal of mankind. It is mightier than the mightiest weapon of destruction devised by the ingenuity of man. Destruction is not the law of humans. Man lives freely

Gandhi, circa 1929

by his readiness to die, if need be, at the hands of his brother, never by killing him. Every murder or other injury, no matter for what cause, committed or inflicted on another is a crime against humanity" (Settel, p. 46).

"It is no nonviolence if we merely love those who love us. It is nonviolence only when we love those who hate us. I know how difficult it is to follow this grand law of love. But are not all great and good things difficult to do? Love of the hater is the most difficult of all. But by the grace of God, even this most difficult thing becomes easy to accomplish if we want to do it" (Settel, p. 53).

Source: Settel, T. (1995). *The Book of Gandhi Wisdom.* New York: Carol Publishing Group.

- Minimize media exposure
- Avoid victimization
- Keep celebrating diversity
- Engage in "bullyproofing"
- Reinforce resilience.

Building on essential humanistic qualities, a number of pathways to peace have been proposed including restorative justice, conflict resolution, and peacemaking criminology.

Box 10.2 Martin Luther King, Jr.

"I believe that unarmed truth and unconditional love will have the final word in reality. That is why right, temporarily defeated, is stronger than evil triumphant" (Classic Quotes, 2010: #9355). Dr. Martin Luther King, Jr. was a United States civil rights leader and minister who stressed pacifism and nonviolence as a means to achieve social justice (1929–1968). Influenced by his father, a prominent Baptist minister of the largest African American church in Atlanta, Ebenezer Baptist Church, and his grandfather, a leader in the early civil rights movement in Atlanta, Dr. King had significant role models for his potential as one of the major leaders in the nonviolent civil rights movement in the United States. After graduating from Morehouse College, he was admitted to Crozer Theological Seminary to pursue a bachelor of divinity degree where he was exposed to Gandhi's philosophy of nonviolence, among others. He went on to earn a doctorate in systematic theology at Boston University.

Dr. Martin Luther King, Jr. in Atlanta, 1966
(AP photo/staff)

King's life like Gandhi's was a journey along a path of collective resistance to injustice, not just for blacks but for all socially oppressed people. Inspired by the principles of nonviolence espoused by Gandhi, Dr. King professed civil disobedience as the best method to fight for civil rights (NAACP website). In his book, *Stride Toward Freedom* (1958) besides talking about the racial conditions in Montgomery, Alabama before, during and after the famous bus boycott where Rosa Parks was arrested and sent to jail on December 1, 1955, King described the book as "the chronicle of 50,000 Negroes who took to heart the principles of non-violence, who learned to fight for their rights with the weapon of love, and who in the process, acquired a new estimate of their own human worth." According to King, the bus boycott worked because the African Americans of Montgomery trusted their leaders' assertion that nonviolence was in essence active Christianity (King, 1958, p. 9). In his chapter "Pilgrimage to Nonviolence" he discusses the intellectual sources of his nonviolent philosophy and his belief that the goal is not to humiliate or defeat an opponent but win them through love to friendship (102).

Among his many great honors, Dr. King received the Nobel Peace Prize in 1964 for his tireless efforts against racial, social and economic injustice in this country and worldwide including war. Many people remember Dr. King for his historic speech, "I Have a Dream," delivered on August 28, 1963 at the Lincoln Memorial in the historic March on Washington for Jobs and Freedom. His speech is credited with mobilizing support for desegregation in the United States and prompted the 1964 Civil Rights Act. Dr. King was shot to death in April, 1968 while visiting Memphis, Tennessee to support the local black sanitary public workers' union. Congress honored him in 1983 by declaring the third Monday of every January as Martin Luther King, Jr. Day (NAACP website).

Table 10.1 Ancient and Current Patterns of Response to Harm and Violations

	Ancient Patterns	Current Patterns
Offense/Harm	Injury to victim and their families in the context of community	Violation of the law, injury to state
Parties	Victims, offenders, families, and community and community authorities	Offenders and government agents acting on behalf of the state
Goal	Repair damage, reestablish right relations, and integrate into community	Reduce future lawbreaking through rehabilitation, punishment, deterrence and/or incapacitation of offender

Source: Adapted from Van Ness and Strong, 1997.

Restorative Justice

Even though the term "restorative justice," which is presumed to have been coined relatively recently by Albert Eglash in 1977 in a piece entitled, "Beyond Restitution: Creative Restitution," it draws its roots from the early legal systems forming the foundation of Western law (i.e., Code of Hammurabi, Mosaic Law, Christian/Judaic Tradition, Roman Law, English Common Law, and American Justice). In their aboriginal forms all of these codes of law include consideration of the need for offenders and their families to settle with victims and their families. Although crime, particularly violent crime, was considered a breach of the common welfare suggesting that the community had an interest in—and responsibility for—addressing the wrong and punishing the offender, the offense was not considered primarily a crime against the state, as it is today (see Table 10.1).

Currently there are a number of definitions of restorative justice. For example, it has been defined broadly as encompassing "a growing social movement to institutionalize peaceful approaches to harm, problem-solving and violations of legal and human rights" that ranges from "international peacemaking tribunals such as Truth and Reconciliation Commission of South Africa to innovations within our criminal justice systems, schools, social services and communities." Further, rather than "privileging the law, professionals and the state, restorative resolutions engage those who are harmed, wrongdoers, and their affected communities in a search for solutions that promote repair, reconciliation and rebuilding relationships (Suffolk University, Center for Restorative Justice, 2007). John Braithwaite and Heather Strang (2001) claim that restorative justice represents a transformation of the values that underpin our typical responses to harms by rejecting vengeance and vindictiveness and supporting healing, reconciliation, and needs-meeting. Restorative justice in its most general formulation has to do with repairing harm caused by crime and the justice system (Calhoun and Pelech, 2010). It has also found utility in other contexts, for example, schools (Wachtel and Mirsky, 2009) and reconciliation among ethnic groups (Haider, 2009).

Restorative justice provides a philosophical and practical framework that has been proposed as an alternative to the traditional criminal justice system and current ways of thinking about offenders and victims. Howard Zehr (1990) writes:

> One of the impediments to our grasping such a concept of justice may be that deeply ingrained idea that what is required to do justice is dictated by natural and universally applicable moral principles. State punishment has become so familiar to us that we fail to realize that it is a *social convention* and that it is only in the past several centuries that people of Western societies have adopted it (p. 90).

Current policies and practices of criminal justice focus almost entirely on the offender as lawbreaker, ignoring almost everything except the questions of legal culpability and punishment. The government enacts laws and punishes those who violate them. To help put the restorative justice approach in context, Table 10.2 depicts the distinguishing characteristic of criminal justice and restorative justice.

In the criminal justice system, the criminal act is an act against the state—the state is officially the victim of a criminal offense. The actual victim, the one who has suffered direct harm or the community, which has also been harmed by the criminal act, do not have formal roles in the proceedings except where the state requires the victim to serve as a witness to bring a case forward.

The relatively powerful position of the state has led to the creation of due process safeguards (such as the presumption of innocence until proven guilty) that have been developed over the centuries to ensure fairness in how offenders are treated. A consequence of these process safeguards is that the alleged offender's posture is defensive (and often passive) during criminal proceedings while the government's posture is on the offensive to prove beyond a reasonable doubt that the defendant is guilty. The court room proceeding gives the state the leading role in proving that a law has been broken by the defendant and in determining what form of punishment should be imposed. This is how the process works, ideally.

The reality of the criminal justice system in the United States is not what is usually portrayed in popular media, in which most criminal cases are tried in formal court proceedings with a judge, jury, and cumbersome legal procedures that protect both victim and offender. The idealized battle is between prosecutor and defense attorney who struggle to convince a jury of the guilt or innocence of the defendant. This is not what occurs, however, in the overwhelming majority of criminal cases in the United States. Most criminal defendants plead guilty (often to a lesser charge) and thus most of the due process protections never come into play (Feinman, 2006).

The culmination of the criminal justice process is punishment, which represents the overriding response of the state and dominates all other alternatives. By ignoring the victim's needs and excluding the victim from the process, the victim is injured twice—once by the offender and then by the state. Moreover, retribution defined as *deserved punishment* for evil done underscores an important aspect of society's response to offenders, but it has two main shortcomings. First, the active party, the punisher, is the government; the offender is merely a passive recipient of punishment. Second, punishment that does not help repair the injuries caused by crime simply creates new injuries; now both the victim and the offender are injured.

This raises some serious questions regarding the effectiveness of the criminal justice system. For example, why does the criminal justice system seem so ineffective in its efforts to prevent criminal violence? From 1980 to 2010 the number of adults incarcerated in the United States has grown from approximately 500,000 to about 2.3 million, which far exceeds the population growth during this period (Glaze, 2011; Bureau of Justice Statistics, 1993; U.S. Census Bureau Abstracts, 2012). There has been an almost three fold increase in the rate of adults under criminal justice system supervision between 1980 and 2010. In 2010, about 5 million were under supervision in addition to the 2.3 million individuals who were incarcerated. The International Centre for Prison Studies in King's College, London found that as of May, 2011, over 10.1 million people are held in penal institutions worldwide. Of those convicted and sentenced, the United States has 2.29 million and China is next with 1.65 million. The United States has the highest prison population rate

Table 10.2 Contrasting Characteristics of Criminal Justice and Restorative Justice

	Criminal Justice	Restorative Justice
Nature of offense	The offense is exclusively defined as a legal violation.	The offense is defined holistically as a harmful act with physical, moral, social, economic, and political implications.
Nature of victim	The state is the official victim; the actual victim does not play a formal role in the proceedings except where the state requires the victim to serve as a witness to bring a case forward or testify against the offender.	The primary victim is the individual(s) that is most impacted by the offense; secondary victims include families, friends, & witnesses as well as the community where the violation occurred.
Focus of proceedings	The main focus is on the offender and the particular "past" offense and on establishing blame or determining guilt in order to determine an appropriate sentence.	The main focus is on repairing injuries and breached relationships with an emphasis on "making things right" and addressing the needs of victims, offenders, families, and the community to prevent "future" harm.
The nature of the proceeding	Criminal proceedings are assumed to be adversarial with action directed by the state and proxy professionals against the accused and where the victim and the community are generally excluded from the proceedings.	Restorative proceedings are assumed to be restorative through addressing the needs of victims and offenders as well as communities emphasizing participation of all those impacted, mutual responsibilities, and mutual aid and support.
Offender accountability	Offender accountability is owed to the state and society and is defined in terms of retribution (just deserts or deserved punishment) with little or no encouragement for repentance or forgiveness. The stigma of crime is not removable	All stakeholders (victims, offenders, and community) share responsibility through partnerships for action. Accountability is defined in terms of genuine understanding of the impact of harmful action, taking responsibility for the harm, apologizing and helping to "make things right." Stigma may be removed through reintegration.
The definition of justice	Justice is defined in terms of processes and procedures and ultimately the punishment of the offender. The CJ system values punishment that deters, rehabilitates, incapacitates, or denounces.	Justice is defined in terms of restitution, mediation, conflict resolution, and meeting the needs of all parties, which is the main goal measured by outcomes such as the relative satisfaction of all parties, degree of involvement of all relevant participants, & assuring safety and peace in the community.

in the world, 743 per 100,000 population, followed by Rwanda with 595 per 100,000 and Russia with 568 per 100,000. More than half of all countries in the study had rates below 150 per 100,000; U.S neighbors, Canada had 117 per 100,000 and Mexico had 200 per

100,000 (Walmsley, 2011). Even though the United States incarcerates more people than ever in its history and more people than any other country, the public at large still expresses fear and concern about crime (Sullivan and Tifft, 2005).

Moreover, we know that prisons actually make people worse, rather than rehabilitating or deterring them. Research evidence suggests that the recidivism rate (repeat offender rate) is significantly higher for those who are sent to prison than for similar offenders who have been placed on probation (Petersilia, Turner & Peterson, 1986; Geerkin and Hayes, 1993; MacKenzie, 1997; Gibbons and Katzenbach, 2006). Clearly the system of corrections does not work. We cannot simply incarcerate our way out of the problem. Winston Churchill in an often cited quotation (1910) said:

> The mood and temper of the public in regard to the treatment of crime and criminals is one of the most unfailing tests of the civilization of any country. A calm, dispassionate recognition of the rights of the accused and even of the convicted criminal against the State; a constant heart-searching of all charged with the deed of punishment; tireless efforts toward the discovery of the regenerative processes; unfailing faith that there is a treasure, if you can find it, in the heart of every individual—these are the symbols, which in the treatment of crime and criminals make and measure the stored-up strength of a nation and are a sign and proof of the living virtue in it.[2]

In contrast to the criminal justice, the aim of restorative justice (RJ) is never retribution or any process that separates or alienates a person from his or her "community." Instead, the aim is to reintegrate or resituate both the victim and the offender within their communities.[3] The question that arises is reintegration into what? Reintegration is possible only in neighborhoods or in "families of care" where a strong sense of belongingness exists and where relationships are based on mutual aid and support. So what is the possibility of social reintegration occurring in a community or family where no prior support existed or exists? How is reintegration possible in neighborhoods such as those described by Nils Christie (1993) as "killed neighborhoods"? Far from possessing reintegrative capabilities, "killed communities" seem to possess the opposite—structural inequalities that are at the root of most interpersonal crime.

For restorative justice to be successful, it must address the repressive structural context, not only in meeting the victim's and offender's needs but in helping people live safe lives and promoting the well-being of the community. To reintegrate victims and offenders into structurally violent conditions is anti-restorative and unjust (Sullivan and Tifft, 2005, p. 84). Mediation and restorative strategies may both be viewed as efforts by third party intervention to resolve conflict, reach an agreement or negotiated settlement, assess damage by one party to another, give and receive apologies, and recompense for damages done. Central to both processes is the informed consent of the participants.

---

2. Found in John Conrad's essay, "What do the Undeserving Deserve?" in Robert Johnson and Hans Toch's (Eds.), *The Pain of Imprisonment* (Beverly Hills: Sage Publications, 1982, p. 325).

3. The following works offer comprehensive descriptions of restorative justice: Braithwaite, J. (1998). Restorative Justice. In M. Tonry, (Ed). The *Handbook of Crime and Punishment*. (Pp. 323–344) Oxford: Oxford University Press. Also Braithwaite, J. (1999). Restorative Justice: Assessing Optimistic and Pessimistic Accounts. In M. Tonry and N. Morris, (Eds.) *Crime and Justice: A Review of the Research*. Chicago, ILL.: (Pp. 1–127) Chicago University Press. Braithwaite, J. (2003). Principles of Restorative Justice. In A. von Hirsh, J. Roberts, A. Bottoms, K. Roach, and M. Schiff, (Eds.) *Restorative Justice and Criminal Justice: Competing or Reconcilable Paradigms?* (Pp. 1–20) Oxford: Hart. Braithwaite, J. (2007). Building Legitimacy through Restorative Justice. In T. Tyler (Ed.) *Legitimacy and Criminal Justice: International Perspectives*. (Pp. 146–162) New York, NY: Russell Sage Foundation.

Mediation is most frequently used in contract disputes (including divorce and child custody) and bears only indirectly on the problem of violence in society. Mediation is an alternative in dispute resolution to litigation. In fact from a practical perspective, many jurisdictions now require alternative dispute resolution (ADR) to be attempted before litigation can occur. The Federal Arbitration Act (FAA) was passed by Congress in 1925. The Act provides for the judicial facilitation and resolution of private disputes through arbitration. In a 1984 Supreme Court case, *Southland v. Keating*, a 7–2 majority ruled that the FAA applied to contracts executed under state law. This contention has come under at least academic scrutiny as an overreach of federal authority and a challenge to due process and state sovereignty (Reuben, 1997; Schwartz, 2004; Schwartz, 2009).

Mediation in the context of restorative justice can take a variety of forms. The roots of restorative justice mediation can be traced to the work of the Mennonites and their commitment to nonviolence (Zehr, 1985; Peachey, 1989). Victim-Offender Reconciliation Programs (VORPs) also referred to as Victim-Offender Mediation Programs (VOMPs) is a restorative justice approach that brings victims face-to-face with their offenders, assisted by a mediator. The crime is made concrete and personalized in this encounter where the offenders learn the human consequences of their actions and the victims are given the opportunity to speak and convey their feelings about the harm they experienced to the person responsible for harming them. For mediation to work, offenders must take responsibility for their actions by agreeing to restitution with the victims and to restore the victims' losses. This can be purely symbolic or it can involve money, work for the victims, community service, or anything else that leads to a sense of justice between the offenders and victims.

There are other forms of mediation besides VORPs. Family Group Conferencing (FGC) was developed in New Zealand and passed into law by the New Zealand Parliament in 1989. FGC has been designed to make decisions about care and protection of children and youth justice outside of formal court proceedings. The family conference process seems to fit well with the values and traditional practices of the indigenous Maori people (Maxwell and Morris, 1993). In the United States, it is currently used primarily as a diversion from the court process for juveniles, but it has also been used after adjudication to address various issues or to arrive at specific terms for restitution. FGC has also been used in a few adult cases and to resolve a variety of offenses such as theft, arson, minor assaults, drug offenses, and vandalism (NIJ, 2007).

A related restorative practice also having its origins in aboriginal practice is the *community sentencing circles* initially developed in the Canadian Northwest. The sentencing circle incorporates three ideas: (1) a crime is a breach of the relationship between the offender and the victim as well as the offender and community; (2) the stability of the community is dependent on healing these breaches; and (3) the community is better positioned to deal with the causes of crime, which often reflect the economic or social structure of the community. This approach is based on principles that are consistent with a restorative justice view of an offense or crime: it is not just an offense against the state but an "injury" to another person and the community that must be healed or repaired. Unlike other restorative justice strategies, the sentencing circle is a part of the court process that may result in convictions and criminal records.

Procedurally, the sentencing circle involves the community (15 to 50 people). The "keeper of the circle" can be the judge or another respected member of the community. Members of the circle introduce themselves and the prosecution and defense make opening remarks. The victim is present and is an equal participant in the circle sentencing process. The circle members address a variety of issues that provide context for the crime that has been committed. The main questions facing the circle are: what needs to be done to heal the victim, the offender and the community; who will take responsibility for carrying out the plan, and who will make sure the plan is successful (Griffiths, 1996).

Victim-offender panels, another restorative justice strategy often used by organizations such as Mothers Against Drunk Driving (MADD), has been developed to give convicted drunk drivers a fuller appreciation of the cost to victims and survivors with the intention of reducing repeat offending. Offender participation is usually court ordered as a condition of probation (Mercer, Lorden, and Lord, 1994).

To prevent harmful acts from reoccurring, John Braithwaite (1998) introduces *reintegrative shaming* as an alternative to stigmatization. Effectively bringing together social control theory (bonding), communitarian theory, labeling theory including Erving Goffman's (1963) concept of stigma, and elements of deterrence theory, Braithwaite provides a formalization of reintegrative shaming. Reintegrative shaming is meant to serve as a constructive guide to restorative justice policy advocates and practitioners. In his view the true reintegration of the offender suggests lifting shame and gaining a preventive effect from positive communitarianism, bonding, and respect. The goal of reintegrating an offender back into the community without stigma transforms shaming into humanitarism.

One of the elements of the restorative process is the *encounter*—the face-to-face meeting of the victim and offender. While this is exceedingly restricted in formal judicial proceedings, it is a key element in restorative processes. Its healing affect has long been recognized. For example, the Greek poet, Homer, in his renowned work, *The Iliad*, memorialized the encounter between Achilles (the great Greek warrior) and Priam (the king of Troy) who were both mourning the deaths of someone very dear to each of them after a bloody battle with heavy casualties on both sides (Achilles mourned the death of his life-long companion, Patroclus, and Priam mourned the death of his son, Hector). After the battle Achilles refused to bury Hector, instead had the body dragged in disgrace around the city. That evening Priam under cover entered the enemy camp to negotiate with Achilles for the release of Hector's body. The two enemies' encounter is meticulously depicted in the poem. They each express their grave loss; they weep together as they reminisce over their loved ones; they share their emotions (fear and anger); they drink and eat; and they come to a resolution. Priam implores Achilles to consider what the loss of a son means to a father and asks him to return Hector's body so that he can bury him properly. Homer's description of the encounter details a broad range of feeling including grief, pity, and understanding as well as mutual respect and admiration. At the end, Achilles safely returns the body and a 12-day moratorium to the fighting is enforced. After Hector's burial the battle continues and both Achilles and Priam are ultimately killed. Homer, however, ends his poem with this extraordinary encounter.

The encounter plays a key role in the restorative process of repairing harm caused by crime. The approach brings victims face-to-face with offenders with the assistance of mediators. In these encounters, the offenders learn the human consequences of their actions and the victims are given the opportunity to convey their feelings about the harm they experienced to the person who harmed them. The offenders must take responsibility for their actions by agreeing to restore the victims' losses either through symbolic or concrete gestures or anything else that leads to a sense of justice being served between the offenders and victims.

Restorative Justice—Measures of Success: There is evidence that restorative justice can be a powerful alternative to traditional criminal justice. Recidivism rates tend to be lower and victim satisfaction typically higher in comparison to similar cases processed by the criminal justice system. The issue it would seem is whether these measures give an accurate assessment of the effectiveness of restorative justice programs and ultimately whether these are good indicators that reconciliation occurs (Lowry, 1993; Umbreit, 1994; Nugent, Williams, and Umbreit, 2004).

Elmar Weitekamp (2003), however, calls for more natural or true experiments to study the effects of various restorative justice approaches. For instance, more research is required to study the relationship of restorative justice with recidivism rates and the levels of satisfaction with respect to restorative justice participation. Relatively little is known regarding any long-term effects of mediation or other RJ practices. He also calls for the establishment of international data sharing of RJ research results as well as best practices, innovations, and quality control strategies. There is also a need for theory development with clear conceptual definitions, propositions, and relational hypotheses that are clearly operationalized and tested as well as holistic reviews of theoretical and methodological works on RJ globally.

Conflict Resolution

Conflict as well as its resolution has always been part of human social life. However, in the late 20th century especially following WWII, work on conflict resolution (CR) was spurred by the specter of nuclear annihilation that the Cold War evoked. Since that time a wide array of new methods to resolve conflicts have been developed and practiced. In fact, many effective approaches from a variety of different disciplines have been steadily constructed and also applied to other spheres of conflicts such as interpersonal conflict and community conflict.

For example, Roger Fisher and William Ury (2006) note that the field of peace studies has particularly influenced the growth of interest in conflict resolution (CR) strategies. Moreover, training in mediation and negotiation has now become a mainstay offering by academic institutions (e.g., Harvard University and Syracuse University). The 1960s and 1970s have become associated with the alternative dispute resolution movement, which sought to provide an alternative to adversarial proceedings and to appealing to the judiciary as a way to reduce the burden on the courts. Since 1986 CR (also referred to as mediation) has increasingly been institutionalized in legal proceedings (e.g., child custody cases and some divorce cases).

Theoretical works in connection with the feminist justice movement, have also contributed to the development of conflict resolution as a viable approach to resolving conflictual situations. The feminist justice movement advocates extending liberal ideals of citizenship and the rights all women and all oppressed groups and more comprehensively calls for a transformation of society (e.g., Harris, 1987; Daly and Stubbs, 2007). Feminist scholarship on law and justice and engagement with restorative justice principles and methods of conflict resolution has taken many forms. Feminist scholarship, for example, has provided a critique of and an alternative to the traditional emphasis on hierarchy and coercive power as the essential forms of decision-making in social life. Feminist theorists have stressed the importance of relationships and the possibility of reaching agreements through consensual decision-making processes. The most emphasized area of feminist RJ and CR is in connection with partner, sexual or family violence.[4] Also, work related to Peacekeeping Criminology, which is discussed in its own section below, has supported the development of RJ and CR.

---

4. Most would agree that the criminal justice system has been less than effective in dealing with violence against women in "domestic violence" situations. Restorative Justice (RJ) has been seen by some proponents as a viable way to deal with this type of violence but others suggest "The principal

Negotiating a Resolution to Conflict: The central idea of conflict resolution (CR) is that conflicts can be redefined as problems that can be solved in ways that satisfy at least some of the concerns of each of the adversaries. Adversaries may be national governments, ethnic communities within a neighborhood or a country, organizations in a city or a neighborhood, or members of a family, or just two individuals. The conflict-resolving approach may be used in each stage of a conflict, including its emergence, escalation, transformation (openness to CR), settlement, and resolution (Fisher and Ury, 2006).

According to Fisher and Ury (2006) any method of negotiation may be judged in terms of fairness using three criteria:

- It should produce a *wise* agreement (if agreement is possible)
- It should be *efficient* (time, cost)
- It should *improve* or at least not damage the *relationship* between the involved parties

A wise agreement can be defined as one that meets the legitimate interests of each side to the extent possible, resolves conflicting interests satisfying all of the parties to a conflict, is durable and takes the larger community interests into account.

Whether a negotiation concerns a contract, a family feud, or a peace settlement among nations, most people routinely use *position bargaining* in which each side takes a position and tries to win over the other side to its position and avoids concessions to reach a conclusion. Position bargaining, however, usually does not succeed in meeting the three criteria of producing a wise agreement, efficiently and amicably. So the first tenet of CR is to avoid position bargaining. Part of the challenge associated with position bargaining is that when people try to impose their positions on others, they may not be able to get beyond those positions. The more one attempts to defend his/her position and attack the opposing position — the more he/she becomes attached to the position and the less likely concessions are made in order to reach agreement. Moreover, as one's ego is invested in the position another challenge arises: "saving face," which makes it less likely that any agreement will wisely reconcile the parties' original interests. In the final analysis, position bargaining fails to meet the three criteria of successful negotiation.

The high costs and ultimate failure of hard position bargaining, has led some negotiators to avoid the hard approach and following a softer approach. The standard posture of the *soft bargaining style* is to be friendly and to make concessions, to trust the other side by disclosing one's bottom line position, to search for a single compromise that will be accepted, which usually necessitates having to concede in order to avoid further confrontation. While the soft method rests on the importance of preserving relationships, the process rarely leads to a wise settlement. Generally a soft form of position bargaining makes one vulnerable to someone who employs the hard strategy in order to dominate the outcome.

Principled negotiation or negotiation on merit is claimed to be the best alternative to position bargaining. According to Fisher and Ury (2006) four elements of principled negotiation or merit negotiation include the following:

---

argument against the use of RJ in men's violence against women is that the power imbalance in violent relationships is too entrenched for RJ to work" (Gelsthorpe, 2012, 398). (See Gelsthorpe, L. (2012). Violence Against Women: Repairing Harm through Kith and Kin. In D.W. Harper, L. Voigt, and W.E. Thornton (Eds.) *Violence: Do We Know It When We See It?* Durham, NC: Carolina Academic Press, 387-406.)

- *People*: Separate people from the problem
- *Interests*: Focus on interests not positions
- *Options*: Avoid having a bottom-line—develop options
- *Criteria*: Assess success/failure on basis of some objective standards

Important skills in resolving conflicts are *empathetic listening* and understanding the issues/facts associated with all sides of the conflict. The ability to appreciate diverse perspectives is often challenging. For example, Peter Senge (2006) using his metaphor of the *ladder of inference* suggests that the problem of miscommunication results from jumping to conclusions without fully understanding others' views, which prevents people from finding the common ground on which to base a resolution. The diagram below represents Senge's ladder of inference:

The Ladder of Inference

Take action on beliefs
Adopt beliefs
Draw conclusions
Add meaning
Select data
Observe data

According to Senge, thinking begins at the bottom of the ladder and moves quickly and uncritically to the top, often moving from selective perceptions to assumptions and meaning added from cultural and personal experiences to drawing erroneous conclusions, adopting beliefs and taking actions based on impressions rather than facts. Senge advocates using the model of the ladder of inference and the tools for inquiry and critical thinking to help people better resolve conflicts, better manage difficult cross-cultural misunderstandings and sensitive and emotional diversity issues.

Peacekeeping Criminology

Harold Pepinsky and Richard Quinney (1991) have proposed a humanistic approach (i.e., mediation and conflict resolution) to resolving the problems of crime and violence and other social problems. Drawing their inspiration from religious and philosophical teachings, they put forward the idea that only through affirming love as the key human quality, not just as an ideal but as a practice, can human beings produce love, peace and happiness in themselves and then begin the process to realize peace in the world. Or, as Gandhi (1957) eloquently put it, "We must be the change we wish to see in the world."[5]

Accordingly, Pepinsky and Quinney argue that the main purpose of criminology should be to promote a peaceful society. They begin by making the distinction between negative

---

5. For an interesting grass roots approach to community peacekeeping, See Parker, L. (2012). Is Community Peace Possible? In D.W. Harper, L. Voigt, and W.E. Thornton (Eds.). *Violence: Do We Know it When We See It?* Durham, NC: Carolina Academic Press, 439-452.

and positive peacekeeping. *Negative peace* comes from a mere absence of overt conflict and *positive peace* stems from humanitarian and mutual understanding. They observe that most practices of the criminal justice system are merely attempts of obtaining negative peacemaking—reactions that serve to suppress, control, or process antisocial acts including acts of violence through threats and applications of force. Positive peace can only become a social reality when the sources of violence, namely alienation, humiliation, shame, inequality, poverty, racism, and sexism are no longer present. They assert that without the construction of positive peace and the establishment of social justice worldwide, the violence of the individual, the family, the community, and the nation-state will continue.

Human Rights and Social Justice

The potential for peace has also been evidenced by world-wide commitment to social justice and the protection of human rights. Beginning with the 1948 United Nations (UN) Universal Declaration of Human Rights, the UN has been on the forefront in trying to ensure basic human rights for all the people on the planet. Following is the Preamble to UN Universal Declaration of Human Rights:

> Whereas recognition of the inherent dignity and of the equal and inalienable rights of all members of the human family is the foundation of freedom, justice and peace in the world,

> Whereas disregard and contempt for human rights have resulted in barbarous acts which have outraged the conscience of mankind, and the advent of a world in which human beings shall enjoy freedom of speech and belief and freedom from fear and want has been proclaimed as the highest aspiration of the common people,

> Whereas it is essential, if man is not to be compelled to have recourse, as a last resort, to rebellion against tyranny and oppression, that human rights should be protected by the rule of law,

> Whereas it is essential to promote the development of friendly relations between nations,

> Whereas the peoples of the United Nations have in the Charter reaffirmed their faith in fundamental human rights, in the dignity and worth of the human person and in the equal rights of men and women and have determined to promote social progress and better standards of life in larger freedom,

> Whereas Member States have pledged themselves to achieve, in co-operation with the United Nations, the promotion of universal respect for and observance of human rights and fundamental freedoms,

> Whereas a common understanding of these rights and freedoms is of the greatest importance for the full realization of this pledge,

> **Now, therefore, the General Assembly Proclaims this Universal Declaration of Human Rights** as a common standard of achievement for all peoples and all nations, to the end that every individual and every organ of society, keeping this Declaration constantly in mind, shall strive by teaching and education to promote respect for these rights and freedoms and by progressive measures, national and international, to secure their universal and effective recognition and observance,

both among the peoples of Member States themselves and among the peoples of territories under their jurisdiction.[6]

Established in 1978, Human Rights Watch (HRW), a non-governmental, nonprofit organization, has been focusing on developing objective and accurate information on human rights violations worldwide. Each year it publishes more than 100 reports and briefings on human rights conditions in some 90 countries, generating coverage in local and international media.

In May of 1996, the 190 nations of the World Health Organization (WHO) passed a resolution declaring violence a worldwide public health problem, urging member states to assess the public health impact of violence and requesting the Director-General of WHO to initiate a science-based public health approach to violence prevention. The results of this resolution have been far-reaching, particularly in the area of developing knowledge about how violence can burden communities in a wide array of health related consequences. WHO has recognized that the health impact of violence is not limited to physical harm alone. Long-term consequences can include depression, mental disorders, suicide attempts, chronic pain, unwanted pregnancy, HIV/AIDS and other sexually transmitted diseases. Children who have been victims of violence are at a higher risk of engaging in high-risk behaviors such as alcohol and drug abuse (p. 32).

The WHO is confident that violence can be prevented. Individual strategies that WHO believes are effective include pre-school enrichment programs for three to five year olds; life skills training and social development programs for older children aged six to 18 and assisting high risk adolescents and young adults to complete school and pursue vocational training and higher education. Other prevention strategies include training parents on child development, non-violent discipline and programs to develop attachments between high-risk youth and caring adults in building social skills and sustained relationships (Krug, et al., 2002, p. 38).

To provide a more activist role for the United Nations in implementing human rights, the Human Rights Council has been created by the UN General Assembly on March 15, 2006 with the main purpose of addressing situations of human rights violations and making recommendations on them. The Council is made up of 47 states responsible for strengthening the promotion and protection of human rights around the globe. On June 18, 2007, the Council promulgated what it called an "institutional-building package" that provides guidance for their future work. Three important elements are the Universal Periodic Review, which assesses human rights situations in all 192 UN member countries, an Advisory committee that provides expertise on human rights issues and a revised Complaints Procedure that allows individuals and organizations an easy mechanism for bringing human rights complaints to the Council (UN Human Rights Council, 2010).

Concluding Comment

Our book, *Why Violence?* ends with "Why not Peace?" As the chapters in this book demonstrate, the problem of violence is complex, which has not lent itself to easy or quick solutions. Yet one observation is certain—we know that we cannot solve the problem of violence with violence. Violence does not bring lasting peace. We also know that respect

---

6. *Source:* http://www.un.org.events.humanrights/2007/hrphotos/declaration%20_eng.pdf.

for and protection of human rights and social justice for all human beings are critical for the realization of peace both within and between nations of the world. Restorative Justice and conflict resolution are among the promising alternative approaches to restore communities or resolve disputes that potentially can result in violence. Practiced in all settings (individual, national, and international), restorative justice and conflict resolution have demonstrated successful outcomes. However, the application of these methods or approaches works best in environments in which human rights and social justice are seriously embraced and continuously sought, not just ideals that are discussed. In order to maximize the effectiveness of restorative justice or conflict resolution methods, we must not only tinker with their application here and there, but we must individually and collectively wholly embrace and commit to transforming our lives and how we think about and do things. Wishing for peace will not bring us closer to realizing peace. Again, as Gandhi so cogently stated: "We must be the change we wish to see in the world."

There are many organizations that are dedicated to peace with millions of supporters from around the world (see Box 10.3).

Box 10.3 Organizations Promoting Peace and Nonviolence
Some historical notes:

The American Friends Service Committee (AFSC) was created by the Religious Society of Friends (Quakers) in 1917 to help conscientious objectors during World War 1 to serve without enlisting in the military or killing people instead they drove ambulances, and worked as medics. The AFSC stayed on in Europe after the war to help rebuild. In 1947 AFSC was a co-recipient along with British Quakers of the Nobel Peace Prize on behalf of all Quakers for their work (AFSC, 2010). Another organization growing out of a similar tradition is the Mennonite Central Committee (MCC) which came into existence in July of 1920 and pledged to help the hungry, including Mennonites, in Russia and the Ukraine. Their purpose and vision statement explicitly identifies justice and peace building and to live and serve non-violently as priorities (MCC, 2010).

The Jewish Peace Fellowship (JPF) was founded in 1941 to assist Jewish conscientious objectors. Initially, the JPF helped educate local draft boards who for the most part were only familiar with Christian roots of conscientious objection and not the Jewish theological basis found in the Torah, Talmud and other religious texts. The JPF renounces participation in war and other forms of violence (JPF, 2010).

In 1945, in the closing days of World War II, a small group of French people met regularly to pray for peace. The concern that kept them coming together was their experience of an agonizing and dreadful fact: French and German Catholics, who professed the same faith, had killed one another by the millions in the 20th century. That could hardly be the will of God, as they understood it. So they prayed for forgiveness, reconciliation, and the peace of Christ. This group evolved into *Pax Christi* a Catholic peace organization. The movement spread quickly throughout Western Europe in the 1950s and was established in the United States in 1972.

Pax Christi USA strives to create a world that reflects the Peace of Christ by exploring, articulating, and witnessing to the call of Christian nonviolence. This work begins in personal life and extends to communities of reflection and action to transform structures of society. Pax Christi USA rejects war, preparations for war, and every form of violence and domination. It advocates primacy of conscience, economic and social justice, and respect for creation.

Pax Christi USA commits itself to peace education and, with the help of its bishop members, promotes the gospel imperative of peacemaking as a priority in the Catholic Church in the United States. Through the efforts of all its members and in cooperation with other groups, Pax Christi USA works toward a more peaceful, just, and sustainable world (*Pax Christi USA*, 2010).

Web links to Pacifist/Peace Organizations

Websites of organizations which support pacifism or anti-war activities:

War Resister's League, New York, NY
International Physicians for the Prevention of Nuclear War, Cambridge, MA
The Peace Abbey, Sherbourne, MA
South Dakota Peace & Justice Center, Watertown, SD
Mt. Diablo Peace Center, Walnut Creek, California
Fellowship of Reconciliation, Nyack, NY
Non-Governmental Organizations Committee on Disarmament, related to the United Nations
The M.K. Gandhi Institute for Non-Violence, Memphis, TN.
Nuclear Age Peace Foundation
Abolition 2000, a global network to eliminate nuclear weapons

Websites of organizations supporting pacifism, having a religious name in their titles:

Quakers (Religious Society of Friends)
Mennonite Central Committee
Friends Committee on National Legislation, Washington, D.C.
Friends Committee on Legislation, Sacramento, CA
American Friends Service Committee
Episcopal Peace Fellowship, Washington, D.C.
Pax Christi USA, Erie, PA
Friends for a Nonviolent World, Minneapolis, MN
Jewish Peace Fellowship, Nyack, NY

Other non violence websites:

Nonviolence USA, http://nonviolenceusa.org
International Center on Nonviolent Conflict, http://www.nonviolent-conflict.org
Nonviolence International, http:/nonviolenceinternationa.net/
Source: Retrieved on 12/17/2010 from http://www.uspacifistparty.org/PacLK.html.
Michigan Peace Team, Lansing, MI
Peace Brigades International, London, UK
Food Not Bombs

It appears that progress is being made at the international level in promoting and guarding human rights. From the 1948 United Nations Universal Declaration of Human Rights to the creation of the Human Rights Council in 2006, the UN has been on the forefront in leading the worldwide movement on affirming and ensuring basic human rights for all the people on the planet. Unless we stand for social justice and demonstrate the collective will to create a more peaceful world, the social problem of violence will continue to wreak havoc in our communities and around the world.

References

Barak, G. (2003). *Violence and Nonviolence: Pathways to Understanding.* Thousand Oaks, CA: Sage Publications.

Barak, G. (2007). *Violence, Conflict, and World Order: Critical Conversations on State-Sanctioned Justice*. Lanham, MD: Rowman and Littlefield Publishers, Inc.

Beck, A. 1999. *Prisoners of Hate: The Cognitive Basis of Anger, Hostility, and Violence*. New York: Perennial.

Braithwaite, J. (1989). *Crime, Shame, and Reintegration*. Cambridge, England: Cambridge University Press.

Braithwaite, J. (1998). Restorative Justice. In M. Tonry, (Ed.). The *Handbook of Crime and Punishment*. Oxford: Oxford University Press, 323–344.

Braithwaite, J. (1999). Restorative Justice: Assessing Optimistic and Pessimistic Accounts. In M. Tonry and N. Morris, (Eds.). *Crime and Justice: A Review of the Research*. Chicago, IL. Chicago University Press, 1–127.

Braithwaite, J. (2003). Principles of Restorative Justice. In A. von Hirsh, J. Roberts, A. Bottoms, K. Roach, and M. Schiff, (Eds.). *Restorative Justice and Criminal Justice: Competing or Reconcilable Paradigms?* Oxford: Hart, 1–20.

Braithwaite, J. (2007). Building Legitimacy through Restorative Justice. In T. Tyler (Ed.) *Legitimacy and Criminal Justice: International Perspectives*. New York, NY: Russell Sage Foundation, 146–162.

Braithwaite, J. and Strang, H. (2001). *Restorative Justice and Civil Society*. Cambridge: Cambridge University Press.

Bureau of Justice Statistics (Executive Summary)/ (1993). *Correctional Populations in the United States, 1980–1993*. U.S. Department of Justice, Office of Justice Programs. Retrieved from: http://www.druglibrary.org/schaffer/govpubs/corr93.html.

Calhoun, A., and Pelech, W. (2010). Responding to young people responsible for harm: A comparative study of restorative and conventional practices. *Contemporary Justice Review*, 13(3), 287–306.

Christie, N. (1993). *Crime Control as Industry*. New York: Routledge, cnn.com/2009-09-15/politics/carter.obama_1_president-jimmy-carter-president-obama-health-care-plan?_s=PM:POLITICS.

Daly, K., and J. Shubbs. (2007). Feminist theory, feminist and anti-racist politics, and restorative justice. In G. Johnstone and D. Van Ness (Eds.). *Handbook of Restorative Justice*. Cullompton, Devon, UK: Willan Publishing.

Dorne, C. (2008). *Restorative Justice in the United States*. Upper Saddle River, NJ: Prentice Hall.

Eglash, A. (1977). Beyond restitution: Creative restitution. In J. Hudson and B. Galaway (Eds.). Restitution in Criminal justice. Lexington, MA: D.C. Heath and Company.

Etzioni, A. (Ed.). 1992. *Rights and the Common Good: The Communitarian Perspective*. NY: St. Martin's Press.

Feinman, J. (2006). *Law 101: Everything You Need to Know About the American Legal System*. Oxford: Oxford University Press.

Fisher, R., and W. Ury. (2006). *Getting to Yes: Negotiating Agreement Without Giving In*. NY: Penguin Press.

Fromm, E. (1989). *The Art of Loving*. New York: Harper and Row.

Gandhi, M. K. (1957). *An Autobiography: The Story of My Experiment with Truth.* (M. Desai, Tr.) Boston: Beacon.

Geerkin, M.R., and Hayes, H.D. (1993). Probation and Parole: Public Risk and the Future of Incarceration Alternatives, *Criminology*, 31, 549–564.

Gelsthorpe, L. (2012). Violence against Women: Repairiing Harm through Kith and Kin. In D.W. Harper, L. Voigt, and W.E. Thornton (Eds.). *Violence: Do We Know It When We See It?* Durham, NC: Carolina Academic Press, 387–406.

Gibbons, J.J., and Katzenbach, N.B. (2006). Confronting Confinement. New York: Vera Institute of Justice. Retrieved from: www.vera.org.

Glaze, L. (2011). United States Bureau of Justice Statistics. *Correctional Populations in the United States, 2010.* Retrieved from: http://bjs.ojp.usdoj.gov/content/pub/pdf/cpus10.pdf.

Goffman, E. (1963). *Stigma: Notes on the Management of Spoiled Identity.* Upper Saddle River, NJ: Prentice Hall.

Griffiths, C. T. (1996). Sanctioning and healing: Restorative justice in Canadian aboriginal communities. *International Journal of Comparative and Applied Criminal Justice, 20*(1&2), 195–208.

Haider, H. (2009). (Re)Imagining Coexistence: Striving for sustainable return reintegration and reconciliation in Bosnia and Herzegovina. *International Journal of Transitional Justice*, 3(1), 91–113.

Harris, M. K. (1987). Moving into the New millennium: toward a feminist vision of justice. *The Prison Journal*, 6712, 27–38.

Henry, S., and D. Milovanovic. (1996). *Constitutive Criminology: Beyond Postmodernism.* Thousand Oaks, CA: Sage.

Heitmeyer, W., and Hagan, J. (2003). Violence: The Difficulties of a Systematic International Review. In W. Heitmeyer and J. Hagan (Eds.). *International Handbook of Violence Research.* Boston, MA: Kluwer Academic Publishers.

HRW. (2005). *Human Rights Watch Witness to Abuse.* Retrieved from: http://www.hrw.org/en/news/2009/12/17/us-court-rules-preventive-detention-un-constitutional.

Iadicola, P., and Shupe, A. (2003). *Violence, Inequality, and Human Freedom.* New York: Rowman and Littlefield Publishers, Inc.

Johnstone, G., and D. Van Ness (Eds.). (2007). *Handbook of Restorative Justice.* Cullompton, Devon, UK: Willan Publishing.

Jones, G. (1968). *A History of the Vikings.* New York: Oxford University Press.

King, Jr., M.L. (1958) *Stride Toward Freedom: The Montgomery Story.* Harper and Brothers Publishers

Krug, E, Dahlberg, L., Mercy, J., Zwi, A., and Lozano, R. (Eds.). (2002). *World Report on Violence and Health.* Geneva: World Health Organization.

Kuhn, T. (1970). *The Structure of Scientific Revolutions.* Chicago: University of Chicago Press.

LaCerva, V. (1996). *Pathways to Peace: Forty Steps to a Less Violent America.* Tesuque, NM: Heartsongs.

Lowry, K. (1993). Evaluation of community justice programs. In S. E. Merry and N. Milner (Eds.). *The Possibility of Popular Justice: A Case Study of Community Mediation in the United States.* Ann Arbor, MI: The University of Michigan Press, 89–122.

Lynch, M., and R. Michalowski. (2006). *Primer in Radical Criminology: Critical Perspectives on Crime, Power and Identity.* (4th Ed.) Monsey, NY: Criminal Justice Press.

MacKenzie, D.L. (1997). Criminal Justice and Crime Prevention. In L. Sherman, D. Gottfredson, D. MacKenzie, J. Eck, P. Reuter, and S. Bushway. *Preventing Crime: What Works, What Doesn't, What's Promising: A Report to United States Congress.* Prepared for the National Institute of Justice by the Department of Criminology and Criminal Justice, University of Maryland. Washington, DC: Office of Justice Programs. Retrieved from: http://www.ncjrs.gov/works/.

Maxwell, G. M., and Morris, A. (1993). *Families, Victims and Culture: Youth Justice in New Zealand.* Wellington: Department of Social Welfare and Institute of Criminology.

Mercer, D., Lorden, R., and Lord, J. (1994). Sharing their stories: What are the benefits? Who is helped? Presentation to the International Society for Traumatic Stress Studies, Chicago, November 8.

Muchembled, R. (2011). *A History of Violence: From the End of the Middle Ages to the Present.* Malden, MA: Polity Press.

National Association of Advancement of Colored People (NAACP). Dr. Martin Luther King, Jr. Retrieved from: http://www.naacp.org.

NIJ. (2007). *Family Group Conferencing.* National Institute of Justice. Retrieved from: http://www.ojp.usdoj.gov/nij/topics/courts/restorative-justice/promisinf-practices/family-group-conferencing.htm.

Nugent, W. R., Williams, M., and Umbreit, M. S. (2004). Participation in victim-offender mediation and the prevalence of subsequent delinquent behavior: A meta-analysis. *Research on Social Work Practice, 14*(6), 408–416.

Peachey, D. E. (1989). The Kitchener experiment. In M. Wright and B. Galaway (Eds.). *Mediation and Criminal Justice.* Thousand Oaks, CA: Sage Publications, 14–26.

Petersilia, J., Turner, S., and Peterson, J. (1986). *Prison versus Probation in California: Implications for Crime and Offender Recidivism.* The Rand Corporation.

Pepinsky, H., and R. Quinney (Eds.). 1991. *Criminology as Peacemaking.* Bloomington: Indiana University Press.

Pinker, S. (2011). *The Better Angels of Our Nature: Why Violence Has Declined.* New York, NY: Viking Press.

Reuben, R. C. (1997). Public justice: Toward a state action theory of alternative dispute resolution. *California Law Review, 85,* 577.

Sawyer, P. H. (1982). *Kings and Vikings: Scandinavia and Europe, A.D. 700–1100.* London: Methuen and Co. Ltd.

Schwartz, D. S. (2004). The Federal Arbitration Act and the power of Congress over state courts. *Oregon Law Review, 83,* 541.

Schwartz, D. S. (2009). Mandatory arbitration and fairness. *Notre Dame Law Review, 84,* 1247.

Senge, P. M. (2006). *The Fifth Discipline: The Art and Politics of the Learning Organization.* NY: Random House (Doubleday) (1st Ed. 1990).

Suffolk University, Center for Restorative Justice. (2007). Retrieved from: http://www.suffolk.edu/colllege.1496.html.

Sullivan, D., and Tifft, L. (2005). *Restorative Justice.* St. Louis, MO: Willow Tree Press

U.S. Census Bureau, Statistical Abstracts of the United States: 2012, Law Enforcement Courts and Prisons, p. 217. Retrieved from: http://www.census.gov/compendia/statab/2012/tables/12s0348.pdf.

Umbreit, M. (1994). *Victim Meets Offender: The Impact of Restorative Justice and Mediation.* Monsey, NY: Willow Tree Press, Inc.

Umbreit, M. S., and Coates, R. B. (1993). Cross-site analysis of victim offender mediation in four states. *Crime and Delinquency, 39*(4), 565–585.

UN Human Rights Council. (2010). The Human Rights Council. Retrieved from: http://www2.ohchr.org/english/bodies/hrcouncil/.

Van Ness, D., and H. Strong. (1997). *Restoring Justice.* Cincinnati, OH: Anderson.

Voigt, L., Thornton, W. Barille, L. and Seaman, G. (1994). *Criminology and Justice.* New York: McGraw Hill.

Wachtel, T., and Mirsky, L. (2009). *Safer Saner Schools: Restorative Practices in Schools and Education.* Bethlehem, PA: International Institute of Restorative Practices

Walsmley, R. (2011). *World Prison Population List.* 8th ed. King's College, London: International Centre for Prison Studies. Retrieved from: http://www.idcr.org.uk/wp-content/uploads/2010/09WPPL-9-22.pdf.

Weitekamp, E., and H. Kerner (Eds.). (2002). *Restorative Justice: Theoretical Foundations.* Cullompton, UK: Willan Publishing.

Zehr, H. (1990). *Changing Lenses: A New Focus for Crime and Justice.* Scottdale, PA: Herald Press.

Index

Titles of books are in italic font. Pages with images are bolded; pages with boxes, tables, figures, or notes are indicated with b, t, f, or n respectively.